HISTORIC HOUSES OF PEMBROKESHIRE
AND THEIR FAMILES

MAJOR FRANCIS JONES

C.V.O., T.D., D.L., F.S.A., M.A., K.St.J.

Late Wales Herald Extraordinary

1908–1993

HISTORIC HOUSES

OF

PEMBROKESHIRE

AND THEIR FAMILIES

Edited by

ROBERT INNES-SMITH

Compiled by

CAROLINE CHARLES-JONES

Biography, Artistic Direction, Marketing

HUGH CHARLES-JONES

Published by

BRAWDY BOOKS, PEMBROKESHIRE

1996

Published by
Brawdy Books, Plas yr Wregin, Dinas, Newport,
Pembrokeshire, SA42 0YH.
Telephone: 01348 811450

ISBN 0 9528344 0 5

Architectural Drawings: David Brunel White.

Front Cover Design: Leon Olin.

Vignettes: Stan Rosenthall.

Typeset in Bembo and printed by
Dinefwr Press, Rawlings Road, Llandybie, Carmarthenshire.

Bound by
Principal Bookbinders, Ystradgynlais, Swansea, SA9 1DT.

IN MEMORIAM
Francis and Ethel Jones.

'A good name is more desirable than great riches,
To be esteemed is better than silver and gold.'
Proverbs, Chap. 3, v. 13-14.

CONTENTS

ACKNOWLEDGEMENTS

Sadly my father did not live to see this book about his home county. It was a labour of love, taking over seventy years to complete.

He believed an historian's duty is to share knowledge. In turn it is mine to honour his wishes. He had not managed to make a list of acknowledgements. So on his behalf I thank all those countless hospitable people who opened their doors and family papers to him.

Robert Innes-Smith's editorial skills are justly renowned, but his Herculanian struggles with medieval and Welsh spelling as he deciphered hand-written notes have my awed admiration and gratitude.

The generous support of kind patron subscribers made this book possible. I am deeply grateful for their warm tribute to my father.

Anne and Mike Eastham of the Pembrokeshire Historical Society have special thanks for their enthusiastic encouragement without which I would not have found the courage to attempt this publication. The Carmarthenshire Antiquarian Society and the London Pembrokeshire Society were also unstinting in their assistance. Also my thanks to the Imperial War Museum in London for permission to use their official war photographs.

My BBC producer Louise Greenberg's belief in my work gave me the hope that I just might be up to the job of writing a short biography of my father. I pray my efforts interest and entertain readers. If so, then most credit goes to Louise.

My thanks also to Tony and Eiry Lewis of Y Siop Lyfrau, Newport, and to Mrs. Pamela Davies of Argoed for unfailing support, kindness, and help which was invaluable.

In finding a printer I found friends too in Donald Martin, Eddie John, and the wonderful Dinefwr printers' workforce. Thank you all.

More thanks go to Mrs. Agnes Gordon and Vanessa Collenette for typing part of the manuscript together with my wife.

The driving force, the inspiration when I faltered, countless hours at the computer, the administration, the compilation, all this was shouldered by my wife Caroline. I simply do not have the words to thank her enough.

This is a family enterprise from cover to cover. A last tribute to beloved parents.

HUGH CHARLES-JONES, 1996

EDITOR'S INTRODUCTION

Long ago Hugh Charles-Jones and I worked for Reuters's in Fleet Street and some time afterwards we found ourselves once more working together for a large publishing house in the Midlands. We little thought that, years later, we would be colleagues yet again.

When he invited me to edit his late father's uncompleted book on Pembrokeshire houses I was very flattered, but that feeling was mixed with a certain amount of trepidation. As a writer on historic houses, heraldry and genealogy myself, the name of Major Francis Jones was well known to me as a giant in those fields and as a prodigious scholar.

Because of my love of Wales, and as a fellow Celt, I accepted the challenge. The first section of the book was typewritten to the letter 'P'. The rest was in the Major's handwriting and not always easy to decipher. Here my travail began. There were thousands of notes on various sized papers and cards. They had been updated over the years, some from the 1930s. Welsh names with different spellings from medieval days were particularly difficult, so I must apologise for the occasional error which may have crept in. Major Jones left copious research material on other Pembrokeshire houses which he did not consider suitable for inclusion. These notes are available for the use of scholars by appointment with the executor.

Whenever I re-visit Pembrokeshire now I see the matchless landscape and the old gentry houses and farmsteads of the County with different eyes. After reading this book I hope that you will too.

The editing and writing involved in the completion of Major Jones's painstaking work has been a great privilege, made even more enjoyable by the unstinted help and encouragement of Hugh and Caroline Charles-Jones and their bountiful Welsh hospitality.

ROBERT INNES-SMITH
March 1996

LIST OF PATRON SUBSCRIBERS

Mrs. M. L. Akehurst, Little Melbreck, Stock, Essex.

Mrs. R. Allen-Mirehouse, The Hall, Angle, Pembs.

Charles Edward Ayres, Fishguard, Pembs.

Dr. D. L. Baker-Jones, Velindre, Dyfed.

P. A. Barker, Swales Music Centre, Haverdowest.

James Barrett, Underdown, Pembroke, Pembs.

Mr. Grahame & Mrs. Pamela Barrett, Carew.

Mr. Grenville Barrett, Cannon Hill Farm, Pembs.

Mr. D. A. Bedford, Greenway House, Narberth.

Mrs. Jane Bell, Druidstone Hotel, Pembs.

Mrs. A. L. Bellan, Dunsfold, Godalming.

Mr. A. R, Bentham, Fron, Whitland, Pembs.

William D. Berry, Roch Castle, Pembs.

Mrs. D. Bevan, Ty Picton, Llansteffan, Carms.

Dr. J. H. L. & Mrs. S. Birchall, Gressingham, Lancaster.

Miss J. Bird, Freshwater East, Pembs.

R. Blacklaw-Jones, Haverfordwest, Pembs.

C. Blundall, Allt-y-Rheini, Cilgerran, Cards.

H. M. Boggis-Rolfe, Plas Pontfaen, Pembs.

J. Booth, Westbury, Wilts.

Miss M. Bowen Evans, Trelech, Carms.

Dr. R. W. Bowen, The Grove, Haverfordwest.

Raymond E. Bowen, Castle Dr., Dinas, Powys.

D. J. Bowen, Ffordd y Gogledd, Aberystwyth.

Mr. & Mrs. M. Boyd, Cwm Eog, Crymych, Pembs.

Mrs. M. Boyes, Allestree, Derby.

Larry Brantinham, Texas, U.S.A.

J. P. Brooke-Little, Lower Heyford, Bicester.

Major W. K. Buckley, Ferryside, Carms.

J. H. Burgess, Kings Heath, Birmingham.

Mr. J. P. Bushell, New Moat, Pembs.

Peter Campbell, Bryn Deri, Cards.

Carmarthen Cultural Services, Carmarthen, Carms.

Ms. Jill Chambers, Castle Cenlas, Mathry, Pembs.

A. W. H. Charles, Henllys, Llanrhian, Pembs.

Dr. B. G. Charles, Aberystwyth, Cards.

Tom Charles, Belmont, California, U.S.A.

Mrs. P. Charles-Jones, Ampney St. Peter, Glos.

J. Charles-Jones, Ampney St. Peter, Glos.

A. Charles-Jones, Fulbrook, Burford, Oxon.

R. Charles-Jones, Oddington, Glos.

G. Charles-Jones, Letcombe Regis, Wilts.

Guy Charles-Jones Wycliffe College Junior School, Stonehouse, Glos.

Miss T. Charles-Jones, Plas yr Wregin, Dinas, Pembs.

Sir Colin Cole, Burstow, Surrey.

Mr. & Mrs. J. Collier, Sutton, Pembs.

Mrs. P. A. Copeman, Robeston House, Robeston Wathen, Pembs.

F. G. Cowley, West Cross, Swansea.

Ms. Elizabeth Cragoe, Trawsmawr, Carmarthen.

Revd. Canon A. Craven, Nolton, Pembs.

Mrs. V. A. Curphey, Sandy Haven Farm, St. Ishmaels.

D. Iwan Dafis, Llandudoch, Aberteifi.

John A. Davies, Herbrandston Hall, Milford Haven, Pembs.

Mr. B. Davies, Trefawr, Llanfyrnach, Pembs.

Mr. R. Parnell Davies, Chesham, Bucks.

Ms. Margaret Davies, Crackwell Fm., Penally, Pembs.

Col. D. L. Davies, Withybrook, Haverfordwest, Pembs.

Mrs. P. J. Davies, Argoed, Felindre Farchog, Pembs.

Mr. T. S. W. Davies, Frochest, Eglwyswrw, Pembs.

G. Davies, Berllan, Eglwyswrw, Pembs.

H. Davies, Brunt Farm, Dale, Pembs.

Dr. Michael Davies, Yelverton, Devon.

Dr. Glan Davies, Nantgaredig, Carms.

Mr. R. Davies, Little Newcastle, Pembs.

Dr. Paul Gillard Davies, Little Dunmow, Essex.

Robin de Wilde, London, WC2.

Mr. H. Devonald, St. Lawrence, Fishguard, Pembs.

Dr. J. R. Dove, Penllergaer, Swansea.

Mrs. P. Drew, New Moat, Pembs.

Elizabeth Dunwell, Glasdir Farm, Nevern, Pembs.

Mr. & Mrs. E. Eastham, Fishguard, Pembs.

Phillip Evans, Llangunnor, Carms.

Mr. Peter Graham Evans, Cheltenham, Victoria, Australia.

Mr. Keith Evans, Langdale, Merthyr Tydfil, Glam.

Canon Conrad Evans, Carmarthen.

Mrs. & Mrs. R. Evans, Box, Llanelli.

Jonathan Firth, Old Priory Road, Carmarthen.

David R. Foreman, Lulworth Pl., Walton le Dale.

D. T. R. Francis, Briar Walk, London.

xii

Mrs. S. Francis, Penbanc, Fishguard.

D. P. Freeman, Maritime Quarter, Swansea.

G. R. Helt, Australian Welsh Friendship Club, Bulli, N.S.W. Australia.

J. Arthur George, The Cottage, Box, Wiltshire.

Constance Mary George, Milton Meadows, Tenby.

W. D. Stanley Gibby, Pyrford, Woking, Surrey.

Col. R. H. Gilbertson, Coed-y-ffynon, Lampeter Vefrey, Pembs.

Mr. R. Giles, Great Mongeham, Deal, Kent.

Rev. C. L. Gillham, Spittal, Pembs.

Mr. & Mrs. C. Goodman, London W9.

Mrs. P. Gould, Tredefaid, Llantood, Cards.

Mr. J. Griffiths, Evesham, Worcs.

Mrs. M. A. Griffiths, St. Clears, Carms.

E. Olwen Griffiths, Pontyberem, Llanelli.

Sir Lincoln Hallinan, Cotham Lodge, Newport.

The Viscount Hampton, Bovey Tracey, Devon.

Mr. S. Hancock, Neyland, Pembs.

Mrs. H. Hawkesworth, Knossington, Oakham.

Mrs. S. Hewitt, Spring Wells, Spittal, Pembs.

Mr. & Mrs. J. Hogg, Pembroke, Pembs.

Mr. H. B. Holt, Newport Castle, Pembs.

Iorwerth Howells, Waunfawr, Aberystwyth.

G. & K. B. Hudson, Begelly, Pembs.

Rev. Herbert Hughes, Llanddewi, Powys.

Mr. J. V. Hughes, Port Talbot, W. Glam.

C. R. Humphery-Smith, Seasalter, Kent.

Francis Hutchinson, Tenby, Pembs.

Mr. Huw Iorwerth, Llansteffan, Carms.

Adrian James & Delys James, Cross Park, Pembroke.

Mrs. M. B. Jenkins, Trearched Farm, Croesgoch.

Mr. P. K. Jenkins, Cefn-Goleu, Llandeilo.

Mr. T. R. V. Johns, Pencnwc Farm, Castlemorris.

Lt. Col. Sir John Johnston, Windsor Great Park, Berks.

Dedwydd Skeel Jones, Bedford.

Miss A. Lawrence Jones, Hendre, Carmarthen.

Mrs. M. Jones, Lochmeyler, Llandeloy, Pembs.

Mr. D. Morris Jones, Aberarth, Aberaeron, Cards.

Valerie Jones, Loveston Cross, Pembs.

Dr. & Mrs. R. T. Jones, Lanstone, Havant.

Mr. & Mrs. Hugh Jones, Rhydgarnwen, Llantood.

Alwyn H. Jones, Longacre Road, Carmarthen.

T. Bleddyn Jones, Llanegwad, Carmarthen.

Dr. Trevor Jones, Llys Hwelon, St. Clears, Carms.

Mrs. Margaret Jones, Stradey Hill, Llanelli.

Mr. & Mrs. E. Jones, Trenichol, Llandeloy.

Howard N. Jones, Yetminster, Sherborne, Dorset.

Mr. Wyn Jones, Blaencilgoed House, Ludchurch, Pembs.

Mr. A. Jones-Lloyd, Lancych, Boncath, Pembs.

Miss C. E. Kelway, Cottesmore, Haverfordwest.

Nigel & Angela Knocker, Cwrt Bach, Newport.

Mr. & Mrs. J. Lane Fox, Bibury, Glos.

Hedd Ladd-Lewis, Cwrt Dinefwr, Llandeilo.

W. E. P. Laxton, Cilgwyn Mill House, Newport.

Mr. & Mrs. S. R. Lewis, Castle Cottage, Amroth.

The Very Revd. B. Lewis, Nevern, Pembs.

R. W. A. P. Lewis, Caermaenau Fawr, Clynderwen.

Mr. D. Lewis, Little Water St., Carmarthen.

Dr. Keith Lewis, Maes-y-Bryn, Gors-Las.

Skyrme Lewis, North Nash, Llangwm, Pembs.

The Hon. T. O. Lewis, Hean Castle, Saundersfoot.

Mrs. R. V. Lilwall, Main St., Pembroke.

M. R. Lippiatt, Priory Court, Haverfordwest, Pembs.

Mrs. E. A. Llewellin, Kilbarth, Rudbaxton, Pembs.

Thomas Lloyd, Freestone Hall, Kilgetty, Pembs.

Sir Ian Lloyd, Priors Dean, Petersfield, Hants.

Mrs. C. Lloyd-Davies, Barn St., Haverfordwest.

Llyfrcell Hugh Owen Library, University of Aberystwyth, Aberystwyth,

The Hon. John Long, Highworth, Wiltshire.

Col. & Mrs. V. Lowe, Ripon, North Yorks.

Dr. & Mrs. Loxdale, Llanilar, Cards.

K. W. Lynch, Hill House, Newport, Pembs.

John Maggs, Williamston Farm, Haverfordwest.

Col. A. M. Man, Castle Croft, Ludchurch, Pembs.

Sir David Mansel-Lewis, Stradey Castle, Llanelli.

Mr. & Mrs. C. Mason-Watts, Newcastle Emlyn.

C. A. Mathias, Ashbourne, Derbyshire.

Roland Mathias, Doffrobani, Brecon, Powys.

Mr. C. Mathias, Hazelbrook Farm, Carew, Pembs.

James Mead, Ashdale House, Llangwm, Pembs.

The Viscountess Melville, Stroud, Glos.

Mr. D. Miles, St. Anthony's Way, Haverfordwest.

M. R. Millington, Ryles Crescent, Macclesfield.

Ms. Catherine Milner, Pencader, Carms.

J. B. Morcom, The Gate House, Stevenage, Herts.

Mr. D. B. Morris, Ramsden Road, London SW12.

Mrs. A. E. Morris, Kingston Farm, Pembroke.

Mrs. C. Murray, Hurstbourne Priors, Hants.

Mr. G. Nash, Fairwater, Cardiff.

National Library of Wales, Aberystwyth.

Mrs. & Mrs. G. Nicolle, Nolton Haven, Pembs.

Mr. M. Noott, Chaddesley Corbett, Worcs.

The Duke of Norfolk, Arundel Castle, W. Sussex.

Mr. G. Oliver, St. Thomas's Green, Haverfordwest.

J. Oswyn Evans, Fferm Pantirion, Llandudoch.

R. Outwin-Flinders, Wycliffe College Junior School, Stonehouse, Glos.

Mr. J. Owen, Cardigan Rd., Haverfordwest.

L. B. Owen, Forge Mill, Templeton, Pembs.

W. A. Owens, Millin Farm, Haverfordwest, Pembs.

R. W. Palmer, Wansworth Plain, London SW18.

P. Dawkins Palmour, Pembroke.

Mrs. B. Parker, Castle Reach, Newport, Pembs.

The Lord Parry, Llangwm, Pembs.

Misses E. A. Y. & L. A. Parry, Ammanford, Carms.

Ms. Maureen Patch, Blackley, Manchester.

Mrs. N. Pearce, Merton Place Hse., Pembroke.
Mr. P. G. V. Pegge, Llwynbedw, Boncath.
Pembrokeshire County Library, Haverfordwest.
D. J. G. Perking, Rhiwbina, Cardiff.
E. H. Perkins, Narberth, Pembs.
G. M. Philipps, Slebech Park, Haverfordwest.
Ms. Margaret F. Phillips, Lamphey, Pembroke.
J. W. Phillips, Cronllwyn, Llanychaer, Pembs.
Ms. Audrey M. Philpin, Little Haven, Pembs.
Mr. & Mrs. T. P. Pocock, Entraygues, France.
Mr. J. Powell, Penmaen, Swansea.
Bryn Price, Fopston Farm, St. Brides, Pembs.
Robert Pugh, Beaufort Mews, Larkhall, Bath.
S. M. Pugh, President Cyfeillion Cymru,
    S. Australia.
Major I. B. Ramsden, Cosheston Hall, Pembroke
    Dock.
Alan Randall, Parade House, Carmarthen.
Major D. Rankin-Hunt, The Royal Collection
    Dept., St. James Palace, London.
Mr. & Mrs. Raymond, Jordanston Hall, Pembs.
J. P. Rayner, Penty Park, Clarbeston Road, Pembs.
Mr. Leonard Rees, Cerbid, Solva, Pembs.
Miss E. Rees, Brynhedydd, Llansteffan, Carms.
B. L. V. Richards, St. Mary St., Carmarthen.
M. P. Richards, Jordanston Farm, Rosemarket,
    Pembs.
Mrs. E. D. Richards, Llanwnwr, Goodwick,
    Pembs.
Mr. D. R. Richardson, Lochturffin, Mathry,
    Pembs.
Mr. J. Roach, Addison Road, Haverfordwest.
Dilwyn Roberts, Pontyates, Llanelli.
D. G. Roberts, Brynaeron, Llandissilio, Pembs.
Mrs. D. P. Robinson, Green Castle, Llangain,
    Carms.
Barbara Rosenfeld, Gallod Fawr, Trefin, Pembs.
Mrs. M. G. Rowlands, Imble Close, Pembroke
    Dock, Pembs.
R. P. Sambrook, Treclyn, Eglwyswrw, Pembs.
Mr. K. B. R. Scale, Musselwick Farm, Marloes,
    Pembs.
Mr. A. Scourfield-Lewis, Colby Lodge, Narberth.
Mr. Eldon Smith, Wellfield House, Carmarthen.
Mr. P. J. K. Speyer, Hill, Narberth, Pembs.
The Viscount St. Davids, Alwyne Place, London
    N1.
Mrs. E. Stanley, Cheltenham, Glos.
B. J. Stewart-Thomas, Haroldston Hall,
    Haverfordwest.
I. T. & J. H. Stokes, Pant Coch Cottage, Carmel,
    Llanelli.
Mr. W. F. Stubbs, Trefasser, Goodwick, Pembs.
Mr. Robert Thomas, Lampit Mawr, Fishguard.

Mr. K. G. Thomas, The Glebe, Tenby, Pembs.
Ms. Sophy Thomas, Pen-yr-Ardd, Llandissilio,
    Pembs.
T. W. G. Thomas, Glasfryn Farm, Fishguard,
    Pembs.
Mrs. S. Thomas-Ferrand, The Leys, Amroth,
    Pembs.
Mr. R. G. Thorne, Little Green St., London NW5.
G. J. & J. H. Tjoonk, Caerforiog Farm, Solva,
    Pembs.
J. Towyn-Jones, Brynsiriol, Carmarthen.
Mrs. N. Tribe, Carn Ganol, Kilgetty, Pembs.
Dr. Roger Turvey, Sycharth, Ammanford, Carms.
Mr. S. C. Van Dulken, Green Road, London N20.
Lady Wagner, Chelsea, London, SW3.
University of Wales, College of Cardiff, Cardiff.
History Dept., University of Wales, Swansea.
The University College of Wales, Aberystwyth.
Karen & Heather Walker, Colby Moor Farmhouse,
    Llawhaden, Pembs.
Dr. H. Walters, Adran y Llyfrau Printiedig,
    Llyfrgell Genedlaethol Cymru, Aberystwyth.
T. B. Warlow, Ffynnongain, Clarbeston Road,
    Pembs.
Mrs. Doreen Warmsley, Newport, Pembs.
E. Warren Davis, Battersea, London SW11.
Mr. & Mrs. S. Watkins, Trewern, Nevern.
Dr. A. A. Watson, Stone Hall, Haverfordwest,
    Pembs.
West Glamorgan County Library, The County
    Archivist, County Hall, Swansea.
D. M. B. White, Longacre Road, Carmarthen,
    Carms.
Mr. M. Whitelock, West Williamston, Pembs.
Mrs. E. M. Williams, Thornton House, Milford
    Haven, Pembs.
Eluned M. Williams, Eton Avenue, Wembley,
    Middx.
A. D. G. Williams, Bancffosfelen, Llanelli.
Sir Glanmor Williams, Grosvenor Road, Sketty.
Margaret & John Williams, Plas-y-Meibion,
    Llangolman, Pembs.
Michael Woakes, Hill Terrace, Fishguard, Pembs.

Estate Agents and Lawyers
Stephen R. Beesley, Price & Son, Haverfordwest,
    Pembs.
J. Hayman-Joyce, Moreton in Marsh, Glos.
P. A. Owen, Owen & Owen, Pembroke, Pembs.
John Roche, Solicitor, 12 Main St., Pembroke,
    Pembs.
John C. Van Bylevelt, The Warren, Saundersfoot,
    Pembs.

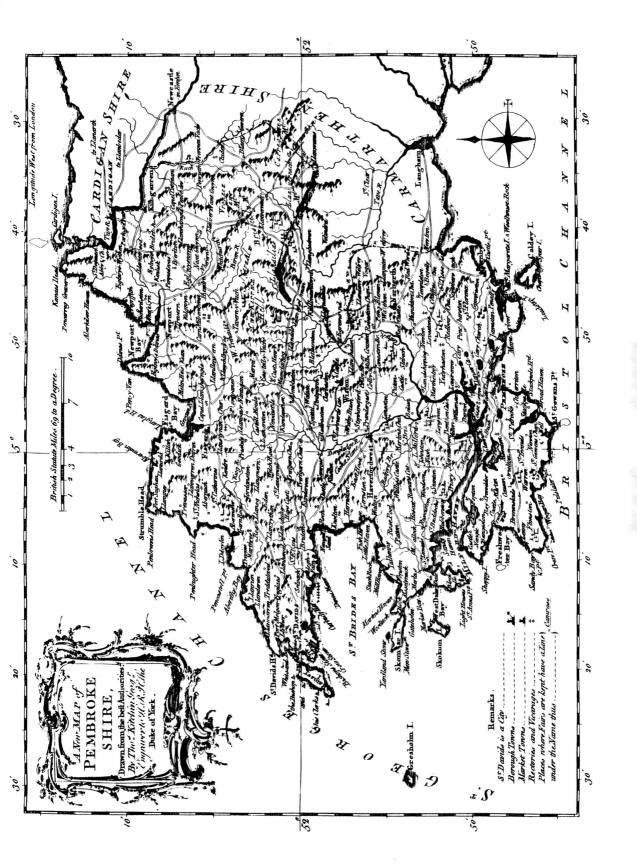

A New MAP of
PEMBROKE
SHIRE,
Drawn from the best Authorities.
By Thos. Kitchin, Senr.
Engraver to H.R.H. the
Duke of York.

British Statute Miles 69 to a Degree.

Remarks.
St Davids is a City
Borough Towns
Market Towns
Rectories and Vicarages
Places where Fairs are kept have a Line
under the Name thus

XV

PARISH MAP INDEX WITH HOUSES
LISTED BY PARISH, AND MAJOR ISLANDS

CARDIGANSHIRE

FISHGUARD
BAY

CARMARTHENSHIRE

ST. BRIDES
BAY

Ambleston 41
HOOK.
RINASTON.
SCOLLOCK.
WOODSTOCK.

Amroth 71
AMROTH
CASTLE. (Earweare).
COLBY LODGE.
EAREWERE.
EASTLAKE.

MERRIXTON.
RHYDLANGOEG.

Angle 126
ANGLE, THE HALL OF.
BANGESTON.

Bayvil 5
RHOS Y BAYVIL.

Begelly 73
BEGELLY HOUSE.
MORGANS.

Langum 88
EAST HOOK.
HOOK.
NASH GREAT.

Lawrenny 86
CRESSWELL.
LAWRENNY.

Letterston 52
HEATHFIELD (LODGE).

Little Newcastle 42
COLSTON.
FFYNNONE.
SUMMERTON.

Llanddewi Felfrey (Velfre)
60
BYRN.
CAERMAENAU FAWR.
FRON.
HENLLAN.
PANTEG. (PANTEAGUE).
PENBLEWYN.
PLAS CRWN.

Llandeilo 25
LLANDEILO

Llandeloy 119
CAERWEN.
HENDRE.
LOCHMEYLER.
LLANDDINOG.
TRENICHOL.

Llandysilio West 37
BRYNAERON.
BRYNDYSIL.

Llanfairnantgwyn 11
PANT Y DERI.
PISTYLL MEUGAN.
TREFACH

Llanfairnantygof 43
CILGELYNEN.
(CILGLYNEN).
NANTYBUGAIL.
TRECWN.

Llanfallteg West 59

Llanfihangel Penbedw 19
BACHENDRE.
CILGADFARCH.

CILRHIWE.
DOLAU LLWYD(ION).
PENBEDW.
PLAS IWERILL (Y WERILL)
WERNDDOFN.

Llanfyrnach 28
BLAEN TÂF.
BLAIDDBWLL.
GRAIG.
PONTYGAFEL.
TREFAWR.
TREHENRY.

Llangan West 61

Llangolman 26
CLYNSAITHMAN.
CWM CERWYN.
GILFACHWRNELL.
LLANGOLMAN.
PLAS Y
MEIBION/MEIBON.

Llanhowell 118
CERBYD.
LECHA.
TREFEUGAN.
TREGLEMAIS.

Llanllawer 30
COURT, CWRT.
TRELLWYN COURT.
TRENEWYDD MANOR.

Llanreithan 116
LLANEY.
LLANREITHAN.

Llanrhian 117
CARTLETT (2).
HENLLYS.
PARK COURT.
PORTHIDDY FAWR or
FACH.
TORBANT.
TREFIN.
TRENEWYDD FAWR.
TREVACOON/
(TREFACCWN).
TREYARCHED.
YNYS BARRY.

Llanstadwell 125
HAYSTON.
HONEYBOROUGH.
JORDANSTON.
NEWTON.

Llanstinan 44
LLANSTINAN.

Llantood 3
RHYDGARNWEN.
TREDEFAID.

Llanwnda 46
CARNE COCH.
DYFFRYN WDIG.
GOODWICK. (Wdig).
LLANWNWR.
PENRHIW.
PENYSGWARN.
TREHOWEL.

Llanycefn 36
LLANDRE.

Llanychaer 31
CILCIFFETH.
GARN.

Llanychllwydog 21
MYNYDDMELYN.
TREDAFYDD.

Llawhaden 57
LLAWHADEN.
RIDGEWAY.
ST. KENNOX.
TALYBONT.
VAYNOR – GREAT

Llysyfran 40
FELINDRE.
SOUTHFIELD.

Loveston 75

Ludchurch 69
HILL.
WESTERTON.

Maenclochog 24
BWLCH Y
CLAWDD/TEMPLE
DRUID.
COTTY.
VORLAN.

Manorbier 140
EAST MOOR.
MANORBIER CASTLE.
NORCHARD.

Manordeifi 14
BLAEN MWRW.

CASTLE MALGWYN
(OLD).
CILAST UCHA.
CILFOWIR, (CILFOWYR).
CILRHIWE FACH.
CLYNFYW.
FFYNNONAU BYCHAN,
later FFYNNONE.
PARC CYNHAETHW (Y).
PENALLTYLLYN.
PENTRE.
VAYNOR.

Manorowen 47
BRWYNANT.
LANGTON.
MANOROWEN.
SCLEDDY.
TREBRITHIN.
TRELEWELYN.

Marloes 108
CRABHOLE.
FOBSTON.
HOOK.
MARLOES COURT.
MUSSELWICK (MUSLICK).
PHILBEACH. (FILBETCH).

Martletwy 77
LANDSHIPPING.
LANDSHIPPING HOUSE.
LANDSHIPPING FERRY.
LANDSHIPPING QUAY.
MARTLETWY HOUSE.

Mathry 49
CARNACHEN WEN
CASTLE CENLAS.
CASTLE MORRIS
LOCHTURFFIN.
LONGHOUSE.
MABWS FAWR.
PRISKILLY.
RHOSLANOG FAWR.
RHYDYDHARDING.
TREFELLYN.
TREWALLTER LWYD.
WAUNBARRY.

Meline 9
BRYANOG FACH.
GLANDUAD.
HAFOD TYDFIL.
HELYGNANT.
HENDRE.
MERIANOG.

GLOSSARY OF USEFUL TERMS

BOVATE: Area an ox can plough in a season.

CARUCATE: 64 acres. See PLOUGHLAND.

COCKROAD: Clear cut road through a wood across which a net is hung from opposite trees to catch woodcock. Cockshoot time is dusk when birds are most likely to fly into the nets.

CULM: The slack of anthracite coal mixed with beaten clay and water and made into 'balls' and used on the fire; it burned very slowly and the fire could be kept in all night.

DEMESNE: Land retained by the lord of the manor for his own use and upon which tenants give free labour as part of their obligations in return for their holdings.

FOREST: Originally used to describe an open area with trees and pasture, moorland and mountain reserved for hunters.

GAVELKIND: Equal succession to land of all heirs.

HUSBANDMAN: Tenant farmer.

INTER ALIA: Among others.

KNIGHT'S FEE: Land held by a knight in return for military service being roughly 640 acres (10 ploughlands).
20 knight's fees held of the King make a Barony.
5 knight's fees held of Earldom of Pembroke make a Barony.

MESNE: Subordinate Lord holding estate from superior feudal Lord.

MESSUAGE: Dwelling house with outbuildings and land assigned to its use.

OXLAND: 8 acres but variable from place to place.

PLOUGHLAND: The amount of land that could be ploughed in a year. It varied from 60-180 acres from place to place.

PROTONOTARY: Chief clerk or registrar in a law court.

STANG: Measure of land, a quarter of a Welsh acre.

SUIT OF COURT: Obligation to attend the lord's court.

TOWNRED: Township or cluster of homesteads.

IURE UXORIS: In right of his wife.

VIDE: See.

Ref: G. Owen, *Elizabethan Pembrokeshire*. Ed. Brian Howells, 1973. Pembs. Record Office.

BIBLIOGRAPHICAL ABBREVIATIONS

Anc. Mon. Pembs.:	Ancient Monuments Commissioners Pembrokeshire.
Arch. Cam.:	Archaeologia Cambrensis.
B.B. St. Davids:	Black Book of St. Davids 1326.
B.G. Charles NCPN:	Non Celtic Place Names, Dr. B.G. Charles, 1938, Ldn. Medieval Studies.
Burkes's L. G. 1850:	Burke's Landed Gentry, 1850 edn.
C of A.:	College of Arms, London.
Carms. RO:	Carmarthenshire Records Office.
Carms. Studies 1974.:	Carmarthenshire Studies, presented to Major Francis Jones, ed. T. Barnes and N. Yates, Carmarthen, published 1974.
Chancery Proc.:	Chancery Proceedings Ser. II 420/40.
DNB:	Dictionary of National Biography, 63 vols., Ldn. 1885-1900, reprinted Oxford 1921-22.
DWB:	Dictionary of Welsh Biography down to 1940 – London 1959.
Dwnn:	Heraldic Visitations see Meyrick, Samuel Rush.
Fenton Tour Pembs.:	An Historical Tour through Pembrokeshire, Richard Fenton. 1811.
Fo.:	Folio.
G.G.Mss:	Golden Grove Manuscripts.
ibid.:	See last reference.
J.B.A.A.:	Journal of British Architectural Association.
L.T.:	Land Tax lists.
Laws Little England:	Laws, Little England beyond Wales, edn. 1888.
Lewis TDW:	Lewis Samuel, A Topographical Dictionary of Wales. Vols. 1 & 2, London 1833, 4th Edn.
Ms:	Manuscript/s.
NLW:	National Library of Wales.
P.R.O.:	Public Record Office.
Papers of G.S.:	Papers of Great Sessions.
Pembs. RO:	Pembrokeshire Records Office.
Pembs. Arch. Svy.:	Pembrokeshire Archaeological Survey.
Pembs. Hist.:	The Pembrokeshire Historian.
Protheroe:	Protheroe Beynon Collection.
R. Comm. on Land in Wales:	Royal Commission on Land in Wales.
RCAM:	Royal Commission for Ancient and Historical Monuments in Wales, An Inventory of the Ancient Monuments in Wales and Monmouthshire, London 1917.
Rees, *Beauties of S. Wales*.:	Rees Thomas, The Beauties of England and Wales, South Wales, Vol. XVIII, London 1815.
S.C. (JF) 1988.:	John Francis Sale Catalogues.
Steegman Portraits:	A Survey of Portraits in Welsh Houses, Vol. II, J. Steegman, Cardiff 1962.
Taylor's Cussion:	George Owen, the Taylor's Cussion, London.
Thos. Lloyd, *Lost Houses*:	T. Lloyd, The Lost Houses of Wales, SAVE London 1986.
Timmins Nooks Pembs.:	Nooks & Corners of Pembrokeshire 1895. Timmins.
Trans. Cymmrodor.:	Transactions of the Honourable Society of Cymmrodorion.
V.L.:	Voter's Lists.
W.W.H.R.:	West Wales Historical Records.

ALLENBROOK. *Dale.*

An interesting 19th century residence in attractive grounds. One part of it was the former vicarage which, with attached houses, has been transformed into a commodious dwelling. It contains a portrait, said to be by Gainsborough, of John Hook Campbell of Bangeston, Lord Lyon King of Arms. Home of Lt. Col. G. B. A. Rind, High Sheriff in 1935, and of his son B. H. G. Rind, High Sheriff in 1966.

ALLESTON. *St. Michael's Pembroke.*

In 1382 it was known as Aylwardiston, which developed into the present form. During the first half of the 17th century it was the home of the Webb family, and in 1640 was held by the brothers Thomas, Richard and Alexander Webb. The original owner was Sir John Carew of Crowcombe Court, Somerset, and in 1605 Edward Webb agreed to surrender a lease on the property to Sir John, but with the right to occupy it till 1608, to preserve deer in the park, to kill two bucks, and to leave '400 sheep with 40 other cattle' to Sir John. Thereafter it was owned by various families such as Davies and Poyer, and in 1904 by the Owens of Withybush, and let to farming tenants.

Refs: B. G. Charles, *Non-Celtic Place-Names in Wales,* p. 24; Rees, *Map of 14th century Pembs.; Land Tax 1786,* and subsequent *Voters' Lists.*

ALLTREINY
– *see* PENRALLTRHEINY

AMROTH CASTLE/EARWERE.
Amroth.

On a low meadow near the sea-shore. The original name Earwere may be derived from a Scandinavian word 'eyrr' denoting a sand or gravel bank. Although superseded about 1800 by the name Amroth Castle, the older name is still used locally, pronounced 'eah-weah'. Seat of the Elliots, from about 1445 it continued in that family for nearly three and a half centuries. They also had residences at Plâs (Narberth), Westerton and Kiffig, the estate lying in the parishes of Amroth, St. Issels, Crunwere, Robeston, Ludchurch and Narberth. In 1597 the herald Dwnn recorded the family pedigree and arms, *argent a fess gules, two bars wavy azure.* In 1670 Earwere contained five hearths. They provided the county with High Sheriffs in 1585, 1609 and 1754. The last of the family, Alexander Elliot, died at Earwere of the gout in 1756. By his wife Elizabeth (widow of Joseph Walter of Rosemarket and Roch, and daughter of John Barlow of Lawrenny) he had no issue. Elizabeth died before 1780, and Earwere became the property of her sister, Mrs. Catherine Owen who was still living at the mansion in 1791. Before 1798 it had been sold to James Acland who built a castellated residence at Earwere, to be named Amroth Castle, which is, substantially, still standing there. Ownership changed a few times during the 19th century, and by 1852 had been converted into a Lunatic Asylum by Dr. Norton, the then owner. In 1897 Amroth Castle was advertised for sale and was bought by Sir Owen Cosby Philipps (created Lord Kylsant in 1923). It remained in the ownership of his descendants until quite recently.

Refs: *Dwnn,* i, pp. 122, 154, 204: Fenton, *Pembs.* 1811; Lewis *TDW* 1840; F. P. Gwynne, *Sketches,* edn 1852; B. G. Charles *NCPN,* p. 91; NLW, Probate Wills; *RCAM Pembs* 1925; Carm. R.O. *Llanstephan docts.* Sale 1897. illstr: Roscoe Howells, *Old Saundersfoot,* 1977, Cat. illustr; *Pembs R.O.,* Deeds *D/LJ, 598* and also Carmarthen deeds in Pembs R.O.

ANGLE, The Hall of.
Just SE of Angle village.

Fenton recorded a local legend that three co-heiresses decided each to build a residence at Angle: one built a castle, the other 'a very handsome building' in the village, and the third built 'a mansion a little way out of the village, to the south-east called the Hall which appears in its day to have been very respectable and belonged till of late years to a family of the name of Kinnar, a name that still exists in the village.' (A similar tale is told of Trefolyne, *vide infra*). The Kinners were engaged in trade and farming at Angle and Haverfordwest, and intermarried with families like the Voyles, and Walter of Roch. In 1587 Sir John Perrot was lord of 'the manor of Hall place in Nangle'. The herald, Dwnn, in 1613 recorded the pedigree of 'William Kiner off the Hawl off Angel'. The family continued at the hall for nearly two more centuries; John Kinner was assessed at four hearths in the Hall in 1670; and William Kinner was mayor of Pembroke in 1703. The house is described in 1739 as 'The Hall alias Court House in Angle'. In 1786 William Kinner was owner-occupier of Hall lands while John Hook Campbell owned a part of the same lands. Early in the 19th century the Hall was purchased by John Mirehouse of Brownslade, and became the main seat of that family. Notably an 'improving landlord' and an enterprising farmer, the new owner was also a J.P., and in 1810 High Sheriff. He improved the Hall as a residence which his descendants still occupy. The Tithe Schedule 1841 describes John Mirehouse as owner of 'Hall Manor', with George Thomas as farming tenant there, one of the fields being known as 'Kiners meadow'. R. W. B. Mirehouse of the Hall was High Sheriff in 1886, owning an estate of 3,450 acres.

Refs: *Dwnn*, i, 109; *Taylors Cussion* fo 98; *Picton Castle Deeds; Cawdor Muniments; Arch. Cam.* 1868, 75; 1877, 311; 1880, 342 (illustr); *Anc Mon Pembs*, 9-10; Steegman, *Portraits (S. Wales)*, 175.

ANASTASLADE. *(now Slade) St. Martins Haverfordwest.*

Now an area between St. Davids Road and Crowhill Road, on the northern skirts of Haverfordwest. In old deeds it is given as Aunsellsland, Ancellislade, Anastaslade, from 1324 to the 17th century, and according to Dr. Charles it was originally 'Ansel's slade' named after the occupier. Colby's map of 1831 shows three farms named Slade and a fouth named Lower Slade, in the area where Slade farm still survives. It was the home of the gentry family of Morgan, the first being

Anthony Morgan of Answerslad, who was followed there by his son Rees Morgan, Esquire, who had married, before 1556, Thomasin Sutton of Haverfordwest. Their son Harry Morgan was living at Hoaton in Roose in 1578. One of the farms was occupied in 1578 by Roger Marcroft described as 'of Ansterslade, gentleman alias mercer.' In 1610-1613 James ap Rice (Price) gentleman, lived there, being followed in 1621 by his son Thomas Price of Anteslade, gentlemen.

In the next century 'Slade otherwise Little Slade otherwise Anastaslade' became the property of Daniel Evans of Peterwell (Cards), and in 1722 was given to his daughter Sarah who had married Marmaduke Gwynne of Garth (Brec). A deed of 1754 mentions the messuage called Great Slade.

Refs: *Pembs Public Records*, vols I and II; *RCAM Pembs*, 309; *Slebech Deeds; Picton Castle Deeds*: NLW, *Papers of Great Sessions, Pembs*; Partition of the Peterwell estate 1722, document loaned to me by the late Major H. Lloyd-Johns.

ANNIKELL. *Steynton.*

A short distance NE from Tiers Cross, and near the road leading to Merlins Bridge and Haverfordwest, now a farmhouse. There are references to the place as early as 1326, but little is known about it, and by the 17th century it formed part of the Picton Castle estate. Lawrence Hore, husbandman, was living at Annikell in 1628. It was later tenanted by the Stokes family. There was a spring on the land, but in 1664 Nicholas Stokes husbandman failed to clear and scour the ditch so the water did not have a free passage to Necell, which led to his appearance in the Court of Great Sessions. By 1670 the Elliots came there and later had a lease from Picton Castle, but this was surrendered to Sir Richard Philipps in the 1760s, and the family moved to St. Botolphs. Annikell was later held by farming tenants.

Refs: *Picton Castle Deeds*; NLW, *Probate Wills.*

ARGOED. *Nevern.*

Now a farmstead, between Wenallt and Pentre Ifan. These are the words of George Owen of Henllys, written in 1603 , 'Argoed, the mansion house of John Bowen ychan, gentleman, beinge a house of long contynuance ... this and much other landes was the portion of Owen vychan sonne to Llewelyn ap Owen [of Pentre Ifan], who had yssue Howell ap Owen ychan, which Howell had two sonnes, Thomas and Llewelyn, between whom he parted his inheritaunce, geaving Argoed and diverse landes with the same to Thomas; and to Llewelyn he gave Trefcoyged and diverse other tenementes neere hande. Thomas of Argoed had yssue James Thomas ap Howell, father to Rees, Gruffith, and Matheas. Rees sould Argoed to Mathaes his younger brother, who, by his will devysed the same to John Bowen ychan who now enjoyeth it ... the armes of the said John Bowen ychan are those of Pentre Ievan with the difference of a fowrthe brother descended of a third. The arms of the yssue of the said Owen vychan is also that of Pentre Ievan.' Over two centuries later, Richard Fenton of Glyn-y-mel reflected, 'Nevern Argoed now sunk to a farm-house, but once the residence of one of the four sons of Llewhellin ap Owen, a wide-spreading branch of the Gwynfardd tree, but long since decayed.' John Bowen ychan who inherited Argoed from Mathias James, married Elizabeth daughter of Owen ap Rhys of Towyn (in Ferwig) but had no issue. He died in 1605, his wife *circa* 1614. His brother Morgan Bowen followed him but the line petered out. In 1634 Elizabeth, daughter of William Bowen of Argoed and widow of George Lloyd of Cwmgloyn lived there and by 1642 Rees Young, gentleman, lived at Argoed, and by 1652 was in the hands of Elizabeth Jones, widow. Thereafter it became a farmstead.

Refs: *George Owen 2nd Book*, 1603-4, p. 275; *Fenton Tour Pembs* 1811; *Land Tax List 1786*; *Golden Grove Ms.* (Gwynfardd); *College of Arms, Protheroe Ms.IV*; *NLW, Pembs Plea Rolls, Bronwydd Deeds*; *Dwnn*, i, 166, 169, 170; *BM Egerton Ms 2586*.

ARNOLDSHILL. *Slebech.*

A farmstead some four miles East of Haverfordwest between Deep Lake and Slebech (new) church.

It once comprised various holdings. From 1331 onwards it was described as Arnolds Hill, doubtless preserving the name of the first or early owner. In 1419 Sir John Wogan owned 1¼ carucates 'in Arnoldshille'; in 1472 it belonged to Philip Alexander, and by 1501 was owned by Rogers of Pentypark, and Stephens. In 1526 Philip Stephen leased 'the manor of Arnoldshill in the barony of Dungleddy' and other properties to Hugh Mansel gentleman and his wife Jane (Wogan) for 60 years.

By 1532 John Husband was in possession, and in that year he mortgaged 'the capital messuage' to the Wogans; seven years later John Wogan of Wiston granted 'the capital messuage of Arnoldeshyle' to his son and heir Richard Wogan and his wife Elizabeth, and in 1577 sold that property and seven other farms to John Barbour of Slebech for £600. Thereafter Arnolds Hill formed part of the Slebech estate whose owners leased it to a series of yeomen – John Tooley from 1619 to 1658 when John Bell who had settled there was assessed for seven hearths in 1670 which shows Arnoldshill to have been commodious. Walter Thornborough, an attorney, tenanted it in 1705, but by 1715 it was leased to a yeoman, George Barzey, whose descendants were granted renewable leases. The Barzeys had lived from 1692 to 1810 at Lecha in Dewsland (vide infra), the last male of the family, Richard, son of Thomas Barzey of Arnoldshill, died there suddenly on 12 February 1814. Afterwards various tenants held the property. Eventually it became property of the De Rutzen family, still owned by descendants.

In 1921 Arnolds Hill farm comprised 265 acres, the dwelling house contained parlour, dining room, two kitchens, larder, pantry, dairy, seven bedrooms, two attics, cellar and outbuildings. I visited the house in 1976: it was a cross-passage house of two storeys and an attic storey: a square house, large chimney at each end, a 'simne fawr' has been closed in: a short wing extends at one end now arranged as dairy and store-room; below the whole is an arched cellar or undercroft built above a rocky outcrop: an extension, 'catslide', now houses a kitchen and dining-room, with a porch entrance: there are some stone corbels supporting oak beams: the main entrance door leads into a hallway: the parlour has an ornamental frieze, probably an 18th century decoration: fine old range of outbuildings and a coach-house with the date 1832 carved on a stone above the entrance: in the farmyard is a well with remains of a cupola, the whole walled: remains of a walled garden and orchards: remains of an avenue of trees and a drive from the house to main road: the house stands on high land, good southward view.

Refs: NLW, *Slebech Deeds*; *Carms R.O. Sale Cat.* No. 460; *WWHR*, vi; *Owen Pembs.* vols II and III.

ASHESTON (TREFASSER).
A large farm in Brawdy parish.
Mentioned in 1326 as Assepiston (Asseriston). From Elizabethan days until the late 18th century it formed part of the estate of the Laugharne family. Described as Treffasser in 1580, as Asheston alias Trevasser in 1632. Among the tenants were Edward Philpin (1630), John Bateman, Thomas Evan and John Charles in 1842. The owner, John Philipps Laugharne of Orlandon, mortgaged Asheston in £600 to Henry John, gentlemen, of Caerwen in 1787; in 1795 the said John Philipps Laugharne and Lettice, widow of the said Henry John, conveyed Asheston to Thomas Raymond, gentleman and in the following year Raymond leased Asheston to Thomas Evan, farmer, and in 1845 he conveyed Asheston to Henry and Anne Harries and William Rees. It was later sold to the Perkins family. The original dwelling house now forms part of the farm outbuildings, and the present dwelling house is of 19th century construction.

AVELLANAU. *Parish of St. Thomas, Haverfordwest, in the outskirts of the town.*
A large, attractive residence, with a pillared porch, built in 1845 by William Evans, solicitor of Haverfordwest, represented today by Mr. James Eaton Evans, the fifth of successive solicitors of the family. Later in the present century it became property of the County Council and until recently was a children's home. The *Western Telegraph*, 13 April 1988, has photographs of the house in 1870-71 and 1949.

Rutzen

BACHENDRE. *In the chapelry of Capel Colman in the parish of Llanfihangel Penbedw.*
Philip Morris, settled at Bachendre in 1650, is said to have been descended from Jenkin Llwyd 'o Cemaes'. John Morris of Bachendre made his will in 1774, and died not long after, leaving an only son Thomas Morris and three daughters, Mary who had married Griffith Jenkins of Cilbronnau (Cards), Elizabeth who had married William Harries of Castlebythe, and Anne Morris, spinster. Anne his widow was living in 1786. The son Thomas bought Trefigin in Monnington parish about 1802 and went to live there. Thereafter Bachendre was let to farmers, and later sold.

Refs: *NLW Pembs Gaol Files,* Great Sessions; *Carms RO, J. Francis Collection* deeds; parish *Tithe Map and Schedule 1849; Pembs RO Land Tax 1786.*

BANGESTON. *Angle.*
The mansion stood about a mile to the east of the village (NB. There are three other places bearing this name – a residence north of Pembroke town, and two farms – south-west of Cheriton and north-east of Kilgetty). It was named after an early owner 'Benger's tun', and families named Beneger are recorded in South Pembrokeshire between 1272 and 1342.

The earliest known family at Bangeston is that of Dawes (first found in the county in 1437), who held the property for six generations. Dwnn called there in 1591 and recorded the family pedigree. Griffith Dawes died in 1592 leaving four children. One, Griffith Dawes, was High Sheriff in 1665, Mayor of Pembroke in 1672 and in 1689, died in 1694 and was buried in Angle church where his memorial is decorated by his coat of arms, *or a fesse dansette ermine between 3 daws proper*. His only child and heiress, Phoebe, married Griffith White of Henllan, and had an only daughter, Elizabeth, last descendant of the family to live at Bangeston. She married four times – Thomas Lort of Eastmoor (died 1687), Richard, Viscount Bulkeley of Anglesey (died 1704), Brigadier Thomas Ferrers (died 1722), and John Hooke. Elizabeth died in 1736, aged 76, and the Bangeston estate passed to her fourth husband who died in 1757, leaving his wife's estate to John Campbell, a younger son of Stackpole Court, Lord Lyon King of Arms, on condition that he took the name and arms of Hooke. The legatee did so and for a time was called John Campbell Hooke, which he later changed to Hooke-Campbell. In 1786 the Lord Lyon sold the Bangeston estate for £52,318 to his nephew John Campbell (later created Lord Cawdor), who sold Bangeston and other properties to his agent John Mirehouse of Brownslade, and it remained in possession of that family down to our times. The old mansion had been improved prior to 1720 by the heiress Elizabeth and her husband Thomas Ferrers, but before the end of the eighteenth century had been abandoned and became ruinous. *Fenton* described it in 1810 as a 'mere shell of a mansion lately remembered as the seat of hospitality, and one of the first of note in Pembrokeshire'. *Timmins* in 1895 wrote, 'Bangeston House proves to be nothing more than the gaunt, dismantled walls of a vast group of buildings'. It is also described by Mrs. M. B. Mirehouse of the Hall of Angle in her book published in 1910.

Refs: *Dwnn*, i, 128, 130: *Fenton, Pembs*, 1811; Timmins, *Nooks and Corners of Pembs*, 1895; *RCAM* 1925; M. B. Mirehouse, *South Pembs*, 1910; *Carms RO, Cawdor Collection; Tithe Map and Schedule* 1841.

BANGESTON. *St. Mary Pembroke.*

The three-storeyed mansion stands to the north of Pembroke town. An 18th century residence, used today as a home for the aged, and, according to the matron, is haunted, and in 1982 she cited some lively occurrences. Described as a yeoman, the first dweller at Bangeston was Morgan Ap Powell (descended from Gwynfardd Dyfed) who had emigrated from north Pembrokeshire where a local plague had broken out. He was living at Bangeston in 1520-21, from which he moved to the town of Pembroke. His descendants continued to live at Bangeston. Lewis Powell and his son Morgan were there in 1578, and the latter moved to nearby Greenhill. It was later owned by the Laugharne family and in 1684 Thomas Laugharne lived there. By 1722 it had been purchased by the Colby family, and in that year was occupied by Lawrence Colby, High Sheriff, and three years later Mayor of Pembroke. The Stokes family were there from 1699 to 1708, for a period, when it reverted to the Colbys. By 1786 it had been sold to Sir Hugh Owen of Orielton. In 1873 the owner was Thomas Meyrick of Bush who lived here after Bush burnt down in 1866. On 20th century maps it is called Bangeston Hall.

Refs: *NLW Bronwydd Deeds, Cwrtmawr Deeds; Pembs RO, LT 1786; Western Telegraph* 22 July 1982 (illustr.).

BARNARDS WELL. *Henrys Moat.*

Now a farm about a mile to the east of the village, on the southern slope of Bernards Well Mountain. The name is said to derive from Brynach. Nearby is Barnards Well near the ruins of an old chapel dedicated to St. Brynach. Among the early owners of the property were the Warlows, and in 1290 it was the home of David Warlagh, who may have been an ancestor of Janet Warlow who married David Gwilym Rees of Llanfairnantygof *circa* 1450. In 1595 George Owen Lord of Cemaes confirmed the right of Owen Jones of Trecwn to 'a capital messuage called Burnaghswill in Harryesmote' parish', and it remained with Owen Jones' descendants to the beginning of this century. The property was divided into two farms, *Ucha* and *Issa*. A rental of the Trecwn estate in 1839 includes Barnardswell-Ucha (230 acres) and Issa (193 acres). From the Joneses of Trecwn, the estate passed through successive heiresses to the families of Vaughan and Barham.

Refs: *PRO, AD, D4057; NLW Bronwydd Deeds; RCAM, Pembs.* 1925; *B. M. Egerton Ms 2586*; Francis Jones, *Holy Wells of Wales,* 1954, p. 203.

BEGELLY HOUSE *Begelly*.

On high ground above Begelly church. Home of a number of yeomen in the 16th century, the house was remodelled later to suit more affluent days. It is now a guest house. The history of the Child family illustrates the rise of yeomen, finally to become leading county landowners. The first member of the family at Begelly, Owen Child, lived there during the years 1540-1569. In the following century they were described as gentlemen, and in 1670 their Begelly home was assessed at four hearths. In 1725 John Child was High Sheriff, thereafter his descendants were described as esquires, and it was during the 18th century that the house assumed its present form. The last of the family, which had been there for some 340 years, was James Mark Philipps Child, Captain in the Royal Pembrokeshire Rifle Corps. who died without issue in 1877. Thereafter the property had several owners and after World War II the house was used as a preparatory school until its closure in 1969 when it was converted into flats.

The Childs family bore *gules a chevron ermine between three eagles proper,* with crest of *an eagle, wings expanded, a snake wrapped around its neck.* The present mansion, built in the first quarter of the 19th century, is a large square building of three storeys, a basement, and attics, but retains older features at the back.

Refs: *NLW, Papers of Great Sessions; PRO, Tay Subsidies* 1543 et seq; *Golden Grove ms; Picton Castle Deeds; Arch Cam,* Ser 2, vol iv, p. 115; Burke's *Commoners,* iii, 692 and *Landed Gentry* 1852; *Western Mail,* 16 August 1986 illustr.

BENTON CASTLE. *Burton.*

On a steep cliff above the western banks of the Cleddau. A small medieval castle which has been ruinous and deserted for many centuries. Little of its history is known. Like many such buildings it had its ghost as shown by the letter written on 22 December 1693 from Nicholas Roberts of St. Davids to Edward Llwyd – 'Benton Castle, formerly said to be haunted, upon which account seldom visited, where they say the Devil would often appear in the shape of a black mastiff dog, and sometimes lie by the fire, but mostly in a vault or cellar, to guard some hidden treasure there.'

The author, R. M. Lockley in *Pembrokeshire 1977,* p. 121, informs us that the castle 'was uninhabited from the time of its reduction by Cromwell until about 1930 when its reconstruction was undertaken by a genial hermit Ernest Pegge, who with his own hands lovingly rebuilt it, using the rock tumbled from its walls by time and Cromwellian cannons, and oak beams from the shipbreakers' yards at Milford Haven. Many a happy hour have I spent with Ernest Pegge, a surprising but sane man and contented as he worked in and about his castle in the lovely wooded estuary. He placed his own mark in concrete over the entrance to the renovated castle'. After World War II it was the home of the late Colonel J. A. Sulivan, High Sheriff of Dyfed in 1974. It is now occupied by his widow, Mrs. Sulivan.

Refs: *RCAM Pembs 1925* (illustr): *Arch Cam* 1865, p. 82.

BERLLAN. *Eglwyswrw.*

On the north side of Pencelei woodland, not far from Eglwyswrw village. A large well-preserved three-storeyed house of double-pile type. Behind it is a much older house (once attached to the larger by a wide passage) doubtless the original Berllan now occupied by a farmer. A number of families lived there in medieval days like the Jordans, but were comparatively short-lived. In the 16th century it became the home of William Owen a natural son of William Owen of Henllys (d.1574) who had bought the Lordship of Cemaes in 1543. William married

Alison daughter of Morgan Bowen of Tre-rickert, and had issue; six generations of the family dwelt there, the last being John Owen, High Sheriff in 1751. The Land Tax for 1786 names the owners as Mrs. Hay and Mrs. Price. Not long afterwards it became the residence of the Reverend David Griffith who had married Anne Bowen of Llwyngwair in 1781. He died in 1834, and his son George David Bowen Griffith succeeded as owner-occupier, being so described in 1838. It was later owned by the Lloyds of Bronwydd and is now owned by Mrs. Hawkesworth, a descendant of Bronwydd.

Refs: *WWHR*, ii, 90-1; *NLW, Vaerdre Book, Bronwydd Deeds, Cwrtmawr Deeds, Morgan-Richardson Deeds; Carms RO, Golden Grove Mss; Pembs RO, Deeds*.

BERRY/BURY. *Nevern.*

On a slope, north-west of Llwynygwair, overlooking the Nevern estuary, Newport, Carn Ingli, and the Preselly foothills. The commodious residence consists of two parts – the main portion is an early 19th century edifice, and to the rear extends a much older wing now used as a farmhouse. In the period 1198-1230 part of the land was granted to the Knights Hospitallers of St. John. The name occurs as Bury during the next three centuries. The tract of Bury formed the demesne of Newport Castle, and in 1523 John Tuckett, Lord of Audley, and Lord of Cemaes, leased part of the land to two yeomen. By 1631 Berry (so called) was the home of George Owen (son of Alban Owen of Henllys, Lord of Cemaes) whose daughter Bridget married Alexander Ford. Their son, Owen Ford of Berry who was assessed at three hearths in 1670, married Anne Barlow of Minwere, and died in 1704 leaving two daughters, co-heiresses, Joan who married William Lloyd of Henllys and Penpedwast and Bridget who married William Gower of Glandoran. In 1731 William Lloyd leased land at Berry 'with a warren and a salmon weir' there, to Evan Rees yeoman and Thomas Lewis gentleman.

In 1786 Berry was owned by George Bowen Esq., of Llwyngwair, described as owner-occupier. He was followed by his son-in-law, the Reverend David Griffith of Berllan, Vicar of Nevern, who died in 1834 leaving the property to his son George David Griffiths Esq. who was still living there in 1854. Mr. Griffith wrote to his daughter Eliza Ann on 10 March 1810 that 'Berry Hill is about to be completed', referring to the main block then being erected. After 1854 the property was alienated.

Refs: *NLW, Bronwydd Deeds, Poyston Deeds, Llwyngwair Collection, Slebech Deeds; Pembs RO Land Tax List 1786; Fenton, Tour Pembs 1811; Pembs Arch Survey Map (1896); Country Quest*, June 1967, contains a photograph of Berry Hill.

BICTON *St. Ishmaels.*

Now a farm between St. Ishmael's village and Sandy Haven. Described as 'terra de Bike-tunia' in 1242, and 'Birkton in Ros' in 1421, John Picton Esq. in 1422 granted to Thomas Perrot and Alice his wife (daughter of grantor) all his messuages, lands, and rents in Bikton at a yearly rent of two greyhounds; the deed has a beautiful seal showing the canting arms of Picton – *three fishes (pikes) in fesse*. The first owner of which I have knowledge is Thomas Lloyd, Esq., of Cilgilynen, who leased for 21 years a messuage and fields of Bicton, to a yeoman, John Roch, who assigned the lease to his son John in 1631. Afterwards the father bought the property and on his death in 1663 left it to his son William. William Roch died in 1689 and left Bicton to his son Nicholas Roch, a draper of Haverfordwest. In 1694 William Allen of Gelliswick brought a Chancery suit to oust Nicholas Roch from Bicton. Seemingly he succeeded, for in the Land tax of 1786 Joshua Allen Esq. is shown as owner of Bicton, with Mr. John Morgans as tenant, and it remained part of the Allen estate down to the present century. In 1915 William Bird Allen of Bicton, grandson of Joshua Julian Allen of Bicton, was High Sheriff, and the same office was filled by Herbert Charles Gordon Allen of Bicton, and of Cwm, Saundersfoot. It is now a farmhouse.

Refs: *Burke's, L. G. 1850* contains a pedigree of the Allens; *PRO, AO*, iii 1723; *Eaton Evans and Williams Deeds; Voters Lists* 1834 et seq.

BIERS POOL. *Near Pembroke Dock.*

On the west banks of Llanion Pill, and just north of Llanion farm – *Colby Map 1831*. 'At Bierspool another farmstead, dating back to a very early period, stands intact'. According to an ancient map this district was in bygone times known as Bayard's Pool. In the grounds of the farm, still to be seen is an old ruined dovecote or pigeon-loft built of limestone, a piece of ancient masonry, but how far back it dates is not known. The earliest occupants within living memory, of the old farmhouse were called Dawkins, and were near relations of the late Mr. William Dawkins of Albion House' – Mrs. Stuart Peters, *History of Pembroke Dock,* 1905, p.4.

BISHOPS' PALACES.

Former residences of the Bishops of St. Davids in medieval times, namely St. Davids, Trevine, Lamphey and Llawhaden (castle). Most were built in Norman and later times, but by today they are all in ruins. Numerous references occur to them in manuscript and printed records, and on maps such as Speed, while they feature in many 18th and early 19th century engravings such as those by Sandby, Gastineau, Sheppard, Wallis, etc.

BLACKALDERN.

About half a mile south-east of Narberth.

Formerly a farmhouse at a place where alder trees grew. In deeds of 1609 it is described as Black Alderne and Black Aldren. It formed part of the estate of the Barlows of Slebech in 1705, but in 1786 its owner was Lord Kensington. During the 19th century a residence was raised near the farmhouse which was tenanted by farmers. In 1858 it was the home of William Gwynne Esq. and afterwards was the seat of a branch of the family of Allen of Cresselly.

Refs: *NLW Bronwydd Deeds; Pembs RO, Deeds DX/148, No. 36; Eaton Evans and Williams Deeds.*

BLAENBYLAN. *Clydey.*

In the northern part of the parish about one and a quarter miles south-west of Ffynnonau. Blaenbylan was part of an estate in north-west Pembrokeshire, and the home of the Morgan family from Elizabethan days to 1768 when it was sold and ceased to be a gentry residence having become ruinous. The first of the family to settle at Blaenbylan was Morgan ap Howel descended from Ednyfed Fychan of Gwynedd whose arms the family bore. Morgan died before 1597. The eighth in descent, Maurice Morgan, was the last of the line to own the property, and in 1768 it was sold.

The house, already ruinous, deteriorated, was finally dismantled, and today no trace of it remains. Maurice Morgan went to London, had a distinguished career, and died there, unmarried, in 1802. Fenton wrote in 1810 – 'Blaenbylan, the inhabited residence within these 60 or 70 years of a most respectable family of the name of Morgan whose possessions in this county were very extensive. The House situated in the most objectionable part of the demesne, was meanly and irregularly built as to its exterior, and within consisted of several small, low, and dismally dark rooms, the whole quite disproportionate to the fortune and rank of the former inhabitants, and the style of architecture even in those days ... The last two of the name, sons of that house, William Morgan and Maurice Morgan, Esquires, I had the pleasure of being well acquainted with ...' When I called there in December 1974 I found that the site and environment in no way justified Fenton's strictures. The farmhouse, built in the 18th century, consisted of a structure of two storeys, with a range of five windows, and on the ground floor an entrance leading to the 'best' part of the house, and other leading to the kitchen and domestic offices. It comprises some 195 acres.

Refs: for a detailed account see Francis Jones's essay in *Ceredigion,* 1976, pp. 307-331; Fenton, *Tour Pembs,* 1811; Rees, *Beauties of South Wales,* 1815.

BLAEN MWRW. *Manordeifi.*

A farm east of Newchapel and south of Pentre. Home of Thomas Jones, illegitimate son of John Morgan of Blaenbylan. He married Elizabeth, daughter of John Harry Lloyd, a descendant of Gwynfardd Dyfed. She was a widow when she made her will on 10 February 1714-15. The son Samuel Jones inherited Blaenmwrw where he was still living in 1727 with his wife Margaret John of Brongwyn, Cards. He had three sisters, but it is not known whether he had any issue.

Refs: *Golden Grove Ms*, vol iv (Ednyfed Fychan); *Carm RO, J. Francis Deeds.*

BLAEN TÂF. *Llanfyrnach.*

This ancient mansion has disappeared without trace. It is marked as Blaen Tâf on the O.S. maps of Mudge (1819) and Colby (1831), and on the Tithe map (1838) as 'Old Blaentaf Cottage', part of Nantydd Ucha farm. It stood on the slope of a small dingle on the south bank of the upper waters of Afon Tâf. Home of a younger son of the Philipps family of Cilsant, and his descendants from 1540 to 1690. Their names appear in six Lay Subsidy Lists between 1543 and 1670, several being Justices of the Peace. By the end of the 17th century the family had slid down the scale, and by 1670 when John Philipps lived at Blaen Tâf, his brother David Philipps farmed at Penrhiw (in 1685) and his sisters Ursula and Margaret, respectively had married James John a fiddler, and John Thomas James of Lletty ffwlbert, farmer. After this, Blaen Tâf was let to farmers, and became part of the estate of the Lloyds of Cilrewe and Bronwydd. In 1750 Rees David of 'Blantafe' was churchwarden and overseer of the parish, and in 1776 Martha Phillips of Blaen Tâf was a petty constable of the parish, a somewhat formidable lady. In time the acreage of Blaen Tâf was reduced and became absorbed into the neighbouring farms, chiefly nearby Nantydd Ucha. The old house was later destroyed. In 1904 only a cottage remained. The Whitland-Cardigan railway passed close to it. Local tradition states that beneath the garden soil 'the ground is paved like a courtyard'.

Refs: *Dwnn*, i, 171; *NLW, Bronwydd Deeds and Mss, Vaerdre Book, Extent of Cemaes, Carms RO Golden Grove Mss;* G. Owen *Second Book,* 282.

BLAIDDBWLL. *(e.p. Bribwll). Llanfyrnach.*

The property is in the eastern part of the parish, bordered by Afon Tâf. The earliest residence, among trees below the farmyard was replaced in 1898 by a modern farmhouse erected to the north of the original buildings. Some remains of the older house have survived. During the Middle Ages it was home of the eminent landowner, Jenkin Lloyd of Cemaes, descended from Gwynfardd Dyfed, who bore the arms *azure a lion rampant within an orle of roses or.* A later descendant at Blaidbwll changed the colour of the roses from *or* to *argent* to denote his adherence to the House of York. The last male of this family, John ap Owen, died a few years before 1570, leaving an only child, Joan heiress of Blaiddbwll, and as she had no issue she left the property to her third cousin, Robert Morris, whose son Philip Robert Morris sold it to Eynon Philipps of Cardigan shortly before 1589. That worthy's grandson, Thomas Philipps, sold Blaiddbwll, then comprising six farms, four tofts, two mills, and 354 acres, to Reynald Morris a local landowner, whose descendants bore the surname Reynolds. The house was assessed for three hearths in 1670. The last male of the family, John Reynolds, died unmarried in 1741 leaving Blaiddbwll to John Parr, son of deceased's sister Sarah Reynolds who had married Thomas Parr of Haverfordwest. John Parr died without issue in 1811, aged 88. In that year Fenton wrote 'I pass by an ancient place called erroneously Bribwll a very powerful man of his time Jenkin Lloyd of Cemaes; having, though long deserted as a residence of a man of fortune, all the remains of ancient consequence from the venerable growth that surrounds it; amongst which I observed two or three remarkably large, sweet chestnuts, always a distinguishing appendage of a great man's residence, it being a tree not commonly cultivated. The demesne appears to be very extensive, and to consist of land of the best quality.' John Parr (died 1811) devised Blaiddbwll to his sister's great-grandson, the Hon. William Henry Yelverton, son of Viscount Avonmore. It remained in that family until 1888 when W. H. M. Yelverton of Whitland Abbey sold the property then consisting of the farms of Blaiddbwll, Blaiddbwll Mill, Troyan, Bryneithin, Penlanfach Ucha, Pantybigny, Plâs y bailey alias Fron Lebon, and a rent charge payable by the Whitland and Cardigan Railway, to John Nicholas, gentleman, of Graig, for £12,400. It is still owned and occupied by John Nicholas's descendants, the Harries family (of Fron).

Refs: *Dwnn*, i, 217; *NLW Mss* 12045 and 12356, George Owen *Second Book* (1603-4) 282; *Tithe Map* Llanfyrnach 1838; *B. M Egerton Ms* 2586; Fenton, *Tour Pembs* (1811); *Carms RO*, Trant/Yelverton Deeds; Francis Jones 'The Families of Blaiddbwll'; *NLW Journal, Summer 1981,* and refs. there.

BLETHERSTON. *Bletherston.*

A large farmstead on the outskirts of the village of Bletherston in the south-west of the parish. The name derives from Bletheri, Blethery, or Bledri, and is known to the Welsh as Trefelen, and is described in 1700 as 'Bledheston or Trevelen'. The earliest family there were the Colbys, who owned it from 1597 to 1786 (and later). In 16th and 17th century deeds they are described as yeomen, later as gentlemen, and in the 18th century blossomed forth as esquires. Younger branches were established at Grondre, Bangeston near Pembroke, and finally Rhosygilwen, Ffynnone, and Pantyderi. The farmstead was described as 'the capital messuage called ye Great House' in 1681 and 1707. It was assessed at three hearths in 1670. In 1786 John Colby, Esquire, was the owner-occupier. Several Colbys held public offices – High Constables of Dungleddy Hundred in 1617, 1623, 1664 and High Sheriffs of the county in 1722, 1770, 1807, 1838, and 1891. The last in the male line, Major John Vaughan Colby of Ffynnone

and the Grenadier Guards, was killed in action in October 1914.

Refs: *Charles, NCPN; NLW, Owen and Colby Estate Deeds, St. David's Episcopal Records, Poyston Deeds, Eaton Evans and Williams Deeds; Carms RO, Golden Grove Mss.*

BOLTON HILL. *Steynton.*

To the north-west of Johnston village. Described as Bolton 1380, Bulton Hill 1515, Bulton 1556, Bowlton Hall 1597, and Boulton Hill 1665. Malkin in 1804 called the house 'an agreeable residence'. In the 18th century, this large property was divided into four farms, all called Bolton Hill. The family of Bolton were in the district in 1324. Philip de Bolton held courts as Steward in Haverfordwest in 1376-78. His son Philip de Bolton junior, was outlawed in 1385 for the manslaughter of Howel ap Griffiths of Llandisilio.

Thomas Bolton (1515-1538) was succeeded by his son David Bolton to whom Sir Gilbert Dethick, Garter King at Arms, granted the following arms on 1 July 1556: *argent on a bend gules 3 leopard faces argent, between 2 fleurs de lys azure; crest, a fawn's head and neck parted per pale indented argent and azure, in its mouth a broad arrow or feathered argent, point downwards.*

In 1670 John Bolton of Bolton Hill was assessed at five hearths. Nine generations of the family lived there until 1740, after which the family became extinct, and the property was sold. In 1760 Essex Devereux Jones, apothecary, is described as of Bolton Hill. In 1786 the four farms called Bolton Hill, and Bolton Hill Mill, were owned by Lord Kensington. An episode in the family history was recorded by S. Lewis in 1840 as follows – 'Bolton Hill an ancient seat formerly belonging to a family of that name, is situated in the northern part of the parish, near an abrupt and lofty eminence called Bolton Beacon. While Cromwell lay at Haverfordwest, two of his soldiers entered this mansion with the intention of plundering it, and Bolton, who had concealed himself, was denied by his wife to the soldiers, who nevertheless, suspecting that he was in the house, one of them took up his child and pretended to throw it on the fire, on which the father rushed from his concealment, and killed the ruffian on the spot; his comrade escaped, and Bolton on reflection deemed it prudent to inform Cromwell of all that had occurred, observing to that General, that the man he had killed had only one eye; the latter replied 'the fellow was a great rascal and you have saved me the trouble of having him executed.'

Refs: *Dwnn*, i, 121, 133; *Pembs Plea Rolls*, 1625, 1665, 1691, 1705; *Picton Castle Deeds*; *NLW, Crosswood Pedigrees* 139A; *PRO Anc. Deeds*, nos. 1079, 4659; *Hare Ms.* 1359; Oxford, *Queen's College Ms 39*.

BONVILLE'S COURT. *St. Issells.*

The old historic residence stood a short distance north-west of Saundersfoot, in what became a coal-mining area; about 600 yards from the above, a modern house, also called Bonvilles's Court, was erected in the 19th century on high ground near the roadway. Both residences are marked on Colby's Map, 1831. The name is derived from the surname Bonville, known in south Pembrokeshire since 1274.

The earliest known owner of the mansion was William ap David who was living there in the 16th century; his eldest son, John Williams, married Ann Bowen of Trefloyne, Penally, by whom he had five daughters, coheiresses. We are told by a contemporary that the eldest co-heiress, Eleanor Williams 'hadd all the Landes assryd her by her father, and the other [sisters] hadd money', and when she married William Jones from Brynygroes near Llanelly, he came to live at his wife's home, Bonville's Court. Both parents and their nine children were living in 1591 when the herald Dwnn called there and recorded the family pedigree which William Jones duly signed. He bore the coat-of-arms of one of his ancestors, Gwynfardd Dyfed. Assessed at seven hearths in 1670. The family remained at Bonville's Court for over a hundred years more, the last being William Jones who died without issue in July 1690. His widow, Lettice Barlow from Creswell, was so deeply grieved, that in the following year she cut her throat with a knife and so died.

Bonville's Court then passed to William Jones's sister Catherine who had married James Philipps of Pentypark. She died in 1724, her husband in 1735 aged 90. Later, Bonville's Court became the property of James Child, described as owner in 1786, and by 1835 it was the residence of Hugh Bowen Mends. Fenton wrote in 1810 that the red mansion retained 'some small remains of a baronial appearance'; by 1861 it had become a 'fragment' with a ruined tower that gives its name to the colliery beside it'; in 1868 it was 'in a vaery neglected condition – the walls however are in tolerable sound condition'; and by 1895 only 'a single dilapidated tower and stair-turret remains'.

Refs: *BM Egerton Ms* 2586; *Dwnn*, i, 122-3; *Golden Grove Mss*; *NLW, Papers of Great Sessions*, 1691; *Crosswood Pedigrees* no. 139; *Picton Castle Deeds*; *Arch Cam* 1868, ilustr; *Pembs Archaeological Survey* 1896-1907; Peter Smith in *Carns Studies*, 1974; *W.W.H.R.*, ii, 76.

BOULSTON. *Boulston.*

An ancient mansion (now a ruin) on the north bank of the Cleddau some three miles below Haverfordwest. Former residence of the Wogans an old Welsh family descended from Gwgan ap Bleddyn of Breconshire whose name became the permanent patronymic of his Pembrokeshire descendants who settled in the county during the 12th century. The first-known occupant of Boulston was Henry Wogan, a younger son of Wiston, who settled there after his marriage to the daughter of Wilcocks Dyer of that place in the 1450s. The Wogans remained there until 1715, having filled the office of High Sheriff on nine occasions, providing a Member of Parliament, besides holding numerous local appointments. The estate was particularly extensive. Among illustrious visitors was the Duke of Beaufort and his retinue in 1684, on their return to Haverfordwest by boat from Picton Castle, 'in the cool of the evening having been well collationed on the way by (Lewis) Wogan Esquire, att the seat of Bolston.' The last of the line at Boulston was Anne Wogan (wife of John Laugharne of St. Brides) who died without issue in 1715 when the property passed to kinsfolk, Wogan of Gawdy Hall, Norfolk. Boulston was then abandoned as a residence.

In 1786 the owner was Elinor Wogan, the mansion being tenanted by Benjamin Phelps, and the home farm by George Morse. In 1797 it was sold by Admiral Sir Charles Cotton, Bart., to Major Dudley Acland, and as the mansion was then in ruins, he built a new residence on high ground to the north, which was named Boulston Manor (now the home of the Llewellin family). The old mansion was a large residence and in 1670 contained thirteen hearths. Part of it was of three storeys, and had large cellars as shown by the surving ruins. Memorials of the Wogans remain in Boulston church which show the family arms as *or, on a chief sable, three martlets or, with a crest of a cockatrice gules jalloped sable, crowned or* (to commemorate an exploit by a Wogan who is said to have slain the creature near Boulston). The surname persisted in the county down to the present century.

Refs: Francis Green in *Y Cymmrodor 1902*, pp. 100-149, illustr; *RCAM, 1925*, illustr; *College of Arms Ms. Fellowes, 1530, Banners (1510-25)* and *Protheroe Ms XII*; Laws, *Little England beyond Wales*, 1888, p 374 and *Sketch of ruins of Boulston*.

BOWOOD. *Castlemartin.*

Name and site lost. A pedigree shows descendants of John Warren of Trewern (1485-6) living at Bristol and at 'Bowood in Castlemartin', and were still at both places in 1638, Mathew Warren at the former and John Warren at the latter.

Refs: *College of Arms Ms, Wagner Ms 3 and 12* (in hand of George Owen, York Herald).

BRAWDY-BREUDETH. *Brawdy.*

Home of the family of Jones the old mansion a four-fronted edifice, stood on a slope immediately below the parish church, about a mile inland from the hamlet of Penycwm above St. Brides Bay. In the same parish also stood the early mansions of Castle Villa, Eweston, Llether, Newgale, and Rickeston. Brawdy was the house of landowning fami-

lies from medieval days. In 1670 it contained four hearths, and an inventory of 1704 mentions The White Chamber, Porch Chamber, Dark Chamber, Dining Room, Parlour, The Hall and kitchen. Two closed-in early windows in the southern gable showed that it had been a three-storeyed building, the upper storey having been removed about 1825. One room, now the parlour, retains its original oak panelling. An ancient arch connected the rear part of the house to the walled garden, the walls continuing in good state of preservation. One of the outbuildings bears the date 1740.

In 1796 Brawdy was let to a George Gwyther whose family bought the freehold in 1919, and whose descendant, Richard Gwyther, still farms there. About 1825 a large part of the dwelling-house was pulled down and the remainder adapted to farming usages. In 1921 a corn-drying kiln collapsed, formerly connected with the house by a gallery leading from a window on the first storey. One of the mansion walls is hollow, said to have been used to hold smuggled wines borne from the cove of Cwm Mawr, along the hidden dingle below Llether.

Brawdy remained in the blood of one family for 17 generations, covering some 530 years. The first known member of the family was David of Brawdy whose son Philip ap David was living there in the years 1400-1437, whose grandson Henry ap David ap Phillip had an only child, Alice sole heiress of Brawdy; who, about 1510, married Richard Jones a younger son of John ap Thomas of Treowen, Monm., and from the Treowen family the family of Herbert Earls of Pembroke descended. By this marriage, Brawdy passed to Richard Jones who died in 1546-7. His descendants improved the estate by marriage with daughters of landowning families – Warren of Trewern, Bowen of Upton Castle, Philipps of Woodstock, Stokes of Cuffern, Reynish of Camrose, Protheroe of Nantyrhebog and Lloyd of Wenallt (both in Carms). By 1600 the Brawdy estate consisted of 30 farms and 1,344 acres, an acreage maintained until 1800.

Dwnn recorded the family pedigree in 1613, duly signed by John Jones. The family filled numerous public offices – commissioners of Acts of Parliament, officers of Train Bands, Grand Jurors, High Constables of Dewsland, Justices of the Peace, a coroner, and two High Sheriffs. William Jones was Standard Bearer to Henry VIII. Cadet branches settled at Llether, Eweston, Grinston, Penbiri, Cruglas, Llangungar Fawr and Ludlow (Salop). Brawdy, Pointz Castle, and Trenarydd formed an episcopal manor of the Bishop of St. Davids, and Joneses of Brawdy were lords of the lay manor of Trefinent (*St. Davids*). The family bore the well-known arms, *per pale azure, and gules, 3 lions rampant, argent, with crest, a woman's head and breast affrontee; Motto Asgre lan diogle ei pherchen.*

Refs: *Dwnn*, i, 196; *PRO Anc Deeds* E210, ms 5173 and 9238; *RCAM Pembs*; deeds and family papers, *penes me*; R. J. H. Lloyd, *Trans Cymmr* 1956.

Editor's Note: Francis Jones was a direct descendant of the Joneses of Brawdy. His earliest memories were of his grandparents and parents telling him of the family's lineage and history. This kindled his life-long love of antiquity and genealogy.

BRIDELL (PLÂS). *Bridell.*

A mile and a quarter south-west of Cilgerran village, and standing just north-east of Bridell parish church. Very little is known of the old farmhouse called Bridell which became known as Plâs y Bridell in the 19th century. In 1786 the owner-occupier was Mary George, widow. On Colby's map of 1831 it is marked as Plâs y Bridell. It became the home of James W. Bowen Q.C. whose estate comprised 1,416 acres in 1873. About that time he completely rebuilt the Plâs

which has survived to the present day. In the early years of the 20th century it was the residence of Walter Francis Roch, Liberal Member of Parliament for the county from 1908 to 1918. Later it became a Carmelite Convent which closed in 1975.

Refs: for plans of the present residence see *NLW Clynfyn Deeds;* a photograph of it occurs in *Allen's Photographs 1871.*

BRITHDIR. *Newport.*

Now a farmstead on the lower eastern slope of Carn Ingli and overlooking the valley of Afon Clydach. In 1540-74 Thomas ap Howell ap Jenkin lived at Brithdir.

In 1584 William Warren of Trewern sold part of the land of Brythtyr to Melchior ap Ieuan ap Newport, yeoman. In the early 17th century it became the residence of Thomas Jones, younger son of John Griffiths Philip Evan ap Clydey. Thomas was also of Pentre Ithel, and his younger brother Stephen Jones was of Rhosygilwen. Thomas Jones was buried in Newport church on 9 June 1654, leaving a son Morris Jones who married Lettice Owen heiress of nearby Wenallt and settled at her home, and had two daughters, Mary Jones who married John Protheroe of Dolwilym, and Elizabeth Jones who married David Morris of Whitchurch. Morris's cousin, Thomas Jones lived at Brithdir in 1670 and was the last of the family there.

For a short time the Ford family lived there, and John Ford of Brithdir died in 1711. Later the property became two farms. In 1786 George Bowen of Llwyngwair owned Brithdir Mawr, tenanted by James Griffiths, and Thomas Nicholas owned Brithdir Bach, tenanted by Benjamin David. In 1834-41 it was occupied by Thomas Rees, farmer. In 1873 the owner-occupier of Brithdir Mawr was the Reverend David George, and the farm then comprised 362 acres. In 1894 Mary George was owner-occupier of Brithdir Mawr, and Thomas Lewis owner-occupier of Brithdir Bach.

Refs: *NLW, Morgan-Richardson Deeds, Pembs. Papers of Great Sessions; Carms RO, Golden Grove Ms.* vol. 1, p. 36.

BROOMHILL *Dale.*

Now a farmstead south of Dale village. The earliest-known owners were the Paynters. In 1599 David Paynter was described as merchant, later to become landowners, and continued to own Broomhill until early in the 19th century. In 1669 Richard and Bridget Walter sold the manor of Dale to David Paynter, and in 1699 he sold the said manor to his son-in-law William Allen of Gelliswick. Evangelism attracted some of the family, like George Paynter of Broomhill who married Eleanor Musgrave of Llanina (Cards), and later emigrated to Haverford, Pennsylvania. In 1743 David Paynter was High Sheriff of the county. Broomhill had been leased to Dr. George Harries of Haverfordwest who held that property in 1786. The last of the family in the male line was David Runwa Paynter, owner of Broomhill in 1823, and three years later lived in Haverfordwest.

Refs: *Pembs RO, Land Tax 1786; Burke's L. G.* 1850, i, 333.

BROWNSLADE *Castlemartin.*

About half a mile south of Castlemartin village, and westwards from the mansion we follow Frains lake (the latter being an old Pembrokeshire word meaning stream) to reach the sea coast at Frainslake Sands. The mansion was set in attractive grounds, and adjoining the grounds is Brownslade Farm, and it would seem that the farmstead was the original dwelling house, for we are informed by Malkin (1804) that 'we find the newly-formed residence of Mr. Mirehouse. The ground now occupied by the house and lawn was a field twenty years ago [c.1784]. Mr. Mirehouse began in the same year with Mr. Johnes; and the present state of the premises evinces the judgment with which his operations have been conducted', and Malkin later states that the new mansion was built about 1800. Plans and illustrations of the proposed house were made in 1783 by William Thomas, architect and surveyor. The property formed part of the estate of Lort of Stackpole Court, which passed to Alexander Campbell by marriage to the Lort heiress. The old house was a commodious building and in 1670 contained eight hearths, the occupier being John Leach. Leach died in 1675, and in 1709 Lady Campbell granted a lease of Brownslade for 21 years, to his son Abraham Leach, yeoman. The family remained until the death of John Leach soon after 1774, and his widow Elizabeth (Prout) surrendered the existing lease to John Campbell of Stackpole Court in 1789 for £3,500. It is clear that another family lived at Brownslade at the same time as that of Leach, which suggests that there may have been two houses there. This was the family of Holcombe.

The will of William Holcombe of Brownslade, dated 1653, was proved in 1662: he was followed by three generations all being described as of Brownslade, and who intermarried with Meares of Eastington, Meyrick of Bush, and Corbett of Nash. The last of the family to live there was Admiral Essex Holcombe, R.N., who died in 1769-70. Not long after this, the Mirehouse family arrived, descended from Mirehouse of Miresdyke, Westmoreland. John Mirehouse, born in 1753, had been at Cambridge University with John Campbell (later created Baron Cawdor), and became his land-agent in Pembrokeshire. In 1786 John Mirehouse, Esq., was tenant of Brownslade, and it was he who built the mansion house, and later bought the freehold. He was High Sheriff in 1810. A progressive farmer and planter of trees, he converted a morass of 2674 neighbouring acres into productive land, for which he received the gold medal of the Society for Encouragement of Arts, Manufacture, and Commerce in 1800. His estate, including Brownslade, eventually passed to R. B. Levett who had married a Mirehouse daughter, and his son R. W. B. Mirehouse, C.M.G., J.P., D.L. of The Hall of Angle, took that surname in 1864. His descendants are still at The Hall.

After the Second World War, Brownslade became a guest-house. Later the area became part of an artillery training range and the house and farm became ruinous. The old ruined house has been demolished.

Refs: Pembs RO, HDX, no. 527, *Report on Brownslade Mansion* made by Mr. A. J. Parkinson in 1976; Wm Thomas, *Original Designs in Architecture*, 1783, with illstr. of the proposed mansions at Brownslade: *NLW Journal* 1980 xxi no. 4; R. G. Thorne, 'History of Leach family' in *Pembs Historian*, 1981; Malkin, *South Wales*, 1804; Stuart Peters, *History of Pembroke Dock*, 1905; *RCAM Pembs*, 1925; *Come to Pembrokeshire, Guide*, c.1936, good illstr. of the house; Mrs R. B. Mirehouse, *South Pembs*, 1910; Thos Lloyd, *Lost Houses of Wales*, 1986, p. 70, illustr. of the ruined mansion.

BRWYNANT. *Manorowen.*

Now a small-holding, it belonged for some time to the Manorowen estate, but was sold after the Second World War by Captain T. G. V. Johns, D.L. It is an interesting small L-shaped house with a wing extending to the front. In earlier times it enjoyed a more august status. In 1326 it was a knight's fee (Welsh tenure). During the 16th century it was owned by Harry David, a younger son of David Thomas, squire of Cilgelynen. He had four daughters, the eldest of whom Jane, married David ap Ieuan Gwallter, who came to live at his wife's home. By this time it had become a farmhouse, and in 1670 its owner, Owen Griffith of Brwynant, was assessed at two hearths. Later it became a small farm, finally a small-holding.

Refs: BM Egerton Ms. 2586; Dwnn, i, 174; *Black Book of St. Davids* 1326.

BRYANOG FACH. *Meline.*

There exists a grant dated 10 May 1412 from Phillip ap Howel ap Jenkyn to Owen ap Gwilym dduy, of a messuage at Brenanog Vawr and four acres at Henllys Morgan with the wood there an exchange of a messuage at Bwlch Seys of fee of Diffrintaffle and of a messuage at Penkelly Vechan (Bronwydd Deeds No. 1283).

In the 1630s James Thomas, his brother and sisters were in possession, children of Thomas Rees of Merianog Issa and his wife Alice, daughter of James Bowen (of Pontgynon) ap Rees ap Rhydderch ap Jenkin ap Rees ap

Gwilym, descendants of Hal Freda. A fairly detailed pedigree exists in the notes and a mass of jottings relevant to this property but difficult to interpret. Ed.

BRYN. *Llanddewi Felfre.*

Marked on *Mudge Map* 1819, and on *Colby's Map* 1831 where the farms of Brynhafod and Brynglas are shown to the south-east of Bryn Mawr. In 1692 Bryn was the house of Philip Mathias, gent. By 1760 it had become property of the Twyning family who settled there, the occupier in that year being Mr. Daniel Twyning and the Reverend Benjamin Twyning, vicar of Henllanamgoed (Carms), both being parliamentary voters. In 1786 it was still owned by the Reverend Benjamin Twyning, while another parson of the family, the Reverend Griffith Twyning owned part of Caermaenan Fach in the same parish. In 1820 it was the home of William Twyning, Esq., J.P., and the family still owned it in 1870, when William Henry Twyning Esq., J.P. lived there, and bore arms: *sable, two bars between two stars of six points or; with canting crest, the twin brothers Castor and Pollux in their infancy* (the stars in the shield represent them after death), and motto, *Stellis aspirate genellis.*

Refs: *NLW, Llwyngwair Deeds, Pembs Gaol Files; Burke's General Armory* 1885.

BRYNAERON. *Llandysilio West.*

An attractive house to the south-east of the parish church, and near the banks of Afon Rhydybennau. In 1769 John Gwynne and the Reverend Morgan Gwynne, clerk, were Tax Commissioners for the county. In 1786 it was owned and occupied by the Reverend John Gwynne, clerk, and in 1788 John Gwynne, J.P., lived there. By 1809 it had passed to David Morgan, J.P. Later it was home of the Reverend Henry Thomas and Mary his wife (they had previously lived at Ty Hen and Bryn). Mary died there in 1843, and three years later was followed by her husband who had been a Baptist member for 73 years. Their son was the Reverend Theophilus Evan Thomas of Trehale, Baptist minister of

Blaenllyn and Newton. In 1904 Brynaeron was owned by Abel Thomas, Q.C., a son of Trehale.

Refs: *NLW, Pembs Papers of Great Sessions; Seren Gomer* 1846, p. 191; *Pembs RO. Voters Lists,* 1894 and 1904.

BRYNDYSIL. *Llandisilio West.*

A large house near the parish church at the north end of Llandisilio village, marked as Bryndissil on Colby's Map 1831. In 1847 it was the home of Reverend Edward Harries. In 1862 it was the home of the Reverend Thomas Harries, clerk, who is said to have built Bryndysil as his residence, and it contains some remnants of ancient stone work taken from Llandisilio church. It is now owned by Mr. Skeel Harries, who has sold Bryndysil house, but retains the land which he farms.

Refs: *RCAM,* 1925, p. 160.

BUCKSPOOL. *Bosheston.*

Now a farmhouse, half a mile south of the parish church. Fenton writes (1810) 'I pass Buck's Pool so called from a small piece of water close to the house ... formerly a residence of a branch of the respectable family of Adams ... It has now no remains of ancient grandeur or of any thing above the condition of a Castle Martin farm-house; all its importance if, as is probable, it possessed any, having left it with its ancient possessors when they migrated to a more desireable situation [Paterchurch] on the banks of Milford Haven.' The family of Adams had been in south Pembrokeshire since the 13th century and had lived at Buckspool until Henry VI (1422-3) when John Adams married Elen, daughter and heiress of David de Paterchurch, and then moved to his wife's home near Pembroke Dock, where his descendants remained until early in the 18th century when they moved to Holyland near Pembroke.

Buckspool remained part of the estate and became a farmstead. By 1786 it had been sold to John Campbell, and became part of the Stackpole estate. Henry Dawkins was tenant in 1786, Henry Hitchings in 1834, and George Hitchings in 1894. The arms of the Adams family were *sable a martlet argent,* and, as crest, *a martlet as in the arms.*

Refs: *Fenton, Tour Pembs,* 1811; *Dwnn,* i, 130-1, 172; *W.W.H.R.* ii, 76.

BULLIBER. *Castlemartin.*

A large farm about half a mile south of Brownslade, formerly part of the Stackpole Court estate, is now within an artillery range. When John Leach of Slade, yeoman, died in 1675, his eldest son Richard Leach had a lease of Bulliber where he died in 1732 and as he had no sons, he left the lease to his wife Elizabeth. On her death the lease passed to her late husband's nephew, Abraham Leach who remained there until 1776. Abraham was followed by his son Nicholas Leach who died in 1811 without issue. In 1834 John Bowling held a lease of Bulliber. Thereafter it was tenanted by farmers. About 300 years to the south-west of Bulliber are the remains of an ancient promontory fort.

Refs: *RCAM Pembs 1925; Pembs RO, Land Tax List,* 1786.

BUNKER'S HILL. *Steynton.*

An attractive small residence, near Milford Haven. It was named after its first owner who probably built the house. Uriah Bunker was living at Bunker's Hill in 1786, and was still living there in 1834. It is marked on Colby's map 1831. Early in the present century it was the home of George Griffith, J.P. In the years 1930-40, R.A.Wheatley, Clerk of the Peace for the county, lived there.

Refs: *Pembs RO, Land Tax 1786; Voters' Lists; Contemporary Biographies of South Wales and Monmouth,* 1907, p. 101 photo of the interior of the house.

BUSH. *St. Mary's Pembroke.*

A large mansion, across the river to the north-west of Pembroke town. Home of the Meyrick family originally from North Wales. The founding ancestor, Cadefael Lord of

Cydywain in Powys, and 8th in descent from him was Llewelyn ap Heylin who fought under Henry Tudor at Bosworth, and was followed by his son Meurig ap Llewelyn, appointed by Henry VIII, Yeoman (later Captain) of the Guard. He was succeeded at Bodwrgan (Anglesey) by his eldest son Richard Meyrick, while his younger son, Rowland Meyrick became Bishop of Bangor. This generation was the first to use the permanent surname, Meyrick. The Bishop (died 1568) married Catherine, daughter of Owen Barrett of Gelliswick, near Milford Haven, and their four sons all settled in Pembrokeshire, one being Sir Francis Meyrick (died 1663) of Fleet, Monkton, from whom the Meyricks of Bush descended.

The family held numerous public offices, Members of Parliament, High Sheriffs, and Justices of the Peace, while one became a Judge. Seventh in descent from Sir Francis was Sophia Jane Meyrick, only child and heiress of Thomas Meyrick of Bush. She died in 1837, having married in 1820 St. John Chiverton Charlton of Apsley Castle, Salop, and their son, Thomas Charlton took the surname Meyrick by R.L. on 31 March 1880, and was created a baronet on 5 May following, the family being now represented by Sir David John Charlton Meyrick, 4th Baronet, of Great Wedlock, Gumfreston.

Fenton writes in 1810 'Bush is a mansion most charmingly situated in a grove … The house and grounds occupy the summit of a gentle acclivity to the north of Pembroke, the pleasure grounds are planned with taste, its gardens unrivalled in their produce …'

On 8 January 1866 the mansion was burnt down, through a beam in a chimney taking fire, but many valuables and portraits were saved. The mansion was largely rebuilt in 1906, with Tudor-style windows. It was said to be haunted by one of its former owners, Judge John Meyrick (d.1732), who was, apparently, amiable. After the departure of the family the house became a Grammar School and later formed part of Bush Comprehensive School. The house is now a Residential Home for the elderly.

Refs: *Dwnn*, i, 136-7, 154, 156, 178, 185; *W.W.H.R.II*, 87-8; *DNB* and *DWB*; Mrs. Stuart Peters, *History of Pembroke Dock*; Burke's *Peerage and Baronetage*; Steegman, II *South Wales (1962)*, 198-200.

BUTTER HILL. *St. Ishmaels.*

About one and a quarter miles north of the village. The earliest family at Butterhill was that of Allen. In 1581 Howell Allen of Butterhill, husbandman, maligned Thomas Bowen, gentleman who brought an action against him in the Great Sessions of the county. He seems to have survived, and in 1604 Howell Allen and William Wolfe, yeoman, were both living at Butterhill. Some three years later, Thomas Roch of Butterhill married Lettice Voyle of Filbeach in the neighbouring parish of Marloes, and their marriage settlement included 'Butterhill alias the Grange of Butterhill'.

The property had been a grange of the Priory of Pill, later of the Priory of Haverfordwest, which owned it until the Dissolution. In 1633 a lease of Butterhill was granted to the then tenant of Sivers Hill for the lives of his sons, John, William and Morris, and the freehold was later acquired by the Roch family, whose descendants owned it until 1906. The family had married several daughters of Dewsland squires – Wilkin of Trefin, Jones of Llether, Laugharne of Llanunwa, Protheroe of Stone Hall. Four held the office of High Sheriff in the period 1760-1901, which the last of the family, Walter Francis Roch, barrister was for some time Liberal M.P. for Pembrokeshire and died without issue in 1963. When sold in 1906,

Butterhill was described as follows: basement, five cellars and larder; ground floor, hall, drawing room, dining room, study, two kitchens, servants' hall, scullery, butler's pantry; first floor, three double bedrooms with dressing rooms, two single bedrooms; second floor ten bedrooms; a main staircase and two back-staircases; numerous outbuildings and an old pigeon house. When I visited Butterhill in 1975, it was empty, becoming dilapidated, a large 3-storeyed double-pile house, with ranges of eight windows in each floor, and a porch-entrance; the fine ornamental ceiling in the drawing room was badly damaged. Miss Lawrence of Tenby in 1950 owned a somewhat unusual relic, namely an early Victorian dolls' house being a replica of the old mansion of Butterhill. The Roch family of Butterhill bore *azure semee of roses or, a lion rampant or.*

Refs: *Fenton, Tour Pembs*, 98-9; *Burke's LG, 1898*, ii, 1267; *Welsh Furniture*, p. 28; *Western Telegraph* 14 Nov. 1984, contains two excellent photographs of Butterhill in 1895 and 1984.

BWLCH Y CLAWDD. *Maenclochog.*

To the east of the village, close to the border of Llandeilo parish, and now represented by a few cottages near Temple David. Home of a yeoman family in the 15th century, and in the later half of the century, the occupier was Griffith Llewelin whose daughter Ellin married Evan Mortimer, a younger son of Richard Mortimer of Coedmore, of Cardigan in 1480. In 1498 Griffith, Howel and David, sons of Howel ap David ap Griffith, granted 'on account of great necessity and poverty' all their lands in Llangolman, and at Bulgh Clawth in Maenclochog, held by Welsh tenure, to Lewis ap David ap Griffith Fychan of Llangolman, Yeoman.

In February 1503-4, Ieun ap Morgan Gwyn of Bulgh y Clawth owned five plots and 100 acres there, three farms in Cemaes, and five properties in Maenclochog, and his sons John, Morgan, and Owen, all being 23 years old and more. Later, Eva verch Peres Broghton, relict of the said Ieuan held properties for her

life at Clenesaithman in Llangolman, Bulghepant, in the lordship of Maenclochog, a farm in the lordship of Cemaes, and Pont Kenan (Pont Gynon) in the demesne of Eglwyswrw. For a period in the years 1543-74, William Griffith ap Howel Fychan was in ward for Bulch y Clawth to William Owen, lord of Cemaes. Later in that century the occupier was Lewis Dedwydd, followed by his son William Lewis Dedwydd, and he by his son William Lewis William Dedwydd, who married Morfydd daughter of John Rees ap Howel of Penybenglog, and had a son, Lewis William, who lived at Bwlch y Clawdd in 1658. He was followed by his son Arthur Lewis who married Mary Beddoe, and had a son Lewis (William) who married Elen Vaughan of Farthingshook. Lewis William, gentleman, was living at Bwlch y Clawdd for which he was assessed at four hearths in 1670.

In 1731 Roger Lewis of Narberth owned 'the capital messuage called Bwlch y Clawdd', and in 1734-5 his brother William Lewis, gentleman, was living there. The antiquary, Lewis Morris, recorded in 1743 that an inscribed stone was found 'in the roadside by Mr. William Lewis's house called Bwlch y Clawdd in ye parish of Maenclochog.' Roger Lewis of Bwlch y Clawdd supported the Picton Castle candidate in the 1760 election, and in 1786 Thomas Lewis, Esquire, of the same place was owner-occupier. Shortly after this the property was sold and a new mansion was built and called Temple David. (vide: Temple David infra). The name Bwlch y Clawdd ceased to be used but still survives locally.

Refs: *Deeds, Baronia de Kemes, Trenewydd Deeds; Carms RO, Golden Grove Mss.* vols II and III; *Arch Camb.* 1896; *Pembs RO,* HDX/695/no.1, *RCAM, Pembs,* 1925.

CAERMAENAU FAWR.
Llanddewi Felfre.

On a gentle slope, a quarter of a mile north of Penblewin crossroads. In early documents the name is spelled variously as Cremina, Cremine and Creminah. In the 17th century the Jones family (descended from Sir Rhys ap

Thomas) lived firstly at Vaynor, Llawhaden, but had moved to Caermaenau by 1687 when John Jones lived there. He was followed by his son William Jones, appointed a Justice of the Peace in 1707, who often served as a Grand Juror, and sealed deeds with the chevron and ravens of his ancestor. He died shortly after making his will in 1738. The estate, which continued to include Vaynor, was substantial, and the family intermarried with landowners like Colby of Rhosygilem, Garnons of Cilgerran, and Adams of Whitland. The last of the family at Caermaenau was Thomas Jones, living there in 1783.

By 1786 the property belonged to John Dunn, with Edward James as tenant. Later it was let to yeomen. It is still an attractive homestead built in the vernacular style. An inventory of Caermaenau made in 1751 names the following rooms: The Blue Room, Dining Room, Study, White Room, Porch Room, Kitchen, Servants' Hall and domestic offices. After the last war it became the seat of Mr. R. W. A. P. Lewis (of Henllan) and Mrs. Lewis, who improved the old house and environs, happily without disturbing traditional features. A tablet on an outbuilding is inscribed 'W. Jones Esq. 1721', and another, 'J. 1744'. Mr. Lewis, a J.P. and D.L., served as High Sheriff in 1972.

Refs: *NLW, Pembs Papers of Great Sessions, Coleman Deeds; Pembs RO, L.T. 1786*; Lewis, *Efailwen to Whitland*, 1978, illustr.

Jones of Brawdy

CAERFORIOG. *Whitchurch.*

Now a farmstead in the north of the parish near the banks of Afon Solfach. Near the buildings are the remains of a moat and a pool called Llyn yr Alarch, while a dovecot stood nearby, but there are no relics of it now. All these were associated with the ancient mansion of Caerforiog. About 30 yards southwards stood a chapel, several parts of which survived as late as 1925. According to Fenton (1811) parts of the chapel remnant were incorporated in an outbuilding; remains of the dovehouse were to be seen in 1856, but were practically destroyed in 1898. Adam Houghton, Bishop of St. Davids 1361-89 is said to have been born here.

The names of previous owners are preserved in a field-name near Caerforiog, Parc Tir Perrot, and in the name of a cottage near Solva, Pant y Perrot. The earliest-known owners were the Perrots of Haroldston who owned lands in Dewsland. By his will dated 1491, Henry desired to be buried in 'the parish church (of Whitchurch) before the image of the blessed Christopher the Martyr', and left all his property to his wife Isabella for life, then to William Perrot of Haroldston and his heirs for ever. In 1498 Isabella granted all the land to the said William Perrot. In 1502 Sir William Perrot made a partition of properties in Dewsland 'whiche sumtyme was Harry Perrotte late of Caerveriocke esquyer'. About 1524 Jenkin Perrot lived at Caerforiog. The 'capital messuage' of Caerforiog was held by Sir James Perrot as of the manor of Trecadwgan, near Solva, in 1613. During the reign of James I (1603-25) David Gwyn, gentleman, described as of Caervoriog, brought an action against Francis Parry of Trecadwgan, gentleman, for forcible entry on Caerforiog. Towards the end of the 17th century it was home of Thomas Williams gentleman, trustee of Dr. Jones's Charity in 1698. In 1718 Rees Price of Tenby, gentleman, and his wife Jane owned Caerforiog, and by his will in 1724 left the property to Jane, who by her will dated 1733 bequeathed it to Anne Wogan of Minwere. The owner in 1740 was John Laugharne of Pontfaen, who in that year sold the property to Samuel Harries of Cruglas, and passed to his son John Harries who owned it in 1786, the then tenant being John James. In 1838 Mary Harries is described as owner (188 acres), with William Meyler as tenant. Thenceforward it continued to be owned by farmers.

Refs: *PRO, ADIII; NLW,* Poyston Deeds; *College of Arms, Wagner Ms no. 2* (AD 1610); *Pembs Arch. Svy* 1896-1908; *Fenton, Tour Pembs,* 1811; Jones and Freeman, *St. Davids,* 1856; *W.W.H.R.,* vols 3 and 8; *RCAM Pembs* 1925.

CAERWEN. *Llandeloy.*

A farm in the western end of Llandeloy parish. In 1512 William Vychan 'of Gaere Wen' also owned lands at Hendre Fach and Tyre Eva (both in Llandeloy parish) Porthiddy Vawr and Trebedw (in Llanrhian parish), which he mortgaged to Howel David Howel Gwilym, for 4 marks. In July 1565, the owner of Caerwen was John Lewys Perkin gentleman, who lived there with his wife Agnes and summoned Thomas Scourfield for £11 due on a bond. The next owner mentioned was David Howell of Caerwen who had died before 1580 when the Caerwen estate was partitioned between his two daughters, co-heirs, Nest and Margaret, the former married David Johnes, husbandman, and was living at Caerwen in 1587, and the latter married Henry James of Treglmais, living there in 1587. In the following year John ap Rees, esquire, of Rickeston agreed to buy a messuage and two tofts, and 74 acres in Caerwen and Llandeloy from David ap John and Nesta his wife, and in 1613 his son, Thomas ap Rees, bought further lands at Caerwen. The family continued to possess the estate until 8 October 1706 when James ap Rhys (Rice) sold it to John Rickson of Pembroke, merchant, and included 'the capital messuage of Caerwen' among other properties in Dewsland.

In 1714 Mrs. Jane Rickson widow, and her son Joseph granted a lease of Caerwen to Francis John, Dorothy his wife and Henry their son, for their lives, at a yearly rent of £15. On 11 May 1754 Henry John of Caerwen bought the farm for £575 from Anne Rickson, and her son William Rickson. Thereafter Caerwen continued to be owned by Henry John's descendants until sold in 1913.

Later it was sold several times and finally to the Pembrokeshire County Council who divided it into two farms.

Refs: *Carms RO,* Sale Ct., 1913; *NLW, Ms* Eaton Evans and Williams Deeds, Maesgwynne Deeds and G.S. Pembs Plea Rolls.

CALDEY ISLAND. *Off the coast of Tenby.*

Although an island, Caldey nevertheless forms an intimate part of the life of Pembrokeshire. During medieval times it maintained a monastery which ended by the Dissolution in 1535-6, afterwards to be inhabited by various farmers and fishermen, and in the 19th century by a landowner who erected a residence attached to the old monastic building. The mansion was later demolished, being in a ruinous condition. The wheel had turned its full circle by 1906 when it once more became a religious centre in the possession of the Roman Catholic church and continues to flourish as such.

Refs: Rev. W. Bushell, *An Island of the Saints,* 1931; and especially Roscoe Howells' well-illustrated *Caldey,* 1984, and references there.

CAMROSE NORTH. *Camrose.*

The earliest-known resident in North Camrose was the Reynish family, descended from Flemings who had settled in the Hundred of Rhos. In 1623 the property called North Camrose was owned by Charles, Prince of Wales, and a Survey made in that year consisted of (1) North Camrose, 72 acres with Jenkin Renish tenant; the house consisted of a hall, five couples, and outshute and two couples, an inner room with loft over it, four couples, a room below the hall door and three couples; all being on a ground floor, and thatched. (2) 24 acres (3) 38 acres (4) 56 acres (5) and several others of very small acreage. John Estmond was tenant of nos 2-4. All were described as North Camrose. Jenkin Reynish was a yeoman, and was succeeded by his son William. When William Reynish's only son and heir Thomas Reynish married Jane daughter of William Jones of Brawdy, gentleman, in 1651 all the Reynish messuages of North Camrose were settled on them.

In 1690 Thomas and Jane settled two messuages, six cottages and 700 acres being the extent of their North Camrose estate. They left two sons, Jenkin and William Reynish. In 1786 messuages and lands in North Camrose owned by John Crowther Reynish, gentleman, and consisting of Wolfsdale (occupied by the said owner) Camrose (by William Reynish) and Mountain Cott (by Thomas John). In 1796 messuages and lands in North Camrose were in occupation of David Reynish. In 1808 he had a lease of Eweston in Brawdy, and was followed there by his son Jenkin Reynish who married Sarah Bennett of Camrose in 1812, and left issue.

Refs: *Jones of Brawdy* deeds; *NLW Journal*, 1980, XXI No. 4; *Pembs RO, L.T. 1786.*

CAMROSE HOUSE. *Camrose.*

To the south of Camrose church, across a little stream, and close to an ancient earthwork, stands the Georgian mansion, a square three-storeyed structure, with ranges of fine windows. Home of the Owen, Webb-Bowen and Penn families. The longest lasting of these was that of Bowen, a branch of the Lochmeyler family, who had settled in Camrose parish in the early 14th century, and also lived at Roblinston (about half a mile northwest of Camrose church) and Wolfsdale. Camrose House was their final home.

Fenton wrote in 1811 'I come to the next mansion of my friend Hugh Webb Bowen, Esq., on whom the property of the last surviving Bowen of this house of Roblinston has dwelt, a mansion enbosomed in wood, in a situation pleasingly retired, and supplying all the elegant comforts of life, which the hospitable possessor has a heart to enjoy.' Almost in front of the house stands an immense tumulus. A deed dated 1722 describes it as 'a capital messuage called Castle, containing six ploughlands.' About thirty years after Fenton, the topographer S. Lewis wrote, 'Camrhos House, the seat of Hugh Webb Bowen, Esq., is the only residence within the parish which is entitled to notice.' Hugh Webb Bowen, who had been High Sheriff in 1806, died in 1833, and his descendants continued at Camrose House until after the Second World War. It was later converted, and in 1970 used as a club for a while. It is still owned and occupied by the family.

Refs: Fenton, *Tour Pembs;* J. R. P. Penn and Green, 'Bowen of Roblinston and Camrose', *W.W.H.R. 1926,* pp37-62; RCAM 1925; NLW, *Morgan-Richardson Deeds; Coastal Cottages of Pembrokeshire,* 1987 illustr.

(GREAT) CANASTON. *Robeston Wathen.*

This residence is believed to have stood where the farmstead of Great Canaston is today. Canaston Bridge, over the highway from Narberth to Haverfordwest, is a short distance northwards. Home of the medieval family of Canaston, whose heiress, Mabel Caneston 'Ladie of Caneston', brought the property to her husband Peter Perrot. According to deeds in the Slebech collection, it was formerly a manor. Marked as Canyston on William Rees' 14th century map. Towards the end of the 17th century the Poyers lived there, and in 1688 was occupied by John Poyer, a wealthy tanner, who founded the fortunes of his family. It was later acquired by the Foleys, and in 1786 was owned by Herbert Foley of Ridgeway, tenanted by Mr. Griffith Gwynne. An estate map of Great Canaston was made by Charles Hassall in 1794.

Refs: *NLW, Slebech Deeds,* nos. 652, 809.

CAPESTON. *Walwynscastle.*

In the southern part of the parish, and named after one of its medieval owners, 'Caprich's tun' which developed into its present form. In 1373 Peter Caprich son and heir of Robert Caprich, granted to Thomas de Hoton, Joan his wife, and Thomas their son, the lands he had inherited from his father at Capriston and Ricordeston in the lordship of Haverford, and dated the deed on 4 August 1373 at Capston. By 1608 it was the home of Francis Noote. On 26 June 1738 Nicholas Roch, Esq., of nearby Rickeston, made his will whereby he stipulated that 'the messuage called Capeston lately purchased by me from Hugh Fowler, esq., (is) to be sold and the proceeds to be paid to my three younger children when 21 years of age.' From deeds of the period 1753-84 we find William Cozens living at Capestone; he died in 1784, and his sons William and John A. Cozens settled at Sandyhaven and Rosepool.

The next at Capeston was William Davies (will dated 1808) whose eldest son Evan Davies became an Indian Army cavalry lieutenant-colonel, known as 'Tiger' Davies for his exploits in hunting that animal, and who was killed in 1827 by disaffected troops of his regiment; and whose younger son Lewis Davies became a naval officer, commanded the sloop 'Rose' at Navarion, being thereafter known as 'Navarion' Davies, rose to the rank of Captain R.N., and was appointed C.B. In the latter half of the 19th century, and up to 1950, the family of Seale of Capeston enjoyed the reputation of being progressive farmers.

Refs: *PRO, Anc Deeds*, nos. 2590 and D6091; NLW, *Pembs Plea Rolls*, 92: *Carms RO, J. Francis Collect.; Pembs RO*, L.T 1786.

CAREW CASTLE. *Carew.*

For architectural details of the castle, with illustrations or plan, see *R.C.A.M. 1925.* The interior arrangements, windows, etc. were made early in the 16th century by Sir Rhys ap Thomas (d.1526). A description of a tournament held by Sir Rhys is contained in *Cambrian Register,* 1795. Leland, writing about 1538 says 'I saw the castel of Carew repaired or magnificently builded by Syr Reese ap Thomas. It stondith by a creke of Milford Haven' (*Tour,* p. 115). Afterwards it became the property of the Carew family, and Sir John Carew and George Carew were High Sheriffs in 1623 and 1640 respectively. In 1670 George Carew of Carew Castle was assessed for six hearths. H. Moll records in 1740: 'A few years ago there was a Law-suit about this Castle and Estate, which was recovered by a worthy Gentleman of Lincoln-Inn of the name of Carew' (*Deser. of Wales,* 1740, p. 261).

Refs: *Dwnn,* i, 78; *Carlisle, TDW,* 1811; *Spurrell, History of Carew;* Laws, *Little England;* W.W.H.R. ii, 71; pedigree in *BLG 1850; Arch Cam,* 1886, p.27.

CAREW RECTORY. *Carew.*

Called The Old Rectory, situated within 100 yards of the parish church. It is possible that it may have been first built when Sir Rhys ap Thomas was modernising the castle. In 1811 Fenton describes it as of a singular appearance, having a square tower on one side through an arched opening, in which, now stopped up, was once the principal residence. It is an irregular building, a great part of considerable antiquity, unroofed, and in ruins.' The low square tower with its corbel table and newel staircase, and also a portion of the sunbathed wall that surrounded the house, have survived. Timmins informs us in 1895, from Carew church 'we make our way to a curious-looking structure known as The Old Rectory.

Though now a mere farm-house the place bears traces of considerable antiquity, and appears to have been built with an eye to defence. The massive walls are corbelled out beneath the eaves of the roof, which is pitched at a steep angle, giving the old structure a picturesque appearance. The house has apparently been formerly enclosed within a walled precinct, and a fast-fading tradition tells of 'the soldiers' having been quartered here in the turbulent days of old.' I visited the house when Mr. Michael Whitelock dwelt there, and who had 'restored' in excellent manner, both internally and externally. He sold the property in 1977.

Refs: *Fenton, Tour Pemb,* 1811; *Arch Cam 1877,* 312; and 1881, 238, illustr; *Timmins, Nooks Pembs.* 1895, illustr; Laws, *Little England* 1888, illustr; *R.C.A.M. Pembs 1925,* illustr.

CARNACHEN WEN. *Mathry.*

An ancient homestead on a gentle slope facing northwards, about a mile inland from Penmorfa and about half a mile north-west of Mathry parish church. During the Middle Ages there were several holdings in the district, and between 1326 and 1630 were variously known as Knachan, Knachan Dawkin, Knachan Thomas Brown, Knachan Castell, Knachan Jenkin, Knachan Tregwynt, Knachan Walter, and from 1630 the form used is Carnachen Wen, alias Carnachan Brown, and only as Carnachen Wen thereafter. In those days Carnachen Wen is also described as a manor. All the other holdings had been absorbed into local farms and their earlier names discontinued.

The first-known family there was that of Brown, descended from Fromand the Fleming, one of whose descendants took the name Perkin. By the early 16th century the family had adopted the Welsh form of nomenclature, so that those living at Tregwynt became known as Harries, and those of Carnachenwen as Perkin. In 1503 David Philip Perkin was lord of the manor of Carnachenwen, and his son Lewis David Perkin occurs in the taxation lists of the 1540s. In 1657 William Tucker of Sealyham bought 'Carnachen wen otherwise called Carnachan Browne', from Owen Perkin who died there about 1668. Thereafter the property formed part of the Sealyham estate and remained in the hands of the Tucker-Edwardes family till the end of the 19th century, during which period Carnachenwen was leased to several gentlemen farmers. In 1740 it was held by the Rogers family from Goodwick, once noted for their successful enterprise as smugglers. The last of the family to hold the lease was Blanche Maria who married David Davies, banker, of Aberystwyth, and their son David Davies of Carnachenwen was High Sheriff in 1832. Blanche Maria was a devout Methodist and the house became the abode of several ministers, and Sunday Schools were held there. Blanche Maria was the last leaseholder, and when she died without heirs in 1846, Carnachenwen reverted to the Sealyham family. Thereafter it was held by several yeomen, and finally sold. It was bought later by the Morgan family of Trewallterlwyd, and is now owned by Miss Jill Morgan who has modernised the old homestead without disturbing its traditional features. The Rogers family had also improved it and the house and buildings have initials and dates engraved on them – 1743, 1754, 1758, 1776 and 1784 and the glass label to a wine bottle is inscribed 'W. Rogers 1762'.

Refs: *Dwnn,* i, 111 (1613 AD); *PRO A.D.,* 2781, 4714, 11066; *College of Arms, Wagner* Ms. No. 2, *Protheroe Ms* X11, 34; *Pembs RO,* Deeds; *W.W.H.R.,* viii, 194; *NLW, Deeds,* Morgan-Richardson, Cwrt Mawr, Sealyham, Lucas, Bronwydd, Eaton Evans and Williams, Pembs Plea Rolls, Gaol Files, and Fines; Francis Jones, The Lay Manor of Carnachenwen in *Journal of Historical Society of the Church in Wales.*

CARNE COCH. *Llanwnda.*

On a slope overlooking Goodwick Bay, and near Ffynnondruidion farm. It was described as a Knight's fee in 1326. In the late 16th century it was the home of William Griffith, gentleman, who also owned Trefayog farm. He married, as his second wife, in November 1610 Ursula daughter of William Warren of Trewern, Nevern. In 1630 in the Great Sessions he claimed 'Ffynnon y grib parcel of the capital messuage called Carney coch' as his property, and he was ordered by aribitrators to build a stone wall at least 4 foot high, and a headstone 'upon the land sear'. By 1640 Carne Coch formed part of the Trelewelyn estate (Phillips). Martha Phillips who married Sparks Martin of Withybush inherited part of that estate, including Carne Coch, after his wife's death. He died in 1787. After this it was held by various yeomen, and in 1978 its owner was Mr. R. V. Johns, a younger son of Manorowen.

Refs: *B.B. of St. Davids;* NLW, *Pembs. Plea Rolls, Spence Colby Deeds; L.T. 1786.*

CARSWELL. *Penally.*

About half a mile eastwards of St. Florence village. Carswell is mentioned in 1348. William Whyte of that place witnessed a deed re Trefloyne in 1397; and Phyllypp Nicoll, husbandman, lived at Carswell in

1543. In 1586 Richard Merydith of Pembroke town, yeomen, left to his fellow townsman, Peter Williams, merchant, the portion of Carswell with the messuage and garden on the hillside; in 1601 the Mayor and Burgesses of Tenby leased their land at Carswell to the Bowens of Trefloyne, for life. The Tenby churchwardens received £6 from William Lewis for rent of Carswell in 1659-60; the Mayor and Burgesses leased Carswell in 1686 to Owen Williams of Tenby, butcher and in the same year Griffith Dawes of Bangeston, Angle and others, representatives of Abra Bowen, spinster, of Gloucester, who had bought a messuage and land at Carswell.

Part of Carswell was owned by Tenby Corporation, and occupied by Frances Ankern in 1786. In 1834 John Keys obtained the lease of the farm of Carswell, with William Llewellin as tenant.

Laws writes – 'Carswell consists of two distinct buildings standing about thirty yards apart; they are not quite in line, but very nearly, and are much of a size. The house to the north consists of a lower chamber vaulted, and an upper one with a curiously high pitched roof. At least the roof was high pitched some twenty years ago, only the gable ends now remain ... At the north end is a huge square chimney. To begin with the lower room, one end is almost taken up with the fire-place, in the right side of which is a large recess, larger than would be required for an oven; a man can well stand up in it. On the left hand of the fireplace is a block of masonry; this Mr. Barnwell suggests, 'was a stone seat, which might also have served for a table' (*Arch Cam.* July 1867, illustr.). There is a square window over the table which is an evident insertion. Another apartment has been built on to the east side, which, as it is not bonded ... may safely be put down as later; the doorway faces the fireplace, and is too mutilated to serve as evidence. The upper chamber is reached by an outside stair; here is a fire-place and two small deeply splayed windows; three others have been closed. The second building consists of three storeys. There is no sign of an original chimney (Ed: this building has been used as a

cottage, and a chimney has been cut in the wall for the first floor; this is clearly recent). The lower chamber is vaulted, lighted by two splayed windows. The vaulting has been cut through for a door, the original of which now leads into another vaulted apartment which blocks the windows. The first floor is reached by an outer stair and lighted by one small splayed window and a modern square one. The attic storey is approached from the same outside steps; these enter the first floor apartment about half-way to the ceiling, from whence I suppose a ladder reached into the roof. In later days the farm seems to have always been divided between two proprietors. Nearer our day we find Carswell farm, 87 acres three roods 14 perches, advertised to be sold on 19 June 1920; the dwelling house, 'recently erected' contains parlour, kitchen, back-kitchen, five bedrooms and outbuildings: $^{17}/_{28}$ths of the farms belong to 'The Tenby Charities (vendors) and $^{11}/_{28}$ths belong to The Church Charities Tenby'.

Refs: Laws, *Little England*, 1888, pp. 189-193, three illustrs, and p 190; *Arch Camb* 1867, illustr.; *RCAM*, 1925; NLW. *Picton Castle Deeds;* Peter Smith, *Houses of the Welsh Countryside*, fig. 8 (133), and also *Land of Dyfed*, p. 31; *Carms RO*, S.C. no. 457.

CARTLETT (1). *Uzmaston.*
Now a suburb of Haverfordwest. Also called Carthlett. Perhaps this is the property later called The Great House. Home of the 14th century family of Gibbon whose seal to a deed of 1342 shows *a lion passant guardant.* In 1786 five properties called Cartlett were owned by Lord Milford, and a similar number by John Campbell Esq. Lord Milford leased the messuage called The Great House in the village of Cartlett, to John Attwood of St. Mary, Haverfordwest, limner, for the lives of lessee Martha Attwood and Thomas Mathewman Attwood, which seems to have been afterwards sold to John Attwood, who, on 29 September 1784 released the messuage called The Great House to Francis Edwardes of Haverfordwest, Esq. On 1 November 1801 the said Francis Edwardes leased it

to Cecile Picton, widow, at a yearly rent of £16.16.0.

Refs: *LT 1786;* Carms RO, Trant Deeds.

CARTLETT (2). *Llanrhian.*
In the village of Trevine. A large commodious house, known to the local folk as Gallod. In the 19th century house of the Thomas and Morgan families. Still inhabited and well-cared for.

CASTLETON. *Monkton.*
Named after the Castle family. The seal of Philip Castlemartin to a deed of 1314 shows: *a fesse between three castles.* Dwnn describes the arms as *gules three castles argent,* and this is also given by George Wm. Griffith of Penyhenglos of Castle or Castletowne. Philip Knethell of Castleton in Monkton, Bailiff of Pembroke in 1546, died in 1587-88 and was father of John Knethell, heir to his grandfather, and aged 23 years in 1587-88. In 1786 Francis Meyrick Esq. owned Upper Castleton, Mrs. Price tenant; in 1834 Evan Evans held a lease of the same property. Both Upper and Lower Castleton are marked on Colby's map of 1831.

CASTLEBYTHE (CASFUWCH).
Castlebythe.
On the lower slope of Mynydd Casfuwch, clustered around an early Celtic fortification, is a small hamlet consisting of two farmsteads, and, until it was recently demolished, the parish church, sheltered by a well grown grove. Both farmsteads are called Castlebythe (Casfuwch). The one at the northern entrance to the hamlet is the ancient home of the former gentry families. It consists of a two-storeyed, stone-built structure with entrance porch, entrance hall, lounge with attractive chimney corner, dining room, kitchen, utility room, W.C. four bedrooms and bathrooms, outbuildings, and farm yard.

The earliest-known family at this farm was that of Philipps, a branch of Picton Castle. During the second half of the 16th century William Philipps, son of Morgan Philipps of Picton, married Elinor daughter of Thomas Lloyd of Cilciffeth, and settled at Castlebythe, and their descendants remained there till towards the end of the 17th century, the last being James Philipps, gentleman, who paid two hearth taxes in 1670. In the 16th century James Lloyd, son of William Lloyd of Cilciffeth came to the lower farm, and was followed there by his son Owen Lloyd who does not seem to have had issue. During the 18th century there were four farms at Castle Bythe, and in 1786 William Wheeler Bowen esquire owned two; (Eliz. Lewis and Griffith Evan tenants), Caesar Mathias Esquire owned the third (William Harris, tenant), and the fourth was owned and occupied by John Harries, gentleman. After this there were several successive owners and tenants, the longest-lasting being the Harries family who continued there till the present century.

Refs: *BM Egerton Ms* 25486, fo. 2909; *College of Arms, Wagner Ms* No. 2; *Land Tax* 1786; *R.C.A.M. Pembs* 1925; *Western Telegraph* 8 Feb. 1984, illustr.

CASTLE CENLAS. *Mathry.*
In a grove on a hill-top 1¼ miles south-west of Mathry village, a commodious attractive house, the front portion of which was built in the late 19th century: the outbuildings to the rear are large. In 1326 it is described as a knight's fee, and in 1342 John ap Robert Goch of Preskilly transferred half a carucate of arable land at 'Berry in the fee of Castle Kynlas' to Philip Cadwgan of Trecadwgan near Solva. By 1566 Castle Cenlas was a manor, and in 1622-25 consisted of the manor and farm of Castlecenlas, and the farms of Castell Rhedyn, Penywern, Mabws Fach and Lochturffin, in all comprising over 587 acres.

Its early owners were the Wyrriots of Orielton, and from them passed by marriage to the Owens of Orielton, from them to the Laugharne family, and from them back to the Owens. On 14 Jan. 1790 Miss Elizabeth Owen granted a lease of Castle Cenlas to the Reverend John Mathias, J.P. of Lochmeyler, and on 15th June of the same year she sold Castle Cenlas, Castle Rhedyn and Mabws

Fach to the same buyer for £840. And so the descendants of the old manorial lords departed. The manorial rights had long ceased.

By his will of 1806 the reverend gentleman left Castle Cenlas to his son Richard Mathias who spent the remainder of his days there. Richard Mathias died in 1846, leaving an only child and heir, Letitia Mathias. She had created a bit of a stir by eloping with the Reverend James Jones, vicar of Mathry, by whom she had four children. In 1859 she leased Castle Cenlas to Henry Tibbetts, and in 1875 to James Griffith. She died on 27 September 1888. As none of her children had married, Castle Cenlas was sold early in the present century to the Rees family of Carnachenlwyd (cousins of my mother) who then settled there, and finally, in 1973 the property was sold.

Refs: *Black Book of St. Davids; NLW, Slebech Deeds*, no. 169; *Poyston Deeds*, no. 240; *Pembs. RO, Land Tax 1786; Tithe Schedule 1842: W.W.H.R.* 1X, 153; see Francis Jones on lay manors in *Journal Hist Soc of the Church in Wales*, 1969 and refs. there.

CASTLE HALL. *Steynton.*

Just east of Milford marked on Colby's map 1831. This residence was built in the 1770s by J. Zephoniah Holwell, sometime Governor of Bengal, who escaped from the Black Hole of Calcutta; he was there in 1786 and soon afterwards moved to Somerset and sold Castle Hall to Robert Farquhar, purser of HMS *Hyena*. In 1797 Robert Robertson, gentleman, was owner-occupier. In 1799 the property was bought by John Warlow, wine merchant, of Haverfordwest, but by 1804 he had become bankrupt, and Castle Hall was conveyed to Benjamin Rotch, a Quaker merchant from Nantucket. He was also a whaler and general trader, and his son, Francis Rotch, established a private bank in Milford. Fenton (*Tour Pembs.*). in 1811 calls it 'a beautiful villa' then owned by 'Mr. Rotch (who) enlarged and beautified the house, grounds and gardens, and raised very extensive hot-houses, conservatories and other necessary appendages of fashionable luxury and taste', and the same author writes further in *Tour in Quest of Genealogies* 'Castle

Hall, the pretty villa of Mr. Rotch … The house is not large, but commodiously elegant, … the demesne (has) a summer-house most judiciously placed. This charming spot once belonged to the former Governor Holwell (but) after the Governor left, it continued long untenanted, but about seven years ago was purchased by a wine-merchant of Haverfordwest … on his failure it was sold to the present proprietor (Mr. Rotch)'.

In 1819 Rotch left Milford, and in 1819 sold Castle Hall to Robert Greville, who died in 1824 and left it to his son Robert Fulke Murray Greville. Owing to difficulties Greville left the county but returned to Castle Hall in the 1850s and was High Sheriff in 1854. He built Black Bridge, a wooden structure across the Pill. About 1857 he employed W. H. Lindsay of Bloomsbury to improve the mansion and he reproduced it in appearance of an Italian Renaissance villa. Greville died in 1867. A London builder and contractor, Sam Lake, came there next, but became bankrupt in 1883.

By 1911 Castle Hall was occupied by Benedictine nuns. They left in 1917, and the next owner was Sir Hugh Thomas, estate agent and landowner of Haverfordwest, who built a new bridge across Castle Pill in 1922. He was High Sheriff in 1924, but died shortly after and in 1925 Castle Hall was advertised for sale. It became deserted, and during the mid-1930s was demolished and the area became a permanent mine depot. This is a tale of woe for house and families, though in the last few years a new interest has been taken in the gardens.

Refs: *Fenton works cited; Pembs RO, Land Tax 1786; Carms RO, Sale Catalogue 1925*; Photo in T. Lloyd, *Lost Houses of Wales, 1986*, pp. 68-9. H. E. Busteed, *Echoes from Old Calentha*, 1908 with portrait of J. F. Holwell.

CASTLE MALGWYN (Old). *Manordeifi.*

This house stood on a high wooded bluff. Today it is a farmhouse with no apparent features to indicate its former status. Originally, a fortified stronghold of the prince Maelgwn, son of Rhys ap Griffith ruler of Deheubarth, and from him derived its name – Castell Maelgwn. Throughout the succeeding centuries a series of different families lived there. About the year 1400 the owner was Ieuan Fychan (descended from Cadifor Fawr of Blaen Cych) whose son Owen followed him at Castle Maelgwyn. Owen ap Ieuan Fychan left two daughters co-heiresses, Eleanor, who married James ap Griffith ap Howell who settled at Castell Maelgwyn, and Angharad, who married Rhys Fychan of Dyffryn Hoffnant in Penbryn (Cards.). James ap Griffith ap Howell, living in the years 1529 to 1555 described in contemporary records as 'domino de Castell Maelgorn in Wallia', has a most remarkable history which I have related elsewhere. On his death Castle Maelgwyn passed to Morgan Jones of Towyn (Cards), grandson of Angharad the other co-heiress.

In 1584 Morgan Jones of Towyn, gentleman, granted a lease for 32 years to David Mortimer (who had been living at Castle Maelgwyn since 1576) gentleman of the capital mansion house called Castle Malgwyn, and a meadow called Dolgamlyn in Llangoedmore, paying a yearly rent of £4, lessor reserving rights of the mill on the Teyvy near Lleghrid bridge 'now in decay'. He was a younger son of Coedmore, and was followed by his son Thomas Mortimer who died in 1613, and was succeeded by his son Edmund who moved to Cilfowyr.

By 1630 the property had passed into the ownership of David Thomas Parry of Noyadd Trefawr (Cards), and in 1634 had passed to his grandson David Parry who in that year mortgaged Castle Maelgwyn to David Jenkins. The Parrys disposed of the property before 1647, and 1680 the 'messuage called Castle Molegwin formed part of the estate of William Jenkins of Blaenpant (Cards). By about 1740 it had ceased to be a residence, and became occupied by tenant-farmers. By 1766 it had been sold to the Symmons family of Llanstinan, and twenty years later 'Castell Malgwyn' was owned by the Pen-y-Gored Company, with Daniel Davies as tenant. In 1792 it was owned by (Sir) Benjamin Hammett (who built the *new* Castle Maelgwyn on the banks of the Teifi) and in 1806 his son sold the old farmstead and lands to A. A. Gower, esq., of Glandovan. It formed part of the Gower estate for over a century. When I called there in the late 1960s it had been bought by Count Munster and farmed by tenants.

Refs: *L. Dwnn*, i, 55; *Golden Grove Ms* vol 2. (Cadifor Fawr) fo. 33; *Land Tax 1786*; *NLW, Muddlescombe Deeds, Noyadd Trefawr Deeds, Eaton-Evans and Williams Deeds*; *W.W.H.R.*, XIV, p. 231; *R.C.A.M.* 1925; Francis Jones, 'Trail of the Fugitive' in *Carms. Historian 1970*.

CASTLE MALGWYN (New). *Cilgerran.*

At the western end of the parish on the banks of the Teifi, close to Manordeifi parish boundary, and about three-quarters of a mile from the old Castle Malgwyn which is in the last-named parish. On or near the site stood the farmhouse of Penygored where an ironworks had been erected, and owned by the Penygored Company in 1786. The Company was bought about 1792 by Sir Benjamin Hammett who, some six years later built the present residence, known locally at that time as 'Ty mawr y gwaith', and named by the builder, Castle Malgwyn. In 1806 the works ceased to operate, and Hammett's son sold the property to Abel Anthony Gower of Glandovan, and it remained the seat of that family until sold after the Second World War. It is now a country hotel and outwardly retains its original form. Described in 1797 by Warner as follows: 'We attended Sir Benjamin Hammett to his house, Castle-Malkwn, a commodious mansion in the immediate neighbourhood of the works ...;' described by Fenton in 1811 as 'an elegant modern building, affording a suite of handsome apartments and most commodious offices'; and by Rees in 1815 as 'a neat modern edifice'. A photograph by Allen of Tenby in 1917 has survived. The mansion is a large square edifice of three storeys each with a range of five windows, with extensions to the rear, renovated in 1978-9.

Refs: *NLW, Coedmore Deeds; Tours* by Warner Lipscombe, 1797, 1802; Fenton 1811: Rees 1815; photo of house in *Western Mail*, 8 June 1979; C. Allen, Tenby, *The Tivy Side Photographic Souvenir*, 1871.

CASTLE MORRIS. *Mathry.*

Locally called Casmorris. A small hamlet to the east of Mathry, clustered around a crossroads on the north side of which on a wooded hillock are the remains of an early fortification, the caput of an episcopal manor, known in medieval times as Le Bailey House, and later as Pencnwc, 'a farmstead which now occupies the site of the destroyed mount of Castell Morris. Within living memory the mound seems to have been fairly intact and to have borne some stone foundations. When removing it from the farmyard, the skeleton of a man was found.' (*RCAM, Pembs,* 1925, p.224). The home and lands were held by the Bishop's leaseholders. The first family that is known at Le Bailey (Pencnwc) was that of Jones. In 1545 William John (later Jones) contributed to a hay subsidy, and in 1571 and again in 1573 William Jones of Castle Morris, gentleman, was High Constable of Dewsland. His coat-of-arms was *argent an eagle sable, armed and langued gules.* The family ceased to hold the property in the early 17th century. During the years 1654-56 John Mathias Esq. of Llangwarren was Steward of Dewsland for the Bishop, and in 1661 he had a lease 'of the manor house called Le Bailey, a fair tenement', and was still holding it when he died about 1683. The next-known holder of the property was a minor squire, John Mathias (with no connection with the Llangwarran family) who had married, prior to 1697, Lettice, daughter of John Ford of Stone Hall and Mary Wogan his wife. The Bishop granted him a lease of 'the manor house called Le Bayle' in Castle Morris in 1746, in 1749 granted a similar lease to Bernard Baine, who granted a lease of the same property in 1749. In 1766 a lease of the manor was granted to Henry Leach of Loveston, and in the following year of the house and land only. The Mathiases continued at Pencnwc (otherwise Le Bailey) until the mid-20th century, and today it is owned and occupied by a descendant, Mr. Johns. The manorial rights had long reverted to the Bishop of the See.

Refs: *Dwnn,* i, 110; *Egerton Ms* 2586; *Chatham Ms;* and *College of Arms, Proth.* IV; Francis Jones, 'Episcopal Manors' in *Journal of the Historical Society of the Church in Wales,* 1967; *Carms RO, Terrier of the Bishop's lands* 1817; *Golden Grove Ms Adv. Pembs.*

CASTLE VILLA (CASWILIA). *Brawdy.*

Now a farmhouse in the northern most corner of the parish, and close to the remains of an ancient castell of the Iron Age, which gives its name Castell Wilia to the spot, a name still used locally in preference to the anglisied version, Castle Villa. From 1400 until the middle of the present century, a period of about five and a half centuries, it was held by various owners.

Henry Morris who was the first owner of this extensive estate, held a high position in the community and bore as his coat-of-arms *argent three towers azure.* His descendants took their wives from the families of Laugharne, Bowen of Pentre Ifan and Wogan.

Last of the line, Anne Morris, sixth in descent from David Morris, married William Scourfield of New Moat about 1550 and was followed by her son John Scourfield, and he in turn by his son Thomas Scourfield. The last named became involved in financial difficulties, and in 1615 sold the Castle Villa estate to his elder brother William Scourfield of New Moat. The canting arms of the family were – *gules three greyhounds courant argent,* with crest of *a greyhound argent, in his mouth a scroll bearing the Welsh word 'Ffyddlon'* (Faithful). The Scourfields never lived at Castle Villa afterwards, and that property was thereafter let to yeomen tenants. Among these yeomen were the following – Bowen from 1621 who left about 1630, Owen there until about 1650, John Protheroe there in 1670 who died in 1697, about 1700 came the Davies family who remained there for four generations, and after Phoebe Davies married Joseph Harries of Trenichol in 1814, that family became tenants of Castle Villa, and their granddaughter Pheobe Davies Harries married Walter Morris of Chapel Farm, Pembroke in 1894. She died in 1897

After World War II Colonel Davies-Scourfield, whose family had owned Castle Villa for some 400 years, sold that property to a Mr. Pettijohn, who after a brief period sold it to a business firm. And so the Pembrokeshire squires and yeomen bid their farewells to their ancient acres. All that is now left of bygone days is the apparition of a medieval owner who, mounted on a spirited horse, gaily clears the entrance gate of Castle Villa in the gloaming.

Refs: *Dwnn*, i, 175; *Golden Grove Ms*,1; *College of Arms Mss; Proth Ms* V, 155; *Wagner Ms* 2 (Geo Owen 1610); *NLW, Recds of the Church in Wales*; Francis Jones, 'Castle Villa', *The Pembrokeshire Historian*, 1981; *PRO, AD.*, E210, D5173; *R.C.A.M. Pembs.* 1925; *B. M. Egerton Ms* 2586.

CEFNYDRE (CYNHEIDRE). *Fishguard.*
This homestead stands one and a quarter miles to the south of the town of Fishguard, on a slope above Criney Brook. The original farm of the name was Cynheidre, but from the early 19th century it took the form Cefnydre, this local pronounciation of which still contains an echo of the earlier form. In 1512 William Dier of Fishguard, gentleman, owned the property and neighbouring properties like Trefbover, Llanest, and Le Escaer (today Esgyrn). John ap Rees ap Owen, gentleman, owned Kynhedre in 1545, and in 1558 Walter Dier of Fishguard, granted Trefbover, Llanest, and Escaer to him. In 1590 Owen ap Rees of Kinhaydref, gentleman, and Margaret Davies his wife were paid the mortgage that they and others had on lands in the township, vill, and fields of Llangloffan in Dewsland. In 1593 Thomas Revell, Esq. and John Garnons, gentleman, were concerned with Owen ap Rees and Margaret his wife and a Fine of 13 messuages, 2 tofts and 720 acres in Kynheidrey, Fishguard and in five other parishes. Kynhaydre and other properties were granted to Thomas Lloyd of Cilciffeth.

By 1637-8 a new name appears when John Owen Jenkin of Trefgroys yeoman, Grace his wife, and Luce Jenkin otherwise Thomas of Kynhaydre widow, mortgaged in £50 on 226 acres in Trefgroys, Treboeth and Clynvinocke, all in Fishguard parish to Thomas Wogan of Llanstinan, gentleman. By 1705

Kevenhydre and Hottypace in Fishguard formed part of the estate of Sir George Barlow of Slebech. The property was again to change owners, when John Vaughan of Trecwn (died 1735) bought Kevenhydre from John Barlow.

Later in the century, the Vaughans sold Kevenhydre to Hugh Harries of Henrysmoat, and in 1786 he was the owner of 'Cinhidre' with David Davies as tenant there. From that time onwards it continued in Harries's descendants, one of whom, Huw Llwyd Williams is the owner-occupier today.

Refs: *NLW, Bronwydd Deeds, Slebech Deeds, Pembs Plea Rolls, Fines in the Great Sessions, Eaton Evans and Williams Deeds; Land Tax 1786; Tithe Schedule, Fishguard*, 1939; *College of Arms Mss, Proth Ms IV and V.*

CERBYD. *Llanhowel.*
A farmstead about a quarter of a mile east of the parish church and about the same distance from Afon Solfach. For many centuries home of yeoman families. In a deed dated at Castro Vilia in 1406, Ieuan ap Ieuan ap David ap Philip Thomas de Kerbyt granted land in

Castro Vilia and Penryn to John son of Henry Morris of Castrovilia (see Castle Villa). We next hear of Cerbyd in Tudor times when Rees ap Owen (Bowen) of Lochmeyler (died 1563) owned, inter alia, two tenements in Kerbit and Treclemes. William Scourfield of New Moat married Katherine, daughter and heiress of the said Rees ap Owen, and in 1622 Scourfield owned two messuages and half a carucate in Kerbett and Treglemes held of Sir John Wogan as of his manor of Treglemes otherwise Carn Fawr. In 1786 Henry Scourfield and Thomas Evans were co-owners of Cerbyd, the last named being also occupier. Not long afterwards Scourfield sold his share of the property to Mr. Evans.

About 1600 Robert John occupied the farm and after his death in 1625 it passed to his daughter Elizabeth who had married Rees ap John (will proved 1650), whose children took the permanent surname of Rees, and whose descendants remained until 1728 when Anne Rees married Thomas Evans who came to live at Cerbyd, and their grand-daughter Anne Evans married William Meyler who came to live there. William died in 1847, and was followed at Cerbyd by his son Thomas Meyler who died in 1861. A branch of the original Rees family bought Cerbyd towards the end of the 19th century. John Rees of Cerbyd was followed by his son John Lewis Davies Rees (died 1952) and Cerbyd passed to his only son Leonard John Rees who has converted the homestead and outbuildings into a holiday centre. Mr. Rees now (1987) lives in Cerbyd which he continues to own and administer.

Refs: *College of Arms Mss, Wagner Ms 2; NLW Mss. Eaton Evans and Williams Deeds, Cwrtmawr Deeds; Land Tax* 1786; *W.W.H.R.* ix, 153.

CILAST UCHA. *Manordeifi.*
To the north of Boncath lay a tract of land called Gwestfa Cilast, consisting of the farmsteads of Cilast Uchaf, Cilast Isaf, Penalltyfelin and Wendros. Cilast Uchaf stood in a field about one and a quarter miles from Boncath, and is marked on Colby's map (1831). Since that time the old farmstead was abandoned and no traces of it remain today, and a new farmstead, also called Cilast Ucha, was built near the roadside about 500 yards to the east of the former building. The name Gwestfa Cilast persisted; a gwestfa was an area whose freemen paid dues to a King.

In the area, too, was Cilast Fawr, but this,

or its remains, have not been located. The first-known family at Cilast Ucha, descended from the princeling Gwynfardd Dyfed, was Rees ap Howel, followed by his son Thomas ap Rees. Thomas's son, James Thomas became an attorney in the Great Sessions and he was followed at Cilast Ucha by his son David James who married in 1625 Janet, daughter of Thomas Lloyd of Cilciffeth one of the most powerful landowners in the county. His son, Thomas James, gentleman, married Bridget, daughter of Ieuan Lloyd of Faerdre, Cards. His children left the area – John James who was a mercer at Newcastle Emlyn in 1685, and Mary James who married John Havard, son of an ale house keeper in the same village. After this, only a few references occur to the property. In 1663 Llewelyn David of Llangolman Penbedw mortgaged a messuage called 'Plâs Kilast' to Thomas Jones of Brithtir.

In 1676 Francis Jones was owner of Cilast. In 1727 Eynon George of 'Cilast Fawr' was churchwarden, and in 1742 David Rees of Cilast Ucha, while in 1743 David William of Cilast Fawr and John Alban of Cilast Issa were churchwardens. After this only Cilast Ucha and Issa are named. For some time the Saunders-Davies family of Pentre owned this property. The highly respected family of George lived at Cilast Ucha and were still there in the first half of the present century. It was later bought by another family of George, from South Pembrokeshire, who held Cilast Ucha until 1980 when they sold the property.

Refs: *NLW, Papers of Great Sessions, Owen and Colby Deeds, S Deeds; Pembs RO, Land Tax,* 1786; *Carms RO, Golden Grove Ms,* (Gwynfardd).

CILCIFFETH. *Llanychaer.*
To the south-east of Fishguard, on high ground overlooking the Gwaun valley and the Pontfaen district, stands the old house of Cilciffeth, now a farmstead within a copse, and further sheltered by the heights of Mynydd Cilciffeth crowned by two cairns. Below the house, within an enclosure of 1½

acres, are the remains of an early fortification called Castell. Although the old mansion has been much reduced it continues to retain relics of earlier days, such as a vaulted basement, and a long window that lit up the staircase. The original name was Cilceithed, which became standardised as Cilciffeth. Fenton wrote in 1811, 'Cilyceithed, the ancient residence of David Ddu, or the Black (whose descendants for centuries were the first men in that county,) falling among three co-heiresses in the time of Charles I, was deserted for the seats of the gentlemen on whom they had bestowed their lands and fortune.

'The possessors of this house were the kings of the mountains and stretched their sway far and wide. Their mansion, as the tradition is, was every way commensurate with their extensive property, command and hospitality; and though at the removal of the heiresses, the fabric was suffered to be dilapidated; amongst the ruins, from time to time, have been discovered much cut stone, vaults, and other relics indicatory of a style of magnificence not common in this country at that period. This part of the estate fell to the share of the daughter who married at Slebech, and came to the late Sir William Hamilton by his first lady Miss Barlow, and is now the property of his nephew, the Hon. Robert Greville.'

David Ddu, the first of his family at Cilciffeth, was descended from Gwynfardd Dyfed. His son, Ieuan Llwyd gave his name to his descendants. Sixth in descent was Thomas Llwyd, born in 1535, the Founder of the Haverfordwest Grammar School, High Sheriff in 1596 and 1613. A patron of the bards, frequent callers at his hospitable house, and owner of a large estate situated in 41 Pembrokeshire parishes. He died at Cilciffeth in 1615, aged 80. His grandson David Lloyd was the last of the male line at Cilciffeth where he died in 1631, leaving three co-heiresses, one of whom Joan (born 1630) had Cilciffeth as part of her share of the 96 properties owned by her father. She married George Barlow of Slebech on whom she settled Cilciffeth.

The Hon. Charles Greville, who inherited the estate from his uncle, Sir William Hamilton, died unmarried in 1809, leaving Cilciffeth to his brother Robert whose son, Robert Fulke Greville, in 1856 sold the house and its demesne to John Meyler, yeoman, who advertised it for sale in 1880, then comprising 781 acres. Some of the previous tenants, such as the Thomases who came there in 1700 held it under leases, being followed by the Gwynnes who left Cilciffeth in 1847. It is still a large farm, occupied today by the owner.

Refs: *Dwnn*, i, 167-8: *NLW, Tynewydd Deeds, Slebech Deeds; R.C.A.M. Pembs*, 1925; Peter Smith, *Houses of the Welsh Countryside* 1975, map 7, p. 373; Francis Jones, 'Lloyd of Cilciffeth, *Pembs Historian*, 1975, *Burke's Peerage.*

CILFOWIR (CILFOWYR). *Manordeifi.*

On high ground, near Carregwen, about a mile due south of Llechryd. A medieval chapel stood here, marked on Dr. Rees's 14th century map, and near it is the farmstead of Gilfowir, also called Capel Cilfowir, and Chapelry of Cilfowir. A Baptist chapel of more modern times stands nearby. In 1493 Thomas ap Griffith ap Howel, a younger son of Castell Malgwyn, was Warden of the chapelry of Cilfowyr. In 1543 Philip ap Ieuan ap Meredydd lived there; in 1593 James ab Eynon of Cilvowyr, gentleman, died, leaving his wife Agnes and his brothers Gruffyd and Morris to inherit a farm in Clydey, and half a close at Cilvowyr. Before 1613 Thomas Mortimer of Castle Malgwyn owned Cilfowir, and was succeeded by his son Edmund Mortimer. Edmund died at Cruglas in Dewsland (will dated 1666) and his daughter Lettice became the ultimate heir of Cilvowir. Lettice Mortimer became a pious Baptist and accepted into membership in 1668. She married Edward James and both were members of the Rhydwilym Baptist Chapel. She died without issue and left Cilfowir to her husband. He had been married previously, his sons by the first wife came to live at Cilfowir.

The last of the Morgan family there was Mary Morgan grand-daughter and heir of James Morgan from whom she inherited Cilfowir in 1736. By 1747 she had married one Julian Courtin, and after mortgaging the property, they had ceased to live in the area by 1762. Cilfowir was bought by Francis Skyrme of Llawhaden in 1762, and in 1807 was bought by Morgan Jones of Cilwendeg, esquire, and thereafter occupied by tenant farmers.

Refs: *NLW, Papers of Great Sessions, Bronwydd Deeds, Spence-Colby Deeds, Owen and Colby Estate Records, Eaton Evans and Williams Deeds, Morgan-Richardson Deeds; Pembs RO, Saunders-Davies Deeds; Carms RO, Golden Grove Ms II; D. Jones, Harries of Bedyddwyr, 1889.*

CILGADFARCH. *Llanfihangel Penbedw.*

This homestead stood on the north-eastern slopes of Frenni Fawr, near Wernddofn farm, and about 1¾ miles south of Llanfihangel Penbedw church. From medieval times, when it was called 'Plâs Ynghil Gatfarch', to the mid 16th century it was the home of a gentry family, then for over two centuries, was occupied by farmers and divided into two farms, Cilgadfarch Ucha and Issa. In 1792 both were incorporated into Wernddofn, that estate being then owned by David Morgan, gentleman. The old property was marked on Colby's map 1831. The Tithe map and Schedule includes 'Cilgedfach cottage' among fields belonging to Wernddofn. The Voters Lists for 1894 lists 'Gilgedfach Farm' (David Evans, tenant), and in 1904 there were two farms of that name, held jointly by Thomas James and Daniel Phillips. According to the local County Councillor, Mr. Thomas George, all that is left today (1981) are some ruins.

Among early owners was Howel ap Llywelin ap Griffith, whose grandson lived at Cilyfforest, Cilrhedyn parish, Carms., who signed for Dwnn in 1591. Another early family was that of Ieuan ap Gwilym, descended from Cadifor Fawr of Blaencych, whose grandson Ieuan Llwyd of Gilgadfarch whose daughter and co-heiress Nest married Rees ap John, descended from the Cardigan-

shire magnate, Rhys Chwith, Esquire of the Body to Edward I, and their descendants lived at Cilrhiwe.

Refs: *Dwnn, i, 103-4148; Dale Castle Pedigrees; W.W.H.R.i, 32-3, s. Crygbychan; College of Arms, Wagner Ms 2; Carms R.O. Golden Grove Ms I (Gwyddno) and II (Cadifor Fawr), and John Francis Deeds.*

CILGELYNEN (CILGLYNEN).
Llanfairnantygof parish.

In the east end of the parish, bordering that of Llanychaer. The homestead stands on high ground overlooking Cronllwyn and the cwm of Esgyru. The earliest forms of the place-name were Cilygolynen and Cilglynen, the latter being the accepted name today. The first known owner was Thomas ap Lewis ap William, grandson of the said William, a blind landowner who lived at Trehros in St. Lawrence. Thomas was followed at Cilgelynen by his son David ap Thomas, who was succeeded by his son Hugh ap David living there in 1591. His son, known as David ap Hugh, and as David Davies, married Elizabeth, daughter of Sir John Wogan of Wiston. Their only child, the heiress, Charity, married in 1609 Thomas Lloyd, son of David Lloyd of nearby Morfil, who came to Cilgelynen where he was living in 1616.

In 1620 David Hugh of Cilgelynen conveyed that estate consisting of the manor of Llanstinan and 27 farms to his son-in-law. The son-in-law, who also held Morfil, died on 2 May 1635, leaving issue to inherit the property and who still owned it in 1705. Thomas Lloyd of Cilgelynen and Morfil was High Sheriff in 1669. It passed to the Owens of Orielton, and in 1786 was owned by Sir Hugh Owen, with John Raymond as tenant at Cilglynen as it was then called, and still owned by the Owens in 1838. Afterwards it passed through several hands and the residence became a farmhouse.

Refs: *Dwnn, i, 174; College of Arms Ms, Proth VI; Pembs RO, HDX.661, no. 2; Tithe Map and Schedule, Llanfairnantygof, 1838; NLW, Papers of Great Sessions, Pembs Plea Rolls, no. 154.*

CILGWYN. *Nevern.*

In the western part of the parish, above the valley of the Clydach and near Carnedd Meibion Owen. There were two farms, Cilgwyn and Cilgwyn Mawr. The area was a chapelry with its own chapel for local folk, and a small Victorian chapel exists there today. Several families dwelt within the chapelry but it is not always clear whether they lived at Cilgwyn or at Cilgwyn Mawr. Among these was Howell ap Rhys ap Llewelyn who left a house and land in the tenement of Cilgwyn to Harry Bowen, a younger son of Llwyngwair, who was followed by a son and grandson in the period 1600-18; Thomas James, (died 1614) followed by his son Griffith James living in 1636, and left two sons, Robert and Thomas James. In 1734 Cilgwyn Mawr was owned by the Warrens of Trewern whose descendants still owned it in 1788, while the Vaughan family was also there in the 18th century. Cilgwyn farm still exists.

Refs: *NLW, Bronwydd Deeds; College of Arms, Wagner Ms No.6 Proth Ms IV; R.C.A.M. 1925. Charles, George Owen, 1973, 46, 53.*

CILRHIWE. *Llanfihangel Penbedw.*

This homestead stands about three-quarters of a mile west of the parish church (the northern transcept being still 'the Kilrhiw'), and the same distance south of Rhosygilwen. Marked on Kitchin's map (1749-1770) as 'Killrhua, Lloyd Esq.', and on Colby's map 1831. I visited Cilrhiwe in 1975 and again in 1983. Built in the 17th century as a double-pile two-storeyed house with an attic storey, and a range of five windows, it has lasted in a fair state of preservation to our time. That it contained eight hearths in 1670 indicates it was commodious. The interior contains a broad Jacobean staircase with balustrades and finials, rising from the hall to the upper storeys; the old parlour is fully panelled as is also one side of the hall. A wing extending to the rear was added in later times and is now used for farming purposes. The attached 275 acres are farmed by Mr. W. D. R. Davies, whose maternal grandfather bought the property from Sir Marteine O. M. Lloyd of Bronwydd in 1911. The drive is sheltered by an avenue of beech trees, and opposite the entrance is a large fishpond.

The mansion, a fine example of the vernacular style of former days, faces north-eastwards, with a view over green pasture fields now used for grazing. The garden was a little distance away, below the outbuildings. The first-known family there, descended from the Cardiganshire magnate Rhys Chwith (or Chwitt), Esquire of the Body to Edward I, and came into the area by the marriage of John ap Meredith to Nest, daughter and co-heiress of Ieuan Lloyd of Cilgadfarch. The great-grandson of the marriage, Owen Phillip, was living at Cilrhiwe in 1567, and also when he signed his pedigree for Dwnn on 22 August 1591. He had two children, David Phillip who died without legitimate issue, and Elizabeth who married Nicholas Bowen of Crugbychan, Verwig, near Cardigan. The family then left Cilrhiwe.

The next family there, Lloyd, came from Montgomeryshire (descended from Bleddyn ap Cynfyn), the first member to come southwards being the Reverend Henry Lloyd, rector of Cilrhedyn. He had two sons, both of whom settled at Cilrhiwe. The elder, John Lloyd, married Cissie, daughter of Hector Philipps of Cardigan Priory, and died at Cilrhiwe on 11 July 1657 in his 36th year, having had no issue. His brother, James Lloyd then succeeded and married Bridget, sister of the said Cissie. In 1661 he was High Sheriff and in 1670 paid tax for eight hearths at Cilrhiwe, died in July 1707 aged 83 and was buried in Cilgerran church. Cilrhiwe passed to his only child Anne who married Lewis Wogan of Wiston. She died in 1703, her husband having predeceased her in 1694. They had one son, Lloyd Wogan who died unmarried, and their mother's estate then passed between three daughters. The eldest daughter Anne Wogan inherited Cilrhiwe mansion and married Thomas Lloyd of Bronwydd (died 1737). His descendants continued to live there from time to time until it was sold in 1910.

In 1752 James Lloyd of Cilrhiwe was

concerned in mine-works at Llandre in Llan-fyrnach and the family took an active part in the silver lead industry there until it closed in 1890. When Sir Marteine Lloyd advertised for sale 'The Kilrhwe Estate' in July 1911, it consisted of the residence of Cilrhiwe (172 acres), and 40 other portions in north Pembrokeshire. The south transept of the parish church is known as 'Cilrhiwe chapel'.

Refs: *Dwnn*, i, 158, 217; *Dale Castle Pedigrees*, p. 25; *W.W.H.R.*, ii, 95; *NLW, Bronwydd, Noyadd Trefawr and Deri Ormond Deeds; Pembs RO, James of Narberth Deeds, Saunders-Davies Colln. Box 10*, Sale Catalogue no.642; I and II *Bleddyn ap Cynfyn fo. 32; R.C.A.M. Pembs.* 1925.

CILRHIWE FACH. *Manordeifi.*

Now a farm, situated between Pentre and Newchapel: marked on Colby's map 1831 as Cilrhiwan fach. The first-known family there descended from Cadifor Fawr of Blaencych, who were living at Rhosychen (Carms.). A later member of that family, Griffith ap Ieuan married Margaret daughter of Sir James Bowen of Pentre Ifan, and their son, Morris married Lucy (living 1613) daughter and heiress of James (living 1539) ap Ieuan Lloyd ap Gwilym ap Philip 'o Gilriweun' which she brought to her husband. Their son David ap Morris settled at Cilrhiwe Fach and was living in 1613. This David married a daughter of Howel ap Morris of Gellydywyll (Carms.), the last-known of the family at Cilrhiwe Fach being their great-grandson John David Thomas. In 1786 it was owned by one Captain Haye, with David Beynon as tenant. In 1894 Sarah Lewis lived there and in 1950 Alwyn and Florrie Lewis.

Refs: *Dwnn*, i, 217 S.A. 'Manordeifi Kilrywenn'; *Golden Grove Ms; Land Tax List 1786; subsequent Voters Lists.* (Pembs).

CILRHIW. *Lampeter Felfrey.*

A Georgian residence sheltered by a copse about four miles east of Narberth, situated between Princes Gate and Treffgarne; marked as Cilrhiw (residence) and nearby Cilrhiw farm, on Slebech estate, and in 1738 John Barlow gave a lease for three lives of this property to William Lewis, yeoman. The property had become part of the possession of William Knox of Slebech by 1786 with Evan Rogers as tenant. In 1834 it was owned by Lancelot Bough Allen, the tenant being Morgan David who enjoyed a lease for 21 years. With the advent of the Allens the house was greatly improved and thereafter was the home of esquires of that family. In 1852 it was described as 'Cil Rhu, lately residence of Launcelot Bough Allan, and passed to his son Gough Bough Allen. The present resident tenant is R. Spranger, Esq.' It continued in the Allen family and in 1948 Bertram Wedgwood Allen of Cilrhiw was High Sheriff and it was occupied by him and Gladice Joyce Allen in 1950. Some time later it was sold.

Refs: *D.W.B.* p.5; *Burke's LG*, for Allen pedigree; *NLW, Slebech Deeds; Pembs RO, Land Tax Lists 1786*; F. P. Gwynne, *Sketches of Tenby etc*, edn. 1852, p.67; *Western Mail*, 2.4.1988 (illustr.)

CILRYDD/CILRYTH.

Also called Coed Cilrydd. Nevern.

This house stood in the woodland of Cilrydd, close to the residence of Pentre Ifan (q.v.). During medieval times it was a seat of the family of Cyhylyn ap Gwynfardd, ancestor of the Bowens of Pentre Ifan, Warren of Trewen, etc. When Pentre Ifan was built it became the main residence, and Coed eventually became a farm. The name is now lost and no trace of Coed remains. One of the first of the family to live there was Eynon ap Gwilym ap Gwrwared, known as 'Eynon Fawr o'r Coed', or 'of Coed Cilrydd'. He was living in 1278-1281, and was followed by his son Owen ap Eynon Fawr, living at Coed about 1302. A descendant, Thomas Bowen of Pentre Ifan, at his death in 1586 owned 'the manor or capital tenement of Pentreyvan and Kilyryth'.

In 1614 William Owen, natural son of William Owen of Henllys, lived at Coed, but his two sons John and George Owen after a few years left Coed and settled at Berllan and at Torbant (Llanrhian) respectively. In 1638 Elizabeth Bowen, widow of Pentre

Ifan, died, owning (inter alia) 'the capital messuage called Pentyre Ievan and 200 acres, and a tenement and 20 acres called Place y Coed'. Both these properties became part of the estate of Warren of Trewern (also descended from Cyhylyn ap Gwynfardd). In 1786 the farm of Coed was owned by Mrs. Jones of Llanina (Cards) and Trewern, with John Thomas as tenant. Mrs. Jones (née Catherine Warren, heiress of the Trewern estate, married Philip Jones of Llanina) and her will was proved in 1793. Coed is not marked on Colby's map 1831.

Refs: *Golden Grove mss (Gwynfardd)*; Francis Jones, 'Warren of Trewern', *Pembs. Historian 1974*, p. 115 and 'Bowen of Pentre Ifan and Llwyngwair, *ibid, 1979*, pp. 27-30, 36.

CILVELGY (KILVELGY). *St. Issels.*

Now a farm just east of Kilgetty. It is marked on Rees's 14th century map as Kilvegy (Kilsketty). In the late 16th century it formed part of the Barlow of Slebech estate, and in 1613 John Barlow owned 'the manor of St. Issells alias Kilvelgy' containing a number of messuages, 500 acres of land, a corn mill, and a fulling mill. The next resident at Kivelgy was Jenkin Thomas, son of Evan Thomas descended from Brychan Brycheiniog. In 1670 he paid five Hearth Taxes, which shows it to have been a commodious residence at that time. He married Mary Barlow of Haverfordwest by whom he had an only child, Anne Thomas, who married Lewis Bowen of Haverfordwest. In 1658 John Bell the elder of Arnolds Hill is described as formerly of Killvelgie, gentleman; in 1679 one Samuel Thomas gentleman was living at Cilvelgy. The property remained in Barlow ownership and finally passed to Sir William Hamilton (who had married the Slebech heiress), who is described as owner in 1786, with John Hodges as tenant, and in 1834 William Hodges was tenant. In 1786 there was also Little Kivelgy owned by Lord Milford with David Welch as tenant.

Refs: *NLW, Pembs Plea Rolls,* nos. 184,226; *W.W.H.R. iii,* 133; *Taylor's Cussion,* p. 97; *Pembs. R.O, Land Tax 1786; Western Mail,* 1 May 1986, illustr. of Kilvelgy farm.

CILWENDEG. *Capel Colman.*

Situated about half a mile east of Capel Colman parish church, and one and a quarter miles to the north-east of Boncath. The first owner of Cilwendeg was Llewelyn ap Howel, descended from Edwyfed Fychan of Gwynedd, Seneschal of Prince Llewelyn the Great. Llewelyn was at Cilwendeg in the early 16th century, and was followed by his son David Llewelyn, and he by his son Llewelyn David. The last-named was followed by his son David Llewelyn living in 1646, and in 1670 paid for two hearth taxes, which suggests that it was a small house at that time. On 17 September 1687 he conveyed the capital messuage of Cilwendeg to his son and heir apparent Jonathan Llewelyn, who in the same year mortgaged the property to one David John, and on 13 January 1698-9 Jonathan assigned the equity of redemption of Place Kilwendeg, Wenros Ucha and Isha, to Miss Mary Skyrme, daughter of William Skyrme of Llawhaden Esq. The mortgage of 1687 held by David John passed to his widow and son who assigned it to Jacob Morgan of Vaynor, Manordeifi, attorney at law, who afterwards acquired the freehold of Cilwendeg and came there to live.

Jacob died in 1732-33, leaving three daughters and the property eventually passed to the youngest daughter, Margaret Morgan who married John Jones of Llanbadarn, Cards., who then settled at his wife's house. Their descendants succeeded to Cilwendeg; Morgan Jones was High Sheriff in 1801 and his nephew of the same name in 1831. The family left Cilwendeg in the second half of the 19th century and were settled at Llwynbedw, Penylan in the Tivyside, and at Llanmilo near Pendine. Morgan Jones of Llanmilo was High Sheriff of Carmarthenshire in 1909. Fenton in his Tour of 1811 writes 'another handsome mansion of modern growth, Cylywendeg, bursts upon the eye, built by the gentleman who now inhabits it, Morgan Jones Esq., owner of the Skerry Lighthouse off the north coast of Anglesey, a property from which he derives a large income.'

Writing in 1840, Lewis says 'Cilwendeg the seat of Morgan Jones Esquire, is an elegant mansion, erected within the last fifty years by the uncle of the present proprietor, ornamented with a handsome receding portico in good taste, and occupies the centre of an extensive demesne beautifully laid out in plantations and pleasure grounds to which are entrances by two handsome lodges, recently added by the present properietor.' A good photograph of the mansion was taken by Allen in 1871. Cilwendeg was advertised for sale in 1931, described as 'a handsome modern mansion' of three storeys, with, on the ground floor, hall, inner hall, double drawing room, dining room, morning room, library, billiard room, two conservatories, domestic offices; on the first floor, twelve bed and dressing rooms and offices; on the second floor, six rooms. It is now used as an old people's home. There is no trace of the earlier residence.

Refs: *Carms R.O., Golden Grove Mss. (Cadifor Fawr, Gwyddno Edwyfed Fychan), John Francis Deeds;* NLW, Morgan-Richardson Deeds, Penally Deeds; Pembs R.O). Saunders-Davies Deeds.

CINNAMON GROVE. *St. Thomas (Haverfordwest).*

Marked on Mudge (1819) and Colby's (1831) maps, two miles south-west of Haverfordwest, above Merlins Brook. Very little has been found about this residence. Cinnamon Hill is mentioned in a deed of 1745, and Robert Prust J.P., senior, of Cinnamon Hill in a deed of 1785. Cinnamon Grove was the residence of Joshua Roch, Esq., in 1795, a kinsman of Hugh Allen of Rickeston. Joshua made his will in 1801. It is recorded that Sparks Martin Walker, aged 13, eldest son of Thomas Walker of Cinnamon Grove, died in 1826. To Malkin, author of *Tour in South Wales,* Cinnamon Grove is 'an agreeable residence'. Now a farm. For photograph of house and description see *Western Telegraph* 10 September 1986.

CLARESTON. *Freystrop.*

Some half a mile south of Freystrop Cross. Fenton (1811) writes 'Clareston, the seat of George Roch Esq., approached by a handsome avenue extending to the road, in midst of a modern but thriving plantation, raised by thick planting, though in an exposed situation and an unfavourable soil;' and S. Lewis (1840) observes, 'Clareston, an elegant modernized mansion, seat of George Clayton Roch, Esq., which was originally the residence of the family of Powel, and came by marriage to the ancestors of the present proprietor; it is pleasantly situated, and the grounds are well laid out'. George Roch, first of his family at Clareston where he was living in 1738, was the son of Nicholas Roch (d. 1745) of Rickeston. By his wife Martha Allen of Gelliswick, George Roch had a son, George Roch who left two sons George Roch of Clareston, High Sheriff 1789, died unmarried in 1820, and Joshua who followed his brother at Clareston where he died in 1827, leaving an only son, George Clayton Roch, High Sheriff 1830, who was burnt to death in his bed on 17 April 1833. He was the last of the line at Clareston.

Later, Clareston was purchased by Thomas Henry Davies, son of Henry Davies of Mullock and Trewarren; he was High Sheriff in 1865, and later sold Clareston to William Ballinger of Swansea who was living at Clareston in 1873, whose family was still there in 1907. A relic of the Roch occupation is an erect stone standing in the grounds, inscribed 'G.R. 1755'. I recall visiting Clareston in the early 1930s when it was the seat of Sir Charles Price, M.P.

Refs: *Contemporary Biographies of South Wales and Monmouth,* 1907 illustr. *R.C.A.M. Pembs,* 1925; D. Miles, *Pembrokeshire Sheriffs,* 1974.

CLEGYR (N). *Jordanston in Dewsland.*

Known as 'Clegyr Mawr otherwise Clegyr Meidrim', and finally just as Clegyr. Today it is locally called Clegyrn and spelled thus on modern OS maps. On the maps of Mudge (1819) and Colby (1831) it is given as Clegyr Mawr. In 1567 William ap John ap Ieuan lived at 'Clegir Meyderym otherwise Clegir Mawr'. Early in the 16th century its owner was William Davids of Dyffryn Wdig, and in 1640, having mortgaged Clegir Mawr otherwise Meidrim he conveyed that property to Ursula Williams widow of Jordanston. In 1697 Thomas Davids of Dyfryn Wdig married Elizabeth daughter and co-heiress of Richard Williams of Clegir Mawr, and so that property returned to the family of the previous owner. Finally, Jane Davids, co-heiress of Dyffryn Wdig married Stephen Colby of Ffynnone, and brought Clegyr Mawr to her husband. In 1784 Jane Colby, then a widow, leased Clegyr Mawr to John Dedwith gentleman, then tenant there. Dedwith, in 1800, married Mary Mathias, daughter of the Squire of Llangwarran. It continued to be owned by the Colbys to the second half of the 19th century. Today it is a farmhouse.

Refs: *NLW, Pembs Plea Rolls, Morgan-Richardson Deeds, Spence-Colby Deeds; Carms R.O., Golden Grove ms. (Gwynfardd); Pembs R.O., Land Tax 1786.*

CLYNFYW. *Manordeifi.*

On a slope to the west of Afon Cych, between Abercych village and the mansion of Pentre. The ancestor of the first-known family at Clynfyw was the Yorkist Jenkin Lloyd of Blaiddbwll, whose great-grandson also named Jenkin Lloyd was living at Clynfyw in 1500. He was followed there by six further generations. The last owner was David Lloyd of Clements Inn, London, whose uncle Griffith Lloyd lived at the mansion. David Lloyd remained in London and on 10 March 1684-5 sold Clynfyw to David Llewelin, gentleman, of Penalltcych, Clydey.

About 1712 the old mansion of the Lloyds was pulled down, and a new one built. David was followed by his son Leoline alias Llewelin Davies who died on 10 April 1747, aged 80, and was succeeded at Clynfyw by his son Owen Davies. Owen's interesting career was spent far from his early home. On 31 October 1729 he was appointed receiver-general of Westminster Abbey, and was also connected with the Augmentation Office.

He and his wife Mary lived in the Little Cloisters until their deaths, Owen on 24 April 1759 in his 60th year, his wife in May 1778, both were buried within the Abbey. Their two children, Anne and Mary died in 1791 and 1786, also buried in the Abbey. Davies was the last of the family to own Clynfyw.

In 1750 he ordered a valuation to be made of Clynfyw so that a sale could be effected. Accordingly the valuation was made in that year. In 1751 a description of the properties was made, which included Clynfyw and properties at Penybont, messuages called Tyr-y-wern ddu alias Tyr-y-ty-hên, three pieces of land at Llwyn-y-Gore called Llain-yn-nhyr-y-Kilgwyn, message called Plâs-gwern-Aaron with three pieces at Kilgwyn, a piece in Gwestra Kilast at a place called Kilvalgen, a piece between lands of William Lloyd Esq. and James Davies, and a piece bounded with a little brook called Gwern Aaron on the west, with lands of Samuel Jones on the north side, with a path from Blaen Morrow to Aberchen on the east side. In 1752 a further valuation was made of the Clynfyw estate and the timber thereon, including some 'hollow trees about the mansion house,' the said Mansion or Capital House well built in stone in or about the year 1712, and covered with slate, and having good orchards and springs of water near thereunto'. Clynfyw was bought in 1753 by Thomas Lewis of Llwyngravis, Cards, and in 1760 Thomas Lewis Esq. is described as living at Clynfyw.

The Lewis family came from the Narberth

area, and were successful businessmen. Thomas Lewis first worked at the Blackpool Iron Forge near Canaston Bridge, and then moved to the Tivyside; in 1714 was living at Llwyngravis, and was associated with the Coedmore Forge near Llechryd, and in 1719 he bought the tools and equipment of that forge. In 1749 he took a lease of the corn mill Melin Abercych, which he converted into an iron-forge. Thomas Lewis was the first at Clynfyw which has remained in the hands of his descendants, the Lewis-Bowens, to this day. During the first half of the 19th century a new mansion of three storeys was erected about 100 yards from the one that had been built in 1712. In 1840 Lewis says 'Clynview the seat of T. Lewis Esq. is a handsome residence pleasingly situated.' The old mansion still survives as an outbuilding, and two delightful water-colours of it painted in its prime in 1845 may be seen in the present residence.

Refs: *N.L.W., Noyadd-Trefawr Deeds; Pembs R.O., Deeds D/JP; Carms R.O., John Francis Deeds, Coedmor Deeds, W.W.H.R., ii, 40-1; Golden Grove ms (Gwynfardd)*; deeds and papers still at Clynfyw (Lewis-Bowen); *C. Allen, Photographs 1871* illustr.; Francis Jones, 'Families of Blaiddbwll', *N.L.W. Journal, Summer 1981*; Phillips, Llofruddiaeth *Shadrach Lewis*, 1986 illustr. opp. p. 84 of Clynfyw as it was in 1840.

CLYN MEREDITH. *Eglwyswen* (*Whitechurch in Cemaes*).
A large farmhouse half a mile south-west of the parish church. Home of yeomen from medieval times. On 8 October 1418 Griffith ap David ap Gwilym ap Rhys granted to Perkyn ap Gwallter ap Rhys ap Rhydderch a messuage, 14 acres, mill and a meadow, and his part of the advowson of the church there, at Clyn Mereduth in the fee of Whitchurch, the messuage and land being near the water of Nevern. In 1507 it was recorded that Gwilym ap Perkyn had died leaving his lands, among them Clene Meredyth at 'Egloyswen'. Before 1574 Morris Lewis ap Ieuan ap Ieuan was in ward to William Owen, Lord of Cemaes, for Clyn Meredyth in Whitechurch, and about 1600 James William Lewis

was in ward to George Owen, Lord of Cemaes, for only half a year, for Clyn Meredyth. Melchior ap Ieuan ap Howel ap Newport, gentleman, died in 1590, and left Clyn Meredith and eight other properties to his son William Melchior (High Constable of Cemaes in 1611). In 1760 Mr. Owen Thomas was tenant of the farm. In the period 1772-82 it was owned by John Symmons of Slebech, with William Davies as tenant-farmer.

In 1786 it was owned by Owen Thomas, gentleman, with William Davies as tenant. In 1839 Mr. Thomas was tenant, the farm then being 90 acres in extent. Later in the century Margaret Thomas of Clyn Meredith (died 1900, aged 65) married George Harries of Castle Villa (died 1908, aged 82) in Dewsland, and their only child Pheobe Davies Harries married Walter Morris of Chapel Farm, Castlemartin.

Refs: *N.L.W., Bronwydd Deeds, Foley of Ridgeway Deeds; Pembs. Land Tax 1786.*

CLYNSAITHMAN. *Llangolman.*
A mile and a quarter south-east of the peak of Moel Cwm Cerwyn, and three-quarters of a mile west of Pentrithel. An old farmstead, alas demolished during military excercises of World War II. Home of the yeoman family of Morris. Griffith Morris of Clynsaithman paid tax for three hearths in 1670. He died in 1684 and was followed by his son Griffith Morris, who married in 1693 as his first wife, Elizabeth Howell of Rushacre and then moved to the farm of Cwm Cerwyn (*vide* infra) where he was living in 1694; by her he had three children. He became a member of Rhydwilym Baptist Chapel in 1689 and religious meetings of that sect were often held at Clynsaithman. His second wife was Dorothy, by whom he had ten children. His will was proved in 1734, and he was followed by his son Stephen Morris. In 1786 Griffith Morris was owner-occupier of Clynsaithman.

Refs: *Pembs R.O., Land Tax 1786; R.C.A.M., Pembs 1925.*

COEDCANLAS. *Coedcanlas.*

In the southernpart of the parish, near the waters of the Cleddau. The name means the woodland of Cenlas or Cynlas, and the name occurs as Castle Cenlas (Mathry) and Coed Canlas (Eglywswen in Cemaes). The farmhouse, a commodious edifice of three stories, retains a number of its earlier features. It is built over a vaulted undercroft, now used as a basement storey, has a large chimney at one gable end, and corbelling at the other gable end, and there are two mullioned windows that have been filled in. Steps lead from the road level to the basement, and there is an exterior flight of stairs from ground level to the first floor. The walls of the house are nine feet thick. Behind the house is a large courtyard, beyond which are farm outbuildings. It was excellently preserved when I visited it on 17 April 1974, the owner-occupiers being the Merriman family who farmed the land.

Coedcanlas was one of Sir John Carew's Knight's fees in 1362, and was then held by John Perceval. The Percevals remained at Coedcanlas until the latter half of the 15th century, when the heiress Elizabeth daughter of Philip Perceval married John Butler, a younger son of the family of Dun. John Butler, described as Lord of Coedcanlas in 1495-6 was succeeded at the mansion by six generations of his descendants. John Butler was a strong supporter of Sir Rhys ap Thomas, Arnold Butler was High Sheriff in 1558, and Member of Parliament in 1554-5. Another John was High Sheriff in 1608, and died in 1629 when he was followed by his namesake who was the last of the family at the old home. John Butler sold Coedcanlas to the Owens of Orielton, and died in 1655. Sir Hugh Owen paid tax for ten hearths in Coedcanlas which shows that it was a large residence. The land had been divided into two messuages in Butler days, mentioned in 1637 as 'Koedkenlas parva, and Magna Koedkanlas'. The Free Chapelry of Coedcanlas had belonged to the Percevals, the Butlers, and finally the Owens. The edifice was 'in decaye' in 1535, restored by the Butlers, fell again into decay about 1660, but in 1718 it was rebuilt on the old foundation and endowed by Sir Arthur Owen, Bt. By 1912 it was again a total ruin.

Refs: *Dwnn*, i, 76; *W.W.H.R.* ii, 72; *O.Pem*, i, 309, ii, 338; *RCAM Pembs*; *NLW, Great Sessions, Pembs Plea Rolls*; *Fenton, Tour*, 1811.

COEDLLWYD. *Clydey.*

On 20 August 1977 I visited Coedllwyd, a 240 acre farm owned by Mrs. Jenkins and her two sons. They told me that the former mansion, 'Rhen Goedllwyd' (old Coedllwyd), had stood in the valley below the farmhouse, on the left bank of a little stream below Penybanc, not far from Star. Old ruined walls and other remains of the Plâs were still visible until 1958 when the Jenkins' bulldozer levelled the site and removed the remains. The site was in fields marked on the parish Tithe Map of 1841 as 1317, and 1326 by the west side of the stream, about half a mile from the hamlet of Star, and a mile south-west of Clydey church.

The gentry family traced to Edwyfed Fychan of Gwynedd. Two of his descendants, the brothers David ap Morgan and Morris ap Morgan were the first to settle in Pembrokeshire, David at Blaenbylan, the last of whom died in 1802, and Morris at Coedllwyd who married Margaret, daughter of John Thomas Lloyd of Clynfywn. Morris Morgan whose will was proved in 1656, left two children – Susan who married her first cousin Morris Morgan of Blaenbylan, and David Morgan who succeeded to Coedllwyd. David was High Sheriff in 1662, and died, leaving a son David Morgan of Coedllwyd, and Elizabeth who married Edwardes of Rhydygors near Carmarthen.

David Morgan was High Sheriff in 1685, paid for four hearths in 1670, and died without issue in 1688, leaving Coedllwyd to his sister Elizabeth Edwardes. She died without issue, and Coedllwyd passed to her aunts, Susan of Blaenbylan (died 1707) and Mrs. Mary Lewes of Pantyrodin (Cards.). Coedllwyd mansion was afterwards owned by the Blaenbylan family until 16 May 1751 when it was sold to William Thomas of Castell Gorfod, and from him passed to the Bowens of Llwyngwair who were the owners in

1786. In 1830 the Bowens sold Coedllwyd and several other properties in Clydey to Thomas Lewis of Clynfyw, and about 1910 Mr. Lewis-Bowen sold it to Mr. Jenkins, whose descendants entertained me when I called. The farmhouse of Coedllwyd is on high ground, over a quarter mile from the site of the old plâs.

Refs: Francis Jones, 'Blaenbylan' in *Ceredigion* 1976, *Carms RO, John Francis Deeds, Trant/Yelverton Deeds; NLW, Tithe Map and Schedule, Clydey parish 1841; Pembs RO, Land Tax 1786.*

COEDWYNOG. *Nevern and Bayvil.*

About midway between the parish churches of Nevern and Bayvil. A few medieval references occur. Thus, in 1331 Jevan elder son of Howe ap Martin granted all his messuages at Coedwinog to his daughter Joan for her life, with reversion to Philip ap Gwilym Lloyd and his heirs; in 1409-10 David ap Philip ap Gwilim Lloyd released lands at Coedwynnocke (held by Joan Verch Howell, their mother, for life) to his brother Perkin ap Phillip ap Gwillim Lloyd; in 1427-8 Wilcoke ap David ap Howell (his mother was Eva Lloyd) granted to his brother David ap David ap Howell a messuage and lands within a carucate at Coyt Wynog on the south of the river Gwithwch; in 1451 Llwelyn ap Perkyn granted to David ap David ap Howel, a third part of a house in which grantee dwells at Coidwinok; and in 1491 Howel ap Jenkyn ap Howel of Nevern and Morgan Dayfor granted to James ap Owen [of Pentre Ifan] their messuages and lands in the two carucates of Coed Wynog in the fee of Bayvill.

In 1516 David ap Gwillim ap Perkin and Jeuan ap David ap Perkin arbitrators in a dispute relating to a messuage lying within the two carucates of Coydewynoke, ordained that 'Thomas ap David ap Perkin and Agnes his wife shall pay 10 shillings to Llewelyn ap Philip ap Oweyn and Isabel his wife before the next Feast of the Saints and Martyrs Civic, and Jubita his mother, and that the said Llewelyn and Isabel shall withdraw their claim to the property in dispute'. In 1547 Agnes verch David Vychan of Nevern,

widow, released a tenement in Koedewnioc to James ap Owen Lloyd. In 1549 'William ap Rees David ap Hoell of Meline parish, gent, and Thomas ap Lewis Yonge gent, of Nyverne,' were arbitrators in a dispute between Jevan ap David ap Eynon, husbandman, and James ap Owen Lloyd merchant, both of Nyvern, relating to a third part of a house called Coydwynocke and an acre on the west side of the house. In 1565 Owen William of Nevarne, husbandman, granted a messuage called Place Koed y Wynock to Jane verch Mathias of Bayvil, spinster, for her life, then to her heirs, and in default to revert to the heirs of grantor. In 1586 George Owen of Henllys bought Coedwynog and lands there from the Pentre Ifan family and others, and in the following year he leased it to Chancellor Richard Edwardes and Mirabella his wife at an annual rent of £4.6.0.

The *Extent of Kemes* for 1 May 1594 recorded 'Coed y Winog. Richard Edwardes, clerk, Chancellor of St. Davids and Mirabella his wife, hold by lease for their lives a chief mansion at Coedywinog to the south of the stream of Gwythwch, in which they live, and also another tenement on the other side of the Gwythwch.' George Owen of Henllys wrote as follows in 1603-4, 'Coedwynok was the mansion house of Mr. Richard Edwardes, Chancelor of St. Davids, deceased, and by him built and about 16 yeares past much beautified, being the first man that caused the place to be acompted or spoken of allthoughe there was some prettie buildings there before his tyme yett nothing to that which he left behind him. This man for his discreete behaviour, Curteouse and liberall Intertaynment in his house, his grave and well advised Counsell to men of all sortes, and for his natural Inclynation, his facyll method in peace makinge, ys not a lyttle myssed in his Countrie; his valye noted fault in his liffe tyme was too much leuytaie in not bearing himselfe as his places and Calling required. This goodman hath made this his house to be in accompt as saith Cicero, *Non dolemus dominum* and *domino domum exornat.'*

David James, gentleman lived at Koedwinock in 1610-11, and Mathew Bowen, gentleman, in 1632. It was owned by George Owen a descendant, Thomas Lloyd esquire of Bronwydd, Cards., in 1786, with David Evans as tenant, and later was owned by Reverend David Griffith of Berllan, clerk, who on 5 July 1831 granted a lease for life of Coedwinog Fawr and Fach to Thomas Davis at an annual rent of £120.

Refs: *B. M.* Egerton Ms 2586: *College of Arms*, Protheroe Ms. N; *NLW* – Bronwydd Deeds, Morgan Richardson Deeds; B. G. Charles 'Second Book of George Owen's Description of Pembrokeshire', in *NLW Journal*, Winter 1948, p. 271.

COLBY. *Wiston.*

Now a farmstead with very large outbuildings 1¼ miles south-east of Wiston village. About half a mile to the north of Colby farm, is the farm called Colby Moor, both being marked on Colby's Map 1831. The first-known owner as Sir John Wogan of Wiston who held a quarter of a Knight's fee in Colby at the time of his death in 1410. Colby and adjacent lands continued in Wogan hands until towards the mid-17th century when Colby was sold to John Vongler described as of Colby, yeoman, in 1649. In 1670 John Vongler was assessed at five hearths, which shows it to have been a substantial house. A few years later he sold Colby to George Owen, D.D., who came there to live. He was described in 1690 as Professor of Theology. In his will dated 1 July 1690, proved 29 January 1690-1, he bequeathed 'Colby which I purchased from John and William Vongler, and the mill belonging thereto' to my wife Mary, with remainder to their eldest son George Owen, who succeeded to the property. George Owen the son was a barrister, a Justice of the Peace, and in 1708 a Land Tax Commissioner for the county. Shortly after on 21 February 1708-9 he sold Colby for £2,300 to John Barlow (of the Slebech family) who came to live at the house. A note made by the Registrar who accompanied Bishop Adam Ottley (1713-1723) on his Visitations in the diocese, records that they called on Mr. John Barlow at Colby, where 'we were entertained there in a London way, everything little but neat, and perfect in the kind; a new house, well seated,

garden, etc.' This suggests that John Barlow erected the 'new house' soon after he acquired it. It remained in that family until 1758 when the heiress Catherine Barlow married (Sir) William Hamilton, and when he died without issue he left the Slebech and Colby estates to his nephew Charles Greville. The residence at Colby had become ruinous, and in 1768 certain improvements were made to it, and Hamilton was warned that the repairs would 'incur considerable expense'. In 1786 the tenant of Colby was one Daniel Roberts. Fenton observed in 1811. 'The ancient mansion has long since been taken down to make room for a farm-house, and its name alone is retained'. In 1838 the owner was Capt. Robert Fulke Greville, and the tenant was Elizabeth Parry.

Refs: NLW, Slebech Deeds, Great Sessions Pembs. Plea Rolls, The Ottley Papers, Bronwydd Deeds, Eaton-Evans and Williams Deeds; Pembs. RO, Deeds D/RTP/P/C, Land Tax 1786; College of Arms, Wagner Ms 2; B. M. Egerton Ms 2586; W.W.H.R. iii and vi.

COLBY LODGE. *Amroth.*

Now an attractive residence in a dell, about half a mile to the west of the parish church. The earliest name of the property was Rhydlangoeg. A farmhouse in the 18th century belonging to the Skyrmes of Vaynor (Llawhaden). In the Land Tax of 1786 it is not specifically named, but as 'New house' owned by Thomas Skyrme, Esq., with Mrs. Brock as tenant. In a description of the Skyrme estate in 1787 it is called 'Rerdlangwig' (13 acres) which was held on a lease of lives by Mrs. Brock (55), Mrs. Bamfield (51) and Miss Thomas (48). On 13 September 1794 the marriage settlement of Jane Bamfield of 'Rhydlangwyg' and James Lewis, mercer, of Carmarthen was executed. The Skyrmes were encountering financial difficulties, and in 1803 parts of the estate were sold by order of Chancery to clear Skyrme debts. Among the properties was the messuage called 'Red Land Wig', which was purchased by John Colby of Ffynnone. Nearby was the 'Redlangoige Colliery' worked by the Colbys in 1806-7. Shortly after its purchase in 1803, a large residence was built, and named after the then owners, Colby Lodge, the building of which was supervised by John Nash's Clerk of the Works. Nash was also concerned with changes to Ffynnone House. In 1834. Lewis wrote 'Colby Lodge, an elegant mansion, seat of Captain Protheroe [later of Dolwilym], is beautifully situated in a romantic dell opening at one extremity towards the sea, of which it commands a fine and interesting view'.

In 1839 Cordelia Maria Colby, widow, granted the 'dwelling house called Rhydlangoeg' to her son John Colby. In 1852 'Mr. Thomas Evans the present resident has lately opened an Hydropathic Establishment at Colby Lodge, the first of its kind in South Wales' – so wrote Miss F. P. Gwynne. The 'freehold mansion and estates called Rhydlangoeg otherwise called Colby Lodge' was advertised for sale in 1855. In 1894 David Thomas and Samuel Kay lived at Colby Lodge and Rhydlangoed respectively. Thereafter it had various tenants and owners. Samuel Kay, J.P., was living at Colby Lodge in 1914 when his daughter Gladys married Lt.-Col. J. C. H. Crosland, who, after the 1914-18 war, came to live at his wife's home, and was there in 1925 when he served as High Sheriff for the county. It was finally sold by Miss E. F. Dixon Mason to the late Mr. I. O. Chance of Christie's, London, in 1965.

The Colby Lodge estate (less the mansion and its 20 acres), comprising 870 acres, was bequeathed to the National Trust by Miss Mason (Miss Crosland's niece). Colby Lodge was excellently looked after by her and Mrs. Chance, who modernized certain interior features, and beautified the garden and grounds. In 1980 they made a gift of the property to the National Trust. Alas, Mrs. Chance died in 1981, and her husband at the end of 1984. The mansion, splendidly maintained by the Trust, still stands. Now occupied by Mr. and Mrs. A. Scourfield-Lewis.

Refs: *NLW,* Owen and Colby Estate Records; *Pembs R.O.,* Land Tax 1786; *Lewis,* Top. Dict. Wales, 1834 edn.; Fanny Price Gwynne, *Sketches of Tenby etc.,* 1852 edn.; *Western Mail* 5 October and 23 November, 1985, Illustrs. of the mansion: Nola D. Davies, *The Story of Amroth, The Church and the Parish,* 1980.

COLSTON. *Little Newcastle.*
Marked as Colston south of Martell farm on Kitchin map 1764, and as Old Coldstone on Colby's Map 1831. Home of the Voyle family in early Tudor days. George Owen in *The Second Book* (p.273) 1603, notes that 'Lewis Yongue [of Glastir, Nevern] the eldest son married Gwenllyan Voel of Colston a gentlewoman and heyre of dyverse landes', and had issue.

In 1500 Jenkyn Voel of Colston granted lands and tenements in Dyffryn Gwayne in the fee of Nantgwyn to John ap Owen ap Rees. The next family there was one Symmons, and in 1670 John Symmons of Colston was assessed at three hearths; the family remained at Colston until 1800. The *Land Tax 1786* lists four farms called Coulstone owned by William Knox of Llanstinan. The *Voters Lists* for 1894 names two farms so-called, while that of 1904 lists the freehold farms of Old Coldstone, New Coldstone and Martell Mill.

Refs: *W.W.H.R.* ii, 41: B. M. Egerton Ms 2586; *NLW,* Bronwydd Deeds; *Pembs RO,* Deeds HDX/562, nos. 34-37.

CORSTON. *Monkton (Pembroke).*
A mansion to the north-east of Castlemartin Village. Marked as Causon on Kitchin's Map 1763-4, as Corston House on Mudge's Map 1819, and as Corsiton on Colby's Map 1831. Home of the Meares family from 1665 to 1770; Francis Meare of Corston was High Sheriff in 1695, and an inventory of his possessions in 1720 gives some particulars about the house at that time; the Ground Floor contained the hall, parlour, kitchen, pantry and an inner cellar; on the Upper Floor were the large chamber, middle chamber, chamber over the kitchen, two lodging rooms, and 'closet of conveniency'; the garrets contained a number of rooms, store-rooms, and the maid's chambers; the 'outer rooms' consisted of outer store room, dairy, outer cellar, brewhouse, cooling house, stables, ox-house, cart house, and other outhouses; and nearby was the haggard. In the Hearth Tax of 1670 Francis Meare is assessed at three and four

hearths, which suggests it was then of moderate size as indicated by the inventory of 1720. In the pre-marriage settlement of Francis Meares junior and Anne Elliot of Pembroke, dated 1726, he settled 'the capital messuage called Corston' to the uses of the marriage. The last of the family William Meares sold Corston in 1770 to John Prout a yeoman of Moor, and after his death about 1780, Corston passed by purchase to Abraham Leach of Pembroke, and it remained the seat of that family until the death without issue of Brig. Gen. H. E. Burleigh Leach, C.B., C.M.G., C.V.O. on 16 August 1936. The widow married Captain Lionel Green and went to live in Herefordshire. In 1940 the mansion was requisitioned by the R.A.F., and afterwards by the County War Agricultural Committee who used it as a Land Girls' Hostel. In 1946 Mrs. Green sold the house. The Leach family produced High Sheriffs in 1797, 1852, 1855 and 1933.

Refs: *Pembs RO*, Deeds 1665-1885; *NLW*, Morgan-Richardson Deeds; R. G. Thorne, 'History of the Leach family' in *Pembs. Hist. 1981*.

COSHESTON (HALL OF). *Cosheston.*

On 26 August 1556 Gelly Barret, gentlemen, of Gellyswick and his wife Mary sold 'a tenement called the Hall of Cosheston' to John Rossant of Nash, husbandman, and Isabel his wife, and it remained in the ownership of the Rossant family for several generations. In 1659 the will of John Rossant of Cosheston, yeoman, mentions the 'house called the Hall of Cosheston'. His son, Francis, was assessed at two hearths in 1670. In 1786 the Hall was owned and occupied by Mr. Abraham Leach. Just north of Cosheston village there was a farm called Snailton owned and occupied by Reverend William Holcombe. For a time the Allen family were in occupation including Seymour Phillips Allen (High Sheriff 1850) and his wife Lady Catherine, daughter of the 4th Earl of Ports-

mouth (*Vide* Burke's Landed Gentry *1969 under* Evans of Cresselly). Later, the name was changed to Woodfield and in 1894 it was occupied by George Stepney Gulston, and shortly afterwards bought by Major Ivor, afterwards Major-General Sir Ivor Philipps, K.C.B., D.S.O., who enlarged the house and gave it the name Cosheston Hall. The General died in 1940, and afterwards it was the seat of his daughter, Mrs. Basil Ramsden, and her son, Major Ivor Ramsden, M.B.E. (High Sheriff 1967) now one of H.M. Gentlemen at Arms, is the present owner-occupier, and is a D.L. The Hall was entirely rebuilt in the mid 19th century.

Refs: *B. M. Egerton MS 2586; R.C.A.M. Pembs. 1925; Pembs. R.O., D/LLC, No. 1;* for portraits at *Cosheston (Mrs. Ramsden) see Steegman Vol. 2. S. Wales (1962).*

COTTESMORE. *Prendergast.*

A mansion about 1 mile north of Prendergast church. The first house there was a farmstead known as Cotts. William Williams was living there in 1731 and his descendants owned the property until 23 December 1801 when it was sold by Francis Williams to Louis Devandes of Cotts, and Mary (Stokes) his wife. In 1814 the new owners assigned Cotts to the Peel family. In 1826 J. H. Peel of Cotts was High Sheriff and described in 1834 as owner of freehold land there. In 1835 his only daughter Helen Peel married Edward Taylor Massy and in 1839 he bought Cotts from his father-in-law, and in that year commenced building a residence, very close to the original house, which was completed in 1841, and given the name Cottesmore. In 1873 E. T. Massy is described in the Landowners' Return as of Cottesmore (231 acres). One of the last of the family at Cottesmore was Lieutenant-General H. R. S. Massy, High Sheriff in 1946. Some years later Cottesmore was purchased by Colonel G. T. Kelway, High Sheriff in 1958 who died in 1990.

Refs: *Cottesmore (Massy) Deeds; Landowners' Return 1873*; Nicholas, *County Families,* 1870 illustr.

COTTY. *Maenclochog.*

Today a farm between Maenclochog village and Rosebush and known as Gotty. During the Tudor era, it was known as Cotty Whiaid. The earliest-known family there was that of Dedwydd, sometimes spelled as Dedwyth. Lewis Dedwydd had two sons, the elder, Griffityh Lewis Dedwydd succeeded to 'Cotty Whyad', who had an only child, Elizabeth who married James ap John Rees David Howel (of the Penybenglog family, descended from Gwynfardd Dyfed), and their son Anthony James settled in Meline where he was living in 1628; the younger son William Lewis Dedwydd had a son Lewis William of Bwlch y Clawdd near Maenclochog who married Morfydd, sister of the above-named James ap John, and had issue (*vide* Bwlch y Clawdd *supra*). In 1786 Cotty was owned by Lord Milford, with William Howell as tenant.

Refs: *Golden Grove Mss. (Gwynfardd); College of Arms, Proth. Ms. IV fo. 50, and XII fo. 44; Land Tax 1786.*

COURT (CWRT). *Eglwyswrw.*

Now a farmstead just over half a mile north of Eglwyswrw. The first family there was that of Cantington. William Cantington, of Eglwyswrw lived at Court in 1199, and died in 1227. His descendants lived there throughout the middle ages and during the Tudor period adopted the Welsh form of nomenclature. Court became part of the Owen of Henllys estate. We are informed in 1594 – 'Coorte Hall the manor house [of the manor of Eglwyswrw]. There was in ould tyme an ancient manor howse or castell called Coorte Hall, nowe commonly called the Coorte, which was seated upon a faire plaine within a square mote standing very commodiously for woodde, water, and other comodities. The howse is now utterly decayed, and the lords kepeth the demeynes in his owne handes.' In 1603 George Owen, Lord of Cemaes wrote, 'The Coorte being this manor house of His lordshipp in tymes past (and as is reported, the mansion house of Bishopp David Martin, bushopp of St. Davids, being lorde of the said

manor) seemeth to have been a house both of accompt and strengthe, for I have seene within the moate there hugh walles and roomes of great breadeth all envyroned within a stronge and deepe mote digged out of the mayne rock fadd with a freshe springe ryshing in the same, and all the greenes there about growen with camamyll.' In 1925, the R.C.A.M. reported that 'nothing except the moat remains of the manorhouse of the lordship of Eglwyswrw, the mansion house of Bishop David Martin [1293-1328].

The site, now part of the modern farmhouse of Court, is about 30 yards by 20 yards; it is surrounded on its north, east and west sides by the remains of a moat 15 feet wide, which, on the east, is cut through rock; here it is seen at its best, the remaining parts being overgrown and largely filled in with soil.' In September 1597 George Owen settled the Court estate on his son Alban Owen who then came to the new house probably built on the site of the old one. Some time after 1615, Alban moved to Henllys. Afterwards it was occupied by several families, the most important being that of Ford, and on their departure at the end of the 17th century, was occupied by farming tenants.

The present edifice was never large, and in 1670 Alexander Ford of Court was assessed at three hearths only. The yeoman family of Devonald held it from 1764, and the last two members, Anne and Martha Devonald died some years before 1845.

Refs: *The Extent of Cemaes* 1594, pp. 59,63; George Owen, *Second Book, 1603-4,* p. 278; *R.C.A.M. Pembs. 1925,* p. 93; Fenton, *Tour Pembs,* 1811, p. 292; George Owen's Elizabethan Pembs in *Pembs Record Series No. 2, 1973,* pp. 32-7, 97-8; *NLW, Bronwydd Deeds; Pembs R.O., Davies-Scourfield Papers; Golden Grove Mss II (Adv. Pembs); College of Arms, Proth. Ms IV (GWG),* p. 143; B. G. Charles, *George Owen,* 1973.

COURT (CWRT). *Llanllawer.*

Originally a farm, until 1800 when the present large mansion was erected. Fenton's description shortly after the mansion had appeared reads as follows: 'Opposite to Bronllwyn on the other side of the river Gwaun, placed on high ground, though well-sheltered from the north, stands Court, a handsome modern mansion belonging to my friend John Gwyn Esq., in the midst of a well-managed demesne, finely sloping to the sun, and commanding pleasing views of the vale where the hospitable genius long exiled from so many deserted houses, and a wanderer, still delighting to hover around the scenes she loved and had once enlivened, has at last found an asylum.'

The old house has a long history. In 1594 Owen Johns, gent., of Brecon held land called Y Coort in Llanllawern, in occupation of Thomas ap Howel ap Gronow and Harry Hugh; and a memorial roll of Cemaes for 9 May 1650 records that among farms on the estate of Owen of Trecwn was Trellwyn and Tir y Court in Llanllawer. Towards the end of the 17th century those two properties became part of the estate of Warren of Trewern. On 1754 an estate map made by John Butcher defines Trellwyn Ucha and Court.

On 14 November 1770 Thomas Williams Esq. of Pope Hill and Haverfordwest, and his wife Anne (née Warren, co-heiress) made a lease of Court to Griffith Gwynne of Cilciffeth, gent. and in 1784 Griffith assigned the lease to his third brother William Gwynne. The Land Tax of 1786 shows 'Esquire Williams' as owner of 'Curt' in Llanllawer. The property changed hands on 5 October 1799 when the said Thomas and Anne Williams sold Court to John Gwynne of Haverfordwest, Attorney at Law and a martyr to the gout. The new owner immediately set about building a mansion on the site of the older house, and it still stands today. In 1847 a detailed map of Court, Trellwynfawr and Ty Cam was made by the Gwynnes. In 1874 and 1875, the last of the Gwynnes, Anne and Martha died unmarried, and Court passed to the next heir, the Revd. Thomas Gwynne Mortimer, whose mother was a Gwynne. During a visit to the Holy Land, he brought back some fig cuttings which were planted in the walled garden at Court where they flourished mightily. He lived the remainder of his life at Court, was Rector of Castlebythe and Rural Dean of Fishguard, and died

in 1903 leaving Court to his kinsman, Mortimer Thomas. It continued in that family until 1956 when it was sold to a local farmer who still owns and occupies it.

Refs: NLW, *Vairdre Book*, Extent of Cemaes 1594; *Bronwydd Deeds, Trenewydd Deeds;* information from the late Mrs. Catherine Royston Brown (née Mortimer Thomas) of Trenewydd, Pencaer; Francis Jones, 'A Pembrokeshire Squarson', *Pembs. Hist. 1974.*

A typical Pembrokeshire farmstead.

CRABHOLE. *Marloes.*

A farmstead close to an inlet, about 6 miles north of Dale. Home of a medieval family who bore the name of the property. In the years 1384-1405 Philip Crabhole lived there, one of whose daughters and co-heirs married Laugharne (late of St. Brides) who later alienated the property. During the 1500's the family of Loughor owned it, and were still there in 1666 when Thomas Loughor of Crabhole, gentleman, is mentioned in legal records. Loughor was probably a tenant, for in 1637 it belonged to Sir John Wogan of Boulston. The Wogans continued to own it, and in 1773 John Wogan of Boulston was the owner of Crabhole (309 acres) with Cornelius Davies (aged 60) as a leaseholder. He was the son of Gilbert Davies (will proved 1739) member of a successful yeomen stock, who also owned Mullock Brownhill, and a descendant, Warren-Davis, were owners of Trewarren, a mansion in the neighbouring parish of St. Ishmael's. Crabhole continued in the hands of successful farmers.

When I visited it on 6 September 1977, I found a large old farmhouse. It once had a gable-end chimney, but this was removed by the present owner-occupiers, Mr. and Mrs. James, who kindly received and assisted me. A walled garden stretched in front of the house, with another, but smaller, walled garden at the side of the house. Earlier, Mr.

and Mrs. Rind now of Allenbrook House, Dale, who once lived at Crabhole have an excellent photograph of the house showing the old gable-end chimney.

Refs: *NLW, G.S. Pembs Plea Rolls, Maesgwynne Deeds; Sale Catalogue* of the estates of John Wogan, 1773; *Fenton, Tour Pembs* 1811, p. 171; *Pembs Co. Land Tax,* 1786; Francis Green, 'Wogan of Boulston' in *Y Cymmrodor*, 1902; Tablets in Marloes parish church.

CRESSELLY. *Jefferston.*

About a mile and a half to the west of the parish church. The original house stood in the middle of a colliery, in the valley below the present mansion. For many generations Cresselly was the home of a yeoman family. The earliest known member was Peter Bartlett, yeoman living at Cresselly in 1564. He was followed by John Bartlett who died just before 1672, leaving his property to his son John Bartlett, junior. On the death of the last-named in 1629, he was succeeded by his son David Bartlett who married Elizabeth Phelps of Carew.

On David's death in 1652, he was succeeded by his son John Bartlett, yeoman, who became agent for John Barlow of Lawrenny. The yeoman's house at this time was a modest one judging from the fact that it was assessed at but two hearths in 1670. His eldest son died unmarried in 1728 leaving Cresselly to his niece Joan, daughter of his brother John Bartlett of Cresswell. In 1729 Joan Bartlett married John Allen of Goodhook, who became the first of that family to settle at Cresselly which from that time has remained in the hands of his descendants who continued to live there.

In 1732 John Allen became High Sheriff of the county, and died in 1752. In 1770 another John Allen pulled down the orginal house which stood on low ground near the coal mines, and erected a new mansion at the present site on the higher ground. It was enlarged in 1869, and still stands today, being the home of the family of the late Mrs. Auriol Evans (née Allen) heiress of Cresselly. Malkin wrote in 1803, 'Cresselly, with its luxurious plantation of firs, seems to possess a comfort-able establishment, but my attention was not directed to anything worth describing'.

Fenton, in 1811, noted 'Cresselly the elegant seat of John Allen Esq., lately my brother circuiteer [barrister, M.P. Pembr. Bor. 1818-26] stands in the midst of a colliery judiciously planted woods skreened those dingy volcanoes from its windows.' Five of the Allens of Cresselly were High Sheriffs.

Refs: *Pembs RO*, Deeds DH/99, no. 8; *NLW, Picton Castle Deeds, Eaton Evans and Williams Deeds;* E. Inglis-Jones, 'A Pembrokeshire County Family in the 18th century' (the Allens of Cresselly) in *NLW Journal, vol. 17, 1971-2* Col. F. S. Allen; Family records of the Allens of Cresselly and some family letters, etc., priv. printed, 1905; Malkin, *Tour, S. Wales;* Fenton, *Tour Pembs.* 1811; Contemporary Biographies, *South Wales and Mon. 1907,* p. 106, illustr. of exterior of Cresselly; T. Nicholas, *County Families,* 1875; C. S. Allen, Tenby, *Photos of Pembs. Mansions,* 1871.

CRESSWELL. *Lawrenny.*

The ruins of this former mansion are engulfed in undergrowth so that it is difficult to examine it. The R.C.A.M. found a similar difficulty when they visited the site in March 1923, but managed to produce a fair description, which may be summarized as follows. The mansion is rectangular in form, 30 ft. by 40 ft., and has a turret at each angle some 16 ft. high. Two, perhaps three of the turrets were vaulted, and one had been used as a dovecot; the courtyard is 15 ft. by 20 ft., and there are remains of a fine porch and doorway on the east front, with a short, broad walk to the banks of the Cresswell river. Beyond the north wall stretched the garden, an almost square enclosure, with a river frontage; there are stables and outbuildings to the east of the house; and about 300 yards west of the house are remains of the domestic chapel; to the north-east of the mansion is Cresswell farm. The mansion was assessed at nine hearths which shows it to have been a commodious building.

The Barlows of Slebech bought numerous lands from the Crown, and it is likely that Cresswell and the chapel was among them for they were owned by John Barlow of

Slebech (d.1600). His younger son William Barlow settled at Cresswell, and married Elizabeth ap Rhys of Rickeston, Brawdy parish. William was High Sheriff in 1612, and died in 1636. His son Lewis Barlow paid taxes for nine hearths at Cresswell in 1670, and is described as of that place in 1679. He was High Sheriff in 1641 and 1668. He also inherited Lawrenny, and died in 1681. His son John Barlow lived for a time at Cresswell, but moved after his father's death to Lawrenny, where he died in 1700-1. The property remained in Barlow ownership. In 1786 Sir William Hamilton (who had married a Barlow) was described as owner of Cresswell, with Mrs. Elizabeth Barlow as occupier. Elizabeth also owned Cresswell Mill. It seems that it was about this time that the mansion was abandoned.

Refs: *R.C.A.M. Pembs, 1925*, p. 144; *W.W.H.R.*, iii, p. 137; *NLW, Slebech Deeds, Spence-Colby Deeds; Pembs RO*, Lawrenny Deeds; *Land tax List*, 1786; T. Nicholas, *County Families*, 1875 edn. p. 909.

CRONLLWYN. *Fishguard.*

Now a farmstead in the Gwaun Valley, about half a mile on high ground to the south of Bont Llanychaer, and near to another old mansion, Cilgelynen. Fenton wrote in 1811, Cronllwyn 'a favourite spot of Sir William Martin as I find it the property of my great-grandfather [John Lewis] of Manorowen soon after his marriage with a daughter of Mortville [Morfil] probably part of his wife's dowry.'

During the 16th and 17th centuries Cronllwyn was the house of local gentry. In 1573 John ap Rees, gent, gave seizin of a tenement and 100 acres at Place y Crwnlloyn and Dolwen, to Griffith John Llewelin, and a few years later we learn that Owain ap Gruffyd ap Llewelin o' Grynllwyn o Abergwn [of Plâs Abergwaun] was married to Marged daughter of John Bateman [of Mynydd Melin], and had two children, Sion ap Owen and Ann, who were living in 1591 when Dwnn called there. The father, Owen (ap) Griffith of Cronllwyn witnessed the will of Lewis Nash of Fishguard on 20 April 1608.

The son John Owen was still living at Cronllwyn in 1657. Thomas Owen of Cronloyne was alive in 1637, and married to a daughter of David Lloyd of Morfil. By the next century Cronllwyn was held by farming tenants. In 1786 it was owned by Thomas Bowen Parry Esq. of Manorowen, with John Williams as tenant, and since then has always been a farm held by local folk.

Refs: Fenton, *Tour Pembs*, 1811: *NLW, Kemes Court Rolls* (Bronwydd colln.), *Great Sessions Papers, Pembs Plea Rolls; Carm RO., Golden Grove mss; Dwnn*, i, 173.

CRUGIAU CEMAES.

Partly in Bayvil and Nevern parishes.

The six Crugian Cemaes tumuli occupy the eastern end of Bayvil parish where it meets those of Nevern and Moylgrove. These sepulchral cairns (or twmps) and the relics found in some have been noted in Gibson's edition of Camden's *Britannia*, 1695 which quotes the views of Edward Lloyd. George Owen of Henllys (O. Pem. 1.108, see also *Second Book* (ed. B. G. Charles) describes the tumuli as 'four little tumps of earth, and yet to been seen 40 miles off, viz from Plynlimon.' The whole area, some 600 feet high occupies a commanding position, and slopes gently westwards. The boundary between Bayvil and Nevern runs through the area along a roadway. North of that road, and in Bayvil, are the tumuli, one of which, just over the further boundary, is in Moylgrove parish, and there are several farms and holdings at Pantgwyn, Trelerni, Pengwndwn, and Pencrugiau on the road-boundary.

South of the boundary, and in Nevern, is the main farmstead of Crugiau, also called Crugiau Cemaes, and the farms of Rhydymaen, Cwm-eog, and Samaria, the cottages of Penuel Cemaes and Post-coch, and due south, across Nant Duad, is historic Coed Pencelli. In earlier days there were several other tenements whose names and locations are now lost – Cwm bychan, Pistsyll y Blaidd, 'the vill of Ryowe Crugie', Caereglwys Mawr, Pantygroes, Crugie yr elyrch (all mentioned 1517), Crugie Ucha (1469) Crugie Issa (1550), and Tir yr Esker in Crugie

Ucha (1594). All the above south of the road-boundary occupied 'the Crugie Quarter' of Nevern parish, and in 1786 'Crugie' farm was owned by John Protheroe, and tenanted by widow Thomas. In 1840 Crigie (171 acres) was owned by James Propert, tenanted by Eynon Havard; in 1894, Eynon, William, Walter and Ellen Havard held the land and farmlands of Crugiau, jointly; in 1909 Crigie farm in Nevern and Bayvil, comprising 213 acres, part of Cwmgloyn estate, tenanted by Eynon and Walter Havard, was advertised for sale. This was the capital messuage of the area, and formerly belonged to Rhys ap Rhydderch, descended from Gwynfardd Dyfed; fifth in descent from Rhys, was·Lewis ab Owen 'who dyverse yeares past pawned the said house and lands of Crigie (Ycha) to Thomas Young of Tredrissy father to Phillip Younge father to John Phillip Young who now dwelleth there' – thus George Owen, Second Book, (1603-4), p.271.

Part, if not all of Crugiau Ucha once belonged to Thomas ap David ap Ievan of Court, Eglwyswrw, descended from the Cantingtons; Thomas was followed by son Owen, who married Avis, daughter of Llewelyn Tew of Cilgwyn, whose only child Avis married James ap Rees a younger son of Penybenglog. Avis's only child and heiress married Thomas Jones of Brawdy, and they in 1582 broke the entail on a messuage and 26 acres in 'Criggie Ycha in Nevarne'.

Crugiau had been purchased by William Owen of Henllys between 1493 and 1508: his son, George Owen, in 1585 bought a further 16 pieces of land from a yeoman, John Lewys Llywelyn who then lived at Crigiau. In 1594 Philip John Howel held lands at Crugiau Ucha lately owned by John Lewis Llewelin, while John Philip Younge held a tenement at Crugiau Issa. In the succeeding years Crugiau changed hands several times, before it was sold with the Cwmgloyn estate in 1909.

Refs: *NLW, Bronwydd Deeds, Kemes Court Rolls, Roll of Wards, G. Owen's Second Book;* B. G. Charles, *George Owen; Cambrian Register,* 1796, ii, 491; *Additional Morris Letters,* p. 109; *Carns RO., Golden Grove Mss.: W.W.H.R.* ii, 91; *B. M. Egerton Ms.,* 1586.

CRUGLAS. *St. Davids.*

Now a farmstead, south of Cwmwdig, on rising ground overlooking Spite Moor, and Pont Cruglas on the main road from St. Davids to Fishguard. For long, home of farming families. In the years 1546-49, William John, husbandman, lived there and in 1562 Maurice ap John ap Ieuan, husbandman. In 1595 the Reverend Walter Thomas, clerk, and Arnold Johnes, gentleman, brought an action in the court of Great Sessions against John Woolcock for trespassing with animals 'at a place called Kriggles' and depasturing there. David John Woolcock of Crickglase, yeoman, made his will on 10 March 1612, in which his three children inherited. Before 1637 it was held by William Jones, younger son of Thomas Jones of Brawdy, on a tenancy granted by the See of St. Davids which owned the property. It later became the home of George Harry, a younger son of David Harry the elder of Llanrhian parish, yeoman. When he made his will on 13 November 1650, George Harry held a lease of Crikeglas farm, and his descendants held renewal leases for six generations, until the death of John Harding Harries (who was High Sheriff 1846) in 1869.

The family whose surname was extended to Harries, were strong Nonconformists. 'Mrs. Harries, Criglas' was a communicant at Trefgarn Owen chapel while 'Mr. John Harries of Kirkglace' and his wife became members of Albany chapel at Haverfordwest. The family gradually added to their possessions and became members of the landed gentry, and left Cruglas in order to live at the nearby mansion of Trefaccwn. The old farmstead of Cruglas was improved, and shortly after 1797 the east front was added to the building. The property has been sold by the See of St. Davids (owner of the freehold), and today is the home of the Evans family, formerly of Trenewydd, Brawdy.

Refs: 'History of Harries of Cruglas and Trevaccoon' by Francis Green in W.W.H.R., VIII a work containing several errors; *Albany Chapel Records,* and *Records of Trefgarn Owen Chapel; NLW, Records of Great Sessions; Carns. RO, Trant Deeds; Pembs RO, Land Tax 1786.*

CUFFERN. *Roch.*

A mansion, some two miles from Roch Gate on the St. Davids-Haverfordwest main road, immediately north of the mansion in the high land called Cuffern mountain, Coffrwm by the Welsh. From early days Cuffern consisted of several farms which continued until modern times. During the years 1150-70 the 'manor of Cuffern' (2 carucates) was granted by Robert fitz Richard fitz Tancred to the Hospitallers of St. John, of Slebech.

In 1392 we find that John Bateman and Margaret his wife occupied lands at Wyddinston and Coffron, held of the manor of Roch, and in the following century Coffron formed part of the possessions of the Knights Hospitallers. The Barrett family owned lands there which were finally inherited by two co-heiresses – Jennet Barrett wife of Nicholas Hurde whose descendants were living in 1592, and Joan Barrett wife of William Roblin whose daughter married John ab Owen of Lochmeyler, from whom descended the Bowens of Roblinston. The will of John Roblin 'of Cuffern' is dated 1434. In 1566 William Yonge 'of Coffrone' yeoman, lived there, and in 1577 John Tankard of East Dudwell and Thomas Bowen of Roblinston held, as assignees of Griffith White, 'a carucate of ploughland' on Goffremont alias Cofferun', being 'but heath grounds, and good for neither pasture nor corn' – this, clearly, being Cuffern mountain.

By 1608 one William David Perkin lived 'at Koffrwm', in 1623 James Young and Francis Stephen lived there. In 1639 Laugharne Young (son of James Young and his wife Maud, née Reynish) died owning lands 'in Cuffern,' and in 1671 Anthony Stokes, gent., claimed a messuage and 190 acres 'in Coffrom'. By will of 1716 James Young of Dale parish bequeathed 'Cyffran alias Cyffrwn', being two ploughlands, in Roch, to his daughter Jane wife of Constant Stokes. Anne Young, the other co-heiress married James Harries, and owned part of Cuffern in 1736, and their son, Francis Harries, by will of 1760 left Cuffern to his wife Elizabeth for life, with remainder to John Rees son of testator's sister Mrs. Anne Rees. This John Rees had adopted the name John Rees Stokes by 1775 when he married Frances Warren of Trewern. Cuffern was still divided into two parts, and in 1786 one was owned by John Rees Stokes, the other by John Jones Esq. of Brawdy. The present mansion at Cuffern was built about 1770 by the said J. R. Stokes, whose descendants remained in possession thereafter. In 1837 his son, John Stokes Stokes owned Cuffern and demesne (240 acres), Cuffern farm (Thos Reynish, tenant) 94 acres, Cuffern Mountain 114 acres, and Start 95 acres. The present mansion is large and commodious, of four storeys, with ranges of seven windows each storey, a pillared Georgian entrance, and gable-end chimneys. Fenton, who was entertained by John Rees Stokes in 1811, states 'Kyffern, the seat of its present proprietor, a handsome modern mansion, well placed with a rising ground to the north … here under this hospitable roof I lose the fatigues of the day, and next morning pursue my route'. In 1986 a hotel and in 1988 renovated and made into a nursing home and is now a home for the elderly.

Refs: Fenton, *Tour Pembs,* 1811; *W.W.H.R.* XI; W. Rees, *History of St. John,* 1947; *Pembs RO, Deeds D/EE/2* and *Saunders-Davis Colln.; Golden Grove mss.;* B. M. *Egerton ms. 2586;* NLW, *Pembs Papers of Great Session;* good photo of mansion in *Western Telegraph* 20 October 1977, and see also 10 August 1988.

CWMBETTWS. *Bridell.*

Now a large old farmhouse, south of Bridell church, and 1¼ miles north-east of Eglwyswrw. Home of the Williams family who later succeeded to the Cwmgloyn estate (q.v.). In 1786 William Williams, Esq. was owner, with John Phillips as tenant.

CWM CERWYN.

Llangolman and Mynachlogddu parishes.

This farmstead stood in Mynachlogddu parish, above the eastern banks of Afon Wern which forms the boundary of that parish with Llangolman. It is on high ground due east of Moel

Cwm Cerwyn ('Precelly Top'). Marked on Rees' 14C map. This district is mentioned in the Mabinogi (Olwen and Culchurch) when Arthur and his retinue hunted the Twrch Trwyth. Land in this area had been granted to St. Dogmaels Abbey and is mentioned in deeds of 1344-5. After the Dissolution the tenement called 'Come Kerwyn', part of the dissolved monastery of St. Dogmaels, was leased for 99 years to David ap Rhys ap Owen, on 12 October 1535, and later assigned to John Bradshaw and his heirs, at an annual rent of 10s.

During the years 1538-44 John ap Ieuan ap Morgan Gwyn of Cwm Kerwyn brought an action in Chancery against David ap. Ieuan ap Jenkyn and Isabel his wife, and William David John and Alison his wife, the said females living daughters and administrators of Ieuan ap Morgan Gwyn and his wife Eva Broughton to properties called Cwmkerwyn, Havod Madog alias Portisepant berth duy, and Tref Loyn, in Kemes. Isabel had a son Piers David (married a daughter of Owen Lloyd of Cwmgloyn) and Alison, had a son Thomas David; this lawsuit involved the custom of gavelkind.

Towards the end of the 17th century, it became the home of Griffith Morris, gent., son of Griffith Morris of Clynsaethmaen, just south of Cwm Cerwyn. Griffith was a Baptist and member of Rhydwilym Chapel, and in 1693 married Elizabeth, daughter of Griffith Howel of Rushacre, Narberth. After the marriage he went to live at Cwm Cerwyn and is described in 1694 as Griffith Morris 'of Cwmckerwyn, gent.' He died between 1732 and 1734, and his son, Griffith Morris, junior, gent., followed him 'at Cwmkerwyn Isha'. In 1726 Griffith Thomas and John Griffith, yeomen, of Mynachlogddu, held a lease of Cwm Kerwyn and adjacent lands, all part of the former monastery of St. Dogmaels.

In 1786 James Bowen Esq. owned Cwm Carun, with John Griffith as tenant. On 5 April 1817 Daniel Owen of Cwmcerwyn was baptized, and on 30 January 1833 ordained Baptist minister of Pope Hill, south of Haverfordwest. Cwm Cerwyn became part of the Cwmgloyn estate, and in 1909, described as a farm of 296 acres, rented by Morris Thomas, was advertised for sale.

Refs: *B. M. Egerton ms., 2586,* folio 352; Lewis, *Early Chancery Proceedings conc. Wales,* 1937, p. 67; Pritchard, *Hist. of St. Dogmaels Abbey,* pp. 28, 45, 64, 109, 121; *Pembs RO., Deeds DB/13/98; NLW, Morgan-Richardson Deed,* No. 2918.

CWMEOG. *Nevern.*

Now a farmstead some two miles to the north-east of Nevern church; to the west of Pencelli wood, and due north from Henllys. At one time it was divided into two messuages called Cwmeog-fawr and -fach, and Cwmeog-ucha and -issa. It eventually became one farm as it now is. The properties were acquired by the Owens of Henllys, and later by their descendants the Lloyds of Bronwydd. In 1470 Owen ap Ieuan ap Oweyn mortgaged a messuage at Cwmhyok in the fee of Bayvil (which Owen's father had of the gift of David ap Ieuan ap Llewelin Vechan), to Thomas ap Howel ap Gwilym ap Phillip: in 1493 Ieuan ap Philip Lloyd mortgaged all his lands at Cwmyok within the ploughland of Tre Vorgan in the fee of Bayvil; in 1503 the messuage in Komeyok was in mortgage from Howel ap Ieuan ap Rees the elder, to Sir Ieuan ap Owen, Knight [of Pentre Ifan] and on 2 June 1503 John ap Howel ap Ieuan ap Rees of Henllys gent., covenanted not to sell any of the properties to anyone except his brother Henry ap Howel when required. In 1542 James ap Howel ap Ieuan ap Rees (descended from Gwynfardd), was owner-occupier of Cwmeog, which he sold in 1548 to William Owen of Henllys. Afterwards it passed to William's son, George Owen of Henllys, and in 1612 he granted Cwmeog Issa to his sons Rees, Thomas, and William, and Cwmeog Ucha to his sons Rees, George, William and Thomas, all to hold the properties at an annual rent; in 1665 Cwmeog was held by George Owen's illegitimate son William Owen of Cwmeog (living 1673) from whom it passed to his son Thomas Owen, barrister, of Grays Inn (will proved 1708) who left three sons, Caleb, Thomas and Richard Owen. Caleb was still living there in 1767.

In 1740 the two farms, Cwmeog-fawr and -fach were sold to Thomas Lloyd of Bronwydd and Anna his wife, and in 1786 it was owned by the said Thomas Lloyd, with David William, tenant. Later the farms were sold, and changed hands several times. When I visited Cwmeog on 4 October 1978, it was owned by Mr. D. Douglas-Osborn. The old farmhouse has been heavily modernised but still retains features of its former days, one of which is its two 'simne fawr' with massive beams over them, one of the beams being forked, a most unusual feature: a small garden bounded one gable end. The owner runs riding-stables there, mainly for visitors.

Refs: *NLW, Bronwydd Deeds, Papers of Great Sessions, Pembs Plea Rolls*; G. Owen, *Extent of Cemais*, 1594; *B. M. Egerton ms.*, 2586 folio 311a; *Golden Grove ms III* (Bradwen); *Bloome's List*, 1673; *Land Tax*, 1786; *B. G. Charles, George Owen*, pp. 5, 18-19, 36, 45.

CWMGLOYN. *Nevern and Bayvil.*

Now a farmstead, about 3/4 of a mile north of Felindre (which is on Afon Nyfer). From Felindre a wooded vale (called Coch Cwmgloyn) runs northwards as far as Cwmgloyn, through which the drive ran from the now ruined lodge along the western bank of the Gloyn, to the old mansion. Fenton states in 1811, 'Cwmgloyne the only mansion of the many in its neighbourhood which is not in ruins or has not been metamorphosed into a farm-house and stripped of its surrounding woods. The principal residence of the Lloyds, a slip of the prolific stock of Gwynvardd prior to its being planted here, was Hendrev near St. Dogmaels ... The late possessor of this place [Cwmgloyn] and the last of his name, in whom his family became extinct, Thomas Lloyd Esq., was a most valuable country gentleman, highly esteemed, deservedly popular, leading an useful life among his neighbours and tenants, and to a taste for general literature added a profound knowledge of the language and antiquities of Wales. Dying a bachelor, he left his estate by

will to Maurice Williams, Esq., the present proprietor'.

The earliest-known owner of the property was Rhys ap Rhydderch (also descended from Gwynfardd). Fifth in descent from him was Jane, daughter and co-heiress of David ap Gwilym ap Perkin of Cwmgloyn, who brought that home and estate to her husband Owen Lloyd a younger son of Hendre, who settled at his wife's home. The marriage took place towards the middle of the 16th century. Cwmgloyn remained in Lloyd ownership for seven succeeding generations until the death of the bachelor squire Thomas Lloyd J.P. (High Sheriff in 1771). Numerous poems of praise to him, as well as his elegy, are contained in *Blodau Dyfed*, 1824. Although the male line became extinct with his death, the property remained in descendants of the Lloyds. Thomas bequeathed Cwmgloyn to his kinsman, Morris Williams of Trellyffant whose grandmother was Frances Lloyd, daughter of Evan Lloyd of Cwmgloyn. It was a commodious house in 1670 when it was assessed at five hearths, but was enlarged since, as its present condition indicates. Morris Williams was followed by his nephew Owen Owen, son of his sister who had married a Mr. Owen. From Owen Owen, Cwmgloyn passed to his son Morris Williams Lloyd Owen, who died without issue in 1908, and in the following year the property was sold.

From Cwmgloyn came five High Sheriffs, and numerous magistrates. After this the property changed hands several times, and an interesting account of its condition in 1940 is given by the author, R. M. Lockley, as follows: 'Cwmgloyn was a noble building even in 1940 when I first saw it as the farmhouse of a derelict farm which I subsequently rented for a song on condition that I would restore the farm. All the land here is up hill or down dale, wild, and near to the bone of the slate rock; not fertile, yet kind to the eye of the naturalist. On each stone pillar of the entrance gate to Cwmgloyn used to be an ancient gargoylish stone face, one of which was lately smashed by a passing lorry. The old house had a great kitchen and cellars under a panelled hall. During my occupation of this

51

house I pulled away a modern stove which had blocked the entrance to a vast hearth in the kitchen. This revealed an old wall-baking oven in which I found books, nearly one hundred and fifty years old; Marshall's *Agriculture* and a farm account book of 1750 with many entries curious to a modern farmer. In the huge chimney (*simne fawr*) could be discerned, above lintel height, a walled-in doorway with, if I remember aright, a pointed arch. We called this the priest's chamber, according to local hearsay it was used as such during the Reformation, as hideouts in several local manors and churches were said to be. The clear spring issuing from the rocks at Cwmgloyn flows through a steep wooded ravine containing a beautiful drive from lodge gates in the hamlet of Velindre, but the woods have lately been felled and the lodge become roofless, and in the general levelling of human society, Cwmgloyn, like many another late medieval manor, is now an ordinary farm.' (Lockley, *Pembrokeshire*, 1957, edn 1977. p. 99). Fenton, thou art fortunate not to be here today! On 4 October 1978 I visited Cwmgloyn and was kindly shown around by Mr. Hugh Thomas, eldest son of the former-owner. It is an excellent example of the vernacular mansions popular in this area, and is now L-shaped, the other wing having been removed, nevertheless still an impressive building. There is a carved medieval head said to represent that of a bishop.

Refs: *R.C.A.M.*, Pembs, 1925; *Dwnn*, i, pp. 246-7; *Carms RO, John Francis Colln; NLW, Bronwydd Deeds, G. Owen Second Book*, p. 271; Francis Jones, *'Lloyd of Hendre and Cwmgloyn'* in *NLW Journal*, 1984.

CWMWDIG. *St. Davids.*

A farmstead on a long slope above Porthriddy and Abereiddy, about three-quarters of a mile from the latter, with a view over the coast from Ynys y Barri towards Penbiri and Penmaendewi. It is an L-shaped building, compact, with small extensions at either end, with dormer windows, fronting northeastwards. The earliest-known proprietors were Philip ap David and his wife Joan (née Sutton) of Brawdy, who owned in 1448 two messuages, and an acre in Eglewscomydik, in tenure of Philip Nicholl, Ieuan ap Rees Menyth, and David ap Philip ap Walter. The name makes it clear that there was a medieval chapel in this remote part of Dewsland. It may have stood within the farmyard below the house near to the holy well, still there, and just below these was a field called Parc y Fynwent, described in Elizabethan deeds as 'Hen Fwnwen' and 'Tir yr hen fynwent'.

Ownership passed from the Brawdy family to that of Voyle of Haverfordwest, and from them to Thomas Canon. In 1607 Thomas Canon sold the two messuages at Cwmwdig, and other properties, to the sitting tenant, William James Harry, who held them in mortgage from Morgan Voyle. The new owner was the son of James Harry son of Harry Hooper, yeoman, living at Ynys y Barry in 1543. William James Harry made a good marriage, his wife Katherine being daughter of Thomas Jones gent., of Brawdy. He died in 1619 leaving ten children. His eldest son, Thomas William James, married in 1632 Alice Tucker of Sealyham, by whom he had an only child, Joan, who inherited Cwmwdig in 1672. The heiress married a yeoman, William Williams of Caerforiog, who came to live at his wife's home. Joan died without issue in 1700, and Cwmwdig passed to her husband's family. The last Williams to own Cwmwdig was Thomas Williams of Pope Hill (d.1810), and Cwmwdig was inherited by his daughter and co-heiress, Mary, who married Samuel Harries of Trefacwm near Croesgoch. Thereafter Cwmwdig was let to farming tenants, until its sale in the present century.

Refs: *Pembs RO, Land Tax 1786, Sale Cat AD 1919; NLW, Morgan-Richardson Deeds, Eaton Evans and Williams Deeds; Dwnn*, i, 113, 193; *W.W.H.R.*, vi, 32; *Browne Willis, Survey of St. Davids*, 1717; *Fenton, Tour Pembs*, 1811; *R.C.A.M. Pembs 1925*.

Dragon of Wales

DALE (CASTLE). *Dale.*

The ancient residence now called Dale Castle, stands on the western fringe of the village of Dale, at the entry into the haven of Milford. The family of de Vale, which suggests that such was the original form of the place-name, held the manor of Dale and several appointments in West Wales during the period 1131-1364. One obtained a royal grant for a weekly market and an annual fair in 1293. The last of the male line died about 1300 and the estate and manor was divided between daughters, co-heiresses. One of these, Ellen de Vale, married Llywelyn ap Owen, a sprig of Welsh royalty, and from that marriage descended the Tudor dynasty, and Owain Glyndwr no less. Nearly two centuries later we find one Richard Walter of Dale owning property there which his widow Isabel sold in 1504. The Walter family, later of Haverfordwest, Roch Castle, Rhosmarket, and Cwmgigfran (Carms) continued to hold Dale in the 17th century, until 1669 when Richard Walter Esq. sold his interest in the manor of Dale to David Paynter. This family lived at nearby Broom-hill farm and acquired wealth. David Paynter's daughter Elizabeth married William Allen of Gelliswick, and in 1705 he granted Dale Castle and the manor to his son-in-law.

A descendant, John Allen of Dale Castle married Mary Stepney, and had an only child, Elinor. On her father's death in 1767 Elinor inherited Dale Castle, manor, and lands, and married in 1776 a Cardiganshire squire, John Llwyd of Ffos-y-bleiddied, Mabws, and Ystrad Teilo, and from them descended the Lloyd-Philipps family who continue to hold Dale Castle to this day. Extensive additions were made to the old residence which was given the official name of Dale Castle. *The Pembrokeshire Archaeological Survey* (1896-1907), states, 'The South Wing of Dale Castle is part, if not the whole, of the original building. The lower part is vaulted: the floor above the vaulting is used as a stable, and the floor above as a corn loft and man-servants' room. Probably the original building was a small oblong block of buildings. The North Wing was built by the late Mr. Lloyd-Philipps.'

An interesting feature is that during the Walter family ownership, a portrait of the sprightly Lucy Walter hung on the wall of the mansion, which came with possession of the succeeding owners, the Paynters, who, after selling Dale to the Allens, moved the portrait to Portclew (q.v.) where it still remained in the years 1896-1907.

Refs: *R.C.A.M. Pembs.*, 1925; *W.W.H.R.* VI, 174-5; *Dwnn*, i, 71; *B. M. Egerton ms. 1586*, fo. 371; H. Owen, *Old Pembroke Families, 1902*; Francis Green, 'Walter of Roch Castle', in *W.W.H.R. V*; Francis Jones 'Gelliswick and its Families', *in Arch Cam. 1980*; Pembs RO, Deeds D/LP; Lewis, *TDW* (1840).

DENANT. *Steynton.*

A pleasant, well-preserved residence, with a farmhouse and outbuildings nearby. Some 300 yards eastwards from the house is Denant Rath, an ancient hill-fort on a tree-clad mount. In 1392 William Malefant held three carucates at Denant by Knights in service and suit of court. In 1535 it was owned by John Wogan; in 1580 the occupier was Richard Browne, yeoman; in 1613 the owner was John Barlow, namely one carucate then held by Sir James Perrott and Thomas Butler, gent; by 1658 it was the home of Patrick Couzens, gent. (brother of Thos Couzens of Robeston Hall) and Alice his wife.

For some time in the 18th century the Packingtons of Westwood (Worcs) owned the property, and in 1786 John Meyrick, Esq. owned Denant with F. Owens, and T. Miller as tenants; the Owens were there at the end of the century, one of whom, Mary Owen, married the Reverend Benjn Davies, Baptist Minister of Molleston, who came to live at his wife's home at Denant; in 1833 Thomas Batine held Denant (525 acres) on a lease of lives; and a yearly rent of £240; by 1844 it had been bought by John Howarth Peel, who was followed by his son Xavier Peel; then came Herbert Fisher and John Thomas Fisher who held Denant jointly in 1894-1904. It is now owned and occupied by Mr. David George and his son.

Refs: *Glam RO, Deeds* (late Cardiff Free Library); *Val. Eccles ; Picton Castle Deeds; Pembs RO,* Land Tax List, 1786; *R.C.A.M. Pembs.* 1925.

DOLAU LLANERCH. *Clydey.*

Now a farmhouse about a mile south-west of Clydey Church, near the hamlet of Star. Of the original mansion, said to have been built in the castellated style, nothing is now visible; it stood immediately south of the present farmhouse, near the present entrance. The old mansion is marked on Colby's map 1831 as Dolau Llanerch, and also buildings where the present farmhouse stands, so that it appears that some remains were still there in 1831.

Fenton in 1811 says that 'not a vestige of the old mansion is left, a nearby farm-house having of later years sprung from its ruins.' Home of the Lloyds, said to descend from Cadifor Fawr of Blaen Cych, from *tempus* Henry VII until the late 17th century. Seventh in descent was Bridget Lloyd, heiress, who married Hugh Lloyd of Ffos-helig, Cards. Their eldest son Morgan Lloyd succeeded to Ffoshelig, and the younger son, Thomas Lloyd, to Dolau Llanerch. Thomas Lloyd was living there in 1738, and died about 1760 when his will was proved. The property eventually passed to Sarah Griffiths (grand-daughter of Hugh and Bridget Llwyd of Ffoshelig), and from them to kinsfolk, Jones, whose descendants Jones-Lloyd of Lancych were the last owners of Dolau Llanerch,

being still owned by Mr. Owen Jones-Lloyd, D. L. of Abercych in 1972, Dolau Llanerch being then let to a farmer. In 1972 I examined the site of the old mansion of which no traces now remain.

Refs: *Golden Grove ms.; W.W.H.R.* ii, 76; *Chatham ms; Fenton, Tour Pembs, 1811;* NLW, *Derwydd Deeds,* no. 705, and *Lancych Deeds.*

DOLAU LLWYD(ION). *Llanfihangel Penbedw.*

Marked as 'Dolellwyddon' just south of Rhyd Howel and to the west of Wern ddofn (Penrith parish) on Colby's Map 1831. The first known owner was Davd Lloyd of Dole Llwyd, descended from the family of Cilgadfarch (vide supra) who traced to Cadifor Fawr. He had five sons and four daughters. The eldest son, Thomas Lloyd had an only son, Morgan Thomas. In the *Clynfyw Deeds,* (NLW), Dolau Llwyd traces back to 1589 when it appears as Place y ddol y Llwyd. In 1786 Dolellwydon was owned by Thomas Lewis Esq. with Sarah Lewis as tenant.

Refs: *Golden Grove MS II (Cadifor Fawr); Tithe Schedule and Map* 1837; *Ex Inf.* Dr. D. B. Charles.

DOLEMAEN. *Mynachlogddu.*

An ancient farmhouse, once centre of a small estate, north-east of Mynachlogddu village, and south-west of Pentre-galar, about half-way between them. It is high in the Preseli mountains, bounded on the east by Afon Cleddau, and on the north by Waun Cleddau. Little has been found about its early history. In 1786 the owner-occupier was Thomas John, gentleman. By 1840 he had died leaving his estate (655 acres) in the hands of trustees, with his widow Elizabeth John as tenant. By the beginning of the 20th century, the property was owned by Arthur Owen Evans and was advertised for sale on 25 June 1907 as 'the Dolemaen Estate' comprising nine farms, a slate quarry, about 630 acres, and rights of pasture over 2000 acres, all in Mynachlogddu parish, as follows – 1. Dolemaen farm (220 acres), 2. Portis-tô (89 acres), 3. Pwll y

Crychydd (cottage and outbuildings, 9 acres), 4. Penddafedd farm (53 acres), 5. Llwyndrain farm (65 acres), 6. Pistyll têg (38 acres), 7. Mountain farm called Foel (64 acres), 8. Llwyneithin (25 acres), 9. Dolemaen Newydd, south of, and adjoining Dolemaen (115 acres). It was a small but compact estate close to the main messuage which the sale map shows as a farmstead with six outbuildings, sheltered on the south side by trees, and to the north was a large pond.

Refs: *Pembs. RO, L.T. 1786; Carms RO, S.C. 633; NLW, Tithe Map 1840.*

DOLPWLL. *Penrith.*

A farmstead on the high slopes on the north of Frenni Fawr, and south of Penrith church. Marked on the maps of Mudge (1819) and Colby (1831). The home of Morris Morgan who died there in 1739. By his wife Frances (Lewis) (1666-1719) he had two children – Morris Morgan (1682-1763) who moved to Wernddofn, married, and had issue, and Bridget Morgan (1689-1763) who married Richard Howell of Ffynnonfelen, Carms. whose grandson was Dr. John Howell M.D. of Tegafynyd in Llanfallteg parish in 1840. In 1786 'Dole Pooll' was owned by Rachel Morgan, with Hannah Thomas as tenant. In 1837 it was owned by Thomas Brightwell Esq. with Rachel Lewis as tenant, then comprising 235 acres. In 1894-1904 it was farmed by James Sandbrook, who had married Margaret daughter of John Griffith George of Cilast, she died in 1899, aged 70.

Refs: *NLW, Croydon Deeds, Tithe Map 1837, L.T. 1786.*

DRUIDSTON. *Nolton.*

About a mile south of the village, on high ground above Druidston Haven: near the sea stands the 19th century residence of Druidston Villa. The name is derived from the surname Drue found in Pembrokeshire in the middle ages. In 1392 Walter Symond is described as 'of Drewyston'. In modern times George Roch, Esq., in 1786 was owner-occupier of 'Druson', who also owned four other tenements called West, South, North and East Druson. In 1859 Druidston Villa was advertised for sale, described as comprising, on the ground floor – dining and drawing rooms, and three best bedrooms, and on the upper floor six bedrooms; butler's pantry, W.C., kitchen, servants' hall, dairy, and cellars, flower and kitchen walled gardens, pleasure grounds, stables, coach house, and outbuildings, with a total of 101 acres. Lord Kensington used it as a residence.

Refs: *PRO, deeds, D, 2503, 2692; Sale Catalogue* June 1859; *L.T. 1786.*

DRYSGOL GOCH. *Clydey.*

A farmstead near Llwynydrain and the stream Pedran a tributary of the Cych. Home of a minor gentry family in earlier days. Thomas ap David ap Howel of 'Trustlegoch' in Clydey, married Eve, daughter of John Mendus, and had a daughter and heiress Elen who married John Thomas Lloyd of Clynfyw, descended from Jenkin Lloyd of Cemais, and their daughter Margaret married Morris Morgan of Coedllwyd. In 1786 the owner-occupier of Drisgol goch was George Bowen, gent.; in 1834 Zephaniah Bowen owned and occupied the property, in 1841 Daniel Bowen, and in 1873 the owner-occupier was Thomas Bowen.

Refs: *Golden Grove MS; College of Arms MS. Protheroe* XII fo. 84; *Manorowen MS.* fo. 149; *W.W.H.R.* ii. 40; *Colby Map 1831.*

DUDWELL. *Camrose.*

A small cluster of farmsteads south of Dudwell Mountain; the most important being East and West Dudwell. A few references occur in medieval times. At his death in 1324 Aymer de Valence, Earl of Pembroke, owned lands in Dodewell; in 1419 a messuage and two carucates at West Dodewall was part of the manor of West Trangar (Trefgarn). The most important family here was that of Tancred who were at Dudwall in 1451, and by 1503 the family also owned Leweston. Eleven generations of Tancreds succeeded to the property, and intermarried with leading families like Wolf of Leweston, Barrett of Filbeach, Philipps of Picton, and Scourfield of New Moat.

In the final generation a deterioration of character seems to have set in. Thus, Griffith Tancred who married Mary Hayward of Fletherhall in 1683 wasted his inheritance, and having mortgaged most of it, fled to Ireland to escape clamorous creditors. His only son, James, became a tailor in Covent Garden, later returned to Haverfordwest, where he died in obscurity in 1698, and he, too, left an only son, the last of the male line of Dudwall, but what became of him remains a mystery. A sister of Griffith Tancred the galloping debtor, married a yeoman, Walter Warlow who came to live at Dudwall and was assessed at two hearths in 1670. His will, dated 1689, shows that he held a lease of Wester Dydwall which he left to his son Walter Warlow, who died intestate in 1700. The Tancred arms were *gules a chevron argent between three escallop shells of the second.* Another family there in late medieval days was that of Barrett who were there for four generations, the last being Peter Barrett who left two daughters, co-heiresses, one of whom, Anne, married Philip Tancred, gent., 'of Dowdwell'. In the 18th century several changes took place. In 1786 East Dudwall was owned by the Haverfordwest Corporation, with James Harries as tenant, and two messuages both called West Dudwall were owned and occupied by John Morse, gent., and Miss Mary Davies. In later times the properties were sold to local farmers.

Refs: *Dwnn,* i, 71, 128; *Pembs RO, Deeds DG/13,* no. 95, *Land.*

DUMPLEDALE. *Burton.*

An ancient mansion, renamed Ashdale in the period 1845-50 by the then owner-occupier George Lort Phillips, later of Lawrenny. The property is at the northern end of the parish, about half a mile from Langwm on the Eastern Cleddau. From the reign of Henry VII it was the home of the Jordan family,

also settled at Jordanston (in Llanstadwell), Honeyborough, Hayston, Neeston, Barrett's Hill, Berllan (in Cemaes), Haverfordwest. John Jordan of Dumpledale was assessed at four hearths in 1670. The family arms were; *Argent a chevron between 3 greyhounds courant gules.* The last of the male line at Dumpledale was the Revd. John Jordan M.A. (Jesus College, Oxon). J.P., who died without issue on 27 April 1808, aged 59. Later in the 19th century Dumpledale was sold to George Lort Phillips, who made alterations to the house, described in 1840 by Lewis (TDW) as 'a handsome modern mansion'. A commodious house in 1670, it was then assessed for four hearths. It changed hands several times after the Lort-Phillips occupation and was bought in 1973 by Mr. William Lees of Haverfordwest who repaired and improved the house. A Sale Catalogue of 1983 describes Ashdale as of two storeys with range of five windows, and an attic storey with three (modern) dormer windows, six bedrooms, three reception rooms, kitchen: the present courtyard at the rear was formerly part of the domestic quarters, and was once a north wing which accommodated the principal rooms. Today called Ashdale, but the old name is perpetuated in the name of an adjoining farm, Little Dumple Dale.

Refs: *Dwnn,* i, 157; *Carms RO, SC 607* (1907); *B. M. Egerton MS 2586; NLW, Slebech Deeds,* No. 11422, *Morgan-Richardson Deeds,* i, GS. *Pembs Plea Rolls.*

DYFFRYN FFILBRO. *Mynachlogddu*.

An abandoned farmstead south-west from Mynachlogddu village; in a little grove on the edge of a windswept moorland; below the homestead flows a tributary of the Glandy brook. It was untenanted when I visited in in 1976. Marked on Eman. Bowen's map 1760, as 'Duffrin Fwlbrocke, Lewis Esq.'; on Kitchin's map 1763 as 'Dyffryn Fwlbrook Lewis, Esq.', as 'Dyffrynfullbrook' on Mudge's map 1819, and as 'Dyffryn Filbro' on Colby's Map 1831. In 1786 the owner-occupier was Stephen Griffith, and also Edward Price, gent., owner, and John Griffith tenant. In 1783 the owner of 'Dyffryn Fulbrook otherwise called Tredwdwr' was Griffith Gwynne, gent, of Cilciffeth. In his will dated 1823, the Revd. John Foley, Vicar of Maenclochog, bequeathed the farm of 'Blaendyffryn Fullbrook alias Tredwdwr' to his five younger children. In 1834 the owner was Nathaniel Rowland of Parke, Henllan Amgoed, Carms. with Edward Owen as tenant.

Refs: *NLW, Tithe Schedule* 1840, shows a cruciform farmhouse, *Trenewydd Deeds,* no. 173.

DYFFRYN WDIG. *Llanwnda parish*.

Now in the township of Goodwick (Wdig). Much of the old mansion has survived despite the fact that it had been used as a farmhouse. The 25 inch O.S.map made in 1888 shows a large house set among trees and orchards with an uninterrupted view of the sea over large sloping meadows; the outbuildings stood a little northwards, and are today mostly ruinous. About 1900 with the coming of the Great Western Railway, and the transformation of the coastal strip into Fishguard Harbour, the modern Goodwick came into being and the pleasant seaward meadows were built over by modern houses such as Plâs y Gamil Road and St. Davids Place, while a railway line was built through the orchard close to the house. Nevertheless, Dyffryn House as it is now called, is still pleasantly situated in well-tended grounds, although its seaward view has been disrupted by the modern buildings.

During my younger days I spoke to numerous people who remembered it before 1900. My younger brother having married the co-heiress, lived in the house till his death in 1990. For several centuries the capital messuage of Dyffryn Wdig and its estate remained in one family. This was that of Davies who were there in 1624 and who intermarried with local gentry families. In 1715 Thomas Davies J.P. was High Sheriff, and not only was he the first to hold that office, but he is the only man in the parish ever to have held it. The last male member of the house, Thomas Davies, J.P. died without issue in 1747, and the estate, consisting of 24 properties and 1010 acres, passed to his sisters, two of whom married sons of the Colby family who became owners of Dyffryn Wdig and most of the estate. The main seat of the Colbys was at Ffynnone, and Dyffryn Wdig was let to a succession of farming tenants, and finally sold in the late 19th century.

Refs: *Pembs RO, Land Tax 1786, Deeds, No. D/RT; NLW, Spence-Colby Deeds, Cwrtmawr Deeds, Papers of Great Sessions, Pembs.*

Pakington, Lord Hampton

E AREWERE.

Amroth, vide Amroth Castle *supra.*

EAST HOOK. *Langum*.

There are three farms in the north of the parish, near the banks of the western Cleddau, viz. East-, West-, and Lower-Hook, all being houses of minor gentry, the most important being East Hook. In 1548 Richard Eynon is described as 'of East Hook, yeoman'; in 1599 Owen Jordan, gent., lived there, and in 1614 his executor Richard Hicks, yeoman, who in

1634, was concerned in sharing one-half of East Hook with John Hicks, gent., by 1656 Richard Eynon, gent., was owner-occupier, and in 1669 was held by John Jones of East Hook gent. Mary, daughter of Owen Hicks, married the said John Jones who was a son of William Jones, a wealthy landowner of Bonville's Court, near Saundersfoot. During the 18th century the owner-occupier was Richard Knethell, Esq. who was there in 1786.

Refs: *Haverfordwest Corporation Deeds; NLW, Papers of G.S., Pembs Plea Rolls; Golden Grove Ms. 1 (Gwynfardd)* fo. 15.

EAST JORDANSTON. *St. Florence.*
About half a mile north-west of St. Florence village, while another farm called West Jordanston is a little farther to the west. I visited this interesting old house on 22 September 1977, being then empty and owned by the Dyfed County Council who were advertising it for sale. It consisted of two storeys and an attic storey, with large rooms, and at the rear of the house – opposite the entrance – is a projection containing a staircase rising to attic height; there was also a wing to the rear. The entrance porch with stone arch consisted of two storeys. Inside the house were several corbels which had once supported the ceiling beams. The style suggests it to have been either Elizabethan or Jacobean in origin. Dr. Charles cites reference to it in 1331, 1376. 1480 etc. In the 17th century it formed part of the Barlow estate. Anne Barlow, daughter of John Barlow, married firstly Nicholas Lewis of Hean Castle, who died without issue, and secondly, in 1663, Lewis Wogan of Wiston. The marriage settlement made on 1 September 1663, mentions 'the manor, mansion, and lanes called Jordanston in the parish of St. Florence'. In 1786 both East and West Jordanston were owned by John Campbell Hooke (of the Stackpole family). About the year 1820 East Jordanston was bought by the tenant George Locke, and in 1873 another of the family, George Locke owned the property and its 244

acres. Afterwards it was bought by Benjamin J. Edwards who sold it to the Pembrokeshire County Council in 1918. It is still used as a farmhouse but the land, some 200 acres, was divided into three small-holdings. The farmhouse was described in 1977 as follows, porch, hall, four reception rooms, two kitchens, dairy, store-room, seven bedrooms, two attic rooms, with stone-built outbuildings.

Refs: *W.W.H.R.* vi, 219; *Land Tax List 1786; Landowners' Returns 1873;* B. G. Charles, *NCPN,* 21 see *Western Mail* 17 and 27 September 1977, illustrs.

EASTLAKE. *Amroth.*
Now a farmstead to the north-east of Amroth Castle. It is called locally, Islick. During the 17th-18th centuries it was the home of the Howell family whose arms were: *sable a lion rampant regardant argent.* John Howell of Eastlake died in 1688 leaving his wife *enciente;* the posthumous child, John Howell Esq. lived there till he died in his 91st year in 1778. The next owner was Edmund Probin, Esq. who let the property to Zacharias Rogers.

EAST MOOR. *Manorbier.*
To the west of Manorbier village, near the coast, above Swanlake Bay. East Moor was the home of the Lorts in the 17th century; near it is another farmstead called West Moor. Sampson Lort, second son of Henry Lort of Stackpole Court, established himself at East Moor. Like his father he served on both sides during the Civil War. His first wife Olive was a daughter of Sir John Philipps of Picton. She died in 1637, and four years later Sampson married Lettice, daughter of Thomas ap Rhys of Rickeston (Brawdy) and Scotsborough. He was High Sheriff in 1650, and died in 1667. His only son, Thomas Lort succeeded to East Moor; he married Elizabeth White of Henllan, but died without issue. A few references have been found to East Moor. In 1670 Thomas Lort was assessed at seven hearths, indicating it to have been a commodious residence.

An inventory of the possessions of Thomas, compiled in 1687 mentions the following rooms in East Moor – hall, the little room within the hall, the little parlour, chamber over the outward kitchen, 'another little room', closet, little room over the entry, chamber over the kitchen, closet within the said chamber, buttery, kitchen, outer kitchen, larder, dairy, and outhouses.

Over a hundred years later, Fenton wrote in 1811 – 'Turn to the left to see Moor, one of the chief mansions of this district about two hundred years ago, of a very irregular form with many ruinous and extensive out-buildings, once entered by a gateway now stopped up, leading to a porter's lodge. With very few exceptions, this may serve as a model of the style of building their houses among the the great of that era in this country which invariably appears to have been surrounded by a high court-wall having a large arched gateway, and essentially differing from the form of the principal houses of the same date, in the upper part of the country ...'

Commissioners of Ancient Monuments who visited the site in 1923 state that in the farmyard to the West of the modern house, were the ruins of a small E-shaped two-storeyed dwelling house 'of no architectural importance'; in its original state it may have consisted of a hall, with North and South wings, and central porch, but most of the features had disappeared leaving only the hall which had been altered almost out of recognition. After the departure of the Lorts the house changed ownership several times. The Land Tax of 1786 names four messuages, each called East Moor, as follows: (1) Sir Hugh Owen, owner, Peter Gwyther tenant, assessed at £3.18.0; (2) Peter Gwyther, owner-occupier, assessed at 7s.5d; (3) Thomas Voyle, owner, Peter Gwyther tenant, assessed at 14s; (4) George Leach, owner, Peter Gwyther, tenant, assessed at 14s 6d. From this it seems that the dwelling of the Lorts was No. 1. The *Pembrokeshire Archaeological Survey* (1896-1907) states that in the farmyard of East Moor is an ancient house now used for farm buildings, probably the dwelling of Sampson Lort.

Refs: Fenton, *Tour Pembs*, 1811; *R.C.A.M. Pembs* 1925; *Land Tax Pemb* 1786.

EASTINGTON. *Rhoscrowther.*

Just over a quarter of a mile northwest of Rhoscrowther village, near the shores of Angle Bay. Today it is bounded by the extensive installations of Texaco Oil Company who also own the buildings and land of Eastington. During medieval times it was a home of the powerful family of Perrot who owned it till the end of the 16th century and in the 17th century, for a brief time, home of Hugh Philipps (d. 1652) younger son of Sir John Philipps of Picton Castle by Anne daughter of Sir John Perrot of Haroldston, and was followed at Eastington by William Meares who was assessed at five hearths in 1670. William, High Sheriff in 1673, died in 1687, and was followed by five generations of his descendants. Finally, John Meares tells us that Eastington had 'fallen to decay and was unfit for habitation', so he bought the Bank Farm estate, Kingston-on-Thames where he died in 1814; his son, John Meares inherited Plâs Llanstephan in 1833, and in 1842 he sold Eastington to Common Serjeant Mirehouse of Angle. It was then let to various tenants.

The later stage in the house's history is depressing. T. F. Holwell had an interest in the place, and on 12 April 1769 he wrote to the attorney, Richard Knethell of Haverfordwest, as follows – 'Sir. I have been to view the premises at Eastington and find them in such a ruinous state that no tenant can possibly enter them in the condition they are, nor engage to keep them in tenantable repair, unless they are previously put into that necessary state. Therefore I beg leave to point out to you what must be absolutely done to make it habitable. The breach in the garden wall of the orchard and the fence of the south court to be made good. The roof of the house which leaks in one place to be tiled and secured; a large breach in the ceiling of what they call the lumber room, another in the ceiling of the back-kitchen, and another through the floor of the south-west bed-chamber, two pairs of stairs where a plank is wanting, and a hole in the ceiling under it to be repaired. The panels in the wainscotting of the dining room are in general loose and falling out, as well as some in the parlour, and both these rooms ought to have at least one coat of paint as well the windows, and the panels secured, and as we are content to become tenants a quarter before the premises are in shape habitable, I will not doubt but you will be so obliging as to order the above absolutely necessary repairs to be done forthwith, as I expect my friend and his lady down the latter end of next week.'

Knethell acted immediately, and on 13th April a mason and two carpenters examined the edifice, and reported that the great part of rafters and laths in the north side of the roof were decayed and ruinous; all other parts of the roof required being pointed with lime mortar; to put this in order would cost £25. They also reported that several beams, the rafters and joints in the roof, and lofts in some of the bed-chambers were ruinous and in danger of tumbling down unless speedily repaired: also, the wooden railing before the court was quite rotten and fallen, and must be entirely new-built; this would cost £45. By November 1769 the repairs had been effected.

The next part of the tale is given by Fenton in 1811 – 'Jestington or as it is commonly called Iseston, for many years the residence of the family of Meares, now property of John Meares Esq ... It seems to have been once castellated, though very little of the original building exists, but that little clearly proves it to have been of a form to entitle it to the name of Castle. The Perrots for some centuries continued to inhabit it till their union with Haroldstone, near Haverfordwest, when they appear to have abandoned this venerable residence on the haven.' A detailed description of the house appears in *Arch Cam.* 1868, 79-80, where it is dated 'temp Edward II', adding that 'The modern house of the Meares, recently removed, abutted on the western wall of the main building, and a farmhouse stands at present on the other side.'

H. Thornhill Timmins describes it more explicitly in 1895 – 'This quaint old homestead of Eastington ... is honeycombed with curious nooks and corners ... crooked passages, and crumbling stairways. The long south front with its homely porch and small-paned windows, is flanked at its western end by a massive medieval structure whose rough, lichen-clad walls are pierced with narrow, deep-set windows, and topped by ruinous battlements ... By a rude steep flight of grass-grown steps we mount to a clumsy door ... we push our way into the interior ... a large and lofty chamber, whose solid concrete floor is prettily marked with lines traced in simple geometrical patterns. Rudely-arched windows admit light at either end, one of them having cusped openings; While a ruined fire-place yawns in the centre of the opposite wall. A small vaulted cell opens from one end of this room, and a narrow stair which has a gangway all around and is pierced with loopholes for defence. The dark vaulted basement of this ancient fabric forms a capital dairy ...' The *R.C.A.M. Pembs, 1925,* describes it as a small ruined manor house of the peel-tower type, probably of the 15th century, now used as a farmhouse; it has a plain vaulted undercroft with two apartments above, to which access is by an exterior flight of steps. From the longer of the two rooms, a short newel stairway leads to the summit of a low lantern or beacon tower; around the roof runs a corbel table and parapet; the windows have been modernized ...'.

Refs: Fenton, *Tour Pembs*, 1811, 218-220; *Arch Camb*, 1868, 79-80, illustr. June 1977, 175; Laws *Little England*, 1888, 207 illustr; H.T. Timmins, *Nooks and Corners of Pembs*, 1895, 85-6, illustr.; *Pembs Arch. Survey* 1897-1907; M. B. Mirehouse, *South Pembs.* 1910, 47; H. Owen, *Old Pembroke Families*, 1902, 52; *R.C.A.M. Pembs*, 1925; *Journal British Arche. Assocn.* XL1, 82; *Dwnn*, i. 89; *Pembrokeshire Magazine*, March 1983, illustr.; *Western Mail* 16 and 28 April 1983, illustr.; *Carns Studies*, 1974, p. 50, fig 6; P. Smith, *Houses of the Welsh Countryside*, 1975, 30, 31, 339, 373; Mr. T. Strickland (descended from the Meares family).

EASTWOOD.

One mile south of the town of Narberth.

Home of the Hassall family, land agents, built towards the end of the 18th century. The house was advertised for sale in 1810 and described as comprising two parlours, vestibule, three principal bed chambers with dressing room and store room, two garret bed chambers, two other garret bed chambers, three lodging rooms for servants, two kitchens, butler's pantry, larder, water closet, cellars, granary, stable for five horses, gardens and grounds. Charles Hassall of Eastwood died in 1814, aged 60. It then became the home of Sir Henry Mannix, Bt., who died at his seat, Eastwood, in 1822, aged 83. The house is marked on the maps of *Mudge, 1819* and *Colby, 1831*.

ESGAIR. *St. Dogmaels.*

Also called Esgyrn. A farm near Ceippyn, north-west of Hendre. Home of a branch of Lloyd of Trefigin (an offshoot of Lloyd of Hendre). George Lloyd of Esgair died some time before 1714, and he was followed by his younger son Evan Lloyd who was living at Esgair in 1733. By 1786 Esgair was owned by William Rowlands, gent, with Lettice Llewelin as tenant. The property was divided into two farms. In 1834 John and Thomas Llewellyn were owner-occupiers of the farms of Esgyrn-fawr and -fach: in 1894 George Llewelyn lived at Esgyrn fawr, and Levi George at Esgyrn fach.

ESGAIR WILYM. *Eglwyswrw.*

Thomas ap Rees of Esgair Wilym was followed there by his son Rees ap Thomas who married Anne daughter of Howell ap Owen of Court (descended from the Cantingtons). Rees died in 1560, his wife Anne in 1590. Their daughter and co-heiress Elizabeth (d.1621) married William Griffith of Penybenglog, Meline (d.1618), whose son and heir was the antiquary George William Griffith. Between 1579 and 1597 George Owen of Henllys bought lands at Esker and in 1594 the following free tenants held land at Esker

Wilêm – Rhydderch Jenkin ap Rees, William Griffith of Penybenglog, gent., and Llewellin Morris. In 1786 there were three farms there – Ysgarwilim Issa owned by Thomas Lloyd Esq. (of Henllys and Bronwydd), Ysgarwilim Ucha by William Jones Esq. (of Llether, Brawdy) and Ysgar Ganol by John Lloyd, gent (of Fagwrgoch in Llantood).

Refs: *College of Arms Mss, Wagner Ms 12,* and *Protheroe Ms XII* (both by G. W. Griffith; NLW, *Llanstephan Ms 101B,* fo. 66-7; *Golden Grove Ms; Bronwydd Deeds.*

EWESTON (TREWEN). *Brawdy.*

About three-quarters of a mile to the east of Brawdy church, are two adjoining farms of this name, neither retaining any early architectural features. Eweston is marked as a knight's fee on Rees' 14th century map. Several references occur to the manorial lords who either held the manor in its entirety or in part. In 1287 William Hu of Owenynstonne granted four messuages, two carucates and half a carucate at Oweynstonne, and a messuage and two bovates in nearby Knareston, to John Howel of Woodstock, absolutely. Some time later, John Cole was lord of the manor. In 1326 William de Rufe held half of the fee, and in 1517 Sir John Wogan of Wiston owned one fourth of certain messuages in Owenston; and in 1581 the manor of 'Owenstone alias Routhditch' was held by the following lords, – Corbett, Henry Longueville, and Morris Wogan of Stone Hall, and the family of Wogan of Stone Hall continued to own part of the manor of Yeweston in 1631. The ownership of the manor of 'Yeweston alias Rowditch' in Brawdy parish, passed by marriage from the Wogans to the family of Ford who settled at Stone Hall, and were the owners in the years 1689-1712. The manorial status seems to have lapsed afterwards, and in 1786 the two properties at Eweston were owned by John Laugharne, with William Hooper and John Thomas as tenants. A doctor, John Thomas, J.P., lived at Eweston, apparently having an aversion to paying taxes, for when Levi Griffith the Collector and Receiver of Taxes for the parish, called at Eweston on 8 August

1816, 'Mr. Thomas did beat, wound, and ill-treat him so that his life was greatly despaired of'. In 1845 both the Eweston farms were owned by a less belligerent person, Mr. George Roch of Llether, the tenants being Stephen Hooper and James Phillips.

Refs: See *Journal Hist. Soc. of Church in Wales*, 1969, pp. 25-7, and refs. there; *Tithe Map Brawdy parish*, 1845.

Welsh love spoon

FARTHING'S HOOK (CLYNFFYRDDIN). *Henry's Moat.*

A farmstead about half a mile south-east of Henry's Moat, and near Afon Syfanwy which enters the northern end of Llys-y-Fran Reservoir. In 1462 the Reverend John Elliot granted lands in Verthinge Shoke, Woodstock and Scollock to John Perrot son of Sir Thomas Perrot. In 1485 Verthyngeshoke was the home of Thomas Yryss and Margaret his wife, as tenants. The property remained in Perrot hands until 1548 when Rees Perrot granted Farthinshock to Morgan ap William Lloyd of Llanstinan, yeoman. From 1590 to 1607 it was home of Edward ap John 'of Klynffyrdhin' who had married Margaret daughter of Henry David of Llanstinan. By 1621 it was owned by William Scourfield of New Moat who also owned the fulling and corn mills attached to the property. About 1627 he sold Farthingshook, its land and mills to Thomas Vaughan, a son of Pontfaen, who then settled there. In 1670 it was assessed at four hearths.

It remained in Thomas Vaughan's direct descendants who were there until 1696 when John Vaughan inherited Trecwn estate from his cousins and went to live at the mansion of Trecwn, and let Farthingshook to the Harding family. The Vaughans continued at Trecwn until the death without issue of Admiral John Vaughan, and the Trecwn and Farthingshook estates passed to his cousins the Barhams (also descended from the Vaughans). It continued in the Barham descendants until 1939 when the estate was advertised for sale, including Farthingshook, then a farm of 293 acres. The property had continued in Vaughans and their descendants for over 300 years.

Refs: *NLW, Coleman Deeds, Poyston Deeds, Bronwydd Deeds;* W.W.H.R., ii, 93, 152; *Golden Grove Mss; P.R.O. Ancient Deeds;* Francis Jones, 'Trecwn' (unpubl. essay).

FELINDRE. *Llysyfran.*

A farmstead on high ground above the east bank of Llys-y-Fran Reservoir, and to the west of New Moat village.

Home of a cadet of Philipps of Pentypark who was a cadet of Picton Castle. By his will dated 26 March 1695 John Philipps of Pentypark bequeathed 'Velindre' to his son Rowland Philipps. Rowland was succeeded at Felindre by seven generations, the last being William Rowland Philipps who was owner-occupier in 1904. Several descendants through marriages with daughters of Felindre still survive in the county.

Refs: *Family wills;* Pembs. R.O., Land Tax Lists 1786; *Mss. of Sir Evan Jones, Bt.,* of Fishguard.

FLIMSTON. *Castlemartin.*

A farmstead near the coast, due north of Eligug Stacks. According to Dr. B. G. Charles the name is found in ancient documents of the period 1324-1331 as variants of Flemisston, i.e. home of a Fleming many of whom settled in the south of the county. From 1600 onwards the form Flimston is usually found, and is thus spelt on Colby's map (1831). Near the house stood an ancient chapel, and on the land is an early earth fortification. Flimston was a long, commodious dwelling, an early vaulted house, with a hall above the undercroft, and a tall round chimney at the main gable end. Many similar houses occur in south Pembrokeshire. In 1786 Flemiston was owned by John Hook Campbell, with Robert Jones as tenant.

Refs: *R.C.A.M. Pembs,* 1925; Charles, *Non-Celtic Place-names in Wales,* 1938; P. Smith, *Houses of the Welsh Countryside,* 1925, Maps nos. 7, 8, 28; Thomas Lloyd, *Lost Houses of Wales,* 1986, illustr.; *Medieval Buildings* Gerald Oliver, 1987, illustr.

FFYNNON CORANAU. *Bridell.*

A farmstead about half a mile to the south-east of Bridell church, marked as Ffynnon Coranau on Colby's Map (1831). The name was anglicised as Crowns Well. In 1642 David Jenkins of Hensol, Glam, Esq. leased the capital messuage called Crownes Well to James Lewis of Cardigan, Esq. and John Parry; in 1746 Margaret, eldest daughter of Jenkin Gwyn of Ffynnon Coranau married John Turner of Crugmor near Cardigan; in 1786 Samuel Lloyd, gent, owned Crowns-hall, with John George a tenant; in 1792 John Colby of Ffynnonau Esq. leased a property in Cilgerran parish to John George of Crowns-well, yeoman.

Refs: *Carms R.O., John Francis Deeds; Land Tax Pembs* 1786.

FFYNNONAU BYCHAN, later
FFYNNONE. *Manordeifi.*

A mansion at the southern extremity of the parish, on high ground above Nant Dulas which joins the river Cych near the residence of Lancych. The mansion was consistently known as Ffynnone Bychan down to 1763 when it became known as Ffynnonau (Ffyn-none). It has been a country residence of three successive families from the early 16th century to 1927.

The first to settle there was Griffith ab Evan, a descendant of Cadifor Fawr of Blaen Cych, and the family (who took the surname Morris) were there for six generations. In 1670 David Morris was assessed at four hearths, so that it was then a commodious residence. The last of the male line, Morris Morris, was High Sheriff in 1710-11, and died without issue, and by will, proved 1730, bequeathed Ffynnonau Bychan to his sister Margaret who married William Morgan of Blaenbylan. They had an only son, Morris Morgan, who had two sons, William Morgan and David Morgan. The elder son, William, gave the property to his brother David in 1746. David died, unmarried about 1750, and Ffynnone reverted to his said brother William, who clearly did not relish the owner-ship, and in 1752 sold it to Captain Stephen Colby, R.N. The captain died without issue circa 1779, and left the property to his cousin John Colby. He was interested in Ffynnone and decided to build a larger and grander residence there, employing Nash as architect. Accounts, vouchers, etc. of Nash's work have been preserved for the period 1792-1799. Very little is known of the older house, and Nicholas tells us in 1875 that the new mansion stood 'a little distance from the site of the old house'; and we learn that on 1 October 1798 John Colby agreed with two masons to build a wall around a fishpond being made in the meadow and grove on the west of 'the old house at Fynone.'

When completed, the mansion consisted of a square block with pediments on each facade, with an east wing of kitchens and domestic quarters which ended in a stable courtyard. Colby also planted many thousands of trees which added to the beauty of the locality. Further work was carried out on the house in the 1820s when it was re-roofed, and in 1827 pillared. A 'Great Doric' portico was added to the main entrance. Further ex-tensions and modellings were made in 1904 by the architect Inigo Thomas, with the result that much of Nash's work was removed, although some of Nash's detail still survives within the mansion. The accounts for the re-building in 1904-8 have survived.

The estate remained in Colby possession until the death of John Vaughan Colby with-out surviving male issue, in 1919 and Ffyn-none passed to his daughter Aline Margaret who married C. J. H. Spence-Jones C.M.G., D.S.O., who took the name of Colby by Royal Licence in 1920. Ffynnone was sold in 1927 to a Glamorganshire business man, Daniel Daniel, High Sheriff of Pembs 1939, who died unmarried in 1952. For some years the mansion was the home of his sister Mrs. Bickerton Edwards, and on her death it reverted to her nephew W. H. C. Daniel, who sold the property. When I visited it on 4 February 1980 I found the mansion in excellent order, owned by a Swansea business man, Mr. Phillips, who sold the property in 1988 to Earl Lloyd George, who greatly improved the house and the environs. It is today the Earl's main residence in West Wales.

Refs: Carms R.O., John Francis Deeds, Trant/Yelverton Deeds; N.L.W., Owen and Colby Estate Accounts, Llwyngwair and Bronwydd Deeds; Nicholas, *County Families 1875* edn.; Fenton, *Tour Pemb. 1811;* Lewis *TDW 1840;* C. Allen 1871 *Tivyside Photographic Souvenier* (illustr.); *Country Quest,* Apr. 1966 (illustr.); J. Hilling, *History of Architecture in Wales,* 1976; (illustr.); D. L. Baker-Jones, Ffynnone, 'Notes on a Country House and its Occupants' in *Trans. Cymmr.* 1965 Part I *(illustr.)* Francis Jones, 'The Hand of Nash in West Wales' in *Trans. Carms Antiq. Soc.,* 1939, and 'Chronical of Blaenbylan' in *Journal Ceredigion Antiq. Soc.* 1976.

FFYNNONE. *Little Newcastle.*

A farmstead south of Little Newcastle village, and near Garn Twrne. Home of yeoman families. The first known family there, that of Symmons whose ancestors were living at nearby Colston in 1670. They continued at Ffynnone until the first part of the 19th century. When Anne Symmons of Ffynnone's will was proved in 1805, the property passed to her brother Thomas Symmons. By 1813 there were two properties there – Old Ffynnone, the original house, and New Ffynnone. By 1840 Old Ffynnone was owned by George Williams of Treyarched, and in 1843 he went to live there. He died in 1849, and left the property to his son, R. M. G. Williams, surgeon, who died at Newport Pembs. in 1910.

Refs: Pembs. *R.O. Deeds HDX/562,* no. 36; wills of Symmons family; Pembs *Land Tax* 1786.

FFYNNON GAIN. *New Moat.*

Now a farmstead to the south of New Moat village, on a steep slope to the north of Bletherston village. In 1326 it was described as a Knight's fee divisible according to Welsh tenure; it was held by Philip Brown who owned Fonnon Keyng and Castel Kymer, being two carucates held of the fee of New Moat. On Rees's 14th century map it is marked as a Welsh knight's fee. It later passed to the Philipps family, a branch of Pentypark. In 1638 John Philipps of Ffynnongain served as High Sheriff. He was inordinately attached to his money which he carried around in a red bag which earned him the nickname 'Shon bwtsh goch' (John of the red pouch). He also owned Haythog, and his son William of that place was High Sheriff in 1646. Ffynnongain was acquired by the Scourfields of New Moat, and Henry Scourfield was owner in 1786. By 1873 the owner of Ffynnongain (132 acres) was W. G. Purser. Some 600 yards from the house was a holy well believed to possess healing qualities.

FERN HILL. *Haroldston St. Issels.*

A modern residence in grounds and trees above a bend of the river Cleddau; Lewis TDW 1840 described it as 'pleasantly situated on the bank of the Cleddau and surrounded by living plantations.' Its most important owner-occupier was Sir Henry Mathias (son of Caesar Mathias of Hook, Freystrop, High Sheriff 1774). He was Mayor of Haverfordwest in 1806, and ten years later was High Sheriff. During his shreivalty he presented an address to the Prince Regent, and was knighted. He was the last Protonotary of the Great Sessions for the Carmarthen circuit. His wife Katherine was the daughter of Philip Jones of Llanina, Cards, by Katherine Warren of Trewern. He died in 1832 aged 75, and his wife in 1848 aged 83. He bore as arms: *or between three lions couchant a chevron engrailed sable thereon five ermine spots argent;* crest: *a boy's head couped at the shoulders, a snake entwined round his neck.* Motto *Spero meliora.*

Refs: *Colby Map 1831;* Sir Henry's first cousin, Rev. Caesar Morgan of Ely, married Mrs. Mary Morgan author of *Tour to Milford Haven,* 1791.

FISHGUARD. *Fishguard.*

The site of the home of the Dyer family is not known. Records refer to the Dyer family as being 'of Fishguard', but whether their home was in the town or elsewhere in the parish is not clear. The two brothers, Walter and William Dyer, both 'of Fishguard', Pembs. were sons of Philip Dyer of Newport Pembs. In 1558 Walter Dyer of Fishguard, gent., granted to John ap Owen of Kynheidre, lands in the vill and fields of Trebover, in Llanust, and Le Escaer, rendering 8s. yearly to the heirs of William Dyer of Haverford who granted the said lands to Walter Dyer in 1512. Janet Dyer of Fishguard, widow, was living in 1552. These facts are entered here in the hope that further research will indicate the site of the Dyer home. The arms of Dyer of Fishguard were *gules an eagle displayed argent beaked and armed or.*

Refs: *Golden Grove ms.* Adv. Pemb. 1, 26: NLW, *Bronwydd Deeds* no. 999; *Pembs Plea Rolls;* G. Owen in *B. M. Egerton ms* 2586.

FLEET. *Monkton St. Nicholas*

Home of the Meyrick family in the late 16th century. Dwnn recorded the pedigree of Sir Francis Meyrick of 'Fleet House in Moncton' Geo. Dwnn mentions Sir Francis Meyrick of 'Muncaton', circa 1608. In the Land Tax of 1786 John Francis Meyrick is recorded as owner of Upper Fleet (Wm Powell, tenant) and Lower Fleet (Jas. Bedford, tenant) in Monkton parish.

Refs: *Dwnn,* i, 137; *Geo Owen Pembs,* iii; *Pembs RO, Land Tax 1786.*

FLETHERHILL *Rudbaxton.*

The scant remains of the old mansion are some distance to the north-east of the present farmstead of Fletherhill, and near the banks of a tributary of the Western Cleddau. Above it is rising land. The old mansion is marked on *Colby's Map 1831.* It was assessed at four hearths in 1670. The name is derived from the Welsh word *llether* (slope) and late 16th century legal records decribe the property as 'Fletherill alias Letherhill' (1584).

From early times Fletherhill was a manor and is described as such down to the 18th century. The manor was held prior to 1349 by Guy de Brisau, in 1592 by Sir John Perrot of Haroldston, in 1606 it was held on a lease by (Sir) John Philipps of Picton Castle, thereafter by four successive generations of the Hayward family. The first known owners of Fletherhill were the Goddard family, descended from the Goddards of Glossop, co. Derby. Two sons were parsons – Henry, rector of Rudbaxton from 1556 to 1563, Edward, vicar of Amroth in 1591; their only sister Alice married William Hayward who settled at Fletherhill. The Haywards intermarried with wealthy landowning families like Llwyd and Morfil and Perrot of Haroldston and amassed a considerable estate in Pembrokeshire and in England. By his will dated 6 November 1646 James Hayward, barrister, younger son of John and Mathilda Hayward of Fletherhill, charged his property in Surrey with an annuity of £20 for the revenue of the 'Hospital of Haverfordwest in St. Martins parish to be paid to the poor chosen and admitted to the Hospital,' and in 1687 the Town Council had trouble in getting the money, and threatened to prosecute Lady Hamilton, daughter and heiress of the said James Hayward, barrister, if she did not pay the £20 annuity regularly.

In 1659-1660 George Hayward served as High Sheriff, and in 1681 Thomas Hayward was returned as M.P. for Haverfordwest, but William Wogan petitioned against the return. The last male member of the family, Thomas Hayward died (unmarried) as the result of a duel, on 9 July 1682, bequeathing the Fletherhill estate to his only sister Mary Hayward. He had mortgaged parts of the estate, but these after redemption, would revert to Mary. She married George Tasker of Castle Pill, Steynton but he died without issue not long after the wedding, and was buried at Steynton on 28 July 1684. The widowed Mary Tasker made her will on 2 August 1684, and left all her estate, including the manors of

Fletherhill, Rudbaxton and St. Ishmaels, the capital messuage of Fletherhill, the rectory of Spittal, and lands in the parishes of Rudbaxton, St. Ishmaels, Bletherston, Camrose, Llandisilio, Llanycefn, and houses in the town and county of Haverfordwest, to the Mayor and Corporation of Haverfordwest in trust, to erect and build an alms house in that town 'for the breeding (sic) and maintenance of poor children of both sexes', and for other charitable uses. And thus was founded the famous Tasker's School that served Haverfordwest and district for many generations, and still flourishes under the name Tasker-Milward School.

A local tale relates that Mary·Tasker had long narrow strips of cloth placed on the road so that she should not soil her shoes when she walked from Fletherhill to Rudbaxton church. These strips were of blue cloth edged with scarlet – colours later used in the early school uniform of the school she had founded. The Haywards bore: *or three lions rampant gules over all a bendlet sable*. Crest: *a lion issuant gules*.

Refs: Fenton, *Tour Pembs.*, 1811; *Golden Grove mss; Dwnn*, i, 179; *Taylor's Cussion* fo. 96b; *Pembs. Magazine*, Feb. 1984; *A. Cam.*, 1888, 132, 1889, 271: *NLW G. S. Pembs, Eaton Evans and Williams Deeds*, no. 3446; Lord Hampton Deeds.

FOBSTON. *Marloes*.

Now a farmstead south of St. Bride's Hill. Formerly home of a cadet branch of Allen of Gelliswick. David Allen was at Fobston in 1702, and his descendants continued there for a further three generations. The last of the male line, David Allen, inherited a heavily encumbered estate, and died an· alcholic in 1797, leaving Fobston to his friend John Gwynne, attorney, of Haverfordwest, a member of the Gwynnes of Cilciffeth and Court. John Gwynne, Esq. is described as owner of the Fobston estate in 1802, with John Stewart as tenant. It was afterwards farmed by yeomen, and became part of the St. Brides estate. A Sale Catalogue of that estate in 1920 describes Fobston as a good stone cement-faced house of eight bedrooms, three sitting rooms, kitchen, back kitchen, dairy, cellar, with substantial farm buildings.

Refs: *NLW, Eaton Evans and Williams Deeds, Brawdy Deeds, Poyston Deeds; M.I. in Marloes church; Pembs RO Deeds D/LP, Land Tax Lists*; see also S.C. (J.F.) 1988, for illustr. description and plans.

FORD. *Carew*.

A farmstead on Ford Pill between Carew Castle and Paskeston. In the 17th and early 18th centuries it belonged to the Philipps family, a branch of Picton Castle. John Philipps of Goodhook (q.v.), agent to his cousin Sir John Philipps, built the residence at Ford. He was agent in 1650 and was still acting as such in 1699. Sir John wrote a 'memorandum of what Privilege my cozen John Philipps had with me from Picton since 1650', and included among them are the following : 'I gave him as much timber as did build two parts of his house at Ford, and the use of my tenants to carry his slates from Llangolman to Picton Key, and my lighyter to carry them from there to Ford, and to carry his limestone from Williamston Park to Goodhook during the time he lived there, and to carry his corn and household stuff from Goodhook to Ford.'

The Philipps family continued to own Ford for most of the first half of the 18th century. Edward Philipps of Ford died leaving a son and four daughters. John Philipps, the son, matriculated at Jesus College, Oxford, in 1722, and in 1735 was High Sheriff of Pembrokeshire. He died without issue, and the Ford estate passed to his sisters, co-heiresses, Elizabeth, married John Smith of Jeffreston, Anne married John Relly of Pembroke, Mary married Reverend James Higgon of Haverfordwest, and Katherine married David Rice of London, apothecary. In 1786 John Smith Esq. is described as owner of Ford.

Ref: *Picton Castle Documents; Haverfordwest Deeds.*

FOLEY HOUSE. *Haverfordwest.*

A large town house built in Goat Street in 1794 by Nash, for Admiral Thomas Foley of Ridgeway. It consisted of three storeys and a basement. The ground floor comprised an entrance hall, drawing room with large bay windows, dining room, smoking room, cloak room; on the first floor, four large bedrooms, dressing room, and two bedrooms in a wing, and bathroom: on the second floor, a large bedroom, two servants bedrooms, bathroom: in the basement, a large kitchen, scullery, store-room, wine cellar, pantries, and larders.

From 1921 to 1947 it was home of the well-known family of George. The property was sold to the Pembrokeshire County Council in 1947, and is used for offices and excellently maintained.

Refs: Francis Jones, 'The Hand of Nash in West Wales' m. Trans. Carms. Antiq. Soc. 1939, pp. 93-96.

FOLKESTON. *Roch.*

A farmstead 1 mile south-west of Roch, above Norton Haven. In 1392 Peter Mossylwyke and Agnes his wife held two carucates at Folkerston by knight service held of the manor of Roch; from about 1413 to 1520 the family of Reynbot held Folkeston. The Perrots were claiming rights to the property, and in 1441 Thomas Perrot of Eastington held some parts of Folkeston which he had from Walter Reynbot of that place, and in 1507 Owen Perrot sued John Reynbot for three messuages in Felkeston. Much later, on 24 February 1664-5 James Philipps of Tregibby, near Cardigan, Esq. granted a lease of Folcaston with creeks, quays, quarries, coal and culm in the townred and fields of Folcaston to Anthony Stokes of Roch parish, gent, for lives. By 1716 Folcaston belonged to Rowland Philipps of St. Brides who gave a lease for lives of that property to Tobias Codd, which lease was surrendered on 14th September 1769 by Dorothy widow of David Codd (grandson of the said Tobias) to Rowland Philipps Laugharne of Orlandon who held, in 1786, three messuages at Folcaston (let to tenants), and still owned them in 1801. The Tithe Schedule of the parish, 1837, shows James Higgon as owner-occupier of Folcaston (279 acres). By 1904 William Stancomb of Bradford, Devizes, Wilts., owned the Folcaston and Southward estates.

Refs: *PRO, Ancient Deeds; NLW, Pembs Plea Rolls, Morgan-Richardson Deeds, Poyston Deeds*

FOREST. *Cilgerran.*

Also called 'Y Plâs ynghefn y drum' (the mansion behind the ridge – a fair topographical description). About three-quarters of a mile north-west of Cilgerran, on high ground above the river Teifi. Phillips wrote in 1867 – 'the old house of Forest stood a little to the north-west of the present dwelling house; and a part of the same exists now incorporated with the outbuildings. From the remains of some ornamental freestone mouldings found among the debris it is presumed that it was an elegant structure. According to the *Pembs. Arch. Survey* (1896-1907) 'of which residence not a vestige is left.' The present building is a farmstead.

In its earlier days Forest was the home of the Revell family who had been mercers and corvisors in Haverfordwest during the early 16th century. Thomas Revell, merchant, of Haverfordwest, married Janet Bowen of Lochmeyler, and was the first of the family to settle at Forest. His son John Revell died in 1546, leaving issue, and his widow Anne (née Walter of Carmarthen) married the eminent Dr. Thomas Phaer (d.1560) who came to live at Forest, and was M.P. for Cardigan Borough (1555-59) and for Carmarthen Borough (1547), and a physician and literateur of merit. John Revell's son, Thomas Revell, J.P., was High Sheriff of Pembrokeshire in 1579, and of Cardiganshire in 1582 and 1593, and M.P. for Pembrokeshire. He died without male issue, and Forest passed to his younger brother, William Revell whose great-grandson, Thomas Revell is said to have 'sold all.'

The next family at Forest was that of Parry, and in 1634 Forest formed part of the Parry of Noyadd Trefawr estate. It later passed to the family of Symmons of Llanstruan, and in 1766 John Symmons conveyed his estates (including Forest) to his son and heir, John Symmons. In 1786 John Symmons Esq. is described as owner of Forest, with John Edwards as tenant, the tax assessment being the largest in the parish. The Symmons estates were sold in 1784, and later we find the owners to be the Lloyds of Coedmore, who owned Forest down to recent times.

Refs: Dwnn, i, 155; Phillips, *Hist. of Cilgerran*, 1867; for Phaer see Dr. John Cule 'Thomas Phaer M.D. of Cilgerran' in *Trans Cymmr* 1880, and also D.N.B., and D.W.B., Golden Grove Ms (Gwynfardd); NLW, Cwrtmawr Deeds, Noyadd Trefawr Deeds, Pembs. Plea Rolls; Pembs Arch Svy, 1896, 1907.

FREESTONE HALL. *Carew.*

A residence on high ground 1¼ miles north-east of Carew Castle. Lewis in 1840 comments on the site as follows – 'Freestone Hall, residence of J. Allen Esq. commanding from the grounds some of the finest views in the county, embracing Lawrenny and its fine estuary, Clareston, and the hundred of Rhos to the west ...' The mansion, built by Roger Allen (1734-1782) second son of John Allen of Cresselly, is a three-storeyed main block with a wing stretching to the rear at one side. A good photo was taken of the house by C. S. Allen of Tenby in 1871. James Allen (son of Roger) presented a paten and flagon 'as a New Years Gift' to the parish of Carew in 1844, and further plate was presented by Thomas Allen of Freeston Hall in 1886 in memory of his eldest son Captain Griffith Allen late of H.M. 98th Regiment. In 1910 Freestone Hall, 'an old House Mansion now used as a farm' was advertised for sale; it comprised a porch, entrance Hall, dining room, parlour, kitchen, pantry, a large back-kitchen, and dairy and outbuildings; there were seven bedrooms, 78 acres were attached.

Refs: Lewis TDW, edns 1834 and 1840; C. S. Allen *Photographs in South Wales*, 1871; J. T. Evans, *Church Plate of Pembs*, 1905.

FROCHEST. *Eglwyswrw.*

A farmstead about half a mile north of Eglwyswrw, and near Court, residence of the Cantington family, lords of Eglwyswrw, a branch of which settled at Frochest in the 14th century. Later descendants adopted the Welsh form of nomenclature. Thomas David ap Evan lived at Frochest in the period 1422-61; another descendant James Morris is described by George William Griffith (1584-1665) as 'now livinge, but neere 100 yeares old.' Frochest was bought by George Owen of Henllys between 1579 – 1597. Thereafter it was let to farming tenants. The Cantington arms were: *gules an eagle displayed argent, a chief chequy argent and vert.* Crest: *a moor's head sable, plumed or.*

Refs: *College of Arms, Wagner Ms 12, Protheroe Ms XIV; Dwnn*, 1, 71; *Golden Grove Ms.*

FRON. *Llanddewi Felfre.*

A large double-pile house on the hillside of Pengawse, overlooking Whitland. It was long empty but is now inhabited again. In the 18th and early 19th centuries it was the home of the Lewis family descended from David Lewis of Fron who married Margaret daughter of Evan Protheroe, Esq., of Dolwilym.

She died in 1749. Their great grandson Evan Protheroe Lewis (b.1792) was the last of the family at Fron, and after 1832 he moved to Narberth. By his wife, Elizabeth Lewis of Whitland (d.1868) he had 14 children. After this, Fron was let to tenant farmers.

Refs: NLW, *Griffith Owen Deeds, Morgan-Richardson Deeds.*

FRONGOCH. *Nevern.*

A farmstead between Nevern and Tredrissi, about three quarters of a mile north of Nevern. An Evan Robin 'de Vrongoch ar lan Nevarne' lived there in the early 16th century. The next occupant, Mathias Bowen died shortly before October 1598, and was followed at Frongoch by his son Thomas Mathias, a minor when his father died. Thomas was succeeded by his son Morgan Thomas who married Jane daughter of Mathias Bowen of Llwyngwair. He had two sons – James Morgan who moved to Tredrissi, and one with the strange name 'Sir Thomas heb achos'.

Refs: *College of Arms Ms, Wagner Ms 5, Protheroe Mss IV and V; Dwnn*, i, 162.

Earl Lloyd-George

Garn. *Llanychaer.*

A farmstead about 400 yards to the northeast of the parish church; an interesting old farmhouse with hall open to the rafters, and an ancient round chimney, once common in the county. I visited it in the company of Mr. Peter Smith F.S.A., of the R.C.A.M. Aberystwyth. The gentry family of Bateman, descended from the Batemans of Honeyborough near Neyland, lived for many years at houses in the Cwm Gwaun area. One of these, John Bateman of Trenewydd (Llanychaer), had an illegitimate son by Margaret daughter of Lewis Llewelin, named Thomas Bateman, who settled at Garn where he was living in 1603. In the second half of the 19th century, Garn formed part of the estate of Mortimer of Court, Llanychaer. The Bateman arms were *argent a chevron between three escallops sable.*

Refs: *College of Arms, Protheroe Ms; Dwnn*, i, 173.

GELLIFOR. *Nevern (Cilgwyn Quarter).*

Now a residence on a slope above the waters of a tributary of the upper river Gwaun, and just over half a mile from Llanerch-y-bleiddied (q.v.) marked on Colby's Map 1831 as Gellyvore, but on modern OS maps as Gelli-fawr. Locally it is still called Gellifôr, but the present proprietors use Gelli Fawr. The farmhouse consists of two parts: the original section is the kitchen area which contains the 'simme fawr' and attached to it is a section which formed the original farmhouse. At one time, the kitchen was extended to include a room. In the last century, a large extention was added, now of two storeys, and an attic storey with a dormer window. Over the outer doorway of the kitchen is a stone tablet which reads 'Rebuilt in 1860 by D. Davies, Esqr., Castle Green, Cardigan.' The property had been owned on 29 September 1860 by the said David Davies. It was advertised for sale by David Davies, son of the said purchaser, and describes 'The Mansion House, which is newly and substantially erected, containing three reception rooms, eight bedrooms, kitchen back kitchen, dairy, pantries, with all necessary out offices, and would make an excellent Shooting Box'; and very fine outbuildings are also described, two cottages on the property, with 241 acres.

The yeoman family of James lived there from early 18th century, for five generations, after which it was sold. In 1860 it was bought by David Davies J.P., D.L., Castle Green, Cardigan, who had served as High Sheriff in 1841. It was advertised for sale by his son in 1889. The present owners have converted the buildings into holiday homes and the house is an hotel. (1993)

Refs: NLW, *Morgan-Richardson Deeds, Croydon Deeds; Carms R.O. Beckingale Colln.; inf. ex Mr. Dillwyn Miles.*

GELLISWICK. *Hubberston.*

Formerly a mansion on high ground above Gelliswick Bay, to the west of the town of Milford Haven, where it stood from Elizabethan days to the second half of the present century. The mansion, facing south-east towards the main gateway, consisted of two storeys, the entrance on the ground floor, with a range of five windows, and on the upper storey a range of seven windows. Its frontage measured 51 feet, its breadth 42 feet. The stairway rose from a room in the rear, where a wing extended. There was a chimney at each gable end, and on the outside some corbelling. In 1670 it was assessed at five hearths. In the 1730s a companion appeared alongside its northern end. Happily, for us, in 1740 John Butcher was employed to make an estate-map-book, where he described 'The Old Building' and 'The New Building', and, what is more, made an admirable sketch of the latter. The new building faced south, and its gable-end was attached to that of the original structure, so that the whole produced an L-shaped residence. The new addition was an impressive building of three storeys built over a basement storey. The entrance was in the centre of the first floor, with a semi-circular fanlight over the door; it had four windows. On the second floor there were two large bedrooms, and a bathroom and a range of five windows. The third floor had three bedrooms each with five windows. The projection to the rear carried the staircase, where a few of the old balustrades could be seen. The basement storey had four windows. The length of the frontage measured some 45 feet, and its breadth over 21 feet. Just to the rear (north) was a large garden of over an acre enclosed with high stone walls. These buildings remained substantially the same to our day.

The extent of the demesne and farmland in 1740 was 266 acres. Gelliswick was the home of the landowning family of Barrett from about 1550 until the death of the ultimate heiress Margaret who had married (as her second husband) George Bowen of Neeston, and towards the middle of the 17th century, her son Henry Bowen (died, probably in 1658) sold Gelliswick to the Canon family of Haverfordwest. The Canons held it until the heiress Elizabeth Canon married Edward Philipps of Picton Castle, and on her death in 1706 the Gelliswick estate became the pro-

perty of her husband's family. The Philippses continued in possession until well into the 19th century. An interesting feature of the history of the occupancy of Gelliswick house and demesne. By 1656 William Allen was tenant, and later held the property under renewal leases. The Allens were wealthy, and during their tenure of Gelliswick two of their number were High Sheriffs, in 1693 and 1742. On the death of John Allen in 1808 Gelliswick reverted to its owners, Philipps of Picton Castle. After this, several families lived there. In 1955 it was sold to the Esso Oil Company who operated in the area. The land was farmed by Mr. Reg Roberts of Haverfordwest, land agent. I visited it in 1978 and 1979, and found the 'old' and 'new' houses in good order. Alas, early in 1981 the house and buildings were razed to the ground by the Esso Oil Company who had 'no further use for it.'

Refs: *Dwnn*, i, 70, 119, 153–4; NLW, *Great Sessions Pembs Plea Rolls, Map Book Picton Castle estate*; *Carms R.O. Golden Grove Ms. (Adv. Dyfed)*; Col. F. S. Allen, *Family Records of the Allens of Cresselly, etc.* pr. 1905; Francis Jones, 'Gelliswick and its Families' in *Arch. Cam. 1980 (illustr.).*

GILFACHWRNELL.

In the free chapelry of Llangolman Penbedw alias Llanfihangel Penbedw.

Marked on Colby's Map 1831 as Gilfach to the east of Capel Colman, and in a deed of 1842 as 'Gilfach alias Kilvach Wrnell'. Home of yeomen and minor gentry. The earliest-known proprietor was Thomas David Morgan of Manordeifi who owned Plâs Kilvach-wrnell at the time of his death in 1655. His daughter Elizabeth married Thomas Lloyd, gent., of Clynfyn, and brought Gilfachwrnell to that family, and was settled on their younger son Jenkin Lloyd who was living there in 1675.

David Lloyd (brother of the preceeding Jenkin) described as 'of Westminster' conveyed Gilfachwrnell in 1694 to Stephen Morris of St. Paul's, Covent Garden, who made his will in 1698. Little has been found about its later history, until 1786 when David Griffiths, gent. is described a owner-occupier of 'Gilfach hwrnell'. In 1798 the said David Griffiths, then of Cilau Wen, Llanstinan parish, by his will bequeathed 'Gilfach' to his sister Mrs. Elizabeth Rees of Cilgwyn, Manordeifi, widow, for her life, with remainder to her eldest son John Rees. In 1813 George Rees of Cilgwyn (eldest son of John and Elizabeth Rees both deceased) broke the entail on the messuage and land called 'Gilfach alias Kilvach Awrnell', formerly held by John Davies gent. afterwards held by David Thomas, yeoman, then by William Davies farmer, and finally by John and George Rees of Cilgwyn. George Rees mortgaged the property, being much in debt, and in his will, made in November 1842, mentions his property called Gilfach alias Kilvach Wrnell.

A plan of the property was made about 1843. The Tithe Map and Schedule of the *Chapelry of Capel Colman in 1849* gives Martha Jane Jones as owner-occupier of 'Gilfach Cottage' and garden and 78 acres. The name and site are now lost.

Refs: *Golden Grove Ms I (Gwynfardd); NLW, Bronwydd Deeds; Pembs R.O. Saunders-Davies papers,* one of which contains the map of Gilfach and genealogical notes.

GLANDOVAN. *Cilgerran.*

Originally Glendyfan, the name became generally rendered as Glandovan. The mansion stands on a wooded slope about a mile south of the town of Cilgerran. It became the home of the Vaughan family descended from the north Wales chieftain Osbwn Wyddel, whose arms, *ermine, on a saltire gules a crescent or,* they bore. The first to be associated with the parish was William Vaughan, supporter of Henry VII, appointed Constable of Cilgerran castle, whose descendant, Robert Vaughan (living 1580) built the house of Glandovan and married Elizabeth daughter of the eminent physician and author Dr. Thomas Phaer of Forest (q.v.). In 1670 Rees Vaughan was assessed at six hearths for Glandovan, the highest assessment in the parish.

In the late 17th century the Vaughan heiress married a Stedman of Strata Florida and the Glandovan estate passed to that family. Eventually, Jane Stedman, daughter and heiress of James Stedman, married the barrister, William Gower of Boughton St. Johns, Worcs., M.P. for Ludlow for 1689, who came to live at Glandovan. There he died in 1723, his wife being sole executrix of his will. They had ten children, the third of whom, Abel Gower, succeeded to Glandovan. Six more generations succeeded, and in 1824 Robert Frederic Gower purchased Castle Malgwyn near Llechryd, which became the main residence. In 1948 Erasmus William Gower sold Castle Malgwyn. The Gower arms were *azure a chevron between three wolf heads erased or.*

Welsh poets of a bygone age sang the praises of some of the early owners of Glandovan, among them Tudwr Aled (fl. 1480-1526) who composed an ode of thanks to William Fychan (who had married Margaret daughter of Sir William Perrot) for presenting him with a 'march glâs'. The house has lasted, and among its features is a fine well-stairway. When I visited it in 1976 in company of Mr. Peter Smith, F.S.A., the owner-occupiers were Mr. and Mrs. Wetherhead, and when I called there in May 1984 it was owned by Mr. David Frost, land-agent, of Haverfordwest.

Refs: *Dwnn,* i, 147-8; *W.W.H.R.* ii, 89; *Carmarthenshire Studies,* 1974, 71 and Plates XII, XIII; P. Smith, *Houses of the Welsh Countryside,* 1975. Plate 90. NLW, *Papers of Great Sessions, Pembs Plea Rolls, Bronwydd Deeds Noyadd Trefawr Deeds, Cwrtmawr Deeds.*

GLANDUAD.
Now called GLANDUAD FAWR. *Meline.*

Also called Glanduad Fawr/Ucha, and there was another nearby farm called Glanduad Fach: in deeds of 1740 and Mudge Map 1819 given as Llandyad. A farmhouse near Afon Duad, quarter of a mile north-west of the parish church, it still possesses the vernacular style of a typical old Welsh gentry house. A large oblong house of two storeys, and an attic storey with three dormer windows. The main entrance leads into a roomy hall, at the rear of which, in a projection, is the main staircase lit by a long window (partly blocked up). On the right is the parlour with perfectly preserved oak panelling with 17th century pillars, and a plaster ceiling with traces of elaborate decoration. The dining room was to the left, today used as a kitchen. At the rear, near the staircase, was the original kitchen with a 'simne fawr', but that and the chimney stack has been removed. An extension to the right of the front had been used as a stable, but in 1975 when I visited Glanduad, this was being converted into a dwelling for a son of the proprietors. On a pane in one of the windows of the house was inscribed 'I lost this day £5000'; on another occurred the name 'Grace Stephens', who died of consumption, and the lines

'My pain, my pleasure, no human tongue
   can tell
Tis heaven to have thee, without thee, hell!

In 1937 I received a letter from Mr. Joseph Thomas, then occupier, about former families, he says '... there was another noted old family, the Stephens, the last of whom, Grace Stephens, died a spinster, and two lines were written on a pane of glass by her lover the day she died, they are to be seen here now,' and then quotes the foregoing distich. All these inscribed panes are gone. Descendants of the chieftain Gwynfardd Dyfed, in direct descent, had lived at Glanduad for four and a quarter centuries, 1325 to 1750. The main line lived at nearby Penybenglog to which estate Glanduad belonged, and later became the seat of a cadet branch who bore Gwynfardd's arms: *azure a lion rampant within an orle of roses or* and adopted the surname Bowen. Fifteenth in descent, Anne Bowen the heiress, married in 1744 John Moore of Muslick, and their daughter Alice Moore married Phillip Powell of Radnorshire, from whom descends Mr. Anthony Powell, the well-known writer of our day. Glanduad afterwards passed through several hands – Lloyd (Carms), Harries, Davies, Stephens,

Colby (1869) and was afterwards owned by gentlemen-farmers.

Refs: Francis Jones 'Griffith of Penybenglog' Trans Cymmr 1939, and 'Bowen of Pentre Ifan and Llwyngwair' in Pembs Historian 1979; B. G. Charles (ed) 'George Owen's 2nd Book', in Journal of NLW, Winter, 1948; W.W.H.R. ii, 38; NLW, Bronwydd Deeds, Morgan-Richardson Deeds, F. Green Deeds and Documents; Pembs R.O. DX/57/35, Sale Catalogue of Glanduad (John Colby Esq., then owner).

GLANRHYD. *Grondre.*

A farmstead south of Clynderwen railway station, and near the road to Penblewin crossroads. The dwelling house is not striking, but there is a very fine range of splendidly built outbuildings. Home of the Griffiths family in the 18th century. The first at Glanrhyd, Evan Griffiths J.P. (brother of Stephen Griffiths of Llangolman) was High Sheriff of Carmarthenshire in 1766, in 1769 he was a Commissioner of Land Tax for Pembrokeshire. An inscribed tablet on an outbuilding reads 'Erected by Evan Griffiths in 1770', he subscribed to Reverend William Evans' English translation of *Cannwyll y Cymry* in 1771, and was a Grand Juror of the Pembrokeshire Great Sessions in 1783, and died not long afterwards. He was unmarried, and his property passed between his sister Catherine, and Mary, wife of John Lewis of Henllan. In 1786 the owner of Glanrhyd was Rowland Edwardes, Esq. with the Reverend Thomas Bowen clerk and James Lewis as tenants. It is still a large and attractive farm.

Refs: Pembs Papers of Great Sessions; Buckley, Carmarthenshire Sheriffs.

GLASTIR. *Nevern.*

Now a farmstead nearly one mile to the north-east of Nevern village. Writing about 1603 George Owen tells us, 'yt was intymes past the personage howse or gleebe of the person of Nevarne before the appropriatinge thereof to the Colledge of Saint Davides [in 1377] ... where it contynued untyll the suppressinge thereof when it was taken into the kinges handes and bought by Matheas Thomas father to Thomas Matheas' [descended from the Youngs]' men tall of person, fair of complexion and gentle of behaviour, but some now decline from the same'. Mathias Thomas was the son of Thomas Lewis who was the son of Lewis Young, eldest son of Howel ap Jenkin Young of Tredrissi. Mathias Thomas' son, Thomas Mathias of Glastir died in 1617 and from him the Mathias family of Llangwarran descend. They all bore the Young arms: *vert a hart trippant between 3 fleurs de lys or*. After settling at Llanwarran c. 1600, the family ceased to use Glasdir as a residence, and it was let to a series of yeomen families and in the 18th century was sold. In 1786 Thomas Keymer was the owner, in 1811 John Evans, Esq. and in 1840 Anne Evans.

Refs: G. Owen, *Second Book of Pembs, c.1603;* Fenton, *Tour Pembs 1811;* NLW, *Poyston Deeds, Bronwydd Deeds;* Golden Grove Mss (adv. Dyfed) i,12; College of Arms, *Protheroe Ms IV, ff. 148-9.*

GLÔG (formerly Glôg-y-frân). *Clydey.*

Now a farmstead on a hill slope between Frenni Fawr and Llanfyrnach, and above the upper waters of Afon Tâf. The building consists of a central block of two storeys, weather-tiled, and a rear wing. The entrance leads to a small oak-panelled hall from which rises a flight of stairs that divides to the right and left. A door from the hall leads to the cellar. On the right of the hall in the parlour, on the left the *neuadd,* with a *simne fawr,* and a kitchen in the rear wing. There is a partly-walled garden, the whole surrounded by pleasant grounds. Thus it was then I called there in 1974.

The family of Owen held the property in the 17th and 18th centuries. Thomas Owen of Glôg, gent, was assessed at four hearths in 1670, and was succeeded by his son John Owen who was a Grand Juror in 1746. John left two sons and four daughters, none of whom had issue. The eldest son, Thomas Owen gent. mortgaged the 'capital messuage called Glogue alias Gloge y vrane' and other lands to Stephen Colby of Ffynnone and W. R. H. Howell of Maesgwynne on 3 April 1767. He died in 1768. His wife Elizabeth, only daughter and heiress of Robinson Lloyd

of Vaynor, afterwards married John Ferrier. He was succeeded by his brother John Owen who settled at Nantuan in Clydey. John died without issue, and in 1786 John Ferrier was the owner-occupier of Glôg (*iure uxoris*).

Not long afterwards Glôg was sold, and in the early 19th century was owned by a gentleman-farmer, John Owen, not related to the earlier family of that name. In 1834 he was owner-occupier of Glôg, then comprising 268 acres. Five generations of this family remained at Glôg. The last male of the family, John Owen, was an innovator and introduced machinery into the local quarries whose output he greatly improved; he also took an active part in establishing the railway from Whitland to Crymych which was opened in 1875, and extended to Cardigan in 1886. This local benefactor died on 30 May 1886, aged 68, and was buried at Llwynyrhwrdd. He left two daughters, co-heiresses of Glôg, namely Anne Mary who married Mr. T. J. Rees, but died without issue; and Miss Anna Louisa Owen. It was Miss Owen and her brother-in-law who welcomed me when my wife and I called there on 10 September 1974.

Refs: Carms R.O. *J. Francis Deeds;* NLW, *Poyston Deeds, Morgan-Richardson Deeds, Pembs Plea Rolls; Tithe Map Clydey, 1841; Land Tax 1786; Trans Carms Antiq. Soc.,* 1908.

GOLDEN. *Pembroke St. Mary's.*

North-east of the town, across the river from the town. From 1603 to 1825 the Cuny family were associated with Golden and for short periods lived at Lamphey, Welston, and Pembroke. The Cunys came from Staffordshire, the first to come to Pembroke being Walter Cuny, whose son and heir, Richard, signed his pedigree for Dwnn in 1613. Some eight generations of the family remained in the county for two and a quarter centuries; seemingly the last in the male line was the Reverend John Powell Cuny, rector of St. Brides who died unmarried in 1820-25. On Colby's map of 1831 are marked Golden Hill and adjacent Golden Farm.

Refs: *Dwnn,* i, 25; NLW, *Poyston Deeds;* Francis Green 'Cuny of Welston and Golden', in *W.W.H.R.,* XII, 169.

GLYN-Y-MÊL. *Fishguard.*

Occasionally called Glyn-aniel. An impressive residence of three storeys and a basement storey, on low ground overlooking Afon Gwaun near its estuary at Cwm (Lower Fishguard). About 1796-7, Richard Fenton the eminent barrister and antiquary, started clearing away the cliffs below Carn-y-Gath, where he made a large alcove for his intended mansion. It was completed by 1779, and the building has survived virtually unchanged to our day. Fenton also created a delightful environment of lawns, gardens, trees, bushes and flowers that attracted admiration; there he spent the last 21 years of his life. Historians will remember him for his *Tour through Pembrokeshire*, 1811. He was a Fellow of the Society of Antiquaries, and wrote poetry. The Fenton family held it until about 1866 when Glyn-y-Mêl was advertised for sale. Afterwards it became the home of John Worthington, a well-known philanthropist, who further developed the attractive grounds. The last of the old squires there was Miss Beatrice Chambers, J.P. active in local life. After her, the property changed ownership and today is an hotel.

Refs: NLW, *Trenewydd Deeds, Tour 1802* (No 17508); *Ferrar Fenton's family history in Pembs Guardian*, c.1896-1900; Coastal cottages of Pembs.,1987 (illustr.)

GOOD HOOK. *Uzmaston.*

A farmstead about two miles east of Haverfordwest. The earliest-known owners of Good Hook were the family of Routh. In 1552 John Philipps of Picton Castle, in his will mentions his daughter Janet Philipps and her husband John Routh, gent. of Good Hook and their son John Routh also of Good Hook. John Routh (the younger) was living there in 1598-1600, but had died before 1629 when his widow Ann was still living there.

In the second half of the 17th century, the Rouths had sold Good Hook, and in 1670 it was owned and occupied by James Wogan (son of John Wogan of Wiston) who had bought Good Hook from Lewis Wogan of Boulston, who was assessed at four hearths. In the late 17th century Good Hook was the home of James Allen, and a descendant, John Allen of Good Hook, married Joan Bartlett heiress of Cresselly and they settled there. John died in 1752. John Bartlett Allen owned the property in 1786, with a widow, Ann Pugh, as tenant. Another change took place in the following century, the owner in 1839 being Sir Richard Bulkeley Philipps of Picton Castle, the acreage of Good Hook then being 207 acres. Near the house stood a tumulus, still commemorated in the field names, Great, and Little Tump Park.

The residence is a good example of vernacular architecture of a modest gentry house. Dating from the 16th century it has retained characteristics of its earlier days. It is cruciform in form, of two storeys, with a chimney at each gable end. The projection in the front contains the main porchway, with a storey above rising to roof height, while the rear projection, also of two storeys, has a large cylindrical stone chimney rising from where it joins the main block. Among its interior attractions are two large alcoves, and a particularly interesting staircase, with decorated balusters. After being empty for 20 years it is being tastefully and carefully renovated by the present owners, Mr. and Mrs. Lewis.

Refs: W.W.H.R., VI, 212, and X, 500;: NLW, Eaton Evans and Williams Deeds; Parish Tithe Map, 1839; Pembrokeshire Magazine, RO 21, 1984, illustr. (interior and exterior).

GOODWICK (WDIG also **ABER GOODICK).** *Llanwnda.*

This house occupied a cliff ledge, overlooking the sea not far from the present main railway station and harbour wharf. Today, the Fishguard Bay Hotel stands on the site of the original house. Fenton in 1811 states that two brothers, 'merchant adventurers from Devonshire' settled at Goodwick and added contraband trade to their legal business, and adds, 'their mansion-house, with a variety of dependent buildings, was nicked like an eagle's nest above the pier, commanding a fine view of the bay and the entrance into the port of Fishguard, and so sheltered from all winds prejudicial to the growth of trees, that it once boasted a most beautiful clothing of wood, remains of which are still visible. Perhaps as a situation for a marine villa, it is not to be equalled by any spot in the kingdom.' Fortunately, an engraving of the old mansion, made in 1814 by the brothers Daniell, has survived, and several pre-1900 photographs showing its conversion into 'Hotel Wyncliffe', and from 1906, showing its final conversion and extension when it became 'Fishguard Bay Hotel', which still functions.

In 1702 a lease for 99 years of the house and the quay below was granted to William Rogers of Minehead, Somerset, merchant, and remained in his descendants throughout the 18th century, until 2 February 1805 when the property and the large farm of Penrhiw was sold to David Harries of Dinas Island, husbandman, and remained in that family until the house and quay were sold to the Great Western Railway early in the present century.

Refs: *For the engraving of 1814 and subsequent photographs, see engraving of the house and quay in Fenton, Tour Pembs, 1811, Daniell's engraving 1814, the Western Telegraph 29 April 1982 and 21 March 1984, The County Echo, 6 September 1983, reproduced on p.189 in A Pembrokeshire Anthology ed. D. Miles, 1983 The Pembrokeshire Magazine, May-June 1984, and February 1985. For a ground outline plan of the old house and outbuildings see 25' O.S. Map 1888; for deeds see collections in Pembs R.O.; for Rogers family see Francis Jones, 'Carnachenwen', unpublished essay. (For another Goodwick mansion see Dyffryn-Wdig.).*

GRAIG. *Llanfyrnach.*

A farmstead about two miles south-west of the parish church, on high ground above the west side of Nant Gafel which joins Afon Tâf near Glandwr. For some 500 years Graig was owned and occupied by the descendant of the Devonald family whose ancestor John Devonald signed his will in 1479. Fifth in descent was Thomas Devonald of Graig, gent., born on 11 August 1570, and in March 1598 married Mary daughter of John Owen Philipps of Blaentaf, grandson of Sir Thomas Philipps of Picton Castle; his son and heir John Devonald of Graig was a member of

the Pembrokeshire Trained Band in 1643, and owner of property in Llanfyrnach, Moylegrove, Monnington, Eglwyswrw, Nantgwgn and Clydey, and his great-grand-daughter Hannah Devonald married in 1761 Thomas Morse of Brinaston, Hayscastle. Her second son, John Morse, settled at Graig and in 1787 married Elizabeth daughter of Henry Skeel of Hayscastle. John died in 1818, Elizabeth in 1841. Their grand-daughter Phoebe Morse (born 1831) married John Nicholas who came to live at her home. Their daughter, Dinah Nicholas, married William Harries of Fron, Llangludwen, whose son Mr. Lloyd Morse Harries now lives at Fron farm.

Thus 16 generations of the family had occupied Graig since 1479, and descendants continue to live in the locality. One of the ancestors, John Devonald, gent., a devout Independent, died on 18 March 1757, aged 76, and over his memorial in Glandwr chapel are his heraldic arms – a rare exhibit to be displayed in a Nonconformist chapel.

Refs: *Haverfordwest Library, Francis Green Mss Vols 19 and 20; Pembs R.O., Deeds D/LJ; NLW, Pembs Papers of Great Sessions Bronwydd Deeds, Maesgwynne Deeds; B. M., Egerton Ms, 2586; College of Arms, Protheroe Ms XIX; J. Lloyd James, Hanes Eglwys Glandwr, 1902.*

GREEN HILL. *Pwllcrochan.*

Now a farmstead on a slope half a mile south of the parish church, and about four miles west of Pembroke town. It was the residence of gentry families from Elizabethan times till the early part of the 18th century, first that of Davies whose pedigree was recorded by Dwnn in 1597, and afterwards that of Powell who came from Court near Eglwyswrw, descended from the ancient family of Cantington. The unusual circumstances leading to the settlement of this north Pembrokeshire family in the English-speaking south, has been minuted by George William Griffith, as follows: 'This Lewis ap Howell ap Owen [descended from the Cantingtons of Court] beinge a younge student in Oxford and understandinge of his father's death and of many others of his ffrendes upon depended his whole hopes, repaired home, and found of his ffrendes left (by reason of a great and infectious [sickness] then raigning in the Countrey) onely his sistere Anne livinge then a wofull widdow and great with child. And perceyvinge the ayre not to be as yet free from these infections, removed himselfe with his sistere into the remotest parte of the Countrey, right unto Pembroke about the 3 of Queen Mary [1555-6]. He married there first one Mary Lloyd, secondly Katherine Hall, one of the daughters and co-heiress of John Hall of Trewent [south-east of Pembroke], and had issue by them both. The said Mary was daughter and co-heiress to Robert Vaughan ap David Lloyd'. Lewis ap Howell was known as Lewis Powell which name was used by his descendants. They bore the Cantington arms: *gules an eagle displayed argent, a chief chequy argent and vert.*

From 1566 Lewis Powell was Mayor of Pembroke on seven occasions. His son, Morgan Powell was Alderman of Pembroke and Mayor in 1591 and 1603, and Morgan's son Lewis Powell of Greenhill and Lamphey was Mayor of Pembroke in 1619 and 1622, Member of Parliament for Pembroke Borough in 1620 and 1625, for Haverford-west Borough in 1634 which he held till his death in 1636. Thomas Powell was assessed for seven hearths at Greenhill in 1670, so that it was a large commodious house at that time. In the 18th century Greenhill became part of the Orielton estate, and in 1786 Greenhill was owned by Sir Hugh Owen and Gwynne Davies of Cwm, Carms., with Elizabeth Webb, widow of John Webb, as tenant. In 1801 Morgan Davies of Cwm sold his 2/3rd share of the capital messuage of Greenhill and of Venny Lake.

Refs: *Golden Grove Mss II*, fos. 229-30; *Pembs R.O., D/Adams no 180*; *NLW, G.S. Pembs Plea Rolls, Poyston Deeds*; *College of Arms, Wagner Ms No 12*; *Dwnn, i*, 90; *J. T. Evans, Church Plate of Pembs.*, 1905, p.75.

GREENWAY. *Narberth (North).*
A large residence in grounds on the eastern fringe of Narberth town. Home of the Davies family for three generations. Francis Davies,

gent., was living at Greenway in the years 1654-1678. He was son of the Reverend Thomas Davies, Rector of Eglwys Cymun. The widow, Anne Davies, was assessed for five hearths in 1670. Francis was followed by his son John Davies, and he by his son, Francis Davies, sometimes called junior, who married Hester Harries daughter and co-heiress of Vicar Harries of Cenarth. In 1708 Francis Davies is described as 'formerly of Greenway, Narberth, but now of Cenarth, Carms'., which suggests that he had gone to live in his wife's home parish. Later he seems to have had trouble concerning the ownership of Greenway, and during the years 1723-25 Francis Davies, gent., brought a suit in Chancery against John Skyrme gent., Dorothy Phillip and Jane Skyrme, re 'the capital messuage and lands called Greenway' and two closes in Narberth parish. By 1753 Greenway formed part of the Elliot estate, and by 1786 the owner was Lord Kensington. After this it continued to pass through several hands. It is still lived in and is in excellent state of preservation.

Refs: *Golden Grove ms. (Gwyddno)* I, 13; *NLW, Slebech Deeds, Cilymaenllwyd Deeds, Great Sessions Pembs Plea Rolls, Ridgway Deeds.*

GRINSTON. *Brawdy.*
About 1¼ miles north-east of the parish church. The manor of Grinton/Grinston was a small but compact unit composed of the following adjoining farms – Easter and Wester Grinton (now two farms called Trefgarn Owen), North Grinton (now called Grinston) the hamlet of Trefgarn Owen, Bwlch Martin, and Pengorse, a total of about 410 acres. In 1326 it was held by free tenants, and in Elizabethan times was listed as a manor belonging to the Ap Rhys family of Rickest-son. In 1687 James ap Rhys mortgaged the manor, and in 1706 sold it to John Rickson, a wealthy tradesman of Pembroke, who sold it in 1754 to the widow Lettice Barlow of Rosepool, daughter of William Jones of Llether, Brawdy. In 1763 she bequeathed the manor to her nephew James Jones. When James died without issue, in 1781, it became

the property of William Jones of Llether, whose daughter and heiress married George Roch of Butter Hill. The Roch owners allowed the manorial rights to lapse. The tenants of both Trefgarns (still called Grinton in 1786) in the 17th-19th centuries were Harries, Bateman, Wilcox, and Charles. North Grinton now Grinston, is the only holding to preserve the old name. It was a small place of about 18 acres, and in 1842 was owned by Blanche Maria Davies of Carnachwen, with William Davies as tenant. In the latter half of the century the tenant was my grandfather, John Jones (died 17 November 1919) and it was there that my father James Jones (died 22 March 1956) was brought up. After the departure of my grandmother in 1926, Grinston was bought by the owners of adjacent Villa farm, and the old dwelling house converted into an outbuilding, alas. (It still stands and continues to be owned by the Castle Villa family).

Refs.: B.B. St. Davids 1326; Francis Jones, *'Trefgarn Owen'* in *Arch Cam* 1961 and *'Lordships and Manors of Dewsland'* in *Journal Hist. Soc. of Church in Wales*, 1969; *Taylor's Cussion; NLW, Great Sessions, Pembs Plea Rolls.*

GROVE. *Narberth.*

Near Molleston, 1¼ miles south-west of Narberth town. Henry Poyer, a rich tanner of Canaston, bought Grove from Richard Hitching, and was assessed at four hearths in the house in 1670. By will dated 1677 Henry left Grove to his son Daniel Poyer who was described in 1701 as a tanner living at Grove. It continued in the family until Anne Poyer, ultimate heiress, died in 1808, leaving Grove to her husband William Callen of Merrixton. Fenton wrote in 1811 '... the respectable old house of Grove, embosomed in trees, seat of the ancient family of Poyer ... and the property was divided by falling to heiresses, and the place has not been inhabited as a family mansion for several years'. Later, the heiress of the Callens brought the property to her husband, J. L. G. P. Lewis of Henllan (q.v.) who was also her first cousin. One of the earlier numbers of the family, Captain

John Poyer of Grove subscribed for 16 copies of the Reverend William Evans's English translation of *Cannwyll y Cymry* in 1771.

Refs: Fenton, *Tour Pembs 1811*; NLW, *Great Sessions Pembs Plea Rolls; Voters' List Pembs 1834.*

GROVE. *Just south of Pembroke town.*

In the late 17th century Grove became the seat of the Lloyds, descended from the ancient family of Lloyd of Morfil, Cilciffeth and Cilgelywen. After Thomas Lloyd married Frances daughter of Hugh Philipps of Eastington, he settled at Grove as his main seat. He was High Sheriff in 1700, and died not long afterwards, being succeeded by his son and heir, also named Thomas Lloyd. The second Thomas served as High Sheriff in 1709, and died in 1711. His widow Mary then married Morgan Davies of Cwm, Carms., and enjoyed Grove until Mary died in 1752, aged 70. Thomas Lloyd left daughters and co-heiresses, one of whom, Elizabeth Lloyd married in 1725 Sir William Owen, 4th Baronet of Orielton. Fenton wrote in 1811 'Grove as well as Morfil, in consequence of the late Sir William Owen becoming entitled to a share of this property by his marriage with one of the co-heiresses, and having purchased the shares of the others, form part of the vast possessions of Orielton.'

Grove thus passed to the Owen family who abandoned it as a residence, and it became a farm. By 1786, Sir Hugh Owen, the then owner had let the property to three tenants.

Refs: Fenton, *Tour Pembs, 1811; W.W.H.R.,* ii, 47; *Land Tax Pembs* 1786; Francis Jones, *Lloyd of Cilciffeth'* in Pembs Historian 1972; *Pembs R.O., Deeds D/LLW/ no. 177.*

GUMPHRESTON. *Gumfreston.*

A large farmstead near the roadside in Gumfreston village, about 1¾ miles west of Tenby.

Timmins wrote in 1895, 'Most visitors to Gumfreston will notice the fine old farmhouse that rises cheek-by-jowl with the carriage-road from Tenby. If we are to believe the tradition of the countryside, this is the most ancient abode in the county. Be that as it may, the place bears traces of no mean antiquity, and is an excellent specimen of a Pembrokeshire homestead of the olden times.' The earliest-known family there was that of Widlock whose members are described as lords of Gumfreston, one of whom John Wydelock the elder, was there in 1372. They bore arms: *sable a chevron between three lions sejant argent*. Afterwards it was held by a Welsh family. Harry Llewelyn of Gumfreston (arms: *sable a falcon argent*) was followed by his son John who left an only daughter and heiress, Janet, who married Owen ap Owen of Pentre Ifan, and Gumfreston was afterwards held by his son Sir James Bowen (died beween 1518 and 1532). Sir James's son, John Bowen had a daughter and heiress, Elizabeth, who married Sir James Williams of Pant Howel (Carms) who is described as Lord of the Manor of Gumfreston, and lay patron of the parish church in 1535. Five successive generations of this family were lords of the manor, until the death of John Williams in 1693, and the manor and freeholds passed to his daughter and heiress Mary who married Judge John Meyrick of Bush who died in 1736, leaving issue. Thereafter, Gumfreston remained part of the Meyrick estate. The *Land Tax of 1786* gives John Meyrick Esq.as owner of Gumfreston (farm), which passed to his descendants.

Refs: *W.W.H.R*, ii, 89; *B. M. Egerton ms. 2586; Chatham ms.* pedigree 42; *College of Arms, Protheroe ms IV; S.C. Hall South Wales*, 1861, p. 443, illustr., and I p. 89 illustr.; *Timmins, Nooks and Corners of Pembs.*, p 27; Francis Jones, 'Bowen of Pentre Ifan and Llwyngwair', in *Pembs. Historian*, 1979; *Come to Pembs Guide*, 1936, p. 21 illustr.; *P.R.O., Ancient Deeds*.

GWERN FFULBROOK.
Eglwyswen, Cemaes/Whitechurch.

Apart from the indisputable fact that this place was in Whitechurch parish, the location of its site is not known. It is possible that it is identical with (Plâs) Eglwyswen, or Whitchurch (q.v.). Contemporary references to Gwern Ffulbrook are as follows: In 1595,

among the properties owned by George Griffith, gent., of Whitechurch, was the following: a messuage called Plâs Gwernfful-brook in occupation of the said George Griffith. The next reference occurs in the prenuptial settlement of Thomas Bowen 'nephew and heir apparent of George Bowen of Gwernffulbrok' in Whitechurch parish, with Joyce Jones of Pantyderi, dated 11 May 1699, and among properties settled was 'the capital messuage called Gwernffulbrooke'. It occurs as 'Gwain Filbrw' on Eman. Bowen's *Map of South Wales 1729*, and c. 1760 edition where it is located south of Pant y Deri, between Rhos Dwarch and 'Volyanog'. Gwain Filbrw occurs in Kitchin's map of Pembrokeshire 1754 and later editions.

Information from deeds and documents among the Bronwydd and Clynfyw deeds, in the National Library of Wales, show that George Bowen of Gwernffulbrook, gent;. left that property to his nephew Thomas Bowen of Gwernffulbrook who married in 1699 Joyce daughter of Thomas Jones of Pantyderi. Their son, George Bowen of Gwernffulbrook, married in 1733 Jane Warren of Trewern; he died in 1740, and Jane married secondly Richard Mathias, agent of Whitchurch. The name no longer occurs in contemporary records, and it seems clear that it was discontinued. It is strange that the property described as a 'capital messuage' and 'plâs' could have vanished as completely. I am inclined to suspect that it is identical with Eglwyswen/Whitechurch (q.v.), a commodious family seat (now a farm) which stands nearby, once home of a family named Bowen, who also owned Gwern Ffulbrook.

Refs: *NLW, Bronwydd, Owen/Colby* and *Clynfyw* Deeds.

HAFOD GROVE. *Moylgrove.*

A farmstead south-east of the village, marked as Hafod on Mudge map 1819, and Hafod Grove on Colby's Map 1831. At one time part of the Henllys estate. In 1725 Anne Corbett of Henllys, widow (of David Owen) granted a lease, for her life, of Henllys to

William Lloyd of Pendpedwast and William Laugharne of Llanreithan [whose mothers were co-heiresses of Henllys estate], with proviso that the tenant of Hafod Fawr, Moylgrove parish, shall retain his lease of that property.

In 1786 George Lloyd, gent, was owner-occupier of Havod (also called Hafod Glandwr in 1841), and gave a mortgage in £6,600 with power of sale to William Rees, gent of Haverfordwest. The property is described as Hafod Glandwr alias Glandwr alias Havod Grove, in 1846. In 1852 the property was sold to Stephen Colby of Ffynone, and afterwards let to farming tenants.

Refs: *NLW, Bronwydd Deeds, Great Sessions Gaol Files of Pembrokeshire; Land Tax 1786.*

Marhall Griffith

HAFOD TYDFIL. *Meline.*

A farmstead, now a complete ruin, on the northern slope of Moel Feddau, and near Bedd yr Afange. One of the earliest owners of this property was Thomas Bowen of Pentre Ifan, who died in 1586, among his possessions being 'a tenement called Hafodtydfil and eight acres'. In the following century it became the property of Lloyd of Trefach, Nevern, who leased it for lives to William Bowen gent who was assessed for two hearths in 1670, and was still there in the 1680s. In November 1682 'the capital messuage and lands called Hafod Tidfil' were included in the post-nuptial settlement of John Lloyd of Trefach and his wife Ruth; and in September 1713 the said John Lloyd conveyed Havod Tydfil, two farms in Moylgrove, and three manors, to his only son

Thomas Lloyd. In 1753 the Reverend William Laugharne of Treprisk and his wife Rebecca (daughter of John Lloyd of Trefach) mortgaged Hafod Tydfil, Treprisk, and Kilsavoi in Meline, Moylgrove, and Fishguard parishes, to Francis Skyrme, gent.

Laugharne died in January 1759, and in the following month, his widow Rebecca granted the three said properties to her nephew John Foley of Colby. In 1786 John Herbert Foley of Ridgeway owned the properties; and in 1827 Emily Mary Anne Foley, widow, granted a lease for life of Hafod Tydfil to the widow Jemima Morris. It was thereafter occupied by farming tenants. Shortly after 1945, the author, Mr. R. M. Lockley, then farming Dinas Island, bought Hafod Tydfil from the widowed Mrs. Nancy Lewis, and farmed there for several years.

Refs: *NLW, Bronwydd Deeds, Foley of Ridgeway Deeds; R. M. Lockley, The Golden Year,* 1948.

HARMESTON. *Steynton.*

A Tudor period farmstead, built in traditional style, a long house with a range of nine windows, and two large gable chimneys, halfway between the villages of Steynton and Johnston. Former home of gentry families. Descended from the Dynevor family, Sir Thomas Jones of Abermarlais (Carms) and of Hermaston was the first High Sheriff of Pembrokeshire, when he served that office in 1541, and his younger brother, Morgan Jones of Hermaston was High Sheriff in 1574. Morgan married Maud daughter of Sir Thomas Philipps of Picton Castle, and was succeeded at Hermaston by his eldest son Thomas Jones, High Sheriff in 1589, who signed the family pedigree for Dwnn on 21 November 1591. He married Elinor, daughter of Sir John Wogan of Wiston, widow of Arnold Baker. In the early part of the 17th century Hermaston passed to the co-heiresses, who had married sons from the Tancred and Bolton families. William Tancred settled at his wife's home.

Elizabeth Tancred, a widow in 1652, conveyed Hermaston to her son Griffith Tancred on his marriage to Mary Howard in that year. Towards the close of the century Hermaston had been bought by a Cardiganshire squire, David Hughes of Vaenog, who was living at Harmeston in 1705. His descendants were still there in 1798, but not long afterwards, the property was sold to another Cardiganshire squire, Thomas Davies of Nantgwylan, who owned it in 1827. Amongst properties settled on the marriage of Thomas Davies of Nantyddwylan (*sic*) Esq., in 1840 were East Harmeston Hall and Harmeston Mill in Steynton parish.

Refs: *Dwnn*, i, 98-9, 189; *NLW, Morgan Richardson Deeds, Griffith Owen Collection, Bronwydd Deeds, Eaton Evans and Williams Deeds, GS.Pembs Plea Rolls; B. M. Egerton* Ms. 2586; Deed in *Cardiff Public Library,* Basil Jones & Sons, auctioneers, Particulars of Property, 1989 (illustr.) News, *Little England beyond Wales,* 1988, p. 72.

HAROLDSTON. *Haroldston St. Issels.*

An ancient mansion, now completely ruined, due south of Haverfordwest Priory ruins, on a slope above the south bank of Merlin's Brook. Some five miles westwards overlooking St. Brides Bay is the parish of Haroldston West. The medieval family of Harold after whom Haroldston St. Issels is named, was the first-known family at the mansion. An undated deed, but pre 1200, concerns William Harold of Haroldyston, and his descendants were still there in the 14th century, until Alice, daughter and heiress of Richard Harold, married Peter Perrot (died 1378), and their descendants remained in possession of Haroldston until 1763 when it was alienated.

High Sheriffs from this house were Sir Thomas Jones, 1541, who held it in right of his wife the widow of Sir Thomas Perrot, Sir John Perrot, 1552 (an ode to him having been written by Dafydd Fynglwyd), he died in the Tower of London 1592, and Sir Herbert Perrot in 1660, who ten years later was assessed for ten hearths in Haroldston, clearly a commodious mansion. Hester, sole daughter and heiress of Sir Herbert, married on 26 August 1700, Sir John Pakington, 3th Baronet of Westwood, Worcs., and the property continued in the hands of their descendants. (see Burke's *Peerage* under Hampton.)

About the years 1707-1762 Addison visited Haroldston, and there at a masked ball met the Countess of Warwick whom he married later. However on 3 May 1763, Sir Herbert Perrot Pakington Bart., whose forebears had owned the property for over five and a half centuries, sold it to Sir John Philipps of Picton Castle; the conveyance describes the property as 'the manor or lordship of Haroldston, the site of the manor or mansion house called Haroldston House, the church or chapelry of Haroldston with patronages thereof, messuage, tenement and lands, consisting of a row of old houses or walls leading from the gate house of Haroldston to Haroldston Dairy, being part of the outhouses and gardens where the old dwelling house stands, fields and closes called the Old Orchard, the Grove, the Water Grove, Water Grove Park, Golf Park, Rath Park, Westfield, Upper Westfield, Oxpark (together 90 acres) and other fields (30 acres), a messuage and land called Church Park and the marsh adjoining; Coney Gare, Hill Park and the marsh adjoining, meadows, Haroldston Marsh with Furzy Hill adjoining, meadow adjoining the old hop garden – all part and parcel of the demesne lands of Haroldston, all in the parish of Haroldston St. Issels'.

An English tourist, calling at Haverfordwest, wrote in his journal in October 1767 – 'Here are two old Houses now in ruins, which have been the seats of good families, and seem built very soon after the fashion of Castles was left off; Prendergast …, and Harriston lately belonging to the Packingtons, but now sold to a man who has pulled down all the materials which were saleable …' A Picton Castle Estate Terrier made in 1773 describes Haroldston (138 acres) owned by Sir Richard Philipps, the tenant being James Lloyd, Esq., and all the fields including 'the ruins of Haroldston House with the Court and gardens' (two acres). One field called Tump Park recalls the days when a tumulus stood there. Land Tax lists for 1786-1798 give Lord Milford as owner of Haroldston and lands. In 1811 the historian Fenton wrote: 'The house [Haroldston] which appears to have been a large and most incoherent aggregate of the building of different ages, and incapable of being traced to any regular plan, is now entirely in ruins; the widow Perrot married Sir Thomas Jones who in order to enlarge the grounds, acquired the dissolved Priory of Haverfordwest; according to George Owen, the vale in which the house stands, was then ornamented with groves and Sir Thomas introduced pheasants from Ireland which he placed in the grove adjoining Harredston House.' In 1834 S. Lewis wrote of Haroldston, 'the ancient mansion is now in a very dilapidated condition'.

A view of the ruins consisting of walls and a tower called the 'Stewards Tower', is given in the frontispiece to Arch. Cam. 1860; this view shows a tower of three storeys (interior 11 feet by 10 feet) with a tiled saddle-back roof, a semi-detached stair rise and garderobes, and terminating in a corbel table and parapet: the lowest storey is vaulted, and the upper storeys show remains of fireplaces and garderobes, the lights are small plain loops; the tower is only a shell, but it said in 1920 to have been inhabited within living memory. It would seem that the house was square in plan, and connected with the tower by an arched doorway. J. H. Parker, in Arch. Cam. 1865, assigned the date of the structure to the 13th century, and says that the hall, lit at each end by a small window of the two trefoil-headed light, occupied the entire first floor, 'the rooms below are vaulted'. The site and its straggling ruins were finally owned by the late Lt.- Col. J. H. V. Higgon of Scolton who presented it to the Town Council of Haverfordwest.

Refs: *PRO Deeds* (1325-1532); *Picton Castle Deeds; RCAM* 1925 (reproduction of Norris' sketch); *Lord Hampton Deeds* (Pakington) in Birmingham Ref. Library; Pembs RO, *Deed D/RTP/H,* 1763 sale; NLW, *Penllergaer Deeds, Noyadd Trefawr Deeds* and Add. Ms. 147C; H. Owen, *Old Pembrokeshire Families,* 1902, pp. 51.66, and refs. there; *Lewis TDW,* edns. 1834 and 1840; *Haverfordwest and its Story,* 1882. Illustrations occur in RCAM 1925, *Arch Cam,* 1860; and D. James, *Sir John Perrott,* 1527-1591, printed 1962.

HAROLDSTON HALL. *Haroldston West.*

A parish, some 6 miles west of Haverfordwest, above the coast of St. Brides' Bay. It is surmised that the Perrots lived here before moving eastwards to Haroldston St. Issels, but there is no proof of this. Little of its earlier history is known. The Land Tax of 1786 gives Hugh Meares Esq. as owner of Haroldston, with John Phillips as tenant. There is a hamlet here where the parish church is located. The parish was one of the few where the rates were still being 'levied and collected by the ploughland' in 1840. On Colby's map of 1831 a house called 'Hall' is marked to the east of the hamlet. It came into prominence in the latter half of the 19th century as the residence of William Howell Walters, son of William Walters who established a bank in Haverfordwest, and a branch at Narberth in 1863. The father was High Sheriff in 1866. The only son, William Howell Walters, born c.1857, a barrister of the Inner Temple, lived at Haroldston Hall; he was High Sheriff in 1898, knighted in 1920, and died in 1934.

Refs: *Carlisle, TDW* 1811; *Lewis, TDW,* 1940; *Kelly's Handbook,* 1887 and 1892.

HASGUARD. *Hasguard.*

The parish lies between St. Ishmaels and Talbenny, to the west of Walwynscastle. There were several farms in the area of the parish church in 1786 when John Philipps Laugharne Esq. owned Hasguard Hall, and two farms called Middle Hasguard, and Francis Meyrick Esq. owned Little Hasguard and Sir William Hamilton and a Mr. Martin owned Lower Hasguard, all let to tenants.

In 1583 a grant of arms was made to Gelby Meyrick of Hasguard, viz: *gules two porcupines in pale passant argent, armed or.* In 1752 Rowland Philipps Laugharne of Pontfaen and Anne his wife, owned one half of 'Haskard otherwise called the Hall of Haskard: he also owned Middle Hasguard which he leased to John Dean of Marloes, farmer, in 1767. George Webb tenant of Hasguard Hall, died in 1792. On Colby's map 1831, the following are marked – Hasguard Hall, Little and Middle Hasguard, and Hasguard village.

Refs: *Land tax*, 1786; NLW, *Poyston Deeds*.

HAVERFORDWEST.

County Town of Pembrokeshire.

In the town are the houses called Hermon's Hill (q.v. infra), Foley House (q.v. supra), both still in good order and inhabited. Several rich tradesmen's families lived here who enjoyed gentry status, such as Keynner, Voyle, Canon, Walter, Bateman, Davids, and Sutton. A few interesting houses have been noted – in High Street (formerly occupied by W. H. Smith's bookshop) in a rear room is a carved stone mantelpiece decorated by five coats of arms (circa 1600); 1. *A boar chained to a holly tree* (Owen of Henllys). 2. Royal Arms, quarterly. 3. *party per pale, dexter, three escallops, sinister, on a bend three escallops.* 4. *On a bend three roses (or escallops).* 5. *A chevron between three ravens.* It is likely that a descendant of the Owens of Henllys was the owner

of this property. Timmins in 1895 describes a house in Quay Street '... we descry a low-bowed entrance opening upon the foot path, the massive nail-studded door, with its giant lion-headed knocker, being enframed by liberally-moulded jambs. Passing beneath this ancient portal, we are admitted to an interior beautified by the rare old oaken stairway shown in our sketch; this stairway gives access to nicely panelled chambers whose fireplaces retain their original blue Dutch tiles painted with scenes of Biblical history.

To the rear of the dwelling-house stands a flour-mill driving a brisk trade in its green old age. Stepping out to the rear we find ourselves upon the riverside quay ...'

Refs: *RCAM Pembs 1925*, p. 112, sketch of mantelpiece: Thornhill Timmins, *Nooks and Corners of Pembs*, 1895, with sketch of stairway.

HAYLETT. *Haroldston St. Issels.*

A residence near the road to Freystrop. A family named Haylot lived in this district in medieval times, but whether the place-name derived its name from them, or vice versa, we do not know. An undated deed, pre 1200, mentions John Heylot de Freystrop; in 1310 William Heyloht son and heir of Walter Heyloht, granted lands in Manorbier to William Harold, lord of Haroldston; and in 1774 Richard Tasker granted to William Perot, Monytharch and High Freystrop, Haroldston – iuxta – Haverford, Trechemanshill, Boydynys, and Heylot, in the lordship of Haverford. Over two centuries later on 8 January 1697-8, Miss Hester Perrott of Haroldston, granted a lease for 29 years of (*inter alia*) Haylett, to Francis Edwardes of Haverfordwest and on 9 May 1725 Sir John Pakington, Bart. of Westwood, Worcs., and his only son Herbert Perrot Pakington, heirs of the Perrotts, granted a lease for 99 years to the said Francis Edwardes of Haylett, Esq., of messuages called Haylett and Boyden (2 ploughlands) in Haroldston St. Issels. However, the lessee who was M.P. for Haverfordwest, did not enjoy the lease for long, for later in this year he died, his will being proved on 16 December 1725. The son, William Edwardes, was created Baron Kensington in 1776, and in the Land Tax of 1786 and 1797 is described as owner of Haylett. Little is known of it afterwards, but a publication of 1882 tells us that Lady Betty Rich resided at 'the country seat of Haylett, every trace of which has now been destroyed.' Later, a fine house was erected there, given the name of Haylett Grange, which is now (1986) a preparatory school.

Refs: *PRO, Ancient Deeds*, nos. 1549 and 1794; Deed in *Cardiff Free Library*; Pembs RO, Deed DX/2; *Haverfordwest and it Story*, 1882, p. 16.

HAYSCASTLE (CASLAI). *Hayscastle.*

Near the parish church there were once three farms, each bearing the names of the tenants in order to distinguish them. They eventually became two farms, known during my youth as 'Caslai Harries' and Caslai Nicholas'. In the vicinity are four ancient burial mounds, called Tumps locally, and the site of an earthwork fortification, which is commemorated in the name of the parish. Hayscastle is mentioned in 1326, and later became a lay manor owned during medieval days by the family of Russell, until Joan Russell, the ultimate heiress, brought the manor to her husband Richard Laugharne of St. Brides, whose descendants held it until about 1800. The farms had several owners from time to time, amongst them William Scourfield of New Moat who in 1745 gave a lease for lives of land in Hayscastle parish to Henry Skeel of Hayscastle, yeoman; in 1760 John Allen of Dale Castle gave a lease for lives of 'the West Tenement of Hayscastle' to Henry Skeel, yeoman; in 1786, one of the farms was in possession of Henry Watts, owner-occupier, and two others of Hays-castle farms, owned by John Lloyd Esq., the tenants being Henry Skeel and John Morse. The main occupiers of the three farms were the Harries family (1597-1764) Watts (1623-1842) and Skeel (1745-1847), and some of those longer than the terminal dates given above. In 1842 one farm (517 acres) was owned by John Allen Lloyd Phillips of Dale Castle, and John Nicholas as tenant, and another farm (448 acres) owned by John Watts and tenanted by Peter Watts, while the third (69 acres) was owned by the executors of William Henry Scourfield, and tenanted by Henry Skeel. Thus they were of extensive acreage. The largest, that tenanted by John Nicholas, whose descendants the Morrises, now own the farm and reside there.

Refs: Black Book of St. Davids 1326; RCAM Pembs. 1925; B. M. Egerton ms. 2586: Pembs RO, Deeds; NLW, Pembs. Plea Rolls and Gaol Files, Morgan-Richardson Deeds: Land tax 1786; Tithe Map and Schedule 1842.

HAYSTON. *Llanstadwell.*

In the northern part of the parish, between Scovaston and Harmeston. There were three properties there, Hayston (Hall), Lower Hayston, and Hayston Mill, marked on Colby's map 1831 and on modern O.S. maps. Hayston was the home of yeomen over the centuries. In 1550 John Mabe was living there, to be followed by his son David Mabe, living there in 1607. David Mabe does not appear to have been wholly desirable, and he was presented in the Great Sessions of 1611 as of Hayston, yeoman 'a most notorious wicked fellow, a fighter, brawler, common gamester of alehouses, sower of sedition, drunkard, ravisher, etc.' Dear me! In 1616 we learn that David Mabe sued John Philipps of Southfield, in respect of a grant he made of 'a capital messuage and land in the vill of Hayston' on 20 September 1613. Later, in 1634, Margaret Collins, widow, complained of David and John Mabe of Hayston, yeo-men, for saying that she was 'an old witch' and would prove that she was just that. In the other messuage of Hayston, John Tasker, yeoman, lived in 1611.

The Mabes seemingly departed before the end of the century, for in 1699, Francis Rossant and John Tasker, gentlemen, re-leased one third of a messuage of 22 acres in 'the townred and fields of Hayston', to Charles Jordan, gent. In 1759 John Jordan of Dumpledale, Esq., conveyed (inter alia) a messuage called Hayston, to the Reverend Owen Philipps of Haverfordwest. In 1785, Herbert Lloyd of Carmarthen and Albany Wallis of London, assignees of certain estates of Marmaduke Gwynne, sold the lordship or manor of Hayston, the capital messuage and lands called Hayston, and a messuage with Hayston Mill, to Richard Mathias of Tiers-ton, Steynton parish. In 1786, three proper-ties at Hayston were owned by Richard Mathias, Reverend Dr. Phillips and Lord Kensington, all let to tenants. Shortly after-wards Richard Mathias and his family came to live there. He died before 1814, and was followed by his son, Richard, who married Justina Needham Harries of Tregwynt by whom he had children.

In 1837 appeared particulars of sale of the mansion house and land called Hayston, late residence of Richard Mathias Esq., deceased, the manor of Hayston, tithes of the whole estate, and the corn grist mill called Hayston Mill, with a newly erected house, in the parishes of Llanstadwell and Rosemarket. Thomas Henry Davies of Hayston Hall, Esq. was living there in 1877-88.

Refs: *NLW, Pembs. Great Sessions; Pembs RO Deeds, D/RTP* (T.H.D.) *Land Tax 1786.*

HAYTHOG. *Spittal.*

About one mile south-east of Spittal parish church, marked on Colby's map 1831 as Upper and Lower Haythog, the latter being the old mansion. The earliest-known family there was that of Barrett, one of whom John Barrett, lived there during the years 1383-1439. Later the property passed to the Sutton family, one of whom, Lewis Sutton of Haythog, was slain there on 18 July 1506. By his wife Gwenllian, natural daughter of Sir Rhys ap Thomas, he had a son, John Sutton of Haythog, and Haverfordwest, who died on 18 August 1551, leaving a daughter and heiress, Thomasin Sutton, who married Rees Morgan, gent. of Haverfordwest.

It later passed to Richard Philipps (descended from Picton Castle), whose son John Philipps, who owned Haythog and Ffynnongain, was High Sheriff in 1638. He was followed by his son William Philipps of Haythog (born ac.1615), a Royalist, High Sheriff in 1645, and M.P. for Haverfordwest in 1660. He was assessed at ten hearths in 1670, which indicates that Haythog was then of considerable size. His daughter and ultimate heiress, Anne, married her kinsman Charles Philipps of Sandyhaven, and Haythog *iure uxoris.* Their son William Philipps inherited Haythog, and was High Sheriff in 1736. His grand-daughter, Anne Philipps, married Joseph John Philipps Laugharne of Orlandon, Pontfaen, and Haythog passed to their descendants, one of whom, William Charles Allen Philipps of St. Brides, was owner of Haythog in 1834. After this it became the home of yeomen and farmers.

Refs: Fenton, *Tour, Pembs,* 1811, 1783 *Pembs Arch. Survey: Pembs RO, Deeds; NLW, Pembs. Plea Rolls, Slebech Deeds; PRO, Anc. Deeds; B. M. Egerton ms. 2586; Haverfordwest Corporation Deeds.*

HEAN CASTLE. *St. Issels.*

The original name was Hên Gastell, the Welsh for old castle, mentioned in 1295; in 1358 'Hengastel' was owned by Laurence de Hastings, Earl of Pembroke. Clearly it was an early Welsh earthen fortification, but it is doubtful whether the Normans used it for military purposes. The first-known reference to it as a residence is in 1636 when its occupiers were Nicholas Lewis Esq. (from Gellydywyll, Carms.), and Katherine Vaughan, widow. It was then called Hencastle. On the death without issue of Nicholas Lewis, the property passed to his widow Anne (née Barlow of Slebech), who married Lewis Wogan of Wiston, and their son, Lewis Wogan junior, married Martha, daughter and co-heiress of David Williams (High Sheriff in 1683) who lived at Hencastle. In this period the residence was commodious, and in 1670 Nicholas Lewis was assessed at eight hearths.

It remained as one of the Wogan residences until the end of the 18th century when it passed to two co-heiresses – Eleanor Wogan who married in 1793 Reverend Thomas Roberts, Methodist minister, and friend of John Wesley, and Susannah Wogan who married in 1794 Thomas Stokes of Haverfordwest, a Quaker. In 1800 Susannah bought out her sister's share for £7200 and Hean Castle passed to her husband. At this time the estate consisted of the mansion, the lordship of St. Issels and Treberth, the castle mill, and 21 farms, all in St. Issel's parish. In 1839 Thomas Stokes was owner occupier of the mansion, and the estate had 52 tenants. Later it was sold by Thomas Stokes' son (by his second wife) also named Thomas Stokes, to his brother-in-law Edward Wilson (High Sheriff in 1861).

In the 1860s Wilson sold the property to a

London solicitor, C. R. Vickerman, who re-built the mansion in the 1870s (immediately in front of the older house) with red sand-stone from Runcorn, Cheshire, brought to Saundersfoot wharf as ballast. A photograph of the original house shows a large tradi-tional two-storeyed building. Vickerman lived at Hean Castle till his death, and in 1899 it was sold to Sir William Thomas Lewis, Bart. (created Lord Merthyr in 1911). It is now owned and occupied by the Hon. Trefor Lewis, son and heir of the second peer.

Refs: *NLW, Noyadd Trefawr Deeds, Pembs. Plea Rolls, Tithe map St. Issels, 1839; Pembs RO, Land Tax 1786:* Fenton, *Tour Pembs,* 1811; *Contemporary Biographies of S. Wales and Mon.,* 1907, illustr.; *South Wales Daily News,* 16 September 1911, illustr.; Roscoe Howells, *Old Saundersfoot,* 1977, illustrs. of the old and present mansions.

HEATHFIELD.
Also called **HEATHFIELD LODGE.**
Letterston.

This Georgian residence was built at the opening of the 19th century by the Harries family of Priskilly, later of Tregwynt. In 1804

it was the home of Margaretta Theodosia Williams, widow of Thomas Williams of Treleddin, St. Davids, and sister of John Hill Harries of Priskilly, High Sheriff in 1805. By 1834 it was tenanted by William Jones (died 1858), father of an only child Anna Jane an extremely extravagant lady who married John Owen Tucker Edwardes of Sealyham. In 1904 it was the home of James Henry

Morton who had married Suzanna Agnes daughter of the owner John Henry Harries of Tregwynt. It was later sold.

Refs: *Pembs RO, James of Narberth Deeds; Lewis TDW,* 1840 *Pembs Voter's List,* 1834; Property Particulars of Heathfield, for Sale, *John Francis, Halifax Property Services,* 1989 illustr.

HELYGANT. *Meline.*

A farmstead marked on Colby's map 1831, as Lignant near Brynberian. The first-known owner was Owen Fysham, descended from Gwynfardd Dyfed, followed by his son Howel, and he by his son Rees ap Howel who was living in 1506 when his seal to a deed shows *a lion rampant within a true-love knot.* It formed two or three tenements held at different times by various owners. In 1597 Thomas Griffith ap Ieuan Jenkin of Mynach-logddu, yeoman, owned Lygnant (Philip Devonald, tenant). In 1614 a tenement (15 acres) called Elygnant formed part of the estate of Thomas James of Cilgwyn, gent., lately deceased and in 1597 William Griffith of Penybenglog, gent., gave a bond in £100 to the Reverend Miles' son Thomas, parson of Meline, for the quiet enjoyment by the latter of 'Plâs Helignant'. The parson's son, the Reverend Lewis Miles, held it in 1632. In 1649 Nathaniel Miles of Meline, gent., and his mother Frances Miles, widow, sold 'Plâs Helignant' to his cousin William Miles of Llanfairnantgwyn for £50. In 1686 it was owned by Owen Miles, gent. and Janet (Bowen) his mother. There were many changes after this, and several owners in 1737 two messuages in Helignant Issa were owned by John Warren of Trewern, in 1786 Thomas Rodger, in 1834 Thomas Lewis of Eglwys-wrw.

Refs: *NLW, Bronwydd Deeds, Picton Castle Deeds.*

HENDRE. *Llandeloy.*

At one time there were two messuages here, Hendre Ucha, and Issa, which still existed in 1865, but by 1894 they had been amalgam-ated to form one unit. In 1625 it was the home of Evan Harry, yeoman, probably a tenant. By 1653 it formed part of the estate of John Laugharne (later of Llanunwas) and Hendre Ucha and Issa (192 acres) continued to form part of the Laugharne estates, and still owned the farm in 1716. Later in the 18th century they were bought by Henry John of Caerwen, a successful estate agent and farmer, who owned it in 1786, the tenant being William Griffith, yeoman. The next owner was William John (Henry's younger son), followed by his only daughter Anne. She married William Scowcroft, a tradesman, of Haverfordwest. They settled at Hendre, and were followed by their daughter, Elizabeth Margaret Scowcroft who married Robert Henry Marshall Yeates. They did not remain long at Hendre, and in 1865 sold the property to a local Baptist minister, the Reverend William Reynolds of Ynys y Barry for £4,600. Mr. Reynolds died in 1908, aged 88.

Refs: *NLW. Williams and Williams Deeds, Fines in G.S., Bronwydd Deeds. Land Tax 1786.*

HENDRE. *Meline.*

A farmstead on the east bank of Nant Brynberian, and near Crosswell. A deed, dated 6 June 1407, is a grant and confirmation from Philip ap Rudderch Cainton, gent. to Howel ap Owen ap Rees, a messuage, lands and woods in Hendref in the fee of Eglwyswrw, bounded by the river Deat, the chapel of Penkelli and the rill of Penkelli *ad magnam' viam de vado leprosoro ad villam de Penkelli.* The next reference is much later.

In 1659 Thomas Reignold of Blaiddbwll, gent. mortgaged three messuages called Hendref alias Pentref in Meline parish, to John Lewis of Henllan Owen, gent. In 1690 Hendre was the home of Sibyl Vaughan, spinster, and in 1699 of another spinster, Elizabeth Vaughan. In 1686 a Fine was suffered between Owen Miles of Llanfairnantgwyn, gent. his mother Janet Bowen, widow, and George Lewis of Meline gent., in respect of Helignant in Meline parish. In 1692 Arthur William of Meline, gent. mortgaged the messuage called Park y Meyruk to George Lewis of Hendre, gent. who was still living there in 1710, but had died by 1727,

when his nephew and heir was another George Lewis. The last gentry family of note there was that of Lewis.

Refs: *College of Arms mss, Wagner ms x11; Bronwydd Deeds, Eaton Evans and Williams Deeds, Ethel Jones Deeds, Penllergaer Deeds, Papers of Great Sessions, Pembs.; Carms RO, Golden Grove Books; Pembs RO, Land Tax 1786; B. G. Charles, George Owen of Henllys, 1973*

HENDRE. *St. Dogmaels.*

A farmstead in the northerly part of the parish, near the coast; on the south of the cove of Pwll Grannant. The first owner-occupiers of Hendre were the Lloyds, descended from the chieftain Gwynfardd Dyfed, who held the property from 1250 down to the 19th century. George Owen of Henllys wrote of Hendre as 'the mansion house of John Lloyd, gentleman, auncientlie descended ... the house of Hendre and manor of Granant came to him by purchase from Rees Lloyd son and heir of his uncle John Lloyd.' Owen called notice to the house as 'caput of Granant alias Hendre to his cousin-german John Lloyd of Cwmgloyn which thereafter was the chief residence of the family.

When Evan Lloyd, son and heir of John Lloyd of Hendre married Mary, daughter of George Owen of Henllys, their marriage settlement dated 1596 included the Hendre estate then consisting of eleven farms in St. Dogmaels parish, one messuage in each of the parishes of Bayvil, Moylegrove and Nevern, and four messuages in Llandygwydd parish, Cards. Hendre was then described as two messuages, -Uch and -Issa. The memorial courts of Hendre alias Granant were held at Hendre down to 1821. Emily Pritchard in her useful work, *St. Dogmael's Abbey*, contains some useful information about the old mansion, quoting the Reverend Henry Vincent in *Arch. Cam.* 1864, as follows – 'Hendre where once was a fine mansion of the Lloyds: a part of the old house, probably an oratory, has been converted into an outhouse; a keystone of the arch of the doorway of what had been the dwelling house is inscribed 'T.LL. Esq. 1744 CW'; the supposed oratory has no entrance from without, and is entered by a door on the north-west. Hendre was once owned by Major Lewis of Clynfiew, who bought the property prior to 1786; the walls are very strong, partly built of seashore pebbles embedded in the hard mortar; the walls and roof of the old chapel at Hendre are in almost perfect condition. Thomas Lloyd of Cwmgloyn (1744) turned the old chapel into a dwelling-house, and when it was later abandoned for the new farmhouse, the old building was turned into a cowhouse and stable. Hendre is now owned by a gentleman from Hereford-shire and administered by a manager; the farmhouse is comparatively modern; the out-buildings are much the same as those described by Mrs. Pritchard.

Refs: George Owen, *Taylor's Cussion, and Second Book*, edited by B. G. Charles; *Dwnn*, i, 246-7; *Fenton Tour Pembs*, 1811; *Arch Camb. Oct. 1864; Pembs. Archaeological Survey 1896-1907;* Francis Jones 'Lloyd of Hendre and Cwmgloyn' in *NLW Journal, winter 1984,* and refs. there; *Francis Green mss, vol. 20,* deed dated 1516.

HENDRE RIFFITH.
Whitchurch/Plwy'r Groes.
A farm to the north of Solva, just beyond Gwarcoed, on the way to Felin Ganol. The earliest reference to it occurs in a deed dated 7 March 1447-8 whereby Elena Adam released a messuage and lands at 'Hendreff ap Griffith ap Oweyn', Whitchurch parish, to David Robyn, clerk. In 1786 Hendreriffith was owned by John Bateman, gent., with John Harries as tenant, paying a Land Tax of 4s. 10. The name occurs as Hendre ruffydd in the Voters List 1904.

Refs: *Eaton Evans and Williams Deeds.*

HENLLAN. *Rhoscrowther.*
There were two properties here – Lower Henllan and Henllan; the former farmlands are flanked on the west and north side by oil storage tanks. The mansion once stood at Upper Henllan. The property is mentioned in a deed of 1273 between John Symon and Sir John de Castro Martin, knight, as a 'caru-cate in Henthlan'. The family of Eynon (descended from Gwynfardd Dyfed) were living there about the year 1400, and bore as arms *gules a chevron or between three towers or.* John Eynon of Henllan fell at the battle of Banbury in 1469. The property finally passed to a daughter, Christine Eynon who married Jenkin White, a rich burgess of Tenby where his ancestors had lived for several generations. Griffith White was living at Henllan before 1550, and died in 1590. During the Civil War in the next century, the Whites supported Parliament, and the historian Fenton quotes a letter of 28 March 1648 which describes an attack by Royalist troops – 'Henllan house was the same day beset, Mr. White, the then possessor, Mr. Roger Lort, Adjutant-General Fleming, and other commissioners meeting there, escaped on ship-board'.

In 1670 Henry White, Esquire, was assessed at eight hearths for Henllan, which shows it to have been a large residence. Thomas White, last of the main male line died in 1680, and the property passed to Elizabeth White who lived mostly at Bangeston. Henllan was abandoned and became a farm-stead at the end of the 17th century. Despite her four marriages, Elizabeth the heiress died without issue in 1736, and Henllan passed to the Campbells of Stackpole Court. The Whites had provided the county with seven High Sheriffs in the period 1561-1658. They bore the following arms: *sable a chevron ermine between three stags' heads caboshed or.*

In 1786 John Hook Campbell owned Lower Hentland (John Meares, Esq. tenant) and Upper Hentland (where the old mansion stood).

In a sale catalogue of 1802, it was advertised for sale by Lord Cawdor, and then comprised of three farms held by tenants – Upper Henllan (165 acres), Lower Henllan (18 acres) and 'part of Henllan farm' (44 acres). It later became part of the Orielton estate. The Tithe Map and Schedule of Rhos-crowther parish in 1838 shows Upper and Lower Henllan as owned by Sir John Owen of Orielton, and tenanted by John Thomas and John Mirehouse. According to the *Pembs*

Archaeological Survey (1896-1907), there were remains of a large brick archway and gable-end of a building, and a place that looks as if it had been a fish-pond. An essay published in 1897 describes Henllan, 'now almost in total ruin, was a mansion of importance.' There were also traces of a walled garden.

Refs: *Dwnn,* i, 129-30; *W.W.H.R.* ii, 50; *Golden Grove mss; B. M.* Egerton ns. 2586; Fenton, *Tour Pembs.* 1811; *Wales Magazine,* Aug 1897; Timmins, Nooks and Corners, 189; Francis Jones 'White of Henllan', in *Pembs. Historian,* 1974.

HENLLAN. *Llanddewi Felfre.*

Between Llanddewi Felfre village and the Penblewin Cross, south of the main road near an ancient earthwork called Caerau and Gaer. Originally it was a small hamlet containing several farms, and an ancient chapel of which no traces now remain. Ever since 1636 when David Lewis, gent, of Henllan, served as a Juror in the Great Sessions, the Lewis family continued as the principal landowners of the parish. In 1670 David Lewis of 'Henllan village' was assessed for two hearths. In 1786, another descendant, described as David Lewis Esquire, was owner-occupier of Upper Henllan, and also owned Lower and Middle Henllan farms, both let to tenants.

The family continued to flourish and in the 19th century produced a Bishop of Llandaff (Rt. Reverend Richard Lewis, 1883-1905) and a Judge (Sir Wilfred Lewis Q.C.). From about 1835 to 1854 the old mansion was untenanted, and 1854 Mr. J. L. G. P. Lewis pulled it down, and built a new mansion, two illustrations of which occur in the 1875 book, *County Families,* by Thomas Nicholas. It lasted until about 1957 when it was pulled down by the present owner of the Henllan estate, Mr. Richard Lewis, J.P., D.L., of Caermaenau Fawr which is now the main residence of the family.

Refs: *Land Tax 1786;* Lewis, *TDW,* 1840; Nicholas, *County Families,* ii, p. 840 (1875 edn. illustr.); C.S. Allen, *Photos of South Wales,* 1871, illustr.; Francis Jones, 'A Victorian Bishop of Llandaff' in *NLW Journal 1975;* Photo taken by C. S. Allen, Tenby, in 1878; copy in N.L.W.

HENLLAN OWEN. *Eglwyswrw.*

A farmstead just over a mile west of Eglwys-wrw, near the border with Meline. Home of a minor gentry family descended from Jenkin ap Howell of Nevern (slain at Banbury 1469). A local record of 1594 mentions 'the land of Richard James where he lives called Henllan Owen'.

In 1603-4 George Owen writes 'Henllan Owen, the mansion house of George Lewis, being his auncient patrimonie, and a brother's share of the old Howell ap Jenkin spoken of before in Nevarne. He is the son of Lewis the son of Richard the sonne of James the sonne of Jeuan ap Jenkin a younger brother of Howell ap Jenkin of Nevarne the younger for there were two of that name in Nevarne, the one grandfather to the other. He beareth the Armes of Pentre Ieuan ...' In 1811 Fenton writes 'At a short distance from this very memorable spot [Cefn Dianel, below Bwlchgwynt] stands the ancient mansion of Henllan Owen, once the residence of my ancestry by my grandmother, daughter of John Lewis Esq of Manorawan, which, with a considerable property that followed it, was a younger brother's portion, of the house of Howel ap Jenkin ap Ropert of Nevern ... It is now but an ordinary farmhouse, and bears no marks of its former consequence.'

According to the *Golden Grove mss,* the last of the family to live there, George Lewis 'sold his inheritauncae of Henllan Owen to George Bowen of Nevarne [Llwyngwair] his cozen, for £145.' Thereafter it was farmed by tenants.

In 1717 James Bowen of Llwyngwair leased it for 21 years to Henry David, yeoman. In 1786, the Reverend James Bowen [of Llwyngwair] owned two farms at Henllan Owen (Thos. Robert, tenant), and the Reverend Mr. Lewis., D.D. owned a third farm there, tenanted by John Thomas.

Refs: *Extent of Cemais 1594;* B. G. Charles (ed) George Owen's *Second Book,* 1603-4; *Golden Grove ms* (Gwynfardd); *College of Arms, Proth. ms IV;* B. M. Egerton ms 2586; NLW, *Bronwydd Deeds.*

HENLLYS.

In the Cruglas Quarter of Nevern parish.

Now a farmstead on a high slope above the river Duad which joins the Nevern at the lower end of the farmlands. It had been a gentry residence throughout the Middle Ages, but it was the Elizabethan antiquary, the celebrated George Owen, that gave Henllys a foremost place among the residences of the county. It was certainly larger than any other similar seat in north Pembrokeshire if we are to judge from the 1670 *Hearth Tax list,* where it was assessed at ten hearths.

Originally, there were two messuages there – Henllys Uch and Issa, the former being the home of the owners. The first-known owners were the family of Pentre Ifan, descended from Gwynfardd, who also owned several properties in the Henllys district. According to Dwnn, Ieuan ap Rees, a younger son, received Henllys as his share, 'a gavas Henllys', called Henllys Ucha in the Golden Grove pedigrees. His son, Howel ap Ieuan (viveus 1499-1520) started selling some of his farms to William Owen, and it was Howel's grandson, Henry Lewis, who sold Henllys Ucha and other properties to William Owen on 7 July 1543, and in 1558 Owen ap William of Cwmeog (whose father was cozen-german to Henry Lewis) sold his lands in Henllys Issa, Cwmeog, Dyffryn and Trefoes to the same William. The new owner, a successful lawyer, was descended from an old north Pembrokeshire family. His father, Rhys ap Owen Fychan was living at Henllys Issa in 1524, and by his marriage in 1487 to Jane, widow of Philip ap Gwilym of Stone Hall, he had William Owen. In addition to acquiring Henllys and other lands in the district, he bought in 1543 the lordship of Cemaes from John Touchet, Lord Audley. William died at Henllys on 29 March 1574, 'being Munday about midnight, and was buried next day at ye church of Nevarn', aged 105 years according to his son and heir, George Owen. As George had been born about 1552, he was 83 years of age when he died. The Henllys estate and the lordship of Cemaes continued in the family until 1681 when William Owen died without issue, and his possessions passed between his two sisters, co-heiresses, namely Elizabeth who married Arthur Laugharne of Llanreithan, and Ann who married Thomas Lloyd of Penpedwast, descended from the Bronwydd family, who in due course, became sole owners of the lordship and estate. After Sir Marteine Lloyd died in 1935, his daughter inherited, and the descent continued in the female line to our day. In the early 18th century, Henllys was abandoned as a residence, thereafter inherited by farming tenants, until sold in the present century. The former mansion was described by George Owen in 1594 – 'The manor place or mansion house of the said manor called Henllys with all houses and buyldinges, coortlages, gardens and orchardes, ys situat in the myddest of the lordes demaine landes and ys buylded of stone, covered or tiled with slate or stone, and there is belonging a fair stable of seven bays long and a barn of 13 bays built and covered as before, with diverse chambers and necessary rooms.' No trace of the original structure remains in the present farmstead.

Refs: B. G. Charles, *George Owen of Henllys,* 1973, a definitive history and refs. there; *NLW, Bronwydd Collection, George Owen's Second Book 1603-4, Extent of Cemais 1594, Pembs Plea Rolls* (Great Sessions); *Carms RO, Golden Grove mss; B. M. Egerton ms 2586; Tithe Map and Schedule, Nevern parish,* 1840; *Fenton Tour Pembs,* 1811; *Dwnn,* i, 60, 156-8; *W.W.H.R.,* ii, 78; *DWB: RCAM,* 1925; *Katherine H. Lloyd, The Lords of Kemes 1087-1914,* 1930.

HENLLYS. *Llanrhian.*

A farmstead about a quarter of a mile north of Llanrhian church, on a slope above a cwm through which a rivulet runs to the sea at Porthgain. The farmlands extend to the coast and includes the islet of Ynys Fach. Henllys together with Longhouse and other properties in the parish were owned in earlier times by the Bishop of St. Davies, and formed part of the episcopal manor of Trevine (Trefin). In the *Black Book of St. Davids,* 1326, the park called Hulles' (Henllys) is named as part of the Bishop's manor of Trevine. In 1554 John David of Trevine sued seven of the parishioners for forcible entry and depasturing on his land at Henlles. In 1640 the Bishop leased lands, including a ploughland called Henllys of 200 acres, to Henry Garnon of Trevine for 21 years. The said Henry Garnon was still tenant in 1660 when a survey of the Bishop's manor was made, including Henllys and a sheep-fold there. On Kitchen's map of 1763, the farm is described as Henllisk. In the Land Tax 1786, the owner of 'Henllys Land' occurs as John Edwardes of Sealyham, Esq., with Peter Harries of neighbouring Felindre as tenant. Edwardes was probably leaseholder, for in 1817 the Bishopric of St. Davids owned Henllys, 164 acres at that time, and in 1845 still owned the farm, then comprising 194 acres, tenanted by Thomas Roch. It was later bought by the Charles family. My wife Ethel was brought up there. It is now owned by Gwilym Charles.

HERBRANDSTON HALL. *Herbrandston.*

Now a residence just south of Herbrandston village. The house, a large modern building, was built in the late 19th century. In 1952 it was bought by Mr. John Davies who now occupies it.

HERMONS HILL. *Haverfordwest.*

An agreeable 18th century residence in Haverfordwest, near the boundaries of St. Mary's and St. Thomas parishes; stands on a hillside overlooking the river Cleddau and the wharves of the county town. The present structure was built in the early half of the 18th century, and was the house of the Williams family, the first of them being Dr. Perrott Williams who had practised in London before returning to settle at Hermons Hill. By his wife Hannah Skyrme of Llanhaden, he had two sons; the elder, Counsellor Williams, J.P., succeeded to Hermons Hill, was High Sheriff in 1767, and died unmarried in 1779, when the property passed to his brother William Williams, officer of the Excise. William died unmarried 1801 and Hermons Hill was bequeathed to his cousin Mrs. Jane Bassett (née Lloyd) of Neath who

lived at Hermons Hill for some years. Dr. Francis Edwardes lived there for some time.

In 1808 Mrs. Bassett, then of Neath, widow, and her kinsman, John Herbert Lloyd of Plâs Cilyhebyth (Glam.) granted a lease of Hermons Hill to Henry Rees, gent., of Haverfordwest at annual rent of £63. Mrs. Bassett died in 1828, and by her will devised Hermons Hill to Samuel Harries of Trefaccwn for life (died 1839) then to his eldest son John Harding Harries who sold Hermons Hill for £1,850 to William Owen of Haverfordwest, a successful cabinet-maker, son of William and Lettice Owen of Llanwnda parish. He continued to prosper, became a J.P. and D.L., and served as High Sheriff in 1859, then living at Poyston, which he had purchased some years previously. After this a succession of owners lived at Hermons Hill, among them Sir Charles Price, M.P.

Refs: *Pembs. RO., D/EE/5, no. 19; Carms RO., Trant Deeds; G.R. Barrett, Deeds; NLW, Griffith Owen Deeds; Brawdy Papers, penes ms; James, Haverfordwest and its Story*, 1957, opp p. 153, illustr. of Haverfordwest with a good view of Hermons Hill.

HILL. *Ludchurch.*

A residence to the north of the parish church. In 1538 William, Abbot of Whitland leased lands called The Hill in the parishes of Ludchurch and Lampeter Felfre, for 99 years, to Lawrence Winterhay gent. and Elizabeth his wife, and in 1593 the said lessees, described as of Hill, leased the said property to Roger Williams of Erreweare, gent. It was home of William Powell, son of Lewis Powell of Lamphey and Greenhill, descended from the medieval Cantingtons of north Pembrokeshire. By his wife Mary, daughter of Richard Vaughan of Cwrt Derllys, Carm. William Powell had a daughter Elinor who married James ap Rice the tumultuous squire of Rickeston (Brawdy) and Scotsborough.

James died in 1692, Elinor in 1700, leaving six children. In the late 18th century it was the home of Charles Swan who was there in 1786. In the second half of the 19th century, Sackville Herbert Edward Gregg Owen lived there, his son, also named Sackville, was High Sheriff in 1911. The house is still well maintained.

Refs: *Golden Grove ms* (Adv. Pembs) fos 229-230; *College of Arms, Gilfach ms; Picton Castle Deeds; Land Tax 1786.*

HILL. *Steynton.*

Exact location unknown; the name hill is included in nine place-names as shown in the Voter List of 1894 – Barretts Hill, Bolton Hill, Bygons Hill, Churchill, Deemshill, Dreenhill, Myrtle Hill, Hill Gate (on Denant mountain) and Sycamore Hill, and the Voters List of 1950 includes an additional seven places containing the element 'hill'. The first of the family at Hill was Rees Lewis William grandson of William ap Llewilin 'a blind man who dwelled at Tre rose in St. Lawrens in Pebidiog.' Rees married Elizabeth Bateman of Honeyborough, by whom he had a son and three daughters. The son, William ap Rees gent. of Hill, married firstly Joan, sister of Owen ap Owen of Pentre Ifan, by whom he had two daughters who married North Pembrokeshire squires, and secondly Elizabeth Barrett. The prenuptial settlement was made on 10 August 1556, and he and his wife were still living at 'le Hill' in 1567. Nothing further has been found about the family.

Refs: *Dwnn*, 1, 70; *B. M. Egerton ms 2586; NLW, Bronwydd Deeds, Pembs. Plea Rolls 1559-1566.*

HILTON. *Roch.*

A residence, marked on Colby's map one mile south of Roch village. Apart from their names little is known of the earlier residents of Hilton, also occasionally known as High Hilton. In 1323 it was the home of Walter de Hilton and his son and heir, William. In 1413 John Mors, and in the years 1436-1445, lands in Hilton and Folcaston were owned by Walter Reynbot (who had received them from his father John Reynbot), who settled them on his sons John, Peter and Geoffrey Reynbot in entail. The family continued in the parish for many generations, and is still commemorated in the name of Rainbotts Hill farm.

During Elizabethan times the Harries family, from Haverfordwest, settled there. Hugh Harries died in 1566, and was followed by his son Thomas Harris gent. who owned the residence and manor of Hilton, and died some time after 1592. It passed to the Butler family of Scovaston, before 1624, in which year the manor of Hilton (200 acres) was owned by Thomas Butler, brother-in-law of the said Thomas Harries. It was later inherited by the heiress Anne Butler. She married William Mordaunt, who *iure uxoris* enjoyed the estates. They were living at Hilton in 1661, and later moved to the main Butler residence, Scovaston. Their sole surviving son, Thomas Mordaunt was living in 1723.

The Grants later lived there; in 1764 the Reverend John Grant, clerk, lived there and in 1766 the Reverend Moses Grant clerk, and John Grant, Esq. were living at Hilton. In 1786 the owner-occupier of Hilton was Francis Edwardes of Haverfordwest. In 1792 he married Martha Williams of Haverfordwest, and among the properties settled on her was 'the messuage and land called Hilton.' Edwardes died without issue, about 1808, and Hilton became the property of Mrs. Jane Bassett of Neath, and by her will dated 1828, the year of her death, she bequeathed Hilton to Samuel Harries of Cryglas and Trefaccwn. He died in 1839, and Hilton passed to his son George Augustus Harries, who settled there and died in 1887. G. A. Harries was followed by his son Samuel Keith Harries, the last of the line to dwell at Hilton.

Refs: *PRO, Ancient Deeds; NLW, Picton Castle Deeds, Coleman Deeds, Pembs. Plea Rolls, Frances Green Deeds, Penpont (Brec) Suppl. Deeds; W.W.H.R. VIII,* (Harries of Trevaccoon).

HOATEN. *St. Ishmaels.*

In the westerly sector of the parish, near the boundary with St. Brides, were the four messuages of Great-, Little-, Middle-Hoaton, and Hoaton Hill, all marked on Colby's map of 1831. The most important of these was Great Hoaton, home of the Morgan family in the 16th and 17th centuries. Descended from the Carmarthenshire family of Morgan of Muddlecomb, Rhys Morgan Esq. married Thomazin, daughter and heiress of John Sutton of Haverfordwest, and had a son and heir, Henry Morgan described as 'of Hoaton' in 1577. Henry is named in documents of 1592-97, 1609, and 1625. He married Janet, daughter of Griffith Wyrriot of Orielton, and had five sons and three daughters. His family arms were *argent three bulls' heads caboshed sable*. According to *Egerton ms*, Henry Morgan died in 1627, but his I.P.M. was taken on 23 January 1636, and showed that he owned extensive properties in the parish. The next reference to the family occurs in legal documents in 1650 and 1656 when John Morgan gent. dwelled at 'Hottowne' in St. Ishmael's parish. It is not known whether Thomas Morgan of Great Hoaton in 1676 was a descendant; he died on 8 November 1715 and administration of his will was granted to his widow Dorothy. His inventory shows a value of £502, among his possessions being a one-fourth share of a barque, and a part of three other boats. By now all the Hoatens were farmed by tenants. In 1786 Great-, Middle-, and Little-, Hoaten were owned by Thomas Skyrme of Vaynor and let to farmers. On the lawn of Great Hoaten rests a huge iron anchor, said to be a relic of the Spanish Armada.

Refs: *Dwnn*, i, 90. 218; *Picton Castle Deeds; NLW, Poyston Deeds, Pembs. Plea Rolls; B. M. Egerton ms 2586; College of Arms , Wagner ms 2; R.C.A.M. Pubs.*

HOLMUS. *Newport.*
A farmstead to the west of Newport near the road leading to Dinas. The name is derived from the old English 'holm', 'holmes', meaning water-meadow. It occurs in Pembrokeshire records of 1276 when Margaret, daughter of William Pecke of Newport granted a house and land at Holmes, Newport. In 1552 David Kethyn is described as of Hollmys. There were three farms there in olden time called Holmhouse-fawr, and -uchaf. In one of these lived William Bowen, son of James Bowen of Llwyngwair, in the 18th century. In 1786, the three farms of 'Rolmouse' (Yr Holmhouse) were owned by George Bowen of Llwyngwair, with Owen Bowen, Thomas Lewis and David George as tenants. By 1894 there were two farms there, Holmhouse-fawr and Holmhouse-uchaf.

Refs: *PRO, Ancient Deeds; NLW, Pembs Plea Rolls*; B. G. Charles, *Non-celtic place-names in Wales*, p. 52.

HOLYLAND. *St. Michael Pembroke.*
A residence, today a hotel, just east of the town of Pembroke and of Golden farm. Home of the Adams family who had moved from Buckspool (q.v.) to Paterchurch (q.v.) in the early 15th century, thence to Holyland towards the end of the 16th century, where they remained till the 1940s. Writing of Paterchurch, Fenton noted in 1811 – 'a cross stood near it ... the remaining ruins of this pious building were removed some years ago in the building of Holy Land, the seat of Joseph Adams Esq.' Holyland formed part of the Adams estate in 1629, possibly earlier, when it was let to farming tenants.

Eighteen generations of the family are known, many taking active part in local affairs, among them John Adams of Paterchurch, in 1448 lieutenant to Henry Wogan, Steward of the Earldom of Pembroke (it was this John who married Elen, daughter and heiress of David Paterchurch and settled at her home), John Adams of Paterchurch M.P. for Pembroke, 1541-44, Henry Adams, M.P. for Pembroke 1547 and 1553, High Sheriff in 1558, Nicholas Adams, M.P. for Pembroke 1589, Mayor of Pembroke five times between 1602-1627 and a J.P., Nicholas Adams, Commissioner of Subsidies for the county in 1661, 1667 and 1669 (he paid tax for seven hearths at Holyland in 1670), Roger Adams, Commissioner of Subsidies 1692, 1695-6 and for Land Tax in 1707. Mayor of Pembroke 1695, he was the last of the family to live at Paterchurch before moving to Holyland. John Adams, J.P. High Sheriff in 1837.

The last male of the family in recent times, John Stephen Adams, was killed in action in the Second World War. Some years after the war, the family left Holyland which was afterwards sold. A curious tale concerns this part of their history. Having moved furniture, etc., orders were given to some local workers to empty what was left in the mansion and to burn it in the adjacent garden. Now, before the family had moved from Paterchurch, a young girl, Agnes Adams, died and was interred in the family burial ground. When they moved to Holyland, they dug up the remains which were placed in a sack which they took with them, and stored in the attic. After the departure from Holyland, one of the family remembered about this, went to Pembroke and asked about the remains. The workmen said that among the 'rubbish' found in the attic were some bones which they had duly consigned to the flames as ordered. And thus was little Agnes finally disposed of. The Adams bore arms: *quarterly, 1 and 4 sable a martlet argent* (for de Paterchurch), *1 and 3, or on a cross gules five pierced mullets or; crest; a martlet argent.*

Refs: *Dwnn*, i, 130.1, 172; *NLW, Poyston Deeds; Pembs RO, Land Tax 1786. Adams Deeds* – see 'Ancient description of Holyland' by John Adams, 1836; Fenton, *Tour Pembs.*, 1811 (2nd edn.) pp. 151, 198, 228, 234; *Laws. Little England*, 307, 428; *Burke's Commoners*, 1837; B. G. Charles, *Non-celtic Place Names in Wales*, p. 23.

HONEYBOROUGH. *Llanstadwell.*

Just to the north of Neyland. There were several farms in the vicinity called Honeyborough, the most important being Great Honeyborough which was the caput of the manor. In 1811 Fenton wrote '... two mansions which formerly were of considerable rank though now nothing is left but their names, Scovaston and Honeyborough, the venerable buildings that, in the remembrance of many living, occupied the site, having being transmuted into farm-houses ... Of the latter, Honeyborough, our ancient deeds make frequent mention, about three centuries ago or earlier, as in the possession of the Batemans, but after that time frequently changing its possessors, till within these forty years it presented extensive ruins of very massive buildings, that to destroy required no small labour.' About 1600, it was

listed as a manor, the lords having been Perrot, Bowen and Scourfield. The earliest family there, the Batemans (arms: *sable a chevron between three escallops argent*) were in possession during the sixteenth century, their pedigree for six generations being recorded by Dwnn and Golden Grove mss. They were still there in 1598. Later Great Honeyborough passed to the Taskers who were there till about 1810. After this it became the home of farming tenants.

Ref: *Dwnn*, i, 173; *Golden Grove mss.;* Fenton, *Tour Pembs,* 1811 (2nd edn.); *Land Tax 1786; Taylor's Cussion,* fo. 98; *W.W.H.R.,* IX, 152.

HONEY HOOK. *Lambston.*

A farmstead a mile to the west of Lambston village. For long, home of yeoman and minor gentry. In 1392 Alice Brown held two Carucates at Honeyhoke and le Walles; in the years 1488-1507 Honeyhook was owned by William Popton; a deed of 1511 had the seal of Thomas Estemond of Honeyhook, son and heir of John Estemond of the same place, deceased. In the late 16th century the Bateman family, wealthy tradesmen, of Haverfordwest, whose arms were recorded in 1530 as *azure, a chevron or between three escallops argent, with three quarterings,* took an interest in Honey Hook, and on 12 March 1602-3 John Bateman of Haverfordwest bought Honey Hook and Wallis from Thomas Bowen of Trefloyne. It remained in Bateman possession for over a century, and the seal of Benjamin Bateman 'late of Haverfordwest but now of Honey Hook' is attached to a Picton Castle deed of 1733. Thereafter the property was sold, and in 1786 the owner was William Davies, with Thomas Gough as the tenant.

Refs: *College of Arms Archives,* Fellowe's Visitation 1530; *PRO, Ancient Deeds; Cardiff Free Library, deeds; Land Tax 1786.*

HOOK. *Ambleston.*

A residence one mile south-west of Ambleston village, standing on a long slope above the northern bank of Spittal Brook. Originally a farmhouse, mentioned in 1592 as 'le

Hooke'. It afterwards formed part of the estate of Sir John Pakington, Bart., who sold it to David Meredith of Haverfordwest, and he, in 1747, sold 'the capital messuage called Great Hook' to Admiral Thomas Tucker Esq., of Sealyham, a distinguished naval officer. He died unmarried in 1766, bequeathing the property to his nephew John Tucker (High Sheriff 1763), who died in 1794 and left it to his eldest daughter and co-heiress, Catherine, who married John Owen Edwardes of Llanmils, Carms. who came to Sealyham, and thereafter Hook remained in the Tucker-Edwardes family.

William Tucker-Edwardes was the father of Mary Tucker-Edwardes (born 1818) who became involved in the interesting 'Madam Rachel' lawsuit involving Lord Ranelagh. Mary married Colonel A. Borrodaile, and their daughter Florence Emma Anna was the last of the family to reside at Hook. She died unmarried in 1934. Some nine years earlier on 1 December 1925, Mrs. H. F. Cope had transferred the capital messuage and demesne of Hook to Thomas Charles Roberts, solicitor, of Perthyterfyn, Flint, and Richard Knight Lucas, estate agent, of Haverfordwest. It was later sold to a farmer. Hook is an excellent example of a traditional Welsh residence, and is in first-class condition. A three-storey main block, with ranges of five windows, a 'wing' in front, and another to the rear. There are eleven bedrooms, several reception rooms, a vaulted cellar, and a fine staircase lit by a long window rising to the top storey. It has been repaired and added to over the years; a massive beam that had been a *simne fawr* bears the date 1732, while a stone in the rear 'wing' has the date 1857. When I saw it in 1979 it was advertised for sale by the owner-occupier, Mrs. Griffiths, who kindly allowed me to inspect the house.

Refs: *NLW, Sealyham Deeds; Pembs RO. Deeds* DB/13/58; *Land Tax 1786;* Francis Green on the Tucker and Edwardes families of Sealyham, in *W.W.H.R. VIII; Western Mail 21 July and 29 September 1979,* illust. and description.

HOOK. *Langum.*

There were three properties – East Hook, West Hook, Lower Hook in the north of the parish, near to the banks of the Western Cleddau, and included on Colby's map of 1831. *East Hook;* the earliest-known owner was Owen Jordan, gent., and when he died Richard Hicks, yeoman of East Hook was his executor in 1614. The heiress was Mary Hicks, whose forebears 'for many generations had been owners of the capital mansion house of East Hook and of a moiety of the said tenement's land.' She married one John Jones, and they had a daughter, sole heiress, Mary Jones, who married Richard Eynon gent., described in 1727 as of 'the capital messuage of East Hook.' Their daughter Elinor Eynon, married a Mr. Knethell and their eldest son, Richard Knethell, attorney, was living at 'the capital messuage of East Hook' in 1760-1786. The property afterwards was acquired by the Powell family. They produced four High Sheriffs of Pembrokeshire – his son John Harcourt Powell, and in 1864, Thomas Harcourt Powell – all being described as of Hook and Drinkstone Park, Suffolk. The last-named was followed by his nephew John Harcourt Powell of Marsh Mills House, Henley-on-Thames, who served the office of High Sheriff for Pembrokeshire in 1910.

Refs: *NLW, Pembs Plea Rolls; Land Tax 1786.*

HOOK. *Marloes.*

On Colby's map 1831, West Hook and East Hook are marked as two adjacent farms, near the coast, on high ground between Musselwick Bay and Martins Haven, both farms being mentioned in a document dated 1307. The properties were owned from 1536 to 1802 by the family of Runwa alias Runwae alias Runway.

Ten successive generations lived at Hook, described in the earliest documents as yeomen, in the late 17th century as gentlemen, and towards the end of the 18th century as esquires. They intermarried with the Voyles of Philbeach, Davis of Crabhall, and Paynter of Dale. In 1786 the owner of both messuages was Benjamin Runwae, the tenants James Jones and John Cooker. Benjamin had a successful naval career, and in his will of 1802 he is described as 'of Hook alias East Hook, Master and Commander R.N. (now) residing in Westbury-upon-Trim, Gloucestershire', who bequeathed the farm of Broomhill and other properties in Dale village to his 'kinsman and godson' David Runwa(e) Paynter of Pembroke town, gentleman. The properties were alienated not long afterwards, and in 1842 Lord Kensington owned East Hook, and C. A. W. Philipps owned West Hook. The family of Runwae became extinct, and few other yeomen families can show an unbroken succession for some 300 years. Fenton in 1811 states that Musselwick (Marloes parish) is 'now inhabited by a respectable freeholder of the name of Runawae.' They also took part in the brewing trade, sending a considerable quantity of ale to Liverpool in the late 18th century. There is still a farm in this parish called Rynaway's Kiln, and on the coast is Runaway's Cove.

Refs: *Dwnn, i, 72; B.M. Egerton ms 2586, fo. 404; NLW, Pembs. Plea Rolls; Land Tax 1786; Fenton Tour Pembs, 1811; Phillips, History of Haverfordwest, p. 180.*

HOWELSTON. *Talbenny.*

A farmstead on high land, a mile east of Talbenny village. During the middle ages from circa 1250 to 1509, seven generations of the family of Howell owned Howelston. Their pedigree, in the hand of G. W. Griffith is in the Wagner Collection in the College of Arms. In the second half of the 15th century Thomas Morris of Castle Villa in Dewsland married Margaret Howell of Howelston, and in 1497 she granted her lands and tenements in Talbenny and Howelston to her son, Henry Morris and they remained in the Morris family till the end of the 16th century, when it passed to the Scourfields of Castle Villa. In 1573 Ann Scourfield married John Meyler of Trewallterwen in St. Edwins parish, and Howelston was settled on her. In 1786 it was owned by the Owens of Orielton.

Thereafter little mention is made of Howelston which was let to farming tenants.

Refs: *Episcopal Registers of St. Davids; College of Arms ms.; Wagner ms. 2, 90 (G. W. Griffiths); N.L.W., Pembs. Plea Rolls, 1609-1614; Francis Jones, 'Castle Villa – Cas Wilia' in The Pembrokeshire Historian.*

John Pavin Phillips

IVY TOWER. *St. Florence.*

A residence a mile north of St. Florence village. The original name seems to have been Tar, meaning a high rock or hill, and about a mile southwards is the farm of Tarr. It was rendered in deeds of 1603-1625 as Ivie Torr and Ivetor. As to the element 'Ivy', the *Cambrian Register* 1706 states it may have been named after Paul Ivy an Elizabethan engineer sent to survey the defences of Milford Haven and Tenby, but 'the latter was not seen by Mr. Ivy nearer than two miles distance at a place, and some pretend to say, called from him Ivy Tower ... where it was believed the voluptuous surveyor found a magnet of more powerful attraction than either Milford or Tenby.' It occurs in the deeds of the Williams family of the years 1727-1778. The farm Ivy Tower is first mentioned in 1771, and is known as such in the following years.

The Williams family descended, by the distaff, from Bishop Robert Ferrer of St. Davids (martyred in 1555), whose only daughter Elizabeth married the Reverend Lewis Williams, Rector of Narberth. Their son Robert Williams bought lands in St. Florence parish, died in 1656 and five generations of his descendants lived at Ivy Tower, which was sold and by 1894 was the home of Colonel H. H. Goodere. Later it was sold again, and today is a holiday park hotel. A well-built Georgian house of two storeys, a range of five windows on the upper floor, with a pillared entrance, flanked by two large windows, on the ground floor.

Refs: *B. G. Charles, N.C.P.N.* pp. 21-2; *Pembs R.O. Williams Deeds, HDX/833, Land Tax List 1786; Cambrian Register* Vol II, 1796, p. 180; *Burke L.G. 1850; C. S. Allen, 'South Wales'* 1871, illustr.; M.I. St. Florence church.

Lewis, Lord Merthyr

JOHNSTON (HALL). *Johnston.*

A village some three miles south of Haverfordwest, on the road to Milford. The mansion on the southern fringe of the village is marked as 'Hall' on modern O.S. maps. In the 15th century it was the home of the family of Tancred, well-known in the medieval history of the county. John Tancred of Johnston (still there in 1499) and died circa 1510, having had the following children – John died young and unmarried, Elizabeth, co-heiress, married pre 1507 Morris Butler who was living at Johnston in 1507, Alicia, co-heiress, married Jenkin ap Owen, and Anne who died unmarried pre-1519. The Tancred arms were *gules a chevron between three escallops argent*. The main seats of the Butlers (descended from the Butlers of Dunraven, Glam.) in Pembrokeshire were Johnston, Coedcanlas, Scovaston, and Tregadwgan; their arms *azure three covered cups or*. Morris Butler, who held several important public offices during the first half of the 16th century, was followed by six generations, and although living in the early 17th century at Scovaston, continued to own Johnston until

Hugh Butler, a Royalist and 'a grand malignant' sold the property to Sir Roger Horsey about 1639. In 1668 Elizabeth Horsey married Arthur Owen (descended from the Orielton family), and he came to live at Johnston.

At that time the manor of Johnston comprised the manor house, and about 200 acres. In 1670 Elizabeth Horsey was assessed at ten hearths for the manor house, which shows it to be have been very large at that time. By 1703 Johnston had been sold to Francis Edwardes (a younger son of the Little Trefgarn family, M.P. for Haverfordwest 1722-1725) and was followed there by his son William Edwardes, prominent in public life, and created Lord Kensington in 1776. He died at Johnston in 1801, aged 90, having represented Haverfordwest in nine Parliaments between 1747 and 1801. Several tourists found it worthy of mention.

A tour written circa 1800, now kept in the archives of the Society of Genealogists, London, contains the following entry: 'Aug. 21. Johnston Hall the seat of Lord Kensington. His Lordship seems an uncommon sloven if the Traveller may judge from the appearance of his House and Garden. Upon enquiry of an old man at the Turnpike, found His Lordship to be a miser, and Her Ladyship a spendthrift'. *Malkin* in his Tour 1804, notes: 'Johnston is an ancient seat belonging to Lord Kensington, which should not be passed by without a visit.' Fenton wrote with some asperity in 1811: 'Johnston, the seat for many years of the Late Lord Kensington, but since his death let to a tenant. There is nothing in the situation to recommend it as an eligible residence as it lies rather low, close to the great road, and in a coal county, therefore a deep clay soil … It is to be lamented that the present nobleman, his son, is obliged to seek a residence in a neighbouring county [Westmead, Carm.]' In the same year, Carlisle writes, 'The only object of note is an old Family Mansion of The Right Honourable Lord Kensington, called Johnston Hall, which is now partly occupied as a Farm-house, and the remainder is in a rapid state of decay': Lewis's *Topographical Dictionary*, (1834, 1840) comments: 'Johnston Hall, an ancient mansion of the family of Edwardes, and for a long time the residence of the late Lord Kensington, is now the property of the present lord, and is in the occupation of Thomas Bowen Esq.'

In 1835 Lord Kensington then living at Noyadd, Llanarth, Cards., sold the estate for £10,000 to the Reverend James Morgan, clerk, of Talgarth, Brec., and on 21 February 1873 the parson's Trustees sold the manor and estate to Richard Carrow. The Carrow family held it for several decades. In 1894 Richard Carrow and his son Charles (owner of the Brickworks at Johnston) were living there. In 1921 the mansion, manor and estate were advertised for sale, the vendor being Howard Gwynne Keppel Palmer, described as 'Beneficial Owner'. The sale catalogue describes Johnston Hall as built around a courtyard, comprising, on the ground floor, a hall, three reception rooms, cloak room, lavatory, servants' hall, kitchen, pantry; on the first floor six family bedrooms: stabling, garages, kennels, tennis court, gardens, orchards; in all 16 acres. The catalogue has two photographs of the house. The Milford Haven family of Brand lived there afterwards, and finally sold it.

Nowadays, the Hall, a double-pile building with a wing to the rear, is set in pleasant grounds; nearby are the old coach-house and other ancient outbuildings, one of which may well have been a dwelling-house (part of the hall) in earlier days, and close to this building is the old walled garden alienated during the 19th century). The owner-occupier the agreeable Lt. Col. H. J. Evans, M.B.E., D.L., retired Gurkha officer, welcomed me when I called there in 1986.

Refs: *Dwnn*, i, 76, 110, 132, 179-80; *Pembs R.O., Land Tax records; N.L.W., Goswood ms. pedigrees, Eaton Evans and Williams Deeds, Floyd ms 1361C; P.R.O., Chancery Proc C5 89/15, Anc. Deeds*, Vol V; *Carms R.O., Golden Grove mss; Picton Castle Deeds.*

JEFFRESTON HOUSE. *Jefferston.*
Originally home of the Nash family, a cadet of Nash of Nash. The Nash heiress, Maud, married David Smith (d.1556), and their descendants continued at Jeffreston until the end of the 18th century. John Smith, High Sheriff in 1753 subscribed to a copy of the Reverend William Evans's translation of Canwyll y Cymry in 1771. He left an only daughter and heiress Anne, who in 1759 married Philipp Philipps of Lampter Felfre House, and their son, Thomas Philipps afterwards lived at both his parents' houses, and had ten children. The *Pembrokeshire Archaeological Survey* calls the house of the Smiths, Great House, Jeffreston.

JORDANSTON (HALL) –
TREWRDAN. *Jordanston in Dewsland.*
An ancient mansion in the vernacular style, with a small grove on a westerly slope overlooking the Western Cleddau, mid-way between the farms of Llangloffan and Trecoed. The mansion is close to the parish church. Nearby is a field called Castell where probably an early fortification had stood. In 1326 Jordanston is described as a knight's fee. In 1411 the living of Jordanston was held by the Bishop of St. Davids, Lord of the Hundred, by reason of the minority of the son and heir of Ieuan ap Roppert ap Meyer [ap Tancred] late lord of Jordanston, deceased.

In the late 14th century the Wogans of Boulston were the lords of the manor, owned the living, and held it throughout the 16th century, but by 1621 the manorial rights had passed to the Gwynn family who owned the mansion and estate. The Gwynns, who came from Llanidloes, Mont., were owners of Jordanston from 1561, until the early half of the 17th century, Matilda Gwynn the ultimate heiress married John Vaughan of Lisswent, Rad., who settled at Jordanston, which their descendants held until the death of Gwynne Gill Vaughan, without issue, on 28 March 1837 in his 60th year. He bequeathed Jordanston to his friend, Major General Sir James Cockburn, Bart., who died in 1852, and the estate passed to his daughter Marianne Cockburn who married Sir James John Hamilton of Plâs Llanstephan, Carms., who died in 1876. Thereafter the mansion became the property of gentleman-farmers, who have maintained the mansion in excellent style. It now belongs to the Raymond family. The mansion was assessed at five hearths in 1670, and in 1709 the estate consisted of the manor, advowson of the parish church, the capital messuage, 17 farms and houses, the wharf at Fishguard, with its royalties, and a water corn mill there. The properties lay in Jordanston parish and nine other parishes in the district. A sale catalogue of 1817 describes the mansion as comprising five reception rooms, two large kitchens, pantries, cellars and domestic offices; eight bedrooms; outhouses; a walled garden (2 acres); two carriage drives.

Refs: *Pembs. R.O., Deeds HDX/661, Land Tax, 1876, Sale Catalogue, 1917; Cardiff Public Library,* Deeds: *N.L.W.,* Cwrtmawr Deeds; *Carms. R.O.,* Golden Grove mss; Francis Jones, 'Jordanston in Dewsland', in *Pembs. Historian,* 1974, and Lay manors of Dewsland in *Journal Hist. Soc. of the Church in Wales,* 1969.

JORDANSTON. *Llanstadwell.*

In the Hundred of Rhos (Roose). A mansion (now a farmhouse) about half a mile southwest of Rosemarket village. I visited it on 19 May 1976 accompanied by Lieutenant Colonel Evans of Johnston Hall. It is a tall three-storeyed house, with ranges of five windows, a fine fanlight over the entrance door; an interesting projection to the rear has a stepped chimney-stack, older than the main block. Originally the home of the Jordan family after whom it is named. A pedigree by George Owen of Henllys starts with Leonard Jordan who married in the second half of the 14th century 'a daughter of John of Doomple Dale' (Dumple Dale was for many years afterwards home of a branch of the Jordans). Leonard's son Thomas Jordan married a daughter of Jenkin Lloyd of Cemaes (Blaidd-bwll, *vide supra*) and had a son John Jordan who married Elizabeth Sturmyn. During the Wars of the Roses, John was an active Yorkist, and in 1469 accompanied Sir Henry Wogan to Banbury where both were slain. His son John Jordan the younger was about eight or nine years old when his father fell. He married Anne Elliot of Earwere. He too was engaged in political warfare, and 'went with the Duke of Buckingham, his master, against the King, and was beheddyd in the castell of Harfordwest, and left his son William Jordan but 4 years old'. Like his immediate forebears William met a mournful end. George Owen notes, 'William Jordan went with Sir John Wogan as capten to Terwin and Turney [in France], and there was slaine, and left his sonne Richard Jordan but 14 yeres of age'. No tragedy attended young Richard's life and he went on to marry Elinor (or Elin) daughter of Henry Morgan of Mudlescwm (H. S. Carms 1544) by, Margaret daughter of Henry Wogan of Wiston. Richard avoided the perils of war, confined his attention to domestic matters with some vigour, and when he died, between 1566 and 1580, he left ten sons and two daughters.

In 1581 David Jordan of Jordanston, gent, descended as son and heir of Richard Jordan deceased, and his widowed mother Elin Jordan alias Morgan, were involved in a lawsuit relating to an annuity of 40s. charged on Dumpledale in Burton parish. David married Anne Lloyd by whom he had issue. His brother Thomas Jordan died suddenly without issue and his wife Alice Thomas was 'burnt in Carmarthen for poysening her husband'. However, the family was not destined to remain much longer at Jordanston. By the middle of the 17th century they had gone, and in the Hearth Tax list for Llanstadwell in 1670 the surname Jordan is not to be found.

In 1734 it was the residence of Thomas Bowen whose forebears lived at Haverfordwest. The Bowens remained at Jordanston until the beginning of the 19th century. By 1834 it was owned by William Henry Wilson of Leics., and they were still in possession in 1904 when Jordanston was owned by William Le Hunt Wilson who was then living at Dulwich.

Refs: *B. M. Egerton ms 2586,* fos 384-5; *Pembs. R.O., Land Tax List,* 1786; *N.L.W., Morgan-Richardson Deeds,* i, 64.

Edwardes, Lord Kensington

KEYSTON (TREGETIN). *Camrose.*

A hamlet near the St. Davids-Haverfordwest highway, between Pelcomb and Roch. Home of the medieval family of Roblin, but the site is not known for certain. A report made of a survey, about 1900, there was in the village a small overgrown ruin, suggested to have been the home of the Keating family who gave name to the place, 'there are three detached buildings, the best preserved, and the largest, a very long narrow structure, 20ft wide and 150 ft. (or thereabouts) long; the greater part is lying prostrate. It is entered by a ruinous semicircular porch. The place is so ruinous and overgrown with brambles that we are unable to take measurements and give the description that is due. When, some 20 years later, the inspectors of *R.C.A.M.* visited it they stated that the few features mentioned above 'have practically vanished'.

George Owen of Henllys, c.1600, gives the following pedigree – William Roblyn de Cestingston married Eleanor, daughter of Sir Walter Malefant and Dame Alice de Roch; their son was David Roblyn who was father of Harry Roblyn. Dr. Charles, who cites the name Ketingeston in 1295, states the name may be derived from Kething, possibly from the Welsh Cethin. The Welsh continue to refer to the village as Tregethin.

Refs: Charles, *Non-Celtic Place Names*, p. 56; *Pembrokeshire Archaeological Survey*, (1896-1907); *R.C.A.M., Pembs.*, 1925, p. 48.

KILBARTH. *Rudbaxton.*

A farmstead about a quarter of a mile west of the parish church. There is a reference to the property in 1326 when Kilbarth, Frowlyn-church, Scolton and Haythog, were counted as a single fee, formerly held by Guy de Brian, but is now in the hands of the Lord Bishop, and for Kilbarth John Symond paid yearly one penny. Much later, in 1566, Hugh Harries of Haverfordwest owned a messuage and a ploughland in 'Gilbawrgh' in Rudbaxton parish. William Phillips lived at Kilbarth in 1650, whose daughter Anne married John Codd who lived at his wife's home in 1669. Six generations of the Phillips family succeeded to Kilbarth, and were there until the first half of the 19th century when its two sons, Edward Picton Phillips (b. 1822) and his brother John William Phillips, solicitor, settled in Haverfordwest. It was afterwards the property of several yeoman families.

Refs: *Black Book of St. Davids*, 1326; *N.L.W. Pembrokeshire Plea Rolls; W.W.H.R. viii*, 107: *Pembs R.O., Land Tax List 1786.*

KILGETTY. *St. Issels.*

Formerly a mansion on high ground just over a mile north of the hamlet of Stepaside. *R.C.A.M. 1925*, p. 375, calls this place 'an ecclesiastical residence of the canons of St. Davids.' Not so. In fact it was the residence of a very secular family, surnamed Canon, whose worldly attachment to commerce in Haverfordwest had enabled its members to purchase landed property and to set up as country gentlefolk. Originally a farm, it was acquired by the Barlow family towards the middle of the 16th century, and about 1620 was sold to Sir Thomas Canon of Haverfordwest. Sir Thomas died in 1639-40 unmarried, and all his real estate passed to his nephew, Morris Canon.

The mansion at Kilgetty was either built by Sir Thomas or the nephew, Morris, who lived at the mansion. He was interested in the coal mines which were around the property, but in January 1655 he fell headlong into one of the pits and died instantly. He was buried with his wife's family, the Wogans, at Wiston. The widow afterwards married Isaac Lloyd who settled at Kilgetty, and in 1670 was assessed at seven hearths. Morris Canon's estate passed to his only son and heir, John Canon, who died in 1690, leaving an only child, Elizabeth, heiress to what was a considerable estate. She married John Philipps of Picton Castle, and on her death, without issue in 1706, Kilgetty passed to the Philipps family in whose possession it has remained to our own days. The Philippses improved and enlarged the mansion and outbuildings in 1725, and a sketch of the mansion and its surrounding fields was made by John Butcher in 1743. It was then a tall house of six storeys, flanked by two long outbuildings, enclosing a large courtyard, from which a gate led to ornamental gardens, at the end of which was a fine belvedere, the ruins of which remain. From the mid 18th century it ceased to be used as a residence, became a ruin, which was removed, so that no traces now remain. Several other features such as the outbuildings, the gardens, and the belvedere, are still to be seen.

Refs: *Francis Jones, 'Kilgetty, A Pembrokeshire Mansion' in Arch. Cam., 1976, pp. 127.139, illustr.; Pembrokeshire Archaeological Survey, 1896-1907; Picton Castle Deeds,: Curtis, Laugharne, 1880, p. 355; N.L.W., Slebech Deeds, Eaton-Evans and Williams Deeds; F. P. Gwynne, Sketches of Tenby, etc., 1852, p. 139; Pembs. R.O., Deeds D/Adams; Fenton, Tour Pembs., 1811.*

KILVELGY. *St. Issels.*

The 'Manor of St. Issels alias Kilvaelgi' was owned by the Barlows of Slebech. The manor house and demesne lands were let to substantial families. In 1636 Nicholas Lewis, esq. lived there, and later in that century Jenkin Thomas, gent., who was assessed at five hearths in 1670. It continued to be owned by the Barlows, and in 1786 the owner is given as Sir William Hamilton who had married the heiress of the Barlows. The house was later transformed into a farmhouse which is its present status. Kilvelgy is close to Kilgetty village, near the road to Stepaside.

Refs: *Taylor's Cussion 1587-88; N.L.W., Edwinsford Deeds, Eaton-Evans and Williams Deeds.*

KINGSTON. *St. Michael's, Pembroke.*

Now a farm, 1¼ miles to the south-east of Pembroke town. In the second half of the 17th century it was held by the Meares family. In the 18th century it was owned by John Campbell Hooke (one of the Stackpole Court family) who is given as the owner in 1786, with Mr. Furlong as tenant.

Refs: *Pembs. R.O., Land Tax List 1786; Meares family pedigree.*

Le Marchant Thomas

LAMPETER VELFREY.

Lampeter Velfrey/Felfre.

Lampeter House, formerly called 'Peniucha'r Dre' and 'Upper End House' due to its position in the village. In the 17th and 18th centuries it was home to the Philipps family (said to be a cadet of Picton Castle). In 1670 Anne Philipps was assessed at six hearths. Towards the end of the 18th century sons of the family moved to Begelly, Jeffreyston, and one son emigrated to South Africa. Another son, the Reverend Edward Philipps (1736-1793) Rector of Lampeter Velfrey, was the father of a daughter who married Nathaniel Phillips of Slebech, and their daughter, Mary Dorothea, married the Baron de Rutzen who afterwards settled at Slebech. Still an attractive residence, Lampeter House consists of an old part and a newer addition. The older part is in the rear, which had chimneys at either end and gables and a chimney (*simne fawr*) on the lateral wall with a massive chimney stack. The house was enlarged by Mr. Tudor Thomas in 1888.

Refs: *N.L.W., Slebech Deeds, Pembs. Plea Rolls; Pembs. R.O., Land Tax Lists.*

LAMPHEY. *Lamphey.*

There were three residences on the north-eastern fringe of Lamphey village, worthy of note, namely:

1. LAMPHEY PALACE.

During medieval centuries this was a residence of the Bishop of St. Davids. Extensive ruins remain; among its noteworthy features are an early 13th century central hall, with an added camera block in the west, which, with its chapel and remodelling belong to the time of Bishop Vaughan (1509-13), and on the east an impressive first-floor hall, and remains of the chapel; a gatehouse and enclosing wall belong to the time of Bishop Gower (1328-47). A detailed inventory of the goods of Bishop Rawling, died 1536, lists the following rooms of the late Bishop 'at his manor place of Lantefey', with their contents, providing an idea of the extent of the building at the Dissolution, as follows – The Bishop's own chamber 'where he was accustomed to take his rest, and where he died'. The Chamberlain's chamber. The Wardrobe. The Checkered chamber. The Great Chamber. The gardine chamber. The Gloucester chamber. The next chamber to the Gloucester chamber. The Parker's chamber. The Steward's chamber. The next chamber. The Porter's chamber. The Cook's chamber. The Painter's chamber. The Barbour's chamber. The Brewer (chamber). The Under Cook's chamber. The Chapel chamber. The second chamber within the Chapel chamber. The Chapel. The Hall. The Parlour. The Wine Cellar. The Buttery. The Pantry. The Kitchen. The Larder House. The Fish Larder House. The Bakehouse. The Brewhouse. The Malthouse. Oxhouse. The Park. List of Books in the study.

Refs: *Arch. Camb.*, 1888, pp. 363-7 which contains the above list and contents, *ibid* 1938, pp. 1-14, *ibid* 1977 p. 174. *RCAM Pembs.*, 1925, No. 362 illustr.; Radford, *Lamphey Place* (official guidebook) illustr.; *Carmarthenshire Studies*, 1974, pp. 47-8; Fenton *Tour Pembs.*, 1811, edn 1903, pp. 236-7 illustr.; *Western Telegraph* 21 April 1983 illustr.

2. LAMPHEY COURT.

A residence just north of the Palace. The area belonged to the Devereux family, but on the attainder of the Earl of Essex late in the reign of Queen Elizabeth, the lands were purchased by Sir Hugh Owen of Orielton and remained in possession of his descendants until about 1821 when they were sold to Charles Mathias of Llangwarran, who, in 1823 commenced to build the residence known as Lamphey Court.

There had been an older house on the site, and according to the *Pembrokeshire Archaeological Survey,* had an outside staircase leading to the upper floor, which was pulled down in 1826. The new Lamphey Court was a large handsome mansion with a fine portico of four Ionic columns. Four of the Mathiases were High Sheriffs – Lewis in 1856, Charles in 1890, Charles Ronald in 1937 and Lewis in 1965. Lewis Mathias was the last of the family at the mansion which he sold in 1978, and now lives in a house in the grounds. The mansion is now an hotel.

Refs: *Lewis, TDW*, 1835 and 1840; *South West Wales, guide*, by Kyrian Rees, 1976, illustr.; Jones, *Wales Illustrated*, 1830, engraving from a drawing by H. Gastineau of the Palace ruins, with part of the new Lamphey Court a short distance away. For illustrations see *Western Telegraph* 4 December 1980, 20 January 1983 and 4 July 1984.

3. LAMPHEY PARK.

A residence just north of Lamphey Court. In 1786 James Thomas was owner-occupier of Lamphey Park, and was still there in 1817 when he was described as gentleman. In 1834 Charles Poyer Callen was the tenant, paying a yearly rent of £50, and Lewis in 1840 states that Lamphey Park, 'the property of Mrs. Thomas occupies a pleasant situation.' It is now derelict.

Refs: Lewis, *TDW*, 1840; *Pembs Vote's List*, 1834; *NLW, Maesgwynne Deeds, no. 59.*

LANCYCH. *Clydey.*

On the banks of Afon Cych, to the east of Ffynnone. A residence built in the first half of the 19th century on the site of an earlier house. The first-known owner was Morgan Llwyd who owned a large estate in the district, and is described as of Lancych in the years 1739-1762, the occupier being Benjamin Davies, tanner. On Morgan Llwyd's death, Lancych passed to Sarah Lloyd his widow. In 1770 she married a second husband, David Griffith of Vaynor, who moved to his wife's home. He was High Sheriff of Pembrokeshire in 1779, and died in 1782-3. Sarah remained there and her will was proved in 1802. Lancych passed to her relation Marianne Jones, who married in 1807 the Reverend Thomas Thomas, Rector of Jordanston in Dewsland, who came to Lancych where he died in 1813. The widowed Marianne continued there till her death in 1831. They had no children and Lancych estate was partitioned.

The next owner was Dr. Walter David Jones, M.D. an antiquary of repute, who died at Lancych in 1869. He left all the estate to his wife Ann for life, then to John Francis Jones 'who shall take and use the name and arms of Lloyd of Ffoeshelig and Dole Llanerch, after the name of Jones.' J. F. Jones Lloyd was followed by his son H. A. Jones Lloyd, solicitor, who died in 1932. He was followed by Mr. Owen Jones Lloyd whose son now lives at Lancych. The irregularity of the plan and survival of some corbelling on the outside walls indicate the antiquity of the earlier residence, but in the 19th century it was reconstructed in the *cottage ornee* style, and the interior radically rearranged.

Refs: *NLW, Lancych Deeds, Owen/Colby Records, Tithe Maps Clydey* 1841; *Pembs R.O., Land Tax List* 1786; B Williams, *Hanes Casnewydd-Emlyn*, 1860, p. 58.

LANDSHIPPING. *Martletwy.*

Landshipping is an area on the banks of the Eastern Cleddau where it meets the Western Cleddau. Landshipping Ferry (a) consists of a small quay with a few houses around it. About half a mile southwards is (b) Landshipping Quay, on an inlet, where ships carried on a lively trade in olden days, and about half a mile eastwards is the small hamlet near which stood an impressive mansion (c) until

its demolition in the early half of the 19th century, marked as 'Landshipping Old House' on Colby's map in 1831.

LANDSHIPPING HOUSE *(see above).*

Caput of the manor of Landshipping was held in the 16th century by the families of Nash and Wyrriot. From the latter it passed to the family of Owen of Orielton early in the 17th century and remained in their hands till its demolition a few years before 1840. The Owens lived there from time to time. It was then a structure of three storeys and in 1670 was assessed as containing twenty hearths, one of the largest Pembrokeshire residences.

A letter from Sir Hugh Owen to Sir John Philipps of Picton Castle, mentions the 'new modelling and a water folly at Landshipping' in 1696-7. Erasmus Philipps in his journal mentions on 3rd September 1729, 'I went to Landshipping, Mr. William Owen and his lady from home.' In the Land tax list of 1786 the house is shown as being held by representatives of 'the late Sir Hugh Owen, Bart'. Thereafter Mr. Owen lived at Orielton, and Landshipping House soon required extensive repair, and an estimate of the work required there, made by Griffith Watkins, 'house builder', on 26th October 1789, mentions (*inter alia*) the following rooms in the mansion – nursery, Blue room, Plad (sic.) room, Lady Owen's room, Dressing room and closet, Plad rooms in the Gallery 'Charset', Yellow room, Gallery corridor, Red and Plad rooms 'on one floor', Sir Hugh's closet, Best Parlour, Hall, Drawing room, Common Parlour, Butler's Pantry, Housekeeper's room, Stewards hall, Servants' hall; a wing on the east side of the house consisting of kitchen, larder, dairy, brewhouse and bedchambers over, being 100 feet long and 20 feet broad; scullery; an old building east of the house, called The Curnal Stable, 22 feet long and 18 feet broad; lime house, coach house, malt house, carpenter's workshop, common stables, middle stables, pigs' yard and cot, pump and cover to the well, garden.

By 1789 the uninhabited mansions of

Orielton and Landshipping were deteriorating rapidly, and the Owen 'Great House' at Tenby, and the Owen house at Haverfordwest, were similarly neglected by the Trustees of the Owen family. Some £2009.16.0 had been spent on repairs at Landshipping, but in January 1790 Lady Owen arranged for the principal rooms to be closed, the furniture to be covered with dust sheets, and dismissed the housekeeper, cook and other domestics, as well as the gardeners and farm hands, retaining only a female caretaker at the mansion. This was the swansong of the old residence, and Fenton noted in 1811 – 'Landshipping, where embosomed 'sacred to social life and social love,' formerly stood a very respectable mansion now unroofed and in ruins, a favourite residence of the late Sir William Owen, where the venerable baronet lived much.' A few remnants of the old mansion are still to be seen near Clare House farm (now belonging to Mr. Eynon). A good deal of the walling of the old mansion's garden still remain, and traces of fish-ponds on the south side below the landscaped and terraced grounds.

LANDSHIPPING FERRY.

Some fifty yards above the shore, a new mansion was built about 1800 by the Owen family, to replace the older, ruined inland mansion. It is marked on Mudge's Map of 1819. In the parish tithe map of 1840, the ground plan of the house is given, then owned by Sir John Owen.

In 1857 it was advertised for sale, and thus described. 'Beautifully situate on the Banks of the River Cleddy and opposite Picton Castle containing sundry 'Bedrooms, Hall Parlour, Dining and drawing Rooms, Library, Nursery, Servants' Offices, Range of Stabling, Coach House, Saddle Room with Granary over, Yard, Extensive Walled Garden, Orchard, works etc'; nearly five acres in all, in hand of the annual value of £30.

When I visited Ferry in 1974, I found the ruined mansion, its walls well preserved, and all the features still well defined. The house consisted of three storeys, and in the front

were two bow windows which rose to roof height, the main entrance was between them. In the rear part was an extension, and to the rear was a wing still inhabited and in excellent condition. It was then owned by Mr. Leavesley of Worcestershire who proposed to renovate the mansion.

LANDSHIPPING QUAY.

This house stood above the old quay. In the 18th century it was the home of William Thomas (will dated 1713) and Mary, his wife. They had three sons and a daughter, namely William Thomas (d. 1734), Hugh Thomas D. D. Master of Pembroke College, Cambridge (d.1780) and Walter Thomas, mining entrepeneur, who settled at Chester. The daughter Sarah Thomas, married in 1723, Henry Leach, mercer, of St. Mary's Pembroke, from whom descended the Leaches of Corston.

Refs: (for the three houses): Taylors Cussion; Fenton Tour Pembs. 1811; Pembs RO, Deeds SMB/HL/C, Land Tax 1786; NLW. Picton Castle Deeds and Papers, Owen/Colby Deeds, Tithe Map Martletwy Parish 1840; Census Return 1851.

LANGTON. *Manorowen.*

A modern residence built at the beginning of the present century by Mr. J. C. Yorke, J.P. descendants of the Yorkes Earls of Hardwick. He was High Sheriff in 1896 then living temporarily at Trecwn. A large house stands on an eminence near Scleddy. The family ceased to live at Langton after World War II. Later it became a Baptist seminary.

LAWRENNY. *Lawrenny.*

The mansion stood on high ground near the confluence of the rivers Cleddau and Cresswell, above the northern bank of the latter. A short distance away is the parish church, the South Transept of which is called 'The Lawrenny chapel'.

In 1587-88, Wogan of Wiston was lord of the manor of Lawrenny, while the freeholds of the district were in possession of the powerful family of Barlow of Slebech, a cadet of which was seated at Cresswell. The first to own Lawrenny appears to have been William Barlow of Cresswell, High Sheriff in 1612, who died in 1636 and was buried at Lawrenny. His son Lewis Barlow of Cresswell and Lawrenny, was High Sheriff in 1641 and 1668. Lewis's son John Barlow was High Sheriff in 1386, and a John Barlow was High Sheriff in 1705. The last named John Barlow was MP for Haverfordwest, and by his wife Anne daughter of Sir Hugh Owen, 2nd Baronet, of Orielton, had issue. Lewis Barlow was assessed at nine hearths in 1670 which denotes that Lawrenny was then one of the largest mansions in the county.

The last male generation of the Barlows, Hugh Barlow, died without issue in 1763, and his wife, Elizabeth, daughter of Sir Arthur Owen of Orielton lived at Lawrenny till her death in 1788, and was buried with her husband in the parish church. Her sister-in-law, Anne Barlow had married Wyrriot Owen of Great Nash, and it was their son Hugh Owen who succeeded to Lawrenny, and took the surname Barlow.

Anne's youngest sister, Dorothy Barlow married John Lort of Pricaston and their daughter Elizabeth Lort married in 1767 George Phillips, MP., of Haverfordwest, and their descendants ultimately succeeded to Lawrenny, namely the Lort-Phillips family who continue to own it to this day. Tourists of the late 18th and early 19th centuries have much to say about Lawrenny. In 1798 Skrine wrote, 'This place (Lawrenny), much improved by the taste of its present owner, Mr. Barlow, may justly be called the finest in Pembrokeshire, both from its internal decoration and its commanding position at the extremity of a high ridge clothed with thick woods'; Barber, in 1803, says much the same; and Fenton in 1811, notes, 'Lawrenny, the charming seat of Hugh Barlow Esq., MP for Pembroke, where he lives for at least seven months of the year ... He boasts a park well stocked with venison, extensive and well managed hot-houses, and has the command of fish.' The house, though of that unpicturesque species of building peculiar to this country about a century ago, a tall cube, and in its external as to form not much entitled to admiration, yet is within disposed of with much taste and convenience, and is well connected with its offices; and from the breakfasting-room you walk into a neat conservatory well furnished with rare plants.'

On 3 June 1809 a notice read, 'To be let, Lawrenny-Hall (late residence of Hugh Barlow, Esq., deceased)', with, on the ground floor, a spacious dining parlour, drawing room, breakfast parlour communicating by a glass door with a conservatory, a library, commodious kitchen, steward's room, housekeeper's room, servants' hall, cellars, and other offices; on the first floor, four bedchambers with dressing rooms; on the second floor, seven bedchambers with three dressing rooms, and a store-room; in the attic storey, ten bedchambers; also coach-houses, stables, walled gardens, hot houses, pleasure grounds, paddock, park, and demesne lands, in all about 388 acres. In 1840, S. Lewis writes, 'Lawrenny Hall, the ancient seat of the late Hugh Barlow Esq. ... and now a ruin. This fine estate is entailed on the family of Lort-Phillips of Haverfordwest'. The historian, Burke, states in 1858 that the original house 'Has lately been pulled down, and another is in the course of being created by Mr. Phillips in the castellated style'. This was George Lort-Phillips, M.P., whose family had inherited the property. This large towered and turreted mansion, typical of the mid 19th century, known as Lawrenny Castle, remained until 1950 when it was demolished. The family continued to live there and to contribute to public life – J. F. Lort-Phillips was High Sheriff in 1880, Lt. Col. Patrick Lort Phillips in 1954, and David Lort-Phillips in 1983. Mr. David Lort-Phillips, the present owner of the estate, lives at nearby Knowles Farm, a commodious farmstead.

Refs: *Pembs R.O. Plan of Lawrenny Demesne* by John Butcher, 1762, *Land Tax List* 1786, and D/Law/2, plan and design for Lawrenny Castle, 1851-58: C. S.Allen, *Photos*, 1871; Thos Lloyd, *Lost Houses*, 1986, illustr; *Western Telegraph*,7 and 14 March 1984, and 7 July 1985, (illustr); *Contemporary Biographies of S. Wales & Mon* 1907, (illustr). Other refs. are included in the text above.

LECHA. *Llanhowell.*

Near Afon Solfach, just north of Caerforiog, and some two miles from the seaside village of Solfach. Lecha is an interesting old farmstead, home of gentlemen-farmers for many generations, and among its features is a pine-panelled room. In 1562 it formed part of the estate of Parry of Trecadwgan, and in the following century was the home of John Jones (whose father was a younger son of Jones of Brawdy) who lived there from 1625 to 1670. By the end of the 17th century ownership had passed to the Barlows of Slebech. In 1741 George Barlow leased the property to Thomas Barzey of Arnolds Hill, for the lives of his three children, George Barzey, Anne, and Sarah. George Barzey, who kept a pack of hounds at Lecha, died without issue in 1810 aged 71, and was followed by his sister Anne Thomas, the last surviving 'life', in 1820.

Ownership passed to (Sir) William Hamilton, in right of his wife heiress of Slebech, and afterwards to the Hon. Robert Fulke Greville of Castle Hall near Milford, who, on 12 August sold Lecha to Stephen Thomas for £3,700. Stephen died in 1889, aged 74, and was followed by his son, the highly respected Dr. Thomas Nash Thomas (known Locally as 'O Lecha'), and finally to Mr. Elfef Martin of Lochmeyler (a great-grandson of Dr. Thomas's sister) who was the last local owner, but died, alas in 1986, having sold Lecha a few years previously.

Refs: *NLW*, Slebech Deeds, Pembs Plea Rolls and Fines (Great Sessions), Williams and Williams, Haverfordwest, Deeds and Eaton Evans and Williams, Haverfordwest, Deeds; *Anc. Mon. Pembs.*

LEWESTON. *Camrose.*

In the east of the parish, between Wolfsdale and Great Treffgarne Mountain, Leweston consists of a group of farmsteads in close proximity. The name derives from Llewelyn and tun, and is marked on Rees's 14th Century map as Leweleston, a lord's demesne, and is included as Lewelyston in the I.P.M. of the owner, Aymer de Valence, Earl of Pembroke in 1324.

There were four farms here, and in the Land Tax of 1786, Upper Leweston was owned by the owner-occupier Thomas Bowen Barry Esq., and the other three called Lower Leweston were owned by the lord, Thomas Bowen, who lived in one of them. Just before 1797, Joseph Fortune was owner-occupier of one farm. The Tancred family were living at Leweston in 1441, and were there in 1591 when Lewys Owen called to record their ancestry. In 1623 one of the farms was owned by the Prince of Wales who had let it to Sir Thomas Canon, an antiquary from Haverfordwest, and his homestead is described in that year as consisting of three principal rooms on the ground floor, '13 couples, and thatched'.

Later in the century it became a residence of the Bowen family from Haverfordwest, and by 1797 one of the farmsteads was owned by Joseph Fortune from the same town, descended from the early Anakers of the county. It was the seat of his descendants until the death in 1925 of Miss Marianne Fortune at the age of 88, her home described in that year as 'a quaint old 17th century house'. One of the Leweston farms became part of the estate of Jones of Brawdy, and was still owned by Frederick William Jones in 1904.

Refs: Essay by J. R. Poyer Penn in *W.W.H.R.1926*, pp. 1-36, and Francis Green 'The Fortunes of Leweston' on pp. 63-76 of the same volume, *Pembs RO*, Deeds 1669-1728, Land Tax Lists; *NLW, Picton Castle Deeds, Morgan-Richardson Deeds*, and *NLW Journal* 1980, xxi, No. 4.

LITTLE MILFORD. *Freystrop.*

To the north-east of Freystrop Cross, near the western banks of the Cleddau, and three miles south of Haverfordwest. This property formed part of the estate of the Perrots of Haroldston from early times. In 1682 Susanna Perrot of Haroldston, widow, granted a lease of a messuage and garden in Freystrop to John Beavans of Little Milford, Yeoman. This is the first reference found to Little Milford.

In 1722 there are references to John Steward of Little Milford, gent, and his son,

Charles. By 1756 it was the home of Caesar Mathias who was Mayor of Pembroke in 1767, and High Sheriff of the county in 1774. He died in 1795, leaving by his wife Alice daughter of Henry Leach of Pembroke, whom he had married in 1754, a son Henry Mathias, who became a lawyer. Henry afterwards moved to nearby Fernhill, was Mayor of Haverfordwest in 1806, and in 1816 was High Sheriff of the county. During his shrievalty he presented an address from the county to the Prince Regent on the marriage of his daughter, Princess Charlotte, and was knighted. Sir Henry was the last protonotary of the Carmarthen circuit. His wife Katherine was daughter of Philip Jones of Llanina by Katherine Warren of Trewern, Nevern, but they had no issue. Sir Henry died in 1832, aged 75, and Katherine in 1848, aged 83. His first-cousin was the Revd Caesar Morgan of Ely, whose wife, Mrs. Mary Morgan wrote her *Tour to Milford Haven in the year 1791*. In 1907 Little Milford, then comprising 319 acres, was the home of Joseph S. Roberts.

Refs: Hampton Deeds (Pakington); *NLW*, Corston Deeds; *Contemporary Biographies of S. Wales and Mon*, 1907, p. 102, illustr.

LINNEY. *Castlemartin.*

Near the coast at the south-western end of the Castlemartin promontary, just south of Linney Burrows, and overlooking the inlet called Black's Cove. Marked as a knight's fee on Rees' 14th century map; as Linney house on George Owen's map, 1603 as residence of 'Row Esq' on the maps of Bowen (1760) and Kitchin (1763). Fenton wrote in 1811, 'Nearer the sea is Linney, an old mansion, formerly the property and residence of the Rows, a family of middling fortune.' It became property of the Lorts, and in 1631 the owner was George Lort of Linney, gent. In 1670 John Leach was assessed at five Hearth taxes for Linney, and his will was proved in 1675. The next was Richard Row, gent, who married Elizabeth Meare. He was High Sheriff of the county in 1729, and died before 1735. His wife died in 1750. They had two children, Francis Row, living at Linney in

1741, who died without issue, and Alice who married in 1721 James Bowen of Llwyn-gwair, and had issue.

The property was afterwards leased to George Phelps, gent., who was there in 1787 (the owner being John Campbell Esq), and was followed by his only son John Phelps who had inherited 10 leaseholds and was living at Linney in 1804. Thomas Jones, gent, lived there in 1834. George Roch, farmer, was at Linney in 1851, and James Roch in 1904.

Refs: *NLW*, Morgan-Richardson Deeds, Eaton Evans and Williams Deeds; Fenton, *Tour Pembs* 1811; *R.G.C. Pembs* 1925.

LOCHMEILIR. *Llandeloy.*

About a mile west of Llandeloy village, and bordered by the farms of Trenichol, Rhos-grannog, Trevanner, and Treiva. Once the residence of landowning families, it is now an ancient commodious farmstead with a ground storey and upper storeys, with attractive dormer windows in the roof, which once formed part of the old residence. It is said to have been named after one Meilir, claiming descent from Bleddyn ap Cynfyn, Prince of Powys. Fenton wrote, '… Llech Meylir, built by a chieftain of the name Meylir of the house of Blethyn ap Cynfyn, who, joining some of the auxiliary armies from Powys, settled in this county and laid the foundation of a family of some consequence of the name of Bowen, whose sole heiress, Catherine, married John Scourfield, Esq, of New Moat, the property of whose descendant, Henry Scourfeld Esq., it now is.'

Meylir's descendants, nine generations of whom lived at Lochmeyler, took the permanent name of Bowen, were there from the 13th century and also owned Robleston Hall in Camrose parish. The last male of the family, Richard Bowen, died in 1564, leaving a daughter and heiress Catherine Bowen who was 24 weeks old when her father died. Margaret mother of Catherine, then married Jenkin Reed of Carmarthen by whom she had 5 sons, and according to a contemporary manuscript 'he had also eightie base children ...' Catherine brought Lochmeyler to her husband, John Scourfield of New Moat, High Sheriff in 1600. She died in 1607, and thereafter Lochmeyler was owned by her descendants, the Scourfields, until 1875 when it was sold by Sir Owen Scourfield to the then tenant Mrs. Harries, who, in 1915 sold it to her son-in-law Mr. Perry Martin, who was succeeded by his son Mr. Elfet Martin, MBE, JP who died in 1986. His widow remained at Lochmeyler. The owners of Lochmeyler enjoyed the privilege of being buried within the church of Llandeloy. In the 19th century the family of Harries, devout Congregationalists, held a lease of the old house, where they used to meet, and in 1838 the historian Dr. Thomas Nicholas preached several sermons there.

The Scourfields continued to live at their original residence, and leased Lochmeyler to responsible tenants. In the 18th century the family of James held it for three generations. On the death of Dr. Richard James in 1771, the property passed to his sister Bridget, surviving lessee. She had married in 1767 the Revd John Mathias, JP, vicar of St. Lawrence, and Lochmeyler passed to him, which he held till his death in 1805. His son, Richard moved to Castle Cenlas, and while there, his daughter, Letitia Mathias, eloped with the Revd James Jones, vicar of Mathry. Meanwhile, Lochmeyler, had been leased to William Harries, a son of near-by Trenichol. Afterwards it became the property of the Martins as mentioned above.

Refs: *Owen Her. vis*, i, 116: *WWHR, XI*, Francis Green 'Bowen of Lochmeyler,' and *WWHR IX*, Francis Green, 'Scourfield of New Moat'; Francis Jones 'Castle Villa' in *Pembrokeshire Historian*, 1981: PRO *Star Chamber Proceedings*: College of Arms, Wagner MS 2: Pembs RO, Land Tax Lists, NLW, Peniarth MS 156, Haverfordwest Deeds, Lucas Deeds, Parish Tithe Map, Llandeloy 1845.

LOCHTURFFIN. *Mathry.*

A large square Georgian building, with a pillared porch entrance leading to a hall, drawing and dining rooms, and inner hall, sitting room, and kitchen on the upper floor; seven bedrooms: from the kitchen there is access to an attached building which was the original farmhouse, containing a hall, dining room, kitchen, an inner hall, and a sitting room, and on the upper floor four bedrooms. Lochturffin stands in grounds with protecting trees, between Castle Cenlas and Treffynnon. From early times, Lochturffin comprised two farms, both farmsteads being on the site of the present building, one of them being attached to the main part. Among the properties forming part of the Lochmeyler estate when the owner, Richard ap Owen, died in 1563, was a tenement and 20 acres in Loughtyrphyn. There were two farms there, one owned by the Scourfields of New Moat, the other by the Owens of Orielton.

In modern days they were combined to make one property. From 1610 to 1727 one of the farms was leased to a local yeoman family named Owen. When widow Owen died in 1727 her son, Henry Owen, 'gave up his bargain, upon which it was rented to Mr. Richard James of Lochmeyler at a rent of four pounds a year'. Richard James died in 1756 and was followed by his son Dr. Richard James who died without issue in 1777 leaving the lease of Lochturffin to his brother-in-law, the Revd John Mathias (died 1805). The other farm was leased by Henry Scourfield to Henry Warlow who died there in 1764, and followed by his son Arthur Warlow.

In 1780 Henry John of Caerwen bought Lochturffin from Hugh Owen of Orielton, and settled there, and thereafter the property remained with his descendants, one of whom, Mary John, married the Baptist Minister, the Revd T. E. Thomas of Trehale, whose son Henry John Thomas lived at Lochturffin when he died in 1893, and is now home of his grand-daughter Mrs. Mary Price (née Thomas), who in 1987 advertised the mansion, grounds, and 21 acres for sale.

Refs: *NLW*, Lochturffin Deeds, Scourfield Deeds, Lucas Deeds, Trenewydd (Pancaer) Deeds, Pembs Plea Rolls; *Pembs RO, LT 1786; G. H Warlow, History of the Warlow Family*, 1926.

LOCHVANE (LOCHFAEN). *Brawdy*.

A farmstead lying in a small vale near the coast, between Pointz Castle and St. Elvis. In early times it had been an episcopal manor belonging to the See of St. Davids. By 1326 it had been amalgamated with the manor of Brawdy, and in 1652 it is recorded that 'the manors of Broodye, Pointz Castle, and Langvoyne' belonged to the Bishop of St. Davids, and much later, in 1861, 'manors of Brawdy, Pointz Castle, and Lloughvane' appears in the episcopal records. By 1613 there were two farmsteads (messuages) at Lochvane. In 1786 one of these farms was owned by John Jones of Brawdy, Esq, with George Howell as tenant, and the other owned by Miss Anne Jones of Llether, with widow Berry as tenant, and 1845 one farm (25 acres) was owned by Benjamin James, the other (95 acres) by George Roch of Llether, with Thomas Beynon as tenant. A descendant of the George Howell of 1786, lives at Newport, Mon, and possesses several

photographs of the old farmhouses and outbuildings (modernised).

Refs: *Black Book of St. Davids 1326: WWHR iii*, 134-5; Francis Jones 'Episcopal Manors of Dewsland' in *Journal Hist. Soc. of Church in Wales*, 1967, No. 22, p. 9 et seq.; *NLW, Slebech Deeds, Pembs Plea Rolls, Tithe Map of Brawdy 1845; Pembs RO, Land Tax List 1786.*

LONGHOOK. *Castlebythe*.

Called Lanwg locally. A farmstead to the south-west of Castlebythe, and separated from the farm of Martel by Afon Anghof. In the 16th century the home of minor gentry families, and afterwards of well-to-do yeomen. The property formed part of the estate of Perrott of Haroldston. In 1625 Sir James Perrott of Haroldston granted (by way of exchange) lands in Upper and Lower Longhook to Margaret Symyns, widow, and John Symyns, gent, both of Martel. These properties are marked on Colby's map of 1831 as Longhook -fawr and -fach.

In 1677 Sir Herbert Perrott granted a lease for 21 years to Thomas Harding of Castlebythe, yeoman, and in 1691 Heather Perrott of Haroldston, spinster, granted a further lease of Longhook and other lands, for 31 years. Longhook was later sold to William Knox of Llanstinian, Esq, and in 1786 he owned both Great and Little Longhook, the former being tenanted by William Myles, the latter by John Thomas. Later, and in 1831 Great Longhook was owned by Hugh Owen Owen, Esq, then of Llanstinan, who leased it to George Miles, farmer, for lives.

Refs: *B. M. Egerton MS 2586; College of Arms, Wagner 71152; Pembs RO*, Deeds; muniments of Lord Hampton, descendant of the Perrotts.

LONGHOUSE. *Mathry*.

A large farm on a headland on the Dewsland coast, between Abercastell and Trevine. The lands of Longhouse lie on the border in Mathry and Llanrhian parishes, the farmhouse being in the former. It formed part of the possessions of successive bishops of St. Davids, and was a grange of importance. Longhouse was situated in the manor of

Trevine which was also owned by the bishops. A survey of the episcopal estates in 1660 states: 'Trevine is a mesne Lordship and therein is a Tenement and lands called Longhouse with the lands called Henllys, being a large ancient house, and the lands appear very good, all worth the sum of £35 per annum, and out of lease in August last 1660. The old tenant is Henry Garnons, the ancient reserved rent is £4.13. 4 which the said Garnons paid and is confirmed in possession.' The charitable attitude of the bishop is shown by a transaction in 1776 when the tithe, corn and grain of Trevine and Longhouse were conveyed to trustees to be used to help poor widows of Mathry parish.

Manorial court roles from 1824 onwards show that a mayor was annually elected for Trevine. Manorial courts were still held in 1896. Longhouse continued to be let on leases. It consisted of 357 acres in 1817, two of fields near the house being Park Maenllwyd and Park Fagwr Hên. The leaseholders from 1695 was the Thomas family, who continued at Longhouse till the death of John William Thomas without issue in 1854. His niece, Ellen Anne Marychurch married H. P. Griffiths, who stayed at Longhouse for a short time before moving to Llanstinan. Then David Perkins of Pwllcawrog settled there, where he was followed by his son Norman, High Sheriff in 1955, and by his grandson Peter who became High Sheriff in 1966.

Refs: *Pembs R.O., Land Tax List 1786; Black Book of St. Davids* (1326); *NLW, Records of the Church in Wales, Bishop's Surveys of 1660 and 1815, Title maps 1842, Trenwydd* (Pencaer) Deeds; Francis Jones, 'The Episcopal Manor of Trevine' in the *Journal of the Hist. Soc. of the Church in Wales*, 1967, No 22, pp 31-35.

LONGRIDGE. *Bletherston*

A large double-pile house, with a wing extending to the rear, on a slope near the confluence of Afon Syfynwy and the Eastern Cleddau. Now a well-maintained farmstead. The name is topographical, 'long ridge', on which the mansion is situated. From medieval times onward Longridge formed part of the temporalities of successive Bishops of St. Davids who leased the property to various gentry and yeomen. In 1292 the Bishop's stud (*equaria*) was kept there. A survey of the episcopal temporalities made about 1660, states: 'Longridge Farm in the Baronry of Llawhaden is a Fair Tenement and dwelling with about 700 acres of land there, in possession of Griffith Twining, gent, undertenant to ye Michels of Harescombe near Gloucester, for 3 lives, in being, and Lawhadden mills for the same lives'. After Griffith Twining came Joseph Twining who was there in 1688 when he was granted a lease for 3 lives of 'The Grange of the Lordship of Llawhadden called Llangrige'. He was followed by John Twining, living there in 1692. The Skyrmes were next at Longridge.

In 1728 John Warren of Trewern married Dorothy Scourfield of Moat; she had previously married William Skyrme of Longridge, and when John Warren died in 1743, she then returned to Longridge. Their son, William Warren married his cousin Jane Skyrme. He died in 1757 and his extensive estates were shared among his four daughters, co-heiresses. Catherine Warren who had married Philip Jones of Llanina (Cards) in 1758, held the lease of Longridge for some years. It afterwards passed to her sister Jane who, in 1773, married Sir Basil Keith, Governor of Jamaica, and in 1786, described in the Hearth Tax List as owner with Benjamin Evans, tenant.

The Terrier of the estate of the Bishop of St. Davids compiled in 1817 shows that he still owned Longridge and adjacent 35 fields comprising 466 acres. The topographer Lewis writing in 1834 and 1840 states that in Bletherston parish is 'an estate called Longridge which belongs to the Bishop of St. Davids'. After this leases were granted to successive farmers.

Refs: *Black Book of St. Davids 1326*; NLW, *Records of the Church in Wales*, Olven and Colby Deeds, Poyston Deeds, F. Green Deeds, Pembs Plea Rolls; Owen's Pembs, vol. 1.; *B. M. Egerton MS 2586: Pembs RO, Deeds (RTP)*; Francis Jones, 'Warrens of Trewern', in *Pembs Historian 1974*.

LOVESTON. *St. Twynells*.

Now a double-pile farmstead about half a mile south of St. Twynells church; to the east is Merrion, to the west is Sampson Cross. For some two centuries home of gentry families. In 1545 Thomas Watkin lived there. By his wife Joan Adams of Paterchurch, he had two daughters, co-heiresses – Elizabeth, married Thomas Adams who was of Loveston, *iure uxoris*, and died before 1562, leaving a son John Adams who lived at Loveston till his death in 1605, leaving a son Thomas who presented a paten to the parish church in 1611, and died in 1626; the other co-heiress, Margaret, married in 1545 Griffith White of Henllan, who died in 1590 leaving a son, Thomas White of Loveston in 1604.

The Whites continued at Loveston, and in 1680 Mary White, widow, paid five hearth taxes, which shows that the house was a commodious structure. The Leach family then came there. Henry Leach (1700-1787) was followed by his son Abraham Leach of Loveston, who bought Corston which became the family's chief residence. Loveston afterwards was let to farming tenants.

Refs: *B. M. Egerton MS 2586; Pembs RO, Land Tax hist 1786; J. T. Evans, Church Plate of Pembrokeshire, 1905.*

LLANDDINOG. *Llandeloy*.

Now a farmhouse standing between Hendre and Caerwen, and to the south of Afon Sol-fach, marked on Rees' 14th century map as Landenank and on Colby's 1831 map as Llandonoch. An interesting commodious old farmhouse, the interior was modernised during the late 1970's, but the exterior is largely unchanged. It was from medieval times a lay manor held of the Bishop of St. Davids as chief Lord of this fee. In 1347 it was held by a local landowner, Philip Cadigan, senior. The manor of Llanddinog was acquired by the Barlows of Slebech, and when it was held by John Barlow in 1613, the manor comprised the following properties – the capital messuage of Llanddinog, a corn mill (Felin Wen), and 21 acres in Hendre Issa, 18 acres in Tyreaberthe and a messuage in Magwr Walter,

both in Whitchurch parish; 2 tenements in Lochfaen and a tenement in Prenscawen, all in Brawdy parish, and two tenements in Croftufty (Whitchurch parish) and Mechelych (St. Davids parish); and the services of certain properties held in Llanddinog manor by knight's service in the parishes of Llandeloy, Whitchurch, St. Davids, Brawdy, Llanrhian, Mathry, St. Lawrence and Llanhowel. Thus, its manorial jurisprudence was extensive. The manor was occasionally united with that of Trecadwgan. In 1629 Griffith Hawkwell of St. Kennox was Seneschall of the manors of Trecadwgan and Llanddinog.

The lords of the manor of Llanddinog continued to be the Barlows of Slebech, and in 1705 the manor and farm of Llanddinog formed part of their estate. In 1715 the farm and the mill was owned by James Harries of Haverfordwest (son of John Harries of Porthiddy) who died in 1719, leaving the properties to his younger brother Dr. George Harries whose eldest daughter Jane Harries inherited and left the properties to her nephew George Harries Griffiths, who died without issue, and the properties passed to the kinsman Dr. George Phillips MD of Haverfordwest in fee simple. Dr. Phillips is described in 1786 as owner of Llanddinog and its mill, with Thomas David (Davies) as tenant. The Davies' remained there for generations, and after them a series of farmers lived there. The manorial rights had long lapsed.

In 1842 George Lort Philips sold Llanddinog and the mill, with it to Thomas John of Carwen for £3225, who later experienced difficulties, and in 1855 granted the property to his creditors. Some local traditions state that – the first issues of the *Pembrokshire Guardian*, then called the *Dewsland and Kemes Gazette*, were printed at Llanddinog before the editor, John Williams, opened offices at Solva; a French emigré Count lived for a time at Llanddinog, and a letter from the Vicar of Llanddinog inviting him to dinner is extant; remains of a building, said to have been a church, were over a field still called 'Wyrglodd y Fynwent,' opposite the farmhouse; and a stone with an incised cross and an inscription, is said to have been a jamb in the gate.

Refs: *W.W.H.R.iii*, 134–6; *RCAM. Pembs.* 1925; Francis Jones on Lay Manors of the Bishopric in *Historical journal of the Church in Wales*, 1969; *NLW, Eaton Evans and Williams Deeds, Williams and Williams (H-west) Deeds*, Court Rolls of the manor of Llanddinog among *Frances Green Deeds*, Poyston Deeds, tithe *map; Pembs RO, land tax 1786; Black Book of St. Davids 1326*.

LLANDIGIGE FACH. *St. Davids.*
Llandigige (fawr) and -Fach, two farmsteads near each other, lying between Berea on the north and Carnedrin Uchaf on the south, marked on Colby's map 1831. In 1326, Daykin and his co-tenants held at Llanegige Vechan three borates of land and paid yearly 3s, and 'suit at the Lord's mill'. Llandigige Fach was owned by John Warlow of Newgate in 1612, a minor gentry family. His son Thomas Warlow of Newgate married Jane daughter of William Jones of Brawdy, and their son John Warlow settled at Llandigige Fach and was living there in 1634. Six generations of Warlows lived there until the early part of the 18th century when Landigige Fach was alienated. The property was then divided into two farms. In 1786 one of the farms was owned by the Widow Nash, with John Warlow (died 1816) as tenant. His brother Henry Warlow died unmarried in 1767; and the other farm was owned by John Parry, gent, with Henry Phillip as tenant. Later it became a unified farm again and thereafter was home of farming tenants.

The last Warlow, the widow Mrs. Mary Warlow (née Martin) died in 1824 leaving Llandigige Fach and Carnedrin to her friend James Froport of St. Davids. Henry Evans was occupier in 1894.

Refs: *Black Book of St. Davids 1326*, p. 104; pedigree of the Warlows (*penes me*)

LLANDIGIGE (FAWR). *St. Davids.*
Location as in preceding entry. The addition *fawr* was discontinued, and the property was usually described as Llandigige. Few references have been found to this place. In 1326 Philip Vaughan, David ap Meilier and their co-tenants held a carucate of land at Llandigige free of rent, from the bishop of St. Davids. In 1559 John Walter is described as of Llandigige. In 1612 Lewis Lloyd of Llandigige Fawr, gent, granted lands in the parishes of St. Davids and Llanhowel, to Thomas Lloyd of Kilkiffeth, Esq. John Harries of Llandigige, Esq., was a J.P and a grand Juror in 1756 and 1767; and in 1786 was the residence of George Harries, Esq with Sir William Williams as tenant. Williams was born in 1755, and in 1782 married Mary Miller and in 1809 – 1824 was described as Esq. and J.P. He died in 1835, and was followed there by his son John Williams who married Jane Makeig of Park y Pratt near Cardigan. He died in 1866, and his wife in 1872. None of their 21 children remained at Llandigige. Daniel Walters was living at Llandigige fawr in 1894

Refs: *Black Book of St. Davids 1325, NLW, Owen of Orielton Deeds, Plea Rolls Pembs. 1612.*

LLANDEILO. *Llandeilo.*
Called Llandeilo Llwydiarth in early days, but earlier in the middle ages Llandeilo, and from about 1750 the farmstead near the old parish church ruin was known as Llandeilo Fach. There were two farms in 1786, both called Llandeilo, and in the Voters' Lists for 1894 and 1904 they were designated Llan-

deilo Uchaf (standing first north of the Llan-golman – Maenclochog road) and Llandeilo Isaf (near the church ruin, the oldest farm-stead in the parish. It stands to the east of Maenclochog, a little south of the ruined church in the farm of Blaenllwydiarth, one of the names applied to the parish in early times.

The parish comprises some 1171 acres, and slopes northward to include the highest point in the Preseli range, namely Moel Carn Cer-wyn. A famous well continues to bubble near the old church; Carlisle, in 1811, calls it 'a fine spring which the credulous still believe will cure coughs when the water is drunk out of the skull of St. Teilo, which is carefully kept clean and shining on the shelf of a farm home just by the well', and Thornhill Tim-mins writes in 1895, 'This curious relic was formerly held in high esteem as a cure for all manner of sickness, water being drawn from the saint's well, and drunk out of the skull .

The virtue of the draught was supposed to consist of its being administered by the eldest son of the house of Melchior, then, as now, the hereditary custodian of St. Teilo's skull.'

The livings of Llandeilo, Llangolman, and Maenclochog, were granted by David de Rupe son and heir of Gilbert de Rupe, to the Abbey of St. Dogmaels. The grant had been made without Royal Licence, but on 30 October 1320, the Abbot received a royal pardon for this omission. Llandeilo later became a lay manor, but in 1898 no emolu-ments were derived from it, and the manor-ial courts discontinued. The parish was united to Maenclochog by Order in Council 11 July 1877. Some ruins of the old church are still to be seen near the farmstead. The earliest-known family there was that of Cadigan who remained till early in the 17th century. Its successor was the Griffith family. Griffith ap Thomas (died c. 1649-52) had some remark-ably enterprising sons who left the old home – John Griffith of London, in 1642 became Treasurer and Solicitor to Thomas Howard, Earl of Arundel who became Earl Marshal in 1646; William Griffith, Groom of His Majesty's Chamber in 1642; Thomas Griffith, ancient of a Company in Ireland in that year, while

another brother Maurice Griffith, *agricola*, stayed at home, and was executor of his father's estate in 1652.

The next family there was that of Melchior, one of whom had married a daughter of Cadigan of Llandeilo in Elizabethan times. The Melchiors, a Welsh family, came from Newport, the first of this unusual name being Melchior ap Ienan ap Howel ap Gwallter, who died on 3 April 1591 and was buried in Newport church on Easter Day. His sons adopted their father's Christian name as their permanent surname. The Melchiors contin-ued to farm Llandeilo until well on in this century. Although they were custodians of St. Teilo's skull, they nevertheless sold the holy relic in 1927, for £50 it's said. In 1950 the Cheetham family lived there.

Refs: *NLW, Bronwydd Deeds, Poyston Deeds, Pembs Plea Rolls; Pembs RO, Land Tax 1786, Voters Lists; Carms RO, Golden Grove MSS, B. M. Egerton MS 2586, C of A MSS, Proth. v,* xii; *Arch Cam* 1889 v, vi 1893; *Bacon, Liber Regis; R Comm on Land in Wales; Lloyd Williams, Craydro Sir Benfro; Carlisle, TDW,* 1811; *Thornhill Timmins, Nooks and Corners of Pembs, 1895.*

LLANDRE. *Llanycefn.*

Not to be confused with nearby Llandre, Egremont, Carmarthenshire. A residence to the west of the village of Lanycefn, near the road leading to Maenclochog. Home of the Twyning family from the late 17th century. Daniel Twyning married Anne Philipps of Southfield, and his son Griffith Twyning of Llandre married Elizabeth Griffith co-heiress of Bjax Griffith of the ancient house of Peny-benglog. Five generations continued to live at Llandre, until William Henry Twyning sold his Llanycefn properties. His sons left Llandre – John Poyer Twyning, William Henry Twyning; James Hamilton Twyning who settled at Evesham as an ironmonger, and Charles Stephen Twyning of Haverford-west, a master mariner, drowned in 1847. In 1786, Thomas Owen, gent, was the owner-occupier, and thereafter it was occupied by several persons.

Refs: Pembs RO, LT 1786, Voters Lists; NLW, Llidiar-dau Deeds.

LLANEY. *Llanreithan*

A large farmstead to the south-east of Croesgoch, and alongside the road to Llanreithan church. The name has been rendered in different ways, but today the local pronunciation is Llan-ey. Home of yeoman families. In 1326 the name is rendered as Llandener, where David Vachan, John ap Henry, and their co-owners lived, holding one carucate of land. In 1459 the seal of David ap David Lloid ap Gwilym de Llandenoe, to a deed of that date, showed a stag. In 1672 John Thomas of Llandenay,gent, served as a juror in Great Sessions; in 1688 William Propert of Llandeney, gent, lived there; in 1786 Llandeny was owned by Samuel Harris Esq., and occupied by John Vaughan. On Colby's Map 1831 it is marked Llandenoi, and in 1838 Llandenoy Farm was owned by Mary Harries, with Captain Hugh Harries, occupier. By 1894 William Williams held the land and tenement of Llanhoy, and in 1950 Margaret and Clifford Thomas lived at Llannoy, who were very kind to me when I called there.

Refs: *Black Book St. Dds, 1326; NLW, Eaton Evans and Williams Deeds, Tithe Schedule of Llanreithan parish 1838.*

LLANGLOFFAN. *Granston.*

Two farmsteads stood here from early days. It is not clear whether part, or whole, of Llangloffan once formed part of a lay manor. In 1587-8 'Stanguaveth alias Llangloffan' was owned by John Wogan, who in that year 'discontinued [the courts] the west part of the town and not the rest'. In 1585 William Griffith was plaintiff in an action with David Rees and his wife Margaret, concerning a messuage and 131 acres in Llangloffan -vawer and -vach. William Jones, and Thomas Lloyd, Esq, were concerned with three messuages, one toft, and 192 acres in Llangloffan -vawr and -vechan. Jenkin Llwyn was plaintiff, and Thomas Lloyd and his wife Charity, defendants, respecting the manors of Jordanston and Stangenavied, and messuages and lands in Llangloffan. Part of the property was later owned by William Tucker of Sealyham, who, in 1666, granted a messuage and lands in Llangloffan to John Owen gent, of Henllan Owen near Eglwyswrw, for £100. The Land Tax of 1786 records Llangloffan Uchaf as being owned by Gwyn Vaughan, Esq, with John Harries tenant, and Langloffan Ishaf owned by William Jones Esq, with David Roberts, tenant. The terms uchaf and ishaf are still used to distinguish the two farms there.

The place is now well-known for its Baptist chapel. During the latter half of the 19th century William Didwith farmed Llangloffan Isha. His name was known in medieval times, and in 1326 Henry Dedewith was a juror of the neighbouring manor of Castlemorris. William Didwith died leaving three daughters only, and the old surname became extinct.

Refs: *NLW, Papers of Great Sessions, Fines; Black Book St. Dds, 1326;* Francis Jones, Lay Manors, in Journal Hist. Soc. of Church in Wales, 1970; *South West Wales, Guide.* by Vywyan Rees, 1986 (*illustr.* Llangloffan farm).

LLANGOLMAN. *Llangolman.*

The parish is on high land of the Preseli, bounded on the north by Mynachlogddu, on the south by Rhydwilym. The farmstead of Llangolman is a short distance south of the parish church. In 1960 the dwelling was described as having a manorial aspect, 'ty-byw manoraidd yr olwg'. The Lewis and Griffith families were among the oldest in the parish. In 1638 Evan John Griffith, gent, served as a juror in Great Sessions.

In 1721 Stephen Lewis was High Sheriff of the county; he married Miss Griffith of Glanrhyd, Cilynaenllwyd, but died without issue. A book-plate of the Revd Maurice Griffith (1721-98) seventh son of Evan Griffith of Llangolman, shows the following arms: *gules a lion rampant regardant argent*, with crest, *on a ducal crown a griffin segreant argent*. In 1786-88 Stephen Griffith of Llangolman is described as a J.P. Stephen Griffith was owner-occupier of Llangolman farm in 1786, also owning Dyffryn Ffullbrook, Rosser's hand, and Troedyrhiw.

In 1805 an inquest was held in the home of Stephen Griffith, before a coroner and jury, respecting the death of Mr. John Griffith, when it was recorded that deceased was found drowned in a pond called Llyn ucha in Llangolman parish. Later the farmstead had a series of occupiers – in 1894-1904 Daniel John, in the 1930s James John who bred black cattle, was an accomplished leader of the local choir which won a prize in the Fishguard National Eisteddfod in 1936. After the Second World War a Pole, Capt. Michalski farmed there with his son Ioan Glyndwr Michalski.

Refs: *NLW, Pembs G. S.; Carms R.O Golden Grove MS (Gwynfardd); Llwyd Williams, Crwydro Sir Benfro,* 1960.

LLANGWARRAN. *Jordanston.*

A mansion within a spinney on a slope above a stream, one mile to the south-east of the parish church. The property was once divided into two messuages, Llangwarran -Fawr and -Fychan, owned in 1543 by Griffith ap Hugh Broughton who bore the arms: *sable a chevron between three owls argent.* The property was sold to the Lloyds of Llanstinan. Llewelyn Lloyd of Llanstinan died in 1588, and Llangwarran passed to his daughter and co-heiress Jane Lloyd. She married, firstly, John Scourfield of Castle Villa, and secondly, Thomas Mathias of Glastir, Nevern. He was eldest son and heir of Mathias Thomas (d. 1588) descended from the ancient family of Young who were at Glastir in the middle ages. Thomas Mathias (born c. 1570) bore the arms of his Young ancestors, namely: *argent a stag trippant gules between three fleurs-de-lys or.*

After his marriage he settled at Llangwarran. Jane died leaving two daughters, and

then Thomas married, secondly, Ursula, daughter of the famous antiquary George Owen of Henllys, Lord of Cemaes, by Elizabeth Philipps of Picton Castle. Thomas Mathias died in 1617 and was buried in the chancel of Jordanston church where he is commemorated by a stone bearing his paternal arms impaling those of Owen and Philipps. His funeral expenses came to £530. By Ursula, he had an only son and heir, John Mathias, who was followed at Llangwarran by 11 generations of his descendants.

The family took a leading part in public life, serving as Justices of the Peace, Deputy Lieutenants, militia officers, they also produced an Eschaetor for Pembrokeshire, a Steward of the Lordship of Dewsland, and eight High Sheriffs of the County. During the Civil War John Mathias was a Roundhead, and towards the end of the century Lewis Mathias was an active Jacobite; during the 18th century the family supported the Methodists and Howell Harris held services in the hall of Llangwarran. Several of the family helped the Moravians and one, David Mathias, became a worthy minister of that denomination. Several entered the armed services, and towards the end of the century, Colonel Henry Mathias, C.B. led the famous charge of the Gordon Highlanders on the heights of Dargai. For some years the mansion was in the hands of strangers, when in 1811 Lewis Mathias granted a lease for lives of Llangwarran to S. M. Phelps, who made improvements to the mansion which in due course reverted to the Mathiases.

In 1810-11 Charles Mathias bought Lamphey Court, and in 1823 commenced to build a new mansion there, which continued with his descendants until a few years ago, when it was sold. After the family returned to Llangwarran, Charles Mathias in the 1880s made extensive alterations and improvements to the ancient home. The last of the male line at Llangwarran was Charles A. S. Mathias, J.P. on whose death the estate passed to his only child and heir, Miss Leslie Mathias who married Mr. John Lloyd-Phillipps a younger son of Dale Castle. He predeceased his wife, and when she died in 1985, Llangwarran passed to her two daughters, who in 1987 advertised for sale the mansion, which the family had owned for nigh on four centuries. Among the Mathias muniments is a drawing of the original mansion made in 1813 by John Tambyn of Haverfordwest, before any extensions and changes were effected.

Refs: *Dwnn*, i, 162, 243 *W.W.H.R.*, ii, 41, *Pembrokeshire Archaeological Survey; Laws, Little England*, 359; *Charles George Owen of Henllys*, 31, 53; *Pembs R.O. Llangwarran Deeds; Cardiff Public Library Deeds; Carms RO, GGMSS; Dale Castle Pedigrees; Manorowen Pedigree MS; College of Arms, Wagner MS No. 3; NLW, Pembs Papers of GS, Colesman Deeds, Tithe Maps 1843.*

LLANION. *St. Mary Pembroke.*

The former residence stood to the north of Pembroke and to the north-east of Pembroke Dock, near Biers Pool farm, and the inlet on the nearby coast called Lanion Pill. An early medieval Welsh manuscript records that at 'Llonyon yn Penvro' beehives and swarms of bees were kept, giving rise to the proverb 'o heid Llonyon'. Another manuscript compiled in 1600-19, mentions the family of Bennet, the last of whom was Hugh, 'There were diverse knightes, as is said, of the Benetts, and their mansion howse was now a decaied howse at Munston, and they were lords of Mirian, Bernards pools in Landian alias Laniell (Lanion) iuxta Pembrook, and in diverse other places in Pembrokeshire'.

The last of the Benetts had three daughters and heiresses: 'the one married James ap Eynon of Kenerth, of whom Mores ap Owen is descended and inherited about 50 pound rent by that descent; the other married Bowen of Roblinston who hath the manor of Llanien; and Lutterell is heire to another daughter, and all three have lands in Merriam'.

For some years Llanion formed part of the estate of the Meares family. George Meares gent was at Llanion in 1665 and five years later was assessed at four hearths. Edward Byam, an Antiguan merchant, finally settled at Llanion where he died in 1768 and was buried in the parish church. His son and heir William moved to Sunny Hill near Manorbier.

The Holcombe family occupied Llanion for a few years in the period 1751-63. It then passed to the well-known family of Meyrick who lived there occasionally. In 1786 J. F. Meyrick, Esq., is described as owner-occupier of Lanion, and the land let to Thomas Kinaston. However, by the first decade of the next century it had fallen into decay. Fenton informs us in 1811. 'Lanion, a seat of John Meyrick Esq., till of late years almost constantly inhabited by a succession of different tenants, temporary residents in the county, but now unroofed and suffered to fall into decay, as Bush, his principal family residence lies so near in a situation much more commanding than the other, though in some respects inferior in point of beauty'. Rees, writing in 1815 describes it as 'now in ruins'.

In 1905 the authoress Mrs. Stuart Peters wrote, 'to the east of Bierspool may be seen the ruined walls of Llanion House, the original country seat of the Meyrick family. Lord Nelson was sometimes a guest at this old house, and it is said that once or twice he was accompanied there by Lady Hamilton.'

On June 5 1846 an uncoffined skeleton was dug up in Llanion Park (now a cricket field).'

Refs: *Myfyrian Archaeology*, 398.b,56; *NLW MS 1602D*, fo 171; *Fenton, Tour Pembs*, 1811; *Rees, Beauties of South Wales*, 1815; *Stuart Peters, History of Pembroke Dock, 1905.*

LLANMARLAIS. *Lampeter Velfrey.*

Marked on Colby's Map 1831, on the eastern bank of Afon Marlais. A memorial in St. Clears parish church to the memory of Mr. John Evans of Llanmarlais in Pembrokeshire states that he married Mrs. Elizabeth Philipps of the House of Llwyn y Crwn, by whom he had surviving issue, three sons and two daughters who had been left motherless at a very helpless age: he died on 1 May 1734, aged 71: the memorial was set up at the sole expense of his son-in-law, Mr. Roger Jones of Laugharne. In the Land Tax List of 1786, Gwynne Vaughan Esq (of Jordanston in Dewsland) was the owner, and John Hall, tenant.

LLANNERCH (Y BLEIDDIE). *Newport.*

Formerly a mansion, now a farmstead, standing in the upper valley of the Gwaun, overlooking a romantic glade at the foot of the northern slope of Carn Ingli. In George Owen's MS *circa* 1600, is a list of houses in 'Leppe, lowe, and close placis', among which is 'Llannercybleidde house'. The name meant 'Glade of the Wolves' but later it became Llannerch only.

The old mansion stood close to the side of the present farmhouse, and together with the outhouses, is said to incorporate some of the mansion. Few traces of the older building remain, but over the doorway of an outhouse is a massive stone with a chamfered lintel. Mr. Vaughan, the owner-occupier, told me that there was a tradition that a church had also stood there, probably the private chapel of the former owners, and that there had been a flight of stairs leading downwards to a room or crypt.

The original gentry family there was that of Bowen descended from Llewellyn y Coed (living 1369) ap Owen (living 1342) 7th in descent from the princeling Gwynfardd Dyfed. The grandson of Llewellyn y Coed, Owen, settled at Llannerch y bleiddie, and was followed there by seven successive generations of his descendants, the last of the family, Owen Bowen (living 1614) had been a ward of George Owen of Henllys. Owen was said to have wasted his inheritance (*omnia devastavit*) and had to depart from his home. After his day, Llannerch was occupied by a series of yeomen farmers. The arms borne by the Bowens were: *azure a lion rampant or, and in chief three roses argent,* based on the arms of Gwynfardd.

Refs: *L. Owen,* vol. i, pp. 34 60-1, 105, 155, 162-3, 170; *Chatham MS Pedigrees: Pembs RO, Land Tax, 1786; Carms RO,* GGMSS (Gwynfardd); *NLW. Bronwydd Deeds, Poyston Deeds, Trenewydd Deeds, Foley of Ridgeway Deeds, AE MS 12356E; Trans Carms Antiq. Soc. 1924-5, vol. xviii,* p. 65.

LLANREITHAN. *Llanreithan.*

Within a sheltering grove in a truly rural spot close to the upper waters of Afon Solfach, between the farms of Clawddcam and Trenichol, stands the parish church and farmstead of Llanreithan. The church stands close to the site of the old mansion which stood near the stream, and had been the home of gentry families from the time of the first Tudor monarch down until 1780, after which it became ruinous, and about 1800 was dismantled and its stone used for enlarging the farmhouse and outbuildings. The walled garden is the only remnant of squirearchal dignity, the site of the mansion being a verdant stretch of pasture.

The farmhouse is an ancient and commodious structure containing some twenty-six rooms. In the early 19th century Nonconformist services and Sunday schools were held there, and the old wooden 'pulpit' is still kept there. The earliest landowning family there was a branch of the Bowens of nearby Lochmeyler, descended from Bleddyn ap Cynfyn, Prince of Powys till his death in 1075. David Bowen of Lochmeyler (living 1506) was father of William Bowen, a second son, who settled at Llanreithan. William was followed by his son David who died without issue, and Llanreithan passed to his sister Crisli who had married Morris David Morgan of Clydey. Crisli's son, Morris ap Morris, was followed by his son Griffith Morris who was living at Llanreithan in 1599. He married Margaret daughter of James Bowen of Llwyngwair, and had James Griffith, High Constable of Dewsland in 1650 and 1652. He died in 1658, leaving an only child and heiress, Anne Griffith, who, before 1641, had married John Laugharne who was the first of that family to settle at Llanreithan. They were an ancient stock, and bore arms: *gules three lions' heads erased or,* which they later quartered with the boar and hollybush of Henllys, as a result of John's son, Arthur Laugharne's marriage, with Elizabeth daughter and coheiress of David Owen of Henllys, in 1678. The Laugharnes' motto was: *ostentare jugulum pro capite alteries,* in memory of their ancestor who had marched to Bosworth with Henry Tudor in 1485.

The family were at Llanreithan for five generations, the most exciting of them being John Laugharne, High Sheriff in 1731. He strongly objected to the marriages of his sisters Anne (to John Lilly, a dancing master), Margaret (to David Benbow, an attorney from Aberystwyth), and Dorothy (to John Ashwall, of Lincoln, described by his brother-in-law as 'a tramp'). John wasted much money in legal proceedings against his sisters and their husbands, while they counterattacked with numerous lawsuits, with the result that John Laugharne found himself heavily in debt, and kept a retinue of armed retainers to protect Llanreithan against attempts to serve further writs on their master. He was then declared an outlaw, and he was captured by a ruse by the High Sheriff and an armed posse and imprisoned in Haverfordwest Castle. He soon obtained his freedom, and is said to have discovered a 'crock of gold' hidden at Llanreithan, which he soon dissipated by supporting the Jacobites of whom he strongly approved. He was the last Pembrokeshire squire to have maintained a jester, known locally as 'ffwl Llanreithan', whose sprightly antics endeared him to his master but proved a sore trial to guests and visitors. The squire had a fierce bout of fisticuffs with the vicar whose views he disliked. In 1751 he was obliged to sell the moiety of the Lordship of Cemaes to his opulent cousin Thomas Lloyd of Bronwydd. Then, suddenly, in 1752 he left for London where he married his concubine, a Mary Parry, and in the following year returned to Llanreithan, with a little baby daughter called Sophia. He did not survive long, and in December 1755 died leaving all his estate to his wife for life, and then to Sophia in fee simple.

Sophia Laugharne was the last of the family to own Llanreithan. She married John Popkin of Trehyon, Carmarthenshire, and died a young woman in 1779 leaving four children none of whom came to live in Pembrokeshire.

In 1790 her widowed husband sold Llanreithan and much of what was left of the estate, thus severing the long connection of the Laugharnes with Llanreithan. The farmstead was owned by a series of yeomen, finally by the Harries family, the present owner, Mr. Mervyn Harries, being the fourth in succession to possess the property.

Refs: Francis Jones, 'Llanreithan' in *Pembs Historian 1970; Carms RO, Trant Deeds, Castell Gorfod Deeds, Plâs Llanstephan Deeds; NLW, Eaton Evans and Williams Deeds, Poyston Deeds, Bronwydd Deeds, Maesgwyne Deeds, St. Davids Diosese Consistory Court Records, Tithe Map 1838-9; College of Arms, Protheroe MS iv,* folio 117.

LLANSTINAN. *Llanstinan.*

A mansion nearly two miles west of Trecwn, in the vale of Nantybugail, and three miles south of Fishguard. At the height of its prosperity the Llanstinan estate included properties in ten Pembrokeshire parishes, the manors of Llanstinan, Llanfairnant-y-gof, and Talbenny, the presentation to Llanstinan curacy, and the Lease of Tithes, and also properties in Cardiganshire and Breconshire. The earliest-known family at Llanstinan were the Lloyds.

At the beginning of the 16th century William Lloyd was owner, succeeded by his son Morgan Lloyd (living 1548) who married the daughter of Thomas Madog, by whom he had a son, Llewelin Lloyd, who died in 1588. Llewelin's daughter and co-heiress, Janet, received Llanstinan as her share, and married Rees Wogan, younger son of Sir John Wogan of Boulston. Rees was the first of the Wogans to settle at Llanstinan, where he was succeeded by five generations of descendants. One of the most successful of them was Sir William Wogan, younger son of Thomas Wogan of Llanstinan by his wife Elizabeth (Owen).

He was a barrister of Grays Inn, appointed King's Sergeant in 1689, and knighted in the same year, and was Chief Justice of the Carmarthen Circuit of Great Sessions from 1689 to 1701. He died in 1708 without issue. An inventory of his possessions made in 1710, enumerates the rooms in Llanstinan, as follows – four garret rooms, Hopkins' room, room over the Oak-room, closet, room over the Little Parlour, withdrawing room, Great Parlour, Hall, Little Parlour, Study (with library), kitchen, dairy, cellar, outer-cellar, cellar under the stairs, servants' Hall, and (probably detached) store-house and brew-house. It seems that Sir William had rebuilt the mansion, and John Lewis tells us 'I remember when my neighbour Sir William Wogan of Llanstinan was pondering where he should erect a new mansion instead of the old, grown ruinous, and was on the point of shifting the old site which was low, near water, and sheltering, to the summit of a hill that would give him a view of the sea, I was the means of prevailing with him to place it where it now stands, a few feet only elevated from the ancient habitation, for which persuasion, the current of fashion rather setting against me, I was much reflected on'. The last of the Wogans of Llanstinan, William, died without issue in 1710, leaving Llanstinan and its large estate to his nephew, John Symmons of Martel. The Symmons' were an old local family, and by the marriage of John Symmons to Agnes daughter and co-heiress of William Prys of Martel, he settled at that mansion, which remained the home of his descendants for several generations. One of them, Thomas Symmons of Martel, married in 1669 Margaret Wogan sister of the Judge Sir William Wogan, and their son John Symmons in 1710 inherited Llanstinan from his cousin William Wogan. John married Martha Harries of Tregwynt, and was High Sheriff in 1713.

The last of the family were two brothers, John Symmons the heir, and the Revd Charles Symmons, D.D., Rector of Narberth, who died in 1826. John the heir, inherited Llanstinan in 1766. About 1773 he married Anne Barlow of Slebech, and afterwards settled at his wife's home. He fell into debt, and in 1783 sold the mansion and estate of Martel to William Knox, and shortly afterwards, Llanstinan, to the same person. William Knox died in 1810, and Llanstinan and other properties were sold to Sir John Owen of Orielton.

Fenton wrote in 1811, 'Llanstinan a mansion which I remember embosomed in majestic woods now, alas! denuded, deserted, and rapidly hurrying to decay – a mansion that ever ranked in this county amongst the first class with regard to its pretensions in every respect'. Lewis, TDW, stated in 1840 that 'The ancient mansion of the family of Symmons, which had been suffered to remain in a neglected state for some time, has been modernised or rebuilt'. It had been repaired by the owner Sir John Owen, Bart, and in 1856 he sold the Llanstinan estate (3,200 acres), and died in 1861. In 1891 it was advertised for sale, with 405 acres, the mansion being described as consisting of an entrance hall, three reception rooms, library, ten bedrooms, dressing room, two water closets, servants' hall, dairy, beer and wine cellars, kitchens, sculleries, outbuildings, and walled garden, and the sale catalogue contains ground plans of the mansion and out-buildings.

Llanstinan Hall is described as, *Ground Floor* – Lounge hall, Library, Study, Dining and Drawing rooms, butler's pantry, WC.; *First Floor:* 5 bedrooms, 2 dressing rooms, linen room, bathroom, lavatory; *Second Floor* 7 bedrooms; *Basement Floor*, servants hall, waiting room, kitchen, larder, scullery, dairy, 2 cellars, boot room, coal house, W.C.; *Outbuildings*: walled kitchen garden.

The mansion was accidentally burnt down in 1940, and today is a gloomy ruin.

Refs: *WWHR*, vii, 7-11, and *xiv, 221-7,*; Fenton, *Tour Pembs.* 1811, p188; Francis Jones, *Journal Hist. Soc. of Church in Wales*, 1969; *Cambrian Register II, 1796, iii*; *College of Arms, Protheroe MS, iv* to 92; *Chatham MS* No 97; *Carm RO, SC no. 914* and *485.*

LLANTEG/LLANTEAGUE. *Crunwear.*
In the small hamlet of Llanteg are two substantial houses, one the seat of the Davies family, the other, of the Hensleighs. Few early references have been found relating to the properties. In the years 1611-17, a farmer called Morris lived in one of the houses. Firstly, let us consider the Davies family, a branch of Davies of Newton, Laugharne parish, descended from the Cardiganshire magnate, Rhys Chwitt (or Chwith), said to

have been Esquire of the Body to King Edward I. Thomas Davies, the first to settle at Llanteg, was assessed at three hearths in 1670. Henry Davies was living at the 'White House in Llanteage in Crunwear' in 1671, and Chancey Davies the elder, was 'of Whitehouse in Llanteague in Crunwear' in 1708. By the mid 18th century they had left Llanteg. They bore as arms: *argent three bulls' heads caboshed sable, horned or*. In 1786 Lord Milford was the owner of three properties at 'Llanteague', and the Revd. Edward Philipps, of one.

We now turn to the Hensleighs who were at Llanteague in the same period as the Davies's. They came from Somerset to Pembrokeshire, and in 1670 John Hensleigh of Llanteg was assessed at two hearths. The last of this line, John Hensleigh, attorney-at-law, died on 28 January 1769, aged 64, at the Red Lion Inn, Carmarthen, and was buried at Llanddewi Felfrey. By his wife Catherine (daughter of the Revd Thomas Philipps, vicar of Laugharne) John Hensleigh had an only child and heiress, Elizabeth, who married John Bartlett Allen of Cresselly and had issue.

Refs: *Picton Castle Deeds; Hearth Tax 1670; Land Tax List 1786*

LLANUNWAS. *Whitchurch.*

A large double-pile mansion on high ground to the west of Solfach Ucha, and overlooking St. Brides Bay. The earliest-known family at Llanunwas was that of Crunn, a name found in western Dewsland from 1326 onwards. In 1597 Thomas William Crunn, yeoman, granted (in consideration of the marriage of his son John to Elizabeth daughter of John Bowen Cadigan of Henry's Moat) to Thomas Symmons of Martel, gent. and William James Harry of St. Davids parish, yeoman, three messuages and lands in the village and fields in Llanunwas-Ucha and -Isha, and Lethgell, and in Whitchurch parish, to be held to grantor for life, and then to the said John and Elizabeth. The said John Crunn had succeeded by 1613 when he held Llanunwas

as of the manor of Llanddinog, the lord being John Barlow of Slebech.

The property afterwards passed to Elizabeth Crunn, widow, whose daughter and heir, Anne Crunn, whose marriage to Francis Laugharne of Llanreithan had been 'Latelie had and solemnized' when their post-nuptial settlement was executed on 1 March 1670, the lands settled 'uppon the Bloved of the said Francis and Anne' were the two messuages of Llanywas -Ucha and -Issa, and Hendre -Ycha and Yssa, in Llandeloy parish. John Wogan of Eweston, Brawdy parish, and Harry Thomas of St. Davids parish, gentry, were trustees. In 1716 the estate consisted of the two messuages of Llanunwas, the mill called Felin Porth-y-rhaw, in Whitchurch, Carnhedryn-Fawr alias -ucha, in St. Davids, and Hendre -Ucha and Isha, in Llandeloy parish.

Francis Laugharne was followed by his son the Revd Arthur Laugharne, rector of Dinas and Prebendary of Caerfai. He married Jane Lloyd of Cards. He died in 1753, Jane in 1757. The Revd Arthur left one son and five daughters, the son, the Revd William Laugharne was rector of Dinas, Manordivy and Llanllawer, and died unmarried in February 1784-5, and was buried at Whitchurch. The inventory attached to his will, names the following rooms at Llanunwas – hall, parlour, closet, study, buffet, room over the parlour. yellow room, middle room, green room, upper room, kitchen, loft over the kitchen, while the outbuildings included carthouse, poultry house, calves house, little stable, stoneloft, barn, malthouse, little loft, brewhouse, and the garden little house.

Llanunwas was sold shortly afterwards, and the owner-occupier in 1786 was Gilbert James, a younger son of John James of Lochmeyler and Dorothy Harries of Priskilly. An attorney at law he had also lived at Holloway near Narberth, and finally at Llanunwas. His wife's identity is unknown. He had two sons, John James who married one Mary Thomas, by whom he had an only child, Jane, and William Ford James, who died without issue, about 1785. John James died in his father's lifetime, and Llanunwas passed to his daughter Jane James, who in 1799 married Joseph Harries of Priskilly, who then settled at Llanunwas. He was High Sheriff in 1821. She died in 1821, her husband in 1824. Their eldest son, Gilbert James Harries, succeeded to Llanunwas, and died in 1856, leaving the estate to his eldest son Cecil Anson Harries who died without issue in 1908, and Llanunwas passed to his nephew Gilbert David Harries who was High Sheriff in 1892, and died in 1916. None of his children lived at Llanunwas.

Refs: Fenton, *Tour Pembs*, p. 76; *WWHR, iii*, p. 135; *Black Book of St. Davids, 1326, NLW, Bronwydd Deeds*; College of Arms, *Wagner MS 2*; *Cardiff Public Library Deeds (now in Glam RO)*; *Brawdy Deeds (Jones)*.

LLANWNWR. *Llanwnda.*

A farmstead in the north-west extremity of Pencaer, just over a quarter of a mile south of Strumble Head light-house, and above the cove of Carregonen. There are traces of a medieval chapel and burial ground near the farm-yard. In 1326 Llanwnwr was described as a knight's fee (Welsh). In 1517 William Tucker of Sealyham granted a lease of a messuage and 40 acres in Llanwnwr, to Rhys ap Lewis William, who, in 1533 alleged that he had received a grant, not a lease, from Tucker. In 1587 Thomas Tucker of Sealyham was described as 'lord of the manor of Llanwnwr in Pencaer'. Later, it changed hands, and the I.P.M. of William Scourfield of New Moat, stated that in 1622 he owned the manor of Llanwnwr. By 1659 Elizabeth Griffith widow, and her son John Griffith, were living at Llanwnwr, when John Vaughan of Jordanston granted properties in the parishes of Jordanston and St. Nicholas to them. The Griffith family continued at Llanwnwr to 1789 when Thomas Griffith, Esq, gave a lease of Llanwnwr (minerals excepted, and certain rooms reserved to lessor) to William Batine of Barretts Hill, Steynton, gent, for the lives of William's wife Dorothy, and their children Thomas and Mary Batine. Thomas Batine the son remained there till his death in 1885. The family of Mortimer (from Trehowel) came to live there, and were followed in the

1890s by J. C. James of Caerlem. In the present century Mr. John Richards settled there, and the present owner-occupier is his son Mr. Morgan Richards of Llanwnwr.

Refs: *B. B. St. Davids 1326; Taylors Cussion*, p. 97b; *RCAM Pembs. 1925*, p. 191; *P.R.O., Early Chancery Proceedings; NLW-Llwyndyrws (Cards) Deeds, Gaol Files Pembs, Poyston Deeds; Pembs RO-DCT Deeds.*

LLAWHADEN. *Llawhaden.*

Formerly a 17th century mansion, now a farmstead near the castle in the village of Llawhaden, contains a 17th century staircase and a panelled room, some stone vaulting; near the house stands a dovecot. Across the road is a large walled garden of former times. Fenton wrote in 1811, 'enter the village and pass the mansion of William Skyrme, Esq, of a most respectable family in this county, whose ancestor, an eminent attorney in the Court of the Marches, settled here about two centuries ago, and laid the foundation of two or three families of that name now centering in this gentleman'.

Rees in 1815 noted 'In the village [Llawhaden] is a handsome mansion, the residence of William Skyrme Esq.' Lewis, in 1840, adds a little more – 'in the village is also a good family house belonging to a descendant of the Skyrmes whose ancestor accompanied Oliver Cromwell into the principality during the parliamentary war, and obtained a settlement at this place.' The Skyrmes came from Shropshire, and in the Pembrokeshire Great Sessions of 1640, William Skyrme of Ludlow, was an attorney in a case. John Skyrme of Llawhaden was High Sheriff in 1716. The Skyrmes left Llawhaden at the end of the 18th century, and thereafter was let to yeomen who used the house for farming purposes.

Refs: Fenton, *Tour Pembs 1811*, 172; Rees, *Beauties of S. Wales 1815*, 807; Lewis TDW 1840, *Pembs RO, LT 1786*; Bucks' Engraving 1740, of Llawhaden Castle, includes a sketch of the mansion (illustr).

LLETHER. *Brawdy.*

About half a mile south of Brawdy church, stands Llether, a large double-pile mansion of three storeys, separated from Brawdy by a small *cwm* through which runs a tributary of Afon Newgale. To the south of the mansion is Newgale farm formerly a manor. In early times Llether was divided into two separate manors – Llether Superior, a manor, also called Llether Ucha (Upper), and Llether Gronw; this is the property described in this entry.

Llether Inferior, a manor, also called Llether Issa (Lower), and Llether David, the lord of the manor in 1568-81 being John Barlow of Slebech; after this, the manor was united to Llether Ucha, the lords and owners being the Jones family of Brawdy.

Later the property included Llether Manor House (mansion), Lether Farm (home farm), and Llether Issa (farm), all in close proximity. The manorial jurisdiction and rights lapsed during the 19th century.

The earliest known reference to Llether Ucha is in 1328 when John ap Philip granted to Adam the clerk (Parson) half of a building and garden, and one-third of a bovate, in Llethergrono, a stang in Roshingern (*sic*) to be held until John ap Philip paid certain money to Adam.

In 1594 part of Llether Ucha was owned by William Jones of Brawdy, and part by the Warlows of Newgale. The lands of William Jones passed to his younger brother Gilbert Jones, and then to Gilbert's son and heir, William Jones. This William married Katherine Hergest of St. Davids, and the property passed in due course to their son and heir Richard Jones who sold it to his cousin William Jones of Brawdy in 1635.

John Warlow of Lower Llether married Catherine Voyle daughter of John Voyle of St. Elvis by his wife Lettice Mortimer, and had two daughters, co-heiresses. The elder daughter, Lettice Warlow had Lower Llether as her share, and in 1652 married James Jones of Upper Llether second son of William Jones of Brawdy, and thence forth their descendants owned both properties. They were succeeded in 1699 by their son William

Jones. The last of their descendants, and eventual heiress, Mary Jones, married George Roch of Butter Hill, and Llether remained in Roch hands. The last to live at Llether was Colonel Thomas James Roch who left Llether for Tenby after the 1st World War.

The Llether estate was advertised for sale in 1919, the main properties being described as

> *Llether Manor House*, consisting of, on the ground floor – entrance hall, dining room, kitchen, scullery, pantry, larder, boot room, and on the first floor, a drawing room, four bedrooms, and dressing room, and on the second floor, three bedrooms, bathroom, and W.C.; the grounds included a large lawn tennis court, a walled garden with access to the first floor of the house by an archway.

> *Upper Llether Farm* (137 acres), the house containing a parlour, sitting room, kitchen, dairy, four bedrooms, with outbuildings, let to William Owen at a yearly rent of £130.

> *Lower Llether*, farm (175 acres), the house containing a parlour, sitting room, kitchen, meal room, dairy, five bedrooms, and outbuildings, let to Henry Williams at a yearly rent of £107. All three houses are in excellent condition.

When I visited Llether in the 1960s, the mansion was owned by the Morris family. When I examined Lower Llether I found a fine painting on the wall over a fireplace, of a mansion (late 17th or early 18th centuries). About 1970-1 it was sold to a Mr. Ling, who during his occupation 'modernised' the house, and by 1975 he was engaged in the sale of the property.

Refs: Francis Jones, Lay Manors of Dewsland, *in Journal of the Hist. Soc. of the Church in Wales, 1969 and 1970*; Fenton, *Tour Pembs 1811*; *Pembs Arch Svy* 1896-1907; *RCAM Pembs 1925*; *NLW Tithe Map 1842* Maesgwyn Deeds; *Pembs RO Land Tax 1786, Deeds DB 13, 30*; PRO, AD. E210, D5520; *Come to Pembs* (guide) c. 1936, *illustr*; History of Jones of Llether (unpublished), penes me.

LLETHER WOGAN.

In North Pembs. Unidentified.

Possibly in the district of Moat. N.B. there is a Llether farm in Mynachlogddu, and called Llether Ucha in the Tithe Map 1840; today they are called Llether Ucha and Issa. The only reference that I have found to Llether Wogan occurs in a Scourfield pedigree assembled by George William Griffith of Penybenglog. The pedigree reads as follows: Harry Scourfield married Etheldred Butler of Trecadwgan in Dewsland, and had a son and heir, John Scourfield of *Llether Wogan* (d.1593) who married Katherine Wogan of Wiston, and had a son and heir John Scourfield, and a younger daughter Mary Scourfield who married Owen ap Evan ap Jenkin, both living in 1591, and had four sons and a daughter, viz. Thomas ap Owen of Mynyddmelin (Llanychllwydog parish) bailiff of Cemaes in 1629, David, James, John, and Catherine. I place the above on record, hoping it will help some future antiquary to identify the elusive Llether Wogan.

Refs: *College of Arms, Protheroe MS nos v and xii* (G. W. Griffith); *LD* i, pp. 110, 176; *Chatham Pedigree MS*, appendix in Laws, *Little England Beyond Wales; Golden Grove MSS; WWHR*, ix, 145 ff.

LLWYN BEDW. *Capel Colman.*

An attractive well-maintained 18th century residence, on a slope just south-west of Capel Colman church, and to the east of Boncath. A short distance northwards is Cilwendeg. The earliest-known owners of Llwynbedw were the families of Morris and Morgan. On the marriage of Morris Morris of Ffynnone, gent to Elizabeth daughter of Jenkin Jones of Rhosygilwen, among the lands settled was Tir Llwgn Bedw (post-nuptial settlement 1692). Jacob Jones (born 1743) youngest son of John Jones of Cilwendeg, settled at Llwynbedw, and died there in 1787. He was followed at Llwynbedw by his son, Revd John Jones (1782-1844) rector of Llanfyrnach and Penrith, from whom descended the Joneses of Penylan and Llanmilo.

Llwynbedw was afterwards occupied by several owners, but their stay was short. Possibly their stay was influenced by the disturbing apparition that haunted the house. It was during the 1890s that Mr. S. Gwilly Davies stayed there as guest of John Daniel Jones, auctioneer, and agent to the Bronwydd estate. The ghost, said to be that of a lady who had been drowned at Glan-pwll-du just below the plâs. In the evening, the sound of a rapidly-driven coach could be heard from the house, then it stopped at the entrance, followed by a ringing of the house bells, and residents could hear the swishing of the ghost's skirts as she darted from room to room. One bedroom was never used as those who had slept there claimed that 'something' disturbed their repose. As a result the occupiers found great difficulty in recruiting house-servants from the district where tales of the 'Lady of Llwynbedw', were well-known. Mr. Peter Gwynne Hughes lived there for many years, his sleeping hours seemingly undisturbed.

Refs: Buckley, *Sheriffs*, 1909; S Gwilly Davies, *Wedi Croesu'r Pedwar Ugain, Atgafion*, 1967, pp. 18-19, 23-27; Monuments in Capel Colmon parish church; *Pembs RO, Land Tax 1786*; NLW, Tithe Map, 1849.

LLWYNGORRAS. *Nevern.*

Now a farmstead on a hillside north of the river Nevern, and between Nevern church and the hamlet of Felindre; marked on Colby's Map as Llwyn-y-goras. At one time the property was divided into several farms – in 1632 we find the capital messuage of Llwyn y Gorres Issa, in 1740 Llwyn y Gorras Ucha, and in the Land Tax of 1786, we find three farms there, namely Llwyngorras [the plâs] owned by Roger Davies Esq, occupied by William Davies, Llwyn y Gorras Fawr owned by Thomas Lloyd Esq of Bronwydd, occupied by John James, and Llwyn y Gorras fach owned by Thomas Lloyd Esq of Cwmgloyn, occupied by Enoch Rees. It was finally united into one property.

The earliest known owners of the property were the Bowen family, of whom George Owen of Henllys wrote about 1608 – 'Lloyn y gorres the mansion house of Morgan Bowen gentleman (b. 1547), standeth for healthe and pleasure fayre upon the topp of a banck over lookinge a fayre and plessant valley, beinge the more pleasant for that it is his ownc. This house was built about 30 yeres past [1578, which is carved on a stone in the wall of the house] by his elder brother Thomas George Bowen, a man who for his good hospitallitie, gentle behaviour amonge his equelles, his good advise to his distressed neyghboures, and other his good partes, was much lamented at his death who havinge yssue but one daughter, sould the same to this her uncle [Morgan Bowen] being third sonne to his father George Bowen, a man in his tyme of noe small rule and estimation who was the naturalle [illegitimate] sonne of John Bowen sonne and heyre to Sir James Bowen knight, and beareth the Armes of Pentre Ieuan with the due difference.' The bard Huw Llŷn (fl c. 1552-1594) wrote an elegy to the above Thomas (ap) George (ap) Owen of Llwyngorras.

In 1595 George Owen Esq of Henllys, confirmed to Morgan Bowen of Llwynygorres, gent, his right in 'a capital messuage called Llwynygorres', a messuage called Plâs Penywayn, and closes called Park yr Ithyn, Tir y vorwyn gloff, and Park Dol yspadrick Issa, all in Nevern parish, messuages called Tythyn Penyrallt, Tythyn yr Escair, and Vron Vawr in Dinas parish, and one-third of a messuage in Mynachlogddu. Morgan Bowen's will was proved in 1612, and not long afterwards his son Owen Bowen and Elizabeth Bowen sold Llwyngorras, to the Webb

family. By her will, proved in 1632, Margaret Webb of Alleston (near Pembroke) bequeathed 'to my son Alexander Webb, the capital messuage of Llwyn y Gorres Issa, late in tenure of Melchior Bowen, and now of mine, in as large a manner as the same was granted to me by Elizabeth Bowen and Owen Bowen.' By the end of the 17th century, the property had been bought by a family named Davies. In 1705 Thomas Davies of Llwyngorras was a Land Tax Commissioner, and in 1715 was a Justice of the Peace. He died in 1730.

In 1762 the owner was Roger Davies, J.P., and still held it in 1786. In 1789 the Llwyngorras estate was sold by the brothers Thomas and Mathew Davies to William Davies (no relation). William, described in several subsequent deeds as of Llwyngorras, Esq., died in 1826 aged 86. His widow, Martha, was described as the owner-occupier in 1840. His descendants, Grace Martha Davies and Jane Davies, were the owner-occupiers in 1894. Among other descendants were Susannah Gwenllian Davies who married Mr. R. T. P. Williams, the well-known solicitor of Haverfordwest, and Captain W. Davies Evans inventor of a move in chess called 'Evans's gambit'. Since 1900 Llwyngorras has had a series of farming owner-occupiers.

Refs: *Journal of Nat. Library of Wales, 19, Geo. Owen Second Book (ed B. G. Charles) WWHR ii, p. 36; NLW, Pembs Great Sessions, Gaol Files, Tithe Map 1840, Bronwydd Collection, manorial court rolls; Pembs RO, Land Tax 1786, Quarter Sessions Order Book 1740, Saunders – Davies Deeds' Carms RO, Golden Grove MSS (Gwynfardd).*

LLWYNGWAIR. Nevern.
A mansion on the north of the river Nevern, and a mile to the east of Newport. The Bowens are one of the oldest of Pembrokeshire gentry. The family settled at Coed in Nevern parish, and continued there until Ifan ab Owen built a residence at nearby Pentre Ifan which bears his name. He was living there in 1409. His great-grandson Sir James ap Owen, a strong adherent of Henry Tudor in 1485, bought Llwyngwair from the Cole

family shortly after 1503, which thereafter became the main seat of the family. Llwyngwair had belonged to the Coles before 1326, one of whom discovered the value of marle as a fertiliser used afterwards for centuries on north Pembrokeshire farms, a productive activity continued by the Bowens such as James Bowen of Llwyngwair (High Sheriff, 1803) who encouraged the use of sea-weed and powdered bone as fertilizers on farms and supported local agricultural societies. Mathew Bowen, a younger son of Sir James, was the first of the family to settle in Llwyngwair, to be followed there by thirteen generations of his descendants. The Bowens of Llwyngwair took an active part in public life, providing seven High Sheriffs, a Lord Lieutenant, and numerous parliamentary commissioners, magistrates, and deputy-lieutenants. In earlier times several bards were guests at Llwyngwair like Ieuan Brechfin, Dafydd Emlyn, and others wrote poems to members of the family in the 16th and 17th centuries.

During the 18th century the Bowens were sympathetic to the Methodists, and many of their leaders were guests at the home and held services there. George Bowen (1722-1810), for his support of this cause became known as 'The Nonconformist Churchman'. Among the visitors were John Wesley, Howel Harris, Daniel Rowland, and Williams Pantycelyn who is said to have composed his famous hymn, 'Dros y Bryniau tywyll niwlog,/Yn dawel f'enaid , edrych draw', while travelling over the Preseli hills to the comforts of Llwyngwair.

It was a commodious house of the traditional type. The antiquarian neighbour, George Owen of Henllys, commented in 1607, 'Llwyn gwair the mansion house of James Bowen gentleman ... the house and demaynes more than halff compassed with the ryver of Neverne yelding as well comoditie fishing as other pleasures. The seat pleasant for wood and water'. In 1670 it had six hearths which placed it among the largest houses in the parish. The tourist Malkin was less impressed when he wrote in 1804, 'Llwn Gwair, seat of George Bowen Esq has the advantage of shelter from some good timber by the side of the Nevern in a country where timber is scarce. In other respects it has nothing to distinguish it from the general style of gentlemen's houses on a small scale', while Fenton in 1811, described it as 'the beautiful seat of George Bowen Esq'. The mansion had been augmented from time to time, and in its heyday had 34 bedrooms. It has survived in excellent state, a long traditional building of two storeys and an attic storey, with ranges each of nine windows, and four dormer windows, with a large entrance porch of three storeys reaching to roof height, with wings extending to the rear.

It had been sold by 1957, and today is a hotel and holiday centre which has altered its outward appearance but very little. Alas, the Bowens have departed, leaving their memorials and coats of arms in Nevern church – *azure a lion rampant or within an orle of eight golden roses*, with the crest of a golden lion holding the well-known Bowen knot in its forepaws – to remind us of the bygone centuries when the benevolent Bowens of Llwyngwair were toasted on the hearths of Cemais.

Refs: *LD,* i, 166-7, *WWHR,* ii, 87; Owen, *Second Book; Baronia de Kemes; PRO, AD,* iii *B. M. Egerton MS 2586; College of Arms, Protheroe mss III, IV, V; Golden Grove MSS (Gwynfardd); Dale Castle Pedigrees; Cardiff Library Deeds ; NLW, Picton Castle Deeds, Llwyngwair Deeds, Bronwydd Coll. Owen of Orielton Deeds, Foley of Ridgeway Deeds, Papers of Pembs Great Sessions, H'West Corporation Deeds, Tithe Map Nevern 1844;* Francis Jones' Bowen of Pentre Ifan and Llwyngwair' in *Pembs Historian* 1979, 25-57, and refs there; B. G. Charles, *Geo. Owen of Henllys 1973,* passim; E. T. Lewis, *North of the Hills* 1973 (illustr); *Western Telegraph,* 15 July 1987 (illustr).

LLWYNI HIRION. *Nevern.*

A farmstead just east of Carnedd Meibion Owen, and about 3¼ miles south-east of Newport. Home of some of the younger sons of Llwyngwair. John Bowen, second son of George Bowen of Llwyngwair, lived at Llwynihirion, and on 4 August 1648 married Elin daughter of George William Griffith of Penybenglog. Their son, George Owen, succeeded to Llwyni Hirion.

LLYSTIN. *Nevern.*

A farmstead south of the river Nevern, about midway between Llwyngwair and Trewern. In 1607 George Owen wrote 'Llistyn sygnifieth in Englishe a full Coort or pallace, a house now alltogether raynated and usid as a dayrie, in tymes past being of great acompt for this was the mansion howse and portion of Rees Llewelyn ap Owen one of the five sonnes of Llewelyn ap Owen aforenamed, and Rees Llewelyn ap Owen had this place called Llistin ... he has also five sonnes ... Gwilym ap Rees his eldest sonne had this house [Llystin] who was first and cheiffe awncester of the family of the Gwillims of this place, and had yssue Rees Gwillim [who] was father to Ellyw his sole heire wieffe to Harry Bowen of Lochmyler ... the house and demeyns come to Owen ap Owen of Pentre Iewan esquior father to Thomas Bowen after whose death it fell to the parte of Jane Bowen [died 1624] youngest daughter and coheire to the saide Thomas Bowen and wieff to William Warren[of Trewern] who now in her right enioyeth the same as a grange or dayrie adjoining to his demeysnes of Trewern. I remember in my tyme a fayer grove of trees about the house which now is roted and the land tilled: out of this house of Lliston yo sprunge forthe dyverse houses of gentlemen'. William Rees ap Gwilym ap Rees of Llystin son of Llewelyn of Coed, lived in 1526 at Llystin Ycha. From the 17th century Llystin was let to a series of farming tenants.

Refs: G. Owen, *Second Book*, 1607, p. 275; *LD*,I, 60, 162-3, 170; Fenton, *Tour Pembs* 1811; *College of Arms, Protheroe MS V; WWHR*, ii, 55.

MABWS FAWR. *Mathry.*

A farmstead in a copse on a slope, a mile to the south of Mathry village, and above the upper waters of Cleddau Wen which borders its northern side. Several adjoined farms bear the names Mabus Fawr, Mabws Fach, Bont Dwr Fabws, and Penlan Fabws. To the east of Mabws Fawr is a hill fort, Castell Llynin Mabws, in a field still called Parc yr hen gastell, and near the house is Parc Ffynnon Dewi whose well was dedicated to the national saint of Wales.

In 1326 'Mabovis' was a fee of which the Bishop of St. Davids was lord; at that time the freeholders were Simon ap Philip, Ieuan ap David, and Rosa Russell who held two carucates and 7½ bovates there, and the Bishop held in his own hand half a bovate and half an acre there. They were to accompany the Bishop and his host in time of war, and to follow the relics of the Blessed David as far as the rocky outcrop of Carn Twrne. In 1560 the brothers William David and John, sons of Ieuan ap Owen of Mabws Fawr lived there, descended from Twdwr, prince of Deheubarth. John left an only child and heir, namely Isabel who married David ap Thomas, gent. David settled at Mabws, and the property in due course passed to his granddaughter Margaret, who married Owen ap Melchior of Newport who settled at his wife's home. They had five sons and four daughters, the eldest of the sons, Charles Owen of Mabws Fawr, was Bailiff of Dewsland in 1631. Lewys Dwnn recorded the family pedigree in 1613, under the heading 'Y Plâs y Mabws'.

The property changed hands after 1634, and about the middle of the century it became part of the estate of the Tucker and Edwardes families of Sealyham, and Mabws Fawr was leased to yeomen families of Dewsland. The best-known of these was that of Evans, who obtained a lease of Mabws Fawr in the first half of the 18th century. John Evans (1715-1775) variously described as 'gentleman' and 'yeoman' was a Land Tax Commissioner in 1768, and was succeeded at

Mabws Fawr by his son, John, who married Martha Mathias of Pencnwc, a descendant of the powerful squirearchal families of Wogan and Ford of Stone Hall, by whom he had a son, John who succeeded to Mabws Fawr.

This John Evans was an enthusiastic Baptist who held services at Mabws Fawr. By his wife Anne Howell of Treddnog he had highly gifted children including John Brown Evans (b. 1831) who emigrated to South Africa where he became an extremely successful farmer and laid the foundations of Angora goat farming in Africa, and to keep his herds under control invented a special wire known as 'Evans Patent Fencing' now called 'Barbed wire'. When he died in 1888, *The Times* described him as 'the largest farmer in the world', his lands extending to 260,000 acres.

His younger brother, Morgan Jones Evans, (1835-1899) succeeded to Mabws Fawr, was a progressive farmer, and produced an improved breed of Welsh Black Cattle, known as 'the Mabws breed', he founded and edited the journal called *The Country Gentleman*, and was a noted contributor to *The Field*, and a well-known poet. He was succeeded at Mabws by his sister, Rebecca Sophia Evans, better known as 'Rebecca Mabws' and was one of the first women to become public lecturers throughout Great Britain. She married the Revd Thomas Williams, and died in 1874. Her only son, H. A. Williams, chemist, Justice of the Peace, County Councillor, died, without issue, at Haverfordwest in 1937 aged 67. In the early 1960s Mabws Fawr was sold to a stranger, who demolished the old house, and erected a new farmhouse.

Refs: *Dwnn*, i, 112; *Black Book of St. Davids*; *RCAM, Pembs* 1925; *Pembs RO, LT 1986*; *NLW, Morgan-Richardson Deeds, Tithe Map Mathry*, 1842 ; Francis Jones Mabws Fawr' in *Trans Cymwr 1970*, 112-129, and refs there.

Holgate

MANORBIER CASTLE. *Manorbier.*

Normally this building, which is mainly a ruin, would not be within the scope of this work but as parts of it have been restored to make it once again a family home then it qualifies on these grounds for inclusion.

Fenton described Manorbier as 'the most perfect residence of an old Norman baron with all its appendages; church, mill, dovehouse, ponds, park and grove, still to be traced'.

It looks today much as depicted by Samuel and Nathaniel Buck in 1740. Nothing much has been added to the building since about 1300 except making part of it habitable again.

Manorbier's greatest claim to fame is as the birthplace the Giraldus de Barri (c. 1146-c. 1220), otherwise known as Giraldus Cambrensis or, more popularly, Gerald of Wales. Gerald was a grandson of Odo de Barri, a Norman who is said to have founded Manorbier. His father, William de Barri, married Angharad, daughter of another Norman, Gerald de Windsor and grand-daughter of Rhys ap Tewdwr (d. 1093), Prince of South Wales.

Gerald wrote (*inter alia*) *The Journey through Wales* and *The Description of Wales*. Both these, written in Latin, are very readable in the late Professor Lewis Thorpe's translation.

Gerald waxes lyrical when describing his birthplace with lavish praise.

The de Barri family (whose arms were: *argent three bars gemels gules*) and their descendants occupied Manorbier for about 200 years, their connexion ending in 1399 when the castle and lands were confiscated by Henry IV. Thereafter the Castle changed hands several times but by the late 1530s it was already in ruins with no one living there. Cromwell's soldiery siezed Manorbier in the Civil War but it was not besieged or slighted. The castle does not have a keep and is built around a large courtyard with a surviving round tower and gatehouse.

Lady Dunsany lived here for a number of years.

MANOROWEN. *Manorowen.*

A mansion within attractive woodland, one mile south-west of Goodwick and two miles from Fishguard, overlooking the road from Goodwick towards St. Davids, and a distant view of Fishguard Bay and the coastline to Pen Dinas. Although the name as spelled at present suggests that of an ancient manor, such was emphatically not the case. Originally it was a *maenor,* an early Welsh tenurial unit, and not to be confused with the later Norman *Manor.*

In 1326 it was a knight's fee called 'May-nornowan'. Local Welsh folk call it 'Farn-awan', more faithful to its origin than the modern 'official' form. The spelling Maen-ornawan occurs in numerous early documents down to the mid 18th century. The latter part is derived from the name of a man called Nawan ap Gnawan, spelled Grawan on the Elizabeth chalice of the parish church.

The Goodwick-St. Davids road passes the present mansion and the church. The original residence stood near the east end of the church, and was flanked on the other side by a large walled garden, which, with a gazebo, has lasted to the present day. In 1665 the estate was bought by John Lewis, lawyer and landowner, of Nantybugail, who soon afterwards, c. 1670-90, erected a new residence across the road on high ground overlooking the church and the gardens.

It was a low two-storeyed edifice with a view over the surrounding countryside, over Fishguard Bay and the coastline to Pen Dinas. The older residence was totally abandoned and not a single stone remains to indicate the site. A history of the life and style of John Lewis in the new mansion was later written by his great-grandson, Richard Fenton the antiquary.

This continued as a family seat until early in the 19th century when the Bowen-Parrys built a completely new residence just in front of Lewis's residence, which was used thereafter for domestic purposes, and continues to be so used to the present day. The new mansion and part of the estate was bought by Dr. Griffith in 1841, and later on he improved and extended the mansion on its western end. This is the excellently maintained mansion (the third at Manorowen) that greets our eyes today. In 1326 it was 'Maynornawan, a knight's fee (English)', but no further references have been found to the property, until the 16th century. From 1550 to 1600 it was the home of the family of Williams, of whom Ievan ap William was a Coroner for the county during those years; William Williams was a Royalist during the Civil War and followed Prince Charles to the continent where he died. Manorowen then passed to a descendant of the Williams family, George Owen of Scleddy who then settled at Manorowen. On 6 December 1665 he sold Manorowen to John Lewis of Nantybugail whose family came from Henllan Owen near Eglwyswrw. John Lewis was an accomplished man: he was a J.P., and mayor of Fishguard on ten occasions between 1641 and 1675, a noted antiquary and archaeologist, builder of the second mansion at Manorowen, and developer of the fishing industry at Fishguard and Goodwick. He died early in the 18th century, leaving by his wife Diana Lloyd of Cilglynen, six daughters. Manorowen was settled on the eldest, Martha, who married, in 1704, Thomas Parry of Pembroke.

The last of the line, Thomas Parry died unmarried in 1768 aged 27, leaving the Manorowen estate to his kinsman, William Bowen of Leweston, whose descendants added the name Parry to their surname. It was during their time that the present mansion replaced the older one at Manorowen.

The last of the line, Richard Parry Bowen, died, heavily in debt, on 9 August 1837, and his heirs and his creditors sold the estate. The capital messuage, demesne, and lands, the home farm, and eight other properties in the vicinity, were sold to Dr. Moses Griffith for £14,000 in 1841. Dr. Griffith, a member of the family of Griffith of Rickeston and Pointz Castle, served for 31 years as an army surgeon, and for several years in India. He never married and died in 1883, aged 94, leaving the Manorowen estate to a son of his bailiff, the Revd Thomas Johns vicar of Manorowen, till his death in 1905. The new owner was followed by his son Mr. V. G. J. Johns, solicitor, who died in 1946, leaving Manorowen to his eldest son Captain Graham Johns, TD, DL.

Refs: *Black Book of St. Davids 1326*; *B. M. Egerton MS 2586*, p. 295; *Fenton, Tour Pembs*, 1811; *Lewis TDW*, 1833 and 1840; *Welsh Port Book*, p. 132.

MARLOES COURT. *Marloes.*

In medieval times there were Marloes of Marloes and later Malephants, but subsequently this has mainly been the home of farming families. David Bevan farmed there in 1753. His son, also David, was Master of H.M. Sloop *Petterell.*

At one time the owner was the Hon. William Edwardes, afterwards 3rd Lord Kensington. His tenant was James Dean Wathen. After the Wathens came the James family who were there between 1885 and the 1920s.

MARTEL. *Puncheston.*

The present farm of Martel is about half a mile east of Little Newcastle and one and a quarter miles south-west of Puncheston. The site of the former mansion is on the northern bank of the stream called Afon Anghof, between Martel Bridge and Allt yr Hwc. A railroad from Letterston passes alongside the site.

The earliest known family here was that of Martel after whom the property was named, John Martel of Martel, living there in the late 15th century. His daughter and heiress, Agnes, married William ap David, member of the family of Llystyn near Newport, who was living at his wife's home in 1557. The estate eventually passed to his three daughters and heirs, one of whom, Agnes had Martel. She married John Symmons, described as 'Husbandman, of Martel' in 1566.

The Symmons were a local family of freeholders, and this marriage brought them within the embrace of landed gentry. John was followed by six generations of his descendants who added considerably to their estates. Among the last of them was John Symmons (1701-1764), a member of the Society of Sea Serjeants, owner of the estates of Martel and Llanstinan (where he went to live), and about 1773 married Maria Philipps of Sandyhaven. He was followed by his son and heir, John Symmons, who was the last of the line as a major landowner. He married Anne Barlow of Slebech and went there to live and rebuilt that residence.

In 1783-4 he sold the estates of Martel, Llanstinan and Slebech, to William Knox (see D.N.B.). The original residence, Martel, had been abandoned, and had become ruinous. By a lease dated 1782, John Symmons leased to Edward Davies of Castlebythe, a turner, part of the messuage called Martel, except a small plot of ground and the old garden on the bank of the brook (Anghof), at a spot between *Old Martell* (mansion), and Martel Mill, and in 1799 William Knox of Llanstinian granted a lease to John Llewellin of Letterston, farmer. In 1811 or shortly after, the trustees of the late William Knox, sold that worthy's estate to Sir John Owen of Orielton. The land of Martel was thereafter owned by successive farmers. The coat of arms of Symmon of Martel are engraved on the chalice (hall-dated 1725) of Puncheston church, namely *party per fesse argent and sable three trefoils two and one counterchanged.*

Refs: Evans *Church plate of Pembs* 1905, 81-2; *Dwnn, i.* 192; *Chatham Pedigrees; W.W.H.R.,ii,44*, XIY pp. 207; Fenton, Tour *Pembs.* 1811; Carlisle *TDW*; Lewis *TDW* 1840; BM *Egerton 2586*; College ot Arms *Proth ms 1X,* 89,99; Pembs RO, *Deeds HDX/686*, No. 2; NLW, *Bronwydd Deeds, Cwrtmawr Deeds; Noyadd Trefawr Deeds, Pembs. Plea Rolls, Eaton Evans and Williams Deeds; Poyston Deeds, F. Green Deeds.*

MARTLETWY HOUSE. *Martletwy.*

Stands to the north of the village, north-east of the parish church, and near to the Vicarage. Home of the Philipps family, derived from Picton Castle, in the 17th Century. On 1 September 1631 John Philipps of Molleston, Thomas Philipps of Martletwy gentlemen, with four others, assigned hogs and swine and 'wild honey' within the forest of Narberth, to John Barlow of Slebech, Esq. On 8 April 1666, the said John Barlow mortgaged 'a capital messuage called Martletwy House' to George Meare of Nangle, gent., and on 12 January 1669-70, the said Meare and Barlow, realised 'the capital messuage and lands called Martletwy House' to Thomas Carpenter of Lincoln's Inn, Esquire, to be held in trust for William Barlow of Mynwear, Esq. In 1670 John Barlow of Slebech paid hearth taxes for seven hearths in Martletwy. In 1682 William Barlow, gent., is described as of Martletwy. By 1786 it was owned by William Knox, with Joseph Davies as tenant.

Refs: NLW, *Slebech Deeds*; Pembs RO, *Land Tax 1786.*

MERIANOG. *Meline.*

On a northern slope of the Preseli, below Carn-alw, and two miles east of Brynberian. Also spelled as Bryianog in earlier documents. There were several farms in the vicinity called Merianog-fawr, -ganol, -fach, and in the nineteenth century the name -west had been added. The name occurs as Breuanog-fawr, (1412), Bryanog (1600), Bryanog fach and issa (1560-1620), and two farms called Vrianog (1786). The earliest notice I have seen occurs in a deed of 10 May 1412 when Philip ap

Howel ap Jenkyn granted the messuage and land of Brenanog-vawr, and four acres at Henllys Morgan with the wood there, to Owen ap Gwilym Ddu (ancestor of the Owens of Henllys, *d. c.* 1447). Thereafter several yeoman families lived there. In 1583 Thomas ap Rees (descended from Howel Gawr, and Gwynfardd Dyfed), described as of Merianock-ycha and yssa was made a ward of George Owen of Henllys, who, nine years later, sold the wardship to William Warren of Trewern. In 1638 Thomas ap Rees and his sons James ap William Thomas (descended from Gwynfardd Dyfed) are described as of Merianog-Issa, and later the said son James Thomas, living at Merianog-fach with his son William Thomas and daughter Chrisley and Margaret. Later the father sold Bryanog. The prenuptial settlement of Griffith Morris gent., of Cwmcerwyn and Catherine Lewis daughter of William Lewis of Rhosymaen, formerly of Vronianog-fawr, was made in 1721, and in 1760 the postnuptial settlement was made between Thomas Morris of Whitechurch and his wife Martha one of the daughters and co-heirs of Thomas Lewis gent., late of Vrianog-fawr, deceased.

The Land Tax of 1786 records Thomas Williams of Treleddyn, St. Davids, as owner of two messuages at Vrianog, and one messuage there owned by John Rees. By 1837 the owners were William Williams of Merianog-fawr, Phoebe Bland of Merianog-fach, and Western-Merianog, and Thomas Rees of Merianog-ganol. The Voters' List of 1950 shows four messuages, viz. Merianog-fawr, -fach -ganol, and -West.

Refs: *Carms RO GGMS.I;* Pembs RO, *LT 1786;* NLW, *Bronwydd Deeds, Tithe Map Meline 1837; College of Arms, Protheroe MS IV and XII.*

MERRION COURT. *Warren.*

Half a mile south-east of the parish church. A manor belonging to Henry Wogan (died in 1499). With the death of John Wogan in 1559 it passed to co-heiresses who sold the property to Thomas Bowen of Roblinston who was lord of the manor in 1587. Some time after 1623 it was sold to the Lorts of Stackpole Court, from whom it descended by marriage to the Campbells (Lords Cawdor). Fenton wrote in 1811 – 'Merian Court, the head of a manor now belonging to Lord Cawdor, and therefore of a still more baronial appearance, as part of the ruin presents a species of masonry of a very superior quality that indicates something more highly finished that what is generally met with'.

Refs: *y Cymmr 1903*, pp. 95-105; *Fenton Tour Pembs.* 1811; Taylor's *Cussion, for 98; B. M. Egerton ms 2586.*

MERRIXTON. *Amroth.*

One and a quarter miles west of the parish church. The original name was Meyrickston. In 1760 it was the home of Evan Williams, Esq., JP., and in 1773 of John Martin Esq., JP. In 1786 William Callen Esq., was the owner-occupier, and his wife Anne (née Poyer), and there was another residence nearby also called Merrixton and owned by H. Skyrme, Esq. with Thomas Cosens, tenant. The tithe map of 1844 gives Sir Richard Bulkeley Philipps as owner, and William Brock Swann as occupier, while a nearby property, East Merrixston was owned by Charles Poyer Callen with David Edwardes tenant. In 1848 William Brock Swann Esq., is described as of Merrixton House.

Refs: *NLW, Slebech Deeds; Morgan-Richardson Deeds; Pembs RO Land Tax 1786.*

MILTON. *Burton.*

Formerly a residence, one and a quarter miles north-west of the parish church; it is now a farm. The earliest known family there was that of Wogan. Richard Wogan of Milton married Maud Philipps of Picton Castle. He died without issue, and his widow then married Morgan Jones who was of Milton (*iure uxoris*) when he was High Sheriff in 1547. Morgan predeceased Maud and was followed at Milton by his son William Jones, gent.

William died in 1577, and his will mentions his brother Thomas Jones of Harmeston, his son Henry Jones, a minor, and his mother Mrs. Maud Philipps Wogan, gentlewoman, who proved the will. Little else is known of Milton, and it was let to farmers. The owner in 1786 was David Hughes Esq. (of Harmeston), and Richard Fields as tenant.

Refs: *Picton Castle Deeds; Pembs RO 1786; L.D. I 229.*

MILTON HOUSE. *Carew.*

A residence, half a mile north-west of Carew Cheriton church, marked on Colby's map as 'Milton House' within grounds on the edge of Milton village. Comparatively modern, it was owned by the Revd. William Holcombe in 1786, with William Phelps as tenant. By the early 1830s William Bowen was living at Milton House, being the first of that family there which was to continue there for nearly a century and a half.

Lewis wrote in 1834: 'Within the parish are several gentlemen's seats of which the principal are Milton House formerly part of the extensive estate of Upton Castle, and now the property and residence of William Bowen Esq., an elegant modern mansion pleasurably situated within grounds …'

William Bowen's sister had married James Summers of Haverfordwest, Clerk of the Peace, and it was to his nephew, James Summers, he left Milton House. James Summers then added Bowen to his name; James Bowen Summers settled there and was High Sheriff in 1874. He was followed by his son, Sutton Bowen Summers, who sold Milton House after the 2nd World War. In 1950 it was the house of Colonel St. L. G. Hawkes.

Refs: *Pembs RO, L.T. 1786; Lewis TDW, 1834 edn.; VL 1904 and 1950.*

MINWERE. *Minwear.*

This consists now of the ruins of a former monastic property and a farmhouse north of the parish church. In 1538 Roger Barlow was living at Slebech but in 1546 he bought with other properties, the manor and rectory of Minwere. In his will dated 1553 he left the dairy house at Minwere with the stock and cattle to his wife Julgan. In 1583 George Barlow of Minwere was admitted to the Inner Temple and afterwards inherited the Slebech estate (q.v.) from his father. Fenton wrote: 'Exactly opposite to the house of Slebech there are considerable remains of a respectable mansion, once inhabited by a brother of the Barlow who resided at Slebech. They are said to have lived in such harmony with each other that their bills of fare were mutually announced by trumpet and the place of dinner fixed by the predominated excellence of the publication'.

In 1613 records show that John Barlow owned (inter alia) 'The manor of Mynwere containing one capital messuage called Sistern House': 290 acres of land; 300 acres of woodland; 10 acres of salt marsh; one corn mill; two messuages in Mynwere and 50 acres; a parcel called Mynwereshill and 100 acres; five cottages and much else. Sistern House was probably a corruption of Sisters' House as there was once a nunnery there, the ruins being in Minwear parish.

The history of Minwere and Slebech are closely linked. The Barlows of Slebech were created baronets (see Burke's *Extinct and Dormant Baronetcies*).

The extensive ruins called Sisters' House are described in detail in *Ancient Monuments* report for Pembrokeshire (1925) pp. 232-4. The main ruin, a building 100' x 25' was not a tithe barn as once suggested. It formed part of the property of the Slebech Hospitallers.

In 1786 Mrs. Ann Barlow was the owner of Minwere but William Knox owned Minwere House.

Major Jones left copious notes about this property. He visited it on April 17th 1974 and noted: 'The farm is still part of the Slebech estate. The ruins of the former mansion are a considerable distance from Minwere Farm which is by the church. The ruins of the mansion are extensive. Part of the dwelling house remains, built over an undercroft. There are remains of large outhouses, the largest being a huge building of two storeys 36 yards by nine yards with slit ventilations. There are two large walled gardens and there is a well with masonry around it and an overflow pool. The ruins are in a woodland and on the bank of the Cleddau opposite Slebech House.'

Minwere latterly belong to the Lewis family and to Baron de Rutzen of Slebech Hall.

MOLLESTON. *Narberth.*

Now a farmstead, called Great Molleston, about two miles south-west of Narberth town. Formerly a gentry residence. Towards the end of the 16th century it was the seat of Owen Philipps, a younger son of Morgan Philipps of the Picton Castle family. He died before 1621, and was survived by his widow, Priscilla Philipps (née Chester), and their son, John Philipps who succeeded to Molleston, married Jane Elliott and they were still living there in 1644. They had a son and heir, Owen Philipps. On 1 December 1635, John Philipps, gent., of Molleston, his mother Priscella Philipps, widow then living, of East Moor, Manorbier, and their son and heir Owen Philipps, agreed to convey the farm of Molleston and pennage of hogs and swine and wild honey in the forest of Narberth, to John Barlow, Esq., of Slebech. Owen Philipps is the last known member of the family at Molleston.

On 14 June 1704 Evan Lewis of Laugharne, yeoman, and Thomas Davies of Molleston, assigned to John Barlow, Esq., of Slebech, for a term of years, a messuage called Molleston, and lands 'near Great Molleston mansion House', and a piece of land called Trebaron in Narberth parish. In 1765 Thomas George and his wife Margaret (formerly widow of Robinson Lloyd of Vaynor), were living at Molleston. In 1786, William Knox of Slebech, is described as owner of Molleston, with William George, tenant there. In 1834 William Hand is described as owner of Great Molleston.

Refs: *Pembs RO, Land Tax 1786, Voters lists, L.T. 1786; NLW, Pembs Pleas Rolls, Bronwydd Deeds, Slebech Deeds.*

MONKTON OLD HALL.
Monkton St. Nicholas.

About one hundred yards south-east of Monkton Priory. In 1811 we are informed by Fenton, 'the prior's mansion, a little to the west of the Cemetery, now converted into a farmhouse, is of a singular form, uniting the architecture of various fashions and ages. It is ascended by a flight of steps, at the foot of which on each side are the remains of very curious pillars. The basement is all vaulted; and the outbuildings, together with the walls that enclosed the whole, give us an idea of the prior's great estate'.

The monastic precinct, or rather prior's liberties, occupying a very large tract, formed a paddock well walled round, commanding a fine view of the estuary, castle, and town of Pembroke, must have been a sumptuous and delightful residence. A dove-house of large dimensions, an inseparable appendage to houses of the first note in this country, still exists entire, just without this paddock. The Priory Farm now rents at £400 per annum;' and Carlisle says, 'There is a building, joining the churchyard on the East, called Monkton Hall; but it is doubtful whether it belonged to the Priory: it has the marks of considerable antiquity, and has long been in the possession of the Owens of Orielton, which is in the parish of St. Nicholas.' *Timmins* describes Monkton Old Hall in detail in 1895, and suggests it may have been the 'hospitium or Prior's dwelling'.

Refs: *Dwnn, i, 137: Fenton, Tour Pembs, 1811, 206; Carlisle, TDW, 1811; Pembs Archaeological Survey 1896-1907; Timmins, Nooks and Corners, 1895, pp. 61-63, illustr.; Laws, Little England, 1888, 119, 143, illustr; Arch. Cam, 1880, 248-252; 1881, 86-7; 1977, p. 172 Carmarthenshire Studies, 1974, essay by Peter Smith, 49.85. figs; Peter Smith, Houses of the Welsh Countryside 1975, pp. 22-0, plans and figures pp. 28-9, photos plates 4 and 5; RCAM Pembs. 1925, 236-7.*

MOOR. *Castlemartin.*
Now a farmstead south-east of the church and marked on Colby's map, *The L.T. Pembs. 1786,* gives Moor and Moor Hays farms, owned by John Campbell, Esq., with Thomas Edwardes, tenant. Fenton writes in 1811, 'Turn to the left (from Castlemartin church), to see Moor, one of the chief mansions of this district about two hundred years ago, of a very irregular form, with many ruinous and extensive outbuildings, once entered by a gateway now stopped up, leading to a porter's lodge. With very few exceptions, this may serve as a model of the style of building their houses among the greatest of that era in this country, which invariably appears to have been surrounded by a high court wall having a large arched gateway, and essentially differing from the form of the principal houses of the date, in the upper part of the country; where, notwithstanding the Norman encroachment, presumptuously called a conquest, as the strongest proof of their never having been subdued, the natives retained their language and the British fashions in everything continued evidently predominant.'

Nearly a century later, Timmins wrote in 1895, '... Moor Farm, where once stood a goodly mansion, of which scarce a stone has been spared.' In the 18th century it was the home of John Prout, (will proved 1780) whose daughter, Elizabeth married John Leach of Brownslade and had issue.

Refs: *Fenton, Tour Pembs, 1811, 223; Timmins Nooks and Corners, 1895, 91, LT 1786, Pembs.*

MOOR. *Walwynscastle.*
Between the villages of Walwynscastle and Tiers Cross, on Colby's map. Home of the family of Summers, descended from William Summers of Moor whose will was proved in 1713. Richard Bowlas of Llanstadwell, and others sold two farms and a ploughshare called Honeyhook Lambrough, in 1718, to John Summers of Moor in Walwynscastle parish, yeoman. In 1786-1797 the owner of Moor was Mr. Thomas Bowlas. The Summers and Bowlas families intermarried and continued to own the property. In 1834 William Bowlas Summers lived at Moor until his death in 1836 and was the last of the family at Moor. His younger brother settled at Rosemoor in the same parish, which became the main seat of the Bowlas-Summers family.

Refs: *NLW, Poyston Deeds; Pembs RO, LT 1796.*

MOOR. *Rosemarket.*

In his will, dated 1696, Thomas Tasker of Moore, Rosemarket parish, gent., mentions 'my capital messuage called Moore' which had been settled in 1688 on the said William on his marriage to Katherine Roch. William died before 1699, and the widowed Katherine then married Philip Rice (who owned lands in the parishes of St. Dogmaels and Moelgrove), who then settled at Moor, *iure uxoris*. In 1712 Mary Tasker, spinster, granted to Sage Tasker, both of Moor, a lease for 21 years of a moiety of Moor in Rosemarket and a moiety of Clareston in Freystrop, at a rent of £15 p.a.

Refs: NLW, *Eaton Evans and Williams Deeds*, No. 43884; *Tithe Map.*

MORFIL. *Morfil.*

Now a farmstead on the lower slopes of Mynydd Morfil, above Pontfaen in the Gwaun valley. The former mansion stood about two hundred yards lower on the slope, due south of the parish church. Towards the end of the 18th century it became a ruin, and only a few mounds and stones remain to indicate the site. Across the vale is Mynydd Casfuwch, and through the vale runs Afon Anghof. From early times this area has been a land of hill-farms, and the environment is still wholly unspoilt. Fenton wrote in 1811: 'Morville, memorable for the gallant stand the Welsh mountaineers made against the Norman usurper, as the portion of a younger son of Cilceithed, whose great-grandson, in compliment to a lowland lady of Castlemartin, whom he married, left his native highland, and there continued to settle, which ... became at last, united to the vast estate of Orielton'.

During the Middle Ages, Morfil was a seat of noblemen descended from Gwynfardd Dyfed.

The first of the family to use the name Lloyd (Llwyd), was Ieuan Llwyd, son of David Ddu of Cilciffeth. The name was borne by twelve generations of his descendants who also lived at Cilciffeth, Morfil, Pen-

gegin, Cilglynen, and finally at Grove near Pembroke. The last in direct descent was Elizabeth Lloyd, daughter and heiress of Thomas Lloyd of Grove, who married in 1725 William Owen of Landshipping, who later became Sir William Owen, 4th Baronet of Orielton. In 1786 Morfil is recorded as the property of Lady Owen, with William Greenish as its tenant. It was a commodious house, and is described as of five hearths in 1670. The family produced several High Sheriffs: Thomas Lloyd of Cilciffith (son of Owen Lloyd of Morfil), in 1596 and 1613, and to mark the last occasion founded and endowed the Haverfordwest Grammar School which lasted to our own times; Thomas Lloyd of Grove in 1700, and his son Thomas Lloyd in 1709. The Lloyd arms were *azure a lion rampant gules within an orle of roses or.* After the gentry ceased to live at Morfil, it was let to farming tenants, William Lewis, yeoman, in 1750, and in 1834-1840 William Williams was tenant of Morfil (then 528 acres).

Refs: *Francis Jones, 'Lloyd of Cilciffeth in Pembs. Historian 1873, 30-62; Fenton Tour Pembs, 1811, 312; Dwnn i, 167-8; Pembs RO, LT. 1786; NLW, Slebech Deeds, Orielton Deeds.*

MORGANS.

Now in Williamston East, but formerly in Begelly.
Earlier deeds describe Morgans as being in the parish of Begelly. From 1291 Williamston East was a chapelry of the rectory of Begelly, and in the 19th century formed into a parish.

Morgans, formerly home of yeomen and minor gentry, is now a farm. In the 17th century, a pedigree shows Thomas Adams of Morgans and his wife Joan, daughter of Stephen Barlow of Arnolds Hill. In 1653, Thomas Adams of Morgans was a freeholder of the manor of Redberth, on the north-west of Williamston East (Colby map 1831). In 1670 Thomas Adams of Begelly parish was assessed at three hearths. In 1676-7 Thomas Adams the elder of Morgans in Begelly, gent., Katherine his wife, and Thomas Adams their son and heir were living. In 1762 John Williams of Morgans, Esq., JP., was a Grand Juror, and in 1769 a Land Tax Commissioner for the county, and was still living there in 1786. John Adams of Loveston St. Twynells (a cadet of Paterchurch), was living in 1591, and had two sons – Thomas Adams of Loveston, (will proved 1627), and John Adams of Morgans in Begelly.

Refs: *RCAM Pembs 1925; W.W.H.R. I 241, IV, 245; Lewis TDW 1840; Picton Castle Deeds; Pembs R.O. Lt 1786; NLW, Pembs Goal Files 1762 and 1772; Tucker MS (peds).*

MORGENAU. *Cilgerran.*

This place is named after a brook called The Morgeney but it was formerly known as Rhosygilwen. In 1904 John Colby of Ffynonne sold Rhosygilwen, Penalltfedw, Cilast Fields and Cnwcgyrn, in all about 200 acres, for £8,000 to Charles Evans Davies Morgan-Richardson, JP., a solicitor. When he occupied the property he re-named it Morgenau.

Morgan-Richardson was the author of the novel *Henry Vaughan, a Story of Pembrokeshire,* set in the west Wales countryside. He died on 28th September 1913 aged 56. His son and heir Charles Lethbridge Ernest Morgan-Richardson (b.1888), succeeded to the property and lived there until his death in 1961, apart from 1914–18 when it was let to tenants. After his death the house and contents were sold.

Refs: *South Wales, Historical Biographical Pictorial, c. 1908, photo; Contemporary Biographies of S. Wales and Mon. 1907, photo of house p. 154.*

THE MOTE. *New Moat.*

The Scourfield family who lived here from the reign of Edward I, produced High Sheriffs of the County in 1600; 1617; 1663. Towards the end of the 18th century the family moved to Robeston Hall (q.v.) and Mote decayed until '... nothing remained save the roofless and time-worn shell ... but phoenix-like and under the refined and cultivated taste of the late William Henry Scourfield Esq., MP. it proudly rose from those hoaried relics and in its increased magnificence and style far surpassed the former building.' (The *Cambrian Journal*, Vol. 5, 1862, p. 241). Fenton, in 1811, notes 'with regret' the roofless shell.

W. H. Scourfield who returned to The Mote about 1830 is said to have employed the architect W. Owen of Haverfordwest. The new house was plain and in classical style.

The house was put on the market in 1925, a bad year for country houses. It failed to find a buyer and was demolished in the following year. Major Francis Jones wrote: 'I visited the ruins on September 27th 1986. A large gable-end chimney still stands as well as near-by outbuildings. Large walled garden and long walls around the house and demesne'. There is a photograph of the building in T. Lloyd's *Lost Houses of Wales*, p. 73.

MULLOCK. *St. Ishmaels.*

A farmstead to the west of Butter Hill mansion. The earliest known reference to it is in 1234-42 when the name is spelled Milnhochdich, and in 1295 as Mulhok. In the late 16th century it was the home of George Jenkins (2nd son of Philip Jenkin of Roch parish), living in 1551-99. In 1610, Sir Walker Rice of Carms, mortgaged a messuage called Lytle Mullock (in tenure of Henry Browne) in £14.10.0. to George Jenkins of Great Mullock, gent. George signed his pedigree for Dwnn in 1613, and was followed at Mullock by his son Philip Jenkins gent., who was there in 1623.

In 1660, Adam Hawkin held the lease of Great and Little Mullock at £33 p.a., and John Davies, miller, held the lease of Mullock Mill at £17 p.a. In the 18th century it formed part of the Stackpole Court estate, and in 1767, the Hon. Pryse Campbell granted to Gilbert Davies of St. Ishmaels parish, yeoman, a lease for three lives, of Great and Little Mullock, Sivershill, and Mullock water grist mill, all in St. Ishmaels Parish.

In 1786 Mullock was owned by John Campbell, Esq., with Mr. Harry Davies, tenant, with the same owner (then Lord Cawdor), in 1797, with Cornelius Davies, tenant. In 1802 the property was advertised for sale by Lord Cawdor, described as

Mullock Farm (254 acres) 'with a convenient dwelling-House, well fitted up suitable for a gentleman farmer, into offices farm-yard, and proper outbuildings', in possession of Henry Davies, aged 39, on lease for his life, at a yearly rent of £60. It was bought by William Bonsfield, Tooley Street, London for £4050.

On 6 September 1813 John Dedwith of Jordanston parish, Dewsland, farmer, 2. John Dedwith Gibbs. 3. Henry Davies of Mullock, and 4. John Philipps Laugharne of Orlandon, assigned a term of years of Southfield and Thornhill, in St. Ishmaels, and on the same date the said properties were conveyed and surrendered to the said Henry Davies and his trustee the Revd. James Summers, cleric, of Haverfordwest.

The first of the Davies (Davis) family at Mullock, was Henry Davis, who was followed by his son, Henry, born c1760. The second Henry Davis of Mullock was High Sheriff in 1819, and died on 16 May 1825, and buried at St. Ishmaels. His eldest son was Thomas Henry Davis, who was followed by his brother Gilbert William Warren Davis, High Sheriff in 1839, JP., who built a new mansion at Trewarren, and about 1842 went to live there. He died in 1886.

Fenton records a local tradition re Mullock Bridge 'under the arch of which the gallant Sir Rhys ap Thomas, in order to fulfil an old prophecy importing that Henry (VII) must go to the crown over this illustrious Welshman's back, condescended to crouch (for it is very low), that his future sovereign might have the full benefit of the prediction'. A sketch of the bridge was made by Timmins in 1895.

Refs: *Fenton, Tour Pembs, 181, p. 96; Timmins, Nooks and Corners, 1895, p. 120; B. G. Charles, Non-Celtic Place-names, 1938, p. 76; Pembs RO DEE.1, Nrs 22-3, 38; LT 1786; NLW, Calendar of Dynevor Documents, 1610.*

MUSSELWICK. *Also called* MUSLICK.
Marloes.

A farmstead to the north of Marloes village, and overlooking Musselwick Bay. Marked on the maps of George Owen (1603) as Muselwick (Marloes); on Kitchin's (1763) as Moselywick, (Marloes), and on Colby's (1831) as Muslewick, (St. Ishmaels), on the coast looking towards Dale.

Although there are several reference to the property in medieval times, there is insufficient information to enable a pedigree of the owners to be made. More such evidence occurs from the 17th century onwards. The first-known family there was that of Moore. John Moore was there around 1650, and was followed by his son Francis Moore who was living there in 1670. In 1714 he was a parliamentary voter, and died about 1744 when his will was proved. Francis's son, John Moore, gent., married in 1744 Anne Bowen of Glanduad, Nevern. He was the last in the male line of his family, and was survived by three co-heiress daughters. The eldest, Alice Moore married Phillip Powell, gent., who then settled at Musselwick, where he died some time after 1793, and the widowed Alice died at Kidwelly, Carms. in September 1828 in her 82nd year. The second sister Anne Moore was unmarried, and went to live in Haverfordwest; the third sister, Elizabeth Moore, married before 1771, the Revd. William Rees, clerk, of Newgale in Brawdy, where he died without issue in 1781, and Elizabeth in 1793. Musselwick, which was mortgaged, became part of the estate of the Philipps Laugharne family of Orlandon, later of St. Brides mansion, and Muselwick was leased to a series of gentlemen farmers – Morse (1802), Bowen (1834) and Scale from 1842 when the owner was Charles Allen William Philipps, with John Scale as tenant. At that time 'Muslick' comprised 236 acres and three of the fields bore the names Beacon Park, Brawdy Park and Church Park.

In 1920 the St. Brides estate was advertised for sale and Muselwick is described as a farm of 225 acres held by George Scale on a twenty-one years lease granted in 1914; the farmhouse was built of stone, and slated, with five bedrooms, three sitting rooms, kitchen, scullery, dairy, and a garden and farm outbuildings. The Scale family continued at Musselwick, and in 1950 the following were living there, Colin Scale, Hugh, Kenneth, William and Mary J. Scale.

Refs: *NLW, Poyston Deeds, J28; Pembs Plea Rolls No. 2884; Pembs R.O., L.T. 1786-1802, v. lists., Deeds hdx 194, nos. 1-3; voters list 1950.*

MYNYDDMELYN. *Llanychllwydog.*

Home of the Bateman family, a cadet of the Batemans of Honeyborough. Thomas Bateman of this place was living in 1591. In 1670 Eynon and Anne Bateman were assessed for three hearths each.

In 1786 Thomas Nicholas was listed as owner-occupier. Later the families of George and Evans were associated with the property.

Dragon of Wales

NANTYBUGAIL *Llanfairnantygof.*

Formerly a substantial farmstead, about half a mile west of Trecwn hamlet. Belonged to the estate of Trecwn, and was leased to yeomen and minor gentry families. In the second half of the 16th century it was owned by the Jones (or Johns) squires of Trecwn, and later the estate passed to the Vaughans (through a distaff descent), and from them to the Foster-Barhams who held the estate till 1933 when Captain C. H. S. Barham and his only son and heir were tragically killed in a road accident near Coventry. Trecwn was afterwards bought by The Admiralty. Nantybugail is included in the Trecwn rentals in the 19th century, but does not appear in the estate sale Catalogue in 1939. Among the earliest folk at

Nantybugail was the yeoman family of Cynfrig who was there in 1595. In 1663 Thomas Owen Esq., of Trecwn granted a lease for 99 years of Nantybugail and Cnwc y Berllan to John Lewis the elder, of Nantybugail.

The Lewis family came from Henllan Owen near Eglwyswrw, and were descended from the ancient owners of Pentre Ifan. John Lewis the elder was the first to settle at Nantybugail, and after his death in 1664, was followed by his son and heir, John Lewis the younger, gent., a solicitor, who played an active part in local life, and was coroner for the county for several years. In 1666 a lease of the farms of Nantybugail and Treforfol was granted to John Lewis and his wife Diana (née Lloyd of Morfil), who had bought the Manorowen estate near Fishguard, and about 1670-80 left Nantybugail and settled at Manorowen. He became a JP. and was Mayor of Fishguard on ten occasions. He died leaving six daughters, one of whom became grandmother of the well known historian Richard Fenton of Glyn y Mêl. In 1739 the leaseholder was Robert Thomas, yeoman, in 1786 James David, in 1859 William Symmons. After this, very few references are found to Nantybugail.

Refs: *NLW, Bronwydd Deeds, Coleman Deeds, Poyston Deeds, Vairdre Book, Extinct of Cemais, Pembs. Papers of Great Sessions, NLW ms 1390D; Pembs RO., LT 1786, Voters lists.*

NANTYLLADRON. *Clydey.*

The name Nantylladron has not been found in post 17th century records. In more modern times appears the farm of Nant-y-lledfron, one and a half miles north of Clydey church, and half a mile west of Dugred-isaf. It is likely that Nant y lledfron represents the earlier name. The will of Griffith ap Evan ap Howell, of Clydey parish dated 22 July 1555, mentions 'my son' and executor Morris Griffith, and my daughters Elizabeth verch Griffith, and Margaret verch Griffith, and the 'tenement where I now dwell called Place Nantylladron'. A pedigree in the Golden Grove mss of Morris ap Griffith ap Ieuan ap

Ieuan ap Howel ap Einon of Rhosychen, Carms, descended from Cadifor Fawr, was followed by his son James who was father of David and Abel James of Werngry in Clydey; this David was followed by his son Morris of Nantylladron in Clydey. James Morris of Nantylladron married Elizabeth daughter of David Parry of Noyadd Trefawr. Morris James of Nantylladron had five sons, one of whom, Thomas Morris was, assessed at four hearths in 1670. The Land Tax for 1786 shows Nant-lladron owned by Thomas Colby Esq., and John Jones MD., with John Mathias as tenant. Nant Lledfron is included on Colby's map in 1831, and is spelled thus in Voters' lists for 1894 and 1904.

Refs: *Carms RO, GGMSS (Cadifor Fawr and Guyddro); Dwnn, i, 217; Pembs RO, LT 1786.*

NARBERTH – PLÂS. (*Narberth*).

The former residence stood on rising ground just above the parish church, within a bow shot of the medieval castle at the southern entrance to the town. It was occupied (perhaps built during Elizabethan days) by John Vaughan a member of the Vaughan family of Pembre (Carm), descended from the Breconshire chieftain, Moreiddig Warwyn. John Vaughan died in 1580-1 leaving six daughters, co-heiresses. His daughter Jane received the mansion as part of her share, and married John Elliot of Earweare (Amroth) who settled at his wife's home which remained in possession of their descendants until the latter half of the 18th century when the estate passed to the Meares family. In legal documents the property is variously called Narberth Place, Narberth Place House, Narberth House and also as Place and Plâs.

In its heyday it had been commodious, and in the Hearth Tax List of 1670, it contained six hearths. The division of the demesne into holdings had been made in the first half of the 18th century. The prenuptial settlement, dated 1743, of the last owner, Alexander Elliot and his wife-to-be, Jane Barlow of Lawrenny, when the names are rendered as 'Narberth Place House'. Alexander died in

1755, without issue, and the widowed Jane moved to Haverfordwest.

The next owners, Meares, did not come there to live, and let the mansion and land to local tenants. In 1786, William Meares was the owner, and the tenants were Gregory Gale, John Roberts, John Evan and Thomas Thomas.

The present Plâs, as it is now called, is a two-storeyed, L-shaped farmhouse, with a projection from the front, at the northern end, while the rear wall, clearly part of the old mansion, contains the remains of a large decorated window in freestone, together with some Elizabethan corbelling. A ground plan of the Plâs made in 1871, includes an extension to the rear of the house, but this has been removed subsequently. In that plan, the property, described as 'the Plâs Demesne (49 acres)' was advertised for sale, and the tenant then was Mrs. Francis Lewis, at a yearly rent of £105. An antiquary recorded his impressions of the house in 1889-1891, as follows. 'An ordinary dwelling house now occupies its site, but a portion of one old wall seems to have been incorporated in the existing house. A small bit of massive masonry and portions of a mullioned window in freestone at the back of the house on the garden side remain to attest the fact that the Plâs was once a mansion of considerable strength and beauty … The last of the Miss Elliots did a very good thing for Narberth by making over to the town for ever a large piece of common, on the edge of which the Board schools are built, on the side of the Haverfordwest road. I think it is commonly called Town Moor'.

The Pembrokeshire Archaeological Society (1896-1907) marked the site of the original mansion in a field to the north of Plâs farm, adding 'Here stood the house of the Elliots: there are only the faintest traces of the house to be seen'. However when I examined the alleged 'site' in 1974 I was unable to discover any trace of a previous building, and neither had the occupier of the land ever heard of any tradition relating to it.

Refs: *Dwnn, i, 122, 204; Picton Castle Deeds; NLW, Slebech Deeds; Carms notes 1889-91. p. 21; Pembs Arch Survey 1896-1907; Pembs RO, LT 1786, Deeds, Sale Cat. 1871.*

NASH, Great. *Langum.*

Marked on Colby's map 1831 are Great Nash near a cross roads about one mile west of Langum village, and about a mile west of Great Nash is Little Nash, and about half a mile south of Great Nash is Nash Mill on the banks of a stream. According to Dr. Charles who quotes numerous examples of the name between the years 1324 and 1566, the name is derived from 'cotton ash'. The mansion house, Great Nash, eventually became an uninhabited ruin. RCAM Pembs. 1925, p. 136 states that a few fragments, including a vaulted cellar of the original mansion, can be traced immediately behind the present building now a large farmhouse probably built in the 17th century; in the farmyard is a 16th century dovecote about 20 feet high.

Great Nash was the residence of four wealthy landowning families. The first was that of Nash, the surname being probably derived from the property. The Nash family lived there in the 15th and the early 16th century. Arnold Nash was followed by his son Richard, and he by another Richard who was the father of the daughter and heiress Jane Nash. She married Alban Philipps third son of Morgan Philipps of Picton Castle. Alban settled at his wife's home, and their son and heir, named Alban after his father, was living at Great Nash in 1648, and he married Dorothy Laugharne. The next owners of the property were the family of Corbett descended from a Merionethshire squire.

Thomas Corbett and his wife Dorothy daughter of William Laugharne, were living at Great Nash in 1670, the house being then assessed at six hearths, so that it was then a commodious dwelling. He was followed by his son, Erasmus Corbett who, in 1681, married Anne Mathias of Llangwarran, and had three daughters and co-heiresses, the eldest of whom, Dorothy Corbett succeeded to Great Nash. She married Charles Owen, son of Sir Hugh Owen of Orielton, and both were living at Great Nash in 1704, and were followed there by their son and heir Wyrriott Owen who married his cousin Ann Barlow of Lawrenny Hall whose surname he adopted in lieu of Owen. The said Wyrriott

Owen (d.1773) had four sons and one daughter. The eldest son, Charles Owen died without issue in 1757, and was succeeded by his next brother Hugh Owen who owned Great Nash in 1786, and died without issue in 1809.

In 1811 Ann Barlow of Lawrenny Hall granted a lease of Great Nash to Thomas George for the lives of his three daughters, Elizabeth, Anne and Cecilia. It was at this stage in the house's history that Richard Fenton commented: 'Less than a mile from the village is the mansion house of Nash, now unroofed and in ruins and perfectly denuded, its woods having been recently cut down. The house, of the most fashionable form of mansions in this county of its date, a sort of cube, was large and habitable within these few years, as it was meant to have been fitted up for his residence by my friend Mr. Wyrriott, late worthy possessor ... what this place was at first called I cannot learn but it took the name of Nash from a family of that name, Advenac, who came into possession of it about two centuries since. It after came to the Corbets, then to the Owens, and now belongs to Hugh Barlow, Esq. the legal representative of the late proprietor.'

Refs: *Dwnn, i, 202; W.W.H.R.,ii, 36,62; Fenton, Tour Pembs, 1811, 134-5; GG mss (Adv. Carm) fo 226; Chatham ms, (No. 102); Pembs R.O., deeds B. G. Charles, Non-Celtic Place Names in Wales 1938.*

NASH, Lower. *Nash.*

Origin of name as in above entry. A small parish situated between Upton and Pembroke town. The main properties were Lower Nash alongside the parish church, and Upper Nash in the east part of the parish: in 1363 the former was called Nether Ash, the latter Over Nash. In 1526 they appear as Lower and Upper Asshe; and in 1607 as Over and Nether Nash, then owned by Henry Bowen of Upton Castle. From the later part of the 16th century the names appear consistently as Nash. The most important property was Lower Nash, today a large farmhouse retaining architectural features of the Tudor period. In 1670 it was assessed at three hearths, the occupier being William Davies, Esq., JP., a member of the ancient family of Davies of Cwm, (Carms) who traced to Rhys Chwith (or Chwitt), Esquire, of the Body to King Edward I. His son, Thomas Davies, was a Grand Juror in 1731, and High Sheriff of Pembrokeshire in 1737. He died on 27 April 1741 in his 71st year; his wife was Jane daughter of David Gwywn of Pentre, Llagathen, Carms. A memorial tablet to Thomas Davies in Nash Church, is engraved with the family Arms: *argent a chevron between three bulls heads caboshed sable.*

The Davies were probably leaseholders, for Lower Nash continued to form part of the Upton Castle estate. In the latter half of the 18th century, Upton was divided between four daughters and co-heiresses, and parts of the estate were sold. In 1786 Henry Leach owned Lower Nash, with John Roch as tenant, while Upper Nash was owned by the Revd. William Holcombe. On 17 October 1800 the will of Mary Roch of 'Lower Nash Farm' was dated, and she mentions 'my brother John Roch of Lower Nash'. In 1840, Lower Nash (then 178 acres), was owned by Abraham Leach, Esq., with Richard Llewelin as tenant.

In 1974 the house was renovated by the new owner, Mr. Eddie Gibby, OBE, JP., D.L. who lived there till his death in 1984. An interesting piece of vernacular architecture is a stone staircase, rising from alongside a fireplace, leading to the upper storey. The building is in excellent state and the home of Mrs. Sheila Gibby.

Refs: *Pembs RO, deeds, LT 1786; NLW, Tithe Map 1840; B. G. Charles, Non-Celtic Place-Names in Wales 1938; Peter Smith, Houses of the Welsh Countryside, 1975, p. 473, and map, No. 33; Francis Jones 'Cwm (Coomb)' in Carm. Historian 1970.*

NEESTON. *Herbrandston.*

Home of the families of Davies and Bowen (Cadet of Upton Castle). Sadly this historic house was demolished by the Esso Oil Company who owned the land upon which it stood.

The Rev. William Davies. LL.B., Parson of Narberth, was father of Griffith Davies of Neeston who died in 1606, his property being described as 'the Great House in the South part of Neeston'. Griffith's granddaughter and heiress, Joan, married in 1635 Henry Bowen. Neeston passed to the Bowens and by descent to the Jordans.

Barrett Bowen Jordan, of Neeston, had three daughters and co-heiresses. Martha, the third daughter, married in 1803 the Rev. William Wilson, of Knowle Hall, Warwickshire. Wilson's mother was a daughter of the Rev. William Harris of Bryn Hyfryd ... The Wilsons, thereafter, quartered Bowen of Neeston in their arms: *gules a lion rampant within an orle of cross crosslets fitchee or.* The Wilson family is recorded in Burke's *Landed Gentry* for 1875.

Barrett Bowen Jordan became heavily in debt, and fled the country. In 1784 he is described as 'late of Neeston' and 'resident of Ghent in Flanders'. Yet two years later he is still recorded as owning Neeston and was assessed for Land Tax. By 1805 the owner was recorded as Thomas Philipps Esq., eldest son and heir of the Rev. Edward Philipps of Lampeter.

NETHERWOOD. *Near Saundersfoot.*

A square house of two storeys with a verandah at one side. It figures in 'Photographs in South Wales 1871'.

Once the home of the Stokes family it belonged to a Mrs. Vickerman in 1852 and later became the home of General Sir George Richards Greaves, GCB, KCMG (b 1831). The General served at Peshawar during the Indian Mutiny, was Chief of Staff in the Ashantee Expedition and was Chief of Staff in Cyprus 1878-9.

Netherwood later became a school.

NEVERN. (Nanhyfer). *Nevern.*

Site unidentified, but it is known that the mansion stood near the parish church at the edge of the village. The Nevern estate was owned by a family descended from Gwynfardd Dyfed. In 1442 Howel ap Jenkin the elder and his wife were living at Nevern. He was followed by his son Jenkin ap Howel who took an active part in the Civil War on the Yorkist side, and was slain at Banbury in 1469.

The estate passed to his son, Howel ap Jenkin the younger, who was living there in the years 1470-1491. George Owen of Henllys was at the townred of Nevern in 1603-4, and wrote – 'Here was the mansion house of Howell ap Jenkin ap Roppert, the younger, the greatest man of lyving in his tyme in all the countrie, and now his heires growen to that povertie that they are scarse knowen who they are, if any be lyvinge. The said Howel ap Jenkin the younger built a fayre house, but died before the same was fynished … He had yssue a sonne named William who consumed the whole inheritaunce, and it is said that Howell ap Jenkin the father, being a learned man, died at the birth of his son William, cast at his nativities, whereby he pesentlied toued his wieffe that she had borne a sonne that should consume and spende all that he and his auncestors had gathered; and thereupon, as it is reported, the said Howell ap Jenkin determyninge to prevent fate, made somme estate of his landes, such as he thought his sonne might not sell the same, and did especiallie repose trust in one Morgan Taylor, a meane and base fellowe mantayned by his almes, and was parishe clerke and wholilie fedd and releeved by the said Howell ap Jenkin, and therefore so much tyed to the said Howell ap Jenkin, that he thought noane might be better trusted than he. After the death of the said Howell ap Jenkin, his sonne William fullfilled his foreseen fotrune and left not one foote of landes unsould, and the said Morgan Taylor do joine in sale of the landes, and this maketh many to muse at this daie to see these ffeoffmentes made by them both, yet well knowen to be Howell ap Jenkin's landes, this being the onelie cause, so that to prevent the determyned will of God no worldlie pollicie can prevaile, and who so trusted base mynded people shalbe served of them in their kynde …' (*Second book, c.1603-4, pp. 273-276*).

It seems that the ruins of the old mansion were still to be seen in 1811 when Fenton mentions among trees near Nevern village are 'the ruins of a venerable old mansion … belonging to and begun to be built by Howel ap Jenkin ap Rotpert, of the princely stock of Gwynvardd Dyfed, and a man then of the greatest property and command in the country, but who died before it was finished … his one son William, who by a most profligatt course of life, dissipated his vast inheritance'. The profligate William married Elen Fychan daughter of Thomas Howel ap Owen Fychan of Argoed in Nevern parish by whom he had three children, – Owen (blind) and Lewis both died unmarried, and Jane who married firstly, Owen nephew of the vicar of Nevern, and secondly, William James. By the first Jane had a daughter Llewen who married twice, and by the second, Owen William, who sold relics of the Nevern estate, Cwm-eog and Trefaes to William Owen of Henllys (father of George Owen). And so the line of the Nevern family was extinct by 1600.

Several bards addressed odes to members of the family. Hywel Surdwal mentions going to the church of Nevern and the mansion nearby: Rhys Nanmor mentions the mansion as being near the river; and Lewis Glyn Cothi who says he looks forward to his meal at Nevern. But one of the family, Howel ap Jenkin ap Robert, seemingly gave short shrift to the bards as shown by his *englyn*:

> Gan Howel gythrel gidag ethrod – gwrdd
> Fe gae gerddor gernod,
> Gan ei dod, gleisiad ei glod
> caid nobol o ad adnabod.

The Squires of Nevern bore the arms of Gwynfardd: *azure a lion rampant within orle of roses or.*

Refs: *NLW, Bronwydd Deeds, Llanstephan ms 38B, B. M. Egerton ms 2586; P.R.O., AD D, No. 827; Chatham ms, ped No. 11; Carms RO, G.G.M.S. (Gwynfardd).*

NEVERN CASTLE (Castell Nanhyfer).
Nevern.

In 1181 Giraldus commented: 'the ancient and chief castle which the princes of Wales possessed in this part of the country was Ceastrum de Lanhever, where still remain the ruins of a very strong hold surrounded on three sides by a very deep moat, evidently cut out at a vast expenditure of labour, which even to this day contains water'. About 1603-4 George Owen of Henllys wrote, 'Nevarne Castle, now utterlie defased, yet doth the seat thereof shewe of what strength yt was in tymes past, being seated on a hieghe hill unacessable on the one parte, and strengthened with a meightie dytck hewen out of the mayne rocke of the other partes, this was the cheiffe house of the lordes of Kemes in the tyme of the lord Rees ... and this is that same Castle called Castle Nanhyver ... which castle of Nanhyver, being see thence utterlie decased and rased, so known but of a few'.

Refs: G. Owen, Second book, p. 276; Arch. Cam. 1859, p. 334; Avc. Mon. Pembs. 1925, p. 260; Laws, Little England, 1888, p. 97.

NEWGALE. *Brawdy.*

Now an ancient farmstead (formerly a manor-house), just below the crest of a high slope, with a fine view over the vale below, Newgale Sands, and St. Brides Bay.

Recorded in 1326 as a 'a knight's fee (English)', and thus marked on Rees's 14th century map. It became a lay manor, its lands in Brawdy parish. The first known family to hold the property was that of Sutton, from about 1430 to 1560. John Sutton, the last of the family in the male line, died leaving his estates to his daughter and heiress Thamoyng who married Rees ap Morgan of Haverfordwest, gent., and on 10 May 1560 they sold estates in Brawdy parish and elsewhere to John Voyle of Haverfordwest, whose I.P.M. taken on 6 May 1681, includes 'Domine Newgale', whose lands were held by William Ieunan and William Jones of Brawdy, tenants.

Later in that year John Voyle of Haverfordwest was described as lord of the manor, and was followed by his son Morgan Voyle who was described in 1588 as Lord of the Manor of Newgale, and of three other manors in Dewsland. Morgan lived mainly in Haverfordwest, was Mayor in 1585, and Sheriff of the town in 1582. His son and heir, John Voyle, mined for silver in St. Elvis in 1624. Some time later the Voyles sold their interest in Newgale manor, which was held by the Owens of Orielton for a short while.

The Warlow family were farming tenants at Newgale as early as 1568, and became lords of its manor in the early 17th century and moved to live at nearby Llether. John Warlow's grand-daughter, and heiress, Lettice Warlow, married, about 1652, James Jones, a younger son of Brawdy. Their descendants remained at Llether, and held the manor of Newgale (*inter alia*), until the first half of the present century, the last manorial lord being Mrs. Nest Massy, daughter of Colonel Roch of Llether.

Refs: NLW, Papers of Great Sessions, Pembs. 1670; Poyston Deeds; Pembs Arch Survey 1896-1907; Dwnn i, p. 177; Francis Jones, 'Records of a 16th Century Pembs. Estate' in B.B.C.S., XIII, May 1949, pp. 93-104.

NEW HOUSE.
(Formerly called Red Castle).
Newton North.

Mudge's Map 1819 and Colby's Map 1831 locate New House on the southern edge of Canaston Wood, and marked as Redcastell on Dincley's Map 1684, and as Redcastle on Speed's Map 1611. Richard Fenton, having left the village of Minwear says 'Hence I pass over a new road carried through very beautiful woods to the ruins of a once very consequential mansion called New House ... It is a large pile of excellent masonry, seems to have been moated, and one of the earliest habitations of the uncastellated form. In some writings, I have seen it briefly noted that New House was formerly called Red Castle ...'; he suggests that it may have been the residence of the Canaston family, and afterwards became part of the Barlow of Slebech estate, (Tour Pembs. 1811, pp. 164-168).

There are several references to the manor of Newhouse in the 16th and 17th century deeds of the Barlows. In 1657, John Barlow Esq., leased to his fifth son, Lewis Barlow, 'a messuage called New House formerly called Redd Castle, in Newton parish' for 99 years. During 1896-1907 the following description of New House ruins was made: 'The basement is 15 yards by 10 yards: there is a fireplace to the east of the stairs on the south-west side; a window on the west, three windows on the north, a door and loophole to the south: the hall had two chimneys on the east, two windows on the south; stairway on the south-west, and three more windows; a part of the building at the east end is cut off by a dividing wall which seems to be of later work: on the east of the basement is a door in a ruined wall, two windows; the wall at the east is gone. A moat encompasses the building'. A more professional description was made by the *Commissioners of Ancient Monuments* in June 1920; 'Castell Coch. About 250 yards north-west of the modern farmstead called Newhouse is a perfect example of the country gentry's residence of the 13th-15th centuries … The moat at Castell Coch, which is an almost exact square of 270 feet, is aligned to the cardinal points … within the square area was built a residence, now a complete ruin, which was succeeded by the Newhouse already mentioned. This was followed, probably in the days of Elizabeth, by a small mansion, which, with many later alterations and additions, can still be traced on a plan executed in 1912, on the occasion of the clearance of the site by the county Ancient Monuments Society. The building then consisted of a large hall (43½ feet by 25 feet internally), and kitchen. The former was of two storeys above the ground floor, the latter of only one. In the north-eastern corner of the hall was a flight of circular stairs. The main entrance was in the centre of the north front, but the smaller room had a separate entrance from the west. The great fireplace was in the partition wall between the hall and the kitchen. The withdrawing rooms were on the first floor above the hall … As the necessity for complete isolation gradually ceased, the mode of entrance and exit was improved, and a roadway made across the moat. To the south-east, just beyond the moat are traces of the fish stew.'

(Plan of moat and house), (*RCAM Pembs.* 1925, pp. 278-9).

Refs: *NLW, Slebech Deeds; Francis Green 'The Barlows of Slebech'. W.W.H.R. III; and refs. given in the text above.*

NEW MOAT. *New Moat.*

A residence in grounds close to the southern side of New Moat, now a complete ruin. The earliest, and main, residence of the Scourfield family from the late 14th century to our time, a period of over 550 years. At the end of the 14th century, John Scourfield lived there, and in a deed of 1438 the parties are described as John Skorffyll the elder of Nova Mota, his wife Isabel, and their son John Skorffyll, junior, and before the end of that century the name was spelled as Scourfield which influenced the family to adopt a canting coat of arms: *gules three greyhounds argent* ('couring the field'), *with a crest of a silver greyhound holding the word 'Ffydlon' in his mouth.* In 1591, the then head of the family signed his name to his pedigree as 'John Schourthefyld'.

That their residence was commodious is indicated by the fact that it contained eight hearths in 1670. The Scourfields owned the New Moat estate for a least fourteen generations. About 1780 William Henry Scourfield went to live at Robeston Hall near Milford, leaving (but still owning) New Moat which became ruinous. On his death in 1805 he was succeeded by his son also named William Henry Scourfield the last member in the male descent of his family. In 1843 he died without issue, leaving the New Moat estate to a descendant of his sister, Elizabeth Anne Scourfield. She had married Col. Own Phillips of Williamston (Burton parish) in 1804, and had a son John Henry Phillips who received New Moat. This John Henry took the surname Scourfield in 1862, and was created Baronet on 18th February 1876 which he enjoyed for a very short time for he died in June of that year. He was succeeded by his son, Sir Owen Henry Phillips Scourfield, 2nd and last Baronet, who died without issue in 1921, leaving the New Moat estate to his cousin Henry George Saunders-Davies, of the Pentre family, who took the name Scourfield by R.L. in 1922. He was followed by his son, Col. David Gwyn Davies-Scourfield, M.C.

The New Moat estate was advertised for sale in 1925, but not sold. At this time the estate consisted of 49 properties. The mansion had become ruinous, and in 1926 was demolished. A few references to the old mansion occur during the 19th century.

In 1811 Fenton wrote: '... Moat, a straggling village, below which I see with regret the shell of one of the most ancient houses in the mountain district, now unroofed, where still within these forty years the family of Scourfield from the time of Edward the First had continued to reside in the midst of a very large contiguous property and a wealthy respectable tenantry. The house of its sort and its age ranked among the very first, and its situation was truly a noble one on an eminence looking down on Haverfordwest about nine miles off ... near a handsome church, the advowson of which was in the family, and in a parish entirely, or with a very small exception, their own property ... Mr. Scourfield now resides at Robeston, about six miles below Haverfordwest, where he had no other property but his demesne with a mansion-house on one side most unpleasantly circumscribed; and, for this, was abandoned the feudal importance of the upland situation'. The next writer, S. Lewis, writes in 1840 – 'Moat: the ancient mansion of the Scourfields who resided here from the reign of Edward I till within the last 60 years when they removed to Robeston Hall near Milford, has been taken down, and is now erecting a spacious and elegant mansion on the same site to which the family will remove when it is competed; the house which is surrounded with thriving plantations and with groves of ancient timber, is delightfully situated at the foot of the southern declivity of the Precelly range of mountains, and commands a fine view over the whole of the lower part of the county.'

Vide: **THE MOAT**

Refs: *Fenton, Tour Pembs, 1811; Lewis TDW 1840; Cambrian Journal 1862, p. 241; L.D. I, 110. 175-6; W.W.H.R. II.64. IX, 145; Carms RO; SC 636, 1925; PRO, Avc Deeds; T. Lloyd, Lost Houses of Wales, 1986, Photo.*

NEWPORT CASTLE. *Newport.*
Standing on the slope of Castle Hill overlooking the town of Newport and Cardigan Bay. Seat of the Martins and their descendants the Owens and Lloyds. This ancient stronghold lies in the old hundred of Kemes invaded and conquered by the Norman Martin de Tours not long after the Norman Conquest of England. Martin first built a castle at Nevern of which only fragments remain, but it was his grandson, Sir William de Martin, who constructed a fairly substantial stone fortress nearer to the sea at Newport. Kemes became a Norman March – defended border territory against the native Welsh. Subsequent owners became known as Lords (or Ladies) of the March of Kemes of Cemaes.

In 1215 Llewellyn the Great captured Newport castle but three years later it was restored to the de Martins and their descendants who lived there quietly until 1357 when another Prince Llewellyn, last of his name, again attacked the place. Thereafter the family was left in peace. William Martin, son of Nicholas, served in the Scottish Wars and was summoned by writ to Parliament in 1295 as Baron Martin. His son, also William succeeded him as second Baron, but on his death in 1324 the barony fell into abeyance. The title of Lord Marcher of Kemes passed to Lord Martin's nephew the 2nd Lord Audley.

Sometime in the 14th century the family moved out of Newport Castle, leaving it in the care of a Constable. The castle had the traditional keep on a motte with a moat and drawbridge. The Great Banqueting Hall still has traces of a 13th century fireplace.

The Lords Audley remained in possession of the now ruined castle until James, 7th Lord Audley, was beheaded in the reign of Henry VI. His estates reverted to the Crown but were restored to Lord Audley's son who sold it to the Owens who were descendants of the Martins, thus as it were, 'keeping it in the family'.

Although for a time the fabric of Newport Castle was kept in order, by the early 15th century it had begun to decay. George Owen (1552-1613) the historian of the County, and author of *Description of Pembrokeshire* and *Cataloge and Genelogie of the Lordes of Kemes* was a Lord Marcher of Kemes and owned the Castle. His father, William Owen (d. 1574), compiler of *Le Bregement de Statutis* (1521), had recovered the Barony of Kemes after a nineteen-year legal battle. Unfortunately for him, George Owen was, for a time, imprisoned in his own dungeon.

From the Owens, Newport passed by descent to the family of Lloyd. Sir Thomas Lloyd was created a baronet in 1863. His son, the second and last baronet, Sir Marteine Owen Mowbray Lloyd, Bt., delineated his descent in *Burke's Peerage and Baronetage* from Martin de Tours and stated that he, by right of tenure, was the 24th Lord of the Barony of Kemes and that 'the Barony of Kemes is the only Lordship Marcher now in existence in the Kingdom, and the lords thereof still exercise a portion of their rights, and annually appoint, under their hands and seals, the Mayors of Newport'.

Sir Marteine's only son and heir fell in the Great War and the baronetcy became extinct. The first baronet had inherited a ruin, but in 1859 he repaired and made habitable part of the Castle, using stone from a demolished gatehouse. For the first time in centuries Newport Castle became a family home again. Sir Marteine's youngest daughter, Joan married Philip Saxon Gregson-Ellis of Bryddyffrin, Denbighshire. The latter's daughter, Mrs. John Gregson-Ellis who died in 1975, was Lady Marcher and has been succeeded by her daughter, Mrs. Hyacinthe Hawkesworth.

The castle has a ghost known as 'The Lavender Lady' with a fondness for children; she carries with her the scent of lavender from a posy she holds. The castle is currently tenanted by Mr. and Mrs. H. B. Holt, who have restored and repaired the building which was in a sad state of decay.

NEWTON. *Llanstadwell.*

Formerly a gentry residence, about three-quarters of a mile east of Newton-ness (now called Newton Noyes), and half a mile south of Waterston village: today Newton is enveloped by an oil refinery. In 1811 Fenton states: 'Newton was once the residence of the princely family of Craddock, lineally descended from Howel Dda, lords of this place, whose descendant Sir Richard married - Emma, daughter and co-heiress of Sir Thomas Perrott of Eastington, and dropping Craddock, took the name of Newton, and was Chief Justice of the Common Pleas. This lead him to settle in England, and dispose of his property in Wales. He died December 14th, 1444 (according to D.W.B., at an advanced age, between 11 November 1448 and 10 June 1449) and lies buried in a chapel on the south side of Bristol Cathedral. This place (Newton), boasting of the most delightful views on the harbour, now the comfortable residence of Lewis Child, Esq., retains nothing of any pristine dignity in point of habitation ... I learn from Mr. Child that in the church-yard of Llanstadwell church there was a sculptured tombstone, bearing an effigy almost overgrown with the turf, which was removed to make place for the internment of his uncle Mr. Bowlas, the late proprietor of Newton, he having directed his body to be laid there, as from tradition he had understood that this was formerly the burial place of the ancient lords of the place; for in a pedigree of that family there is mention made of one buried at Newton, meant I presume for Lanstadwell'. The judge married, firstly, Emma daughter of Sir Thomas Perrott of Haroldston St. Issels, Pembs., and secondly, Emmota, daughter of John Harvey of London, and had issue by both. Emmota survived him, and died in 1475; in the church of Yatton, Somerset, is an altar tomb with the effigy of a judge, wearing the collar of SS, and his lady by his side

(D.N.B.). Sir Richard owned lands in Somerset and Gloucestershire.

Among his descendants was John Newton of Gonerby, Lincolnshire, from whom descended the illustrious Sir Isaac Newton. Sir John Wynn recorded, 'William alias Wilcocke Crados married an inheretrix in Pembrokeshire where his posteritie remained ever since. Havinge by the house called Newton named themselves Newton Cradocke both in Pembrookeshire and Somersettshire.' The next family at Newton was that of Bowlas, a minor gentry family, who were there from 1554 (possibly earlier), until 1795 when it passed to their kinsfolk the Child family by will of Samuel Bowlas in 1794, to Lewis Child, Esq., who was living at Newton in 1795.

The last of the family at Newton was Elizabeth Bowlas Child who, by will dated 16 October 1861, proved 13 June 1862, left all her realty and personalty to her sister Jane Child, and the said Jane Child (sister of William James of Fishguard, Esq.,) whose will dated 27 May 1865 (with three codicils), was proved on 4th May 1871, the executors being the Revd. Henry Lewis of Stowmarket, Suffolk, and John Child of Roch. Particulars of sale of the Newton estate appeared in 1871. A sale catalogue offered the Newton estate in Llanstadwell parish for sale on 21 August 1900; the estate was on the shores of Milford Haven, with a frontage of nearly two miles: the family Mansion of Newton House, with lawn, garden, conservatory, wash house, stables, farm building, cottages and lime kilns (416 acres, on shores of the said Haven), with four other pieces of land, all in occupation of Roch Davies, Esq.

Refs: *Pembs R.O., Newton Deeds and documents 1554-1871, L.T. 1786, NLW, Poyston Deeds, Pembs. Plea Rolls 1686, Dwnn, pp. 44-5, 274-5: Fenton, Tour Pembs. 1811, p. 152; Lewis TDW 1840; Sir John Wynn, History of the Gwydir Family, 1927 edn. pp. 32-3.*

NEWTON. *Rudbaxton.*

A residence about 1¼ miles south of Scolton mansion, and about half a mile north of The Rath. Near The Rath are Newton Hall and Little Rath farms marked on Colby's Map 1831. The mesne manors of Newton and Rudbaxton were held in 1587 by the lords Stanley and Havard as of the manor of Fletherhill. In 1631-2 Owen Edwardes of Little Treffgarn bought Newton manor from Thomas Stanley of Knockin. At the time of his death, pre Oct. 1649, Owen owned four messuages and 495 acres in Newton, as part of the large Little Treffgarn estate, and in 1786 William Mortimer Edwardes owned Newton Hall and Newton Lodge near The Rath, and Rowland Edwardes was owner-occupier of Newton. Today (1987), the owner-occupier of Newton is Mr. Peter Higgon, son of the late Col. Higgon of Scolton.

Refs: *Picton Castle Deeds; W.W.H.R. VIII, p. 194; Owens Pembs ii, pp. 400, 519; Pembs. RO, Land Tax 1786; Voters List 1894, 1950; Taylor's Cussion (1587-88) p. 96a.*

NOLTON. *Nolton.*

A coastal parish overlooking St. Brides Bay, between Newgale on the north and Broadhaven on the south. The village and parish church are located about three quarters of a mile inland. Fenton has written of two ancient houses:

1. The glebe house is situated exactly opposite the church separated by a road only; and with no pretensions above the character of a cottage, yet furnishes most unexpected and comfortable accommodations. It has marks of great antiquity, being vaulted; and was formerly approached by a gateway opening into a quadrangle, walls five feet thick, and cement as hard as a rock ... It is remarkable that a family of the name of Grant from Scotland, in the time of the unfortunate Mary, settled in this mansion, and that his descendant now occupies part of the property: the only large enclosure in the parish was called Grant's Park before the whole parish was enclosed, 1750 ...'

2. 'On the north side of the church-yard was the old manor-house, the mansion of the lord of the vill ... of which, perhaps, not a vestige would have remained but for a water-closet entered from the first floor, as at the

145

parsonage, a peculiarity in the old mansions of the country. The property of Nolton, of which this old mansion was the head, before the great rebellion, was in the family of Crowe, but being forfeited, it was bought by the City of London, under condition of paying the usual quit rent to the Crown, still paid; of the city a Mr. Cozens of Robeston West bought it; from this purchaser it devolved on Thomas Kymer, Esq., who sold it to Mr. Barlow of Lawrenny; and Hugh Barlow, Esq., member for the town of Pembroke, is now the possessor'.

Refs: *Fenton, Tour Pembs. 1811, pp. 87-8; RCAM, Pembs 1925, s.n. Nolton.*

NORCHARD. *Manorbier.*

Just south of The Ridgeway, and north of Lydstep. Formerly a commodious residence of an ancient landowning family, built over a continuous vault. It is now a farmhouse. The earliest residence of which we have any record was that of Looney, also spelled as Lynny and Lang. Thomas Looney left no sons and Norchard passed to his daughter and heiress Isabel who married Lawrence Marychurch who settled at his wife's home. Between 1400 and 1600, eleven generations of his descendants lived at Norchard. The origin of the family is unknown, and the name was often rendered as St. Marychurch by Dwnn. Five of the name served as Mayors of Tenby in the period 1501-1526. When Dwnn recorded the pedigree and arms (*a fawn couchant*) on 10 November 1591, John Marychurch signed, and gave five shillings to the herald for his travail.

The family remained at Norchard until the latter half of the 19th century. In 1670 William Marychurch was assessed at seven hearths for Norchard, and Maud Marychurch and Francis Marychurch were each assessed at one hearth apiece. The male line seems to have failed shortly afterwards, and when Mary Marychurch married on 1673, John Williams of Gumfreston, and Pant Howel (Carms), who then settled at Norchard which passed to Mary's descendants. Mrs. Mary Meyrick had two daughters who

married two brothers – Mary to John Meyrick (d.1732), and Alice who married Francis Meyrick (d.1741). In 1786 Norchard was owned by John Meyrick Esq. (of Bush), with Nicholas Roch as tenant. Thereafter Norchard was farmed by a series of tenants.

Refs: *Dwnn, i, 124; W.W.H.R. ii, 37; Chatham Pedigree in Laws, Little England; Picton Castle Deeds; Pembs R.O., L.T. 1786; Peter Smith, Houses of the Welsh Countryside, p. 23; B.M. Egerton Ms 2586; Come to Pembs. Guide, (c. 1936) p. 28 illus.*

NOTE: A family of Marychurch lived in Haverfordwest from the 17th century, where they were successful tradesmen, mercers and glovers. William Marychurch, a Royalist, was elected Mayor of the town in 1653, but was fined and ousted from the post at a suit in Haberdashers' Hall, London. In 1694 William Marychurch was Sheriff of Haverfordwest, and Mayor in 1694; in 1829 Joseph Marychurch was town sheriff, and in 1865, Mayor of the town. The family also owned property at Llawhaden.

NORTH DOWN. *Lamphey.*

In 1840 this was described as a 'genteel residence' occupied by the Rev. B. Byers.

Major Jones's notes are sketchy, but he gives a rough pedigree of the Rowe family. Henry Rowe of Lamphey, who died in 1705 had a son Lewis described as 'of Northdown'. Lewis's eldest son John inherited. His second son (b.1699) was the Rev. Henry Rowe, Vicar of St. Petrox. John's son Richard, inherited North Down and was Mayor of Pembroke in 1766, 1775, 1781 and 1786.

Lloyd, Baronet

ORIELTON. *Hundleton.*

Formerly in St. Nicholas, Monkton parish. A mansion on high ground one mile south of

Hundleton village, and three-quarters of a mile north of St. Twynnells. Pembroke town is 2¹/₂ miles to the north-east. Fenton wrote in 1811, '... Orielton, a mansion that has maintained high rank for centuries ... probable that it was originally inhabited by some powerful follower of Arnugh de Montgomery, of the name of Oriel, a name now almost worn out, and only found among the vulgar ... in the reign of Henry the second, it was possessed by a man of note, of the name of Wyrriott, whose descendants continued to occupy it till the reign of Queen Elizabeth, when, by the marriage of Sir Hugh Owen, Knt, with the sole heiress of that great estate, Elizabeth Wyrriott, it changed the name of its owner. Sir Hugh was a younger son of the ancient house of Bodeon, Anglesea. Orielton continued to be their chief residence, where they intermarried with the first families and shared the highest honours of the county'. While a fair amount of evidence exists concerning the owners, little has been found about the early edifice. George Wyrriott was in residence in 1188 when Gerald of Wales called and mentions the ghostly visitants at the house.

In 1300 Sir David Wyrriott of Orielton attended the court of Joan de Valence, Countess of Pembroke, and was living in 1323, and may have been Sheriff of Carmarthen in 1314 and 1317. In 1384 Richard Wyrriott of Orielton was instructed to deliver Manorbier Castle to the King's hands; and his great-grandson Thomas Wyrriott was Sheriff of Pembroke in 1459. Thomas Wyrriott had been an officer in the bodyguard of Hum-phrey, Duke of Gloucester, and on the arrest and murder of the Duke in 1447, Thomas was imprisoned in London, but later released. The next owner, Henry Wyrriott, married Margaret natural daughter of Sir Rhys ap Thomas K.G. of Dynevor. He led troops during Henry VIII's war in France, and became High Sheriff of Pembrokeshire in 1549 and 1559.

When the herald, Fellows, called at Orielton in 1530 he recorded the arms of 'Harry Weryote of Oryalton' as: *argent a lion passant sable*, with several quarterings, and the Crest: *a hairy man holding a branch on his shoulder.*

The last of the family at Orielton, in the male succession, George Wyrriott, was a JP. and High Sheriff in 1577; by his wife, Jane Philipps of Picton Castle, he had a daughter and heiress, Elizabeth Wyrriott, who married in 1591, Hugh Owen, a younger son of the Owens of Bodeon, Anglesey, who settled at Orielton. At the time of her marriage the Orielton estate comprised four manors, eighty farms, four water corn mills, a fulling mill and 5,200 acres in south and mid-Pembrokeshire, to which Hugh Owen added many more properties. Hugh was a JP., High Sheriff in 1583, was later knighted, died on 8 February 1613-14; and buried in Monkton churchyard.

His successor, also named Hugh Owen, was created a Baronet on 4th August 1641. The Owen arms were: *gules a chevron between three lions rampant or.* Orielton was a large commodious mansion, assessed for seventeen hearths for taxation in 1670. A tourist in 1802 wrote of Orielton – 'The house is neither ancient nor modern, being fronted with brick, and the frames of the windows and the corner stones of freestone; somewhat in the stile (*sic*) of Llanvorda (Denbs.) before it was burnt. The house has plantations up to its very front ...' The Owens of Orielton were a family of considerable distinction producing several Justices of the Peace, Lords Lieutenant, High Sheriffs, an ADC. to Queen Victoria and Members of Parliament, and were rewarded with baronetcies and governmental appointments. The first baronetcy, granted in 1641, was borne by successive descendants until 1851 when Sir William Owen, 8th Baronet, died without issue. However, Corbetta Owen, sister of the 7th Baronet, had married John Lord, of Pembroke in 1774, and their eldest son, John Lord, inherited the Orielton estate in 1809, when he adopted the name and arms of Owen and was created a baronet (of the 2nd creation) on 12 January 1813. About 1809 he took down the old edifice, and erected a new mansion. Unfortunately he became heavily in debt, and in 1857 Orielton and what was left of the landed estate was sold to M. A. Saurin of Cilwendeg, sometime a Gentleman Usher of the Privy Chancellor. However his baronetcy survives in the person of Sir Hugh Owen, 5th Baronet.

Orielton had remained in possession of descendants of the Wyrriots for some seven hundred and fifty years, and it was the first time that it had ever been sold. Among the descendants living today is Captain Mark Phillips, first husband of Princess Anne, the Princess Royal.

At the time of the sale in 1857, Orielton had been deserted by Sir John Owen and becoming ruinous, the new owner made several improvements, and restored it as a residence. Mark Anthony Saurin of Orielton was High Sheriff in 1867, and his son Morgan James Saurin held the same office in 1883. One of the later owners of Orielton was A.G. Gaddum, High Sheriff in 1943. The property was later sold, and is today a field Centre.

Refs: *Dwnn, i, 247-8, ii, 95; W.W.H.R., ii, 95; Peter Smith, Houses of the Welsh Countryside, 1975; Francis Jones, 'Owen of Orielton in Pembs. Hist. 1974; Timmins, Nooks and Corners, 1895, 74, illus.; Black's Guide 1851, p. 304; Fenton, Tour Pembs., 1811, p. 216; Phillips, Memoirs of the Owen Family; C.S. Allen, S.W. Photographs, 1871, illus.; The Welshman Newspaper, 26 Aug. 1842; S.W. Daily News, 7 Jan. 1911; NLW Journal, 1968, illus.; NLW Maps, prints and Drawings, Orielton c 1810; Pembs. Arch Survey 1896-1907; NLW, Pembs. Plea Rolls 1544; ms 1730, Tour (AD 1802); B. M. Egerton ms 2586.*

ORLANDON. *St. Brides.*

About a mile to the south-east of St. Brides inlet. It was also called Humprey. In 1603 there is reference to 'the lands of Hugh Butler, Esq., at Humproughe'; and in 1668 John Hopkins, gent., instituted a law-suit against Walter Roch, Yeoman of Humpra in the parish of St. Brides. It afterwards became a property and residence of the Laugharnes descended from William Laugharne who had married the daughter and heiress of the family of John de St. Brides, and in 1832 'the capital messuage and demesne called Orlandon alias Humprey', belonged to the Laugharne family.

During his Pembrokeshire tour, Fenton reached 'Orlandon or as it was formerly called, Humprey, the seat of my old friends, J.P. Laugharne, Esq., whose hospitality I was engaged to share for a few days, and from whose inexhaustible source of ancient lore I was permitted to draw largely ... After experiencing the most hospitable reception from my friend, and a night of such refreshment as the antiquarian traveller can but seldom command ... I set out ...' Some seventy years later, in 1882, a local historian wrote, '... where stood till of late an old mansion worthy of note, Orlandon, once the seat of the Laugharnes' ... The Orlandon property, which was once the most extensive in the county, has all been sold. It was at one time the boast of the family that they could ride from sunrise to sunset without going outside it ...' Thornhill Timmins, who called there about 1895, had this to say, '... Orlandon, where the skeleton of a large old mansion rises grimly above a group of wayside cottages. In its palmy days Orlandon was the home of the Laugharnes, a family of some celebrity in their time, but now extinct in this locality.' The Laugharnes had been established in Haverfordwest in medieval times, and later became landowners with seats at Pontfaen, Llanunwas, Llanreithan, St. Brides Hill, and Orlandon.

In the late Middle Ages, William Laugharne married the daughter and sole heiress of John de St. Brides, and settled at St. Brides Hill and Orlandon, both in that parish. They bore arms: *gules three lions heads erased or.* In 1762 Rowland Philipps Laugharne of Orlandon, was High Sheriff; John Philipps Laugharne of Orlandon was High Sheriff in 1788 and 1797.

On 15 April 1835, Sir William Laugharne Philipps of Haverfordwest, Bart., released in trust for sale 'Orlandon otherwise Humprey' in St. Brides parish, and lands elsewhere in Pembrokeshire. The Tithe Schedule for the parish, in 1839, records William Charles Allen Philipps as owner-occupier of Orlandon, and a ground-plan of the commodious mansion is also given. The family abandoned it, and a sale catalogue of 1920 of the St. Brides Estate includes, 'Orlandon, the mansion, now in ruins, was the early home of the Laugharnes'.

Refs: *Dwnn i, 73, 184; Fenton, Tour Pembs. 1811, 96-7; Timmins, Nooks and Corners, 1895, 119, sketch of the ruins; Phillips, Haverfordwest and its Story, 1882, 29-30; Pembs. RO, Deeds HDX 194, No. 17; NLW, Papers of Great Sessions, Pembs. Plea Rolls 1668; Poyston Deeds.*

*John Phillips Laugharne,
Inner Temple*

PANTEG. (Panteague).
Llanddewi Felfre.

A residence in a dingle east of Plâs Crwn, south-east of Llanddewi Felfre, and about a mile from the A40 road from Whitland to Haverfordwest. A photograph taken in 1987, shows Panteg, a large commodious double-pile Georgian house of two storeys and an attic storey; ranges of five windows, set within lawns and attractive grounds; now called Panteg Farm (309 acres).

The first known owners were the Stepneys of Prendergast near Haverfordwest. In 1619 Sir John Stepney sold Panteg to Henry Hensleigh whose family had come to Pembrokeshire from Paxton, Somerset. Five generations of the Hensleighs remained at Panteg, until 1763, when Elizabeth only

daughter and heir of John Hensleigh, married John Bartlett Allen of Cresselly, and their descendants took the surname of Hensleigh Allen. The Hensleighs had been quickly successful, and by the 18th Century had become Esquires. They took little part in local life apart from supporting worthy causes. Thus, John Hensleigh subscribed for four copies of the Revd. William Evan's translation of Canwyll y Cymry in 1771.

In the following century, Panteg was let to tenants. The house was bought in 1987 by Mr. Plowden formerly of Vron (qv).

Refs: *Pembs. RO, LT 1786; NLW, ms 6462 (George Owen); College of Arms, Protheroe ms IV, ff. 84, 86.*

PANTIRION. *St. Dogmaels.*

A residence to the north-west of St. Dogmaels village, between Granant and Ffonnon Feddyg; marked on Colby's Map 1831. Little has been discovered about it in early times. In the second half of the 18th century Pantirion was the home of Richard Jones, described as Land Surveyor, and owner-occupier in 1786; Later it became home of the Jenkins family, a branch of the Cilbronnan family. In 1875, Richard Jenkins, JP of Pantirion (son of Griffith Jenkins), lived there, took an active part in local life, and was 13 times Mayor of Cardigan. By the end of that century Pantirion had passed from the Jenkins' and in 1904 was the home of one Griffith Lewis.

Refs: *T. Nicholas, County Families, 1875 edn, p. 903; NLW, Bronwydd Deeds No. 2093.*

PANTSAESON. *Also* PANTSAISON
Monington.

The residence is marked on Colby's Map of 1831 among woodland on a long southerly slope, three-quarters of a mile north of Monington parish church, one and a half miles north of Glandwr farm, and one and a half miles north-east of Moylgrove village. About ten years ago Plâs Pantsaison was described by Mr. Hugh Lloyd Howell (of the Glaspant family) as follows: 'The approach to Pantsaison is well wooded with trees on both sides of the drive, which through neglect is now rough and uneven. This Georgian mansion has a pillared portico, with scroll-work on the wall above. A stone staircase with metal banisters goes down to a tiled entrance hall; several spacious reception rooms open on to the hall, with a smaller room that has a moulded ceiling of floral design; most of the bedrooms are large and sunny with ample head-room; while the servants' quarters at the back of the house are extensive with stairs leading to the upper floors. Traces exist near the present residence of an older house, probably Jacobean'.

The industrious Thomas Nicholas recorded the history of the family and residence in 1875, as follows: 'This family (James) has been resident at and in possession of, Pantsaison beyond any record to the contrary. There is a tradition in the family that there were thirteen William James's in succession before the last two Johns: Col. John James (d.1819), and John T. W. James (b.1812), but it does not seem to have had very extensive possessions or to have arrogated to itself a place among the chief families of the county ... At the west end of Pantsaison there is a scarped earthwork ... The present house of Pantsaison is of the Italian villa style, and was built in the year 1836. Two or three (probably more) successive houses have been standing on or near the same spot'.

The 6" OS Map of 1904 marks 'The site of manor house', to the north-west of the present residence, and near a cluster of outbuildings. *The Pembrokeshire Archaeological Survey* (1896-1907) reported, 'a farmyard and building of no archaeological import occupies the site of old Pantsaison house. The property has been in the James family for many generations. Their predecessors were the Peverils, who lived in a house between Pantsaison and the sea, the very site of which is in dispute'; the foregoing is noted in *RCAM Pembs.*, 1925, p. 235, but adds no further information.

The Peverils were a well-known family in the district in medieval times, but no connection with Pantsaison has been found. My own researches reveal no early connection with the James family. They show that Thomas Lloyd of Pantsaison was living there on 13th July 1614; and in 1615 Thomas William Lloyd, yeoman was living there; later in the century William Rowland of Pant y Sayson, who was assessed at two hearths in the Hearth Tax List of 1670. The eldest daughter of Thomas Rowland, Mary, married William Garnons, member of a well-known landowning family in North Pembrokeshire. In 1721-22 a Mary Rowland married William James, and their prenuptial settlement, dated 28 February 1721-22, includes the following properties settled on the couple:- Trevarrld-Ucha and -Issa, and other lands in the parishes of Monington, Llantood, and Bayvill. Although the bridegroom is described as of Pantsaison, it was not included among the properties settled. From this marriage onwards, six generations of their descendants continued at Pantsaison. One of the family, Col. John James, in 1799 fought a duel on the field called Fortune's Frolic, killed his opponent, and had to flee to the continent. He returned to Pantsaison, and died in 1819.

The last owner, William Frederick Lloyd James (b.1872) sold Pantsaison to Mr. and Mrs. Robertson Williams, and left the district to live in Herefordshire. His sister, Mary Ellen James (b.1874) married Mr. J. M. Philipps of Treffith, JP, C.C. She died at Tenby in 1924; she was author of 'The Fishguard Invasion'. The arms of James of Pantsaison as given by Nicholas are as follows: *Sable a dolphin naiant, embowed or, between three cross crosslets or*, quartering those of Bateman, Vaughan and Taubman; Crest: *a demi bull rampant sable, horned and hoofed or*; motto, *Ffyddlon et y gorffen*, (faithful to the end).

Refs: *Thos. Nicholas, County Families 1875 edn. p. 902; BLG, 1850; RCAM, Pembs. 1925, p. 235; Pembs. Arch Survey (1867-1907); Alumni Oxoniensis; Pembs. R.O. LT 1786; VL 1894 and 1904, Deeds 1808 and 1813; Landowners Return 1873; NLW, Tyllwyd Deeds; Mrs. Ethel Jones Deeds, Morgan Richardson Deeds, Alwyn Evans ms 12357 E, p. 14 - 16, Papers of G.S.*

PANTYDERI. *Llanfair Nantgwyn.*

A mansion, three-quarters of a mile to the east of the parish church. Commodious, built in the traditional Welsh style, it is of three storeys with ranges of five windows, and still has the original oak-beams, and a fine oak staircase; it overlooks a well-tended lawn and a trout pool. The earliest mansion is said to have occupied a site at a place called Hendy, a short distance away. Nicholas noted that the present building contains parts of considerable age, that several additions were made, the last about 1840 being the most extensive.

For over seven successive centuries Pantyderi was a residence of gentry families. The first descended from Gwynfardd Dyfed, and by the distaff from the Cantingtons of Eglwyswrw. Madoc ap Hywel was living at Pantyderi in 1289, and from him descended Canvey John, son of John ap Gruffyrd or 'Gnts', whose descendants finally adopted the permanent patronymic of Jones. Thomas Jones, solicitor and coroner, was at Pantyderi in 1694, and married to Grace Lewes of Llysnewydd, and had (*inter alia*) a son and heir, John Jones, also a coroner for the county. John died without issue, and by his will (2 Feb. 1721) and codicil (6 Dec. 1728) left Pantyderi to his unmarried sister Anne for her life and then to testator's nephew, Thomas Bowen, second son of Joyce Jones by her husband, Thomas Bowen of Gwern Ffulbrook in Llanfair Nantgwyn parish. Their descendants, the Bowens succeeded to the Pantyderi estate.

In 1786, Thomas Bowen was owner-occupier of the mansion. From the Bowens, the property passed to the well-known Colby family of north Pembrokeshire. In 1837 Thomas Frederick Colby was the owner-occupier of Pantyderi, the mansion and lawns, and demesne of 147 acres, two of the fields being known as Park Castell Coch, and Park Ffynnon Goch. The last of the Colbys at Pantyderi was a notable character, Thomas, usually known as 'Twm Colby', some of whose idiosyncrasies have been recorded by H. M. Vaughan in *The South Wales Squires*, pp. 89-90. The eccentric squire died on 4 April 1912, aged 82. The present owner occupier is Mr. E. L. Jones and his family. The house is in excellent condition, and well maintained and used as a holiday centre.

Refs: *Dales Castle ms; Manorowen ms; Nicholas County Families 1875 edn; Lewis TDW 1840; H. M. Vaughan, S. Wales Squires, 1926; Carms R.O. Golden Grove ms (Gwynfardd); Pembs RO; LT 1786; Voters Lists; Deeds D.RTP; Saunders-Davies Col.; College of Arms col.; Protheroe ms IV fo 155; NLW, Morgan Richardson Deeds, Cwrtmawr Deeds, Alwyn Evans Ped.*

PARC CYNHAETHW(Y). *Manordeifi.*

Now a farmstead about half a mile southwest of Cilfowyr. Little is known of its early history. In the 15th Century and the early 16th century it was owned and occupied by freeholding families, from whom the property passed by marriage to one of the leading gentry families of south-west Wales.

On 15 October 1543, Llewelin ap William Thomas of Cilrhedyn (Carms), released a tenement and land at 'Perthkynaythoo' (*sic*) in Cilgerran Hundred, to Philip ap Ieuan ap Meredydd of Kilvowyr. It became the property of David of Park Kynhathwy son of Griffith ab Ieuan. He was followed by his son, Thomas ap David, who married a daughter of Griffith of Whitechurch parish, by whom he had two daughters, co-heiresses; the elder co-heiress, Janet, married Thomas Philipps son of William Philipps son of Sir Thomas Philipps of Picton Castle, descended from Cadifor Fawr of Blaen Cych. After the marriage Thomas Philipps moved to Parc Cynhaethwy, and was living there in 1587-1591, and later. He was followed by his son Eynon Philipps whose name appears in the Manordivy Muster Roll in 1613. The will of a neighbour, John Beynon, son of Eynon ap Griffith of Cilfowyr, dated 3 April 1615, left two messuages called Tythynod Park Kynhoethwy within the territories of Kilvowir (formerly in tenure of Thomas Philipps, gent., deceased) to testator's nephew, William White. Very few references have been found to Parc Cynhaethwy in later times.

Refs: *L.D.I., 105; WWHR, ii, 85; Pembs. RO; LT 1786; VL 1834; Carms RO; GGMS (Adven. Perw) fo. 231 NLW; Great Sessions, Pembs. Plea Rolls, Nos. 52, 59; Eaton Evans and Williams Deeds, No. 34.*

PARK COURT. *Trefin.*

Today a farmstead within the village of Trefin. From medieval times Trefin has been an Episcopal manor, directly under the governance of the Bishop of St. Davids, who is said to have had a residence here which, according to local tradition, stood on the site of the present Park Court, a name said to derive its name from the manorial court held there from time to time; the courts were held in different houses in Trefin, occasionally – in 1720 it was held in the house of John Thomas, in 1722, in the house of David Thomas, in 1824-28 in the house of Sarah Francis, and in 1895 at the Ship Inn, Trefin.

In 1686 in the John Thomas, of Trefin, gent., sued John ap Rice of Rickeston, Brawdy, Esq., for £20 damages , for entering with force of arms on a messuage of plaintiff called *le Court* and on an acre called *le Orchard* (now Old Orchard, a farm adjacent to Park Court), and departed with cattle, took away trees and traves, (i.e. beams), and six couples. Total value of the manor in 1306 was £16.

From the records of the court we learn that the animal fair was held in the village on the feast of St. Martin, and lasted for three days, a mayor was appointed annually. The court was still held in 1898 under the Bishop's authority, to whom tolls and dues were paid. The Bishop held the adjacent farms of Longhouse and Henllys where he kept cattle and horses, and grew harvests of corn and other grain. Park Court was leased to the family of Garnon for many years. Latterly owned by the Davies Family.

Refs: *Black Book of St. Davids 1326, pp. 57, 71, 105; Fenton Tour Pembs. 1811, pp. 19, 55; NLW, Archives of Courts of Great Sessions; Francis Jones, Journal of Hist. So. of Church in Wales. 1967, pp. 31-5.*

PARK GLAS. *Crinow.*

'The parish, with the exception of a very small portion, belongs to Roger Eaton, Esq., whose elegant mansion of Park Glas is situated within its limits' (Lewis TDW 1840). Eaton left daughters and co-heiresses. His wife, Mrs. Dorothea Eaton, presented a

chalice to Crinow church in 1844. The house had been built by an earlier Roger Eaton, of Clynpathal in 1743.

Memorials in Crinow church give clues to the subsequent descent and ownership of the estate. Charles Delabere Prichett Jones of Park Glas was the only son of the Rev. David Jones, Rector of the Parish. He died in 1867. Algernon Romilly Jenner of Park Glas died in 1872 and Charles Eaton Vaughan Shield, only son of H. R. and A. M. Shield of Park Glas died at sea in 1900 aged 25.

Major Jones has drawn a sketch of the house and notes that there is a photograph of it by C. S. Allen, of Tenby in 'Photographs in South Wales 1871'.

PARK Y PRATT. *St. Dogmaels.*

About a mile south of Cardigan town bridge, and near the Cardigan – Eglwyswrw road. The earlier mansion stood in a grove to the north of the present residence. Near the earlier site stood a cottage in later days known as Hen Park y Pratt. The first family to own the property was that of Pratt who gave the name to it. According to *Pembs. Arch. Survey, 1896,* 'the old house stood some 300 yards below the present homestead, and was surrounded by trees, several of which still remain. There is nothing left of the mansion but some rough walling, and an out-house which has been converted into a cottage'. Little is known of the earliest owners, the Pratts, except that Geoffrey Pratt was living there in 1292, and that the family gave its name to the property. By the 15th century Elen Pratt heiress of

Park y Pratt, married John Cole of St. Dogmaels, and had a son Philip Cole, who was followed by his sole daughter and heiress Janet Cole, who married Owen ap Rhys of Llystin, 10th in descent from Einin Fawr o'r Coed in Cemais who traced back to Gwynfardd Dyfed, an eminent landowner of the county in medieval days ...

This Rees had five sons, between whom their father's estate was divided by gavelkind. Gwilym who had Llystin, Owen who had Llanwerda y Blerddied, James who had Henllys Ysha, John who had Cryngal his mother's property, and Howell.

The Cole family also became owners of Llwyngwair in Nevern parish. Owen ap Rhys who married Janet, eventual heiress of Park y Pratt, was followed by his son Jenkin ap Owen, and he was succeeded by Thomas ap Jenkin. This Thomas married Elen, daughter of Howel Young ap Jenkin, and had a son and heir, David ap Thomas who enlisted in the army, served at Bologne, and elsewhere in France in the reign of Henry VIII, and signed his pedigree for Dwnn on 21 January 1588.

In 1559, Rice Vychan ap Rhydderch of St. Dogmaels vill, Esq., his wife Engharaud, and Rhydderch ap Rees Vychan of Selyham, gent., granted three pieces of land at Tir yrv hengoed, in Bridell, to David Thomas Jenkin ap Owen of Park y Pratt, gent. He was a much loved landowner, interested in genealogies and antiquities. Bards were welcome at Park y Pratt, and Sirn Mawddwg sang his elegy when he died at a very advanced age on 10th May 1601. By his wife, Janet, daughter of Sir James ab Owen ap William ab Owen of Pentre Ifan, he had three sons: Einion, living 1588; Nicholas, of Park y Pratt; the Rev. Nicholas David the younger, vicar of St. Dogmaels, 1601. The eldest son, Einion, married Margaret John of Trefaes Issa, 'and , as thei saye was devorsed and then married one Hugh Phe ap Ieuan Jenkin in the liff of her husband Eynon David, and had by him a son named David, and then she died, the said Eynon David surviving her' ... so wrote her contemporary, George Owen of Henllys. Nicholas, the second son, entered the Church, became Vicar of St. Dogmaels, and

according to George Owen, 'Park y Pratt the mansion house now of Nicholas David, cleric, second sonne to his ffather, David Thomas who in his tyme lyved and dyed in the love and likeinge of all his acquaintance, and who greathe beauwtified the place ...'

Few references have been found of the David family afterwards, and it is clear that they had left Park y Pratt before the end of the first half of the 18th century; the post nuptial references dated 25th September 1666, of Thomas Bowen gent., of Cilgerran, and Ann David second daughter of Stephen David of Park y Pratt, gent., mention some 23 properties were settled, in the parishes of Cilgerran, Bridell, and Emlyn Is Cych.

The last reference I have seen to the family mentions William Morris of Park y Pratt, gent., living there in 1716. In 1760, Mr. Thomas Morris of Park y Pratt is listed as a parliamentary voter. The Land Tax of 1786 states that Mr. Thomas Morris was the owner-occupier. In the period 1815-1875 the Jenkins family lived there, and in 1858 William Griffith George was the occupier. An ms. of 1860 states, 'Park y Pratt was, during the last century and part of this in the possession of a family named Morris, the last of whom, dying without issue, left the estate to a cousin of his living in Bristol who resided for some time at Park y Pratt accompanied by a person named Sumner in whose favour he made his will. Sumner sold the estate to Thomas Davies, Esq., of the Bridge, Cardigan and ere he left the country erected a monumental stone in memory of his friend'. Henry Graham Partridge, owner-occupier of Park y Pratt, was High Sheriff in 1971.

Refs: NLW Mostyn ms Nos. 50 (c 1592), No. 3033B and 5603; Bronwydd ms No. 50 c 1601-2; Eaton Evans and Williams Deeds Nos. 49 & 1275, Noyadd Trefawr Deed No. 874, George Owen 'second book' 1269, and ms 5603, fos 84-5; Carms RO, Golden Grove Books (Adv. Pembs) I, fo 1239; Pembs. RO Deeds MDX, 615, No. 1; College of Arms mss, Wagner Ms 2 (by G. Owen); Pembs. Arch. Svy, 1896; L. Dwnn, i, 60; WWHR, II, p. 55; Nicholas 1875 edn.

PARSELE. *St. Edwins.*

A farmstead on high ground about a mile east of the parish church. Home for many generations of yeoman families. On 29 December 1559, Jenkyn Morgan ap John of Penderyn (Brec.), yeoman, stole cattle from John Llewellyn David ap Gwilym at Pursellay, Pembs. He was apprehended, and in June 1560, with others, was tried, pleaded guilty, and placed in Haverfordwest goal, whence he managed to escape.

In 1596 John Wogan, gent., sued Thomas David Morgan and his wife Margaret, re three messuages, two tofts and 34 acres in Perselick and St. Edwins, and in 1598 the said John Wogan sued Thomas Bowen, Gent., and his wife Janet, concerning three messuages, two tofts and 34 acres and a rent charge of 1s 10d. in Treddirg, Perselly, and St. Edwins. In 1601 John Wogan sued Richard Howel and Thomas David Morris of St. Edwins parish, yeoman, for trespass and depasturing on Wogan's lands at Persellick in St. Edwins, to the value of 40s. In 1613 John Wogan, gent., gave 6s 8d to agree with Thomas David Morris and his wife Margaret, re a messuage and 33 acres in Persellick.

Nothing further is heard of the property, until 18 November 1765 when Julien John of Parselle, widow, signed her will, leaving a chest to Lettice daughter of John Harry of Little Newcastle parish, and the residue of her goods 'to my nephew by law, George Evan and my niece Jane Harry, they to be executors of my will'; which was proved on 25th December 1765. At this time the Morse family lived at Parsele, descended from the Morses of Treindeg. Three generations lived at Parsele, one of whom, Henry Morse, gent., was described as a parliamentary voter, of St. Edwins parish, in 1760, and as owner-occupier of Parselle in 1786. The Evans family came from Scleddy, and were interested in antiquities. Edward Evans of Parselle died in 1914, leaving a son George Morgan Evans (*d. unm.* in 1960), and Margaret Evans d.1939, aged 56, having married Edwin Morse son of Thomas Morse of Pantybrwyn.

Edwin Morse who held Parselle *iure uxoris*,

sold the property and retired to Letterston where he died in 1960, whose son Edward Llewelyn Morse married Lily Scale of Trewallterwen, and whose daughter, Elizabeth, married Owen Reynish of Churchlands. Edward Evans of Parsele kept an interesting diary full of information about farming at Parsele and the surrounding district; he was the first to draw attention to an inscribed stone in the farmyard of Llangwarran in 1896.

Refs: *PRO. Cal Pat.Rols 1560-63, p. 522; NLW Paper of Great Sessions 1596-1613; Pembs RO L.T. 1786. Survey by Henry John, Head Surveyor 1787.*

PASKESTON. *Cosheston.*

A residence about a mile north-west of Milton village, built in the Georgian style, with a modern extension to one gable end. The first-known folk at Paskeston were yeomen, probably tenants, namely David Scurlock, yeoman (1559), George Ellys, gent. (1617), and William Jermin, gent. (1626) son of Rees Jermin, yeoman, after which came John Rossant, (1659) son and heir of James Rossant of Cosheston, yeoman. The Rossants belonged to the minor gentry and lived at Paskeston during the period 1659-1780, and acquired a small estate, the last of whom we find at Paskeston, being John Lewes Rossant, gent., and Mary his wife and John Rossant and John Lewes Rossant, gent., all of whom were living there in 1780.

It is likely that there was a farm as well as the mansion there, as early as 1724; Nicholas Roch of Paskeston, was High Sheriff in 1729, and in his will, proved in 1759, he mentions his sons, Nicholas, Mark, and George, and 'my kinsman' Thomas Roch of Butterhill. He was succeeded by his son Nicholas Roch of Cosheston, who succeeded his uncle (who was still there in 1815). Nicholas Roch of Paskeston died there in 1866, and was followed by his son, also named Nicholas Roch who is included in the Landowners' Return of 1873 as owning 944 acres.

The next gentry family there was that of Allen (kinsman of the Cressely stock), who were mentioned at Paskeston in 1894. Newton Seymour Allen, DSO. of Paskeston was High Sheriff in 1919 and died in 1934.

Refs: *Pembs. R.O., L.T. 1786; Deeds LLC/1, and D/LLC; NLW Picton Castle Deeds; Rogers of Pembs. G.J., Plea Rolls; RCAM Pembs. 1925; D. Miles, Sheriffs of County of Pembs.*

PATERCHURCH. *St. Mary, Pembroke.*

The former residence on the west of the town, overlooking the estuary, and in the 19th century became included within the area of the Pembroke dockyard. The earliest families there were known by the name of the property.

This was the main residence of the Adams family. The earliest known resident there was David de Paterchurch whose daughter and heiress, Elen, married in 1422-3 John Adams, son of Nicholas Adams of Buckspool (q.v.) in Bosherston parish. John settled at his wife's home, and became Lieutenant to Henry Wogan, Steward to the Earl of Pembroke and in 1448, was followed by his son, William Adams who married Alice, daughter of Sir William Herbert of Troy, Mon., Steward of Pembroke, natural son of William Earl of Pembroke. William's grandson, John Adams, served as MP. for Pembroke Borough in 1541-44, and was still living in 1553; his wife was Catherine daughter of Thomas ap David Goch ap Meredith ap Madoc, Baron of Stapleton Castle, near Presteigne, Rad.; the bard, Lewis Glyn Cothi addressed a poem to David Goch whose ancestry he traced to Rhodri Mawr, a prince of Wales.

'Breiniawl wyt o'r barwnwaed
barwm ystelptwn nos deed'. (dud?)

David Goch was a noted Lancastrian who raided all Yorkists within range until eventually slain at Pennal field near Pennal, Mer.

The last of the family there was Rhys Adams whose will was proved in 1698. The house was not used as a residence after that date, having passed to his son, also Rhys, who sold it to Richard Gwynne of Gevenifa,

Carms., who made his will on 9th September 1702, and states ... 'I have lately purchased of Rice Adams, gent. a capital messuage or mansion house called Paterchurch, heretofore mortgaged unto John Owen late of Berllan, Esquire, deceased, upon which mortgage there is still £1,350: Paterchurch is to go to my grandson, Thomas Gwynne'. The demesne of the old mansion contained the private cemetery of the Adams family, the last to be buried there, 'in their own burial ground', being Roger Adams, son of William Adams, on 11 January, 1731-32. Many bones and skulls were disinterred later, especially when the foundations of the Royal Dockyard were made in the year 1820-1844, and again in 1889. The Gwynne family alienated the property before 1731, when it was owned by the Owens of Orielton who held it until part of their estate was sold by Sir William Owen to the Government by Act of Parliament of 1757, and thereafter remained Crown Property.

The Adams line seems to have wilted towards the end of the 17th century as Rhys's two brothers, William and Nicholas, were apprentices in London in 1698 and nothing further was heard of them. However some members of the family still had connections with Paterchurch in 1731, after which they exchanged land there with the Meyrick family, it is said as a result of gambling, and on the Meyrick land they built Holyland (qv) early in the 18th century, and it became the chief residence of the family.

The old mansion was decaying fast and was offered to the Hon. Charles Fulke Grenville, who in a letter on 1 September 1802 wrote to Lady Cawdor that he was '... surprised at the dilapidation, the house has neither roof, doors, or windows; the wind and thieves have been so diligent since my last visit that I do not know how my villa will become elegant', and the idea of purchase was abandoned. In Mrs. Stuart Peters' *History of Pembroke Dock* (1905) it tells us that: 'In 1854 the crumbling walls of the old ruined mansion of Paterchurch were pulled down with the exception of the tower. The old place had served many purposes: it had been a residence and later had been used as a store and also as a modeller's shop'. The gateway to Pembroke Dockyard was part of the old mansion. Much of Pembroke Docks now cover the site of the house and park.

In 1900, Allen noted, 'The gate tower of the old house (by some mistaken for the belfry of a church), was enclosed within the royal dockyard at the south-west corner'. It can still be seen there.

Refs: Dwnn, i, pp. 92, 130, 172; WWHR, ii, 76; Pembs. Arch Survey 1896-1907; Sketch by Norris in Cardiff Public Library; Parish reg. St. Mary, Pemb. Mr. & Mrs. S.C. Hall, Tenby, p. 9; Mrs. E, Stuart Peters, His. Pemb. Dock. 1905, pp. 1-4, 12 and plan and photo. RCAM Pembs. 1925, Allen Sheriff of Pembs. 1900, p. 18. Pembs. RO, VL; Deeds HDX 589, Nos. 9-10, 12 plan & Sketches. Mrs. Barbara Gordon, (née Adams of Holyland) has a good water-colour of old Paterchurch c.1800 which she kindly showed to me when I called on her in April 1974. For photo and account of the Tower see W. Tel. 6. Jan. 1983.

PEMBROKE CASTLE. *Pembroke.*

It is not strictly within the scope of this work to include the great ruined fortresses of the County but we feel that an exception must be made in this case. Not only is Pembroke Castle the largest Norman stronghold in Pembrokeshire, it is also of great historic importance as the birthplace of Henry Tudor, later Earl of Richmond and eventually King Henry VII, first of the Tudor Monarchs.

Gerald of Wales writes authoritatively about the Castle as his grandfather, Gerald of Windsor, was appointed castellan by Arnulph, son of Roger de Montgomery who founded the Castle in 1093.

King Stephen created the first earldom of Pembroke, a title which passed to some of the most powerful magnates of the period including William Marshal and Aymer de Valence.

Jasper Tudor became Earl of Pembroke in 1454. He was second son of Owan Tewdwr and Queen Catherine of France and therefore half-brother of Henry VI. Jasper made parts of the Castle into more comfortable living quarters. His older brother, Edmund Earl of Richmond, married Lady Margaret Beau-

fort, a descendant of Edward III and it was here that Edmund's widow gave birth to Henry Tewdwr who was to change the dynastic history of England and Wales. You can see the actual room. For a fuller account there are many sources but Robert Innes-Smith's *Pembroke Castle* (Pilgrim Press, Derby), the Castle's guidebook, gives a succinct summary of its history and architecture.

Oliver Cromwell did his best to demolish the Castle but it was too big a task. A great deal of damage was done and the local people used the ruins as a quarry for stone.

Pembroke castle remained a romantic ruin until 1880 when J. R. Cobb of Brecon carried out a scheme of restoration. Nothing further was done until 1928 when Major-General Sir Ivor Philipps, KCB., DSO, bought the ruins and began further extensive restorations. After the death of the Major-General his daughter, Mrs. Basil Ramsden, inherited the building and in 1959 handed over its administration to trustees who open the Castle regularly to the public. At the time of writing the trustees are represented by Major Ivor Ramsden, M.B.E., the Major-General's grandson. (*Vide* COSHESTON HALL).

PENALLT CADWGAN. *Cilgerran.*

Lewis Wogan of Wiston married, as his second wife, Anne, daughter of James Lloyd of Cilrhiwe. She died in 1703, then living at Penallt Cadwgan. By Anne, Lewis Wogan had four children – Lloyd Wogan, baptised 1786, died young, Anne married Thomas Lloyd of Bronwydd, Bridget married Lewis Powell of Greenhill, and Katherine married John Warren of Trewern. In 1894 one Ivor Evans held the land and was tenant of Penallt Cadwgan.

Refs: WWHR, vi p. 217; VL 1894.

PENALLT CYCH. *Clydey.*

Sometimes also called Penrallt Cych, and so marked on modern maps. Now a farmstead on high land to the west of Pont Cych and the hamlet of Aber Cych. The first known family there was David ap David 'alias Dwbl Dys' of Penallt Kych, who married Mary, daughter of Lewis Philips Howel of Blaenythan Cards, but nothing further is known of them.

Towards the middle of the 17th century David Llewelyn, gent., a minor squire, owned the property, and in 1684 he bought the nearby mansion of Clynfyw and went there to live. He died about 1716, having made his will on 30th April of that year. His eldest son, Thomas Davies, succeeded to Penallt Cych, and his second son Llewelin (Lerline) Davies succeeded to Clynfyw. Thomas married Elizabeth Bowen daughter of Canon James Bowen MA., member of the Bowens of Pontgynon, and was followed at Penallt Cych by his son, James Davies. James married Anne, daughter of Thomas Howell of Bryn y Ceirch and Llether Moel, and Cynwyl Elfed, and had two daughters and co-heiresses.

On her death in 1731, she was followed at Penallt Cych by her daughter, Anne Davies, who married Henry Williams of Trelech, son of Andrew and Janet Williams. Henry then settled at his wife's home, and died there before April 1764. On 9 April 1764, the widowed Anne let Penallt Cych to Evan Humphrey of Cynwyl Elfed farm at a rent of £20 yearly, 6 fat hens, two fat geese, to carry three horse loads of coal yearly to Penallt-Cych, the lessor to have liberty to graze a horse there. The Williamses had three children, Henry Williams (died 1773), Thomas Williams (d. 1778), and Margaret (heir of the brothers), who married Thomas Howell of Cynwyl Elfed who came to live at Penallt Cych, and died in 1816. Margaret died in 1815, aged 72, and Penallt passed to their heir Thomas Howell who built a mansion at 'Glaspont otherwise Tythinpobyog' where he went to live, and the family remained there until some two decades ago when it was sold by the head of the family, Mr. H. W. Ll. Howell, JP.

After the departure of the Howell family, Penralltcych was leased to the Revd. John Morse, BA., Fellow of Hertford College, Oxon., who kept a school there where pupils paid 18 guineas per annum and one guinea entrance fee. During some alterations to the house a number of horse heads were found beneath one of the floors, believed to have been placed there as protection against an 'echo' in the room.

Refs: Carms. RO, G.G. MS i, fo 12, J. Francis Deeds, No. 567; Carms. Ant. Soc. Deeds. Pembs R.O. L.T. 1786. NLW. Griffith Owen Deeds, No. 6229, 7789, Tithe Map, Pembs. WWHR ii, 40-1, Manorowen ms p. 149, Curtis Laugharne p. 124, The Cambrian 1.2. 1806., Francis Jones, 'Diary of a Doctor's Wife' Carms. Hist. 1981. Ms Hanes Cisdal Capel Iwan. gan. Parch. D.G. Roberts 1970 in Carms. RO, Maps Mudge 1819 and Colby 1831.

PENALLT Y LLYN. *Manordeifi.*

Spelt as Penralltyllyn on modern maps. A farmstead on a slope just south of Cilfowyr, and flanked by the farms of Parc Cyneithw and Cilast Issaf. Home of the family of Lloyd, descended from Lloyd of Dolan Llanerch, Clydey, tracing to Cadifor Fawr of Blaen Cych. Six generations lived at Penalltyllyn from Elizabethan days to 1685. They were minor gentry and the estate was a modest one. The family deteriorated and shortly after 1685 sold the property.

Griffith Lloyd married a daughter of Thomas Lloyd of Trewern, by whom he had three sons, none of whom were able to forward the fortunes of the family; namely Jonathan Lloyd, a weaver, living at Penrith in 1685, Jenkin and John of whom nothing is known after their departure from Penalltyllyn. The downward trek had started as early as 1622 when John Lloyd and his wife Jane, mortgaged a quarter of Penalltyllyn, where they dwelt, also called Plâs Pen Allt y Llyn, and a messuage call Tirt y Skybor hên, and a quarter of a close called Park Dawkins, all in the territory of Cilfowyr. After the eventual sale of the property the farm was let to farmers.

Refs: Dwnn, ii, p. 45; Dale Castle Deeds ms fo 127; Manorowen ms p. 154; Pembs. RO, LT 1786, & VL 1834, 1894, 1904; Carms. RO G.G. MS; NLW, Morgan Richardson Deeds and ms 12356, p. 154.

PENALLY ABBEY. *Penally.*

This fine mansion built in the Gothick style in the 1790s adjacent to the church and with fine views over Carmarthen Bay has abbatial remains in the grounds including a ruined 13th century chapel dedicated to St. Deneilol and a Flemish chimney. Its early history is obscure but from 1916 to 1924 it belonged to the Jameson whiskey family. It has been restored and sensitively converted into a country house hotel by Steven and Elleen Warren.

PENALLY COURT. *Penally.*

The earliest known owner of this property was Lord Milford in 1786, with Thomas Rowe as tenant. Thomas Rowe died in 1791 aged 64, and by his wife Anne daughter of the Revd. Philip Elliott of Annikell, he had a son, Revd. Thomas Rowe who succeeded to Penally Court, and died in 1810. Thomas's son, George Rowe, became a doctor at Haverfordwest. In 1834 William Wakes was living at the Court, and in 1852 R. Waters, Esq., lived there and was Mayor of Tenby. The next owner was John M. Griffith, a yeoman, progressive farmer, breeder, show judge, and member of the Welsh Land Commission. His daughter, Mary May Griffiths, when aged 25, was appointed by Queen Victoria, Superintendent of the Royal Dairy at Balmoral, in 1896. Now tenanted by Mr. Evans, and known as Penally Court Farm, the ruins of the old Court can still be seen.

PENARTHUR. *St. Davids.*

A farmstead to the north-west from St. Davids, near the road leading to Porthmawr. In earlier days there were three farms here, Penarthur (also known as Maen Arthur), Penarthur-Ucha and -Issa; owned by yeomen and minor gentry. In 1608 Thomas Price, Esq., agreed with David John Howell, Theodore Howell and Thomas John Howell, in respect of two messuages, two tofts and 176 acres in Maenarthyr Ycha alias Penarthur, Treleddyd Fawr, St. Davids, and Carnedryn Issa.

Thomas John Howell succeeded to Penarthur-Ucha, and later owned Penarthur-Ucha and -Issa, Trelethed Fawr, Tir y Gof, Trewellwall (*sic*), Carnedren-Issa, Llanvwgar, Caerfarchell, and Clegyr Owen. By his wife, Jane Mathias (a widow in 1637) he had three sons and two daughters. Towards the end of the century, Thomas Howell lived at Penarthur Issa and on his death in 1695 was succeeded by his eldest son, John Howell, who settled at Penarthur Ucha, where he died in 1703, leaving two daughters, co-heiresses, Elizabeth who married Evan Davies of St. Davids, Esq., and Esther who married a Mr. Colby. The said Evan Davies, Esq., was described as of Penarthur in 1739 when he was a Grand Juror. Some of the family seems to have slipped down in the social scale, such as James Howell of St. Davids, blacksmith (*faber lignarius*), described in 1710 as administrator of the goods and chattels of John Howell of Penarthur, husbandman, who had died intestate. In 1725 Esther Howells the elder, widow, lived at Penarthur-Usha. By about the mid century the Howell family had left the area. In 1786 William Davies, gent., owned Penarthur, with the Revd. Canon Holcomb as tenant. Thomas Colby, Esq., was owner of Penarthur-Ucha, the tenant being John Lewis. A little after this, William Davies left Penarthur and established himself at Barry Island which formed part of his estate.

On 3rd November 1798, William Davies of Barry Island, Esq., granted a lease of messuages called Penarthur-Ucha, -Issa, and Penarthur, two cottages at Trelethid Fawr, a field called Six Acres, and the Bishop's lands in Penarthur called Tyr Lleech, Arthur's Stone, and Penygroes, to William Nash. Thomas Nash died in 1825, leaving his widow Dorothy and their three daughters. In 1848, the widow sold her share of Penarthur to her relatives, Henry and Margaret Harries and their children.

In 1862 Penarthur and its adjacent lands, were offered for sale (title to commence with the will of William Davies of Barry Island, dated 19th October 1800). The property was described as Penarthur, 126 acres (Ebenezer

Williams, tenant held by lease dated 27th September 1850), and a leasehold interest in three pieces of ground called Tyrneach, Penygroes and Arthur's Stone (Maen Arthur) containing five acres.

At one time, the Hergest family of St. Davids, held one of the three messuages called Penarthur, but references are rare. Towards the mid-17th century, Thomas Hergest, vicar-choral of St. Davids, is described as of Penarthur; and later, one Margaret Hergest of Penarthur (living 1696), married Gilbert Tegan of St. Davids parish, by whom she had Thomas Tegan, yeoman, John, and Margaret Tegan, all living in 1703.

Refs: *Pembs. RO, LT 1786, Sale Cat. 1862, NLW Papers of GS (Pembs), William and Williams (HW) Deeds, Spence Colby Deeds.*

PENBEDW. *Llanfihangel Penbedw.*

Penbedw farmstead marked immediately south of the church on Colby's map 1831. Home of the antiquary George Owen Harry in late Elizabethan times, rector of Eglwyswrw and Llanfihangel Penbedw. He was a well known historian and genealogist, author of *The Genealogy of King James 1* (1604), and *The Well Springs of True Nobility*. A manuscript in the hand of David Edwards, kept in the College of Arms, contains a pedigree of Hopkin of Gower which states 'this pedigree was drawn by George Owen (Harry) of Pen Bedowe ye 18th day of November anno domini 1603'. By his will, proved in 1655, Thomas David Morgan, gent., of Manordeifi parish, bequeathed to his grandson John Llwyd. 'My capital messuage called Penbedwin Llanfihangel Penbedw parish, and lands within the free chapel of Llangolman Penbedw called Plâs Cilvachwrnele and Tir y Ffynon Fawr, now in my occupation, to my son in law Thomas Lloyd and Elizabeth his wife, my daughter.' Grandson Griffith Lloyd is also named. The Lloyds remained there till the end of the century. The Land Tax List of 1786 gives James Bowen Esq., as owner, with Revd. Lewis Walters as tenant. The follow-

ing are commemorated on a tombstone in Eglwyswrw churchyard – Evan Protheroe of Penbedw in Llanfihangel Penbedw parish, died 4th January 1831, aged 88; and the Revd. David Protheroe, vicar of Eglwyswrw, died 28th September 1855, aged 86. During the years 1894-1904, William Thomas lived at Penbedw.

Refs: *College of Arms ms Box 36/X; WWHR ii, pp. 242-4; DWB, p. 343 s.n. Geo. Owen Harry; B. G. Charles, George Owen of Henllys, 1973*

PENBERI. *St. Davids.*

Marked on Colby's Map of 1831 as Penberry. A farmstead on the east side of Carn Beri, a carn on the coast near Penclegyr. The earliest known resident was Arnold Jones, gent., younger son of William Jones of Brawdy by his wife Mary Warren. He was there prior to 1584, and married Anne Wogan of Stone Hall. He was High Constable of Dewsland in 1605, and was still living in 1615. He was followed by his son Henry Jones of Penberi. In 1599, Thomas James of Penbury, yeoman, sued one David Harry for trespassing and depasturing at Portheiddy Fawr in Llanrhian parish.

Thomas James (Harries) of Penbury made his will on 7th March 1616, which was proved in the following year, left four sons and one daughter, all surnamed James, one of whom Lewis James, gent., owned Penbiryvawr, Penbiry Golman, Rosegolwyn, Tregweyth, Tir Prior, Herglodd Ycha, Whitchurch, and Trevadog, in 1631. It was owned by John Harries in 1776, when John Warlow surveyed Penberry and in 1811 an amended table of acreages of fields was made by John Tamlyn, surveyor. The Land Tax list of 1786 records John Harries, Esq., as owner of Penberry, with Phillip Beynon as tenant; the widower Margaret Beynon and her two sons John and William were still there in 1807-11. In the first decade of the present century, William Propert Williams lived at Penberry (1904).

Refs: *Pembs. RO; Deeds HDX 1588, No. 1 Land Tax 1786; NLW Papers of Great Sessions. Plea Rolls and Fines.*

PENBLEWYN. *Llanddewi Felfrey.*

Now an abandoned ancient farmhouse at Penblewin crossroads; a modern farmhouse has been built nearby. For several generations the old house was the residence of the Jones family who also owned Caermaenau and other local properties. In 1656 it was the home of John Jones, gent., who married a daughter of John Philipps of Woodstock locally called 'Shon butsh goch'. By 1786 it was owned by John Dunn, gent., with Edward James and David Jones, tenants.

Photo of Penblewyn in W. Mail, 18 Feb., 1987.

PENCELLI FAWR. *Eglwyswrw.*

A farmstead to the north-west of the village and near to Pencelli forest. The name is rendered in earlier legal documents as Pencellivor. Although several references occur to the property, insufficient evidence has survived to enable a coherent genealogy of the folk who dwelt there. Between the years 1579 and 1597, George Owen of Henllys bought Pencelli fawr which lay within Owen's manor of Eglwyswrw. In 1786 Cefn Pencelli and Pencelli fawr were owned by 'Mrs. Hay and Mrs. Price', with Llewelyn Williams as tenant; through marriage to an heiress of Henllys the property passed to Lloyd of Bronwydd, Cards, and in 1834 Thomas Lloyd of Bronwydd was described as owner. In 1894, Pencelli was held by William Morgan, and in 1950 by Guildford M. Morgan, when it was spelled as Pengelly.

Refs: *B. G. Charles, G. Owen of Henllys, 1973, pp. 33-4, 37, 39, 46, 56, 69, 71; G. Owen; Second Book of Pembs., NLW Journal, 1948, p. 2791., NLW, Bronwydd Mun. Kemes Court Rolls.; College of Arms, Protheroe ms iv, fo. 89 and Wagner ms No. 12.*

PENCELLI FYCHAN or FACH.
Eglwyswrw.

Near Pencelli Fawr, into which it was later absorbed: the name is now lost. George Bowen was father of Robert Bowen who lived at Pencelli Fychan in late Elizabethan times, where he was succeeded by his son

John ap Robert Bowen, who married Mary daughter of William Griffith of Penybenglôg. John died early in 1615 owned two messuages called Pencelly Fychan, two other messuages called Cippill Gwynt, and a messuage called Ty Mawr, and 500 acres. He died c. 1615 and left two daughters co-heiresses, called Jane Robert alias Bowen, and Joanna Robert alias Bowen, aged respectively six and three years, who became wards of George Owen of Henllys, lord of the manor of Eglwyswrw.

During the 16th century the Youngs who came from Tregamen, held Pencelli Fychan; John Young married Margaret Bowen, and their son Philip settled at Pencelli Fychan, where he was followed by his son, John Young, whose daughter and co-heiress married Owen ap Owen of Glanduad. Very few references occur to the property after this, and as it no longer exists, it is likely that its lands were absorbed into neighbouring farms.

Refs: *WWHR, ii, 92 s.n. Pencelli fach. NLW, Kemes Court Rolls, 4 May 1615.; Dale Cas. Ped. Book. fo 163; B. M. Egerton ms no. 2586; Bronwydd Deeds ms 699.*

PENCELLI CAPEL. *Eglwyswrw.*

There was a chapel called, in 1612, 'the chapel of Penkethllie Vaughan', attached to the benefice of Eglwyswrw. In a deed dated 6 June 1407, it is described as 'the chapel of Pencelli', *ad magnam viam de vadu leprorsuro ad villam de Pencelli. (College of Arms, Wagner MS No. 12).* It stood between Pencelli and Trewilyn Uchaf, but became a ruin, and is described in 1914 as 'heavily covered with undergrowth.' *RCAM Pembs. 1925, p. 94).*

PENCELLI FOREST. *Eglwyswrw.*

Just north of the village, in the manor of Eglwyswrw. In George Owen's time it enclosed 500 acres, within which were 13 'glades or cockshuts' where woodcocks nested. By 1786 it had passed to the Lloyds of Bronwydd.

Refs: *Fenton, Tour Pembs. 1811, p. 293; B. G. Charles, George Owen of Henllys 1973, and refs. there.*

PENPEDWAST. *Meline.*

A farmstead to the north-east of the parish church, on high ground above the valley of the rivers Cynon and Nanhyfer. The house, now an empty ruin, was built on a rocky outcrop and faced eastwards. George Owen of Henllys purchased a house and some lands at Penpedwast in 1578, and added to it by further purchases there in 1584 and 1595. What had been a remote hamlet of two or three households became a single holding which Owen leased in 1584 to the Revd Miles Thomas, rector of Meline, who built 'about 20 years past' a mansion house wherein he now dwells'.

Originally, the property was owned by local freeholders; on 20th October 1465 Lewis ap Gwilym ap Res (*sic*), Res ap Gwilym ap Res, and David ap Gwilym ap Res, granted to John ap Howel ap Jenkyn, a moiety of a messuage and lands on Pant Bedewas in the fee of Meline, which lately belonged to Oweyn Person: on 21 September 1577 Melchior ap Ievan ap Howell of Newport, yeoman, granted to Owen Johnes of Trekoner, gent, a messuage at Pant bedwast then in tenure of Owen Lewis, and on 10 March 1577-78, Owen Johnes released to George Owen [of Henllys] a messuage at Pantbedwast and a close and two acres at Allt y claffe in Meline parish. On 5 May 1584 George Owen granted a lease for 21 years of three messuages and lands at Pantbedwast to the Revd Miles Thomas. Thus the conglomeration of dwellings and lands became a single holding.

By 1612 the parson had departed, and in that year George Owen settled Penpedwast and Henllys-issa on his sons George, William, and Evan. Penpedwast continued with the descendants of George Owen [d.1613] until the death, without issue, of William Owen of Henllys, c.1681, when the estate passed to his two sisters, co-heiresses – Elizabeth who married Arthur Laugharne of Llanreithan (d. 1699) and Anne who married Thomas Lloyd of the Bronwydd family who settled at Penpedwast. The eldest Lloyd grand-daughter and heir Anne (born c.1738) daughter of William Lloyd of Penpedwast, married, c.1737, her kinsman Thomas Lloyd of Bronwydd, who, in 1750 purchased the moiety of the Barony of Cemaes from his wife's cousin, John Laugharne of Llanreithan. Thereafter it continued as property of the Lloyd family. Thomas lived mainly at Bronwydd, and Penpedwast was leased to tenants. In 1834 William Jones, gent, held it under a lease for lives. In 1883, plans and specifications were produced for 'the new buildings at Penpedwast farm'. By 1894 it had been sold to Morris James, described as owner-occupier of Penpedwast.

When I called at Penpedwast in April 1986, it was owned by Mr. Phillips who farmed the land, but lived at Tremain near Cardigan. The house was empty and would become ruinous in due course; the hallway was still panelled, as was the *neuadd* – relics of bygone gentry times. There were four bedrooms. The nearby outbuildings were still in use. The old orchard was on the slope close to the house.

Refs: *NLW, Bronwydd Deeds and Documents, George Owen's Second Book, Llwyngwair Deeds, Hampton Deeds, Tithe map Meline 1838, B. G Charles, George Owen of Henllys,* 1973.

PENRALLTRHEINY. *Cilgerran.*

Today the name used is Alltreiny. A commodious residence built in the traditional Welsh style, a short distance to the south-east of Cilgerran. About 12-15 yards away is a two storeyed building, once a dwelling house, probably 16th century, and now used for lumber, at the top end of it a modern garage has been added. The present mansion is of two storeys and a spacious attic storey, all in excellent state. When I called there in May 1983 it was the home of a retired banker, Mr. P. L. M. Davies, O.B.E. and his wife, kindly hosts, who later sold the place and in 1985 moved to Fishguard.

The first family of any note at Penralltrheiny was that of Garnons, an English Border family, they settled in Cilgerran parish 1559-69, and in Elizabethan days John Garnons, Attorney of the Great Sessions, became M.P. for Haverfordwest in 1571, and of the county of Pembroke in 1574. He was Clerk of the Peace for the county in 1575. He married Elen daughter and co-heiress of John Davids of Trefin and Penralltreiny by his wife Alice Revell daughter of Thomas Revell. By Elen (d.1618-19) he had nine children.

The Garnons left Penralltreiny towards the end of the 17th century; in the first half of the 18th century it passed to a Miss Garnons, heiress of her two brothers who had died without issue; she married William Phillips of Fagwr Eynon, Monington, gent., who moved prior to October 1766 to his wife's home, and was described as owner-occupier in 1784. Their eldest son, William Phillip married Francis Maria Gower of Glandovan by whom he had two sons and two daughters. On William's death in 1803, he left the estate to his *second* son, John, to the exclusion of the eldest son William who was allowed

an annuity of only £25. The reason for this somewhat unusual procedure, is, that William, shortly after birth, had been put out to be nursed with a woman who had a baby son of her own, and it was believed that she had substituted her own child for that of Penralltreiny.

John Phillips, a major in the Royal Pembs. Militia, died unmarried in 1848, leaving the property to his sister's son, William E. Williams, commander of a steam vessel on the Ganges for many years, who, on inheriting, resigned the post and returned to live at Penralltreiny; he married and had issue.

The family of Howells of Ffynnonfelen, (Carms) owned Penralltreiny for a short while in the mid-18th century (about 1753-1764). During the 18th and 19th centuries, the mansion was enlarged and improved. When it was advertised for sale in July 1917, the Particulars and Plan described it as 'a Gentleman's residence', with 84 acres attached. It was approached by a wooded drive, at the entrance of which stood the Marine Lodge. The mansion contained, on the Ground Floor, entrance hall, drawing, dining and breakfast rooms, and domestic offices; on the first floor, the East Wing contained a sitting room, two double bedrooms, bathroom, housemaid's closet, cupboards, and in the West Wing, a double bedroom and two smaller bedrooms. On the second floor, were four bedrooms and two attics. There was adequate stabling including a dairy 'fitted with slate shelves'. The pleasure garden and grounds included tennis lawn, herbaceous borders and shrubs, and a walled kitchen garden with fruit trees. Also for sale, was a modern farm house 'erected about 20 years ago' (c. 1897), with, on the ground floor, a small sitting room, large kitchen, scullery, pantry, and on the first floor, three bedrooms, and outhouses.

PENRHIW. *Llanwnda.*

A farmstead on high ground called Pencw, overlooking Fishguard Bay. The modern village called Harbour Village was built on Pencw at the beginning of the present century.

The earliest known owner of Penrhiw was Jonathan Thomas living then in 1699. Jonathan and Anne his wife gave a lease of 'Goodig' in 1702 to William Rogers. He moved to Haverfordwest, then to Natt's Hook, Walton West parish, where he made his will in 1722. He was succeeded by his son and heir John Thomas who married Margaret Brazell of St. Ishmaels parish, and by their post-nuptial settlement, dated 5 Feb. 1716-17, the two messuages called Penrhiw, and Goodwick, were settled to uses of the marriage. John left two daughters and coheiresses.

The first daughter, Anna Thomas, married William Rogers of Goodwick, and on 16 January 1744-5, they mortgaged their moiety of Penrhiw to Miss Margaret Thomas of Cilciffeth; the mortgage was assigned on 29 May 1759 to Lewis Dedwith of St. Nicholas, husbandman, who, on 3 Jan 1760, assigned the mortgage to William Lewis, gent, of Penyrallt, Nevern, and on 16 November 1767 William Rogers and Anne (owners) sold the premises of Penrhiw (comprising a moiety of two messuages, one orchard, four gardens, 130 acres) to Sparks Martin Esq. of Withybush. In 1786 Sparks Martin is described as owner, with Thomas Thomas as tenant. Finally, the moiety of Penrhiw was sold on 15 December 1804 to David Harries of Dinas Island.

The second daughter, Elizabeth Thomas, married in 1742 William Moore of Haverfordwest; their son Edward Moore, who on 2 February 1803, sold the moiety of Penrhiw to the said David Harries who, in the following year, purchased the other moiety, so that the whole of Penrhiw became his property, where he came to live. His daughter Dinah Harries married G. B. Meager of Oystermouth, near Swansea, and their great-grandson Captain John Francis of Carmarthen, is living.

Today Penrhiw, still a flourishing farm, as owned by Mr. Arthur Perkins, now of Penysgwern, Llanwnda parish.

Refs: LT 1786; wills; *Trenwydd Deeds;* pedigree *penes me; RCAM Pembs 1925 ...* p. 185.

PENTOUR (PENTOWER). *Fishguard.*

A wholly modern residence of the late Sir Evan Davies Jones, Bart., JP., High Sheriff in 1911, Lord Lieutenant of Pembrokeshire. It was sold after the second World War, by his son and heir, Sir Thomas Jones, Bart, and described as comprising, on the *Ground Floor:* a tiled Entrance Hall, Dining Room, Lounge, Morning Room, Sitting Room, Kitchen, and domestic offices; *Half-Landing:* Drawing Room; *First Floor:* – six bedrooms, bathroom. In the early 1960s it was used as a hotel; in the early 1970s it was sold to Mr. Wynford Vaughan Thomas, the television personality, who died in 1987. It stands on high ground with a view over Fishguard Bay, Dinas Head, Pen Morfa, Cwm Gwaun, and part of the river Gwaun. In the distance northwards the Preseli Hills.

PENTRE. *Manordeifi.*

A residence in the south-eastern part of the parish, on high ground overlooking Cwm Cwch. Its original name was Pentre Ifan, and is thus described in deeds and legal records of the 16th and 17th centuries. Not far away is Castellan called Castellan Ifan in the first half of the 17th century. Pentre has been the home of three gentry families from the late Elizabethan period down to the present century. The earliest of these was the family of Parry descended from Harry ap Philip of Blaen Cych and his wife Anne Clement.

The first of the Parrys at Pentre was John Thomas Parry (ap Harry) who was living there in 1610, and died about 1625. Thomas's grandson, David Parry of Pentre (living 1643), married Mary daughter of Jason Lewes by Temperance Saunders daughter and heiress of Nicholas Saunders, and had a son and heir Thomas Parry of Pentre who was assessed at three hearths in 1670, so that the house was then of modest size. By this time the Parrys had slipped down the slope a little. Thomas, by his wife Anne Voyle of Llanelly, had three sons – 1. Rowland Parry, a tanner, 2. David Parry, 'in service at Cilrhiwe' in 1698, and Roger Parry of whom nothing is known. By this time the property belonged to the

Saunders family. David Saunders, third son of Tobias Saunders of Ceyn-y-Felin, Cilrhedyn, weaver (died 1719), lived at Pentre where he died in 1750. David was succeeded by Erasmus Saunders who married in 1746 Jane Phillips of Moelifor, Cards. Erasmus died in 1759, aged 40, and left Pentre to his three daughters, co-heiresses – Bridget and Magdalen, both died unmarried, and Susanna, ultimate sole heiress. Susanna (1755-1823) married Dr. David Davies, MD., Doctor of physic, of Carmarthen, son of Rhys Davies of Llandovery. After the marriage Dr. Davies moved to live at Pentre, and took the surname Saunders-Davies. He died in 1829, aged 74.

Five successive generations of the doctor succeeded to Pentre. After the mid-20th century, they left Pentre, which was sold. For a time it became a girls' private school, known as 'Pentre Manor School'. Later, Pentre was purchased by Mr. Parkes-Gibbon, a tradesman of Carmarthen.

Little is known of the mansion until we come to the 19th century. Rees wrote in *Beauties of South Wales*, 1815, 'a new mansion is now erecting on the site of the old by Dr. Davies, the present occupier who married the only surviving heiress of this house ... its gardens and walls are on the old style and greatly admired. The grounds are pretty, surrounded with woods and thriving plantations' (p. 870). Alterations were made by C. R. Cockerill, in 1824-5. To Lewis, author of the *Topographical Dictionary of Wales*, 1840, it was 'a handsome and substantial modern edifice erected on the site of the old mansion'. In Francis Green's admirable account of '*The Saunders of Pentre*', W.W.H.R. ii, p. 161 ff. there is an illustration, (opp. p. 181) made in 1853 of Pentre, but since that time further additions and changes have been made. *The Tivyside Photographic Souvenir*, 1871, by C. Allen, contains a photograph showing Pentre as a low two-storeyed house, with ranges of five windows and a pillared porch-entrance. It was enlarged, and stone-cased in 1879, and an attic storey added. See Thomas Lloyd, *The Lost Houses of Wales* (1986) with photograph on p. 73.

PENTRE ITHEL. *Mynachlogddu*.
Marked as Pentrithel, to the west of Mynachlogddu parish church, and north-west from Dyffryn Filbro farm. Now a farmstead. Both name the ancestor of the first family at Pentre Ithel, as Griffith John Llewellin of Blaenygroes, succeeded by his son Thomas Gitto, and he, in turn, by Lewis Thomas Gitto who lived at Pentre Ithel until he was 'kill'd by a gret mischaunce with a gunne'. His wife was Catherine daughter of Lewis Philipps of Pentre Ifan (Mayor of Newport 1588-90); She married secondly Thomas Jones who was living with his wife at Pentre Ithel in 1622. A younger son of Pentre Ithel, Stephen Jones, moved to Rhosygilwen. The Jones family remained at Pentre Ithel until the latter part of the 17th century.

The property was owned in 1786 by 'the heirs of Morris Bowen, Esq., of Upton Castle; in 1840 Morris Morris and Griffith Morris owned it, being then 148 acres, the tenant being Benjamin Thomas; in 1894 one Evan Thomas lived there; in 1904 Stephen Davies of Dyffryn Fylbro owned $\frac{1}{6}$th part of Pentre Ithel, and soon afterwards it passed to the Owens of Cwmglôyn. The Cwmglôyn estate, owned by Morris Williams Lloyd Owen, then of Haverfordwest, advertised the estate for public auction, including Pentre Ithel (144 acres). During the 18th century Baptists held religious meetings at the house.

Refs: *Pembs. R.O., Deeds BD, 13, 98; LT 1786; VL, 1894, 1904, Carms RO; Golden Grove ms (Gwynfardd). NLW, Tithe map 1840, Mudge's Map 1819, and Colby map 1831. College of Arms, Protheroe ms iv.*

PENTYPARK. *Walton East*.
A mansion on a spur about five miles north-west of Haverfordwest, and just over one mile south-west of the parish church of Walton East. For nearly 500 years from 1500 to the present day, Pentypark was the seat of landowning families. The first known family there, that of Rogers, were there in the late 15th century, and John Rogers and his three children, John, Jenkin and Alice, was living at 'Bentclergh' in 1501-03. Jenkin

was followed by his son, Jenkin Rogers junior, who may have been the father of Thomas ap Jenkin Rogers. This Thomas and Isabella his wife, were described as of 'Bentyberche' in 1554, being the last of the line of Rogers. Shortly afterwards James Philipps son of William Philipps second son of Sir Thomas Philipps (d. c.1519) of Picton Castle, was seated at Pentypark. He was called variously James William and James Williams Philipps, according to the Welsh custom of nomenclature. He married Jane, daughter of Edmund Griffith of Cichele, a north Wales landowner. James died before 1572 when Jane Williams of Bentiborth, widow, alias Jane Philipps then of Woodstock and her son, John Williams Philipps, administrators of the goods of James William of Bentyborth, gent., who died intestate.

The said son John succeeded to Pentypark, became a JP., and was High Sheriff in 1622. He married Grace, daughter and heiress of Richard Vaughan of Carsygedol, by whom he had four sons and two daughters; the eldest son James Philipps succeeded to Pentypark, and their male descendants continued there until the death of James Philipps JP. (H.S. 1787), who left an only daughter, Mary Philipps, who married Sir Richard Philipps of Picton Castle, created Lord Milford. She died, in 1815, her husband in 1823, without issue.

It was during this period that Fenton wrote about Pentypark, (1811): 'Pentypark, a mansion embosomed in woods, since the death of the late possessor (James Philipps, d. 1794) now seldom inhabited but by servants placed there to air it, belonged to a branch of the ancient family of Kilsant ... finally inherited by Lady Milford (d.1815) and her sister Mrs. Jane Philipps'. The property passed to the Lloyd family of Ffosybleiddied, Cards, one of whom, John Lloyd, had married Mary only sister of James Philipps of Pentypark (father of Lady Milford). It was inherited by Colonel James Philipps Lloyd who came to live at Pentypark where he died in 1837. The property afterwards passed again to the Lloyds, the last in the male line being Richard Llewellin Lloyd (H.S. Pembs. 1912, d.1938), who left three daughters, one of whom, Grace, married Mr. Trevelyan Jones who still lives at Pentypark.

The earlier mansion was destroyed by fire in the 18th century, and the present residence was built in 1810: during the early 1870s it was restored and enlarged by Capt. F. L. Lloyd-Philipps (High Sheriff in 1877). When I called there last in 1981, the house was in excellent state, but what amused me was to find that one of the attics housed a large colony of bats. The walled garden, originally comprising three acres, had been reduced in size.

Refs: *WWHR. ii, p. 67; Fenton, Tour Pembs. 1811, p. 178; Lewis TDW, 1840; Lloyd, Family Pedigrees and Records 1913, p xxvii; S. Wales, Hist. Bio. Pictorial, c.1908, illust. of Pentypark; D. Miles, Sheriffs of Pembs. 1541-1974; J. Steegman, Portraits in Welsh Houses, S. Wales Vol. II, 1962, Illustr. of some 30 portraits in Pentypark; NLW, Slebech Deeds, Papers of G.S. Pembs, Pleas Rolls Pembs; Noyadd Trefawr Deeds.*

PENYBENGLOG. *Meline*

The mansion of Penybenglog stood on a bluff above Afon Nantyfer, between the ancient fortifications of Castell Penybenglog and Castell Clwyd. It continued as a gentry seat from the Middle Ages until the end of the 18th century. Fenton, in 1811, wrote '... another mansion, Penybenglog, ranked with the first in its day; which, though it has long ceased to be inhabited by any of the descendants of its ancient possessors and has often changed masters, yet by having had the good fortune to find a succession of respectable tenants, it has been kept in a state of decent

Old Penybenglog

repair, and till within these few years one of its windows exhibited the pride of ancestry in painted glass ...' Fortunately, a poem describing the heraldic window on 23 April 1642, has survived, while the long window, lighting the main staircase in the house, has also survived, but without the coats of arms. The house mentioned by George Owen of Henllys about 1611 – 'in Is Nevarne standeth Penybenglog the mansion house of William Griffith' (died on 24 March 1608). William was followed by his son George, who greatly improved the property and of whom it was written by a contemporary, 'George William Griffith, after the death of his father, lived at Penybenglog: repayred the Ruines of the decayed buyldinges, erected and bestowed charge upon ffences, hedges, and moundes upon the demesne thereof, and for enlargeinge the same demesne purchased certeyne tenements and lands in Meliney and Nevarne, amountinge to the value of £300 and upwards ...' (NLW *Llanstephen* ms 138E fo. 33).

The earliest owners of Penybenglog descended from the 11th century chieftains Gwynfardd Dyfed and Cyhylyn Fardd. Howel Gawr held the property in 1342, and his grandson Rhys (living 1370) owned Penybenglog, Glanduad Ucha, Cwmgloyn and Cruglass Issa; he was followed by his son Llewelyn (living 1451-1481), whose son and heir, David ap Llewelyn, who left an only daughter and heiress, Dyddgu (died 1538), married Rees of Dyffryn Tâf, son of David ap Howel ap Jenkin Lloyd of Blaiddbwll who, in her right, succeeded to Penybenglog. The said Jenkin Lloyd descended from Cyhylyn Fardd and bore arms: *azure a lion rampant or within an orle of roses or*, but as 'he was a zealous partisan of the House of York, changed the colour of the roses to *argent*'. Rhys of Penybenglog died in 1520, and his wife Dyddgu in 1538; their grandson Griffith inherited Penybenglog where he died on 28th November 1569, and was followed there by five generations of his descendants who all bore the permanent surname of Griffith. Of these the best known was George William Griffith, JP. (b. 1584) noted scholar, historian, antiquary and genealogist, who married Maud Bowen of Llwyngwair in 1605. He died in 1654-55, and many of his manuscripts have survived among the Bronwydd Archives (now in N.L.W.), in the British Museum, and in the College of Arms.

His great-grandson, Robert Griffith, was the last male of the family at Penybenglog where he died without issue in 1737, when the estate passed to his three sisters, co-heiresses, each enjoying a share, namely Anne married Thomas Merchant, gent., of Manorbier-Newton; she died on 26 November 1761, aged 74; Elizabeth who married Griffith Twyning of Llandre, Llanycefn, gent., had issue; and Lettice who married John Williams of Cardigan. Over the succeeding years the co-heiresses sold their shares of the estate to various buyers, mostly from West Wales. The mansion of Penybenglog, and its demesne continued intact. The mansion was commodious and in 1670 contained six hearths, and in 1744 Thomas and Anne Marchant conveyed one-third of the estate with other properties

in Meline and Nevern, to Thomas Parry of Aberystwyth; by 1756 Penybenglog was owned by George Summers of Haverfordwest, who, in that year sold it to his only daughter, Mrs. Elizabeth Parry, widow.

During the years 1759-1771 the tenant of Penybenglog was the rector of Meline, the Revd. Watkin Lewes (father of Sir Watkin, Lord Mayor of London, M.P.). In 1773 the Revd. John Lewes of Whippingham, Isle of Wight, Doctor of Laws, sold Penybenglog, probably for a term of years, to the Revd. James Bowen rector of Meline. The freehold continued in the Parry family until the death of George Parry of Scovaston, near Milford, solicitor, who by will made in August, 1816, bequeathed 'my messuage called Penybenglog' in Meline, and a house and garden in Haverfordwest, to his housekeeper (and paramour), Miss Elizabeth Elson, widow. She did not keep it long, and by 1828 Penybenglog had been bought by John Hughes, Esq., of Alltcwyd (Cards), who still owned it in 1837 with a Thomas Hughes as tenant. In the early part of the 19th century the old house seems to have become ruinous. Over the kitchen door is a stone inscribed 'Rebuilt 1828 J. Hughes Esq. (owner), William Lewis tenant'. Whether this meant it was totally or partly rebuilt is not clear, probably the latter, for the house with its ancient cellars and other features, clearly survives still on the original site. A local farming family of Hughes owned it at this time.

Penybenglog was bought by Mr. Stuart Wilson (its owner-occupier when Major Jones visited in 1986), who improved and repaired the three-storeyed house, retaining the long window that once contained ancestral coats-of-arms, tastefully extending and improving surrounding lawns, flower beds, grassy ground and walks, retaining the ancient style of historic Penybenglog.

The last 'official' notices of the house were made by *The Pembrokeshire Archaeological Survey* (1896-1907), as follows: 'Penybenglog mansion. An old pedigree house. The existing house is of the 18th century. It has good panelled ceilings, a charming old china Closet, dados etc. A hideous new wing was added some time ago and the old entrance (relic of an earlier house) destroyed. Overhead was a beam, fortunately preserved, on it the date 1623, and in a vase-shaped figure the initials G.G. Outside is a nicely carved pew-back brought from Meliney Church when this edifice was restored, on it is the following legend: SED: MATHILD:UX: GEO: PER (resti GRI) PENYBENGLOG: G.E. 1626, 'At the rebuilding of the church (1865) this pew-back was removed to Penybenglog'. (visited 1920, *RCAM*, 1925, p. 226).

Refs: *Geo. Owen, 2nd Book p. 227, edited by Dr. B. G. Charles, in NLW Journal 1948, L.D. i, pp. 151, 184, WWHR ii, p. 54; Fenton Tour Pembs. 1811, pp. 309-310, Francis Jones, 'Griffith of Penybenglog' in Trans. Cymmr. 1939, pp. 125-153; NLW Llanstephan ms 138E, fo. 35; Alltlwyd Deeds; E. T. Lewis, North of the Hills, 1973, contains a photo of Penybenglog.*

PENYRALLT. *St. Dogmaels (Llandudoch).*
A farmstead marked on Colby's map as Pen'rallt, on the northern outskirts of St. Dogmaels village. Once the home of minor gentry families. In the 15th century it was owned by John Philip Thomas David, who was succeeded by his two daughters, co-heiresses, one of whom married Rees Young son of Howel Young of Cemaes, and the other married Morris ap Owen ap Howel ap Jenkin Lloyd of Cenarth. Later, the owner was one William Young, who, by his wife Elizabeth Morgan, had two sons, one of whom, Rees Young, 'sold Penyrallt to Thomas Young of Tregamon' (*Golden Grove ms*). Afterwards it passed to the Davies family, and in 1670 Nicholas Davies was assessed at five hearths, which indicates that Penyrallt was then a commodious residence.

In 1739 John Ladd, only son of Dr. James Ladd, MD., is described as 'late of London but now of Penyrallt', unmarried, he had three sisters – Martha Ladd died young, Jane Ladd married after January 1724, Rice Lloyd of Chancery Lane, and Elizabeth Ladd who married about May 1727, James Lloyd of Cilrhiwe. In 1786 the owner was Sir Watkin Lewes who let Penyrallt to a tenant farmer.

PENYRALLT. *Nevern.*

In the Cilgwyn quarter of the parish. Early in the 17th century it was the home of Thomas Vaughan son of Lewis Vaughan of Fagur Goch in Morfil, branch of the medieval family of Vaughan of Bredwardine, Herefordshire, whose arms were: *Sable a chevron argent between three boys' heads affrontee proper each with a snake vert entwined round his neck.* The arms are described in one of Lewis Glyn Ceothi's poems before 1450. The chevron is sometimes omitted. Thomas Vaughan of Penyrallt married Margaret Mathias daughter of Thomas Mathias of Glastir. He was followed by three successive generations of Vaughans who were still living at Penyrallt in 1689. By 1786 Penyrallt had become the property of the Le Hunte family.

Refs: Carms RO, Golden Grove ms I fo. 3; College of Arms Mss, Protheroe Ms IV fos. 148-9.

PENYSGWARN. *Llanwnda.*

Now a large farmstead alongside the highway from Goodwick to Harmony (Pencaer) and sits within a well-grown protecting copse, and formerly a minor gentry residence … In 1326 Pensgwarn is described as a Knights fee (Welsh). In 1636 Pensgwarn (then comprising two farms), formed part of the estate of Philips of Trelewelyn, and continued as such until 1814 when shortly afterwards it was sold to the Mortimer family. In 1748 the tenant was Peter Meyler, husbandman, whose eldest son James Meyler of Pensgwarn married Ann daughter of Morris Davids of Llanwnda parish in 1748.

In 1786 the tenant was William George. After 1814, it was sold to John Morgan Mortimer gent., described as owner in 1834. However he was somewhat improvident, and on 16 November 1849 he was obliged to grant Pensgwarn and four other farms in Llanwnda parish, two farms in Fishguard parish, as well as properties in Nantcwnlle and Llanddewi brefi parishes (Cards) to trustees to provide funds for payment of grantors debts. The Mortimers left Pensgwarn, and in 1894 Edward Perkins held the messuage and lands, and today it is owned and occupied by his grandchildren Mr. Arthur Perkins and his sister Miss Nesta Perkins JP. The farmhouse is commodious and well kept, as are the attractive well-preserved outbuildings.

Refs: Black book St. Davids 1326; NLW, Trenewydd Deeds; LT 1786; Francis Jones, 'Trelewelyn' (unpublished essay).

PHILBEACH. *Also rendered as* FILBETCH. *Marloes.*

In the Dale peninsula, between Marloes village and Crabhole, about a mile from the sea-coast. From about 1200 to about 1800, Philbeach was the residence of gentry families, but was later adapted to farming purposes. In the 13th century it belonged to the De Vale family overlords of the Dale district. The earliest spelling is Filbech and Fulbuche, which later is rendered as Filbeach, Fulbech and finally Philbeach. Dr. Charles suggests that the meaning of the name was 'hay field', which well describes the residence which stands on high ground overlooking a small valley. Robert de Vale, Lord of Dale, had a daughter Sara, who married William (de) Ffilbech, and had a son Sir William Ffilbech, knight. The knight was followed by an only son, Henry Ffilbech, who had an only child, Joanna, the last of the line to live at Philbeach. She married David Barrett of Dudwall, Camrose parish, who settled at his wife's home. They were followed at Philbeach by their son Peter Barrett who was living there in the reign of King Henry VI.

Peter had two daughters, co-heiresses; Margaret Barrett the elder daughter inherited Philbeach and married William Voyle, and Agnes Barrett the younger daughter inherited Dudwall and married Philip Tancred, whose descendants were still at Dudwall in 1591. William Voyle settled at his wife's home and was the first of the Voyle family at Philbeach which remained there till the latter end of the 17th century. The last of the main line there was William Voyle, living in 1647 and his wife Barbara daughter of Sir William Chancey, knight. They had no children and the estate passed to William's brother, Matthew Voyle who married Grace, described as widow in 1706; they had two daughters only, and Philbeach was sold to the Wogan family of Boulston.

In 1773 it was owned by John Wogan, with Alice Davids, aged 80, as tenant and comprised 197 acres ... The last Wogan owner was Elizabeth Wogan described as owner-occupier in 1786. By 1790 it had passed to a Mr. Cotton; in 1802 Major Robert James Acland was owner, with Evan Parry as tenant; in 1840 Robert James Acland was owner, with William Cale as tenant.

Thereafter the property was occupied by farmers, and was occupied by the owners, Mr. and Mrs. James to whom I am grateful for their kind welcome when I called there in 1977. The old mansion is now empty, and its interior partly ruined, and the owners live in a house built on the hillside a short distance away.

In 1811, the antiquary Fenton noted '... near Dale ... Pass by Crabhole an ancient mansion where once lived Phillip de Crabhole ... and farther on by another venerable house, William de Filbatch by marrying Sarah daughter of Robert de Vale of Dale, became possessed of a vast addition to his own property ... In this old house till very lately remained the old baronial hall, with a long oak table placed across the floor at the upper end, raised as in college halls, on a dais or steep'. *The Pembs. Archaeological Survey* (1896-1907) states, 'A round chimney and some portions of the old house are still standing', and continue to the present day. When I visited Philbeach on 6th September 1977, I found the old house empty, and in one part the ceiling over 'the best room', the bedrooms and the main staircase had been removed; the cellar below had been covered and cemented over. It was a large house extended on to a higher level in later times. The large old chimney at the end of the older part still survives, as does the walled garden nearby.

Refs: *Francis Green 'Wogan of Boulston' 1902, illustr.; Sale Cat. June 1733; Anc Mon Pembs 1925, p. 218 , photo showing the round chimney; Peter Smith, Houses of the Welsh Countryside, 1975, maps 8, 9, 28,; Dwnn i, 71-2; WWHR, ii, 58; Dale Castle Pedigrees No. 137; Carms. RO, G.G.Ms (Adv Pembs); Pembs RO, deeds; B. M. Egerton ms 2586,* 398-399; *PRO, Anc Deeds; NLW Papers of Great Sessions, Plea Rolls, Goal Files, Tithe map (Marloes) 1842, Cwmgwili Deeds; Cardiff Library, Deeds.*

PICTON CASTLE. *Slebech.*

Seat of the families of Wogan and Philipps. This is undoubtedly one of the premier country houses in Pembrokeshire, if not in the whole of Wales. It was a fortified house in the reign of William ll and from that time to the present has been occupied by families in direct succession from the Norman owners, the de Pictons, whose heiress, Joan, married Sir John Wogan of Wiston with Picton Castle and estate as her dowry. Joan was the only daughter of Sir William Picton who, however, had a brother Philip who had descendants in the male line including the celebrated Sir Thomas Picton who fell at Waterloo.

Major Jones's account differs from the above. He states that Henry I granted the property to Wizo the Fleming who immediately built a fortification. About a century and a half later a new castle was constructed on a lower site where it still stands, though much altered. And it was the heirs of Wizo's family which brought the property to the Wogans. The Wogans took a prominent part in the subjugation of Ireland and Sir John Wogan was Justiciar of that country from 1295. Six successive generations of the family lived at Picton.

From the Wogans Picton passed by descent

through another heiress to Sir Henry Donne who was killed at the Battle of Banbury in 1469. One of Sir Henry's two daughters, Jane, married Thomas ap Philip and brought to his family the Picton estate, with which family it has remained ever since. Thomas's descendants took the name of Philipps. They descend from the princely stock of Cadifor ap Collwyn who was Lord of Pembrokeshire and died in 1089. The Philips/Philipps family produced numerous cadet lines and many distinguished public servants including two Lords Lieutenant, 35 High Sheriffs, several Members of Parliament, innumerable JPs, military and naval officers, barristers and other important posts and several were granted knighthoods, baronetcies and peerages.

During the Civil War Sir Richard Philipps garrisoned Picton for the King and the Castle sustained a long siege. It collapsed as the result of a typical dirty Parliamentary trick. Sir Richard's baby son, Erasmus, was being nursed by a maid-servant. As the maid watched through the window at the besieging forces she was spotted by a trooper who approached the window, which was on the lower floor, carrying a flag of truce and brandishing a letter. In good faith the girl opened the window, still holding the child, to receive the letter. Suddenly the trooper lunged forward and snatched Sir Richard's heir and rode off. A genuine message was then sent threatening that if the Castle was not immediately surrendered the child would be killed. Sir Richard had no alternative but to give in. The Parliamentary general's conscience was so stricken that he refused to give the order for the Castle to be demolished, which is why it still stands today. Sir Richard's father, Sir John, was created a baronet in 1621. The 7th Baronet, another Sir Richard, was raised to the peerage as Lord Milford in 1766. As he died without issue the barony became extinct and the baronetcy passed to a cousin. The Rev. Sir James Erasmus Philipps, 12th baronet of Picton, had six sons. The eldest succeeded as 13th Baronet and was elevated to the peerage as Viscount St. Davids. The second son,

Sir Ivor was a distinguished soldier and Governor of Pembroke Castle which he bought and restored. His only daughter, Marjorie, married Lt.Col. Vincent Basil Ramsden and their son, Major Ivor Ramsden, of Cosheston Hall (q.v.) at the time of writing, represents the trustees of Pembroke Castle. The third son, Owen, was created Lord Kylsant, a title which became extinct at his death. The sixth son, Sir Laurence, was created a baronet and had the barony of Milford re-created for him. His son, the 2nd Baron was well-known for his eccentricites and sat in the House of Lords as a Communist!

The earliest surviving picture of the Castle was sketched in 1684 when the Duke of Beaufort called there. It shows a building within a walled enclosure. The entrance to the front of the Castle was between the two main flanking towers. The 18th century Lord Milford made several changes and built a dining room and drawing room at the east end. He swept away the old portcullised entrance, the moat and the drawbridge and replaced them with a classical portico with Grecian columns. However, in 1840 the portico was replaced by a 'Norman' doorway which remains today and is more in keeping. Many visitors to Picton have left descriptions of it but space precludes all but a few comments. Fenton was allowed to see over the Castle and, in the manner of the time, was refreshed with fruit and wine. Another who feasted on peaches and nectarines and took some away was Sir T. Cullum who commented on a strange horned owl which not only hatched its own eggs but also sat on chicken's eggs, hatched them, ate them and was 'rather savage to strangers'! At the time of writing the Castle is occupied by the Hon. Hanning Philipps, a younger son of the 1st Lord Milford of the second creation.

PIERSTON. *St. Brides.*
A farmstead in the headland south of St. Brides Bay, to the east of St. Brides, and near to Hoaton farm. The villages of Marloes and Dale are situated to the south-west of Piers-

ton farm. In medieval times Pierston was a manor forming part of the possessions of the De Brian family. In 1270 an agreement was made whereby one-third of the manors of Pererston (Pierston) and Popleton were granted to Andrew Wake and his wife Johanna, for their lives, with ultimate reversion to the heirs of Guy de Brian. Few references occur to Pierston thereafter.

In the years 1717-1726 Pierston was the home of Thomas Bowen, gent., and his son and daughter, Henry and Frances. By 1756 it was owned by George Lloyd Meares, High Sheriff in that year, and in 1769 Hugh Meares of Pierston was a Commissioner of Land Tax for the county.

In the years 1786-1797 George Meares Esq., was the owner, with James Roch, gent., as tenant, and later it was bought by Lord Kensington of St. Brides mansion. The topographer Carlisle noted in 1811, 'the manor belongs to Lord Kensington in right of his purchase of Pierston, although Mr. Laugharne contends to have a mesne lordship in the single tenement of Little Marloes only, where he claims a jurisdiction exclusive of the Lord paramount'; and in the same year, Fenton noted in his *Tour* that he 'passed Pearston, once the residence of a family of considerable respectability in the county, Meares, but by purchase now the property of Lord Kensington'. Thereafter the house and attached lands were leased to farmers.

In the sale catalogue of the St. Brides estate (Lord Kensington) in 1920, Pearson Farm (282 acres) is described as 'The spacious, stone built, rough cast and slated house', sheltered by plantations, and containing five bedrooms, two sitting rooms, kitchen, back kitchen, dairy, and offices, and 'charming old walled and well timbered gardens', together with farm outbuildings, held on 21 year's lease by W. P. Richards.

Refs: *Carlisle T.D.W. 1811; Fenton Tour 1811; Pembs. RO; Land Tax 1786; NLW Maesgwynne Deeds No. 96; Dr. Rees, 14th century maps; H. Owens, Old Pembroke Families 1902, p. 83.*

PISTYLL MEUGAN. *Llanfairnantgwyn.*
A large three-storeyed house, with eight bedrooms in the heartland of Cemaes, near the road from Eglwyswrw to Boncath, are three farms whose names commemorate a local saint – Pistyll Meugan, Dyffryn Meugan and Penanmeugan – about half a mile eastwards of the parish church. The most important of them is Pistyll Meugan, marked on Rees' 14th century map as the chapel of 'Llan Meugan'. As will be shown later, Pistyll Meugan was divided into two farms.

The chapel and holy well continued to function down to the close of the 16th century, but the bell was tolling on 14 July 1592 when the following letter was dispatched: 'These are to will and requier you being gentlemen to us knowne to be well affected and forwarde in her Majestie's service and good of the countrie, forthwith with all convenient spede to repaire to the place called St. Meugans where somtyme offringes and superstitious pilgrymages have been used, and there to cause to be pulled downe and utterlie defaced all religues and monuments of that chappell, not leaving one stone therof upon an other, and from tyme to tyme to cause to be apprehended all such persone and persones of what sexe, kinde, or sorte whatsoever that shall presume hereafter continue to the tenor and purporte of the said honourable commission, to repaire either by night or daie to the said chappell or well in superstitious maner, and them to bring or sende before us or envie of us'. Signed by 'your very loving ffrends George Owen (of Henllys), Alban Stepneth (Prendergast), John ap Rees, Haverfordwest'.

When the Commissioners of Ancient Monuments called there in 1914, they reported 'a strong spring still flows in the foldyard of Pistyll Meugan Farm, but no trace of the chapel remains above ground'. In 1618 it was reported that 'at Saint Meigan yng-Hennys fair are said to have been held on Ascension Day, the Thursday after Trinity Sunday, and the Monday after St. Martin's Day'. Tolls from St. Meugan's fair were paid to the Lord of Cemaes; in 1600 George Owen received £3.15s.7d and in another relic of

Elizabethan times was noted by George Owen of Henllys who tells us that two games of Cnapan were annually played at St. Meugans on Ascension Day and Corpus Christi Day, between the men of Cemaes against the men of Emlyn (hundred) and the men of Cardiganshire.

Few references have been found to the property in more modern times. In the 18th century it was part of the estate of the Bowens of Llwyngwair. In 1726 James Bowen, Esq., granted a lease for 21 years of 'Pistill Moygen otherwise called Llanvoigan', to John Evan, mercer, and in 1758 George Bowen Esq., owned the property. Not long after it was sold. In 1786 there were two farms called Pistillmoyan, one owned by John Jones, gent., with Daniel Evans, tenant, the other by Thomas Lloyd, Esq., with David Bowen tenant; and Llanvoygan by Walter Rice, Esq., with David Morris tenant.

In 837 Pistill Megan was owned by Mrs. Anne Evans, with Morris Williams tenant; two of the field names 'Castell Coch' may commemorate an early Celtic fortification and 'Park Pensylvanea' which suggests 18th century Quaker associations.

In 1894 Thomas and John Vaughan held Pistill Meigan, jointly. When Pistyll Meigan was put up for sale in 1981-82, the sale catalogue showed a commodious three-storeyed 19th century house with a projection to the front rising to roof height, with an entrance porchway leading to a hall, drawing, dining, and breakfast rooms, study, two kitchens and offices; on the first floor, five bedrooms, and on the second floor three bedrooms; to the rear were outbuildings, stables, cattle sheds etc.

The house is surrounded by two acres of grounds, and included an orchard, and sheltered by a small grove of mature trees. It can be seen from the roadway. When I gazed at it I thought of earlier days when Pistyll Meugan's hallmarks were the chapel, holy well, pilgrimages, gaiety, and pugilistic endeavours.

Refs: *Geo. Owen, Vairdre Book ms in NLW; Llyfr Phygain, 1618; Owens Pembrokeshire I 271, note 7; B.G. Charles, George Owen of Henllys, 1973, and The second Book of Geo.*

Owen's Description of Pembs. in Journal NLW Vol. V, No. 4 winter 1948; Dillwyn Miles, A Pembs. Anthology 1983, p. 220. Fenton, Tour Pembs. 1811, p. 282; Pembs. RO, LT list 1786; Western Mail, 4 June 1981 and 15 April 1982 (illustr.); Francis Jones, The Holy Wells of Wales, 1954, p. 209; NLW Llwyngwair Deeds; Western Mail, 15 April 1872.

PLÂS CRWN. *Llanddewi Felfrey.*
A mansion in a wooded countryside south-east of the village of Llanddewi Felfrey. Sometimes called Poys-cwm. The first known owner, Philip Lewis Thomas, was living there in 1613-1647. His son and heir John succeeded and left an only daughter the heiress Elizabeth, who married Reynold Lewis (descended from Gwynfardd) of Clynpottal, High Sheriff in 1678, who settled at his wife's home, where he was still living in 1693. His two sons died without issue, and Plâs Crwn passed to his daughter Elizabeth Lewis who married James Woolley and had five daughters. The property continued in the family until about 1733 when they made arrangements for selling the estate. The next owner was Thomas George, gent., who was at Plâs Crwn in 1759 and made improvements to the old mansion.

His son and heir, Evan George, succeeded and died in 1859, leaving Plâs Crwn to his son, Owen William George who married Catherine Margaret Beynon of Trewern; Evan had two daughters, Frances Margaret who married Dr. Thomas Rees-Thomas of Lampeter House, and Catherine Mary George who remained unmarried. Frances had issue, and Plâs Crwn passed to her son Frank James Gordon Thomas who married Katherine Geraldine eldest daughter of Col. Lewis W. Penn, C.B., of Camrose, by whom he had a son, Frank Griffith Thomas, who spent part of his childhood at Plâs Crwn, which he left about 1910, when Plâs Crwn was advertised for sale. F. G. Thomas had a daughter Pamela Thomas who married a Mr. Brownrigg, and were living at Little Marcle, Oxfordshire, in 1981 when I had the pleasure of meeting them.

The sale catalogue, dated 1910 describes Plâs Crwn as having a tiled floor conservatory with a doorway in the centre, and at each end passes by means of French windows into a dining and drawing rooms, hall, and smoke room; pantry, kitchen, scullery, servants' hall, housemaids' pantry, dairy, with passage to the back door; there were two cellars; a staircase led to the first floor. On the half-landing was a bathroom and convenience; on the first floor were five bedrooms, and on the second floor two bedrooms, nursery, and china pantry. There was a walled garden, outbuildings, stables etc. In front of the house a 'ha ha' separated the house from the field beyond. When I called there in 1976, it was empty, falling into ruin.

Refs: Carms. RO, Golden Grove ms LT 1786; Sale Cat. 1910; Pembs. RO, Deeds; College of Arms ms, Protheroe ms; Landowners' Return 1873; information ex inf. Mrs. Brownrigg, and Revd. M. G. R. Morris, vicar of the parish; NLW Llwyngwair Deeds.

PLÂS Y MEIBON/MEIBON. *Llangolman.*

A farmstead on a slope just north of Pont-howel bridge built over the upper waters of the Eastern Cleddau. The house sometimes called Ponthowel. The property came to prominence for the first time during the 18th century when it became the home of the yeoman family of Gwynne. The Plâs is a commodious building of two storeys with a range of four windows; at the side extends a lower two-storeyed building which seems much older, and may well have been part of the original structure. It is used as the kitchen and other domestic purposes, and is entered through a large traditional porch; a tablet in the outside wall is inscribed 'G.G. A.D. 1756'. (i.e. Griffith Gwynne), and on another tablet are the words 'Rebuilt by T. James AD 1871'

I visited it in 1973 and made a sketch of the house. In 1786 Thomas Gwynne is recorded as owner-occupier. On 21 June 1797, Richard Jones made a survey of Plâs Meibon demesne and adjoining farms, (Pont Howell Mill, Cnwe y Deryn, Plâs Hwdog, Tir Coch, and Wern), being the estate of Thomas Gwynne Esq.

The estate was put up for sale at Narberth on 3rd August 1797. However, Plâs Meibon was not sold then, and in 1801 it was owned and occupied by Thomas Gwynne. However the Gwynne family moved to Cilciffeth, and Court Llanychaer. Plâs Meibon was occupied by several yeoman families in the 19th century; in 1834 James Gibby was living at 'Place Meibon'; in 1873 Daniel James was owner-occupier; in 1894 David Griffith and William Philips were occupiers; and in 1904 Benjamin Davies was of Plâs y Meibon.

Refs: Pembs RO, LT 1786; NLW, Mrs. Thomas (Pencaer) deeds; Landowners' Return 1873; Griffith Gwynne, Place y Meibon, subscribed for a copy of Revd. Wm. Evan's English Translation of Cannwyll y Cymry 1771.

PLÂS IWERILL (Y WERILL).
Llanfihangel Penbedw.

In the wooded glen of Iwerill. The site of the Plâs is now unknown. There were several other farms in the near vicinity; Tythyn Dyfryn ywerill and Tythyn Gwaun Ywerill (1640), all in Gwestfa Iwerill (1640-2), and Dyffrin Rhiwerill. In 1634 Philip Gruffydd ap Edward, gent., of Eglwyswen parish released the messuage and lands called Plâs y Werill to Rutherch ap Richard of Llanfihangel Penbedw.

In 1642 James Davids of Eglwyswrw parish (grandson of Rutherch ap Richard) and his mother Ellen Davids, owned Plâs Blaen Iwerill, and other properties in the parish and chapelry of Llanfihangel Penbedw, and in Gwentfa Iwerill in the said parish. In 1659 James David of Llanfihangel Penbedw, gent., owned Plâs y Werill. In 1662 the said James David and Temperance his wife, mortgaged Plâs Ywerill in £50 to Thomas Jones of Brith-dir, gent., to be held in as large a manner as Rutherch ap Richard (grandfather of John Davids) purchased the same from Phillip Griffith ap Edwards; and on 3 October 1663 James Davids gent., and Ellen Davids, widow, both of Llanfihangel Penbedw, in consideration of £70 released Plâs Iwerill to Thomas Jones of Brithdir, gent. In 1665 James Davids then of Eglwyswrw parish, held a mortgage in £28 on Plâs Blaen Iwerill and two other properties in Gwestva Iwerill.

The property passed from Jones of Brithdir to Jones of Cilwendeg, but the name Plâs Iwerill was no longer used. In 1786 Dyffryn Rhiwerill was owned and occupied by Anne Morris. In the parish Tithes Schedule of 1837 Dyffryn Rhiwerill was owned and occupied by Morgan Jones, (of Cilwendeg). No traditions of the Plâs have been found, and its very site is unknown.

Refs: *NLW, Bronwydd Deeds; Tithe Schedule 1837; Pembs. RO, LT 1786.*

PLÂS NEWYDD. *St. Dogmaels.*

Situated just south-east of St. Dogmaels village. The property was originally owned by the Lords of Towyn, a district to the northwest of the town of Cardigan, on the Cardiganshire side of the Teifi estuary. About 1560-70 Margaret, daughter and heiress of Rhydderch ap Rhys Fychan, lord of Towyn (descended from the chieftain Gwynfardd Dyfed), married Thomas ap Harry of Blaenpant and Neuadd Trefawr, Cards, and brought to him Plâs Newydd as part of her dowry. Their son, Stephen Parry, settled at Plâs Newydd, and was High Sheriff of Cardiganshire in 1629. His grandson, Stephen Parry was living at Plâs Newydd in 1646, died unmarried, and Plâs Newydd passed to his sister Elizabeth. This Elizabeth was assessed at seven hearths in the Hearth Tax List of 1670 ... She married her second-cousin, David Parry of Newydd Trefawr (will proved in 1666), by whom she had a son, David Parry of Noyadd Trefawr, High Sheriff of Cards. in 1684, died a bachelor in 1711, buried at Llandywydd.

Later, Plâs Newydd was sold, and in 1786 the owner occupier was Sir Watkin Lewes (Lord Mayor of London 1780). Fenton noted in 1811, 'on a pleasant eminence stands Plâs Newydd, *new mansion,* a name perfectly appropriate, being a later creation of my countryman and old friend Sir Watkin Lewes, as a temporary residence whenever he found leisure from City duties to visit his native country'. Sir Watkin had an only daughter, Justina Bann Lewes. In 1824 Herbert Evans of Highmead, Cards, Esq., is described as heir

at law of Sir Watkin Lewes. The author Rees states in his *Beauties of South Wales,* 1815, p. 868, '... a modern mansion called Plâs Newydd, built by Sir Watkin Lewes'. No trace of the earlier plâs has survived.

Refs: *Carms RO, John Francis Deeds, Golden Grove mss; Pembs. RO, LT List 1786 and deeds; Fenton Tour Pembs. 1811, p. 282; Pritchard, History of St. Dogmaels Abbey, pp. 185-6; NLW, Great Session, Pembs. Plea Rolls, Griffith Owen Deeds No. 2594.*

POINTZ CASTLE (CAS BWNSH).
Brawdy.

A farmstead on high land near the road from Haverfordwest to St. Davids. The farmland slopes to the coast washed by the waters of St. Brides Bay. On the western side lies the parish of St. Elvis (Llansilo) and just beyond is the picturesque village of Solfach.

Pointz Castle is named after an early owner, Pointz, whose name suggests Norman or Flemish origin. Near the entrance to the farm is a mound called Pointz Castle, which probably marks the remains of an earthwork fortification; the field abutting it on the west side is known as Parc y Castell. It guarded the entry to the dwelling house which stands a hundred yards or so beyond.

It was a large commodious long house built in the vernacular style, and around its front was a wall enclosing a courtyard. It was a capitular manor belonging to the Bishop of St. Davids, who kept livestock there, the demesne land and the house being let to yeomen.

A record dated 1292-3 shows that the Bishop possessed 280 cattle and sheep and grain at Pointz Castle, valued at £46. 17s 2d, a considerable sum in those days. By 1326 it was united with the neighbouring manor of Tynevydd, and the combined manors were united to that of Brawdy whose caput stood alongside the parish church a short distance away. In 1326 the manors of 'Castrum Poncins and Nova Vida' are given as one manor; the demesne consisted of four carucates, each of 89 acres; there was a water grain mill; among the tenants were David Bowen, David Parys, David and Adam the millers, Cadifor ap David, Daykyn ap Howel, John Fawr; the Lord (Bishop) owned 24 cattle, 7 horses, and 500 sheep; the tenants had to wash the sheep; they were also to follow the relics of the Blessed David so far as Garn Twrne, and pay duties and attend courts, etc. Most of the lands specified were part of the manor of Pointz Castle, where the Bishop possessed 280 sheep, cattle, and grain. In 1588 both manors were amalgamated with that of Brawdy which was also one of the Bishop's manors. In 1545-6 Walter Wythyn, husbandman, held Pointz Castle, and in 1582 it was let to John ap Rhys of Rickeston, and in 1584-88 William Martin lived at Pointz Castle. Afterwards it was held by various members of the Rickerston family of Rhys, and were succeeded by the family of Griffith, old highly respected yeoman stock who lived at Hendre in Llandeloy parish.

Evan Griffith of Hendre had a lease of Rickerston in 1745 and came there to live. His son, Samuel Griffith, was the first member of the family to live at Pointz castle, and was succeeded there as leaseholders by four successive generations of his descendants. Finally, on 29 July 1940 Pointz Castle was transferred from the Bishopric to the University of Wales who are now the owners. The tenants (at the time of Major Jones's visit. – Ed.) are Mr. and Mrs. Leslie Raymond. The ancient family of Griffith was, at the time of writing represented by three ladies, the daughters of Mr. and Mrs. George Griffiths of Pointz Castle namely: Mrs. Mabel Thomas, Mrs. Iris Morgan, and Miss Dorothy Griffith.

It is a pity to have to end on a sad note. During a violent storm the roof of the historic manor house of Pointz Castle was badly damaged and the University decided that the best thing to do was to demolish the house that for many centuries had been a landmark of Dewsland, and to build, some distance away, a new house with no trace of the vernacular in its appearance.

Refs: *The Black Book of St. Davids, 1326; NLW, Tithe Map, LT, and Church in Wales Records; information from Griffiths of Pointz Castle family papers; Francis Jones, The Lordships and Manors of Dewsland.*

PONTFAEN. *Pontfaen.*

An attractive commodious mansion standing near the parish church on a steep slope above the upper waters of the river Gwaun which flows for some seven miles to reach the sea at Fishguard. Behind the mansion, the land rises to the north-east, to the hill tops of Mynydd Morfil and Mynydd Cilciffeth, and before it, across the river the land rises to Mynydd Melyn in Llanychlwydog and Mynydd Dinas in the parish of that name. The original mansion stood there in early medieval days, and, with a few architectural changes, has retained its status to the present day. The house is protected by a copse of well grown trees.

In 1811 Fenton observed: 'Pontvaen which was inhabited by a family of considerable influence in this country within these sixty years, of the name of Laugharne, the heiress of which married Rowland Philipps Esq., of Orlandon, whose son John Philipps Laugharne Esq., my old friend and school-fellow, is the present proprietor'. Some thirty years afterwards S. Lewis wrote, 'Pontvaen House, formerly residence of the Laugharnes, and now, by purchase, together with the estate, including the whole of the parish, the property of Henry Rees, Esq., is a handsome mansion, pleasantly situated and surrounded with thriving plantations'. In 1863 the Pontfaen estate in Pontfaen, Morfil, Llanychlwydog, and Llanychaer parishes, was advertised for sale, and we are informed the demesne having been in the proprietor's (Henry Rees) own hands for some years, has been farmed, drained, and improved at a very considerable outlay, under the best system of husbandry, and is now in splendid condition. The mansion and offices having been built of late years and in thorough repair ...'

Pontfaen had been the house of three successive families for many centuries. The first known proprietors descended from the Dyfed princeling, Gwynfardd Dyfed, whose arms were: *azure a lion rampant or between an orle of eight roses of the second,* was borne by his descendants.

In the years 1350-1400 the owner was Rhys ap Robert ap Owen, said to have been the first of his line to settle at Pontfaen, and was followed by his son Gwilym Vychan who was there in the 1440s. His son Llewelyn, succeeded him and the estate passed to his only child, the heiress, Llenca. She married shortly before 1491, John Vaughan of Abergavenny descended from the Breconshire chieftain, Moreiddig Warwyn concerning whose coat of arms: *gules three boys' heads each with a snake proper entwined around each neck,* a strange tale is told. John settled at his wife's house, and was the first of the Vaughans there. In those days Pontfaen was a substantial building, and in 1670 contained five hearths. Six generations of Vaughans continued at Pontfaen which eventually passed to the ultimate heiress, Lettice Vaughan who married in 1625 Francis Laugharne, younger brother of Major General Rowland Laugharne, who

took a prominent part in the Civil War in West Wales. Ann Vaughan, grand-daughter and heir of the said John and Llenca, married her kinsman, John Laugharne of St. Brides. Six generations of Laugharne lived at Pontfaen until the marriage of the ultimate heiress, Anne Laugharne in 1750, to Rowland Philipps of Orlandon a cadet of the Picton Castle family, who there upon adopted the surname Philipps Laugharne. Later descendants inherited the baronetcy of the Picton Castle family, the last of them being Sir Godwin Philipps who died aged 17 in 1857.

Most of the properties of the Laugharnes lay in St. Brides and Haverfordwest, and the later generations took little interest in their Pontfaen inheritance and in 1823 the Pontfaen estate was sold to Henry Rees of Roch parish. Thus after over five and a half centuries, Pontfaen passed to a stranger. Some time after 1845, Henry Rees sold Pontfaen to the Gowers of Castle Maelgwyn in North Pembrokeshire. In 1863 it was sold to Richard Arden, a wealthy London lawyer. It eventually came to the Buckinghamshire family called Camm. In 1941 C.B. Camm sold Pontfaen and part of the estate to Major John Francis D.L. of Carmarthen, father of Captain John Francis, O.B.E., D.L. whose daughter is the owner at the time of writing.

Refs: *Pembs. RO, LT 1786; Dwnn, ii, 172-3, 244; NLW, Poyston Deeds; Francis Jones, 'Pontfaen' in Journal NLW 1977; Fenton Tour Pembs. 1811; S. Lewis Top. Dictionary of Wales. 1835 and 1840.*

PONTGYNON. *Meline.*

The farmhouse of Pontgynon stands at the northern end of the parish, on the lower slopes of the Preseli, above the waters of Afon Nanhyfer, between Eglwyswrw and Crosswell. On Dr. Rees's 14th century map it is marked as Trefgynon, a knights fee (Welsh). When my wife drove me there on 2nd January, 1977, a beautiful sunny day, we found a picturesque old two storeyed structure with a range of three windows, very vernacular in appearance. The floors of the rooms slope with the terrain, and walking through them we approach the eastern banks of Afon Nanhyfer; ceilings are low, there are massive well-preserved old oak-beams. Mr. John Williams, the present owner-occupier, is a descendant, through his mother, of the Rees family who had claimed a lease of Pontgynon in 1786 and later acquired the freehold.

Originally the residence of gentry, we are told by the antiquary George Owen, in 1603-04: 'At Pontgynon upon Nevarne banke dwelleth William Bowen, second sonne of Mathias Bowen of Lloyn gwayer ... the house he dwelleth in was builded by himself about 28 years past (c.1575), the lands thereof was partlie geaven him by his father, but much amplified by his own purchases'.

The Bowens remained there till the end of the 17th century, and a document of the period describes the Pontgynon estate as follows: the capital messuage and mansion called Plâs Pontgynon; a messuage west of Pontgynon Bridge; a messuage known variously as Eskybor Fawr alias Eskybor Pontgynon; a field called Park y Tynkr; a messuage called Tythyn Pantyrhiw fechan alias Tyther yr Allt grach; a water corn mill called Pontgywn Mill alias Felin Newydd alias Felin Killallyn; these were mortgages and for a time were owned by Griffith of Penybenglog which thereafter became the home of farmers who held it on leases for lives.

John Warren of Trewern was the owner in 1736. Early in 1786 it was owned by Rees Stokes, and later in that year John Rees Stokes and his wife Frances (née Warren of Trewern), Catherine Warren his sister-in-law granted a lease of Pontgynon to the then tenant, Thomas Rees, for the lives of lessors, and of John Rees (aged 7), son of Henry Rees of Pennffordd, and another John Rees (aged 6) son of Evan Rees of Rhosmaen fach. In the early 19th century, the property was owned by the Lloyds and Williamses of Cwmglôyn, while the Reeses remained as tenants. The Rees family continued at Pontgynon as occupiers, James Rees in 1834 and by 1894 by William Rees, and was bought by them shortly afterwards. By 1950 it was owned by David R. Williams, a kinsman.

Refs: Pembs RO, LT 1786; Carms RO Golden Grove Gwynfardd, NLW, Bronwydd Deeds, Tithe Map Meline 1837; WWHR ii, 37; G. Owen 2nd Book of Pembs. 1603, p. 276, PRO, Chancery Suits 5, 451/85.

PONTYGAFEL. *Llanfyrnach.*

The valley of the Tâf, through which that river runs, forms the boundary between the shires of Pembroke and Carmarthen. The vale was well known for its gentry and yeoman families some of which have survived to the present time.

The residence of Pontygafel stands near the hamlet of Glandwr, whose nonconformist chapel contains a memorial tablet adorned with the coat of arms of John Devonald of Graig who lived there in 1479 – an unusual exhibit in a nonconformist chapel. Nearby also is Derlwyn owned by later owners of Pontygafel and used by them as a residence for the widows of the family. During medieval times Pontygafel was a residence of descendants of Jenkin Lloyd of Blaiddbwll who derived from the Chieftain Gwynfardd Dyfed.

Nine successive generations of the lineage of Jenkin ap Llewelyn held Pontygafel from early medieval times down to the latter part of the 17th century. Morris ap Howel of Graig married Morfydd daughter of Rhys ap David ap Hywel Jenkin Lloyd of Blaiddbwll, and their daughter Janet married John ap Eynon of Pontygafel, whose descendants continued there for four generations, the last members of the line adopting the surname Evans in the late 17th century.

The property passed to William James whose son John James lived at Aberelwyn from 1702 to 1767, and with Pontygafel continued in the James family until the 1970s when it was sold by the then owner, Mr. E. O. James. From circa 1700, seven successive generations of Jameses continued there, highly respected, the last generations were eminent solicitors, barristers, senior civil servants, and local government officers.

Refs: Golden Grove ms; Protheroe ms xix, fos. 48, 53; mss of H. E. James BA; deeds in Pembs RO, HDX; Colby Map 1831.

POPEHILL. *Johnston.*

A tall commodious residence in a rural area, near the roadway leading from Haverfordwest to the town of Milford. To the north of the residence is Dredgeman Hill, and to the south, the village of Johnston. From time to time several gentry families lived at Popehill, but none remained there for long. In 1431 William Aftecote, described as son and heir of Margaret Cadell 'late of Apehill in Wallia', quit claimed all his lands in Treenhill (now Dreenhill) in the lordship of Haverfordwest, once owned by Phillip Lloyde, Rector of Herbrandston, Co. Pembs. In the following century the property passed to the family of Lewis.

In 1566 Hugh Lewis lived at Popehill, having married Maud, widow of Thomas Butler, gent. (son of Arnold Butler of Johnston), daughter of John Harries of Haverfordwest. Hugh held the property in 1597, after which it passed to Thomas Canon, gent., who was still there in 1604. Afterwards it passed through several hands. In 1725-6 Popehill was owned by William Bowen, gent., later of Mullinger, a cadet of the Bowen family of Upton Castle. In 1762 it was held by Mary, described as widow of Thomas Williams gent., of St. Davids parish, and since 1733 of Popehill and at Haverfordwest, where she was then living with her eldest son, Thomas Williams.

By 1773 the owner-occupier was Thomas Wright, still there in 1807. It changed hands again, when bought by William Edwardes of Johnston Hall (created Baron Kensington in the peerage of Ireland on 20th July 1776), descended from the chieftain Tudor Trevor of North Wales. He died in 1801 and was succeeded by his son and heir, the second Baron, who left Popehill, and settled in the neighbouring county of Carmarthenshire where he died in 1861. Thereafter Popehill became home to local yeomen; one of them was deacon of Bethesda Baptist Chapel who permitted religious services to be held at Popehill before Horeb Chapel was built in 1817.

Refs: *Picton Castle Deeds; Carms. RO, Trant Deeds. Lucas Deeds; Pembs. RO, Papers of Great Sessions, Plea Rolls; LT lists 1786 and 1797; NLW, Francis Green Deeds No. 3; Roberts, Baptist Hist. Sketches in Co,. Pembs. 1907, p. 34.*

PORTCLEW. *Lamphrey.*

An imposing house in the southern end of the parish on high ground overlooking the cove of Freshwater East and the waters of the Bristol Channel beyond. Lewis in 1840 speaks of 'Portclew, a modern mansion, the residence of Thomas Parry Esq., is beautifully situated on an eminence commanding a fine view of the sea.' In 1326 Thomas Wettar of Portclew was described as a landowner in the fee of Lamphey, part of the temporalities of the See of St. Davids. In 1560 Edmund Poyer and John Philips are described as 'of Portclew'. By 1595 it was held by Lewis Bishop whose descendants remained there until the death of Lewis Bishop after 1771.

The Bishop family had come to Pembrokeshire in about 1600 and bore arms: *argent on a bend cotised gules three plates (or besants)*. The well-known family of West Wales landowners, the Parrys, succeeded the Bishops when John Parry married Margaret, daughter and heiress of Lewis Bishop and came to live at his wife's home. John became High Sheriff in 1772. Their son William Parry married Ann Kemm, second daughter of Henry Kemm of Northdown, their marriage settlement having been made on October 22 1801. Their daughter, Mary Ann Parry, married at Lamphey on Jan 26 1830 the Rev.

Francis George Leach, son of Abraham and Catherine Leach of Corston. Francis died in 1876 aged 80 and his wife died in 1894 aged 86. By the mid-19th century the Parrys had left Portclew and Portclew House became the home of Col. William Morrison whose descendants were still there in 1904. The district around Portclew had a number of properties which bore the name. In 1786 John Parry was owner-occupier; Sir Hugh Owen owned East Portclew; Sarah Bastin owned Little Portclew and Abraham Leach owned another farm of the same name. In 1894 there were four properties in the area: Portclew; Portclew Burrows; Upper Portclew and Little Portclew. By 1950 most of these properties remained including Portclew House, occupied by the Uphill family.

PORTH CLAIS. *St. Davids.*

The cove and the farm are situated on the coast south of the cathedral city. In 1326 Porth Clais was a lay manor of the See of St. Davids. In 1587 and 1599 John Garnons was lord of the manor. The Garnons family held lands at Trevine and also Cilgerran. John was successful attorney at law, and was Clerk of the Peace for Pembrokeshire in 1575; MP. for Haverfordwest in 1571. He held the manor of Porth Clais, and in 1603 a Final Concord was made of the manor and lands between John Phillip and John Owen, plaintiffs, and John Garnon and Ellen his wife. Ellen (also called Ellin), was a daughter and co-heiress of John David of Trevine. John died in the first decade of the 17th century, and was followed by Ellen in 1618. Very few references have been found to Porth Clais in later records. In 1786 Porth Clais was owned by the Revd. M. Williams, the tenant being Henry Arnold.

Refs: B.B. of St. Davids 1326; Taylor's Cussion; PRO Records Wales , 3 0214; see Francis Jones, Lordships and Manors of Dewsland in Journal hist. Soc. of Church in Wales. 1970, p. 9.

PORTHIDDY FAWR and FACH.

Llanrhian.

A large farmstead on the boundary separating the parishes of Llanrhian and St. Davids, with lands in both parishes. The capital messuage was Porthiddy Fawr, with Porthiddy Fach, the small adjacent farm forming part of the larger property The lands are on the coast near the cove called Abereiddy, bordered on the northern side by Ynys y Barry, and on the southern by Cwmwdig.

Several references to the property occur in medieval deeds and documents. In 1383 Philip ap Philip Meugan granted lands at Porthiddy fawr, Llanmyon Frân, and 'Trefftheyaw', all in the lordship of Pebidiog to Margaret daughter of William ap Philpyn. In 1450, Walter ap Jenkin Lloyd owned lands in Porthiddy fawr and two years later he released to John ap Ieun Gwyn ap Rhys four stangs at Porthiddy Fawr, called Tyrhende, Penvrce, Martle and Fford Fychan, and several other properties within the lordship of Pebidiog; and in the same year he released to John ap Oweyn of Porthiddy Fawr, 'lands in Porthiddy Fawr where the hall of John ap Oweyn is'.

In 1459 David ap David Lloyd of Llanderoe (now Llaney near Croesgoch), released 16 virgates in Porthiddy Fawr to John ap Oweyn. In 1523 Dafydd ap Ievan ap Meredydd granted to his daughter Margaret a messuage and lands in Porthiddy Fawr and Fach.

The property seems to have changed hands fairly regularly during these early days, but in the 16th century it passed to a local yeoman, and remained in successive generations of his descendants for nearly two centuries. This was the family of Harry, later known as Harries.

The first known ancestor was David Harry James the elder of Porthiddy Fawr who was there during the period 1588-1630, and is variously described as yeoman and husbandman. Of his wife all that is known of her is her Christian name, Margaret. They had two sons, David Harry (James) the younger who was at Porthiddy Fawr from 1637 till about 1679 when he died. He had a brother, George Harry; described in contemporary deeds as 'gentleman', he married a member of a well known gentry family; Grace daughter of Thomas Jones of Brawdy, and sister of John Jones. Their prenuptial settlement was made on 30th March 1629. Their two sons, David and John adopted the surname Harries, and their daughter Elizabeth married David Perkins of Trefaccwa (d. 1694). John succeeded to the property and is described in 1663 as 'gentleman'. He was assessed for four hearths in Porthiddy Fawr in 1670. His will, dated in 1685, was proved in the year following. John Harries married Jane daughter of a wealthy landowner, Thomas Phillip of Trelewelyn near Manorowen, their marriage settlement being dated 25th July 1658. He died in 1686, and Jane died about 1716-17.

They had three sons and five daughters. The eldest son, David Harries, received only £10 under his father's will, while Porthiddy and Treglemais, with other properties were left to his widow absolutely. David moved to London where he married a lady much in debt for which he was arrested. After this he went to Holland and became a favourite of the Prince of Orange, who became King William III of Great Britain in 1694. David continued to enjoy Royal Favour, and in 1701 is described as a Page of the Bedchamber in Ordinary. He lived in London but little is known about him or his wife. He had two sons, the younger being John Harries, a Colonel in the Army, but neither had any association with Porthiddy or the county. James Harries, the second son went to live in London where he fought a duel. As a result, he returned to his native county, and married Elizabeth Harries, widow of Haverfordwest. He lived at Haverfordwest for the remainder of his life, and died in 1719. He had no issue.

The third son, George Harries, entered the medical profession and practised as a physician in London. On the death of his brother James, he inherited the paternal estate of Porthiddy, and then settled in Haverfordwest. Very little is known of him or his wife; their two children were Jane and Caroline Harries; the elder daughter lived in Carmarthen, and died unmarried some time after 1763; the second married Thomas Griffiths of Coed, Llandyfeilog, Carms., and had a son and a daughter. The five daughters of John Harries and his wife Jane (Phillips) were Elinor, Mary, Ursula, Anne and Elizabeth, all of whom married Pembrokeshire landowners and clergymen. Elinor, the eldest daughter, married firstly, Thomas Higgon, and secondly, Owen Phillips of Haverfordwest (d.1740), by who she had three sons, from one of whom, George Phillips, a clergyman, descend the well-known county family of Lort-Phillips.

The Porthiddy estate passed eventually to Lort-Phillips; in 1786 George Phillips, Esq., was the owner, and in 1801 John Lort-Phillips is described as owner of Porthiddy Fawr and Fach, and continued in possession of that family until finally sold.

Refs: *Pembs. RO., LT 1786 et seq.; NLW, Morgan-Richardson Deeds; Eaton Evan and Williams Deeds; Papers of Great Sessions, Plea Rolls; WWHR, VIII, pp. 141-146, essay by Francis Green who erroneously ascribes the origin of the Porthiddy Fawr family to the Harries of Cruglas.*

PRENDERGAST. *Prendergast.*
The ancient residences, known as Prendergast House and Place, stood on low ground on the western bank of the river Cleddau which divides Prendergast parish from the Borough of Haverfordwest. The property derived its name from the medieval owners, the last of whom to reside there, Maurice de Prendergast, accompanied Strongbow to Ireland where his descendants remained for successive generations and had no further connection with Pembrokeshire.

Prendergast manor and its accompanying estate passed to the family of Joce (or Joyce), then to the Wogans, and in early Tudor times to the family of Cadarn or Catharne. Henry Catharne of Prendergast became Constable of the Pelidiog Hundred (now Dewsland), and Clerk of the Courts of Haverfordwest and Roose. His will, dated 17th April 1525, was proved in the following year. He was succeeded by his son Thomas Catharne, High Sheriff of Pembrokeshire in 1565, and MP for the county for a long period before he died on 24 February 1567-8. By his wife Jane, daughter of Sir John Wogan, he had four daughters, co-heiresses, and Prendergast House passed to his daughter Margaret (b.1546), who married in 1565 Alban Stepney, the first of an English family from London and East Anglia to settle in West Wales.

On 31st December 1561 the Bishop of St. Davids appointed Alban to be Receiver-General of the diocese for life. By his marriage he acquired Prendergast House and other portions of the estate which Margaret his wife had enjoyed as daughter and co-heiress of Thomas Catharne. She died before 1573, and by that year Alban had married his second wife, Mary, daughter of William Philipps of Picton Castle. Alban was also High Sheriff of the county in that year, an appointment he held again in 1590 and 1605. Active in public affairs, he was MP for Haverfordwest in 1584 and 1586, for Cardigan county in 1589, for Carmarthen County in 1597, and for Pembroke County in 1603. He added to his estate in 1579 by purchasing lands near Prendergast, and in Haverfordwest, and in the parish of Roch. Alban Stepney, died in 1611, was survived by his wife, Mary (Philipps), by whom he had four sons and two daughters. His will, recited in detail by Mr. Francis Green, shows that he owned an extensive estate in Pembrokeshire and Carmarthenshire. His eldest son and heir, John Stepney, born in 1600, received a knighthood in 1621, and on 10 November of the same year, advanced to a baronetcy. The baronetcy was borne by his descendants, and terminated with the death of Sir Thomas Stepney, 9th Baronet, on 12 September 1825, without issue. Sir Thomas had been Groom of the Bedchamber to Frederick, Duke of York, for thirty years.

The family property then passed to descendants on the female side who had married into the Gulston family who lived at Derwydd, Carms. They took the name of Stepney-Gulston, and later Cowell-Stepney. On 22nd September, 1871, John Cowell-Stepney was created a baronet, and left two sons. James Charles Murray Cowell-Stepney,

Page of Honour to King William IV, was a Lieutenant-Colonel in the Coldstream Guards, and was killed at the Battle of Inkerman in 1854, aged thirty. His brother, Emile Algernon Arthur Keppel Cowell-Stepney, succeeded to the estate, and on the death of his father Sir John Cowell-Stepney on 15th May 1877, Emile succeeded to the baronetcy. He was somewhat eccentric, dropped his title, and emigrated to the United States where he died in 1909.

No remains of Prendergast House have survived, and few references to it in earlier sources have been found. In 1530, we learn that Henry Catharne, Esq., Lord of the Manor of Prendergast, kept a gaol under the tower of his house. there is a long gap to the next reference. This is in June 1662 when John Ray speaks of a fair house of Sir John Stepney. In 1670, Prendergast then the house of Sir John Stepney, is described as containing nine hearths. During the 18th century the Stepneys spent most of their time in Carmarthenshire, and ceased to reside at Prendergast which became ruinous, finally derelict. A tourist who saw it in October 1767 speaks of it as 'now in ruins'. A few parts of it continued to exist in 1811 when Richard Fenton notes '... I descend to the margin of the rich meadows whose banks the Cleddau washes, to see the small remains of the mansion called Prendergast Place ... where nothing is left but the shell of a spacious barn, and one fragment of a portion of the old house, with a few small apertures by way of window cased with freestone, and part of a lofty garden or orchard walk ... (after the departure of the Stepneys) the old mansion of Prendergast was suffered to fall into decay, and the property annexed to it sold'.

Samuel Lewis, the topographer, found little there of interest in 1840, when he noted as follows '... of whose mansion some remains may still be traced ... (on the family moving to Carmarthenshire) 'the ancient seat, being deserted soon fell into decay.'

The only relic of the early days to have survived is 'The Lady of the Ghyll', a ghost in the form of a vaporous cloud, said to walk along a footpath in Prendergast; the small tract of land that harbours her is called 'The Ghyll'.

Refs: *Dwnn, i, pp. 89, 135, 180. G. G. ms (Pembs. Pedigrees), R. Fenton, Tour Pembs., 1811. p. 120. Samuel Lewis TDW 1840. NLW – LT 1786, Poyston Deeds No. 157, Burke's Landed Gentry 1969 (Stepney-Gulston).*

PRISKILLY. *Mathry.*

John, son of Robert Goch of Preskyli (*sic*) held land in the manor of Castle Cenlas in 1342. In 1661 the Bishop of St. David's granted a lease to John Owen, of Priskilly, of lands including the wood or forest of Priskilly. The parcel consisted of about 400 acres and Owen '... hath built a pretty litle tyled house thereon'. Major Jones's notes contain an Owen pedigree of four generations. Later the area seems to have been divided into three sections: Priskilly Forest, Priskilly Fach and Priskilly Fawr. In the 18th century ownership was divided between the Bishop of St. Davids, the Scourfields, the Vaughans, the Lloyds, the Morses and the Howells. In 1815 297 acres of Priskilly Forest was held by Moses Mathias and 520 acres of Priskilly demesne by J. H. Harries Esq. 'The ancient

mansion of the family of Harries of Priskilly Forest is now the property of John Hill Harries Esq.' (*Lewis TDW.* 1840). 'The house is of no regular order of architecture, and when the present occupier came into possession of it, had grown much dilapidated by age. He

immediately set about repairing and improving it, and it now presents the appearance of a comfortable country residence such as befits the habits and requirements of a private gentleman of fortune. It stands embosomed in wood and skirted by the Western Clwyd (*sic*) (The Cleddau). The grounds are extensive and, like the gardens, kept in the best possible order.' (Burke's Visitations, ii, 231 (1853). The Harries family were in possession in the 1880s (*Vide* Walford's *County Families*).

Philipps
Lord Milford

RAMSEY ISLAND (YNYS DEWI and YNYS TYFANOG).

Lying off the St. Davids Peninsula, across Ramsey Sound. Home of the Whitton family – Thomas Whitton (d.1673/4) married a Wogan of Stone Hall. In 1543-4 Nicholas Jenkins, Philip Lewes, Thomas Blethryn, Geffrey Walter, John Vechan, Thomas Gwilym Owen, Thomas Walter, John Voyard, all of City of St. Davids, mariners, were summoned to answer William Browne of St. Davids, for 'taking his goods at Ramsey, on 23 May, 1543, viz. 50 puffins eggs, 60 puffins, and 500 gulls at Ramsey, to the value of £10'.

The Revd. James Summers (1822) leased it to John Mathias and David Morgan; and in 1832 there is record of a lease from the Bishop of St. Davids to William Bowlas Summers of Walywnscastle (son of James Summers, deceased), of Ramsey Island, and in 1833 he instituted an action that the lease to John Mathias and David Morgan be set aside; and in 1848 J. B. Summers had leased the Island to the family of George Phillips, farmers of Rosepool for life of Elvi, wife of George

Phillips at £226.10s. 6d rent p.a., but he surrendered the lease in 1851. On 20 June 1891 William Williams of Grove Hotel, St. Davids, Innkeeper, granted a lease to Luther Bowen Rees of Clegyr, farmer of Ramsey alias Ynys Trevanog, and the small islands called the Bishop and his Six Chicks; being the prenuptial settlement of said L. B. Rees and Elizabeth Mary Williams daughter of William Williams. On 1 February 1901 there was a notice in the 'County Guardian' – 'Ramsey Island to let, together with the outlying islands of North Bishop, South Bishops, Cantwr, and Walltog. Ramsey is well stocked with rabbits and feathered game of every description. The area of Ramsey is about 600 acres, arable and grazing, and is well watered and fenced. For further particulars apply to Mrs. Martha Williams, Grove House Hotel, St. Davids, or to Mr. John Reynolds, Treglemais, Croesgoch'.

The Black Book of St. Davids (1326) states 'They say that the Lord (Bishop) has in the Island of Ramsey two carucates of Land containing 100 acres and each acre worth to let 2d per year, and there can be kept there 10 horses, 100 head of great cattle and 300 sheep and the pasture for each head of great cattle is 2d and for every 10 sheep 2d, and they say that the Lord is able to take thence 100 loads of rushes and heath; each load is worth 3d and the Lord is able to take there, without injury to the stock, 500 rabbits for cooking and they are in actual value worth 33s 4d. Total 75 shillings'.

Fenton's Tour records: 'The old house where I have formerly made one of many a pleasant party is in ruins, and a new farmhouse is built near'. The Cambrian Travellers Guide' (1813), says that the place is the home of the peregrine falcon, that puffins were few and that the local cheese was 'excellent'. The Queen and her family picnicked on the island on August 9th 1977, when *Britannia* put in on her way to Northern Ireland.

RHOSDWARCH. *Meline.*
South of Rhosmaen, shown on Colby's map of 1831. In 1746 Lewis Morris found an ins-

cribed stone near Rhos Dewyrch, the seat of John Howells, gent. In the 1786 Land Tax the Rev. John Howels is shown as owner and the tenant as John Griffiths. In 1809 a George Howell was of Spanish Town in Jamaica. There is a pedigree in Francis Jones's notes.

RHOSLANOG FAWR. *Mathry.*
Home of the Hergest and Wogan families. John Hergest was assessed at one hearth in 1670. Lewis Wogan of Boulston, (d.1702) names Thomas Wogan of 'Treslanog' as a remainderman to his estate. The arms of Hergest: *argent a dragon passant, wings raised sable langued or.* The arms of Wogan: *or on a chief sable three martlets of the first.* Crest: *A cockatrice.* In 1326 Rhoslanog Fawr was a knight's fee. (*Black Book St. Davids*). In 1786 Thomas Williams of Rhoslanog Vach, yeoman bought the estate for £654. He bequeathed moeity to his natural daughter Mary Bateman (1829). In 1839 the property (also called Treslannog Vawr) was owned by Sir James Cockburn, Bt. with James Roch as tenant.

RHOS Y BAYVIL. *Bayvil.*
Shown in Colby's Map of 1831. Home of the Peverill and Mathias families. These Peverills are descended from the great but now extinct Norman house. George Owen in his second book says '... now the dwellinge place of Thomas Mathias ap Owen. The house is now more simple in vyor than the partie is auncient by descent as heyre male to the auncient famylie of the Peveralls whose auncestor was of those of Devon who was one of the knights that came with Martyn Toures to the Conquest of Kemes and had to him geaven this, Tregamman and diverse other landes, but tyme had greatlie dessinguished the lyving and estimasion of this famylie. His father Mathias was sonne to William sonne to Gwillim sonne to Owen Peverill third sonne to John Peverill.'

John Peverill in 1427/8 divided his large estate between his three sons. The youngest, Owen Peverill received Rhos y Bayvil, (amongst other lands), from him descended paternally Mathias ab Owen of Rhosbayvil whose children adopted the permanent surname Mathias. The arms are: *quarterly gules and vair, a lion rampant argent.* George Owen finds a later version of the Peverill arms as: *Sable four besants in chief, on an escutcheon of pretence gyronny argent and gules.*

RHOSYGILWEN. *Cilgerran.*

Home of the Lloyd, Jones, Colby and Morgan-Richardson families. In 1670 Jenkin Jones, grandson of Howel ap Jenkin Lloyd, was assessed at three hearths. His son Theophilus died 1697 leaving a daughter, Anne married to Jonathan Colby.

'Rhos y Gilwen the elegant modern mansion of John Humphreys Esq., who obtained this estate by marriage with Catherine daughter of the late Thomas Colby Esq., of Fynnonea and erected the present house' – *Lewis TDW 1840 and 1834.*

J. R. Phillips in *History of Cilgerran 1867*, pp. 125-6, says, 'The old house which at the present day would hardly merit to be called a respectable farmhouse, stood a little below the present edifice which was erected about 35 years ago by Mr. Humphreys, a brother-in-law of the present Mrs. Colby. This house is a neat specimen of what is generally termed domestic Gothic, and its interior arrangements are commodious and well arranged.

In 1904 Morgan-Richardson bought Rhosygilwen from the Colbys for £8,000. He died

in 1913 and C. L. E. Morgan-Richardson who followed died in 1961. In 1983 when Major Jones visited it, the owner-occupier was Mrs. Jane Cresswell Evans, who lived there alone with a tenant in part of the house. The Colby arms were shown in a painted glass window overlooking the stairs. It was offered for sale in July 1984, and later sold and was destroyed by fire in 1985. A photograph of the exterior in *Contemporary. Biog. S. Wales and Mon.*, C. Morgan-Richardson, 1907, p. 154.

RHOSYMAEN. *Meline.*

In the will of Lewis Rees, Gent., of Newport, Pembrokeshire: 'To my nephew John Owen of Rhosymaen, Nevern, a house in Newport now in occupation of Evan Owen, officer. Residue to my said nephew, William Owen of Newport, and make him executor'. 24 November 1786.

'Rhosymaen … the mansion house of Thomas Bowen, an infant now in ward, the sonne of Owen James, son to James Lewis, natural son to Lewis David, son to David ap Griffith ap Evan ap Madoke ap Howell ap Owen ap Gwillim Dew ap Gwillim ap Gwrwared of Kemes and so paternally descended of the ancestors of Pentre Ivan gave the coats (of arms) of that house with the due difference. The mother of the said Thomas was the natural daughter of Thomas Lloyd, Esq., his grandmother paternal was daughter to George Owen, gent. The inheritance of this house was in our father's age accounted next the best sort of livings though now lately many new purchases have left him behind, and yet is the same not diminished'. G. Owen, Second Book, p. 278. The spelling has been modernised.

Major Jones left further notes on this house and sketchy pedigrees.

RHYDGARNWEN. *Llantood.*

In the 17th and 18th centuries this was the home of the Morgan family. In the will of Rowland Jenkins of Bayvil dated June 19th 1657 he leaves land called Rhyd y Garne in

Llantood to his sons. In 1786, William James, gent., was owner and David Richard was tenant. In 1873, William Griffiths George was owner with 138 acres. His descendant, John Picton Meredith George, solicitor of Cardigan, died in 1934.

In 1975 it was the home of Dr. and Mrs. Browlie. In 1988 it was bought by Mr. and Mrs. Hugh Jones, owner-occupiers. The present house was built in the early 19th century near the older farmhouse of which no trace now remains.

RHYDLANGOEG. *Amroth.*
Vide **Colby Lodge** *supra.*

RHYD Y DRISSI . *Whitchurch-in-Cemaes.*
This does not appear in VL 1904, nor in LT 1786 nor in VL 1834 nor on the Colby Map. Major Jones provides a rough pedigree of owners from Madoc Gwilym (1289) to the early 18th century.

RHYDYDHARDING. *Mathry.*
Major Jones worked out a pedigree for the Thomas family and their descendants who owned this property from David Thomas assessed for one hearth in 1670, until the present century. There is no mention of the property in the Land Tax returns for 1786.

RICKESTON. *Brawdy.*
Home of the Le Maen family from the early 14th century, and from the 16th century the ap Rhys family. In 1326 it was a Knights fee (English), and in the *Black Book of St. Davids* it is recorded that 'Wenllion Martyn holds the manor of Ricardiston, pays 12d, and service, follow(ing) the relics to Garnturney'.

The old mansion, of which not a trace remains above ground, stood about 100 yards south of the present house of the boundary of the Brawdy airfield and is marked on 6" O.S. maps as 'site of Rickeston manor house'. '… a large old mansion called Rickeston demands our notice in a high exposed situation yet embosomed in a grove of no mean growth … It has a court in front entered by a gateway over which are the arms of Urien Rheged bespeaking its former possessor to be of that stock'. The owners, later visiting Scots-borough near Tenby and preferring that place, they became gradually estranged, and issue failing, it (Rickeston) was sold about the beginning of the last century and has never since maintained a higher rank than that of a farmhouse, the principal part of the building having long since fallen into decay. When I visited it about twenty years ago I was told by some of the old inhabitants who had heard it from their fathers, that in that court (yard) had often been seen three or four coaches-and-six at a time, and the family were known to attend the parish church in Brawdy in such an equipage.' *Fenton's Tour Pembs.* 1811, p. 23.

The following were High Sheriffs: John Ap Rhys 1582 and 1593, James ap Rhys 1655, and James ap Rhys in 1688. The arms of Le Maen or Moigne: *or six martlets gules, three, two, one.* The arms of Ap Rhys: *argent, a chevron between three ravens sable, over all a bend sinister gules.*

On 8 December 1601 Thomas Phillips of Picton, gent., and Thomas ap Rice of Rickarston, gent., were assigned of lease for lives of pennage of hogs, swine, and wild honey within the forest of Narberth and also the rents and farms of the tenure of Molston, parish and Lordship of Narberth, each a possession of Rees Griffith, Esq. attainted of high treason, which pennage and lands held of the Queen by a lease for lives of Owen Phillips, Alban Phillips and the said Thomas Phillips of Picton. (Slebech Deeds No. 236).

Anne Lewis, widow, was assessed at five hearths for Rickeston in 1670. A stone, once a gatepost on Rickeston Hall farm inscribed 'Briaci fil … V … G.' is now in Brawdy church. Sir Ivo Rhys extends the reading to Briaci fili Evalengi. One of the fields on Rickeston is called Parc Garreg Lwyd, which may refer to it. (*Anc. Mon. Pem.* p. 29) In 1787 William Jones is shown in the Land Tax lists as owner and Samuel Griffith as tenant. In 1842 William Griffith is the owner, Levi

Griffith tenant, of fields named as Gwaun Cile, Park Carreg lwyd, Park y Windy, Park'r Orchard, Rhos Munck, and the cottage at Gwaun Spilsea. For a history of Rickeston Manor see Francis Jones, *Rickeston and Scotsborough – Pembrokeshire Historical Society 1966.*

RICKESTON. *Robeston West.*

Home of the Roch and Harries families. The Roch family provided two High Sheriffs for the county, Nicholas Roch in 1675 and a namesake in 1733. On 3 October 1611 a grant from Thomas Lloyd of Kilkethed Esq., to Robert Bowen of Llanchaelt, gent., and Thomas ap Owen James of Meline, gent., of the following properties – four tenements called Great and Little Richardston in Robeston Park in Rowse, in tenure of John Fortune, Nicholas Rotch and Patrick Sinett; and Richarston Myllne, on trust for said Thomas Lloyd for life with remainders. In 1683 Thomas Roch of Rickerston was murdered by Vaughan Phillips, gent., probably in a duel; in 1689 the owner was George Roch. In 1738 is recorded a prenuptial settlement between George Roch of Riccaston, gent, and Martha Allen daughter of William Allen of Gelliswick, and Rickeston was the home of the Allen family from the early 19th century. Charles Allen of Rickeston Hall is recorded on the 1904 Voters' List.

RIDGEWAY. *Llawhaden.*

Home of the Fawly or Foley family. On 30 August 1711, Richard Fawly the elder of Ridgeway, gent., Sir George Barlow of Slebech, Bt., and William Phillips of Haythog, Esq., and Richard Fawley the younger of Ridgeway, gent., agreed the release of lands in Pembrokeshire, including the capital messuage called Ridgeway alias Lletherston, to trustees to the use of Richard Fawley the younger to enable him to make 'a competent settlement on any woman he may happen to marry and may bring a Fortune into the family' (*ref. CRO Glasbrook DD. No. 9*).

The original house, for which Richard

Foley was assessed for three hearths in 1670, stood at some distance from the present mansion which was built in the 18th century by John Foley, and is a plain house on high ground (Burke's *Visitation of Seats*, iv, 1858, p. 40). The modern Ridgeway house was completed in 1741 – the ancient mansion having stood in the now stable yard. – (Nicholas, *County Families* ii, p. 950, 1875). Fenton in his *Tour Pembs.* 1811 describes it as '… the elegant residence of my estimable friend, J. H. Foley, esq., crowning it amidst groves chiefly of his own planting'. John Herbert Foley was High Sheriff in 1795. Ridgeway was advertised to let in 1809 with a full description of the accommodation including eight bedrooms, library, large drawing room, servants hall, coach house, stables, walled garden, pleasure grounds and plantations – in all about 350 acres.

In 1871 it was the seat of R. P. Davies, and a photograph appeared in *Photographs in South Wales 1871* by C. S. Allen of Tenby.

Major Jones visited the house in 1981 and wrote of it: 'The front of the house is surrounded by a ha-ha. In the rear is a dog graveyard, one of the stones bearing the date 1887. The west wing of the house seems much older than the rest, and has a large old chimney stock of stone which is clearly very old. There are some drip labels in the wall alongside the chimney. The mansion is empty but in excellent state, and divided into flats, and is internally much changed.

It is now a home for aged people'.

RINASTON. *Ambleston.*

Due west from Ambleston village, near the road to Little Newcastle. Called Tre Reina or Tre Rina in 1566, and called today by Welsh, Tre-einer. In 1230 there is mention of Capella de villa Reineri Chapel of the House (*A. Carm. Ser. II., iii, p. 261*), and the remains of the church can be seen in an enclosure 120' x 100' now within the yard of the farmhouse, and a burial took place within the church in 1789 a few years before it was abandoned. There is an old tombstone in the farmyard inscribed 'David Morse of Reneaston, died

30 July 1785, Martha his wife died 11 January 1789'. In 1308 the house was called Villa Reyneri, and in 1315 John Reyner was tenant.

In the 15th century this was the seat of the Cole family, and in 1503 Jane Cole of Rhinaston married Harry Howel of Llysyfran, and their daughter Jane married John Scourfield of Moat. In 1384, Henry son of John Cole of Reineriston was owner. By the 17th century Wogans and Powells were associated with the property, and after them the Morse family. Phoebe Morse, daughter of David and Martha Morse married John Evans of Trevayog, St. Nicholas, farmer (prenuptial settlement 21 December 1776), and they had three sons the youngest of whom, John Evans is described as 'of Rinaston'. By 1786 in the Land Tax lists, William Phillips Esq., is shown as owner, with John Evans as tenant. The house is now a farm.

RHOSMOELED. *St. Dogmaels.*

Lewis Griffiths (no dates given), died seized of Rosymoylad, (*sic*), and his three daughters and co-heiresses held the lands jointly in co-parcenary. Two of the daughters married: Elen to William Thomas Woodcock and then to William Powell. Thomas Powell, son of the second marriage, inherited his mother's moiety and sold it to William Thomas Griffith. Jane married Morris ap Howell Ddu whose son Thomas Morris sold *his* moiety to his cousin Jenkin William.

In 1786 LT., William Rowland, gent., was the owner-occupier and in 1894, Owen James.

ROBESTON HALL. *Robeston West.*

Fenton in his *Tour Pembs. 1811,* describes '... Robertson Hall is about five miles from Milford, in a pleasant English like looking country and we understood in a good neighbourhood. The garden is extensive, but this year except in the Peach and grape Houses, quite destitute of fruit. It seems well sheltered and has high Quick edges to break the force of the wind, but it seems the blights from the sea are so injurious to the trees, that a crop except under glass cannot be depended upon'.

In Carmarthen Museum is the frieze of a mantelpiece from Robeston Hall of late 18th century work. It bears the carved arms of Fowler: *quarterly azure and or, in the first quarter a hawk's lure and string or. Crest: an ostrich head or between two wings argent, the beak holding a horseshoe azure.* Hugh Fowler, who presented the parish church with bells in 1719, inherited the estate from his mother, Martha, née Cozens whose father, Thomas Cozens of Robeston Hall, was assessed for six hearths in 1670.

Hugh Fowler, of Grays Inn died without issue and the property went to his nephew Thomas Keymer (b. 16 July 1722) who sold Robeston to William Scourfield in c. 1783. The latter was High Sheriff in 1812, the year in which he sold Robeston. The particulars of sale give a fairly detailed description of the estate which comprised 338 acres including 12 acres of plantation, hothouses, peach houses and a conservatory. 'The mansion house is a substantial stone building containing spacious breakfast, dining and drawing rooms, servants' apartments, extensive offices, stabling, coach houses ...' and so on.

For four years the house was leased to Charles Fulke Greville, at £20 per annum, (perhaps the same Charles Fulke Greville who married Lady Charlotte Bentinck, daughter of the 3rd Duke of Portland – Ed).

The house was destroyed by fire on 24th August 1921 – a barn and an ice-house survive. *Vide* T. Lloyd's *Lost Houses of Wales,* 1986, p. 73 (illust.).

ROBESTON WATHAN HOUSE.
Robeston Wathan.

On an eminence close to the church and village. The mansion of Robeston Wathen was erected about 1815 – (Nicholas, *County Families* 1875 edn p. 897). In 1840 this was the seat of the Rev. J. W. James, and in 1867, the home of Ven. George Clark, Archdeacon and Prebendary of St. Davids. It had many owners including the families of Barlow, Rice, Colby, Phillips and Lord Kensington.

Sale particulars give details in 1866 and 1929. There were seven principal bedrooms on the first floor and some grand reception rooms and a conservatory. From 1977 it has been a country house hotel.

ROBLINSTON. *Camrose.*

The ruins stood about half a mile north-west of Camrose Church. Original home of the Roblin family. William Robelyn having held half a Knight's fee in 1251/2. In the reign of Henry IV, Jane Roblin, daughter and heiress of Alexander Roblin married John ap Owen whose son Morris Bowen was ancestor of the Bowens of Roblinston. Morgan Bowen murdered John ap Rice but was pardoned and died in 1609. Fenton in his *Tour Pembs* (1811), writes '... a large ruinous shell of a house called Roblinston of a plan and dimensions much exceeding what was generally the character and size of the mansions of this county at the time when we may venture to date its erection about two centuries ago, inducing us to form a very respectable opinion of the builders spirit and taste ...I have called it a shell, as it appears never to have been finished, or at least never inhabited as I could learn, no memorial of it in that state having been preserved anywhere.'.

In 1926 it was recorded that nothing remained of the house and that the site was occupied by a modern house. It seems that the Bowens never occupied their house and moved to Wolfsdale.

ROCH. *Roch.*

Former home of the Walter and Stokes families. This was probably the house near the castle now used as a farm house and formerly part of the castle demesne. The castle itself, a mere tower, was restored, and an extension added for domestic purposes by Lord St. Davids in the early 1900s, and Major Jones and his family leased the tower for a period after W.W.2.

In about 1601 William Walter bought from the de Longueville family the manor of Roch and the advowson of the church plus a quarter share in Dale Castle and the manor of Eweston and an eighth share in the manors of Hodgeston and Barton. The Walter family were shoemakers and tradesmen in Haverfordwest and the said William was, in 1611, described as 'yeoman'. William Walter, died 1650, married Elizabeth Protheroe niece of 1st Earl of Carbery, and his daughter, Lucy b. 1630, was the mistress of Charles II. On 6 September 1665, Richard Walter of Ravensdale, Carms, and Bridget his wife, mortgaged the capital messuage called the Demesne of Roch, and another messuage in Roch (containing three and a half ploughlands to Anthony Stokes of Roch, gent., for £433. 6s. 8d; and on 15th May 1725 Sir Richard Walter leased the capital messuage called 'the Demesne of Roch to Constant Stokes for 21 years at £52. p.a. In 1732 Joseph Walter is given as being 'of Rosemarket'.

In 1735 Joseph Walter of St. Thomas, Haverfordwest gave a lease of possession to William Owen of Landshipping and Lewis Barlow of Lawrenny, of the Manor of Roch, the capital messuage called Roch Castle and Trevrane, and other lands in Co. Pembroke. This Joseph's sister, Bridget Walter, married Anthony Stokes of Haverfordwest, and left (*inter alia*), a daughter Thomazina Stokes who married John Jones of Brawdy. The said Joseph's widow, Elizabeth (née Barlow), married secondly, Alexander Elliott of Earwere and Narberth. Alexander Elliott and Elizabeth his wife released to Benjamin Stokes of Haverfordwest the capital messuage and demesne of Roch with the castle or site called Roch castle for £1300 and one third of coal and culm during lives of said Alexander and Elizabeth in survivorship.

Major Jones left copious notes on this property and of the various owners and tenants. Mr. William Berry bought Roch in 1971 and part of the castle is now rented as holiday accommodation.

ROSEMARKET. *Rosemarket.*
Home of the Walter family, although they ceased living there before 1670. Sir Richard Walter was High Sheriff in 1727. On 12th August 1735 Joseph Walter gave a lease of possession to William Owen of Landshipping of (inter alia) the capital messuages called Walter's Hall and the Hall of Rosemarket. Fenton in his *Tour Pembs.* 1811, '... here Sir Richard Walter had a mansion whose remains speak it to have been highly respectable about a century ago, and possessing all the appendages of a great man's house in those days'. Again ' The ruins of this mansion are now the property of Mrs. Owen Barlow who is the principal proprietor of land in the parish.' – *Lewis TDW 1840.*

Francis Jones visited the ruins on 19th May 1976. He described them as extensive with a massive chimney stack. 'Mr. Sidney Pawlett of Cross Farm remembered it well and had played in the ruins when a child. About twenty years ago the ruins were swept away and the present farmhouse erected partly on the site of the old mansion. It stands on a rise at the edge of the village and in an adjoining field the old dovecote still stands'. He goes on to say: 'Cross Farm, adjoining the parish church, is an interesting survival. It has an undercroft (once used as a dairy) and above it was the main chamber, now the parlour. This is very ancient. The owner-occupier, (1976) is Sidney Pawlett, an agreeable person'.

ROSEMOOR. *Walwynscastle.*
This stands near the road about half-a-mile south of Walwynscastle church. In 1786 Thomas Bowlas was owner and later it was the home of James Bowlas Summers,

(d.1878), with 1540 acres worth £2355. (*Landowners Returns* 1873). He was the son of John Summers of Moor (qv). J. B. Summer's, daughter, Alice May Summers, was married in Cawnpore to Capt. R. W. H. Ronaldson, only son of J. T. Ronaldson of Hawick Grange, Northumberland.

ROSEPOOL. *Walwynscastle.*
This originally belonged to a family called Row, but later became the home of the Bateman and Barlow families. In 1541 William Bateman (of the Honeyborough family) is described in the Picton Castle archives as of 'Rowispole'.

In the 17th century this was the seat of a younger branch of the Barlows of Slebech. The last of the male line there was William Barlow who married Lettice Jones of Brawdy parish in 1723. He died without issue and his will proved 8th October 1744. His widow enjoyed the property until her death in 1769 when it reverted to the Barlows of Lawrenny. The house had a fine walled garden. In Colby's map 1831 a colliery is marked just east of Rosepool house and demesne.

RUDBAXTON, GREAT. *Rudbaxton.*
Close to the parish church, just east of the house is a 'motte'; c.1150-1200 Rudbaxton was the fee of Alexander Rudebac. The Welsh called (and still do) the place, Rydbac.

It was probably Great Rudbaxton which the Haywards acquired by marriage with the Goddard heiress, and later went to Fletherhill. Fenton (*Tour Pembs.* 1811), describes Great Rudbaxton as 'one of the largest tenements in the county and in the best condition'.

Sir William Lewis was the owner of Rudbaxton in 1786 Land Tax lists, with Mr. Charles Gibbon, tenant, as was James Llewellin in 1834 at a rent of £50 p.a. James Williams occupied Rudbaxton farm in 1904 (Voters' List).

RUSHACRE. *Narberth.*

The local Welsh folk call this 'Rhydsiacer'. Griffiths Howells, gent., owned extensive lands here (no date given). His mother had been born there and was probably the daughter of William Jones of Cartellgarw, Llanglydwen Park.

Philipps, Viscount St. Davids

ST. BOTOLPHS. *Steynton.*

The earliest reference to this residence is in the will of William Howell of Huberston Park 'to be buried in the Park chapel, ... my sons William and David Howell, my daughters Rebecca and Jennet (to be kept at school till she can read the bible). ... To my son William Howell all my lands at Booth-ockes in the parish of Hubberton, and to be executor', will proved 14 November 1656. (*ref. PCC Berkeley 385*). Home of the Elliot, le Hunte and Stokes families. '... a newly erected mansion built on the site of the old chapel of St. Budock by Mr. le Hunte, a gentleman of Ireland who, since the troubles in that country, has resided in Pembrokeshire where he possesses a valuable property inherited from an ancestor in the time of Charles I, who married an heiress in this county though none of it lies in the neighbourhood of his residence'. Fenton's *Tour* 1811. General le Hunte acquired the mansion through the marriage of a forefather to a co-heiress of Lloyd of Kilkiffeth.

The Elliots, in the person of the Revd. Philip Elliot, obtained St. Botolphs through his marriage to a cousin, Mary, daughter of John Howell, of St. Botolphs. Philip's son, Dr. George Elliot, M.D., left two sons who each married a daughter of John Letsom, a fashionable 18th century doctor (*vide: English Speaking Students of Medicine at the University of Leyden* by R. W. Innes Smith).

Lewis (TDW) says that ' In the western part of Steynton parish is St. Botolph's the seat of A. L. Stokes, Esq., by one of whose relatives it was purchased in 1826 from the representatives of General le Hunte. The present mansion was built in 1800, about a hundred yards to the west of the ancient edifice, and partly on the site of a monastery ... and part of the walls of the ancient monastery, which are still remaining, have been incorporated with the out-buildings of the modern mansion'.

Anthony Innys Stokes, was High Sheriff in 1827, and Major A. V. W. Stokes (d.1947) was a distinguished sportsman of the old school and once rode in the Grand National. He was born at St. Botolphs and lived there all his life. After his death the property was bought in the following year by his cousin, Mrs. Lee Roberts. The house was, in 1976 a hotel. See *Burke's L. G.* 1937 Stokes of St. Botolphs.

A word must be said about the name St. Botolphs. There was, on the property, an old chapel dedicated to St. Budoc, rendered in the vernacular as 'St. Buttock'. When the private house was built this name did not seem appropriate so it was re-named St. Botolphs!

ST. BRIDES. *St. Brides.*

Called le Hill in 1298, and home of the St. Brides, then by marriage to Russell, then by marriage to Laugharne, the name is often rendered as 'Lacharn', being the Welsh form of Laugharne in Carmarthenshire, whence doubtless the family came. Fenton in his *Tour Pembs.* p. 96-7 wrote '... rode to visit the old mansion of St. Bride's formerly the residence of John de St. Bride's ... whose daughter and sole heiress enriched the family of the Laugh-arnes who came into Pembrokeshire from Cornwall. There is a tradition that he was shipwrecked on the coast and that the lady who afterwards honoured him with her hand, discovered him almost lifeless on the shore, and had him removed to her father's mansion not far off, where he experienced the most hospitable treatment and being a handsome man soon captivated the lady ...'

The habitable house, exclusive of offices, seemed at one time to have formed the sides of a quadrangle enclosed by a high embattled wall, with a walk all round at top, having an arched gateway in front, and another leading to a walled garden of considerable extent. In front of the house was a paddock, including a bowling green and fish-ponds, and bearing marks of having been laid out in walks between venerable oak trees of large girth, though of stunted growth in point of height, and bending under the pressure of age and the western almost irresistible breeze, for it faces that aspect of the ocean that here almost washes the walls of this enclosure'.

The pedigree given in *Dwnn*, i,73, and signed by John Laugharne in 1597, begins with the 14th century Thomas Lacharn who married Siwain, daughter and co-heir of Krabol. The Laugharnes were for several centuries burgesses and merchants in Haverfordwest. Francis Laugharne was High Sheriff in 1568 and 1578; Rowland in 1586, and John in 1631. Branches of the family settled at Fenton, Llanreithan, Llanunwas, Walwynscastle and Pontfaen. Rowland Laugharne of St. Brides was assessed at eleven hearths in 1670 suggesting that St. Brides was, even then, a very large house. The last of the family, John died without issue, and the estate passed to his sisters and co-heiresses. Albania inherited the mansion as part of her share, and married William Philipps of Sandyhaven and Haythog (High Sheriff in 1736), and he became owner in right of his wife. Finding the situation of the mansion too low, he built a completely new one on high ground to the west to which the name of St. Brides Hill (q.v.) or just Hill was given. He died in 1739. William's son, Charles Philipps died in 1750 leaving three sons and two daughters. All but Anne died without issue. She became the heiress and married Joseph Allen who assumed the name of Allen-Philipps and was High Sheriff in 1809. His son William was also High Sheriff in 1844 and, having no issue devised St. Brides Hill to his nephew, the Revd. Gilbert Harries, a member of the Harries family of Llanunwas, near Solva.

The 4th Baron Kensington purchased the castle in 1880, and the 6th Baron Kensington sold the estate in 1920. It then consisted of a baronial residence, Skomer Island, Midland and Grassholm and Gateholm Islands, twelve farms, 22 small holdings, 40 cottages, manorial and foreshore rights, in all 3,662 acres; the rents were recorded at £2,901. 15s. 7d. It was for a while known as Kensington Hospital. It is now holiday apartments.

R. M. Lockley, *Pembrokeshire* (1977 reprint), p. 21, says that: 'St. Brides was formerly the site of a local herring fishery'. A chapel stood on its shore but 'When St. Bride's chapel a salt house was made/St. Bride's lost the herring trade. More than that, the sea swept in and devoured the chapel and much of its graveyard, so that even today the odd gravestone is seen peering out of the eroded shore, near the ancient lime kiln'.

ST. DOGMAELS. *St. Dogmaels.*

In the 16th century this was the property of the Bradshaws, a Lancashire family who settled first at Presteigne, Radnorshire. In 1536/7 John Bradshaw described as 'of Ludlow' was granted a Crown lease of St. Dogmaels Abbey and Caldey. On 10th November 1543 he received a grant in fee of both properties for the sum of £512. 2. 10d. His son John sold Caldey to Walter Philips of Tenby. John's two sons, Edward and John, were both captains in the army and were captured at Pill in 1643. Their sisters married into the families of Owen ap Henllys, Gwynne of Taliasio and Lloyd of Llanstephan. The arms of Bradshaw are: *argent two bendlets sable, a martlet in chief.* However, the seal to a bond from William Bradshaw to Thomas Canon of Haverfordwest in 1607 shows a shield charged between what seem to be three martlets (*Picton Castle archives*).

By 1670 St. Dogmaels Abbey had become the property of Thomas Parry who was assessed at six hearths in that year. The actual monastery was suppressed in 1535 and the church adapted for parochial use. Most of the Abbey buildings fell into ruins and the secular mansion house was probably where the vicarage now stands.

ST. ELVIS. *St. Elvis.*

For several generations this was the home of the Voel family, descended from Dafydd Voel ('The Bald') of Trewern, Nevern. In 1670 Margaret Voyle, a widow, was assessed for three hearths. St. Elvis became the property of the Williams family of Trelethyn. In 1788 Thomas Williams leased to David Morris of St. Elvis, yeoman, the farm of St. Elvis (except the store house near Quadan), with power to build a 'wear' in some part of St. Elvis river, to be reserved for lessor, and lessor also to have engress and egress, and to cut down and 'stoak furze' if necessary for life of lessee, Jane his wife, and Ann their daughter at the rent of £70 p.a. and six fat hens at Christmas.

Ref: *W&W Cttw No. 23318.*

ST. KENNOX. *Llawhaden.*

'A farmhouse set amidst ancient trees on the west bank of the Eastern Cleddau'. (*Avc. Mon. Pem.*, p. 143).

Former home of the Hawkwells and the Owens, cadets of Henllys. It is now a farmhouse standing on the site of what was once known as The Chancellor's House where once lived the Revd. Rhys Pritchard when Chancellor of St. David's (1620). The house had been annexed to that dignity. According to *Eminent Welshmen* (p. 425) the Vicar used to preach from 'the rocky eminence near the house to an audience which no church could contain'. In 1551 William Hawkwell, yeoman, was summoned to answer for a debt of £34. The Hawkwells were still in possession in 1702. In 1786 Sir William Hamilton was owner. Lord Nelson took the opportunity to visit the Royal Dockyards at Milford Haven whilst being entertained here by Lady Hamilton. Sir William Hamilton was a true patriot, even being prepared to lay down his wife for England. In 1843 the Revd. William Houghston was owner. The property was sometimes called 'St. Enochs'.

SANDYHAVEN. *St. Ishmaels.*

Home of the Rhys, Button and Philipps families. William Rhys was High Sheriff in 1557. On October 28th 1641 Miles Button, of Cotterell, Glamorgan was owner in fee and granted a lease to Thomas Stepney (brother of Sir John Stepney, 2nd Baronet) for life at £30 p.a. The arms of Button are: *argent a chevron between three tuns gules.* Thomas Stepney was still living at Sandyhaven in 1649 and his will was proved on July 5th 1669. His son, John, eventually succeeded to his uncle's baronetcy, now long extinct. Sir John Stepney married a daughter of Sir Anthony Van Dyke, the portrait painter. In 1786 John Campbell, afterwards lst Lord Cawdor, was owner with William Cozens as tenant. In 1802 Lord Cawdor sold the property, then a substantial farmhouse, with the Cozens family still as tenants at a yearly rent of £130 for the sum of £4556. In the sale catalogue it was described as 'Sandy Haven Farm ... with a roomy farm house and offices, garden, large farm yard and convenient buildings for the Husbandry Business.' They were still tenants in 1839 when Thomas Lloyd owned the estate, then 348 acres. From the 1850s to the 1870s the Philipps family (a cadet of Picton Castle) were owners. Major Jones visited Sandyhaven in 1974 and again in 1976. He was disappointed to see that the outer walls had been cemented. A Mr. Beer, a farmer, was in residence at that time.

SCLEDDY. *Manorowen.*

Home of the Owen family, a cadet of Trewern, probably the farmhouse near the crossroads of the smithy. Colby's map of 1831 shows Scleddy Ucha and Issa. Very little information in Major Jones's notes. In 1731 George Owen Esq., was in possession of Scleddy Ucha, but the property was let to a number of tenants. In the Land Tax lists of 1786 Dr. Edwards is shown as owner, Thomas B. Parry, Esq., as tenant. The Voters' Lists of 1834 shows Timothy David of Sklethy, lease of lives of part of Sklethy Issa; Daniel Francis of Sklethy Ganol, lease of lives of house and lands of Sklethy Ganol; David Griffith of Sklethy, lease for lives of Sklethy Ucha Farm.

SCOLLOCK. *Ambleston.*
This could not have been a large house as in 1670 the highest number of hearths in the parish was only two. The Joyces were in possession during the Middle Ages followed by the Gwylims – Richard Gwylim being an 'Alderman of Pembroke'. In 1786 Thomas Picton is listed as owner. In 1834 Thomas Llewellyn had a lease of Scollock farm. On Colby's Map of 1831 New Scollock, Old Scollock, Scollock Cross and Scollock Bill are all shown.

SCOLTON MANOR. *Spittal.*
Now well known as the Scolton Manor Museum and Country Park. The museum is devoted to Pembrokeshire and serves as a local history research centre.

The Higgon family have lived hereabouts since at least the 16th century. On February 6th 1609/10 William Higgon of Scolton gave evidence in a case against one George Wadin. Higgon and his neighbours said that they had long suspected Wadin was 'a sheepe stealer and did lead a lewde life'. The case showed him to be, indeed, a very bad lot! Thomas Higgon was assessed for four hearths in 1670 but it is not certain whether he lived at Scol-

ton. The first recorded member of that family to live there was James Higgon (d.1732). The old house was destroyed by fire in the mid-18th century and the Higgons went to live in Haverfordwest. They did not rebuild the house until 1840 at a cost of £3,000. John Higgon was High Sheriff in 1793; John Donald George Higgon in 1889 and Lt.-Col. J. H. V. Higgon in 1951. The Colonel sold the estate in 1972 to Pembrokeshire County Council who converted it to a museum. The pedigree is outlined in Burke's L.G. 1972 and the Scolton portraits are listed in Steegman II South Wales (1962).

SCOTCHWELL. *Prendergast.*
Originally a farm, marked on Colby's Map 1831.

Home of the Surman and Stokes families. Thomas Surman of Scotchwell is described as 'gentleman' in 1754 and Simon Surman served as a Grand Juror in 1783 (in 1788 he was Surveyor of Highways in Prendergast Parish). In 1786 he was assessed for Land Tax at 4s. On January 15th 1794 Paul Surman conveyed Scotchwell to Thomas Stokes. Henry Stokes of Scotchwell, who married Anne, daughter of Dr. George Phillips, M.D., died in 1823. His second son, John Lort Stokes, born 1812, achieved fame as an Admiral who served on *H.M.S. Beagle* with Charles Darwin and was badly injured by an aboriginal who speared him. Admiral Stokes not only helped Darwin chart various areas of Australia but was later to command his own ship and sailed to New Zealand. The name 'Cptn Stokes' is carved on the trunk of an old tree in the grounds. It is ironic that Simon Surman was Surveyor of Highways in 1788. Exactly two centuries later there was a battle against building an eastern by-pass for Haverfordwest. The then owner, Mr. Steven Llewellyn, who inherited Scotchwell from his father, tried to stop the by-pass which would have cut through the property and be about 25 yards from the house. Having, in the 1970s, been an hotel and caravan park, it was destined to become an old people's home.

SCOTSBOROUGH. *Tenby.*

Stood on the eastern shore of the eastern branch of an inlet called Ritec (also Hoyleswater).

Once the home of the Perrot and ap Rhys families. John Perrot was High Sheriff in 1551; Thomas ap Rhys in 1610; James ap Rhys in 1655 and another James ap Rhys in 1688. This house has long been a ruin. In *Archaeologia Cambrensis* (6th Series, Vol. VI, part II, April 1906) a full and graphic description of the building as it then was is given: 'During the first quarter of the nineteenth century this old mansion was in a ruinous condition, but the west front had been patched up and converted into cottages. A terrible epidemic of confluent smallpox broke out in these tenements in or about the year 1824 and such of the occupants who did not die fled in panic … Since that time Scotsborough has not been inhabited and for many years after the smallpox outbreak was looked on as an accursed place.'

It was described in *The Book of South Wales*, London, 1861, pp. 441-2, as 'Scotsborough – whence its imported name we cannot say – is merely the picturesque ruin of an ancient house, which belonged to the honourable and far-descended family of Ap Rhys whose monuments are in Tenby church. The ruin consists of crumbling walls, many of them held together by twisting fronds of ivy – the ivy being remarkably fine. As an example of the strong dwelling of a period when, although defences of domestic buildings had become less a necessity than they had been, it was still a policy and a duty to be always prepared for attacks; the old house of Scotsborough will be examined with interest.'

In 1906 the huge growth of ivy was removed to reveal the original building and there are illustrations in this monograph of what the ruins looked like at that time. Between 1930 and 1934 when Major Jones lived in Tenby he visited the ruins many times and they were then much as they were in the 1906 illustrations. Further information can be gleaned from Francis Jones's '*Rickeston and Scotsborough*' in *The Pembrokeshire Historian* for 1966.

SCOVASTON. *Steynton.*

Marked with three dwellings on Colby's map 1831; Upper, Middle and Lower Scovaston.

Home of several families including the Butlers and Mordaunts. Thomas Butler was High Sheriff in 1644. In 1670 William Mordaunt was assessed at seven hearths. Scovaston was formerly a considerable mansion. '… the venerable buildings, that, in the remembrance of many living, occupied the site, having been transmuted into a farmhouse' *Fenton's Tour*. The last Mordaunt to own Scovaston is said to have had 21 children! This family was probably a branch of the Mordaunts who were formerly Earls of Peterborough. In 1685 William Mordaunt brought an action against Rice Gibbon for saying to Mordaunt's servant 'Your master is but a poor pitiful knave and has nothing but what he picks out of other men's pockets'. By 1863 the house had been rebuilt and was occupied by William Rees who was High Sheriff in that year. Just before Christmas in 1985 tragedy struck Scovaston. The then owners, Richard Thomas and his sister Miss Helen Thomas were brutally murdered and the house set alight. It was completely gutted. These gruesome events were covered in illustrated articles in the *Western Telegraph* (1 Jan. 1986) and the *Western Mail* (28th Dec. 1985). The estate and ruins were put up for sale in May 1986.

SEALYHAM. *St. Dogwells.*

Situated in woodland in a small valley through which runs the Afon Anghof which fills a small lake.

Home of the Tucker family and world famous as the place where Sealyham terriers were first bred. The first of the family to be associated with Sealyham was John Tocker, otherwise Tucker, described as 'gentleman' in 1560. An eighteenth century Tucker – Admiral Thomas Tucker, R.N. achieved renown by killing the notorious pirate 'Blackbeard' in the West Indies. He went on to capture Spanish ships with rich cargoes and died in 1766. An heiress married an Edwardes, descendant of Owen Edwardes, grandfather of the lst Lord Kensington, and they took the name of Tucker-Edwardes (*Vide Burke's Peerage*). In 1840 the house was described as 'an elegant modernised mansion'. The ghost of a woman in white used to haunt the drive, the tradition being that a daughter of the house, Grace Tucker, had fallen in love with the coachman. Her angry father is said to have built a small cottage off the drive with barred windows in which he consigned his daughter 'to cool her off'. This little building, Major Jones reports, became a ruin but had for a time been used by Captain John Owen Tucker-Edwardes as kennels for his hounds. He was the first man to breed Sealyham terriers. Mrs. C. O. Higgon once told Major Jones that she and a friend had actually seen the ghost gliding across the drive on a winter's evening in 1987.

The Tucker-Edwardes family sold Sealyham in 1920 and it was transformed into a tuberculosis hospital. It eventually ceased to be a hospital and changed hands again in 1970 and again in 1988 when New Zealanders Sam and Valerie Richards bought it and now run it as a sports centre for children.

SIMPSTON. *Roch.*

In the Autumn of 1604, Morgan Bowen, described as 'of Symston, gent.' was granted a pardon for killing John Rees of Roblinston, yeoman, in a duel at Haverfordwest. In 1724 Thomas Jones of Cremina, Llanddewi Felfrey purchased absolutely the Simpston estate in Roch parish for a large sum from Ralph Price and others. The Land Tax returns for 1786 give Francis Meyrick Esq., as owner. Very little other information is available about this property.

SION HOUSE. *St. Mary's, Tenby.*

Here we have a lost Nash house. The architect designed it for William Routh in about the year 1792. In 1810 it was the home of Mrs. C. Routh who put the property up for sale '... built within the last 18 years under the direction of a very eminent architect and no expense spared ...' Originally a high, three-storeyed classical house it was enlarged and its symmetry spoiled later in the 19th century. It even had a change of name as Wooferton Grange and was for a time a girls' school. On March 24th 1938 the house was totally gutted by fire. The site is now a block of flats. A photograph of the ruin can be seen in Thomas Lloyd's *Lost Houses of Wales*.

SLEBECH. *Slebech.*

Home of the families of Barlow, Symmons, Knox, Phillips and de Rutzen. Mrs. Morgan writes in her *Tour of Milford Haven*, 1791 (pp. 296-7): 'It is an exceedingly handsome house and has accommodations for a vast many people (*sic*). I think they told us there were 25 bedrooms with each a dressing-room adjoining; and likewise two parlours, a study, a drawing room, a dining room and a billiard room, besides offices and accommodations of every other kind'. A more precise description appears in May 1792 when the estate, of over 7,000 acres, was put up for sale by public auction by 'Mr. Christie at his Great Room, Pall Mall'. The sale particulars are very detailed both of the house, its interiors and the curtilage. The mansion had three regular fronts with flights of stone steps to the principal floor. The north and south fronts each extending to 88 feet with uniform semi-circular bows. Roger Barlow and his brother Thomas bought the Commandery of Slebech from the Crown. John Barlow of Slebech was High Sheriff in 1562 and 1575; George Barlow in 1618; Sir John Barlow in 1681; George Barlow in 1752. Several later owners also held this post including Baron de Rutzen. In 1773 Anne, daughter and heiress of George Barlow married John Symmons of Llanstinan but had no issue. Symmons sold the estate to William Knox of Soho Square, W.1. for £70,000. In 1792 Knox sold the mansion to Nathaniel Phillips of Gloucester Place.

Mary Dorothea Phillips, the eventual co-heiress of the estate, married in 1822 Baron de Rutzen and it stayed with that family until

John, Baron de Rutzen fell in action in 1944. His widow later married the 19th Lord Dunsany and his daughter married Sir Francis Dashwood, Bt., of West Wycombe. Lady Dunsany inherited Slebech and eventually sold it to the Hon. William Philipps, C.B.E., who made some interior alterations. Mr. Philipps, who died in 1974, was the fourth son of the lst Lord Milford. He was High Sheriff in 1968. Major Jones left copious notes on this house.

SODSTON HOUSE. *Narberth.*
Called Sottisdoune in 1282. Marked on Colby's map 1831 and Mudge's Map 1819. Sodston House enjoys a quiet rural setting a few miles north of Narberth. In 1702 the messuage and land called Sottston was part of the Barlow of Slebech estate. On 7th November 1768 Ann Trevanion of Slebech, widow, mortgaged Sodson and other messuages to Bridget Foley of Ridgeway, widow. (*Slebech Deeds,* No. 727).

Home of the James family. In 1786 William James, gent. is described as owner-occupier. This is a T-shaped house. A sale notice in *Cambrian* 9 June 1808 describes the house as a substantial modern mansion house with three spacious parlours, eight bedchambers, garrets and closets. There were, of course, the usual outhouses and gardens and about 100 acres in all. Major Jones lists many transactions connected with the estate. In 1905 Webb Bowen conveyed Sodston to Colonel Bernard Robert Ward, R.E. Latterly it was owned by W. Benyon Evans of Narberth who sold it to David Davis who conveyed it to Anthony Ward of Lower Broadmoor. Mr. Ward lent the deeds to Major Jones in 1976. In 1985 the estate was up for sale again as a whole or in lots.

SOUTHFIELD. *Llysyfran.*
One Henry Jones bought Southfield in 1562. His grandson, Thomas Jones, died in about 1633 leaving two daughters and co-heiresses Anne and Elizabeth. The former married Thomas Philipps, of Felindre and their son,

James Philipps is described as 'of Southfield'. His descendant, John Philipps of Southfield, was a prominent Methodist and died in 1894 and is buried at Llysyfran. Although married thrice he left no issue and Southfield went to a Miss Melchior, daughter of his sister Letitia who had married William Melchior of Llanseilo. Miss Melchior married David James (d.1919) and their son, William Melchior James (1868-1963) inherited Southfield. His elder son David Melchior James (1898-1978) inherited but died childless. The notes describe him as 'an odd fish with delusions of grandeur'. Major Jones visited Southfield in 1974 and described it as being now two farmhouses one the older house containing the kitchen and servants' staircase and the other, at right-angles to it, a newer building with a fireplace bearing the date 1842.

STACKPOLE COURT. *St. Petrox.*
This, without doubt, was one of the grandest houses in Pembrokeshire, if not all Wales. The earliest known owner was a Crusader, Sir Leonard de Stackpole (his effigy is in the local church). His family did not remain long at Stackpole and the estate passed through an heiress to the Vernon family, of Haddon Hall in Derbyshire. The Vernons preferred the comforts of Haddon to the then fortified house which was built by the Normans to keep out the Welsh. The family's steward, George Lort, was left in charge. Lort in the mid-16th century bought Stackpole from his employers and took up residence. His descendants became baronets and were Royalists in the Civil War and garrisoned Stackpole for the King but they were forced to surrender. The Lorts regained their influence at the Restoration but on the death of Sir Gilbert Lort, Bt., in 1698 Stackpole passed to his sister and heiress, Elizabeth who was married to a Scot – Sir Alexander Campbell, yr. of Cawdor. Her husband was descended from the 3rd son of the 2nd Earl of Argyll who had married the heiress of the old Thanes of Cawdor in Scotland. Through her marriage the Campbells thus attained substantial estates in Wales which remained

with their descendants until recent times. She died in 1714 and her great-grandson, John Campbell, was created Baron Cawdor of Castlemartin, Co. Pembroke, he having represented Cardigan in Parliament. His son was elevated to an earldom in 1827 as Earl Cawdor, of Castlemartin. The Campbells rebuilt Stackpole and further enlargements were made in 1821 by George IV's architect Sir John Wyattville and his assistant Henry Ashton. The 5th Earl Cawdor spent most of his time on his Scottish estates and after the War his son decided that the 150-roomed house would have to go, largely because of the confiscatory Socialist taxation in force at the time. The sale of contents in 1962 was one of the most important ever to be held in South Wales. The great house itself was demolished in the same year – a needless and wanton act. The National Trust now owns the park and the Cawdors have divested themselves of all their Welsh property.

STONE HALL. *St. Lawrence.*

Set in ten acres of gardens and woodland near the village of Welsh Hook.

The first known family seated here was descended from Gwynfardd Dyfed of Cemaes in the person of Evan ap Philip ap Gwilym who was in possession in 1465. Gwilym ap Philip inherited from his father in 1487. By his wife Margery Tancred he had an only daughter and heiress Anne. Anne Tancred married Sir John Wogan of Wyston who was a Gentleman Usher of the King's Chamber also Bailey Itinerant of the Lordship of Haverfordwest and in 1525 was appointed Bailiff of the Manor of Roose in consideration of his services in England and abroad. He was High Sheriff of the county in 1543, 1550 and 1554, and of Cardiganshire in 1541 and 1555. He died in 1557 and was succeeded by his second son Morris Wogan. The Wogans remained at Stone Hall for a further four generations, the last to live there being William Wogan whose only son died young and his two daughters Dorothy and Mary became co-heiresses. Dorothy married William Ford, of Crewkerne, Somerset without

consent of her mother who regarded Ford as unsuitable as a consort for a Pembrokeshire heiress of high degree. Mary, however, approved of her sister's choice, and to emphasis this married his brother Richard Ford. The estate was partitioned and the Hall formed part of Dorothy's portion. The Fords remained at Stone until the last of the male line, William, died in 1793 aged 76 leaving the estate to a relation by marriage, one of the Protheroes of Dolwelyn. The Revd. William Ford Protheroe died heavily in debt in 1823, his only daughter having married George Roch of Butter Hill.

Stone Hall eventually became the home of Thomas Bowen who, in 1824, had a lease from Sir John Pakington (*Vide Burke's Peerage – Hampton B.*) of coal pits and storehouses at Little Milford Quay. Later it belonged to John Entwistle Peel but in 1873 he sold it to the Revd. Edward Peacock, son of the Revd. Edward Peacock by his wife Anne, daughter of William Lort Mansel, Bishop of Bristol. There have been several owners since then, among them the Revd. Murray Mather, author of *The Birds of Pembrokeshire and its Islands* (1904), and the Seton family who sold out to Dr. McGeoch in about 1951. Dr. McGeoch sold what remained of the estate to Richard Lloyd, an antiques dealer who was living there in 1981. He eventually sold it to Dr. and Mrs. Alan Watson who converted the house into an hotel and restaurant in 1985.

SUMMER HILL. *Roch.*

Nearly one mile south of Cuffern – Colby's Map 1831.

'... pass by Summerhill once the residence of a respectable branch of the family of Edwards, descended from Tudor Trevor' (Fenton's Tour). 'There are some walls of this old house incorporated in the comparatively modern farm.' (*Pemb. Arch. Survey*). In the 14th century 'Somerhill' was owned by the Knights Hospitallers. In the latter half of the 16th century this was the property of a family called Hurd(e). By 1613 John Barlow of Slebech owned the Manor of Summerhill and the services of two carucates there. By 1642 we find Thomas Edwards, gent., described as 'of Somerhill'. He died intestate. At the end of the 18th century the Revd. Owen Edwards was owner but by the beginning of the next century the seat had become a farmhouse. In 1838 the tenant was Thomas Owen. It was occupied by the Owen family, throughout the 1800s and in the 1894 and 1904 Voters' Lists. the tenant was William J. Owen who held a lease for lives, he died in April 1957, his wife was Annie Owen, née Rees.

SUMMERTON. *Little Newcastle.*

On the 6" O.S. map, Summerton House otherwise known as East Summerton is marked, and close on the West side is Summerton Farm, about a mile north-east of the village of Little Newcastle.

There is an early earth castle on the land of this farm. James ap Rees of Sommerton was sued for 10/- in 1594/5. The property is mentioned in the will of Laurence Hyer, farmer, of Sommerton in 1606. In 1786 Sparks Martin is listed as owner with Martha Mathias as his tenant. In 1894, one Daniel Luke was owner. At that time the house was described as '... originally a mansion and is still very commodious and with little expense could be renovated'.

SUTTON LODGE. *Portfield Gate, Haverfordwest.*

William Summers, of Sutton, gent., was assessed at £1. 6. 3d. in Land Tax in 1786. John Arthur Allen (b.1802), son of John Allen of Gelliswick, settled at Sutton Lodge and married Mary, daughter of Stephen Thomas of Lower Haythog. In the mid-19th century it was the residence of John Perry Jones, J.P., D.L. (d.1872) descended from the Penrys family of Llanedy, Carmarthenshire (*Vide Burke's L.G. 1898*). In the 1980s it had become a country house hotel.

TALYBONT. *Llawhaden.*

Home of the Hawkwell family, the first of whom came to Pembrokeshire as an official of Bishop Barlow who first settled him at St. Kennox. From there they moved across the Cleddau to Talybont. In 1551 William Hawkwell of Llawhaden, yeoman was summoned by John Snyy of Bristol, gent., administrator of Martin Pollard, gent., for £34. John and Katherine Hawkwell were assessed at two and three hearths respectively in 1670. Griffith Hawkwell was High Sheriff in 1663 and 1690. Fenton wrote: 'The mansion of Talybont, almost facing the church on the oppoite bank of the river, and now belonging to John Meares Esq., was first built and inhabited by a family of Hawkwell ... None of that respectable family to whom it now belongs (Meares) have resided there for these forty or fifty years; and like many of the deserted houses in this county too good to be pulled down, it has experienced in that time a fluctuating succession of occasional tenants'. The Meares family, of Eastington, acquired Talybont by marriage and but preferred living at Eastington and the deserted house deteriorated accordingly.

In 1770 William Hawkwell Meares carried out considerable repair work to the building. This was because a Dr. Berkenhout from London had, the year before, approached the family with a view to renting the place. The rent was to be £10 p.a. and the lease to run for six years but the Doctor stipulated that the considerable repair work required was to be carried out by the owners. The ground floor rooms had suffered badly as a result of flooding when the river burst its banks. Fifteen loads of slate were delivered for rerofing, at a cost of £2.7s. 0d., and 20 deal boards costing £2. 10. 0d. The following were tiled – outer kitchen and malthouses, kilnhouse (one side new), one side of the parlour new, pigs cott all new, part of the mansion on the leads and part of the half roof, the south side of the mansion on the leads and part of the half roof, the south side of the mansion and the half roof: the following were painted – outside of the parlour, staircase, front of the mansion, stable, dairy, coach house, and one side of the kiln house; and 17 feet of glass costing 17 shillings was used.

In the Land Tax List of 1786, Upper and Lower Talybont both owned by John Meares Esq., and both tenanted by Issac Ormond, assessed at £1.4s.7d. and 17s 4½d respectively. In the Voters' List of 1894 Daniel Davies of Talybont, dwelling house, and Henry Thomas James of Talybont, dwelling house are recorded.

Campbell, Earl Cawdor

TALBENNY HALL. *Talbenny.*
South of Talbenny village. The Howell family lived here in the 14th century and were still there in the early 16th century. According to the Land Tax records of 1786 Hugh Owen Barlow Esq., was owner but in 1797 one Adam Wathen described as 'gent.' was owner occupier. In 1805 James Wathen was of Middle Hasguard and Adam Wathen was of Talbenny Hall but by 1834 William Cole, of Philbeach was owner of the freehold.

TANCREDSTON. *Brawdy.*
About a quarter of a mile east of Tancredston. For an account of the lay manor of Tancredston, Major Jones refers us to his essay in the *Journal of the Historical Society of the Church in Wales. 1970.* This covers the years 1326 to 1860. In the *Black Book of St. David's*, William Martyn in 1326 '... holds at Tankardiston a fee from the Lord in Chief and services. Mistress Wenthliana Martyn holds one fee at Tankardyston'. The name has been spelt in

several different ways. In 1550 John Griffith senior of Tankerdston, husbandman, was accused of an assault. In 1683 Owen David, yeoman, and his wife Katherine, of Tankerston were both sued for stealing 10 ash trees worth £20. In 1699, in his will of that date Griffith Hawkwell (*Vide* TALYBONT) left Tancredston to his wife. In the Land Tax records of 1786 Henry Scourfield is listed as owner, with Thomas Hicks and George Evan as tenants. The Scourfields owned The Moat which had been their principal residence since the reign of Edward I. Sir Fulke Scourfield married Jane de Vere, daughter of an Earl of Oxford. Their eventual heiress married Owen Philipps of Williamston and their son John assumed the name and arms of Scourfield and was created a baronet in 1876. This became extinct on the death of his son the 2nd baronet. The Scourfields were still in possession of Tancredston in 1842.

TARR. *Penally.*
A substantial house, standing in a prominent south facing position overlooking the castle, beach and headland, just south-east of the hamlet of St. Florence. Home of the Dunn family (branch of Dunn of Crickwarren). John Dunn of Tarr (1810-1889) owned Crickwarren, Maidenwells, and lands in St. Mary and St. Michaels, Pembroke, in Llanddewi Felfrey, Narberth, St. Florence and Penally; he was succeeded by children of his next brother Thomas Dunn. In 1786 Tarr and West Tarr were owned by Lord Milford with John Dunn occupier, and West Tarr with Henry Evans as occupier.

In the Voters' List of 1834, John Gwyther is of Tarr, with lease of lives of Tarr and West Tarr farm, an old tower-house. In 1894, Thomas David Bowen is of Tarr Farm tenant; and by 1986 Tarr Farm is offered for sale as a substantial 19th country house, with three reception rooms and six bedrooms and two bathrooms, also offered were two cottages and six acres of land then being used as holiday accommodation.

TEMPLE DRUID/ BWLCH Y CLAWDD. *Maenclochog.*

This was one of several houses in South Wales designed by John Nash (1752-1835), one of George IV's architects. It was built in the 1790s for Henry Bulkeley (1760-1821). The original name was Bwlch y Clawdd. When Bulkeley died the property was put up for sale. It had eight principal bedrooms and some fine reception rooms 'fitted up with

statuary, marble chimneypieces and correspondingly finished' as the sales particulars described it. The house was drastically altered so that little of Nash's work remains and it became a hunting lodge early in 19th century and its name was changed to Temple Druid. Nearby was a prehistoric cromlech said to have been a druids' temple. This no longer exists, only the house's name reminds us of the fact. The Temple Druid estate became part of the Trecwn (Barham) estate between 1819-39. In the 1839 Trecwn rental we have Temple Druid, with Revd. J. Davies, tenant, Temple Druid farm, Ebenezor Meyler, tenant, and Temple Druid cottage, W. Rees, tenant. There were several owners over the years and there was even a rumour that the place had been bought on behalf of Nelson as a retreat for himself and Lady Hamilton. Among other owners were a Mr. Pryce who had made his fortune in India, Leo Walmsley, the author, who lived there during the last war and recently it was the home of Mr. and Mrs. Harry Furmstone who lived there for

over 20 years. In 1989 Temple Druid was put up for sale with 88 acres of woodland, pasture, a lake and a trout stream.

THORNE. *St. Twynells.*

This is one of the houses in danger mentioned in Thomas Lloyd's *The Lost Houses of Wales*. It is, he says, '... a small but very sturdy late medieval hall with stone screen passage, pointed doorways and massive chimneys'. He goes on to say that it was (1986) 'empty and in disrepair'. In the late 18th century John Moody was listed as owner, and in 1894 John Vaughan.

THORNTON HOUSE. *Steynton.*

A three-storeyed house about two miles north of Milford. First mentioned in 1618 with John Scone of Thornton, yeoman; in 1623 David Baten, yeoman is of Thornton. Francis Andrew, described as 'gent.' whose father was a farmer, lived at Thornton and his family was succeeded by the Crymes family in the person of Captain John Crymes, R.N., who lived at Thornton at the beginning of the 19th century. He was son of the Revd. Amos Crymes of Buckland Monachorum, Devon. The house was for sale in 1818, described as a 'desirable and modern built residence'. The vendor was the Captain's son, the Revd. Amos John Crymes (d.1856). His agent was his brother-in-law, Morgan Rice James, a solicitor and County Treasurer. Of Mr. Crymes's children, his son John became a naval officer and one of his daughters married in 1849 Lt. Col. Anthony Bowen Owen Stokes of St. Botolphs. Mr. Crymes lived at Haverfordwest and let Thornton first to a family of O'Grady from Ireland and then to the Revd. Thomas Richards, M.A., who ran a boys' school there. After Emmelin Crymes had married Colonel Stokes the couple moved into Thornton but they left when the Colonel became Chief Constable of Pembrokeshire.

Thornton was again let and eventually sold to William Rees who built Thornton Baptist Chapel in 1867. Major Jones gives a long list of tenants and owners; Richard Poyer Lewis Penn of Camrose lived there in the 1880s, and Captain Charles Lewis William Allen Penn was born there in 1887. Other residents were Joseph Thomas of Haverfordwest and Broad Haven, another Baptist stalwart who passed it on to his daughter, Mrs. Colborne wife of a Congregationalist Minister, and including E. Picton Bamkin (d. 1927). Mr. Bamkin's sisters, Mrs. Cole and Mrs. Daysh eventually sold up in 1948. These two ladies used to show visitors a table in their sitting room 'upon which Lord Nelson placed his hat'. The purchaser in 1948 was the Milford Dock Manager, J. C. Ward whose widow sold it to Dr. Williams, of Haverfordwest who was living there in 1976.

TORBANT. *Llanrhian.*

A farm house now very much altered with modern metal windows and a rather hideous porch it serves as a ten-bedroomed guest house. In 1624 Torbant first comes to notice. On 15th June 1624 John Morgan of Cilgwyn, labourer, stole from Torbant in Llanrhian, five white lambs the property of Elizabeth Owen of Llanryan, widow; and in 1631 David Lewis of Llanrhian, labourer, servant, of William Laugharne of Jordanston, gent., was in charge of sowing his mother's corn. He took a peck of wheat to Haverfordwest and sold it for 22d. He also confessed that he took from his master's house at Torbant, a 'plow chippe' belonging to his master, and sold it for 4d. Sadly, there is no record of the punishment for these lightfingered employees.

In the early 17th-century George Owen and Elizabeth, née Gwillim, were the owners but there is a lease dated 25th July 1678 from Timothy Halton, D.D., Archdeacon of Brecknock to William Skyrme, gent. for the lives of the said lessee and of his daughters Mary and Elizabeth Skyrme. In the Land Tax returns of 1786 Francis Skyrme Esq. is listed as owner with Thomas James his tenant. In 1842 the Revd. Richard Davies, Archdeacon of Brecon was the owner. In recent times it belonged to Captain Cecil Charles.

TREBRITHIN. *Manorowen.*

Now a farm house this was, in Tudor times, the home of the family of William Walker Glyn whose descendants moved to Plâs Manorowen near the parish church and took the permanent surname of Williams. In old deeds this place is sometimes referred to as Tre Aberithin.

In the *Cwrtmawr deeds No. 1121* on 25th May 1602. David Hugh of Kilyglynen, gent., and William Williams of Manernawan, gent., there is a bond for possession of a decayed messuage and land in townred and fields of Tre David, Park y Baython, and Trebreythyn, in Manernawan. Lawley Phillips is shown as 'of Trebrithin' by his Will dated 4 February, 1688, proved 28th May 1689; in the Tax Tax list of 1786, Mrs. Joan Mathias owner, John Morris, tenant; and in the Voter's List of 1834, William Francis of Trebrithin, has a lease for lives of Trebrithin Farm.

TRECADWGAN. *Whitchurch.*

Home of the Butler and Parry families. Major Jones refers us to the period 1147-1635 in his essay on the manor in the journal of the *History Society of the Church in Wales,* 1970 (pp. 26-33). For instance in 1332 a grant is recorded from John ap Henry ap Robyn to Philip Cadogan, Lord of the town of Cadogan in Pebydianck, of all the grantor's lands in the town of Cadogan in the tenement of Pebydianck to be held of the chief lord of the fee by the accustomed rents and services. Thomas Parry is recorded as owner in 1622. He was a merchant of St. David's. Francis Parry was there in 1668. From the 18th century onwards it served as a farm house and changed hands several times. Dr. George Phillips was owner in 1786 and John Lort Philips Esq. is described as owning 'the capital messuage called Trecoedwogan' in 1809. The family was still in possession in 1838. Major Jones left rough notes on this property apart from his published monographs.

TRECLYN. *Eglwyswrw*.

Just to the east of the village. In 1678 Thomas Griffith of Treclyn, great-grandson of William Griffith of Penybenglog was involved in a long Chancery case. Mrs. Hay and Mrs. Price were joint owners in 1786 (*Land Tax returns*) and they had a tenant – Mr. James Bowen. In 1894 William Rees was the free-holder and David Rees in 1904. The house is now a farm house.

TRECWN. *Llanfairnantygof*.

Known as 'Homestead of the hounds', at the foot of a steep slope, on the northern banks of the Nantybugail brook. Richard Fenton writes in his *Historical Tour* (1811) ' Trecoon, a mansion ... in point of situation yields to very few spots in the county, as possessing every ingredient of fine scenery, being situated on the edge of a steep hill, having a higher at its back, sheltering it from the north above the narrow vale which the little river Cyllell rises in and runs through, hav-ing the boundaries on each side nobly wooded, till where the vale terminates in a bold craggy rock that projects from a tract of healthy upland affording ample room and subject for amusement to the sportsman ... under this roof I pass the night, enjoy com-pany and conversation rarely to be met with in so retired a situation, and experience the same kind and hospitable reception (from the Barhams), as I have been accustomed to meet with in that house from my childhood in the time of its former possessors (the Vaughans).'

In 1595 there is a confirmatory document concerning Owen Johns' right in 'a capital messuage called Trekoone'. In 1670 John Owen paid tax on seven hearths.

The Vaughans were succeeded by a Hamp-shire family called Barham – John Foster Barham being High Sheriff in 1834. The tithe map drawn in 1838 shows the mansion and outbuildings much the same as they were until the third decade of the present century. According to the Pembrokeshire Archaeo-logical Survey Map made about 1900, the site of the original mansion was about 150 yards to the south-west of the present one, but the

Ancient Monuments Commissioners Report for Pembrokeshire (1915) calls Trecwn 'a modern mansion on the site of the one visited by Fenton'. The earlier house must have been of substantial proportions, for in the hearth tax of 1670 it is listed as possessing seven hearths. That has completely gone. A photo-graph of the later house taken in 1871, shows a large double-pile structure of three storeys with attics above, a range of seven windows on each storey, with the main entrance at one gable end adorned by a pillared porch. By 1889 a long wing projecting westwards had been added to the mansion, while the grounds on the north side are marked as 'aviary'.

The earliest known family at Trecwn was that of Owen. After the tenure of the Owens the property passed to kinsfolk, the Vaughans of Farthingshook. By 1786 John Vaughan Esq., was the owner-occupier – Admiral Vaughan, according to John Wesley in his Journal (18 Aug. 1784) who tells of life at the old mansion 'where the Admiral governs his family as he did his ship – with utmost punct-uality. The bell rings and all attend without delay whether at meals or at morning or evening prayers.'; John Wesley preached here under an oak tree in 1777. He consid-ered it to be one of the loveliest places in Great Britain. Latterly the Admiral suffered severely from gout which hastened the end of his days. Still, he lived to a good age, and a memorial in the parish church commemor-ates the 'Admiral of the Blue whose earthly tabernacle was dissolved on 2nd November, 1789 aged 76 years'.

As he was last male heir of the line of Vaughan the succession devolved on descen-dants through the female line, the Foster Barhams. Each of these families descended from its predecessor at Trecwn, so that the property had remained in possession of the same kin for nearly four centuries until sold in 1939 for the first time in its recorded history. The next heirs of Trecwn derived descent from a Northumberland border clan whose name was variously rendered as Forester, Forster and Foster. From this line came Col. John Foster, a wealthy planter settled in Jamaica where he owned large properties which he administered with the help of his brother Thomas. The Colonel married Elizabeth Smith of Barbados, and two years after her husband's death in 1731, at the age of 50, she married Dr. Henry Barham, a physician, and also a Jamaican planter, son of Dr. Henry Barham F.R.S. descended from the Barhams of Barham Court, Kent. Elizabeth and Col. Foster had several children, the fifth son Joseph, born in Jamaica, inherited extensive estates from his father, uncle Thomas, and his step-father, Dr. Henry Barham who required him to take his surname, which he did by Act of Parliament in 1750 being thereafter known as Joseph Foster Barham. His estates in Jamaica then amounted to 6,496 acres. On 1 July 1754 Joseph Foster Barham married Dorothea Vaughan, younger daughter of John Vaughan of Trecwn, and in her descendants, ultimate heiress to that estate. Trecwn became the main family home from 1803, and the Barhams continued there until 1933 when Captain and Mrs. Barham and their two elder children were killed while motoring from Trecwn towards Oxford where the two children were at University. Near Coventry they stopped to visit a hostelry, and when crossing the road a motor-car ran into them with the result that Captain Barham, his wife and children were killed.

As a result of this tragic event the house was sold to the Admiralty. Trecwn was a very fine-looking seat, but relatively modern. Magnificent tapestries hung in the Drawing Room and the house's destruction by the Admiralty was a tragedy. The house is illustrated in *Photographs in South Wales* 1871 by C. S. Allen and also in Thomas Lloyd's *The Lost Houses of Wales*. There is a sketch made by Major Jones in his notes on the house, and there are extensive articles regarding the history of Trecwn.

A typical Pembrokeshire farmstead

TREDAFYDD. *Llanychllwydog.*

This property is mentioned in a document dated 13 April 1464. Phillip ap Ievan granted to Ievan ap Gwilym ap Eynon 'all his messuage in Teffdavid in fee of Menyth Melyn'. The latter's descendants are mentioned in a charter of 19 November 1519 – 'Gwilym ap Ievan ap Gwilim ap Eynon of Trefllan in Kemeys, yeoman, and his son James, ap Gwilym ap Ievan ab Gwilim ab Eynon, Grant of three messuages viz – one called Trefddavid Yssa, the other lying at the upper head of Trefddavid, and the third called Plâs y dyffryn, and also six acres which he lately had of the gift of Ievan ab Rees ab Lln ap Phillip between Gwern Pennyll on the west and the way called Forthsayson on the east, and also the wood which he had between Pant y Moch on the west and the water of Cwm lvelyn on the east, in parish of Llannchloydock in the fee of Menethmelyn'. (*Bronwydd Deeds No. 1173*).

Tredafydd was owned by inheritance by Ursula, wife of John Owen of St. Kennox, and on April 3 1684 they sold it to John Higgon. The Higgon family were still in possession in 1822. In the Voters' List of 1834 William Higgon is shown 'of Tredavid, freehold house and land'; he was a J.P. in 1820. However in 1828 William David Esq., J.P. was owner. In the Voters' List of 1894, John Gwynne is of Tredavid Uchaf, land and tenement there, and John Phillips of Tredavid Isaf.

TREDEFAID. *Llantood.*

Home of the Parry and Lewes families. In Major Jones's notes he has worked out a pedigree of the Parry family for several generations though with only one date given. The will of John Parry of Tredefaid was proved in 1641. He married Jane, daughter of Griffith David of Llanarth and had four daughters and co-heiresses. The youngest, Elizabeth, married John Griffith or Griffiths and David Griffiths, gent. is described as 'of Tredefaid' in 1685. However, another daughter, Lettice, married Thomas Lewes and in 1705 we find a John Lewis, gent. 'of Tredefaid'. In the late

18th century the Revd. William Lewes, Rector of Newport, was in occupation. His son, Sir Watkin Lewes, became Lord Mayor of London and in 1809 was living at Belvedere House in Southwark. In 1975 Major Jones and his wife visited Tredefaid. In that year the owners, Mr. and Mrs. John Woodhead, sold to a Mr. and Mrs. Gould, of Kent. There is a date of 1698 on the house.

TREDDUOG. *St. Edrins.*
In the 17th century Owens and Meylers and in 1622 William Scourfield of The Mote (*Vide Burke's Landed Gentry*) owned a messuage and 12 acres in Tredduog. For a full account of this manor (1332-1863), Major Jones refers to his essay in *Journal Hist. Soc. of Church in Wales 1970*. Henry Scourfield was listed as owner in 1782, his tenants being James James and Thomas Howells. In 1833 Daniel Davies of Foxhill and Lettice his wife gave a lease of Tredduog (136 acres) to George Harris of Tredduog for the lessee's life. On 20th October, 1847 Lettice Davies late of Foxhill, widow, now of The Burrows in Walton West, mortgaged to William John of Prendergast, gent., Tredduog in £500. On 7th October 1844, John Phillip of Mathry, farmer, mortgaged to Phoebe John of Trehale, widow, the messuage in the parish of St. Edrins called Clyn ffwon, being part of the messuage of Tredduog purchased by John Howell gent from William Ford Protheroe, clerk.

In 1984 the property was sold with 211 acres, outhouses and farm buildings. The vendors were Col. and Mrs. Chaldecot. Mrs. Chaldecot had inherited the estate from her mother, Mrs. Thomas, heiress of the Trehale estate (q.v.).

TREDRISSI. *Nevern.*
Home of the Young family. Howel ap Jenkin Young who had inherited Tredrissi (no date given) had five natural sons, who, in spite of their illegitimacy, married well and established families. Howel, after the birth of his fifth son, married his paramour but she produced only one daughter, Elen who, being the only legitimate child, inherited Tredrissi on her father's death. Elen married David ap Evan David by whom she had a son, Rhydderch, who sold the property to his uncle Thomas Young, the fifth natural son of Howel, and his descendants continued there into the 17th century. 'This famylie of the Youngues were in tymes past noted to be men tall of person, fayer of complexion and gentle of behavioure but now declyne from the same' – G. *Owen Second Book (p. 273)*. The arms of Young of Nevern were: *azure three bulls' heads caboshed or*. From the Youngs descended the Mathias family, and James Mathias is recorded in 1840 as owner-occupier with 65 acres.

TREFACH. *Nevern.*
Home of the Lloyd family in the 17th and 18th centuries. John Lloyd was assessed for five hearths in 1670. In 1638 he had placed his daughter Elizabeth with Richard and Dorothy Jones to be educated but was sued by the latter in 1642 for refusing to pay the tuition fees. Major Jones's notes contain pedigrees of the Lloyds and their close relations. In the 18th century the Bowen family were in possession – Lewis Bowen of Trefach is mentioned in 1743. His daughter and heiress married firstly John Lewis of Egremont and secondly Thomas Lewis who was 'of Trefach' in right of his wife. David Lewis, son of the first marriage succeeded. In 1771 Stephen Lewis of Trefach subscribed towards two copies of the Revd. William Evans's translation of *Canwyll y Cywry*. By 1840 Thomas Davies is listed as owner-occupier.

TREFACH. *Llanfairnantgwyn.*
This is another Trefach. It lies S.E. of Pantyderi and was the home of the Lloyd and Williams families. On 17th July 1723 William Williams, Baptist Minister, J.P. for Pembrokeshire and Cards., and for the Borough of Cardigan who was nineteen at the time of his first marriage to Jane, sister of James Bowen of Llwyngwair, she died within a year of her marriage; William Williams

became Minister of Blaenywain chapel. By 1768 Ebenzer Chapel was built on the Trefach estate. He helped to start the Baptist mission in North Wales in 1776, of which he was Treasurer and organiser. About 1774 he went to live in Cardigan and founded a Baptist chapel there in 1775-6, and another in Verwig in 1797. Published several religious tracts and pamphlets; died 13th August 1799; buried in Ebenzer chapel burial ground. He had married secondly, Eleanora, daughter of Revd. D. Morgan of Garragh, Co. Londonderry, and one of the heirs at law of Revd. Thomas Pardoe of Jesus College, Oxford. She died without issue 1780 and he married Dorothy, daughter of Thomas Lewis of Llwyngrawys, Cards in October 1784 and they had four children; the eldest William Morgan Williams of Trefach, died without issue in 1820 and his estate passed to his nephew James Bowen, son of Mary Anne Williams who married Thomas Bowen of Pantyderi, Captain 10th Hussars.

Now a farmhouse it is a long square building with protruding stepped chimneys at each gable end. A slate stone in the wall states: 'Trevach built by J.W.B. Esqr. 1872. A datestone on an outhouse has '1853 J.W.B.' (James William Bowen, Esq., shown on the Tithe Schedule of 1837 as owner of Trefach, tenanted by Thomas Harries). There is a photograph of it as it was in 1972 in E. T. Lewis's *Mynachlogddu: A Guide to its Antiquities (1972)*. Major Jones visited the house in 1985, a Mr. Jones being the owner.

TREFAES. *Moylgrove.*
In 1602 James Perrott of Haroldston, Esq., sued Ievan ap Rees of Trefaes for trespass and in 1614 and 1615 and yet again in 1635 the Reeses of Moylgrove were involved in litigation for trespass. Major Jones left an unfinished and undated pedigree of the family of John Phillip Thomas, who by his second wife Janet, daughter of Hugh Harry of Haverford, had two children, Margaret John who married David Perkin of Menevia who had a son Thomas Perkins whose only son William was hanged for murder.

John Phillip Thomas's younger daughter called Margaret John Junior married Eynon David Thomas of Park y Pratt, and 'and as thei saye was devorsed and then married one Hughe Phe ap Ievan Jenkin in the liff of her husband Eynon David, and had by him a son named David and then she died, the said Eynon David surviving her' (*Wagner ms 2*). After this unfortunate saga the house became the home of Jenkin Lloyd who was assessed for six hearths in 1670. The property passed to the James family, William James being the owner in 1786. This family still had the property in 1904, William Frederick Lloyd James being the owner.

TREFAWR. *Llanfyrnach.*
The land formerly belonged to Whitland Abbey in Carmarthenshire. This building, standing S.E. of the parish church is now a farm. The Gwilyms owned this property in the 16th century; David Gwilym, married twice, the name of his first wife being unknown, he had by her six children, and by his second, Llenen verch Philip Weith of Trehendy, four more, one, Katherine, 'had a base daughter by Morgan Bowen, now sowing in Havfordwest 1592, a semster', and John his son, had 'a daughter yt goeth abeging'. His eldest son by his first marriage, Morris (d.1570) inherited Trefawr and the family remained at Trefawr for several further generations; they were followed by the Lloyds (no dates given). In 1786 Thomas Jones was owner-occupier. William Jones, probably his son, was the freeholder in 1834.

TREFAYOG. *St. Nicholas.*
Now a farmhouse, Evan Griffith is mentioned as owner in the 1610 *Plea Rolls,* he had one son, William, who married Ursula Warren of Trewern, and they had three children, However by 1732-3 the will of Peter Watts shows him to be of Trevayog. By 1670 it had passed to the Mathiases, John Mathias having been assessed for two hearths in 1670. In 1756 and 1759 John Mathias of Trefayog was a Grand Juror, and in 1773 John

Mathias Esq was a Justice of the Peace. Other owners include the families of William David – Voters' List 1834; in the late 18th/early 19th century the family of Evans and, in the Voters' List of 1894, James Perkins is of Trevayog, house and land. When Major Jones recorded his findings the owner was Mr. Idris Davies.

TREFELLYN. *Mathry.*

The earliest reference in the Major's notes is in 1326 when David ap Ievan ap Gr' (*sic*) held four bovates at Trefellyn. In 1632 Jenkin Gwynne of Jordanston bought a number of properties, some 1,555 acres in all, which included Trefellyn, from David Hughes. Thus this property merged with the others as part of the Jordanston estate which passed from the Gwynnes to their kinsfolk the Vaughans. The manors remained in their possession until well into the 19th century, except for a short period when Trefellyn was owned by a member of the Martin family but by 1786 the Vaughans were back in possession. In 1842 Sir James Cockburn was the owner and subsequent owners were Protheroes and Thomases. Trefellyn was put up for sale in 1983 and described as 'An outstanding and substantial dairy and arable farm.' An aerial view shows the modest six-bedroomed Georgian house dwarfed by huge ranges of modern outbuildings.

TREFEUGAN. *Llanhowel.*

In the 16th century the armigerous family of Propert lived here, and the line descended from Harry William Propert, 1546, through six generations to William Propert who was assessed for land tax here in 1769. In 1838 the property was part of the marriage settlement of William Evans when he married Mrs. Jane Mathias.

TREFFGARN HALL. *Treffgarne.*

Home of the Evans family in the 19th century until 1914. The house has been the home of several prominent personalities, the present building having been constructed for Dr. David Evans in 1824. The previous house had belonged to Rhys Evans, described as 'a

substantial yeoman', and another Evans, John, established a number of Baptist chapels in the county. In 1931 Mr. Victor Higgon, a relation of the Evans family, lived here and was High Sheriff in that year. In recent years the Hall has been an hotel and restaurant and was up for sale again in 1985. This handsome symmetrical Georgian house has six principal bedrooms with a particularly attractive coach house.

TREFFGARN (LITTLE). *St. Dogwells.*

Also known as Trowgarn Fach – one of the supposed homes of Thomas ap Owain, scion of the royal house of Deheubarth. For the early history of this manor see the author's essay Trefgarn Owen in *Arch. Cam.*, 1961, pp. 102-128. Fenton wrote: 'Little Trefgarn, a single mansion-house on the top of the hill, the east side of the vale, is held under lease from the Precentor of St. David's by John Edwards Esq., whose ancestor, when he fillest stall in the cathedral, having made it his residence, his descendants for near two centuries continue to inhabit it and in my remembrance, in a style of great hospitality, till the present possessor, leaving it for Sealyham (q.v.), the seat of his lady in the neighbourhood, it has dwindled into a farm-house'.

The first to lease it was Thomas Edwardes. In about 1777 his descendant, John Owen Edwardes, having married one of the co-heiresses of John Tucker of Sealyham, moved there to live. It is one of the rare instances of a county family living on leased premises for over three centuries and owning considerable property elsewhere in the county. The property was finally bought from the Ecclesiastical Commissioners in 1880 for £12,300. Charles Rice Saunders, of Hazel Grove owned the house and land in 1904. In Law's *Little England* (1888, p. 192) there is a description: 'Little Trefgarn ... a long narrow building still stands though in a very ruinous state, which may have served as a gentleman's residence in the 14th century, for though there are no architectural details such as windows or arches, the masonry appears to be of very great antiquity. This building in now used as a cattle shed.' In the G.W.R. publication *South Wales, the County of Castles* (1924 – p. 47), a photograph shows Little Treffgarn as a substantial farmhouse with a courtyard in front and a wing attached to the rear portion.

TREFIN. *Llanrhian.*

Home of the Richard family. Henry Richard of Trefin (1732-1812) was circulating Minister and C.M. preacher for 60 years. By his second wife he had a son, the Revd. Ebenezer Richard (1781-1837) who became private tutor in 1806 to one of the Bowen family. He was ordained in 1811 and retired from the ministry in 1830. His brother, the Revd. Thomas Richard (1783-1858) published two volumes of his sermons in 1866. Ebenezer's son, Henry Richard (1812-1888), was M.P. for Merthyr Tydfil from 1868 to the year of his death. He died without issue and is buried at Abney Park, London. Recent distinguished owners of Trefin were Mr. Edgar Phillips, member of the Gorsedd of Bards and Archdruid of Wales, and the Revd. Lloyd Evans – schoolmaster, poet and author. When he retired from the ministry he became a priest in the Anglican Church.

TREFLOYNE. *Penally.*

Home of seven generations of the Bowen family, descendants of Pentre Ifan. Thomas ap Owen (son of Owen ap Owen ap Pentre Ifan) was the first to settle at Trefloyne in the latter half of the 15th century and was still there in 1501. The last of the main line, Thomas Bowen, married Anne, daughter of Sir Erasmus Philipps of Picton Castle, and when he died without issue in 1679 the estate became the possession of his widow's family. The Philippses lived only occasionally at Trefloyne which they let to tenants.

During the Civil War the Royalist commander, the Earl of Carbery, used the house as his HQ and garrisoned it for the King. It was beseiged in 1644 and captured by the Parliamentarians after a cannonade. In 1646 leading men in County Pembroke petitioned Parliament for consideration to be extended to Thomas Bowen of Trefloyne, 'a gentleman of a very fayre and eminent fortune in the country', whose house and estate had suffered greatly in the war.

The mansion contained eight hearths in 1670.

In 1714 Sir John Philipps gave a lease of Trefloyne, with the hall part of the dwelling house and the loft over it, the outer kitchen, the room called 'Mr. Philipps' Chamber' and the room over it ... and the barn, stable, ox-houses, carthouse ... orchards, gardens and the marsh adjoining to Margaret Marchant, widow, of Penally. In 1754 Sir John Philipps leased the mansion to Revd. John Williams at a rent of £50 p.a.; Anne Williams of Penally, widow, by will dated 28th January, 1765, left to 'George Williams, Clerk, son of my husband, John Williams, clerk, the freehold lease of Treloyn in Penally parish which I hold under lease from Sir John Philipps, Bt., and after his decease to his sister Anne, wife of George Scawe, mariner; will proved at Carmarthen 24th May 1769'.

A water colour made about 1800-1810 shows part of the old house, then mainly in ruins. Materials from the old house were used to build the farmhouse and in 1800 a crude figure of a Virgin and Child was found in the rubble. Over the fireplace in the principal apartment was a carved escutcheon: *a chevron between three escallops.* * All that now remains is a fragment of a gable containing a pointed window, and near the house is the base of a dovecot.

F. P. Gwynne, in *Sketches of Tenby,* 1852, says 'It is now a desolate ruin, entered by an archway; some parts of it have been repaired, and are now tenanted by two labouring families. A good view of this extensive ruin is obtained by ascending the hillside at the back of the courtyard. There is an old well halfway up this hill, hidden by a clump of trees and shrubs'.

* These arms do not seem to relate to any of the named owners or tenants. They could be Bateman, Colby or Tancred.

TREFRAN. *Roch.*

In 1441 there was a grant by Thomas son of Walter Jurdan to Sir Richard Newton, Chief Justice of the Common Pleas and Robert Hoggetyn, clerk, of lands in Capriston, Bikton, Sutton and Trevrane in the Lordship of Haverfordwest. William Walter, yeoman, is listed as 'of Trevrane' in 1612. In that year a case was brought against his wife, Elizabeth Harries for abuses towards Jane Walter, alias Laugharne wife of William Walter of Roch Castle.

Elizabeth is said to have come from Trefran near to the house of William Walter at Roch, where the common pound was situated, crying loudly 'Where are the thieves, the servants of Jane Walter who have stolen my cattle?' She then fell on her knees and prayed that the curse of God might fall on Jane Walter. Next she climbed into the pound shouting 'God's wounds I will kill all the cattle'. At this point William Walter, bailiff of the manor, stopped her but she still rounded on him shouting that he and all the others present were thieves and rogues. On another occasion this harridan again fell on her knees and cursed Jane Walker and used 'many execrations and wild and indecent speeches'.

The family of Walter were still there in 1733 when Dame Thomazine Walter, a widow, and Joseph Walter leased Upper Trefran (three ploughlands) to Stephen Thomas, husbandman. In 1804, Stephen Thomas (junior) surrendered the lease to John Higgon, the then owner. The Tithe map of Roch parish 1837 shows James Higgon, Esq., owner of Trevrane, with John Thomas, tenant, of 48 acres; Crick-a-franc, James Higgon, Esq., owner, John Nicholas tenant, 23 acres, and Trevrane, James Higgon, Esq., owner, Richard Tew tenant of 181 acres.

A chapel subordinate to Roch parish is said to have stood at Trefran – *'Parochiale Wallicanum' in Y. Cymmr. XXii,* p. 26. The site is shown on 6" OS map to be on Newgale Sands, about half a mile north of Trefran Colliery, and close to the culm pits which have practically obliterated the site. It is probably to be identified with a shallow oblong depression traceable in dry weather. This was St. Caradoc's Chapel mentioned by Giraldus. Fenton mentions 'the triffling ruins of Cradock's Chapel'.

TREGAMAN. *Nevern.*

Tregaman derives its name from the river Gaman which flows past it.

Home of the Peverell and Young families. Tregaman formed part of the estate of the family of Peverell. John Peverell in 1427 divided the estate between his three sons, Howell, Jenkin and Owen. The eldest, Howell, received Tregaman which was inherited by his only child Eva who married Rees Morgan of Cardiganshire. By him Eva had two daughters and co-heiresses: Nest married to John Cole and Morfydd married to William Thomas Philpin. Their issue, after inheriting, sold Tregaman to Thomas Peter. Thomas Peter's daughter, Sage, inherited. She was married to Thomas Philip Young who, says George Owen (Second Book – p. 272) '… likelie hath builded a new house upon the same'. William Young was assessed for four hearths in 1670 and the Youngs remained in possession until the 1760s. In 1764 we find John Morris of Haverfordwest, drover, listed as owner. He was then in financial straits and and wrote to a cousin asking for help. He died in that year unmarried. Owen Owen was owner in 1840, with John Owen occupier; in 1908-9 Tregaman in the parish of Bayvil, Moylgrove, and Nevern formed part of the Cwmglôyn estate; the tenant being Mr. Thomas Lloyd at rent of £148 p.a.

Major Jones records an event in 1602 which deserves mention: 'Thomas Young; killed at Eglswywrw Faire upon Ascension day 13th May 1602 by John Bowen and Hugh Bowen the sonnes of James Bowen his uncle, brother to his mother, who were both executed for the same act at Haverford West XVIIIth of July anno prd'. (*Protheroe IV*)

[It would be interesting to speculate what relationship, if any, the original owners, the Peverells, had with the great Norman house of Peverell which flourished in Derbyshire after the Conquest – Ed.]

TREGLEMAIS. *Llanhowel.*
Treglemais, alias Cern Fawr, was an episcopal manor, becoming a lay manor at the end of the 16th century. For further notes on this house see Francis Jones's essay in *Journ. Hist. Soc. Church in Wales 1967.* In 1654 William ap Rice was in possession but a century later it belonged to the Phillipses, George Phillips, Esq., being assessed for land tax in 1786. In 1737 David Reynolds was living in the parish. He got a lease of Treglemais and his descendants eventually bought the freehold and lived there for five generations and the family sold it after the Second World War.

TREGROES. *Fishguard.*
Between Fishguard and Manorowen on Colby's map 1831, about one and a quarter miles south-west of Fishguard town.

The Courts Leet of the Royal Manor of Fishguard were held at Tregroes, probably for the Welshery. The manor was originally held by the Abbots of St. Dogmaels, but in 1536–40 came to the Crown and was divided into two: the Manor of English Fishguard and the Manor of Welsh Fishguard. In 1653 a Court Leet was held in the house of William Phillips 'neare ffishguard'. In 1814 the Steward of the Manor was Lord Kensington and a map of the Manor which was made in that year shows a group of three buildings at Tregroes, one of which is called 'Manor House'. Courts were still held there in 1859 (*Vide: Fishguard and Goodwick Silver Jubilee Tribute* 1977, pp. 4 -7).

In 1568 – 1600 John Phillips was of Tregroes, and on 19 August 1616, James Phillips stated in a law suit, he then living in the parish of St. Edrins, a husbandman, '… has known manor of Fishguard for last 48 years. Born at Tregroes, when 20 years old he moved to St. Edrins … about 40 years ago' – Law suit PRO (*Vide: History of St. Dogmaels Abbey*).

Ann Williams was owner-occupier in the Land Tax List 1786. The families of George and Gwynne were also sometime occupiers of Tregroes. They were all strong supporters of the Hermon Baptist Chapel – the first to be built in Fishguard in 1776 by the Revd. John Williams and Henry Morgan Esq., of Tregroes. Henry Morgan always gave a sovereign in the collection which he modestly covered with a penny.

TREGWYNT. *Tregwynt, Granston.*
The year was 1797 and a grand ball was in full swing in this handsome Georgian house. Suddenly a breathless messenger arrived to announce that a French force had landed at Llanwnda, not far off. Music and dancing stopped immediately and the women hurriedly removed their jewellery and hid it before being taken by carriages to Narberth. One old servant remained, loaded all the muskets he could find and awaited the siege – which never came as the invaders soon surrendered. The house might be Georgian but its origins go back much further.

Tregwynt is one of the earliest inhabited sites in the area. A 14th century map designates it as a manor house. The Lady Nesta, one of the descendants and co-heiress of Wizo the Fleming, who had come to Pem-

brokeshire in the 12th Century married Fromand Brown (1300-1350) and their descendants in the female line remained in possession for six centuries. Their name changed to Harries and they made good local matches with the neighbouring gentry families of Phillips of Woodstock, Haythog and St. Brides, Bowen of Llwyngwair, Owen of Priskilly, Jordan of Neeston and Jones of Llether, and Symons of Llanstinan, and produced four High Sheriffs of the county, and numerous magistrates. (*Vide: Burke's Landed Gentry for 1921*). Richard Llewellin was owner for a short time, and High Sheriff in 1840; the estate was sold in 1877, and bought back by descendants of the original family; the *Cambrian Tourist, 5th edn.* 1799, says '... we passed a neat house called Caergwent (Tregwynt), belonging to Mrs. Harries'. Mr. John Harries Burrington, descended from the distaff side of the family, died in 1984 and left the estate to his relations the Gabbs. In 1986 it was put up for sale and much of the land was acquired by the National Trust.

TREHAL. *St. Edrins.*
This property formed part of the estate of Scourfield of Castle Villa and Trewilyn, and in 1611 a fine was suffered of two messuages and 99 acres in 'Trehayle' between James and Thomas Scourfield and the latter's wife. It remained a farm but at the end of the 17th century it was the home of Dr. Thomas Williams, descendant of an old Cardiganshire family, who, being a nonconformist,

emigrated to Pennsylvania in 1725. It became the property of Hugh Owen by 1787 and of John Roberts by 1799. By the beginning of the 19th century it was bought by Abel John of Caerwen whose only daughter, Mary, married, in 1839, the Revd. Theophilus Evan Thomas (1802-1874) a Baptist minister eminent for his piety and charitable disposition. The present house was erected by him in about 1844 or 1845 on or near the older farmhouse and was in recent times the home of the minister's descendant Mrs. Chaldecot. The property included a chapel and yard and amounted in all to 270 acres. The arms of Thomas of Trehal are: *argent on a chevron engrailed azure two griffons passant. On a chief azure three cinquefoils.* Major Jones left a quantity of rough notes about details of this estate.

TREHENRY. *Llanfyrnach.*
Shown on Colby's Map 1831 as about three-quarters of a mile south-west of Llanfyrnach church. Home of the father and grandfather of the famous Jenkin Lloyd of Blaiddbwll in the same parish. The father, Ievan Fychan (or Lloyd) ap Ievan Llwyd, described as of 'Pentre Henry in Trayan Caroe in the fee of Dyffryntaf' is mentioned in a deed of 14 Richard II (1390-1) – (*Protheroe ms*).

Philip John ap Rees settled here in 1584. The prenuptial settlement of Lewis Philip John (son of Philip John ap Rees of Llanfyrnach ar dafe, gent), and Jane Phillipp, daughter of John Phillipp of Llanvirnach, gent. details: 'The said Lewis Philip John grants to Reginald Lewis of Llanvirnach ar dafe, and Llewelin ap Morris of the same place, yeoman, my messuage called Tre Henry in Ll'virnach, a messuage called Frynondeg and lands, being an entail on the prospective bride and bridgegroom and the heirs of their bodies'. Reginald Lewis died without issue.

According to the Land Tax records of 1786 Trehenry was owned by Lady Keith wife of Sir Basil Keith (*Vide:* LONGRIDGE).

TREHOWEL. *Llanwnda.*

The families associated with this property include Lloyd, Williams, Harries and Mortimer. In 1603 William Thomas Lloyd had an interest in Trehowel. On May 30th 1638 Jenkin David of Trevasser Clethee Coch, yeoman, granted Rice William Lloyd and his son, both of Trehowel, all their title and claim to two messuages and other lands around. William Williams, gent., was 'of Trehowel' in 1748 and William Mortimer, gent., in Land Tax List of 1786, and the Voters' List of 1834. *The Cambrian Tourist* (1822 edn. p. 136), says '... we passed a neat house called Caergwynt (Tregwynt) belonging to Mrs. Harris. The kind attentions of a farmer in the neighbourhood of this memorable spot, claim our warmest acknowledgements. Having finished a most comfortable meal at Mr. Mortimer's house, Trehowel (which, during the confusion, was considered the headquarters of the French), he explained all the minutiae respecting this circumference, and very obligyingly printed out the situation of their camp, and related many entertaining and interesting anecdotes. Deeply impressed with gratitude towards Mr. M. for his facilities, we soon arrived at Goodric sands'.

TRELEDDYN. *St. Davids.*

A double-pile 17th century house with a smugglers' tunnel allegedly leading to Porth Seli. For many years this was the property of the Williams family but other families such as Bleddyn, (1529) Tuckers, and Blands were connected with it. On January 16th 1799

Thomas Williams of Treleddyn, owner of the sloop *Phoebe,* of the Port of Solva, proved ... that ten hundred or 33 bushels of salt taken on board for the curing of herrings were lost through stormy and tempestuous weather. One of the Williams family, a merchant farmer, is said to have been the first man to sight the French fleet in 1797 as it approached the coast of Pembrokeshire in its vain attempt at invasion. In the late 18th century the famous actress, Mrs. Jordan, leased the house and was regularly visited by the Duke of Clarence, her lover, afterwards King William IV. It is said that one of the ceilings was emblazoned with the royal coat of arms, but this has disappeared, if it ever existed. The property was put up for sale in 1884. The house, then Upper Treleddyn, was mentioned in the *Black Book of St. Davids.*

TRELEWELYN. *Manorowen.*

Home of the Phillips family, descended from the dynasty of Rhys ap Tewdwr.

In 1558-9 David ap Lewis and Thomas Llewelyn granted and confirmed to David Morris Rees, all messuages and lands in the vill and fields of Fynnon y gribe, Tref Lewelyn, Penmeythyn, Kaergowill and Pant Yago, in parishes of Llanwnda and Maneruawan, for life of said David Morris Rees, then to Maurice ap David his son, and to the children of the said Maurice ap David by Lleycue verch Thomas Morris legitimately procreated. By 1672 Trelewelyn was part of the prenuptial settlement of David Paynter of Broomhill, Dale, and Ursula Phillips of Trelewhelin, spinister, and the property stayed in the Phillips family. In the Land Tax of 1786 Sparks Martin Esq., is owner, and John Richard, tenant assessed at £1.1.6.

It is shown in a lease on 9th June 1795 between Elvi Martin of Withybush House, widow, 2. John Phelps of same, her son, and 3. Miles Meyler of Manorowen parish farmer, lease for three lives of the capital messuage and land called Trellewhelin in the parish of Manorowen.

Fenton wrote: 'Within a field or two of the

above mansion (Manorowen) occurs another called Trelwelyn, formerly embosomed in a fine wood, though now denuded, and once the residence of a family as noted for their talent for sordidly accumulating wealth as their neighbours were for a liberal circulation of it'. One of this family, Thomas Phillips 'as noted for his avarice as his usury' became High Sheriff in 1667 on the recommendation of the Duke of Beaufort. In 1670 he was assessed for five hearths.

Major Jones's notes say 'The old tree-lined drive to the mansion is now cut by a railway line and disused. The present farmhouse is a substantial building but the former residence stood a little distance below in the woods, so I was informed by the owner, Captain T. V. G. Johns, of Manorowen, but no trace remains'. He later revises his opinion by considering that the present building is, in fact, on the site of the old and might even incorporate parts of the original (see Mudge Map 1819 & Tithe Map 1837).

TRELLWYN COURT. *Llanllawer.*
Trellwyn Fawr and Fach, about one and a quarter miles east of Llanllawer on the southern slopes of Mynydd Dinas overlooking Cwm Gwaun, marked on Mudge Map 1819 and Colby Map 1831.

The earliest reference shown by Major Jones is in 1394-5; 'A grant by Howell ap Griffith ap Henry of Trellwyn, Dinas to David Mille, chaplain, of lands in Penrynzovy, Penmonethvawr, and Treflloyn – dated at Penrynzovy, Tuesday next after the feast of St. Clement the Pope 18 Richard I' – *PRO Ave Deeds* D 4932.

17th century home of the Lloyd family, descended from the Lloyds of Cilciffeth and Morfil. Morris Lloyd of Trellwyn, living 1613, was foster father of his cousin Thomas Lloyd of Penygegin who later succeeded to Cilciffeth.

At one time the Batemans (descended from the Honeyborough stock) lived here. Life did not always go according to plan – 'Disposition of Margaret Williams of parish of Dinas, widow, taken at Trewern 20 November 1837,

and another, Ellen Young of Nevern, widow, said she was in a place with Mr. Robert Prichard, Bachelor of Divinity, Vicar of Nevern, on 30th October last, when Margaret Williams, widow and Owen Battman of Llanllawer, yeoman, were contracted for matrimony, and they then delivered themselves to give and pledge their troth, and as they were going to church to be married, Thomas Perkin drew the said Margaret away and would not suffer her to be married with Owen Battman'.

In the 1894 Voters' List, Martha Phillips is shown as of Trellyn Fawr and in 1904 Voters' Lists, James Phillips and David Phillips of Trellwyn Fawr are shown as joint owners of land and tenement, and the Phillips family still farm there.

TRELLYFFANT. *Nevern.*
Home of the Picton family. 'Trellyfain is the mansion howse of Owen Picton as yt hath ben to 3 or 4 of his auncestors before, and in auncient times the landes of Howell ap Jenkin of Nevarne … The coate of the Pictons is: gules three pikes nayant argent. (G. Owen, *Second Book* p. 273). Fenton writes: '… I proceed to Trellyffan … to see the figure of a toad, well sculptured in black marble, which is introduced into a chimneypiece and was formerly covered with glass to preserve it from any injury. It is said to have been brought from Italy, the work of a foreign artist. My enquiries as to the date of its introduction here were fruitless, and all I could learn was, that it had filled its present station for some centuries … Whether the present occupiers of Trellyffant are descendants of the original family, one of whom was the unfortunate victim of Giraldus's account, I cannot pretend to say, but they have lived there for some generations, and as the respectable clergyman, our companion (The Revd. Mr. Owen, visiting his native county after 21 years) informed me, who traces to the same stock, bear a toad for their crest … He says that if bodily peculiarities are hereditary, then the present proprietors may be descended from Syssyllt Esgair who became a meal for

the toads ... there can be few instances adduced of tallness being continued in a family so long as this, every one of the present as well as the former generation being upward of six feet and even a female of only nineteen years of age nearly as tall'. Giraldus tells a story of a toad and as a memento there was a carving in dark green veined marble about the size of a woman's hand and reputed to have been the work of an Italian artist, brought back from Italy by Sir Richard Mason, Knight of the Green Cloth in the time of James II to his relatives at Trellyffant who bore a toad as their crest. In the 1890s the owner was Morris Owen Lloyd Williams who lived at Haverfordwest. His widow died in 1942 and Major Jones was unable to trace the whereabouts of the toad.

TRENEWYDD. *Crunwear.*

Home of the Howell family descended from Cadefor Fawr of Blaencych. Reginald Howell bought Trenewydd in 1686. Of his sons, John the eldest inherited the estate but *d.s.p.* in 1795, having been a bankrupt; Court records dated 15 July 1756, detail: 1. Creditors of John Howell of Trenwydd, Pembs, a bankrupt, 2. George Howell. Ratification of Release of real and personal estate of John Howell in return for £2,272; by 1772 John Howell was living in Haverfordwest on an annuity of £70 raised on his estates.

George Howell, of Haverfordwest was a surgeon. One of his daughters married the Revd. John Phillips, Rector of Talbenny, and the other married a surgeon with the splendid name of Essex Devereaux Jones. By 1786 The Revd. John Phillips was the owner but 60 years later Robert Morgan is described as 'of Trenewyd'. His relation, Frances Elizabeth Morgan, was born in 1843 and died in Brighton in 1927. She was the first woman in Wales to become a doctor.

TRENEWYDD MANOR. *Llanllawer.*

In 1586 John Bateman owned this property. He was a son of Philip Bateman of Honeyborough by his wife Jane, daughter of Sir

John Wogan of Wiston. John married Jane, daughter of John ap David ap Gwilym ap Rees of 'Llystyn' in the parish of Nevern. The family steadily declined in the social scale and the last of his line, Price Bateman was a husbandman whose will was proved on July 8th 1745. He left an only daughter, Martha. In more prosperous days the Batemans made alliances with old local families such as the Mortimers of Coedmore, the Wilkins and the Bowens of Trefloyne. In 1985 the Manor was put up for sale. Its core dates from Tudor times and it contains some attractive Gothick features. On high ground above the house are the remains of a prehistoric fort while below are the ramparts of Castell Cleddyf and the holy well of St. Degan. On a cliff not far off overlooking St. George's Channel is a stone commemorating the abortive French invasion of 1797.

TRENEWYDD FAWR. *Llanrhian.*

A traditional stone farmhouse, the centre of a large dairy farm. Records go back to 1326 when the place was known as Froches or Vrothes. In 1424 Sir Henry Wogan of Boulston acquired the property and married Elizabeth, one of the sisters of Sir James Bowen of Pentre Ifan. On Sir Henry's death the estate went to Sir Richard Wogan in 1541 though before his death his son, another Sir Richard, took over and demised the lands to Meilir Lloyd of Dewsland, his then servant, to be held at will. Sir John Wogan appointed him his reeve or rent gatherer. Meilir died in possession of Trenewydd Fawr and his son Rowland Lloyd continued his father's duties. The latter died leaving a natural son Robert who, together with Morris Howell 'by colour of having by casual and indirect means gotten into their hands the ancient entail made by Henry Wogan Esq., and other deeds, and in August 17 James I (1619) entered on Vroches and expelled Sir John Wogan's tenants therefrom. (From the *Chancery Proceedings James I H31. No. 18 16 Nov. 1620 Bill of Complaint*). This was one of many law suits concerning this estate and carefully recorded in Major Jones's notes. In 1975 the owner-occupier was George Richards and his son Morgan Richards. In 1982 Trenewydd Fawr was on the market with 365 acres. The farmhouse is described as 'traditional' and has two reception rooms and five bedrooms.

TRENICHOL. *Llandeloy.*

Henry ap Owen is recorded as owner in 1545. Trenichol was the subject of bitter legal battles from 1596 to 1622. 'Jenkin Reade of Loghmeylor, gent., and Richard David of Loghmeylor, labourer, defendants v. William James Peter for forcible entry and depasturing at Trenycknoll Ysha, parish of Llandeloy, ad. val. £10.' and in 1598 Rice ap Ievan, (will dated 24 Jan. 1602, proved 1603), 'of Trenicholl Yssa, yeoman plaintiff sued Richard David for forcible entry on a toft, and 24 acres in Trenicholl Yssa, which Jenkin Reade gent., and Margaret his wife on 18 August 1598 deseised to said Rice for a term not yet ended, and ejected him.'

In 1611, William Scourfield plaintiff sued John David re 20 acres in Llandeloy parish which John David had diseised him. John David in defence says that James Peter gent., held the land in fee, and when he died it descended to William James Peter his son and heir. William James Peter then enfeoffed Owen Yonge gent., in the lands to the use of said William James Peter for his life, and afterwards to use of James Williams and his heirs for ever. The said William Peter died at Trenichol and then James Williams entered and was seised in fee, and James Williams at Trenichol demised the lands to John David. But William Scourfield under colour of a supposed enfeoffment from said Owen Yonge entered and expelled James David.

William Scourfield says that the lands were owned by Richard Bowen in fee; and Richard Bowen died in Llandeloy parish on 1st August 1560, and the lands descended to his daughter and heir Margaret Scourfield. On 24th August 1560, Katherine assigned the lands to Margaret Bowen relict of said Richard Bowen to hold for Margaret's life as dower. On 20 December 1563 the said Margaret married at Llan-

deloy to Thomas Scourfield. On 20 May 1566 the said Thomas Scourfield and Margaret his wife deseised the tenement to James Peeler for the lives of grantors, and said James Peeler died in Llandeloy parish so seised. On 20 July 1568 Thomas Scourfield died and Katherine died on 16 October 1608, and the lands descended to said William Scourfield plaintiff. On 12 September 1610 Margaret granted her inheritance in the said lands to the said William Scourfield. The case was still in dispute in 1616, but by 1622 William Scourfield of New Moat was owner of a messuage and land in Trenichol. It was assessed at one hearth in 1670, John Harry, owner, and in 1786 Mr. Callen was owner, with William Harries tenant.

James Harries of Trenichol made a will on September 4th 1823 leaving a lease of Trenichol to his wife with remainder to his children Joseph, Thomas, George, Mary and John. The *Pembroke Telegraph* for December 2nd 1943 records a funeral in St. Brynach's churchyard, Dinas, of John Harries, son of the Trenichol family and described as a 'sportsman and follower of hounds'.

TREPRISK. *Moylgrove.*

'… the mansion house of Mr. John Bradshawe is by him newly built. It was in auncient tyme the inheritance of Phillip ap David whose son Griffith Philip had issue Owen ap Griffith who sold it and his other landes to John Bradshawe of St. Dogmaels Esq. who gave it to this John Bradshawe as a younger son's portion' (G. *Owen Second Book*, p. 268). In the *Pembrokeshire Plea Rolls* No. 48 John Bradshawe, gent., is described as 'of Treprisk'. At the end of the 18th century the estate had passed to the James family. William James's will dated 26 April 1830 devised his farm of Treprisk to use of his sons William and David. At the beginning of the 20th century James Williams Williams of Cambray House, The Parade, Carmarthen, owned the freehold of the house and land of Treprisk.

TRERHOS. *St. Lawrence.*

Also called Patrickford. In the 16th century William Llewelin 'a blind man dwelled at Trerose in S. Lawrens ...' On 26 December 1719 a prenuptial settlement of William Allen, the younger, and Martha Fowler (d. of Martin Fowler of Haverfordwest, and mother of Hugh Fowler) described lands in St. Issells, Reynaldston, Hayscastle, three messuages and land in the townred of Trerose, messuage and land called Bonner, moiety of water corn mill called Stone Hall Mill, in St. Lawrence, Goorid in St. Davids, messuage and land at Solva, and a messuage and land called Half Ploughland in Hubberston with a corn grist mill and brewhouse lately built on it, and a one third of a messuage and land called John Webb's Tenement in Llanstadwell. By 1792 Trerhos had passed to Thomas Morse, given as of Lower House, St. Lawrence. On 28 May 1748 John Allen of Gelliswick, Esq., and Mary his wife gave a lease to David Morse of Trerhos, of the messuage and land called Pen Issa yr Dref in Trerose, for lease of lives, and of Thomas and David Morse the two sons of Joseph Morse of Brimaston Hall, yeoman at £17 p.a.

In the 18th century the Lloyds lived here and were succeeded by the Vaughans and the Edwardes family of Sealyham (q.v.) The last mentioned let Trerhos to James Harries as recorded in 1834 and another James Harries was still the tenant in 1904.

TRERICKERT. *Nevern.*

'Ricardston (*sic*) being of late the mansion house of the Bowens of that place was, as I finde in auncient wryttinges called Hoodes town of the Hoodes the first owner thereof, for this was the auncient inherytaunce of Lucas de Hoda ... (who) having lost Bury and other landes were forced to take this Ricardston and Jordenson, being a village next adjoyninge, for his mansion place; which Lucas de Hoda had yssue ii sonnes Ricard and Jorden, who, partinge their father's patrimonie betweene them called each part after their owne names: Ricard de Hoda callinge his parte Ricardston and Jorden Jordenston, which names contynue to this day. Ricardston contynued in the name of Hoode untyl it descended unto one Perkyn Hoode, the particulare descendes I cannot lay downe, thie Perkyn had yssue Llewellyn, father to Griffith ... (his) one daughter maried a gentleman of Cardigan sheere called David ap Owen ap Meredidd of Corrws in Iskoed whose daughter and coheire Dythgy maryed Matheas ap Bowen third brother to Sir James Bowen of Pentre Ievan, Knight, whose sonne Owen ap Mathias ap Owen was father to Morgan, father to Rees whose yssue being extinct the inheritance fell to his iii sisters: Agnes wieffe to John Owen Phillips Esquier; Alison wieffe to William Owen; Margaret wieffe to John Phillips, younger ... between which sisters and their heires at this instant there is no small trouble for the quartering of this house and demeisne, and great sommes of money allreadie spent ...' (G. Owen, *Second Book,* p. 272). Rees Morgan died in 1577 leaving Elizabeth his daughter and sole heiress '... after whose decease the whole inheritance of the above named Rees Morgan her father was enjoyed by John ap Owen .... uncle to the foresaid Rees by force of some fraudulent estate, which inheritance, after great expenses in law, was recovered by the sisters of the said Rees, being his next heirs whose issue enjoy most part of the said inheritance' (Proth. IV GWG fo. 105). Elizabeth Owen died in 1587; in John Owen's Vairdre Book, 1684, he says: 'Rees Bowen of Richardston, gent., died ye 3rd of October 19 Elizabeth 1577. Elizabeth sole child and heiress of said Rees (Bowen) was but a month old at her father's death, and died a virgin, (ye greatest fortune in her time in ye whole county of Pembrock being ye valued to be worth five thousand pounds) 15th December 1587, whereby her said Aunts, ye sisters of ye said Rees Bowen came to be heirs to her ample and large possessions, and the said John Owen in ye right of his mother was entitled to six tenements in Meliney parish, four in Nevarn, two in Bayvil, two in Eglosserow, two in Monachcloddy, five in Llanfyrnach, five in Penrith parish, three in Clydey, two tenements and a burgage in St. Dogmells, two in Llanychlloiddog, and one in Manclohogg, ye lordship of Monington, wich in all amounts to 36 tenements in Kemes over ye above 14 burgages and two closes in Cardigan, Tregibby and Haledare in Verwich and Penyralt in Langoedmore, being 19 more'.

In 1589 Henry Stidman is shown as of Richardstowne, near Newport, gent., in the Plea Rolls, and in the 1786 Land Tax list, Mrs. Hay is owner with David Harry tenant assessed at ½. In 1840 Anne Evans was owner.

TRESISSYLLT. *Granston.*

Home of the Griffith and Harries (*Vide* Tregwynt) families. Its original name was Tresissyllt ap Cynrig and was a Knight's Fee in 1326. In the Black Book of St. Davids 1326 it is detailed: 'Ievan ap Moylmoroa, Orweyn ap Morice and their co-tenants hold two carucates at Trefseysilk an episicopal manor of Villa Grandi: note that the Lord bought at Trefseyssell a certain liberty called 'Hauancia' that is from 6½ bovates formerly of Mawr ap Ithel, from which was a customary rent to be paid to the Lord at Pentecost of a 1d and one needle. Llewelin ap Kedivor and his co-tenants hold at Trefseysil one carucate, and pay yearly at Michaelmas 4½d and 1lb of wax and do services'.

In 1578 William Griffith of Tresissyllt married Anne, daughter of John Scourfield of Moat and had issue: John, James and David. In the following century members of the Phillips, Lewis and Scourfield families had interests in the property. John Harries was assessed for tax on Tresissyllt in 1786. The family still owned it in 1839 but it was let to Samuel Thomas who had inherited the lease from his father, farmer John Thomas who died in 1813. In his will, proved at Carmarthen 28 February 1814 and sworn under £1000, he leaves: 'To my eldest son James Thomas, my lease of Tregydd, and stock on it. To my eldest daughter, Pheby Thomas, now living with said James Thomas, £200, maintenance and choice of best bed at Tregydd, furniture, blankets, etc., and a horse. To my wife Lettice and my son Samuel Thomas, joint exors, all

stock etc., at Tresissillt and mill under the late George Harries of Priskilly, Esq., dated 12 November 1803, being a lease for lives of John Thomas, Samuel Thomas, and Mary Thomas: and another lease of tithes of Tresissillt from George Harries of Tregwynt, Esq., for three lives. To my son James Thomas £400, choice of best horse, and maintenance at Tresissillt. To my eldest daughter Pheby Thomas £50 from Tresissillt. To my daughter Mary Thomas £300, a horse, chest, blankets etc., and maintenance, a horse and saddle, while she is unmarried at Tresissillt, and also my part of the good sloop 'Endeavour'.'

In 1862 the Revd. Henry Davies is described as 'of Tresissillt' He was married to Samuel Thomas's sister Mary, Samuel having died unmarried and intestate. In the will of Revd. Henry Davies, he left his personalty to his wife Mary Davies. To trustees of Harmony Baptist Chapel, Ll'wnda, £400, the yearly interest to go to the ministry of that chapel of £300 and the interest of the remaining £100 towards carrying on a day school in connection with that chapel. To treasurers of Baptist college at Llangollen in North Wales, and to Treasurer of Baptist College, Delhi, India, £100 apiece. To trustees of Hill Park Baptist Chapel, Haverfordwest, £50. In 1904 David Harries Bowen was in possession.

TREVACCOON – TREFACCWN.
Llanrhian.

In the second half of the 17th Century the Perkin family lived at Trevaccoon. It was not at that time a large house, for David Perkin (described as 'gentleman') was assessed at only two hearths in 1670. His wife, Elizabeth, was the daughter of David Harries of Porthiddyfawr by Grace Jones of Brawdy, by whom he had six children. His will was proved on 26th July 1694. John, his only son, succeeded to Trevaccoon. In 1695 he married Mary, eldest daughter of George Williams of Treyarched by whom he had an only child, Dorothy Perkin. How Trevaccoon passed to the next owners, the Hardings, is not known, but it is possible that Dorothy Perkin, the heiress, married Richard Harding, who was living at Trevaccoon before 1728. Richard had an only daughter called Grace who married in May 1730, the Revd. William Propert, son of David Propert of Trevigan. Grace inherited the property, bringing it to the Properts. William and Grace had a son and daughter. The son, Richard, died in his father's lifetime in 1762 without issue. The daughter, Elizabeth, inherited. She had married in 1756 John Harries of Cryglas. The Harries family remained at Trevaccoon until it was sold sometime during the 20th century. The late Mr. Francis Green, whose mother was a Harries told Major Jones of a tradition that one of the Hardings had ploughed up a 'rich treasure' in a field on Porthiddy land afterwards known as 'Parc Harding'. What the nature of this treasure was and what became of it is not mentioned. The house was enlarged by the Harrieses. Major Jones has left a handwritten list of repairs required to Trevaccoon mansion and its outbuildings.

TREWALLTER LWYD. *Mathry*.

In 1654 John Williams obtained a mortgage on this property of £25 which was not redeemed until 1675. In 1703 Lewis Mathias gent., leased Trewallter Lwyd to George Williams for 99 years at £5 p.a. and two couple of pullets at Shrovetide.

On 1 March 1727 James Williams of Treyarched, gent., granted a lease of Richard Reed of parish of Mathry, carpenter of Walterston, otherwise Trewallter, (now in possession of Samuel Williams, leaseholder) for 21 years at £10 p.a. and eight hens at Candlemas. On 3rd May, 1751 Francis Skyrme of Llawhaden, Esq., released to Bridget James of parish of St. Edrins, spinster for £125, Trewallter Llwyd in the parish Mathry, (late in tenancy of James Williams, gent.,) in as large a manner as the same was purchased from Lewis Mathais late of Ll'gwarran by James Skyrme deceased, father of the said Francis Skyrme. Bridget James married William Higgon of Spittle, and in 1759 they sold Bridget's share in Trewallter Llwyd.

In 1787 Lord Kensington leased a house and garden and ten pieces, (two acres, two stangs, 20 yards) of Trewallter Llwyd to Dorothy Williams of Treyerched, widow for 21 years at 20/- p.a. rent. In the late 19th century this house was the home of Thomas Charles, father of Joseph John Charles who was father of Ethel Charles, wife of Major Francis Jones.

TREWALLTERWEN. *St. Edrens*.

Home of the families of Meyler, Skeel and James. A grant of land is recorded in 1406 by William and Isabella Russell and Major Jones refers the reader to 'my essay *A Tale of Three Homesteads*' ... John Meyler had this property in 1593. He married a Scourfield and had five children. In the 18th century the estate belonged to the James family. James James had been ailing and infirm and hardly able to walk. However, he insisted on going to see his reapers in the fields. On September 15th 1789 he set out as usual but was later found dead in a field. At the inquest the verdict was that he had died of his infirmities by visitation of God. The last of the line, James James J.P. (1791-1838) sold Trewallterwen to George Parry of Haverfordwest in 1815. James married Anna Louisa Maria, daughter of John Philipps Laugharne by whom he had an only child Anna Maria Cordelia, married to John Entwisle Peel of Haverfordwest. The estate was sold in 1831 and afterwards the Benyon family owned it. There is a local tradition that a cairn once stood in Park Cerrig Llwydion on Trewallterwen farm near to the Clunffwan stone. The old house was taken down. There was a wall where, it was said, treasure was concealed and at night some heard strange knocking sounds. Some tenants are supposed to have found money from time to time.

TREWARREN. *St. Dogmaels*.

Home of the Warren-Davis family and built towards the middle of the 19th century. The Davis family formerly lived at Mullock. Gilbert Warren-Davis built the present house in the early 1840s. He married Margaret Biddulph and had two sons and six daughters, one of whom, Margaret Alice, kept diaries.

His elder son Henry Warren-Davis of Tre-warren married Christabel Rolson and died in 1924. His widow died in 1940 and the estate was sold. In 1977 the owner-occupier is recorded as David Llewellin.

TREWELLWELL. *St. Davids.*

Home of the yeoman family of Mortimer in the 18th and early 19th centuries, being then a farmhouse. Thomas Colby is listed as owner in 1786 with David Mortimer as tenant. Thomas Mortimer acquired the freehold in 1835. The last of the family, Thomas Mortimer, had an only daughter, Eleanor, who married the Revd. Thomas William Jones, Vicar of Llanybri and his son the Revd. Mortimer Lloyd Jones (b.1828) was a graduate of Corpus Christi, Cambridge. The estate was sold but Mr. Lloyd Jones bought it back in 1875 and assumed the name of Mortimer. The place was again sold at the end of the 19th century and bought by Colonel Howell who built the present mansion, incorporating the old farm into the rear of the premises. Trewellwell was advertised for sale in 1931 by Captain John Hamilton Howell. It had eight bedrooms on the first floor and farm outbuildings. In the early 1970s the remaining part of the original farm, built in 1776 and incorporated by Colonel Howell into his new house, was replaced by a modern extension.

TREWERN. *Nevern.*

Situated in a small valley under the shadow of Carnedd Meibon Owen.

Home of the Warren family descended from Gwaring ap Dafyddfell. 'Trewern, the mansion hosue of William Warren Esquier … called in auncient wrythynges Trewern-waylod. It is the auncient inheritaunce of the said William Warren for diverse hundred yeares past, how auncient it is not well knowne …' (G. Owen, *Second Book.* p. 275) … Major Jones first mentions a reference to Trewern in 1344, 'Thomas son and heir of William Picton of Newburgh granted land within the precincts of the burgages of Fiscard, called 'Tyr Roys', for two years, to William Warin ap David Voil (*Pro Avc Deeds,* iii, E210. D1233).

In 1430 Haverfordwest Corporation Deeds show 'Joan formerly wife of Lewis Wareyn of Traverne, widow'. In the mid 1550s William Jones of Brawdy married Mary Warren, daughter of William Warren, of Trewern. In 1614 Dafydd Emlyn wrote an Ode on the wedding of Thomas Warin of Trewern and Elizabeth daughter of Thomas Lloyd of Cwmglôyn; and Gwffydd Hafren also wrote an Ode in praise of Thomas Warin of Trewern. The following Warrens served as High Sheriffs: Thomas Warren 1639; William Warren 1674; John Warren 1712, and William Warren 1740. The south transept in Nevern Church is known as the Warren Chapel.

Fenton wrote: 'The line ended in four co-heiresses, the present Dowager Lady Kensington (Elizabeth, daughter of William Warren. She died in 1801 aged 90 – Ed.), the late Lady Keith who died in Switzerland, and Mrs. Jones of Llanina, Cardiganshire. Trewern fell to the share of the latter, and is now the property of Edward Warren Jones Esq.' (Fenton's *Tour,* p. 308).

This Edward Warren Jones left the Llanina and Trewern estates to his friend Captain Longcroft, R.N., whose daughter, a ward of E. W. Jones and heiress brought them to her husband, Thomas Lloyd of Coedmore. The lands were willed to Peter Walter Warren Lloyd in his infancy, by Elizabeth Mary Lloyd (who died aged 94) on her death bed in 1947. Peter Walter Warren Lloyd is a collateral descendant of the Warrens of Trewern, and he later sold the Trewern estate to his sister, Susan Watkins (née Warren Lloyd), and her husband Stephen Watkins, JP, now living at Trewern (1996).

The present house dates from the Tudor period c.1578, and for generations has been a farmhouse. It is E-plan having a hall and two wings and a central porch. The house is entered through a massive oak door with wrought-iron hinges and bar-holes. This leads to a large room once used as a kitchen, but from its size and panelled ceiling it was probably one of the principal apartments. This opens into a hall from which a broad oak staircase leads to the oak-panelled bedrooms on the first floor.

In 1670 it was assessed for five hearths. A small building near the house is said to have been a cockpit and the late Mr. Francis Green told Major Jones that the tenant had told him that in this building 'the Warrens kept their vermin'.

In the Voters' List of 1834 it is recorded that the house was let to a parson, the Revd. David George who farmed Trewern then 200 acres, for thirty one years (at £50 p.a.). He was an enthusiastic liberal and addressed numerous meetings to further that cause, and consequently his landlord gave him notice to leave. He moved to the nearby farm of Brithdir Mawr (q.v.), where he was living in 1872-74 when he served two years as Mayor of Newport. He was an eminent local figure who helped and counselled all folk in the locality. He died on 15 May, 1892, aged 82. One morning, during his tenancy, after a bad storm, some damage was discovered to a chimney-stack. When a mason was sent to investigate and do repairs he had to climb up the kitchen chimney but lost his way and ended up in a secret chamber above the porch which was filled with treasure – silver plate and valuables probably hidden there at the time of the Reformation and forgotten. It is said that the parson and the workman made a pact and from time to time the parson would take a piece up to London, sell it and divide the proceeds with the mason. The story is told in more detail in Herbert M. Vaughan's *The South Wales Squires*.

TREWENT HALL. *Trewent Point.*
Home of the Hall family in the 16th and 17th centuries. Their arms were: *argent a fesse between three griffons' heads erased or*. In 1551 John Hall, alias Howell of Trewent, gent., was summoned to answer Sir John Wogan. An heiress brought it to the Owen family and Sir Hugh Owen was owner in 1786. The Cradock family had connexions here (*Vide* George Owen's list of Pembrokeshire gentry).

TREWRACH. *Fishguard.*
This is near the coast about half a mile north of the village of Dinas. Records go back to the 14th century when Griffith ap Ievan ap Llewellyn ap Eynon is described as being 'of Trefwrach'. In 1348 Walter Deyer of Dynas and Margaret uxor ... lands in Trefwrach and Cylgenawan in Lordship of Fishgard. Major Jones lists various names associated with the lands. A Mrs. James was owner in 1786 and John Ritharch owned the freehold house and lands of Trewarch in 1834. James Rees James was owner in 1904.

TREWILYM. *Eglwyswrw.*
Home of the Cantington family variously spelt as Cantrington, Cantinton, Cainton and Canton. The house is on a slope of the east side of Nant Duad. The family descended from Sir William Cantrington, Lord of Eglwyswrw who died in 1227/8. His son, William, lived at Trewilym 'which by scite and ruines yet to be seene seemeth to have been inhabited with divers dwellings'. Griffith Cantrington sold the Lordship of Eglwyswrw to Robert Martin but his line continued at Trewilym Issa and ended in an heiress, Elizabeth. She married Rees David Howell who died at his wife's home in 1538. His grandson, father of G.W. Griffith the genealogist, sold Trewilym to George Owen of Henllys. The arms of the Cantringtons were: *gules an eagle displayed argent armed or, a chief chequy gules and vert*. In 1834 the estate was mentioned in the will of the then owner, the Revd. David Griffith who left everything for the benefit of his children.

TREYARCHED. *Llanrhian.*
Home of the Williams family from 1518 to about 1900. George Williams was owner in 1769. In 1796 the old hall was taken down and partly rebuilt. In the following year a garden hedge was laid and in the next year a kitchen was built. A garden wall was made in 1802. These facts come from an account of his early life written by John Williams of Treyarched (1770-1847). The last Williams owner, Dr. P. M. G. Williams, died at Newport, Pembrokeshire in 1910.

TY GWYN. *Bridell.*

One chronicler wrote of the area that '... the only gentlemen's seats are Tygwyn and Plas-y-Bridell. James Bowen was owner in 1786 and during the last quarter of the 19th century it was the home of William Bowen, J.P., D.L., barrister-at-law and Patron of the Living of Llanfair Nantgwyn. He also succeeded to the estates, through his mother, daughter of William Morgan Williams. J. W. Bowen was still in possession in 1904. The house was described in sale particulars in that year as '... large and commodious and of residential character' in its own grounds, planted with ornamental trees and surrounded 'by park-like fields'. Estate agents' jargon does not change much.

UNDERDOWN. *Near Pembroke.*

In the 16th century this was home of the Voyle family. In 1788 Captain Charles Tyler, R.N. lived here with his wife Margaret, daughter of Abraham Leach of Pembroke with their large family. He ended up being Admiral Sir Charles Tyler of Cotterell, Glamorganshire, and died in 1835. Colonel Owen Lowless was living here in 1977 but sold it in the following year to Mr. James Barrett who turned it into a private hotel.

UPTON CASTLE. *Upton.*

Home of the Malefant and Bowen families. A description in 1810 said: 'The castellated mansion here, which is now in ruins, was the ancient residence of the Malyfants'. From the Malyfants, the estate passed by descent through the female line to the Bowens, originally of Cwrt Bryn y Beirdd, Carmarthenshire, of the same family as Sir Rhys ap Thomas, K.G.

Morris Bowen, in his will of 1706, left Upton to his 'Welsh uncle', John Bowen of Benton, and after the last male in the main line, Morris Bowen, died in 1758, the estate was partitioned between his four daughters:

Mrs. Mary Skyrme of Pembroke; Mrs. Anne McCormick of Truro; Mrs. Martha Tayleur of Buntingsdale, Shropshire, and Miss Lettice Bowen. The house and its lands were eventually bought by a Captain John Tasker, formerly of Bombay. On Tasker's death in 1800 at the age of only 58, the Castle passed to his niece, Maria, married to the Revd. William Evans. The last of this line was Vice-Admiral Richard Evans J.P., who died in 1927. The property was then sold to a Mr. Stanley Neale, of Cardiff whose widow lived there until her death in 1973. The earliest illustration of Upton Castle dates from 1800 but since then many changes have been made. By 1835 the remains of the old Castle had been incorporated in the present building. These consist of the entrance gateway and the two circular towers by which it was defended. One of these now forms a projecting window. High Sheriffs from Upton Castle include Rees Bowen (1564); Hugh Bowen (1698); Morris Bowen (1746) and John Tasker (1798). Sketches and further details are in the Pembrokeshire section of the Royal Commission on Ancient Monuments in Wales and Monmouthshire (pp. 401 *et seq.*).

VAYNOR. (*Great*) *Llawhaden.*

Major Jones visited this house in 1972. He describes it as a 'Long single pile house with a doorway with stone Corinthian columns in the wall. In the centre of a broken pediment are the arms of Skyrme: *a chevron between three escallop shells impaling a lion rampant* – about 1650-1700. The crest missing'. Over the back door is a stone inscribed 'W.S. 1707', doubtless for William Skyrme.

Thomas Skyrme was High Sheriff in 1769. Records go back to 1365. In 1586 Evan Phillip Gwrwared, yeoman, was in possession. His wife Margaret was the 'reputed daughter of Sir John Morgan, Knight'. In 1612 these two sold certain lands in 'Vaynor Llawhadden' to Thomas Cannon Esq. After the death of William Skyrme in 1787 the mansion house and lands of Vaynor were put up for sale.

The sale particulars state that the tenant was Mr. Thomas James, who 'had a lease for life of Thomas James, aged 39, his wife aged 35 and his daughter aged 13 years'; the freehold was offered of 'All that capital Messuage, or dwelling house and lands, with the barns, stables, outhouses, building, gardens, orchards, and watercorn grift mill thereunto adjoining and belonging, called and known by the names of Vaynor and Pontshane Mill. In the 'Remarks' it states ... 'The timber on this farm is worth £1501, the Landlord coventants to keep the roof of the mansion house in repair, and to furnish the tenant with 60 barrels of Culm, yearly or 36s in Lieu. The tenant allowed Timber, growing on the premises for the use of the farm. About fifteen Bishop's acres of Church land, lies intermixed with this land, for which £4.10s.0 is paid to the Bishop of Saint Davids. A valuable Limestone quarry on this lot.'

In the 19th and 20th centuries the Harries family owned Vaynor. There is a pedigree in Major Jones's notes bringing the family up to the 1980s. The house was owned by Mr. Pemberton.

VAYNOR. *Manordeifi.*
Marked as 'Fainor' on Mudge's map 1819. The Lloyds of the Bronwydd family were here for a short time in the 18th century. Marked on Bowen's map 1760 as 'Vaynor Vawr', it is now a farmhouse with no trace of its former status. Vaynor was part of the estate of Brigstocke of Blaenpark, Cards., in 1763.

Thomas Lloyd sold Bronwydd and settled at Vaynor and died there in 1737. He was succeeded by Robinson Lloyd (died December 1742), who had a daughter and heiress Elizabeth who married firstly Thomas Owen second son of James Owen of Glôg, died 1768, and secondly John Ferrier living in 1810. In 1785 John Ferrier and Elizabeth his wife, heir of Robinson Lloyd, are of Cardigan town.

In 1787, Vaynor is shown in the prenuptial settlement of Mary Davies of Penhendrew, and Benjamin Griffiths of Vaynor, Manor-

deifi, settled on him in an Agreement of Feb. 7-8 1787, by David Griffiths his father, of Vaynor, gent.; Rees Griffiths, son and heir of Benjamin Griffiths inherited the tenancy in 1848. In 1972 when Major Jones visited, the owner was Mr. D. Gibbon. He described it as '... a small agreeable residence, and seems to comprise two houses, the older one being in the rear. The newer part was built in the first half of the 19th century, and most of its reception rooms and bedrooms have shallow arched alcoves in them. There is a small hall. The house stands on a slope with a fine southerly view'.

Major Jones's notes on this house are complex.

Percival Lewis

VORLAN. *Vorlan*
(now in Maenclochog parish).
Home of the Vaughans descended from the Pontfaen family. Thomas Vaughan was assessed for three hearths in 1670. Thomas Vaughan, the last of the line at Vorlan, made a will in 1711. He left three daughters and co-heiresses: Mary, married to Roger Lewis, Elinor married to Richard Lewis, and Lettice married to John Thomas of Cilciffeth. They all had issue. In 1786 Vorland belonged to Lord Milford. This was Lord Milford of the first creation. He was Sir Richard Phillips, 7th Baronet, who was an MP and raised to the peerage in 1766. He died childless and the peerage became extinct.

On Colby's Map 1831 are Forland Moat and Forlan fach; just east of Moat mansion, and Forlan and Castell Forlan, a promontory earthwork, south of Maenclochog hamlet. In the 1894 Voters' List Elias Jenkins and Catherine Jenkins are listed as tenants of Vorlan Farm, and in 1904, G. Jenkins has the house and land.

Herbert Vaughan
of Llangoedmore

WALWYNSCASTLE. *Walwynscastle.*

Home of the Holland and Laugharne families. The Holland family go back to Hugh Holland (d.1584). He married in 1543 Jane, daughter of Hugh Conway. Their son Robert was Rector of Prendergast and author of *The Holy Historie.* His son Nicholas, living in 1635 was 'of Walwynscastle'. His son, another Nicholas Holland was an attorney in Haverfordwest and died at a great age in 1718. John Laugharne was assessed for four hearths in 1670. The notes are rather patchy and do not tell us very much.

WATERWINCH. *Tenby.*

This villa is sited in a deep dell near the coast just north of Tenby. In the mid-19th century the house belonged to the Norris family, C. Norris Esq., being in occupation in 1852. In 1921 Waterwinch was the country seat of Sir Edward Ridsdale, G.B.E. (b.1864) who was M.P. for Brighton (1906-1910) and Vice-Chairman of the Council of the British Red Cross Society. A Mr. Griffiths was in occupation in 1980 and he and his wife took in bed and breakfast visitors. They later sold the house.

WAUNBARRY. *Mathry.*

Records date back to 1342 but in the 17th century the family which lived there was called John but in 1786 it belonged to the Scourfields. This family had connexions with Waunbarry also going back to the 17th century. In 1622 William Scourfield of New Moat owned 30 acres there.

WAUNGRON. *Lampeter Velfrey.*

Home of the Philipps and Northey families. There are two houses, the mansion and Waugron Isaf which is a farm. Francis Philipps Esq., who died in 1682, was described as 'of both the Waungrons'. His daughter Mary married Hugh Jones who died young in 1719 aged under 30. His widow lived on until 1757 dying at the age of 78. The couple's two children, Francis and his sister Elizabeth raised a monument to their parents and grandparents in 1759. Mr. Jones and a Miss Hancorne (a relation of the Philippses) were owners. In 1876 Thomas Rees Oliver Powell died at Waungron. He was a barrister and Deputy Judge of the County Court but in the 1890s the property belonged to Major Augustus J. W. Northey of the 41st Regiment and of Eaton Square, S.W.1. He was son of Col. Lewis Augustus Northey and grandson of Sir William Paxton of Middleton Hall, Carmarthenshire. The arms of Northey are: *argent a pansy or between 2 lilies argent.* In a catalogue of 1918 when the estate was put up for sale the house is described as being within half a mile of the town of Whitland. There were eight bedrooms and dresssing rooms, four reception rooms and numerous 'offices'. The farm was also included in the sale. The main house probably dates from 1840-1850.

WEDLOCK. *Gumfreston.*

Home of the family of Wedlock, also spelt Widlock or Wedlake. In 1359 John Widelock was a juror at Tenby and in 1362 he held two messuages in Gumfreston and Widelock worth 10 marks, held of John de Carew. The family were described as 'Lords of Gumfreston'. The arms of Wedlock were: *sable a chevron between three lions sejant argent.* The Williams family of Porthcawl owned Wedlock in the 17th century, and the Meyricks in 1786. Thomas Williams owned it in 1904. Wedlock is now a farmhouse.

WELSH HOOK. *St. Dogwells.*
Home of the Wogan family originally, and now a farmhouse. Records go back to 1140 when it was owned by the de Kemeys family who were still owners in 1535. The next proprietor was William Jones who had it in 1575 and sold to the Cornock family but in 1619 it belonged to the Wogans of Stone Hall. It was described as a manor in 1758 and again in 1770 when it was united with other manors and the property of the Barlows. It changed hands again several times to *inter alia* the Tuckers and the Georges. Major Jones refers to his 'The Squires of Stone Hall' in NLW Journal 1987. In the early 1970s Welsh Hook was extensively modernised internally by the owner Mr. J. S. Roberts, of Newton West.

WELSTON. *Carew.*
Home of the Cuny family. The present house stands on the site of an earlier house of the same name occupied by a member of the Cuny family in the middle of the 17th century. It was pulled down early in the 19th century. When Cromwell was besieging Pembroke he made Welston his HQ. According to Fenton '... there is a quilted counterpane of white linen that covered Cromwell's bed still in the possession of a lady, a descendant of that house, stained with ink spilled as he was writing one of his despatches during his confinement'. The 'confinement' refers to the tyrant's attack of gout which obliged him to stay in bed for a few days. In the will of Richard Cuny of Pembroke dated 24th October 1627 he mentioned four of his farms which he left to his son Walter Cuny including 'Welshtowne' (Welston). Walter was still in possession in 1638, and it was in Walter's time that Cromwell commandeered the house. Walter was Mayor of Pembroke

when he died. His daughter married Francis Parry to whom there is a marble tablet in St. Mary's Church, Pembroke (*Vide* Thomas Roscoe's *Wanderings and Excursions in South Wales*, 1836, p. 154). By the 18th century the Cunys had moved to Golden near Pembroke. In 1834 the property, described as 'a substantial modern house' was the seat of George Donne (or Dunn) Esq. The Dunns still had it in 1873 but in 1904 John Evans was owner of the freehold. Major Jones's notes include a pedigree of the Cuny family.

WENALLT. *Nevern.*
Home of the Warren, Jones and Knolles families. This property is south-east of Ponty-Baldan in the valley of the Nyfer not far from the confluence with the Duad. Anthony Warren, was the third son of William Warren of Trewern by his wife Janet, daughter of Sir Rhys ap Thomas. Anthony lived at Wenallt and married Katherine Bowen of Trerickart by whom he had a son John Warren of Wenallt who 'fledd out of the countery and died sans issue'. No dates are given in the notes. Thomas Jones of Wenallt was High Sheriff in 1680. His daughter Lettice married Thomas Jones. Fenton wrote: '... I come to the ruined house of Wenallt, formerly of great respectability, in the possession of the several families of Johnes, Knowles and Bowen, though after it became the property of the last which resided at Upton Castle (q.v.) ... was soon abandoned and the estate, falling among heiresses, was sold and suffered to go into decay'.

WERNDDOFN. *Llanfihangel Penbedw.*
This large estate belonged to the Morgan family in the first half of the 17th century. The last in the male line was Colonel David Morgan who died unmarried and intestate in 1825. Wernddofn passed to his next of kin, two brothers John and Richard Howell of Llanwilio, Carmarthenshire, great-grandsons of Bridgit Morgan of Wernddofn (1689-1763) who had married Richard Howell. Shortly after inheriting, the brothers sold the

estate to Thomas Brightwell, of Norwich (*Vide* Dolpwll). In 1837 John Colby is listed as owner and the estate consisted of 318 acres.

WESTERTON. *Ludchurch.*
In 1600 Owen Elliot of Narberth, who became High Sheriff in 1609, granted a lease to his brother Morgan Elliot and his wife Anne, of his 'great new house lately built by John Elliot Esquire'. This John (d.1586) was the father of Morgan and Owen and had himself been High Sheriff in 1585 and the house, in Ludchurch parish, was called Westerton and was accompanied by four decayed messuages adjoining as well as other properties in the same parish. Morgan was educated at Oxford and died in 1628 without surviving issue when Westerton reverted to the grantor. By 1786 the property belonged to Lord Kensington and in 1839 the Hon. William Edwardes was the owner. He later became the 4th Lord Kensington and was Lord Lieutenant of the county, M.P. for Haverfordwest and Comptroller to the Household of Queen Victoria. In July 1974 Major Jones visited the house at the invitation of the then owner, Mr. Lawrence, who had put the estate on the market for £100,000.

WESTFIELD. *Rosemarket.*
Home of the Davies and Bowen families. William Davies (the name is sometimes rendered as 'Davids') was assessed for three hearths in 1670. In the Pembrokeshire Plea Rolls he is described as 'gent'. William Davies made an inventory of his house in 1728 listing 14 rooms, all identifiable today. His goods were valued at £142.17.0d including an old Norwegian boat. He made his will in the same year. He cut his elder sons off with the proverbial shilling '... to my eldest son John who had married a woman of ill fame and character – 1/-' and also 'to my idle and extravagant son William – 1/-'. He left the bulk of his estate to another son Charles and a lesser share to his next son Thomas who went into the Church. At least he had two out of four who were not duds. One of Charles's

descendants, William Davies, was the freeholder in 1904.

WHITECHURCH. *Whitechuch-in-Cemaes.*
Fenton wrote: 'In a wood almost opposite to the church is a respectable mansion called by the name of the parish where, perhaps, the original founder may have resided, ancestor of the present proprietor, an offset of the prolific stock of Gwynfardd to whom all the gentry of this district, forming a perfect clan, trace their lineage. This parish has even had the reputation of being free from adders ...' This was probably the home of Nicholas Morgan, assessed for three hearths in 1670. James Bowen was the owner-occupier in 1786. In 1839 the Misses Margaret, Elizabeth, Frances and Joyce Bowen were the owner-occupiers with 219 acres. The last of them died in 1856. After that a clergyman, the Revd. Evan Thomas lived in the house. Major Jones visited Whitechurch in 1974 and again in 1986. He describes it in his notes as '... a large gentry residence with a walled garden and nicely laid-out grounds still well cared for. Now the home of a farmer, Mr. J. B. Vaughan Thomas.'

WHITEWELL. *Penally.*
A ruined house, described by Fenton as 'above the rank of such as farmers might have been supposed to inhabit'. These remains, according to an account written in 1922 'must have been an important house at one time. They are situated within the bounds of Whitehall Farm, about 1½ miles west of Penally village. It was L-shaped, having a hall and a wing. The hall had a fireplace at the south end and it stood over a vaulted undercroft. The east wall has disappeared. The wing, apparently of two storeys, was also built over a vaulted cellar; it retains several ruined lancets and remains of fireplaces. The walls are heavily clothed with ivy and the interior is choked with undergrowth. The ruins of an outbuilding adjacent to the main structure comprise a gable pierced by a single lancet with a range of pigeon holes above.'

Anc. Mon. Pem., p. 291. In 1786 one Madam Barlow was owner with William Powell as her tenant.

WILLIAMSTON. *Burton.*

Home of the Bowen and Scourfield families. Fenton described it as an 'old baronial residence' and it was certainly at one time an Elizabethan manor house. He goes on 'Williamston, where for many years a family of the name of Bowen, an offset from the family tree at Upton, flourished, but which is now the residence of the Revd. Dr. John Philipps. This house I conceive to have sprung up in consequence of Benton Castle being abandoned as a habitation from the thorough change in the state of the country and the modes of life. The land at its back, between it and the haven, was in Queen Elizabeth's time noted as a park having deer, an addition it still retains, together with a very parkish appearance'. There are, in fact, two houses joined together.

John Bowen was assessed at four hearths in 1670 and William Bowen was High Sheriff in 1761. Other owners who served in this office were John Henry Philipps (1833) and Sir Owen Scourfield (1881). Colonel Owen Philipps of Williamston (Pembrokeshire Militia) inherited Williamston through his wife Janet, daughter of Thomas Bowen. He married Anne Elizabeth daughter of Henry Scourfield of Moat. Their son, John (b.1808), assumed the name of Scourfield and inherited the property. He was created a baronet by Disraeli in 1876 and married Augusta Lort Phillips of Lawrenny Park. A prominent Tory politician he in later life became a recluse who imagined himself to be a pauper. His son, Sir Owen, 2nd Baronet died without issue and the title became extinct. Sir Owen, by all accounts, was also something of an eccentric. He was over generous to the poor and whenever he visited Haverfordwest handed out coins galore to the populace. He had a passion for steam trains. A few years ago this handsome mansion was bought by Mr. Richard Fairclough, a trained nurse and psychologist. He converted the house into a nursing home and provided a high quality life to the chronically sick. In 1989 the property, with its park now reduced to but 4½ acres was for sale as a going concern.

WISTON. *Wiston.*

Home of the Wogan family. The first proven Wogan at Wiston was Walter who owned a moeity of two fees there in 1324 but it is possible that others of his family preceded him there. Therefore 21 generations of the family owned the Wiston estate until it failed in the male line in 1793 and in the following year the estate was sold. It had been owned by the Wogans for some 570 years without a break and members of the family served as High Sheriffs for Pembrokeshire and Cardiganshire 11 times from 1543 to 1745. Poems of praise were written to Sir John Wogan of Wiston, (d.1483) by Rhys Nanmor; a poem to Sir John Wogan (d.1557) by Lewis Morganog; and other poems were written by Rhisiart Torwerth and Lewis Morganwg amongst others.

Fenton (1810) described the house as 'a large and awkward pile'. He goes on to mention a sketch which was made of the old near-by castle by the Buck brothers but it was never published. The castle in Fenton's time had been in ruins for about a century. The house and estate eventually were acquired by Lord Cawdor but even by 1900 little of the old house remained. In that year Francis Green paid a visit and wrote: 'Practically nothing is left of the old mansion of the Wogans at Wiston except for a portion of the old offices which has been incorporated into the modern farmhouse. The tenant, Elizabeth Jones, who was possibly some 60 to 70 years of age, said that her family had occupied the place for three generations.' The following information was given by Mrs. Jones who remembered the old mansion before it was pulled down. 'It had two sitting rooms and part of the kitchen (on the ground floor) of the present farmhouse was formerly the laundry of the old mansion and the wall between the sitting room and the stairs 2 ft. 6 ins. thick.' There is much else given and for this fuller account the *West Wales Historical Records VI,* pp. 229-231, should be consulted.

WITHYBUSH. *Rudbaxton.*

Home of the Martin, Phelps and Owen families. The Sparks family were tradesmen in Haverfordwest from the first half of the 17th century and had bought Withybush in the previous century. The first to live there was Sparks Martin (b.1713) who was High Sheriff in 1750. He left the estate to his sister Elizabeth who had married John Phelps who assumed the name and arms of Martin. The arms of Martin of Withybush were granted in 1788 as: *argent a marten proper collared gules.* The Revd. Thomas Martin 'late of Withybush' died in 1865 aged 82, and the last male member of the family was the Revd. C. M. Phelps (he did not adopt the name of Martin) who died in 1907. Well before his death the estate had been bought by William Owen, four times Mayor of Haverfordwest, who became High Sheriff in 1859. His sons, George Leader Owen and Dr. Henry Owen were also High Sheriffs (in 1894 and 1902 respectively). The Owens played a prominent part in Pembrokeshire affairs on the Bench and in civic realms. Dr. Henry Owen, mentioned above, was a considerable historian and the author of many works including *Old Pembrokeshire Families* and *Gerald the Welshman.* He was the first Treasurer of the National Library of Wales and bequeathed his own library to it. During the last War the house was taken over by the R.A.F. and afterwards left empty and derelict. A photograph taken in 1947 shows Withybush in a parlous state and it was demolished not long afterwards, its present site obliterated by a modern housing estate.

WOLFSDALE. *Camrose.*

Home of the families of Mortimer, Pencaer, Bowen, Reynish and Crowther. 'At Wolfsdale is an old manor house, home of the Bowens'. In 1763 John Bowen and Sarah his mother sold the lordship of Wolfsdale to William Couzins of Sandy Haven. In 1832

the manor was repurchased from the Couzins family by C. W. T. Webb-Bowen, of Camrose. Richard Pencaer was lord of the manor in about 1500 and his daughter Joan married John Warren of Trewern. In 1662 it was conveyed by order of the Court in Chancery from Owen Edwards of Treffarn to John Bowen of Wolfsdale.

In 1217 Llewellyn the Great, campaigning in South Wales, met Bishop Iowerth of St. Davids at Wolfsdale, with the result that Llewellyn agreed to retire, having first extracted hostages from the men of Roose as a pledge of their willingness to accept his rule.' – *W.W.H.R. XI,* 1926, pp. 14-15. In 1620 Morgan ap Owen (Bowen) of Wolfsdale was committed at Haverfordwest Sessions by Sir John Stepney the Mayor and Thomas Cannon for making an assault and an affray on his own father and William Jones with his 'sword drawn in a very outrageous manner'. Other members of this family also appear to have been in trouble one way or another over the years.

The arms of the Pencaers, lords of Wolfsdale in the time of Henry VII were: *Gules on a fess engrailed between three bucks' heads caboshed, as many crescents.*

There were two houses here in 1786, one owned and occupied by John Crowther Reynish, gent., the other owned and occupied by William Bennett, gent. John Bennett (1817-1884), married Lettice, daughter of John Reynish of Wolfsdale and their son, John Crowther Bennett (1842-1882) was described as 'of Wolfsdale'. In 1873 he owned 685 acres.

WOODSTOCK. *Ambleston.*

Woodstock was the home of several important families. The first known owner was Hywel Fychan, descended from Cadifor Fawr of Blaencych which was there *circa* 1300. He left two sons, John Howell of Woodstock and Philip Howell of Lysyfran. John Howell married Jane Joyce of Prendergast, and had two sons, John of Woodstock and Hugh Howell who was knighted and whose son Richard was appointed Constable of Pembroke Castle on 16th February 1390. The said John Howell is named in several early records. On Monday after the Assumpton 1381, David Drew of Wyllyamstoun granted a messuage 'in Wylliamystoun near Tankardystoun in the Lordship of Pebidyauk (Trewilym in Lawrence parish) to John Howell of Wodystok'. His daughter and sole heiress married Stephen Perrott.

The Perrott arms were: *azure a dove volant argent*. The Perrotts were succeeded by a cadet branch of the Philipps family of Picton Castle.

Richard Philipps settled at Woodstock and was living in 1615. Various other families were associated with Woodstock as tenants principally the Williamses who tenanted Woodstock from the Perrotts from 1678 until the mid 1700s. The Land Tax List 1786 shows 'Two tenements called Woodstock, both owned by John Tucker, Esq., one tenanted by John Williams, the other by Francis Llewelyn, assessed at 18s and £1.4s.0d respectively, and a third called Woodstock, James Phillipps, Esq., owner, James Morgan occupier assessed at £2. 2s 0d' in the same list.

In 1904 Land Tax, Benjamin David Thomas was shown as of Woodstock, Hugh F. Evans of Woodstock East, Thomas H. Phillips of Woodstock House and land joint, Thomas Price of Woodstock house and land. *Colby's Map* 1831 shows, Woodstock, Upper Woodstock, Woodstock Slop, and Woodstock Mill. Fenton in *Tour Pembs*. 2nd. edn. 'At Woodstock there was a chapel of ease to Ambleston parish, but has long been down, and even the cemetery has been ploughed over. Since then, a Methodist chapel has been raised there.'

Y NYS BARRY. (BARRY ISLAND).
Llanrhian.

This literally means Barry Island and records go back at least to 1342. It was from this place 'where there always hath been and yet will be wild birds of the sea, gulls, mews and divers other birds' – (part of profits of Archdeaconry of Carmarthen), that the family of the celebrated Giraldus Cambrensis – Gerald of Wales, took their surname (see *Gerald of Wales* translated and edited by Professor Lewis Thorpe – Penguin Classics).

On 16th July 1550, Henry Hoper of Iland, of the parish of Llanrhian gave Jannet verch James David Gove a Bond for payment of £5, in default of which Jannet can enter on lands in Trevoughllwyd and Tyrevellwr gwynt in parish of Llanhowell. In 1662 J. Barlow widow of George Barlow Esq., seised of one third of certain lands in Llanrhian parish, which included 'the island called Ynnys y Barry'. (*Slebech Deeds*, No. 405). In 1784 William Davies, gent was the owner. His seal bore: *a garb erect amongst stubble*. In 1789 he subscribed ten guineas towards the repair of St. David's Cathedral. In 1805 Richard Le Hunte of St. Botolphs gave a lease of 21 years of Ynys y Barry to Francis Fortune of Haverfordwest for £220 rent p.a. On Colby's Map 1831, the whole area of the headland of Porthgain – Abereiddy is called Ynys y Barry, and the farmhouse is called Barry Island, and in 1848 the marriage settlement of William Reynolds of Barry Island, Minister of the Gospel, and Margaret Anne Thomas, settles Barry Island, otherwise Island y Barry (313 acres). In 1882 they made over the property in favour of their son James William Reynolds. In 1989 Ynys Barry became a country house hotel.

FRANCIS JONES (1908-1994)
A BIOGRAPHICAL PROFILE

by H.C.-J.

In 1974 the late Sir Anthony Wagner, KCVO, KCB, D.Litt. (Oxon.), Garter King of Arms, wrote of my father in the Foreword of a book dedicated to him: 'To lead in a special field is a great but no in-ordinately great distinction, but to conquer for oneself from scratch a whole field is rarer. This is what Francis Jones has done for Welsh history and family genealogy. As an old friend may perhaps be permitted to say, how in himself no less than in his work Francis embodies and transmits that singular charm and excellency of the immortal Welsh bardic tradition he so worthily represents'.

Sadly my father did not live to see this, his last book, in print. He believed an historian's duty is to make his findings known to all. So it is now my duty to publish this volume.

Millions of words flowed from his pen but none gave him greater pleasure than these about his beloved home county where our family have lived for over eight hundred years.

This is a literary 'coming home' in a life cycle of unique achievements taking over 70 years of research.

To honour such a father is hard, but I feel this book is incomplete without a pen portrait of the man behind the words and the woman behind that man. I have tried to be dispassionate, but if I err on the side of admiration and affection I hope you will understand. My aim is to give an insight into the man whose words will take you down the ages to the homes and people of bygone Pembrokeshire.

The story began when the Norman Conquest was a nearer memory than the Battle of Waterloo is to us today. For 730 years our family held the Brawdy estate through seventeen generations before it was dispersed. Francis Jones's parents were steeped in family history and genealogy. It was only two generations since an ancestor was High Sheriff in 1773; of the House of Brawdy, only the old drive pillars remain, and sheep graze over the site of the old mansion where William Jones, standard bearer to Henry VIII lived.

Francis Jones was born in 1908 in the windswept village of Trevine perched high above the Celtic Sea on the St. Davids peninsula. The Wicklow hills in Ireland are seen on a clear day outlined by the setting sun. Inland are the sweeping curves of the Preseli hills which gave Stonehenge their bluestone pillars. Bishop Asser came from Trevine to go with his friend King Alfred the Great to found Oxford University.

As soon as he could walk and talk Francis Jones was immersed in family history, of coats of arms, and genealogies handed down orally in the old Welsh tradition. Such tales had also fired his own father, James's, imagination, and this adventurous teenager, my grandfather, emigrated to his uncle's ranch in the Welsh Patagonian colony in the 1880s to make his fortune. Maybe he hoped to return in triumph to reclaim the old Brawdy estate. He became ranch manager and horse breaker, and trekked herds of horses over the Andes to sell them to warring factions. One night he was attacked by a mountain lion, but in killing it with his knife he was badly mauled. He was found by Indians who nursed him back to health. On another expedition his companion died

Riding the Patagonian Pampas.

Tales of Chivalry.

and James got lost trying to round up the horses on his own. He finally staggered home, a skeletal wreck having survived on wild berries and snakes he caught and ate. Later an accident crippled him, and his days of riding the pampas ended. He returned home for a long convalescence, married and scratched a living where he could. He was a natural linguist, and during his twelve year adventure he learned three more languages. During the two world wars he was often called on to act as an interpreter at Fishguard Harbour. His gun belt, a mummified paw of the lion he killed, a book of heraldry from *his* father, and his own essays and poems in Welsh are now heirlooms grouped round my desk as they were at my father's.

Francis Jones was the eldest of four children. He learned to speak Welsh and English when very young. An ability to remember long pedigrees showed a remarkable memory. He displayed intense curiosity at the hearths of relations the family often visited to talk about the old days. He told me that his earliest memories were in his first year, and I believe him still. The family moved to the quaintly named 'Stop and Call' hill-top area of Goodwick, where he went to primary school. When he was about six the family visited Haverfordwest Market. The boy wandered away into St. Mary's church, and in that ancient empty place he was captivated by monuments with gaily painted coats of arms. As he stared up, sunlight streamed through stained glass windows to light up a knight's crested helmet high on the wall. That solitary moment decided his life. Inspiration, revelation, vocation or whatever, from then on he was dedicated to historical studies. It flowered in him till his death some eighty years later.

He started school before roads were tarmacadamed, cars were a rarity, when people read by candles at night, and golden guineas were in circulation; the sun never set on the British Empire, and the Boer War was a fading memory. The approaching holocaust of the Great War did not mute the laughter in school playgrounds then. He effortlessly won a scholarship to Fishguard County School. It was a long walk, with a glorious view over Cardigan Bay up to the hills of Snowdonia, and the unspoilt countryside provided a treasure trove of evidence of its continual occupation from the Stone Age. Cromlechs, castles, druid stone circles, the ports where Vikings and Normans landed, were around as he walked down to school. The next short years would decide many careers in this quiet backwater with its scanty opportunities. The schoolteachers were dedicated and well trained with a deserved status in the small community. They taught large classes of pupils whose families encouraged them to learn. All knew the key to opportunity was education.

Then, as always, one of Wales's biggest exports was its brightest and most adventurous youth. It seems the ABCDE of education was Ambition, Blackboard, Chalk, Discipline and Enthusiasm. Those teachers rarely complained of being under resourced. Their resources were between their ears. Resourcefulness was their watch word. There were prizes for neat handwriting and fastidious presentation inspiring intense competition amongst pupils.

Francis kept a list of his fellow pupils' progress. Many strode out of the isolation of rural Pembrokeshire to become judges, professors, doctors, service officers, and captains of merchant ships. The class system was rigid then, but doors were open to all. The keys were talent and initiative, curiously two qualities that can be nurtured but never taught. These pupils learned long poems by heart, learned their multiplication tables by singing them, and excelled at mental arithmetic. They were always set holiday tasks.

I now have many of my father's notebooks; considering they were compiled by a boy barely in his teens their content range is astonishing. There are poems and essays for Eisteddfods in Welsh; also many maps of Pembrokeshire and the UK meticulously drawn some even depicting the railway network. Masses of pencil and water-colour drawings of castles, historic houses of all types, churches and idyllic rural vignettes. There are cartoons of fellow pupils and masters, little articles and notes on Pembrokeshire families, legends and episodes from history. Snippets from the laws of Hywel Dda jostle with snatches of poetry from Blake, Keats and Shakespeare. There are carefully drawn copies of Egyptian hieroglyphics, the Morse code, maps of star constellations, the Braille alphabet, the Greek alphabet and drawings of the Zodiac signs. There are excerpts in old Greek and Latin, and even navigation tables copied from his seafaring grandfather's charts that he used when rounding the Horn in the days of sail. I was most touched to see the address of the College of Arms and a list of the boys' books on heraldry. There are over a hundred note books, and it is easy to see that they evidently honed his natural gift for memory, which is a family trait.

Being a loner he didn't play in team sports, though he was a good runner and swimmer and enjoyed fishing from the harbour. He longed to catch a giant conger eel, but left no record of

This is the stone commented upon by Mr. G.E. Evans, in a field by Stones. In the background is a little hillock with some stones on its top. This might contain some historical story

The old Tower of Penysgwarne

Research notes when 14 years old.

Francis Jones's parents.

doing so. It was a rare failure in his life. I often think of the lad pushing his way to school through the frequent Pembrokeshire gales. When the storms were spectacularly violent the school would arrange for a horse and cart to get the drenched pupils home.

I see from my father's reports that he was making steady progress at the top of his class. As a teenager he was writing poetry, essays and recording the histories of houses and families. He won prizes in school debates, and recitations in chapel competitions. There was a rich and lively cultural life then, and talent emerged early. A chair he won at an Eisteddfod in 1922 is in my hall today. Other events were plentiful like fairs, open air boxing, pony racing on beaches, and agricultural shows.

Throughout his life my father needed little sleep. I came across a synopsis for a 38-chapter novel, and copies of letters to English publishers sending them his articles. So in addition to his examination work, he was already happily burning the midnight oil. Every day had purpose for him, even holidays. Whenever he could borrow a pony he would visit distant parishes as his interests widened to make further researches. More often than not, he walked great distances, spending nights with relations in cottages and farm houses. He would listen and fill his note books in English and Welsh as he sat on settles in front of open log and culm fires on the stone flagged floors as bards and poets have done round the 'Simne fawr' for centuries. He often left by way of a thank you, a poem usually written in Welsh, many of which are prized today. Evidently he managed his time with the precision of a computer. His fastidiousness showed in his personal neatness, and he loved being well dressed, a trait that stayed with him all his life. I never once saw him unshaven.

His mother took him for his first trip to England. They stayed with a relation who had been a General in the Indian Army, and lived in some state in the Georgian spa town of Bath. It made a huge impression on the boy. So did the advice he was given; if he was to succeed in life outside Wales, he would be wise to flatten his vowels. He attended to this immediately, and with the naturally attractive timbre of his voice, his immaculate diction made him a compelling broadcaster, lecturer and raconteur for the rest of his life.

The short slim youth with the steady blue eyes became a familiar figure calling on local vicars to comb through parish records, to decipher names and dates from long fallen tomb stones. He also consulted the Pembrokeshire parish pump pamphleteers who abounded then as they do now, to track down more information. They were generous in their help and encouragement, as were many of the gentry. Most were not the bucolic lechers as portrayed in 'Tom Jones', in fact they were capable managers, knowing better than most that a fool and his money are soon parted. Many had a tradition of culture, having libraries full of family and estate records. They opened their doors to the young scholar and soon my father was deep into ancient records and books, pioneering through archaic ledgers and copying old manuscripts and deciphering old seals. Lawyers records offices gave him the same challenge, and dusty manuscript would give him a clue to some historical jig saw. He would plan his route; then with a map, note book, apple and sandwich he would tramp off to view some far off ruin, often setting out at dawn.

He ate sparingly all his life. The tools of his profession were just pen and paper, but what a brilliant intellect directed them. He was uniquely self-sufficient in his lonely quest.

The early morning countryside was full of interest for him. His powers of acute observation picking out landmarks, houses, and wildlife as he walked or rode in the valleys along the coast. Patronage then did not have today's spiteful meaning. Francis Jones's charm, good manners, and his enthusiasm endeared him to the vicars, landowners and local historians of those far off days, and he had an instinctive feel of how the establishment worked.

Many of the family went to sea. One of my father's uncles owned a coastal trader plying its wares to Liverpool, Bristol and Cardiff. My father set sail in the summer holidays aboard the 'Ben Rein' as unpaid cabin boy. He loved those voyages particularly the drama of heavy seas. His uncle's first mate (another relation), was a drunk soured by losing his Captain's ticket after being convicted of gun running in the Far East. My father wrote a particularly poignant story about one of his voyages. I long to find more notes about those days at sea when there were so many ships under sail, and when the bodies of poor sailors were often washed up on Pembrokeshire beaches.

Many of my mother's family were seafarers, her brother brought home fine silks from Japan which were made into dresses for the girls to wear to chapel.

Francis easily passed his Higher School Certificate, *cum laude*. It was time for him to make a living. Not having the money to go to University, he made an wise decision. He became a student teacher acting as an apprentice to qualified schoolmasters. After years of practical experience and more examinations he in turn would qualify. He was posted to schools all over Pembroke-shire, St. Nicholas, Haverfordwest, Saundersfoot and Tenby. One of his brightest pupils was a boy who became the actor Kenneth Griffiths. Importantly, the school holidays gave him time for research and writing. Soon he was having so many articles published in local papers that he had to use a range of pen names. De Loy, Some One Else, Audax, Essex Harries, Dewisland, Ygrr and others. It was as well that he did not go to university as there is no substitute for experience, and that he was having in abundance. Many historians encouraged him, particularly Herbert Vaughan, author of *The South Wales Squires*, who became a life long friend.

My father wrote on a wide variety of subjects, so avoiding narrow specialisation, and the petty jealousies that abound in academe. It was a lonely path, as all his published work had to stand public scrutiny by experts. He also knew failure. I found some of his articles with a terse comment, 'Rejected by' ... Evidently these spurred him on to turn obstacles into stepping stones. The deductive powers he applied to his output was such, that within a few years he built up a huge network of fellow scholars all over the UK and world-wide, and many consulted him. I have trunks filled with their letters in the huge archives he left.

In his early twenties he was already an authority on many subjects. He also found time for politics, becoming a speaker for the Primrose League. As a good traditional Tory he attacked a

Mr. David Lloyd George ferociously, and his note books are full of anti-liberal barbs. His flashing ripostes put down many a heckler at the hustings so I have been told.

My father was twenty-three when he married my mother. She was the perfect match for this unusual man. She was tiny, vivacious, brown-eyed, brown-haired, the daughter of the Charles family of Llanrhian, well-to-do farmers. She was educated at the Hill House Lady's College in Haverfordwest, spoke Welsh, wrote well, painted in water-colours, played the piano, and she was an excellent horsewoman. Her parents having died young, she also had practical experience in running the farms they owned.

Ethel Charles of Henllys, Llanrhian.

Ethel Charles was of old Pembrokeshire stock first recorded in 1242 and one of her ancestors, David Didwith, was Rector of Freystrop in 1390. She bought a small but useful dowry to their marriage. Her personality exuded warmth and kindness, and she had a terrific sense of humour, and we learned from her to find fun and laughter in the smallest unexpected things. They had four children in rapid succession, of whom I am the eldest. Mamma ran our home with meticulous thoroughness, and the house was charming and always welcoming. What warm unforgettable memories she left her family! She devoted her life to my father's work and yet gave us an idyllic childhood. My father sensibly, not having the slightest interest in money, left all those matters to her. They went on sketching expeditions, she helped read his proofs, he read his articles to her often acting on her suggestions. Yet she always had time for her children.

After marriage my father's interest in politics waned. Whether my mother being related to Mr. David Lloyd George had anything to do with it I do not know.

In the late 1920s my father discovered all Haverfordwest's old records, including medieval manuscripts rotting away in the Castle gaol cells. He volunteered to rescue and classify them. He started work wearing an old cassock to save his clothes from the dirt and dust. As he was forever rushing to and from his new treasure trove, he needed a key. So for official access he was made a Special Constable, and he founded the present Record Office. It was resolved at a council meeting that he would be paid a small sum for this work. At this an historically challenged councillor banged off a newspaper letter saying what a waste of time and money this was. My father got his induction as an archivist, self taught and off his own bat. He was soon wearing another uniform when, in 1931, he was commissioned into the 4th Welch Regiment to start his third career.

He threw himself into soldiering with the same dynamism he gave to teaching and writing. Drill nights, lectures, weapon courses, week-end camps, summer camps, and more exams. Yet this did not stem his flow of articles which were now being more widely published in learned journals all over the UK as his reputation grew and his researches took him all over Wales and the borders. All my life I saw him writing late into the night. Even if we got up early, there he was, writing at his desk before going to work. Four or five hours sleep a night sufficed him, yet strangely I never saw him doze in the day. The older I get, the cleverer my father gets in my memory. The proverb that 'The hours before daybreak are sent from Paradise', comes to me now as in the early dawn I look out from my home high on the Preseli slopes and see across Fishguard Harbour up to Goodwick where my father's career began.

In 1936 he made a big career move, applying for a post in the National Library in Aberystwyth.

Bath time for officers of the 'Fighting Fourth' Welch Regiment by Fred May.

Applicants needed a university degree, but this he blithely ignored. He travelled up for an interview with an old school friend Bertie Charles (later Dr. B. G. Charles), in an Austin Seven. They were both successful. My father then moved the family up to Cardiganshire. We lived at first in a delightful remote mansion, Plas Broginin, rented from the Pryse estates. A trout stream ran at the bottom of the drive. As we enjoyed breakfasts of freshly caught trout he landed, it seems this had been a factor in our going to live there. He loved the countryside all his life. He cycled to work some ten miles away, and his salary was £150 p.a. His fertile mind explored the new medium called 'The Wireless'. The BBC broadcast his scripts in 1938 and he mastered the microphone as easily as he had the pen. That is to say he would have an original idea, write it, check, double check it, revise, polish, present it, then rehearsal, rehearsal, and more rehearsal. The thoroughness of his early education was paying off, and the advice he got during his visit to Bath. So fortune favours the prepared mind.

My father's teachers taught him that talent is useless without discipline and dedication. These ethics are neatly observed in one of his essays which I found. 'A man with strong discipline,' he wrote, 'will impose a strong discipline on himself. If he is to realise his ambition he realises he will have to do certain things, things that will involve hard work which will often be unpalatable. Yet he will do them because it is essential if he is to advance. He will remain in his study on a fine day when all his instincts urge he should be enjoying himself with friends on a bowling green or in convivial company at a cocktail party. He will write not merely when the spirit moves him, but will buckle down to the task even when he is not in the mood to do so. He will not wait for inspiration, he will work for it. He who works in fits and starts is not likely to receive the laurels.' My father saw life as a race, in which the only thing that interested him was first place.

When I was small he used to take my brother and me out for long walks. I now realise these were mini route marches. Once I collapsed with fatigue. His words of advice echo in my memory. 'Remember,' he said, 'the weak fall out and die.' I got home under my own steam. However, I was grateful for my father's training when I was one of a small band to pass a mountain warfare course in Scotland. It lead my brother to be captain of rugby, boxing and cricket of the British Army teams in Berlin. My brother and I both did two years National Service on active service, and now it occurs to me that Mamma had a total of nine years in her life when her men were away and every telegram that came to her home could have been bad news.

My parents moved to Aberystwyth so that we children could go to school. Our new home was a wonderful choice, its back garden led to gorse covered hills of the open countryside and the sea

Family group.

was only a few hundred yards down the quiet road. They kept up their links with Pembroke-shire, my father having transferred to the Pembroke Yeomanry. Getting back for regimental duties (combined with researching) was easy then by GWR trains or by Crossville buses on uncrowded roads. The Yeomanry of those days continued the tradition of being rather like a county club where land-owners and the professional classes filled the Officers' Mess. Many of their fathers had died in the Great War serving the same regiment, and sometimes there would be three generations of the same family during mess nights, all of whom had served or were in the regiment.

As the balmy days of the thirties unfolded so pleasantly, we went on family outings to picnics in the Cardiganshire hills, on river banks and on beaches. My father taught us to put up tents. He taught my brother and me to draw and to fish for trout, to box, and took us out to sea in a small boat. He and a friend sailed it up to Barmouth which gave my mother some anxiety as they had originally intended to go to Ireland but my mother vetoed that. Although my father's salary was small, he made it up with fees from articles, broadcasts and his army pay.

Hitler's savage blitzkrieg in Poland cut short our family unity. War was declared and a few days later we saw my uniformed father off at Aberystwyth station. The platform was crowded with families saying goodbye to their men. We waved to him through the clouds of steam from the engine as they all went out of sight into the darker fog of war. For the next five years my mother brought up four children on her own.

My father was posted to an experimental regiment of field artillery, every man of whom had a high IQ. After intensive training they took part in an army gunnery competition, winning the Silver Gun trophy by a huge margin. This elite regiment was then dispersed, the men promoted and posted to other regiments to pass on their expertise. My father was promoted to Major. There survives from this time, an article he wrote, 'The History of Cockfighting in Wales' sub-titled, 'written on active service'. Even in the Battle of Britain he found time to write.

Orders for overseas arrived and his regiment boarded troop ships in the Clyde, and the convoy sailed for North Africa. I wonder if they sailed down the West coast to avoid the Channel U-

236

Boats or whether as they rounded the Pembrokeshire peninsula, my father leaned on the ship's rail trying to catch a sight of his home county as they sailed for battle. The ships were crammed with ammunition, high explosive, and motor fuel. Knowing they might be torpedoed any minute cannot have made it a pleasure cruise. Memories of the Ben Rian and mackerel fishing might have passed through his mind. Safely past Gibraltar they steamed for an amphibious landing in North Africa.

They were soon in action, when a daring Panzer attack overran the infantry they supported. The regiment was then embroiled in a muzzle-to-muzzle engagement. It was the Battle of Beja and they beat off the tanks in one of Rommel's last full scale attacks of the desert war. During the melee a shell exploded as he was standing between his signaller and a young officer. When he got up, both companions lay dead. My father told me that during a lull in a battle, a soldier was shouting for his officer, 'Mr. Smythe, where are you, where are you?' The Germans then attacked shouting, 'Meester Smythe vo bist du.' Mr. Smythe and his men then gave them a hot reception which broke up the assault. The scholar had been tried and tested in the carnage of war and had not been found wanting. He also knew the elation of victory in the desert in contrast to being drawn up on ceremonial parades on Tenby sands.

One of my father's keenest and best young officers was a Keith Joseph, later Lord Joseph. With the triumphant end of the Africa campaign, the regiment went to Palestine via Cairo for rest from the ferocity of modern battle to the calm of ancient pyramids and the Sphinx. My father then visited historical sights whenever he could in Jerusalem, Damascus and the places familiar to him by name from his Sunday School days. Unfortunately his writings of that period were later lost in the destruction of war. The regiment then set sail for the Allied landings in Sicily.

25 pdr. guns of F.J.'s regiment in action.
(Imperial War Museum official photograph. Ref. NA581).

Direct hit on German MK.4 tank.
(I.W.M. official photograph. Ref. NA757).

Unloading guns onto Salerno beachhead.
(I.W.M. official photograph. Ref. NA6632).

Aftermath of the Battle of Beja.
(I.W.M. official photograph. Ref. NA1042).

F.J. after Salerno.

My father wrote of his whereabouts despite censorship, in coded letters which he had arranged with my mother. After the Sicilian campaign his regiment was once again on Royal Navy ships for their third landing. This time on the Italian mainland at Salerno. This was viciously contested, with landing craft being blown out of the water. Those who managed to reach the beaches were immediately under close quarter attack. My father being second in command of his regiment, was a forward observation officer. He was in the first wave and made his way through the hurricane of exploding shells, mines and raking machine gun fire.

The Division then laboriously fought the bitter campaign up Italy through tough terrain, foul weather and heavy casualties to Monte Casino. During a lull in 1944, he met Baron de Rutzen, a good friend who had often entertained my father at his home in Picton Castle. They had lunch together, no doubt talking of the far off Pembrokeshire days. The Baron went up to lead his Welsh Guardsmen in an attack. A short time later he was killed.

A happier story about my father is that he was sketching an old building, and the Brigadier, in passing, asked him to hurry up as he was holding up the attack. The battle went on and the building he had sketched was blown to smithereens.

My father was obviously being groomed to take over command of a fighting regiment of his own, when he was unexpectedly posted to the War Office in London as a staff officer. He was to join the Cabinet Office to write the official history of the Sicilian and Italian campaigns. He skipped off to Naples and cadged a lift home in an American plane.

Visiting ancient monuments between battles, 1944.

Francis and Ethel Jones
outside their
South Kensington home.

Post war. In the
Surrey Yeomanry
(QMR).

Lifelong friend from
school days,
F.J. and B. G. Charles.

Although he had his London job, he wanted to return to Pembrokeshire. So he leased Roch Castle, and we moved in and he used it as a base from doodle-bombed London, and while he went job hunting locally. None was suitable so we all moved up to London, where my mother went house hunting and found us a large flat in Queens Gate Place in South Kensington. It was ideal, quiet, but central, in the West End, and Kensington Gardens were only a short walk away. He often walked to the War Office through what he called his four park walk. In the early mornings of course, through Kensington Gardens, Hyde Park, across to St. James's Park via The Green Park. My brother and I had previously been boarders at Haverfordwest Grammar School. He found us public schools in London and I never forget that our education was paid from his army salary, much of it earned on active service in the front line. My brother Dedwydd won a place at Oxford as well as being a star athlete. Of our sisters, Anne won an art scholarship, Elizabeth became a nurse. I had a nice side line: witnessing a brutal smash and grab raid in Hammersmith. I reported it to the *Daily Mail*, and got a fee. After that I would prowl London for news stories, and Hyde Park Corner was a good source for gang fights and violent battles among coster-mongers. I was uninterested in history being more concerned with up-to-date news. If this dis-appointed Daddy he never showed it.

My parents led a very busy social life, visits from Welsh relatives, scholars and professors, and I don't know how my mother coped with all the entertaining and us four children, but she seemed to thrive on it. My father was also back in the Territorial Army in the Surrey Yeomanry. Of course he immediately wrote the regimental history. He poured out a stream of articles, and planned several more books, of which this is one. He had just put down his sword and picked up his pen and carried on where Mr. Hitler had interrupted him.

By far the most significant calls he made were at the College of Arms, where he found a treasure trove of ancient Welsh records concerning Welsh families and genealogy. They were as unclassified and muddled as those he had found in Haverfordwest. He made friends with a Herald, Anthony Wagner, a direct descendant of Owain Glyndwr, and an authority on Welsh history himself. They got permission for my father to classify the Welsh records. The volunteer archivist was back at work. Some of his articles appeared regularly in the Hon. Society of the Cymmrodorion. In all its long history only one man had more articles published by them. He was also writing for *The Times, Burke's Peerage*, and many national magazines. In 1953, his book, *The Holy Wells of Wales*, was published to become a pioneering classic, still selling well today. It brought him a Honorary MA from the University of Wales. He was also a military commentator of the Coronation route which gave him his first experience of a royal ceremony and involved him in its administration. He and my mother still spoke Welsh at home, and found it most useful in making quiet asides to each other at the many meetings and parties they attended.

He belonged to many London societies and clubs, and there is a story about him remarking to a bearded brown faced man next to him at a St. James's club, 'You look as if you've just come from the North Pole.' The reply was, 'Actually it was the South Pole.' My father drew himself up and said, 'Well *I* come from South Kensington.'

So passed fourteen years of family life, full of humour, excitement and interest. My parents often remarked on how happy those London days had been. He then finished his huge task at the War Office. He stayed on for over a year writing and researching particularly in the College of Arms. He then took the post of County Archivist at Carmarthen, and the last of his gratuity paid for the move. It was a finely balanced act, not without concern for my mother. My parents were then aged 52, when many look forward to retirement. For them the best was yet to come, and lots of it.

Then came momentous family news in 1963. The Royal appointment of my father to Wales Herald of Arms Extraordinary. The post was last occupied in the days of the Black Prince in the 14th century. In retrospect, I think it was a case of the job finding the man, and not the other way round. At his first official appearance he was clad in court dress and the fabulous tabard which had been eighteen months in the making by the Royal College of Needlework. His debut was processing with his colleagues of the Royal Household leading the Royal party at the State Opening of Parliament. Afterwards he was presented to Her Majesty. When we asked him what his impressions were, he was very cool about it. But then after Salerno there was little left to overawe him. He kindly got me a seat in St. George's Chapel, Windsor for his first appearance in the Knights of the Garter service.

After the ceremony the procession returned to Windsor Castle. Lord Cobham who had been installed that day approached my father. A snatch of a programme about Lord Cobham I had made had just been repeated on 'Pick of the Week'. The new Knight of the Garter told the new herald that the BBC interviewer resembled him. He was tickled to hear it was indeed the herald's son. The Duke of Edinburgh then clapped Lord Cobham's shoulder and congratulated him on the programme. My brother, Dedwydd, had recently had two of his plays on at West End theatres so my mother had some reason to be proud of her three men.

Like many others in 1965, my father received a code word that triggered off the greatest State Funeral since Queen Victoria was buried. Sir Winston Churchill had died. Plans for this of course, had been drawn up for some years, and officials proceeded with the meticulous organisation matched only by the sincerity of the nation's grief. Thousands of soldiers, sailors, airmen, court officials, the Royal Family, civil servants, politicians, the Foreign Office, the Home Office, the world press, and television all co-operated under the direction of the maestro of ceremonial Bernard, Duke of Norfolk.

The ensuing display astonished the world with its dignity and solemn grandeur. Even the candles round the coffin were those last used for the Duke of Wellington's funeral. It was the climax of nearly a thousand years of ceremonial experience. The heralds stood like statues flanking the catafalque at St. Paul's high altar, as pictures were flashed to every corner of the

Farewell to Sir Winston Churchill from St. Paul's steps. F.J. on the left of the picture.

globe. I wonder if, as my father looked down the length of the Cathedral at the gathering of royal families, presidents, prime ministers and heads of state whether he thought back to his Trevine childhood when his parents told him of the lives of great heroes? Did he think back to that instant when he gazed up at the knight's helmet in St. Mary's Church in far off Haverfordwest? Sadly, I will never know now.

It would not be honest of me to depict my father as a saintly figure, perfect in every way. He was human with shortcomings, but such was his iron self control they rarely surfaced in public. I don't think his intellect ever rested; he planned and analysed before he spoke or acted. He always kept his aims firmly in mind. To achieve them he learned to dissemble and to conceal his true thoughts. He despised failure, and had an unerring instinct for people's weaknesses. He kept in with those who could become useful to him, as they did with him too. He knew the old boy network at a high level and operated it with subtlety. His charm was a useful asset as his success mounted.

One episode neatly illustrates this. He unwisely mentioned an outline of an idea for a book to another scholar. Later I saw him really angry for about the only time in my life. The man had coolly stolen my father's cherished idea. Now this person was a Power in the Land, so my father calmed down. Afterwards he went out of his way to help the man with the project which turned out to be a great success. That a tacit understanding then existed was proved by the enormous support this man gave my father in far more important undertakings from then on. I doubt though that Daddy ever dropped his guard again.

He kept his inner circle of friends for life, from school days, battlefield and Court. They lived in cottages, farm houses, mansions, great castles and London flats. The obituaries in *The Times*, *Daily Telegraph* and *Observer* among others attest to his gift of friendship. He kept his mother's photograph by his bedside for as long as I can remember.

The only person he ever shared his innermost thoughts with was my mother. During the war years he was away, and it may have been a shock for him to find boisterous children instead of the tots he had left, but I don't think that affected him much in his attitude to us. The household kept silent when he was at his desk, pretty much as before. Our mother dealt with the children's problems.

When I came out of the army, he put me into a job that he thought suitable. I left it after a short while, but he made no comment. After that he never offered to influence my career again. Neither did he ever praise my successes, nor condemn my failures. He left me to sink or swim on my own, as indeed he had done all his own life. The common ground we all had was humour. There he revelled in amusing stories and jokes, though he was scathing if our wit was not up to scratch. He never gave quarter, and most certainly never asked for it. To be cut down by his sarcasm was a withering experience, and most certainly to be avoided at all costs as I remember it. It was cobra quick and stabbed like a rapier. We were always slightly afraid of him and anxious to please. I think he played on this sometimes. He would mildly shepherd our thoughts into an opinion which, wanting to please, we would gladly adopt. Too late, we would find ourselves between a rock and a hard place, with no way out. The hasty opinion would then be dissected with remorseless precision. Not nice at all. It is called mind games today I think; whatever it is – he was very good at it. For his sons he saw success in terms of a professional or a structured career, ignoring the fact that his own career was entirely self-motivated.

Bursting with pride I told him of a big freelance BBC contract I had landed , 'Ah,' he languidly remarked, 'the BBC is full of left-wing queers.' Once my brother disagreed with his opinion, and quoted chapter and verse proving his point. Father dismissed him saying, 'Anyway, boy,. your legs are too short for your body.'

For many years I lived in a pretty Cotswold hamlet halfway between Carmarthen and Windsor. My parents in their pre car-owning days used to come up for they loved the area, to stay with us, and I would drive them up to Windsor for the Garter ceremonies. They took me to parties after the ceremony, and great fun it was too. At one I overheard an interesting bit of conversation. It was addressed to a court official by a business tycoon. 'Listen, you get me that knighthood and I'll give you a yacht.' The courtier gave a wintry smile, and slid away. The last I heard was 'Now hang on, I mean what I say. She's forty-five feet long.' I told my father about this, he said, 'Ah, he's still at it then.' He quoted Napoleon to me: 'Men are easily won by ribbons and trinkets'. Daddy was frequently approached by worthies pressing to be included in the Honours List. He had a set drill, he would say he would do what he could, and usually do nothing. If they were included they were, he said, grateful for life. If not, he would advise them to keep on trying.

It is no surprise that history was deeply ingrained in my father's subconscious. Living in old dwellings with historical connections throughout his life, from ancient farmhouses, the little mansion Plas Broginin, to castles such as Roch and Carmarthen, and stately Queens Gate there were some curious episodes.

Once he was puzzled about the whereabouts of a particular gravestone he had searched for. On going for a long walk he was approached by a figure who told him to look in a particular spot. Considering he had told nobody about the grave stone my father was puzzled, and thought it might have been a day dream. He visited the graveyard the following day. The head stone was exactly where the apparition had told him. He wrote up the experience and it was broadcast on BBC radio. Whilst living in the little house inside Carmarthen Castle, he had a series of strangely macabre dreams which he wrote down. One about a missing gold coin which he also wrote about and broadcast. I would be most intrigued if when we lived at Roch Castle he was ever visited by the royal mistress (who is a distant ancestress), Lucy Walter who once lived there. Maybe there are some things best left alone.

A herald's life appeared to me to consist of parading in gorgeous uniforms, solemn marching in ceremonies, and circulating at official parties such as the Buckingham Palace Garden party exuding charm. I soon knew better as I saw the work behind the scenes. He was, I think responsible for all queries on Welsh genealogy that flowed into the College of Arms endlessly from all over the world. These included some bizarre and amusing letters from cranks. He advised and helped draw up coats of arms for ennobled Welshmen, for clubs, insignia for town corporations, regiments, High Sheriffs, Royal Mail stamps and commercial companies. He replied to thousands of people from all over the world wanting family and heraldic information about their Welsh ancestors. Photographs of coats of arms on pottery, silver, book plates, crests on fireplaces, old coach panels, paintings of gravestones and church plaques came even from China. He handled all these queries with meticulous thoroughness in addition to his duties as an archivist and historian. He was in constant demand to join committees, to become president of historical societies, to be a governor of many bodies, to lecture, to make presentations. This as well as writing for radio, newspapers, TV, and advising on Post Office stamp designs. A steady stream of overseas visitors visiting Wales to trace their ancestry appeared at his house. He still wrote articles and researched his coming books. All this would have been impossible without my mother's help. She was not only his secretary, but still advised on his creative writings.

They started each day with a cup of tea at six o'clock. We often heard them laughing together as they prepared for their day. How lucky he was to have fallen in love with a woman who was equal to the big demands his work made on their partnership. Their research trips needed to be more time effective; having no car they relied on friends and public transport. My father claimed he couldn't drive. Actually he could, but his attention was easily distracted by fine views and houses in the country. He once took over the wheel of his army jeep from his driver in London. This man told me later it was the most frightening experience he'd had since being on active service in Italy. Although she could not drive my mother bought a small car, and passed her driving test at the first attempt. She was then over sixty. The instructor said she was the best pupil he ever saw. Afterwards my parents planned their excursions with the exactitude of military landings, clocking up many thousands of happy miles delighting in each other's company. My father referred to his chauffeuse as 'Boadica'; she never had a single accident.

Although public honours clustered to my father's name he never became pompous. I never once saw him stand on his dignity, and he still delighted in collecting bizarre, outrageous stories and jokes. That he kept his sense of proportion is well expressed on a piece of paper I found on which he had written 'One of the most severe trials to which the head and heart of man can be put is great and rapid elevation. Some prove equal to their new dignity imposed on their conduct and attitudes. Others are unable to carry their corn. It is also a trial for one's friends and acquaintances, for few men are completely devoid of a measure of envy when they realise that they have been lapped in the race of life'. Well, hold his corn my father did, he was ever courteous and was kind to everybody. He still found time to help and encourage young students and fellow scholars, so carrying on the tradition of kindness shown to him when he started his career in Pembrokeshire.

He went out of his way to be kind to one eccentric who thought he was a peer and visited his imagined estates (which was most of Industrial South Wales) to collect rents from his 'tenants'. He only got abuse. He then asked my father to have a quiet word with the Queen about his treatment. My father then arranged for a friendly eye to be kept out for this deluded man. Closer to home, a bumptious man with grandiose ambitions was arriving with fanciful ideas for ceremonials. We wondered why my father tolerated him. My exasperated mother suggested banning his visits; my father looked at her with enormous reproach 'Ethel, how could you be so cruel as to deprive me of my private jester,' he said. The visits continued, and a family joke ran, and ran, to laughter over many years.

Grandson Gareth Charles-Jones (No. 24) clears Beecher's Brook in the Grand National. (Photo: Bernard Parkin).

My parents always loved racing. They had great excitement in seeing my jockey son, Gareth, on TV winning at Cheltenham and Chepstow, and completing the Grand National. Maybe the youngster inherited some of his grandfather's winning ways. He once received an invitation to dinner by a man he rode for. The little gathering waited for the guest of honour, but no name was mentioned. Her Majesty the Queen Mother arrived, and Gareth took her into dinner. Not even Wales Herald topped that!

My father got great amusement from the little ditty I composed to the tune of 'My old man's a dustman'. He loved it and often used to ask me to sing it to him. It went: 'My old man's an 'erald, 'e wears an 'erald's 'at. E's got an 'erald's baton … and 'ee knows what he can do with that'. He called it his Herald's Anthem.

The Investiture Procession. F.J. leading front left.

The Queen presents the new Prince of Wales. Pictured directly above the Prince is Sir Anthony Wagner. F.J. to his right.

Soon another great State occasion was on him, this time he had a major role. It was the Investiture of the Prince of Wales in Caernarfon Castle in 1965. The Duke of Norfolk was Supremo, and the Earl of Snowdon and my father completed the trio organising the event.

I was a green staff officer at the Investiture, leading the peers and gentlemen of the Prince's party in the procession. I was nervously standing at the start line when my father found time to wish me luck. So did Mamma, there's family for you!

Everything went without a hitch in the meticulous time table. The only discordant note being some nationalists who tried to throw eggs at the royal carriages. We inside the castle were puzzled to hear the ugly rumblings of the crowd bent on tearing the egg bombers apart. They were rescued by the police and normal cheering service was resumed. After the ceremonies Her Majesty presented the new Prince of Wales to the people from a balcony of the ancient ramparts to tumultuous cheering from the huge crowd. My father stood behind the Royals clutching his ivory wand of office. It was the peak of his career, and later he was made a Commander of the Royal Victorian Order, an honour bestowed by the Monarch's personal command. It really was the day from which dreams are made.

The most graphic example of my father's indifference to money came about during the Investiture. He got a letter from an agent offering a huge sum of money to do a lecture tour in America. He showed it to my mother, who said 'You had better answer it don't you think'. He

245

F.J. in his element – research visit to an historic Welsh house, 1971.

carried on working at his desk. A week later it was still lying there. Again Mamma drew his attention to it, 'Ah yes,' he said, 'I'm too busy to answer it, will you just say no for me.' The sum offered would have bought a nice house.

Many hundreds of his articles appeared in newspapers, magazines and learned journals all over the world, and many books published. Yet in his huge archives I did not find a single author's contract. He would see his work in print never knowing what the fee was until it dropped through his letter box. Human nature being what it is he was sometimes not paid at all. This never ruffled him as he lived frugally, spending little on himself. On one occasion an Editor of *The Times* had him paid in cash. The money never got home, but he 'arrived' in a taxi full of

246

Francis and Ethel Jones at Buckingham Palace after his being made Commander of the Royal Victorian Order.

antiquarian books he had bought. My mother cut down his pocket money for a while after that.

My parents life settled down to an even tenor, and if anything his work output increased. Their little car clocked up thousands more miles, as they began the gigantic task of collating material for a series of books, county by county of historic homes and families in Wales. They started with Pembrokeshire, Carmarthenshire and Cardiganshire. By now my father was a Fellow of the Society of Antiquaries, an Honorary MA, a Deputy Lieutenant of Carmarthenshire, a Director of the National Trust, a Governor of the National Library of Wales, a Freeman of Haverfordwest, and a Knight of the Order of St. John, and president of various historical associations; he was even made an honorary member of the Mark Twain Society in America.

My parents always enjoyed having people to stay at their home, and once entertained my BBC producer, David Glencross. David came down complaining of not feeling well and casting a gloom over our breakfast table. He apologised to my parents, 'Not at all,' said my father, 'you are a guest here, and you may cast as much gloom as you like.'

They seemed to get busier as they got older, my father's diary being full for months ahead, He found a pause to retire as County Archivist, and then aged sixty-five in 1974, charged on with his work enjoying every minute of it. I never in my life ever heard him say he was tired. He and my mother were now working in harness full time, and she was able to keep up with him too. What a couple. She also had her amusing episodes; once at a rehearsal for some royal event she became a stand in for the Monarch. From then on she was affectionately known as Mrs. Wales. For us children nobody could ever be a stand-in for Mamma.

One of the most pleasant official invitations my parents had was to the wedding service of Prince Charles at St. Paul's Cathedral. My mother bought a new hat. I saw it on television, when a camera panned across five ex-prime Ministers in the congregation, Macmillan, Wilson, Callaghan, Home and Heath. It also picked out my parents sitting behind them. Although it was an ill starred marriage it was a spectacularly brilliant occasion, and neither of my parents lived to see the marriage break-up.

My father developed angina, but apart from a change of diet it made not the slightest difference to his work, and curtailed the official duties not one iota. He even worked on a new ceremonial order, a corps of Welsh gentlemen to attend the Prince of Wales, called the Teilo of the Order of St. David. Maybe another will now take up the cause.

Catastrophe hit our family in 1985. My mother died suddenly after fifty-four years of marriage to my father. Her memory lives with us all in every waking day. Shortly afterwards I returned to Pembrokeshire from the Cotswolds, and was able to see more of my father. In 1987 his Carmarthenshire book was published. It

F.J. with guard dog, Ben.

F.J.'s last Knights of the Garter Ceremonial Parade at Windsor, 1988.

contained descriptions of no less than 600 properties, and over two thousand families that lived in them down the ages. It was a tour de force, ran into two quick editions and sold out.

Then, in his late seventies, he developed cancer of the stomach, and half was removed. A few days later whist I visited him, he insisted on getting out of bed and shaving himself. I doubt if I will ever see such will-power again. By way of convalescing he continued writing and researching this book. Many kind friends especially Thomas Lloyd and David Brunel White drove him about West Wales. With enormous determination he attended his last Garden Party at Buckingham Palace in a wheel chair. Is it any wonder that I feel compelled to publish his book? He suffered another misfortune when up in Aberystwyth for research work at the National Library, he fell and broke his hip. He had an immediate hip replacement in the nearby hospital, and later told my brother, 'I was lucky, they caught me while I was still warm.'

He, who had loved walking so much, adjusted to a new hip slowly. He courageously struggled on, in spite of the deterioration of his health and immaculate handwriting. The desire to impart his knowledge of Pembrokeshire urged his frail fingers to work. After handling his pen and sword with such distinction he finally grew tired. My mother, the only person who had shared his innermost thoughts and supported him with her constancy and encouragement was gone. He was in his 86th year.

I wrote in the service sheet for his Memorial Service in St. David's Cathedral, 'Death came gently to my father. He died in his own home after years of loving care from my sister Anne.

'We children, Dedwydd, Elizabeth, Anne and I were around him as he slipped painlessly away as if one of the pages of his own books had been gently closed.'

My father had never been physically demonstrative apart from the odd handshake or clap on the shoulder. I kissed him then for the first and last time in my adult life.

I organised our final tribute in St. David's Cathedral on the date of our Mamma's death. It is a place they loved, near to their birth places and Brawdy. There was a large and distinguished congregation. We all listened to the wonderful harp music of Susan Drake, and to the rich voice of our cousin, Aerwyn Charles singing 'David of the White Rock'. For the first time three Garter Kings of Arms attended together. My father's richly coloured tabard was displayed near the High Altar for its only appearance in Pembrokeshire.

That is how we said goodbye to our parents.

HUGH CHARLES-JONES
April 1996

249

STRANGE SEQUELS

Shortly after my mother died, I took my father to London for the State Opening of Parliament. Spectator tickets are eagerly sought, peers and heralds getting one each. My father always gave my mother his allotted ticket. I had never attended the ceremony.

Through a series of inexplicable coincidences totally unconnected with my father, I was given a ticket. Being late I only just got a place, but was able to see my father on parade, and he spotted me.

Some months later in my father's house I thumbed through a book called *Royal Ceremonies of State*. I spotted Mamma quite plainly in a photograph of the State Opening of Parliament. The strangest thing was that she was in the exact spot where I stood on the first time she was absent. It was where she could see my father. (Broadcast in full BBC Radio 4, 1994.).

After my father's death, I was involved in some overseas business, and as a result was invited to the Opening of Parliament again, and for lunch at the House of Lords afterwards.

This meant that for over 30 consecutive years a member of our family was present. I felt I was representing my parents in a closing chapter in the family history which began so long ago in a Pembrokeshire house. *H.C.-J.*

State Opening of Parliament.

FAMILY INDEX

Trewern